NO MAN'S LAND 2 · SEXCHANGES

Other Yale University Press books by Sandra M. Gilbert and Susan Gubar

The Madwoman in the Attic (1979)

No Man's Land, Volume 1, The War of the Words (1988)

No Man's Land, Volume 3, Letters from the Front (1994)

Also edited by Sandra M. Gilbert and Susan Gubar

Shakespeare's Sisters (Indiana University Press, 1979)

The Norton Anthology of Literature by Women (W. W. Norton, 1985)

NO MAN'S LAND

The Place of the Woman Writer
in the Twentieth Century

Volume 2 · Sexchanges

SANDRA M. GILBERT AND SUSAN GUBAR

Yale University Press · New Haven and London

Published with assistance from the foundation established in memory of Philip Hamilton McMillan of the Class of 1894, Yale College.

Set in Baskerville type and printed in the United States of America by Vail-Ballou Press, Binghamton, New York.

Library of Congress Cataloging-in-Publication Data
(Revised for vol. 2)

Gilbert, Sandra M.
  No man's land.

  Includes bibliographies and indexes.
  Contents: v. 1. The war of the words—v. 2. Sexchanges.
  1. English literature—Women authors—History and criticism. 2. English literature—20th century—History and criticism.   3. American literature—Women authors—History and criticism. 4. American literature—20th century—History and criticism.   5. Women and literature—Great Britain—History—20th century.   6. Women and literature—United States—History—20th century.   7. Feminism and literature—Great Britain. 8. Feminism and literature—United States. I. Gubar, Susan, 1944– II. Title
PR116.G5   1988   820'.9'9287   87–10560
ISBN 0–300–04375–9 (v. 2 : alk. paper)
       0–300–05025–9 (v. 2 : pbk.: alk. paper)

The paper in this book meets the guidelines for permanence and durability of the Committee on Production Guidelines for Book Longevity of the Council on Library Resources.

10   9   8   7   6   5   4

For Valentine

We may not know exactly what sex is; but we do know that it is mutable, with the possibility of one sex being changed into the other sex, that its frontiers are often uncertain, and that there are many stages between a complete male and a complete female.

—Havelock Ellis

[T]he company of Amazons which nineteenth-century America produced among its many prodigies [included] not-men, not-women, answerable to no function in either sex, whose careers were carried on, and how successfully, in whatever field they chose: they were educators, writers, editors, politicians, artists, world travelers, and international hostesses, who lived in public and by the public and played out their self-assumed, self-created rôles in such masterly freedom as only a few early medieval queens had equaled. Freedom to them meant precisely freedom from men and their stuffy rules for women.

—Katherine Anne Porter

So we have been invited, all of us, to install ourselves in a very dim Venusberg indeed; but Venus has become an introverted matriarch, brooding over a subterraneous "stream of consciousness"—a feminine phenomenon after all—and we are a pretty sorry set of knights too, it must be confessed.

—Wyndham Lewis

I was tired of being a woman,
tired of the spoons and the pots,
tired of my mouth and my breasts,
tired of the cosmetics and the silks.
There were still men who sat at my table,
circled around the bowl I offered up.
The bowl was filled with purple grapes
and the flies hovered in for the scent
and even my father came with his white bone.
But I was tired of the gender of things.

—Anne Sexton

Contents

Preface

"Make it new," Ezra Pound famously exhorted his contemporaries as he struggled to fashion a modernist aesthetic for a modern world. The statement would appear to be gender-free, but elsewhere the "Sage Homme" who acted as midwife to *The Waste Land* strikingly sexualized his definitions of what was new and who could make it. Explaining in his translator's postscript to Remy de Gourmont's *Natural Philosophy of Love* (1931) that "the brain itself [is] only a sort of great clot of genital fluid,"[1] Pound went on to conceptualize originality as "the phallus or spermatozoid charging, head-on, the female chaos," adding in a confessional aside, "Even oneself has felt it, driving any new idea into the great passive vulva of London." Indeed, to the extent that he believed that the "mind is an up-spurt of sperm" (172), which is "the form-creator" (173), Pound linked modernity with masculinity: "Without any digression on feminism, . . . one offers woman as the accumulation of her hereditary aptitudes, . . . but to man, given what we have of history, the 'inventions,' the *new* gestures, the extravagance, the wild shots, the *new* bathing of the cerebral tissues." (170; emphasis ours).

How and why did this acolyte of the new happen to engender such apparently eccentric ideas? In this, the second installment of our three-volume *No Man's Land; The Place of the Woman Writer in the Twentieth Century*, we will expand on our claim that the sexual battles we explored in volume 1, *The War of the Words*, were inevitably associated with radical "sexchanges," as well as with notably sexualized visions of change and exchange, in the lives and works of both literary men and literary women. Specifically, we will argue here that this is the case for two interrelated reasons: the sexes battle because sex roles change, but, when the sexes battle, sex itself (that is, eroticism) changes.

Chronologically, this book begins in the fin de siècle and primarily covers a period from the 1880s to the end of the First World War and the decades—the twenties and thirties—generally associated with the flowering of high modernism. Thematically, it elaborates upon a number of issues we also addressed in *The War of the Words*. We will continue to study, for instance, the relationship between female dreams of a powerful Herland and male fears of a debilitating no man's land, showing that the rise of the New Woman was not matched by the coming of a New Man but instead was identified (in the imaginations of both men and women) with a crisis of masculinity that we have imaged through the figure of the no-man. As a corollary of this, moreover, we will pursue our earlier analysis of the discrepancy between men's hostility toward what they perceived as threatening female autonomy and women's anxiety about what they saw as the fragility or even the fictionality of such autonomy. In addition, we will continue to examine the dilemma of twentieth-century literary daughterhood that we have called the female affiliation complex and to consider the sometimes striking, sometimes subtle connections between gender and genre.

At the same time, however, we will discuss in detail a number of matters that we only touched on briefly in *The War of the Words*. We will explore, for example, the sexual imagery associated with imperialism and its decline, with the intensified consumerism of Gilded Age America, and with the opening as well as the closing of the American frontier; we will examine the evolution of turn-of-the-century and modernist women's revisionary mythic and religious ideas; we will analyze the relationship of the feminist and the free love movements to the female imagination; we will consider the emergence of a lesbian literary tradition constructed by English and American women writers; and we will study the asymmetrical impact of the Great War on men and women. Throughout the book, though, our principal focus will be on changing definitions of sex and sex roles as they evolve through three phases: the repudiation or revision of the Victorian ideology of femininity that marked both feminism and fantasy during what we might call the overturning of the century; the antiutopian skepticism that characterized the thought of such writers as Edith Wharton and Willa Cather, who dramatized their discontent with what they saw as a crippling but inexorable feminization of women; the virtually apocalyptic engendering of the new for both literary men and literary women that was, at least in part, fostered by the fin de siècle formation of a visible lesbian community, even more shockingly triggered by the traumas of World War I, and perhaps most radically shaped by an unprecedented confrontation (by both sexes) with the artifice of gender and its consequent discontents.

"We may not know exactly what sex is," wrote Havelock Ellis in a passage from the *Psychology of Sex* (1933) that we have used as an epigraph for this volume, "but we do know that it is mutable, with the possibility of one sex being changed into the other sex, that its frontiers are often uncertain, and that there are many stages between a complete male and a complete female."[2] He was here drawing on the views of his visionary compatriot Edward Carpenter, who argued in a utopian meditation on "the Intermediate Sex" at the center of his controversial but widely influential treatise *Love's Coming of Age* (1896) that "In late years (and since the arrival of the New Woman amongst us) . . . there are some remarkable and (we think) indispensable types of character, in whom there is such a union or balance of the feminine and masculine qualities that these people become to a great extent the interpretors of men and women to each other." And both Ellis and Carpenter were clearly responding to the transformative impact of the suffrage movement, whose role in changing definitions of sexuality was succinctly summarized by George Bernard Shaw, a friend and contemporary of both men. "People are still full of the old idea that woman is a special creation," commented Shaw in 1927, but, he noted, "I am bound to say that of late years she has been working extremely hard to eradicate that impression, and make one understand that a woman is really only a man in petticoats, or if you like, that a man is a woman without petticoats."[3]

But the optimism implicit in Ellis's, Carpenter's, and Shaw's remarks was not shared by all their contemporaries, even though most agreed that they were living through a time of what George Gissing called "sexual anarchy"[4] and that we might now define as a sexual revolution. Some, like Thomas Hardy, the creator of that vexed and vexing New Woman Sue Bridehead, were skeptical about the ameliorative possibilities for change in a civilization that had "never succeeded in creating that homely thing, a satisfactory scheme for the conjunction of the sexes."[5] Others, from the conservative novelist Mrs. Lynn Linton and the misogynistic theorist Anthony M. Ludovici in England to the popular columnist H. L. Mencken in America, conceded that in the sexual realm, as Mencken parodically put it, "the old order changeth and giveth place to the new. The sun do move," but deplored the horrifying transformations they felt they were observing.[6]

In a well-known series of articles in the periodical *Nineteenth Century*, Mrs. Linton castigated "Wild Women" for "warring as they do against the best traditions, the holiest functions, and the sweetest qualities of their sex," and several decades later Ludovici warned that "the continuous expression and assertion of male elements in a woman, and of female elements in a man, . . . result in nothing but misery, both mental and physical."[7] Similarly, Mencken expressed his distaste for women who are "almost male in their violent earnestness" and who "range from the man-eating suffragettes to such preachers of free motherhood as Ellen Key and such professional boob-shockers and martyrs as Margaret Sanger."[8] Conservative as these thinkers were, their ideas were paradoxically comparable to those of the avant-garde Ezra Pound, who sought to reconstitute in the guise of the new the old Aristotelian "verities" of the "active" spermatozoic male and the "passive" ovoid female. All, in fact, would have agreed with the antisuffragist zoologist Walter Heape, author of *Sex Antagonism* (1913), who claimed in a statement radically antithetical to the views of Carpenter and Ellis that the "reproductive system is not only structurally but functionally fundamentally different in the Male and the Female; and since all other organs and systems of organs are affected by this system, it is certain that the Male and Female are essentially different throughout," adding that "the accurate adjustment of society depends on proper observation of this fact."[9]

To most of the women whose works we study in this volume, however, early twentieth-century society's sexchanges offered at least a modicum of hope for the destruction of old sexual rules and the redemptive construction of new social roles. Many, of course, were conscious of the intensity with which some of their brothers (and, indeed, some of their sisters) waged a war of words against what Adrienne Rich calls "the will to change," and—because such consciousness frequently inhibited or qualified feminist aspirations—the map of female metamorphic imaginings that we will trace here is a convoluted one. Although, as critics from Mario Praz to Nina Auerbach and Bram Dijkstra have shown, turn-of-the-century male writers represented female desire as unnervingly ascendant in the figure of the femme fatale,[10] fin-de-siècle and modernist women of letters were often hesitant, recalcitrant, or ironic in their depiction of feminine eroticism. In various ways, such writers as Olive Schreiner and Charlotte Perkins Gilman sought to erase, reform, or redirect New Womanly sexuality, while Kate Chopin implied that there might be no place for female desire in her culture, and Edith Wharton, along with Willa Cather, made the problem of such desire a central issue.

Nevertheless, in visions of an art of love liberated from the constraints of gender, modernist women from Amy Lowell and Gertrude Stein to Virginia Woolf and H. D. questioned the very concept of a "natural" philosophy of love and art. Their fantasies of sexual transformation simultaneously derived from and reformulated a series of crucial questions that are at the heart of this book. What might sex be and what could sex roles be in the midst of, or after, a war between men and women? Who or what is a woman, a man, an androgyne? Such queries, which preoccupied theorists from the 1880s on, persistently haunt the work of all the literary women whose texts we will examine here. But perhaps because these questions were so frighteningly central, many modernist women of letters could only answer them in oblique, sometimes fragmentary, sometimes contradictory, often guarded ways. In a world of sex wars and sexchanges, the new was often literally and literarily unspeakable, even by those who yearned to bring it into being.

Even at their most elliptical, though, these women were confronting issues that are still crucial for theorists of sexuality and textuality, issues that we ourselves, as feminist literary critics, have continually had to reexamine. During our own fin de siècle, after all, as during the last, a heightened consciousness of gender as a social construct has generated heated debates about the place of biology in the formation of sex roles and sex differences, about the relationship between anatomy and destiny. At times, in fact, these debates replicate the distinction between Havelock Ellis's sense that sex is "mutable . . . its frontiers are often uncertain," and Walter Heape's belief that "Male and Female are essentially different throughout."

To be sure, most feminist thinkers today assume that nurture, at the very least, qualifies nature. Recently, however, a number of poststructuralist theorists—deploying both male and female signatures—have claimed that there is no gendered "reality," that the concepts "man" and "woman" are, as some would put it, "always already" fictive since human identity is itself a tenuous, textually produced epiphenomenon. Arguing that the appeal to gendered experience is as naive as an appeal to biological essentials, such thinkers as Toril Moi in England and Mary Jacobus in America would detach the literary text from both the sociocultural context and the (delusively male or female) authorial name in order to affirm the infinitely equivocal nature of reading and writing, of being read and being written.[11]

In one important way, of course, these radical claims are salutary, for they remind us that, as Monique Wittig once put it (alluding to Simone de Beauvoir's philosophic position), "woman is made, not born" just as "man" is.[12] They are problematic, though, to the extent that they deny the possibility that the "woman" or "man" who is made makes (what we ordinarily call) texts. Paradoxically, in other words, although poststructuralist feminists rightly view "female" and "male" as arbitrary constructs, some refuse to acknowledge the possibility that these powerful constructs inexorably make and mark the products of the imagination. Moreover, although such thinkers rightly seek to disentangle sexuality and gender, the sexual body and the sex role, some appear to overlook the obvious fact that the constructs "female" and "male" are shaped by varying cultural interpretations of anatomical distinctions between the sexes even while these arbitrary constructs are used to perpetuate cultural evaluations of such distinctions.

When we ourselves use the words "woman" and "man," "female" and "male," "feminine" and "masculine," therefore, we are always deploying what we, too, understand as artificial, socially determined signifiers. But we are also always using these terms both to explore their changing resonances and to examine the ways in which such changes in meaning affected the lives and art of the writers we have chosen to study. On the one hand, therefore, we do not regard biographical speculations as irrelevant to our enterprise, since we assume that the concepts "female" and "male" have an impact on human experience, which has always—at least so far—been gendered. On the other hand, we seek to locate the text in its sociocultural context, since we believe, too, that the concepts "female" and "male" are inextricably enmeshed in the materiality and mythology of history, which has also, we have found, almost always been experienced as gendered. Finally, we trace the varying themes that collect around the concepts "female" and "male" at moments when those ideas are just as much in flux as they are today, since we think that compelling leitmotifs—the femme fatale, the New Woman, the crisis in scripts of virility, the image of the frontier, the metaphor of transvestism—reveal drastic sociocultural changes at least as forcefully as revolutions in poetic language do.

Perhaps, therefore, because in this book we are dealing with a time of cultural extremity and sexual experimentation, some of the works as well as some of the themes we have chosen to analyze may themselves appear extreme or extraordinary. But it is our view—not an unusual one—that the ordinary is often constituted out of the odd. Thus, such works as Rider Haggard's *She*, Bram Stoker's *Dracula*, Charlotte Perkins Gilman's *Herland*, Virginia Woolf's *Orlando*, and Djuna Barnes's *Nightwood*, all of which may seem idiosyncratic, actually function to illuminate key aspects of the historical moments in which they were produced. Similarly, apparently eccentric subjects like necrophilia, parthenogenesis, and transvestism can offer important psychic and social truths into a particular generation, insights that (as our transatlantic choice of authors indicates) frequently cross political and geographic boundaries.

Such insights may, of course, appear not only eccentric but painful. Three cases in point: first, our examinations of both imperialist xenophobia and suffragist racism necessarily lay bare grievous wrongs that we must all nevertheless confront as we come to terms with the forces that shaped, respectively, modernism and feminism; second, our study of the strategies lesbian writers constructed to deal with their alienation from an overwhelmingly heterosexual literary history must take into account the loneliness of artists who felt themselves to be expatriated from their own culture as well as their entanglement in the terms provided by that culture; third, our analysis of the asymmetrical responses of literary men and literary women to the Great War that haunts modern memory inevitably uncovers a distressing sexual competition which seems to have allowed at least some women to profit from male pain, a competition we must nevertheless acknowledge if we are to understand the dynamics of gender difference in the twentieth century. About such disturbing material, all we can finally say is, Reader, we felt we had to write it, but please don't kill the messenger.

In our next volume, we should add, we will deal in greater depth with a number of important issues that we do not discuss here: with, for example, the major literary experiments of Virginia Woolf; with the poetic themes and strategies of Edna St. Vincent Millay, Marianne Moore, and H. D.; and with the emergence of a black female literary tradition in the works of Jessie Fauset, Nella Larsen, Zora Neale Hurston, and others. In addition, we will there trace the fate of modernist "sexperimentation" in the writings of women who record and respond to the pain of World War II and in the sexchanges of a generation caught up in a second wave of feminism. But, like both this volume and its predecessor, *Letters from the Front* will also continue our investigation of the relationships between feminism and modernism, politics and poetics, gender and genre, old rules and new roles, during a period of notable cultural conflict.

In approaching these complex issues in this book, we should note here, we have, as often in the past, divided our responsibilities: Sandra Gilbert drafted chapter 1 (on "The Agon of the Femme Fatale"), chapter 3 (on "Kate Chopin's Fantasy of Desire"), chapter 4 (on Edith Wharton and "the Arts of the Enslaved"), and chapter 7 (on "Literary Men, Literary Women, and the Great War"); Susan Gubar drafted chapter 2 (on "the Colonies of the New Woman"), chapter 5 (on "Willa Cather's Lost Horizons"), and chapter 6 (on "Lesbian Double Talk"); each of us drafted portions of chapter 8 (on "Transvestism as Metaphor"), but its final version is really a jointly created text. As always, however, we have continually exchanged, discussed, and revised each other's work so that we feel this book is fully collaborative.

Besides learning from each other, we have as always learned a great deal from many others. Among our most valuable advisers as we worked on this volume were such colleagues and friends as Elyse Blankley, Richard Bridgman, Charles Carrington, Shehira Davezac, Joanne Feit Diehl, Susan Stanford Friedman, Barbara Gelpi, Donald Gray, Carolyn Heilbrun, Samuel Hynes, Terence Martin, Esther Newton, Elaine Showalter, Carroll Smith-Rosenberg, Garrett Stewart, Ruth Stone, and Mary Jo Weaver. In addition, as we noted in our preface to *The War of the Words,* all of our work on feminism and modernism is indebted to discussions we have had with participants in our 1981 NEH Summer Seminar for College Teachers, in a seminar at the School of Criticism and Theory in 1984, and in classes at Indiana University, at the University of California, Davis, and at Princeton University.

We are grateful, moreover, for research support from the National Endowment for the Humanities, the Rockefeller Foundation, the Guggenheim Foundation, the Indiana Foundation for the Humanities, Indiana University, the University of California Humanities Institute (Davis), and Princeton University. And we are, of course, grateful too for invaluable research assistance from Alice Falk (Indiana University), Marjorie Howes (Princeton University), and Judy Peck (University of California, Davis), the last of whom also gave us invaluable help with our index, as well as for the usual splendid copyediting from Judith Calvert at Yale University Press. To Ellen Graham, our tirelessly encouraging editor at the Press, we again offer love and friendship, as we do, also, to such members of our inner circle as Joan Bennett, Gina Campbell, Elizabeth Parr, Jayne Spencer, and Catherine Thompson, all of whom helped enrich our lives and, we hope, our writing.

Our families, too, have in many ways aided and abetted our work on sexchanges. As in the past, we must thank our mothers—Angela Mortola and Luise David—and our children—Roger, Katherine, and Susanna Gilbert, Molly and Simone Gubar—for the pleasure of their company during the composition process, and we must thank, too, our husbands—Elliot Gilbert and Edward Gubar—for being two very different but equally important models of "the masculine," from whom we ceaselessly learned. But with special love and hope we dedicate this book to Valentine, a new child and a child of the new.

I
Feminism and Fantasy

1 Heart of Darkness: The Agon of The Femme Fatale

[She is] beautiful always beyond desire and cruel beyond words; fairer than heaven and more terrible than hell; pale with pride and weary with wrong-doing; a silent anger against God and man burns, white and repressed, through her clear features.

—A. C. Swinburne

Man's timid heart is bursting with the things he must not say,
For the Woman that God gave him isn't his to give away;
But when hunter meets with husband, each confirms the other's tale—
The female of the species is more deadly than the male.

—Rudyard Kipling

I give you mom. I give you the destroying mother. . . . I give you Medusa and Stheno and Euryale . . . I give you the woman in pants, and the new religion: she-popery. I give you Pandora. I give you Proserpine, the Queen of Hell. The five-and-ten-cent-store Lilith.

—Phillip Wylie

Queen Victoria, there's a woman . . . when one encounters a toothed vagina of such exceptional size. . . .

—Jacques Lacan

What is the relationship between the feminine and the modern, or between the feminist and the modernist? In 1936 William Butler Yeats offered as the opening "poem" in his *Oxford Book of Modern Verse* an extraordinary selection, a text which suggests that, at least in one part of himself, the Irish visionary believed that woman had some originatory connection with modernity in general and with modern literature in particular. For, in Yeats's view, the first modern poem was not a work in verse by Swinburne or Rossetti, Hardy or Housman. Instead, it was a prose passage about a femme fatale—the famous description of "La Gioconda" from Walter Pater's *Studies in the History of the Renaissance* (1873), which Yeats excerpted, versified, and offered as a discrete work under the title "Mona Lisa":

> She is older than the rocks among which she sits;
> Like the Vampire,
> She has been dead many times,
> And learned the secrets of the grave;
> And has been a diver in deep seas,
> And keeps their fallen day about her;
> And trafficked for strange webs with Eastern merchants;
> And, as Leda,
> Was the mother of Helen of Troy,
> And, as St Anne,
> Was the mother of Mary;
> And all this has been to her but as the sound of lyres
>   and flutes,
> And lives
> Only in the delicacy
> With which it has moulded the changing lineaments
> And tinged the eyelids and the hands.[1]

Though Yeats radically decontextualized this passage—cutting it free from Pater's speculations about both the painter Leonardo and his real-life subject—the Irish poet (who was not ordinarily in the habit of fashioning poems *trouvé*) clearly shaped "his" text to emphasize what he saw as the crux of Pater's fascination with Leonardo's famous portrait: the fact that "Lady Lisa might stand as the embodiment of the old fancy" of "a perpetual life" and "the symbol of the modern idea" of "humanity as wrought upon by, and summing up in itself, all modes of thought and life."[2] In doing so, he followed the lead of his sometime mentor Oscar Wilde, who cited the same passage from Pater in his crucial "The Critic as Artist" (1884) in order to justify the authority of the interpretor (as against that of the creator) with the explanation that "it is . . . the beholder who lends the beautiful thing its myriad meanings . . . and sets it in some new relation to the age so that it becomes a vital portion of our lives and a symbol of what we pray for, or perhaps, of what"—tellingly—"*we fear that we may receive*" (emphasis ours).[3]

Of course, it may be argued that (as James Longenbach has claimed) Yeats, even more than Wilde, privileged Pater's meditation by beginning his anthology with a strange collaboration between himself, Pater, and Leonardo because he wanted to stress the paradox that for him, as "for Pater, what is modern is nothing more than the sum of everything that has preceded it."[4] But how had it come about that for Yeats—as for Pater and Wilde—both prehistory (in Yeats's first line, "She is older than the rocks among which she sits") and history (in the line that precedes Yeats's first line, she represents "the animalism of Greece, the lust of Rome, the mysticism of the Middle Age") are incarnated in a female figure who has become what Wilde called "a vital portion of our lives"? We are accustomed to a Yeatsian mysticism that locates history's turning points in the bodies of such mythic heroines as Leda, Helen, and Mary, but it is nevertheless surprising to find that this major modernist introduces and defines the canon of the new with an evocation of female priority and primacy that, at least covertly, figures history itself as feminine.[5]

We will argue here, however, that male writers from Pater to Wilde to Yeats, along with many of their descendants, linked a new perception of what they saw as the archaic power of the feminine with the reactive urgency of the modern aesthetic they were themselves defining, because, as we suggested in *The War of the Words*, women were in some sense what one journalist called "the cause of modernism."[6] In our first volume, we argued that sophisticated avant-garde strategies of linguistic experimentation need to be understood in terms of male anxiety about unprecedented female achievement in both the social sphere and the literary marketplace. But if this point is subtly articulated in many of the major monuments of unaging intellect produced by fin-de-siècle and twentieth-century literary men, it is even more flamboyantly dramatized in a number of widely-read popular works, works that include *She* and *King Solomon's Mines*, the most famous "hits" by Rider Haggard, late Victorian England's "King Romance," as well as George MacDonald's *Lilith*, Wilde's *Salome*, Bram Stoker's *Dracula*, and Stoker's less well-known *The Lair of the White Worm*.

Though some of these fantasies and romances might seem at first radically different from the far more complex and ambitious works that form the usual canon of this period's masterpieces, in fact the sexual imperatives that, say, Haggard and Stoker transcribe can be said to shape writings by such diverse contemporaries as Sigmund Freud and Joseph Conrad as well as by a number of other major protomodernist and modernist thinkers. Thus an analysis of *She*—whose terse pronominal title suggests that the book might be an abstruse treatise on the female gender or a fictive exploration of the ontology of womanhood—can function as a paradigmatic reading of the turn of the century's bestselling, masculinist mythology.

Speculating in 1942 on the horrors of what he called "Momism," Phillip Wylie declared in *Generation of Vipers* that "Mom," the "five-and-ten-cent store Lilith," is "the consequence of *She*."[7] He was referring, of course, to one of the most charismatic works of the late nineteenth century: published in 1887, *She* sold a nearly record-breaking 30,000 copies within a few months, and though the novel no doubt owed some of its popularity to Haggard's reputation as the author of another exciting bestseller, *King Solomon's Mines,* and some to its exotic African setting, most of its charisma seems to have come from the compelling mystery incarnated in its eponymous heroine. The formal title of this woman—*She-who-must-be-obeyed*—was hardly less ontological-sounding than the title of the novel in which She starred, yet it was as crucial to the book's power as it was in representing Her power. For Haggard's heroine was in many ways a definitive embodiment of fantasies that preoccupied countless male writers who had come of age during a literary period in which, as Mario Praz remarked some fifty years ago in *The Romantic Agony,* "sex"—and specifically the female sex—had been "obviously the mainspring of works of imagination."[8]

Unlike the women earlier Victorian writers had idealized or excoriated, She was neither an angel nor a monster. Rather, *She-who-must-be-obeyed* was an odd blend of the two types—an angelically chaste woman with monstrous powers, a monstrously passionate woman with angelic charms. Just as importantly, however, She was in certain ways an entirely New Woman: the all-knowing, all-powerful ruler of a matriarchal society. But unlike such other symbolic New Women as Tennyson's (or Gilbert and Sullivan's) Princess Ida, She was a mythic figure, a classic femme fatale whose charms and claims were enigmatically fantastic. Though the plot of Her story in some sense recapitulates the plot of both *The Princess* and *Princess Ida*—three dauntless male explorers penetrate the secret fastness of a female country—Haggard's romance is therefore significantly revisionary, echoing Wilde's use of the Pater passage as a hermeneutic touchstone and prefiguring Yeats's use of Pater to define modernism as much as it recalls Gilbert and Sullivan's use of Tennyson to repudiate feminism.

To be sure, though Gilbert and Sullivan's runaway princess is comically ineffectual, Tennyson's imperious Ida, "Robed in the long night of her deep hair," does often seem like a femme fatale.[9] Yet, despite the Victorian poet's depiction of the battle in which Ida is engaged as fundamentally irrational, her demands are themselves rational: she and her female acolytes seek simply "To unfurl the maiden banner of our rights" (IV.483), and, when they are defeated by their own tender femininity, Tennyson shows them quite reasonably (or so he implies) submitting to the inevitability of their domestication. Haggard's She, however, is a female of a very different species, for, as we shall see, even while Her powers allusively evoke the urgency of suffragists unfurling the "maiden banner" of their rights, they function, more fabulously, as objectifications of the primordial female otherness which may have been the real source of male anxieties about New Women. New Womanly as She in some sense is, in other words, *She-who-must-be-obeyed* is also an ontological Old Woman—at least figuratively "older than the rocks among which she sits"—whose mysterious autonomy brings to the surface everyman's worry about *all* women.

We will argue that it is especially because of this last point that Haggard's portrait of Her was so popular, and so popular with male readers in particular, and we will show that because of this last point, too, Her story was both a summary and a paradigm of the story told by a number of similar contemporary tales: all were to varying degrees just the kinds of fictive explorations of female authority that Haggard's title promised and his novel delivered, and many solved what their authors implicitly defined as the problem of female power through denouements analogous to—perhaps even drawn from—the one that Haggard devised for *She*. Finally, we will demonstrate that both the fascination of Haggard's semidivine femme fatale and the compulsiveness with which he and his contemporaries made Her "the mainspring of works of imagination" were symptoms of a complex of late Victorian anxieties that were exacerbated not just by the battle of the sexes that we have already analyzed but also by a series of other key cultural changes, including the feared "recessional" of the British empire, the intensified development of such fields as anthropology and embryology, and the rise of a host of alternative theologies.

The idea of a land ruled by ferocious women is, of course, as old and as enduring as the idea of the Amazons. Long after the Greeks and Romans had elaborated fantastic visions of Penthesilea and her female troops, Sir John Mandeville declared in his *Travels* that

> Another Yle is there towards the Northe, in the See Ocean, where that ben fulle cruele and ful evele Wommen of Nature: and thei han precious Stones in hire Eyen; and thei ben of that Kynde, that yif thei beholden ony man with wratthe, thei slen him anon with the beyoldyne, as dothe the Basilisk.[10]

Such a Medusan queendom has always haunted the western literary imagination. Yet, in the detail and intensity with which Rider Haggard imagines Her, She is a notable nineteenth-century phenomenon, a creature who, metaphorically speaking, first appears around the beginning of the era, a few decades before Haggard himself was born, almost as if Her birth were a dramatic symbol of the birth of Romanticism.[11]

Before and after Haggard claims Her and names Her, She is called La Belle Dame sans Merci, Geraldine, Moneta, Venus, La Gioconda, Cleopatra, Faustine, Dolores, Carmilla, Lilith, Salome, and Helen. As the allusiveness of so many of Her names suggests, She is from the first a version of the divine sorceress, one of those magical daughters of the Goddess—Morgan Le Faye, Duessa, Isolde of the White Hands, Medea, Circe—whose mystical powers deprive man of *his* powers. But She is a different being now from the woman She was in medieval France or ancient Greece or for John Mandeville. Almost completely absent from literary history for some hundred years or more, She is gradually reimagined by the nineteenth century in response to circumstances that drastically revise Her nature.

For one thing, though She is thought to be immortal or nearly so, She is now located far more specifically in and through history than before. Indeed, She is now characteristically described in such a way that writer and reader seem to discover, almost simultaneously, that (even if invisible or unrecognized) She has always been there, making history or quietly subverting it. As the Paterian icon on whom Wilde and Yeats brooded, after all, "she has been dead many times, and learned the secrets of the grave; . . . and, as Leda, was the mother of Helen of Troy, and, as Saint Anne, the mother of Mary." But considerably earlier, as Keats's Belle Dame, She evokes visionary generations of "death pale" kings and princes, and later, as Yeats's own female "Rose of the World," She has endured while, because of Her, "Troy passed away in one high funeral gleam, / And Usna's children died." As Swinburne's Faustine, too, She is a woman whose "bitter and vicious loveliness" suggests "the transmigration of a single soul . . . through many ages and forms"; as his Venus, She is traced through ancient times to the Renaissance; and as his Cleopatra, "Under those low large lids of hers / She hath the histories of all time" while "her lips / Hold fast the face of things to be." Thus, as Harold Bloom has observed about Pater's Gioconda, in a remark that helps illuminate her significance to Yeats, She customarily "carries the seal of a terrible priority" so that She is perceived in and behind the forces of history like a half-concealed fatality, a secret cause that transcends and transforms the currents of events.[12]

Paradoxically concealed and revealed by history, Her power and Her secrecy are also manifested by Her command of an enigmatic language. Coleridge's Geraldine communicates with ghosts and hypnotizes Christabel with "shrunken serpent eyes." Swinburne's Cleopatra reads "the ravelled riddle of the skies" as well as "the shape and shadow of mystic things." Macdonald's Lilith tells "a tale about herself, in a language so strange and in forms so shadowy, that I [the narrator] could but here and there understand a little." Keats's Belle Dame speaks, of course, a "language strange," and even Pater's silent Gioconda becomes, herself, a term in an untranslatable vocabulary, for her "unfathomable" smile graphically expresses "strange thoughts and fantastic reveries and exquisite passions."[13] Because She expresses such passions, however, She often stalks apart "in joyless reverie," and thus She becomes a kind of neo-Byronic heroine, tormented by a wounded consciousness, a mysterious inner hell from which, given Her apparent immortality, She can find no release.[14]

Such suffering is first dramatized by the "stricken look" and "sick assay" of Coleridge's Geraldine and then by the tears and sighs of Keats's Belle Dame as well as by the darting ferocity of her "wild wild eyes." But among Romantic figures it is perhaps most strikingly revealed by Keats's unveiled Moneta, who incarnates a sickness that *is* an alien consciousness, a "high tragedy / In the dark secret chambers of her skull." Later in the century, however, Swinburne's, Macdonald's, and Wilde's heroines experience equally dreadful agonies of the spirit. Perverse desires torment Swinburne's Faustine, his Dolores, and the Sappho of his "Anactoria," while powerful memories afflict his Cleopatra. Terrible hungers obsess Macdonald's Lilith; and such morbid passions rage in Wilde's Salome that her deeds seem to guarantee the dangers implicit in Sappho's words and Faustine's face. By the fin de siècle, in fact, as Wilde's *Salome* suggests, She has become a creature burdened by a consciousness so brimming with its own excess that She can only express the torment of self-awareness in a willed erotic annihilation of Her beloved. Thus, although, as Keats observes of Moneta, She Herself experiences "an immortal sickness which kills not," it does often rouse Her to destroy or devour precisely that obdurate otherness which first awakened Her desire.[15]

Because Her consciousness is not only fierce but alien, though, and because She speaks a "language strange" while appearing in history only obliquely, She is almost always understood to inhabit odd spaces— underground caverns, shadowy corners, and labyrinthine passages— the interstices of "reality." Venus, of course, lives "under the hill," as Swinburne and Beardsley learned most notably from Wagner, but La Belle Dame also inhabits "An elfin grot," which, as Praz observed, adumbrates the geography of *Tannhäuser*,[16] while even Lilith, Salome, and Swinburne's many perverse heroines dwell just on the other side of the ordinary world. The earth beneath which Venus, La Belle Dame, and their lovers move, moreover, is really no more than a kind of veil, a dark but prosaic surface that conceals them from everyone but the initiate. Thus, this deceptive outer layer is analogous to the "silken robe" that clothes the "mark" of Geraldine's "shame," the veils that shroud Moneta, the (punningly) "great grave beauty" that "covers" Cleopatra, the face that "suits" Faustine "for her soul's screen," and the "cold eye-lids that hide like a jewel" the strange "hard eyes" of Dolores.[17] At the same time, however, the apparent innocence, or anyway neutrality, of all these surfaces, veils, and screens links them to the doors, mirrors, and bookshelves which open to admit Macdonald to Lilith's realm; to the secret drawers that let him into the predominantly female fairyland of *Phantastes;* and to the cistern from which Wilde's John the Baptist emerges into Salome's murderous, moon-haunted realm.

She is there, say Wilde and Keats, Pater and Swinburne, Macdonald and Beardsley, on the other side of mirrors, paintings, bookcases: un-der the hill of reality. And She is there in continents that during the nineteenth century became increasingly accessible to European explor-ers, "underdeveloped" continents where ordinary trade and compar-atively ordinary geographical research inevitably became entwined with Her extraordinary existence. Rider Haggard located Her under a mountain in the heart of an African darkness. As we shall see, his por-trait of Her strikingly integrates all the details we have outlined here even while his plot neutralizes Her powers through a defensive maneu-ver that was to become a common strategy with which turn-of-the-cen-tury male writers confronted and combated Her land, Her language, Her history.

Though the most extraordinary events of *She* occur in Africa, the novel that tells Her story opens, prosaically enough, in an English uni-versity town "which for the purposes of this history we will call Cam-bridge,"[18] and opens, too, by presenting a series of just the kinds of ancient manuscripts that scholars study in English university towns. Starting with an "editor" who claims once to have seen the fabulously handsome Leo Vincey and his homely guardian Ludwig Horace Holly on a "Cambridge" street, the novelist authenticates his narrative through the traditional device of reporting the mysterious appearance of a manuscript in his morning mail. Even from the first pages of the "Ed-itor's Introduction," however, Haggard's contrivance of the fictional-ized scholarly apparatus with which he surrounds this manuscript is especially expert. Informational footnotes to Holly's narrative, illustra-tive diagrams, sample quotations, and realistically representative typographies create an illusion of historicity so intricate that the reader is quickly entangled in the web of alternative history that is Her story. In particular, though, this illusion is created by the tracing of Leo Vin-cey's lineage to an ancestor mentioned in Herodotus's account of the *Persian Wars,* and by the successive translations of the ancestral tale inscribed on the so-called "sherd of Amenartas" with which Holly and

Leo are ceremonially presented on the young man's twenty-fifth birthday.

The story the sherd tells is about the ill-fated romance of an Egyptian priest of Isis called Kallikrates, whose "grandfather or greatgrandfather . . . was that very Kallikrates mentioned by Herodotus" (9). And as if to demonstrate Holly's (and his own) ability to deploy an expert *patrius sermo* or "father speech" which might ward off from the start the onslaughts of the female "other," Haggard repeats the account in uncial Greek, cursive Greek, "medieval Black-Letter Latin," "Expanded" medieval Latin, and modern English.[19] That in Book IX of his chronicle Herodotus really does mention a "Callicrates" who was "the most beautiful man . . . in the whole Greek camp" gives uncanny solidity to Leo's heritage.[20] That the misadventures of this grandson or greatgrandson of Callicrates have been recorded in every major western classical language makes them appear even more compellingly substantial. Moreover, the secondary texts that surround Leo's history, mainly philological analyses and historical commentaries, further guarantee the tale's authenticity. In a conversation with Holly, for instance, Leo's dying father traces the etymology of the name "Vincey" from the Greek "Tisisthenes," meaning "Mighty Avenger," through "the cognomen of Vindex" to its modern form of Vincey, "the final corruption of the name after its bearers took root in English soil" (11). Just as impressively, a series of signatures and inscriptions on the sherd and on some parchments that Leo inherits along with it express the feelings of Kallikrates' descendants in Latin, Old English, Elizabethan English, and various other scripts.

Earlier, Holly had remarked that "It is curious to observe how this hereditary duty of revenge, bequeathed by an Egyptian who lived before the time of Christ, is . . . , as it were, embalmed in an English family name" (34). But in this novel where embalming frequently becomes both theme and subject, it is not just "the hereditary duty of revenge" that is embalmed in language. Rather, given the elaborate parodic scholarship and self-reflexive historicity with which Haggard presents his tale, it is the story itself which (or so we are persuaded) has been embalmed in received history and conventional language. Encountering the "sherd of Amenartas," therefore, we pass to the other side of *The Persian Wars* and discover an alternative history that has all along been mummified in Herodotus's official chronicle. With Leo Vincey and Horace Holly, we learn that implicit in the patriarchal account of battles that shook (or seem to have shaped) "the dawn" of modern civilization was this disquieting history of another force: a country ruled by a passionate and murderous woman.

To be accurate, the story the sherd tells is the record of a struggle between *two* women—the Egyptian princess Amenartas and the powerful white queen Ayesha, also known as *She-who-must-be-obeyed*—for the love of "Kallikrates (the Beautiful in Strength)." This descendant of Herodotus's handsome soldier broke his vows of celibacy to Isis in order to elope with Amenartas, but after a shipwreck and many other misadventures he and his lover found themselves in the domain of Ayesha, who is described in the sherd as being, mysteriously enough, "the Queen of the people who place pots upon the heads of strangers" as well as "a magician having knowledge of all things, and life and loveliness that does not die" (31). When Ayesha, too, falls in love with Kallikrates, the two women enter into a struggle that does not end until all three have journeyed to the secret place of "the rolling Pillar of Life," where Kallikrates definitively rejects Ayesha, and She, in a rage, "smites [and kills] him by her magic" (32). Amenartas's own "magic" has made her impervious to the queen's murderous impulses, so that Ayesha, in fear, sends her back into the world, where she gives birth to the first vengeful Tisisthenes and finally dies in Athens, after inscribing her history on the potsherd that Leo Vincey will inherit more than two thousand years later.

The mission he receives along with this extraordinary heirloom is both dramatic and unequivocal: "seek out the woman, and learn the secret of Life, and if thou mayest find a way slay her" (34). But it is also surely significant that Leo's quest is not only *for* a woman, it is in behalf of a woman. Both his goal and its impetus, therefore, suggest his secondariness and instrumentality. Indeed, even the male lineage whose burden (and beauty) Leo inherits implies his own potential impotence, for he is obliged to undertake this quest only because all of his forefathers, throughout most of recorded history, have failed in it. This last point is particularly emphasized by a haunting letter that Leo receives from his dead father when he opens the casket containing the sherd and attendant parchments: "Through this link of pen and paper . . . my voice speaks to you from the silence of the grave" (28), Leo's father has written, and he goes on to confess both his failure in the quest and his decision to commit suicide in grief over the death of yet another woman, Leo's mother.

At first, however, as Leo and his aggressively misogynistic guardian, Horace Holly, begin their journey, they do not seem to be adventuring into a realm whose strangeness inheres primarily in its femaleness. Certainly a conventional enough shipwreck flings the pair, along with their servant Job and an Arab named Mahomed, onto just the shore where Kallikrates and Amenartas had been cast twenty-two centuries earlier. And the coast itself offers a standard adventure story setting, complete with wild beasts, fever-inducing mists, and mysterious ruins. One of these ruins, though, is "a great rock carven like the head of an Ethiopian" (31) mentioned both by Amenartas and Leo's father. Monumental as Egypt's Sphinx, this object looms over the harbor like an emblem of strange thought that looks "devilish" to the xenophobic travelers, suggesting that they are about to enter a perverse and satanic domain.

As the men make their way inland, through vaporous marshes and stagnant canals, the landscape across which they journey seems increasingly like a Freudianly female *paysage moralisé*. When they are finally captured by a band of natives whose leader is a biblical-looking Arab called "Father," the explorers are lifted into litters in which, captives though they are, they yield to a "pleasant swaying motion" (82) and, in a symbolic return to the womb, they are carried up ancient swampy birth canals through a rocky defile into "a vast cup of earth" (82) that is ruled by *She-who-must-be-obeyed* and inhabited by a people called the Amahaggar. About these people, moreover, they soon learn that

> in direct opposition to the habits of almost every other savage race in the world, women among the Amahaggar live upon conditions of perfect equality with the men, and are not held to them by any binding ties. Descent is traced only through the line of the mother, and while individuals are as proud of a long and superior female ancestry as we are of our families in Europe, they never pay attention to, or even acknowledge, any man as their father, even when their male parentage is perfectly well known. [85]

Given the brief appearance of Leo's ancestor, Callicrates, in Herodotus's history of the Persian Wars, it is notable that there is an eerie correspondence between the strange land of the Amahaggar and the perverse Egypt Herodotus describes, a country whose people,

> in most of their manners and customs, exactly reverse the common practice of mankind. The women attend the markets and trade, while the men sit at home at the loom; and here, while the rest of the world works the woof up the warp, the Egyptians work it down; the women, likewise, carry burdens upon their shoulders, while the men carry them upon their heads. Women stand up to urinate, men sit down.[21]

Though the details of Egyptian and Amahaggar peculiarities are not the same, in each case the country is described as uniquely alien, and alien in particular because relations between its men and women inhabitants are antithetical to those that prevail in "normal" civilized societies. Thus both Egypt and Kôr, as Haggard's explorers learn the Amahaggar land is called, are realms where the matriarchal rule that most cultures define as disorderly, indeed "unnatural," has been shockingly legitimized.

The alarming misrule that the Amahaggar share with Herodotus's ancient Egyptians reminds us that Callicrates' grandson or greatgrandson, Kallikrates, was a priest bound by terrible vows to the Egyptian goddess Isis. When he escaped those vows, moreover, he journeyed from one alien country into a realm of even fiercer misrule, almost as though the vengeance of the goddess were pursuing him. That Leo is soon seen not only as an heir but as a reincarnation of this Kallikrates strengthens our sense of his secondariness: in coming to Kôr he has fallen into the power of women, becoming, like so many men before him, a helpless stranger in Her strange land. When he is chosen as a husband by an aristocratic Amahaggar woman who seems in both her nature and her culture like a reincarnation of the royal Amenartas, we are persuaded of the ineradicability of his family's doom. Not only must the female be obeyed, so must the fate that makes the Vinceys her victims. Periodically returning these male travelers to the womb of Africa, the wheel of reincarnation enforces a sort of hideous repetition compulsion, a masculine inability to struggle free of woman's power.

She-who-must-be-obeyed, however, manifests the severity of Her misrule only after some delay. At first, it is Her subjects who express the murderous female sexuality that She Herself tends to deny. Thus we learn before meeting Her what it means for Her to be the queen of a people who, bizarrely, "place pots upon the heads of strangers" (31), for shortly after the explorers arrive in Kôr they are invited to a feast at which a group of the Amahaggar try to kill the Englishmen's Arab guide, Mahomed, by putting a red hot earthen pot on his head. This astonishing mode of execution, a cross between cooking and decapitation which seems to have had no real anthropological precedent, is such a vivid enactment of both castration fears and birth anxieties that it is hardly necessary to rehearse all its psychosymbolic overtones. Yet the sexual symbolism becomes almost comical, as if Haggard had deliberately transcribed a nightmare vision of sexual intercourse, when—just before the victim's head is supposed to be devoured by a fiery female symbol—the cannibalistic Amahaggar ceremony prescribes that he should be seduced into submission by a particularly voluptuous woman, who must "pretend . . . that he [is] the object of love and admiration [and thereby] cause him to expire in a happy and contented frame of mind" (106).[22]

But if the hotpotting episode is grotesquely sexual in its elaboration of the ways in which female misrule can cause a vessel associated with domesticity to become as deadly as woman's anatomy seems in the worst male nightmares, the inner landscape of Kôr itself is both more melodramatically sexual and more unnervingly historical. *She-who-must-be-obeyed* inhabits a great cave in the wall of an extinct volcano whose "vast ancient crater" holds countless exotic birds, beasts, and flowers as well as the "colossal ruins" of the city of Kôr. As Holly describes it, moreover, entering her domain is at least as symbolic as being hotpotted, though (in several senses) graver. Blindfolded, the explorers are carried (again) on litters "into the bowels of the great mountain . . . an eerie sensation, that of being borne into the dead heart of the rock we knew not whither" (137). Their destination is just as eerie, for the cavern palace where She dwells is both luxurious and sepulchral, half a set of elegant apartments "under the hill," like the Venusberg of Wagner's *Tannhäuser* or Swinburne's "Laus Veneris," and half a set of "vast catacombs," a sort of Hades where "the mortal remains of the great extinct race whose monuments surrounded us had been first preserved, with an art and a completeness that have never since been equalled, and then hidden away for all time" (142).

She Herself, therefore, turns out to be an interesting cross between Venus and Persephone. As Venus, for instance, She commands the absolute erotic devotion of any man who looks upon Her unveiled. When She removes her wrappings, Holly sees Her as "Venus Victrix" (163), as Circe (167), and as "Aphrodite triumphing" in "that dear pleasure which is [Her] sex's only right" (199)—the pleasure of bringing a man to his knees in adoration of Her sexuality. But even swathed in ghostly white, She has the Circean power of transforming human males into animals. Visitors are supposed to crawl in Her presence, and though the Englishmen refuse to abase themselves, they are reduced to their beastly essences by new, animal names that they are given during their stay in Her land. Holly becomes "the Baboon," Leo "the Lion," and the servant Job "the Pig," and their animalism is further emphasized by the fact that they eat meat and milk while She sustains Herself only on fruit and water.

While She is as voluptuous as Venus, however, She is also a Persephone, married to death and queen in a country of shadows. Shrouded in a "white and gauzy material" that makes Her look like "a corpse in its grave-clothes" (149), She judges and condemns the hapless Amahaggar with the lucid indifference of eternity, explaining that "those who live long . . . have no passions save where they have interests" (185). For recreation, She takes Her visitors on a tour of Her domain, a "whole mountain peopled with the dead, and nearly all of them perfect" (179). Besides commanding a realm of tombs and ruins, She has spent, it soon appears, more than twenty necrophiliac centuries watching, praying, cursing, and sleeping by the side of the dead Kallikrates, who has been miraculously preserved in a secret catacomb. Finally Kôr, the name of the dead city she rules, links Her even more definitively to the bride of Dis, for Persephone is also, after all, called *Koré* or *Kora*. But the ambiguity of the word *Kôr* emphasizes in addition the crucial ambiguity of the city's queen. Ruling this domain which is at the *core* or heart of the earth, *She-who-must-be-obeyed* is part a *Kore* collecting *corpses* in the "dead heart of the rock" and part a Venus collecting *coeurs* or hearts, and seducing or enchanting the flesh that is the living *corpus* of the earth.

In Her striking duality, then, She transcends the traditional archetypes of Venus and Persephone to become a resonant amalgam of their collective attributes. Such early and middle twentieth-century psychoanalysts as Jung, Freud, and Nandor Fodor responded to Her enigmatic complexity by arguing in ahistorical terms that She is a perfect incarnation of the "anima," a type of the "Ewig-Weibliche," or a fantasy vision of the "Beloved" extrapolated from prenatal memories. More recent critics, among them Henry Miller, Morton Cohen, Norman Etherington and Nina Auerbach, have made similar, if sometimes more historical, arguments, relating Her to fin de siècle visions of the unconscious or to eternal male desires for eternal female beauty.[23] But precisely the contradictions and complexities that interest so many of these readers suggest that She is primarily an avatar of the femme fatale who haunted writers from Coleridge, Keats, and Swinburne to Pater, Wilde, Macdonald, and ultimately Yeats, so much so that Her character in a sense summarizes and intensifies all the key traits these artists brooded on.

Having lived under the hill of ordinary reality since classical antiquity, for instance, She chats familiarly about Greek and Arab philosophers with the bemused Holly; clearly, like Pater's Gioconda, She has "learned the secrets of the grave . . . and trafficked . . . with Eastern merchants." Wherever she studied, moreover, She acquired strange herbal wisdom, esoteric healing powers, and arcane alchemical knowledge. In addition, because She is a connoisseur of a language strange as that spoken by Keats's Belle Dame, only She can decipher the writing on the walls of the tombs among which She lives, and She has surrounded Herself with mute servants whose handicap She Herself has bred, depriving an entire lineage of language so that no one will speak Her secrets. Nevertheless, despite Her supernatural powers, She is tormented by desire and regret, burdened like Macdonald's Lilith, Swinburne's Sappho, or Wilde's Salome by an alien consciousness. Like Moneta, moreover, She is condemned to the perpetual repetition of a terrible psychodrama in the "dark secret chambers of her skull," while, as Henry Miller puts it, "Jealousy, manifesting itself in a tyrannical will, in an insatiable love of power, burns in her with the brightness of a funeral

pyre."[24] Finally, indeed, one suspects that just as the name *Kôr* applies
at least as much to Her as to the lost city She rules, the name *Kallikrates*
has as much to do with Her as with the dead priest who was Her victim.
For, like *Kali*, the Indian goddess of destruction, She is murderous:
She condemns men quickly and casually to death by torture and is capable of "blasting" those she dislikes with a Medusan glance. In Kallikrates' first incarnation, She murdered him, and now, in his second,
She murders the Amahaggar woman who seems to be a reincarnation
of Her hated rival.

Like the Indian god Brahm, however, or like the Great Mother as
Neumann and others have defined her, She is not merely a destroyer;
because She is a combined Persephone and Venus, She is a destroyer
and a preserver.[25] In fact, She has evidently learned many of Her techniques of preservation from the dead priests of Kôr, and perhaps the
most peculiar feature of Haggard's discussion of Her kingdom is his
ruminative, obsessive, even at times necrophiliac interest in the mummies that surround Her as well as the embalming techniques through
which they have been preserved. From the royal tombs She and Her
visitors tour to the little white mummified foot the servile Arab "Father" Billali carries with him everywhere like an erotic good luck charm,
the dead are ubiquitous in Kôr. The Englishmen are shown a "pit about
the size of the space beneath the dome of St. Paul's" (190) filled with
the bones of Kôr-dwellers, and they peer voyeuristically into chambers
occupied by beautiful embalmed bodies, including a pair of lovers clasped
in a quasi-sexual embrace beneath the inscription "Wedded in Death"
(194). Even more bizarrely, they regularly dine in a cave decorated by
bas-reliefs that show it was used by the priests of Kôr for embalming as
well as eating, and they are invited to a ceremonial feast at which the
torches are flaming human mummies as well as the severed limbs of
those mummies. In Kôr, even the arms and legs of the dead become
significant fragments with which She illuminates Her ruins.

The literal as well as metaphorical piling up of all this dead flesh
reminds us, of course, that the womb of the Great Mother is also a
tomb. But such mysterious preservation of the flesh also implies other
and perhaps more uncanny points, for, as Haggard presents it
throughout *She,* the very idea of embalming paradoxically evokes anxieties about both the ordinary world the Englishmen represent and the
extraordinary realm She rules. The mummy-crowded tombs of Kôr,
for instance, hint that dead history may still be willfully present in the
living moment. Just as Amenartas's vengeful imperative was "embalmed" in the apparently ordinary modern name of Vincey, so the
quests and failures of Leo's "ordinary" ancestors are embalmed in Leo.
In a sense, indeed, the mountain of death in which he finds himself is

like a huge vessel on which the message of the sherd has been rein-scribed: tombs full of enigmatic corpses and indecipherable hiero-glyphs suggest the haunting persistence of the past, the affliction of history, the burden of ancestry. Worse still, like the wheel of reincar-nation, with its perpetual repetition of the same characters and the same messages, the mummies evoke the dread associated with the imagined persistence of the self through history and thus the nausea of belatedness.

At the same time, however, the unnatural practices that have pre-served the mummies evoke an unnatural culture—not just Herodotus's peculiar Egypt but also the strange Egypt that was being diligently studied in the nineteenth century. More metaphysically, the alien opac-ity, inertness and silence of the lifelike but embalmed bodies quite lit-erally incarnate the horror of otherness and specifically the horror of the body that is other than one's own and therefore opaque to one's thought. Indeed, Haggard's romance of the Great Mother may secretly imagine the same connection between mummies (as bodies) and mum-mies (as mothers) that Mary Shelley's *Frankenstein* makes.[26] Certainly Ayesha is both powerful Mother Goddess and shrouded mummy. In fact, She Herself seems to be the most theatrical example of unnatural preservation that we encounter in the book that tells Her story. More than two thousand years old, She has been embalmed alive. Herself both destroyer and preserver, She has been spectacularly preserved. But She lacks the crucial third ability of creation, and She lacks the ultimate power of *self*-preservation. Implicit in such lacks is the spectac-ular moment of Her destruction, a sexual climax that can be defined as a sort of apocalyptic primal scene.

Perhaps inevitably, She is destroyed by the very flame of life that has heretofore preserved Her (and which at one time presumably created Her). Ironically, too, She is destroyed because of her lover, though not—at least not overtly—because of any ill will on his part. Wishing to share her magic longevity, She has brought the Englishmen on a quasi-sexual journey even more perilous than the approach to Her kingdom or to Her palace at Kôr. After crossing a terrible abyss and crawling down narrow winding passages, the explorers have at last reached the secret "place of Life," a rosily glowing cavern that is "the very womb of the Earth, wherein she doth conceive the Life that ye see brought forth in man and beast" (299). Here, She promises the Englishmen, "ye shall be born anew!" And here, quite unexpectedly, in a consummation that seems to be the opposite of what anyone would wish, She is annihilated by the "rolling pillar of Life" that has previously preserved Her.

Wishes for Ayesha's destruction, however, have been carefully cultivated in the chapters that precede the catastrophe in the "place of Life," for Her actions and ambitions are shown to become increasingly Satanic as the novel progresses and Her fatal attraction to Her lover, as well as Her willful desire for complete possession of him, gathers energy. In the chapter called "Triumph," for instance, She "blasts" Leo's Amahaggar wife Ustane, and when he protests Her deed, She "blasts" him too, with slightly less force but fiercely enough so that he feels "utterly cowed, as if all the manhood had been taken out of him" (234). Worse still, She follows up this sexual insult by tearing away her veils and seducing the unwilling Leo, so that, "with the corpse of his dead love for an altar [he plights] his troth to [this] red-handed murderess . . . for ever and a day" (239). Worst of all, within twenty-four hours of this grisly seduction scene, She is planning, like some monstrous anti-Victoria, to "assume absolute rule over the British dominions and probably over the whole earth" (267). "It might be possible to control her for a while," speculates Holly,

> but her proud ambitious spirit would be certain to break loose and avenge itself for the long centuries of solitude . . . [She] was now about to be used by Providence as a means to change the order of the world . . . by the building up of a power that could no more be rebelled against or questioned than the decrees of Fate. [267–268]

This "power," as Holly and Leo soon learn, is not only in its aims but in its origin illegitimate, because, like most diabolical capabilities, it has been usurped. En route to the "place of Life," Ayesha reveals that it was actually a hermit-philosopher called Noot who discovered the miraculous fire, and She, then authentically young and beautiful, charmed him into sharing its secrets.[27] The terrible punishment in store for such a transgression begins to emerge when She and Her companions reach an abyss that they must cross on a narrow plank. Plunged into darkness for most of every day, this gulf can only be bridged when, passing though a cleft in the rock, "like a great sword of flame, a beam from the setting sun [pierces] the Stygian gloom" (285). The moment of illumination that follows, says Holly, is exhilarating, for "Right through the heart of the darkness that flaming sword was stabbed" (285). Prefiguring phallic weapons of light and hearts of darkness in works by Haggard's literary descendants from Conrad to Lawrence, Holly's imagery also both illuminates and foreshadows Ayesha's doom. For She is, metaphorically speaking, destroyed during a moment of unholy intercourse with the phallic "pillar of Life" whose sexual comings and goings, the Englishmen now discover, eternally shake the secret "womb of Earth." Thus

She Herself represents a "heart of darkness" into which the flaming sword of patriarchal justice must be ritually stabbed.[28]

The "rolling pillar of Life" that brings Haggard's romance to its apocalyptic climax is an almost theatrically rich sexual symbol. At regular intervals, it appears with a "grinding and crashing noise . . . rolling down like all the thunderwheels of heaven behind the horses of the lightning" (300–301) and, as it enters the cave, it flames out "an awful cloud or pillar of fire, like a rainbow many colored," whose very presence causes Holly to rejoice "in [the] splendid vigor of a new-found self" (301). Both Alexander Grinstein and Nandor Fodor claim that (for obvious reasons) it represents the sexual energy of the Father, with Fodor going so far as to argue that its powerfully persistent, rhythmic return into the rosy cave draws upon prenatal memories to depict parental sexuality from the point of view of the unborn child.[29] Be this as it may, it seems clear from the pillar's celestial radiance and regenerative power that this perpetually erect symbol of masculinity is not just a Freudian penis but a Lacanian phallus, a fiery signifier whose eternal thundering return speaks the inexorability of the patriarchal law She has violated in Her Satanically overreaching ambition.

Like the stars whose imperturbable order defeats Lucifer in George Meredith's "Lucifer in Starlight," this phallus comes and goes on an "ancient track," indifferent, omnipotent.[30] Like the "pillar of fire by night" that helps Moses lead the children of Israel out of an Egypt even more perverse than Herodotus's, it expresses the will of the divine Father, and in doing so it will lead Holly and Leo out of Her degrading land back into the kingdom of their own proper masculinity.[31] Flaming out "like a rainbow many colored," it also recalls the covenantal rainbow of Genesis, and thus it becomes, in a sense, the pillar of society, an incarnate sign of the covenant among men (and between men and a symbolic Father) that is the founding gesture of patriarchal culture.[32] In addition, as a powerful male sexual symbol, it comments dramatically upon the less powerful female symbols deployed by the Amahaggar in the earlier hotpotting episode, for it is radiant, insubstantial, transcendent, where the hot pots were inert, earthen, grotesque. In fact, the novelist Henry Miller grasps the purpose of this pillar of fire more accurately than those psychoanalysts who have emphasized its Freudian function at the expense of its Lacanian signification, perhaps because of his belief (which we discussed in *The War of the Words*) that "the eternal battle with women . . . enlarges the scope of our cultural achievements."[33] Ayesha's fate, Miller notes, "is not death, indeed . . . but reduction," and he adds that "one is privileged, as it were, to assist at the spectacle of Nature reclaiming . . . the secret which had been stolen."[34] As Harold Bloom observes of Pater's Gioconda, Ayesha "incarnates too much, both for her own good and [from a masculinist point of view] for ours."[35] Finally, therefore, naked and ecstatic, in all the pride of Her femaleness, She must be fucked to death by the "unalterable law" of the Father.

As Miller also notes, however, Ayesha's defeat is not really a death or even a "reduction" but, quite literally, a "devolution."[36] If She has incarnated "more than was good for her, or for us," Her very flesh is punished for such presumption. As She passes through the stages of Her unlived life, aging two thousand years in a few minutes, the language strange of Her beauty shreds and flakes away, Her power wrinkles, Her magic dries up, and the meaning of Her "terrible priority" is revealed as degeneration rather than generativity. The Mosaic reality behind the false commandments of *She-who-must-be-obeyed*, Holly and Leo learn, is and always was a bald, blind, naked, shapeless, infinitely wrinkled female animal, "no larger than a big ape," who raises herself "upon her bony hands . . . swaying her head slowly from side to side as does a tortoise" (308). More terrible than the transformations of Dr. Jekyll or Dorian Gray, this reduction or devolution of goddess to beast is the final judgment upon Her pride and ambition. "Thus She opposed herself to the eternal law," concludes Holly, "and, strong though she was, by it was swept back into nothingness—swept back with shame and hideous mockery" (309).

In Ayesha's shame and in fate's mockery of Her, Holly also observes, he sees "the finger of Providence." For—and here he begins to articulate the secret fear that really energizes Haggard's fantasy—"Ayesha locked up in her living tomb, waiting from age to age for the coming of her lover, worked but a small change in the order of the world. But Ayesha strong and happy in her love, clothed with immortal youth, godlike beauty, and power, and the wisdom of the centuries, would have revolutionised society, and even perchance have changed the destinies of Mankind" (309). As Miller, again most astutely, puts it: with Ayesha's defeat, "Isis, to whom she had sworn eternal devotion, will be no more."[37] When She dies, therefore, Holly and Leo—and Haggard—bear witness not just to the death of a mortal woman but to the annihilation of the goddess, the deconstruction even of the idea of the goddess.[38]

———

She was not only a turn-of-the-century bestseller but also, in a number of dramatic ways, one of the century's literary turning points, a pivot on which the ideas and anxieties of the Victorians began to swivel into what has come to be called "the modern." Most obviously, this is because Haggard's novel both summarized and transformed the history of the femme fatale whose character so preoccupied the nineteenth century. For although She is a conventionally romantic Belle Dame sans Merci, the stony waste land that She rules is modern in its air of sexual and historical extremity. One of the outposts of "death's dream kingdom," it threatens the living empire of England with dismemberment, fragmentation, incoherence. Ultimately, in fact, it can only be redeemed through a sexual conflagration that is not merely an appropriate but also, for the explorers, a secretly desired climax of the combat that has set so many men and women of this novel so violently against each other.

Like the extreme perversity of Her land, however, this erotic apocalypse represents a crucial revision of earlier depictions of the femme fatale, in which it had become a sort of nineteenth-century tradition for the Circean woman to survive and triumph. Even Flaubert's notorious Salammbô only swoons to death *after* she has witnessed the hideous torture-execution of her lover, Mâtho. On the surface, indeed, it seems as if most of Haggard's precursors could barely begin to imagine the death of the goddess, so enthralled were they by her magic and so dependent on her charms. But perhaps, too, those charms, sinister as they often seemed, had not yet become so threatening that a serious defense against them was required: the *femmes* of Keats and Swinburne may not have seemed quite *fatale* enough to be condemned to death themselves. *She,* however, was associated with a new era in the fictionalizing of female power. Certainly in England the ceremonial sexual act that brought about Her "reduction" or "devolution" was followed by a number of similar scenes in fin-de-siècle and modernist tales.[39]

Most striking, because most shocking in their late Victorian context, are the ritual slaughters that conclude some of the fantasies about female power that were published in the decade after *She* appeared. The most theatrical of these is no doubt the climactic moment in Bram Stoker's *Dracula* (1897), when, on what would have been the first day of their marriage, the noble Englishman Arthur Holmwood drives a phallic stake into the dark heart of his "Un-Dead" fiancée Lucy Westenra. The body, Stoker tells us in what emerges as a masterpiece of double entendre, "shook and quivered and twisted in wild contortions; the sharp white teeth champed together till the lips were cut and the mouth was smeared with a crimson foam."[40] But finally, a "holy calm" succeeds the tumult in the coffin. In thrall to Dracula, Lucy was also an emissary of the goddess, for the body of the Transylvanian count had been borne mysteriously back and forth across the English Channel in ships called the *Demeter* and the *Czarina Catherine,* as if he were an embalmed inhabitant of Kôr, part of the cargo that *She-who-must-be-obeyed* would import if She could reach the British Isles. Staked, beheaded, and stuffed with garlic like some savory roast meat, however, Lucy is definitively screwed into her coffin, neutralized. Now "No longer is she the devil's Un-Dead," murmurs kindly Dr. Van Helsing. "She is God's true dead, whose soul is with Him!"[41]

Similarly, in Macdonald's *Lilith* (1895) the vampire princess Lilith must be mutilated—specifically, she must have her hand chopped off—in a symbolic defloration-and-castration scene, so that she can "sleep the sleep."[42] Preternaturally gleaming, Adam's ancient sword is as Lacanian a phallus as the "rolling pillar of Life," for, explains the Father of mankind, "the angel gave it me when he left the gate."[43] After it flashes toward Lilith, therefore, there is "one little gush of blood" and in a minute this archetypal female rebel is both peaceful and powerless.

Again, though it is far more self-reflexive and ironic, Wilde's *Salome* (1894) hints at such a denouement, for after the depraved daughter of Herodias destroys two men—the "young Syrian" and John the Baptist—another man avenges their wrongs and restores patriarchal order, in a crucial swerve from the story outlined in the New Testament.[44] "Kill that woman!" exclaims the hitherto unkingly Herod in the last line of the play and, just as Salome is indulging her unholy desire for the head of Jokanaan, "the soldiers rush forward" and "crush beneath their shields Salome, daughter of Herodias, Princess of Judaea."[45] Salome's unnatural power is expressed in the qualifying phrase that emphasizes her matrilineal descent—"*daughter* of *Herodias*"—as if to explain precisely what must be crushed out of her, and why. And significantly, though her destruction is commanded by one man it is finally a communal act, performed not by a single executioner but by a band of men acting in unison.

Perhaps the most apocalyptic act of this sort, an act of destruction more divine than communal, is the quasi-scientific but really cosmic annihilation of the femme fatale that concludes Bram Stoker's *The Lair of the White Worm* (1911), a fantasy far less well-known (and less skillful) than *Dracula* which nevertheless reiterates the themes of the earlier novel and of *She* in, if possible, even more flagrantly "Freudian" terms. Like Ayesha, like Keats's Lamia and dozens of other femmes fatales, Lady Arabella March, the villainess of this book, has strange and deadly powers. Specifically, she has become an avatar of a gigantic White Worm, a "monster of the early days of the world" that lives in a well-hole on her ancient estate, Diana's Grove, and "be she woman or snake or devil" she must be destroyed.[46] But the task is not an easy one. A paradigmatic phallic woman, Lady Arabella is seductively feminine, with, in her human guise, a "sinuous figure" (29) and a voice of hissing sweetness, and, at the same time, monstrously masculine, appearing in her White Worm form as "a long white pole, . . . an immense towering mass . . . tall and thin, . . . a tall white shaft" (143). Admits Stoker's hero, who is (appropriately enough) named Adam,

> I never thought this fighting an antediluvian monster would be such a complicated job. This one is a woman, with all a woman's wit, combined with the heartlessness of a *cocotte*. She has the strength and impregnability of a diplodocus. We may be sure that in the fight that is before us there will be no semblance of fair-play . . . [135]

His comrades-in-arms agree, and one offers a battle plan that succinctly summarizes the strategies deployed by the heroes of all these books: "Now, Adam, it strikes me that, as we have to protect ourselves and others against feminine nature, our strong game will be to play our masculine against her feminine" (135).

Ultimately, "play[ing] our masculine against her feminine" is what Stoker's heroes do, at least in a symbolic sense, for Lady Arabella as both worm and woman is destroyed by a Jovian bolt of lightning which ignites a load of dynamite that her male antagonists have inserted into "her" well-hole. Listening outside Diana's Grove at the height of the retributive thunder storm, Adam and his young bride realize that "*Something* was going on close to them, mysterious, terrible, deadly!" Then, when Lady Arabella's stately home explodes, they witness a virtual orgasm of death as they gaze voyeuristically toward "where the well-hole yawned, a deep narrow circular chasm" from which "agonised shrieks were rising, growing ever more terrible with each second that passed":

> The seething contents of the hole rose, after the manner of a bubbling spring, and Adam saw part of the thin form of Lady Arabella, forced up to the top amid a mass of slime, and what looked as if it had been a monster torn into shreds. . . . At last the explosive power . . . reached the main store of dynamite. . . . The result was appalling. The ground for far around quivered and opened in long, deep chasms. . . . The hole . . . sent up clouds of dust and steam and fine sand mingled . . . which carried an appalling stench. . . . Then almost as quickly as it had begun, the whole cataclysm ceased. [186–187][47]

In the end, Adam and two male mentors victoriously inspect the "hell-broth in the hole." The worm/woman has been swallowed up, and one of the older men declares that "it is quite time" the hero and his bride departed for a postponed honeymoon. As in so many turn-of-the-century fantasies, a group of men have bonded in order to achieve a ceremonial assertion of phallic authority that should free all men from the unmanning enslavement of Her land and return the relations between the sexes to the "proper" balance of male dominance, female submission.[48]

<hr>

To identify the fictionalized anxieties that impel the stories of Ayesha, Lucy, Lilith, Salome, Lady Arabella, and many other powerful women toward a common and uncommonly ferocious denouement is not, however, to understand the history of the psychological and social anxieties that underlie all these texts. What, after all, worried Rider Haggard so much that he was driven to create his extraordinarily complex fantasy about Her and Her realm in just six volcanically energetic weeks? Why did thousands and thousands of English and American readers respond to his dreamlike story of Her with as much fervor as if he had been narrating their own dreams for them and to them? Within a few months after *She* made its first appearance in bookstores, Haggard was *the* literary celebrity of his day both in England and the United States. The critic Walter Besant confessed that he had read the book "in a single night . . . it was impossible while [it] was in my hand to take my eyes from a single page." "Ten thousand readers . . . demand imperatively to know the colour of Mr. Haggard's eyes," reported the American *Literary World*. "Many a provincial lad," recalled J. P. Collins, "rashly [mortgaged] the income of months in order to burst into a bookshop and buy *She*."[49] Why and how did Haggard's romance inspire such enthusiasm?

Of course, like any writer, Haggard had personal reasons for fantasizing the way he did. As a child, for instance, he had actually owned a fierce-looking rag doll that was used by "an unscrupulous nurse" to frighten and bully the terrified boy, who therefore called it *"She-who-must-be-obeyed."* In any case, the young Rider seems to have been shy, dreamy, dull, all qualities that would trigger later anxieties. Of seven sons in his family, only he "was denied a 'proper' schooling" because even his mother, herself a published writer, thought him "as heavy as lead in body and mind."[50] As a young man, moreover, he was painfully jilted by the woman he always considered his true love, the beautiful Lily Jackson, whom members of the Haggard family nicknamed "Lilith." Because such a complex of early private humiliations might well lead to later fantasies about power and powerlessness, it is comparatively easy to trace the personal dynamics that transformed She-the-doll into She-the-goddess or the real man called *Haggard* into the fictional people called the *Amahaggar*. It is easy, too, to see why such a man would have had to convince himself that, like his imperious doll, both his icy beloved and his arrogant goddess might ultimately be nothing more than the collection of pathetic fragments his friend Rudyard Kipling—in a poem tellingly entitled "The Vampire" (1897)—declared that even the most fatal woman was: "a rag and a bone and a hank of hair."[51]

What comparable public dynamics, however, affected not only Haggard himself but *She*'s throngs of eager readers? We want to suggest that the charisma of this novel arose from the fact that the work itself explored and exploited three subtly interrelated late Victorian phenomena: an interest in Egypt and, more generally, a preoccupation with colonized countries and imperial decline; a fascination with spiritualism; and an obsession not just with the so-called New Woman but with striking new visions and re-visions of female power.

As Edward Said has noted, Egypt in the nineteenth century became more than ever a focal point for imperialist anxieties and passions.[52] In the alien, barely decipherable hieroglyphs of its history and in the many mysteries of its ancient and modern religious practices, it must always have seemed to many Europeans to summarize and symbolize, as it had for Herodotus and as—together with Kôr—it did for Haggard, the mystifyingly obdurate power of what we might call geopolitical otherness.[53] But now such otherness was being notably redefined. To begin with, philological analyses undertaken by Champollion on the Rosetta Stone and carried forward by other nineteenth-century Egyptologists started to make definitively clear the range and sophistication of linguistic experience possible even among supposedly "barbaric" races. Similarly, increasingly aggressive exploration of Egyptian and Nubian tombs and pyramids was uncovering the startling extent of what one writer has characterized as "the vast underground network of caverns and burial chambers" in, say, the Theban necropolis and other elaborate burial sites.[54]

No doubt because of this intensified archaeological activity, the practice and processes of mummification—which Europeans had in any case always regarded with awe—had now become subjects of respectful scientific analysis as well as, more than ever before, material for plot and metaphor. In popular literature, tales of mummies' curses and other ancient spells proliferated, while more elite artists, from Giuseppe Verdi (*Aida*, 1871) to Anatole France (*Thaïs*, 1890) and W. B. Yeats, drew in various ways on comparable Egyptian lore. Even in the 1920s and 1930s, Yeats was elaborating Egyptian imagery: the powerful spiritual consciousness he longed to have would be, he wrote, "wound in mind's pondering / As mummies in the mummy cloth are wound," and he metaphorized apocalyptic transformation as "a crop of mummy wheat!"[55]

Finally, as if to reinforce the fascination that such artists felt, the translations of the *Egyptian Book of the Dead* and similar sacred texts that had been begun by E. Wallis Budge and other scholars were also emphasizing the richness of what had long seemed a hopelessly opaque or chaotic theological system, while the new orientalists' studies of Islam clarified what they saw as the dangerous coherence of a creed that had been traditionally defined as "barbaric" and confused. By 1911, former prime minister Arthur James Balfour was lecturing Parliament on the greatness of Egypt and asserting, "We know the civilization of Egypt better than we know the civilization of any other country. We know it further back. . . . It goes far beyond the petty span of the history of our race. . . . Look at all the Oriental countries. Do not talk about superiority or inferiority."[56]

Such attention to ancient Egypt and modern Islam was not an isolated phenomenon. Rather, it was part of a larger surge of philological, archaeological, and anthropological scholarship that was throughout the nineteenth century drastically revising western notions of prehistory, of comparative religion, and of "primitive" social structures. To be sure, as Morse Peckham has observed, a good deal of early scholarship in these fields was based—as Darwin's theory of evolution also was—on an implicitly ethnocentric "chain of being" that subordinated the "primitive" native to the "civilized" westerner so that "the value of anthropology for imperial management should not be underestimated."[57] At the same time, though, Peckham notes that the studies of, for instance, Edward Tylor (whose *Primitive Culture: Researches into the Development of Mythology, Philosophy, Religion, Language, Art, and Custom* [1871] essentially founded modern anthropology) revealed significant similarities between the supposedly primitive and the ostensibly civilized: such a man was well on his way to becoming a cultural relativist, as were many of his contemporaries and descendants.[58] Moreover, as Frances Mannsaker has observed, meditating on anxieties about imperial decline, "the idea of evolution . . . was open to many different interpretations. What, for instance, did 'fittest' mean? It might not necessarily be equated with a western European definition of 'best'; the civilised might not be those most fitted to survive."[59]

Thus, increasingly revealing the complexity (or at least the potency) of cultures that had been thought simple and the sophistication of societies that had been thought crude, anthropological and archaeological researches dramatized the haunting enigma of human otherness that might not be, as many Europeans still struggled to believe, inferior, but merely different. In the 1840s, in "Locksley Hall," Alfred Lord Tennyson had created a representative young man who declared "Better fifty years of Europe than a cycle of Cathay."[60] But within a few decades it was becoming obvious that a cycle of Cathay (or, indeed, Egypt) might be just as eventful and important as a cycle of Europe, despite the radical distinctions between the two civilizations.

As both Morton Cohen and Norman Etherington have noted, Rider Haggard was both a dedicated amateur Egyptologist and, through his friendship with Andrew Lang, a student of anthropology.[61] In January 1888, just after *She* was published, Haggard sailed for Egypt, which was, in Cohen's words, "the land of his dreams," and in 1907 he replied to a query from *The Bookman* about the volume he had most enjoyed that year by choosing Breasted's *Ancient Egyptian Records*.[62] In his autobiography, moreover, he claimed to have had four recurring visions of his own previous incarnations as a "primitive" man:

> In the first, he is a young man dressed in skins at a cooking fire in a setting very like the Bath Hills of England. In the second he is a black man fending off an attack on his black family. An Egyptian palace is the setting of the third, in which he greets a furtive lover with violet eyes. A slightly taller version of Violet Eyes crops up in the fourth fantasy. She leaps up from her seat in a Viking Hall and throws her sobbing self on Haggard's armor-clad breast.[63]

Together, Etherington wittily comments, these might constitute "tableux from the ethnographic section of a museum." In addition, Haggard knew about the discovery in 1871 of the mysterious stone ruins at Great Zimbabwe, traveled extensively in Africa, and assiduously studied goddess worship among the Zulus and in "ancient Arabic religion."[64] It is significant, therefore, that *She* broods on one manifestation of the newly haunting enigma of geopolitical otherness not only in Haggard's use of the preclassical goddess Isis but in his naming of Her and Her land: *Ayesha* or *Aisha* was the second and favorite wife of the Islamic prophet Mohammed, to Christian readers the incarnation of alien theology, and Her strange land of *Kôr*, besides recalling hearts of darkness, corpses, and the pagan goddess *Koré*, evokes the *Kor-an*, the Islamic holy book which is in its essence Other than the "good" (western) book of the Bible.[65]

But the wisdom of other cultures, and specifically the wisdom of ancient Egypt, was also gradually emerging in the nineteenth century through the sermons and séances of spiritualist "adepts" like Madame Blavatsky and her disciples, for spiritualism, with its different but equally serious emphasis on a realm of otherness, was the second contemporary phenomenon that Haggard's romance exploited through its construction of a 2,000-year-old heroine and through its flirtation with the concept of reincarnation. The novelist himself had been an active spir-

itualist in his youth, attending séances in the London homes of Lady
Poulett and Lady Caithness, events which impressed him so deeply that
he described them in vivid detail thirty-five years later. "At one," says
Morton Cohen, "he saw a massive table that skipped like a lamb and a
lady spirit with an elongated neck like Alice's in Wonderland."[66] Moreover, his novel *Stella Fregelius* (1904) begins, as Etherington puts it, "in
the world of Jules Verne's science fiction and ends in the realms of
Madame Blavatsky's theosophy" while in 1912 he explained his "ethnographic" visions of earlier incarnations by advancing a full-fledged
Victorian theory of metempsychosis.[67] But such destabilizations of orthodox Christianity, originating with the disruptions of reality enacted
at séances that were presided over—even enacted—by women, must
have dramatized yet again the fragility of the control the rational western mind had supposedly achieved over a world which might at any
moment uncannily assert itself. Where both materialistic science and
traditional Christian theology declared that there was nothing (for the
dead were, if anywhere, elsewhere), spiritualism seemed to prove that
there was something, a realm of insistent consciousness pressing against
the far side of appearances and straining to be spoken.[68]

When theosophy, fostered by spiritualist experiences and ideas, sys-
tematized a set of radical, hermeticist propositions about reality, re-
minding readers that, as Madame Blavatsky argued, such mysticism
had always flowed below western thought like an underground river,
the hegemony of patriarchal rationalism was even more seriously shaken.
Certainly the appearance of Blavatsky's *Isis Unveiled* (1877), as well as
the charisma and notoriety of its female author and of her quasi-fem-
inist disciple the birth-controller Annie Besant, must have not only ce-
mented the connections between the "adepts" of the orient and such
challenges to a commonly agreed-upon "reality," but also emphasized
the link between, on the one hand, the alternative historical and theological possibilities propounded by spiritualism and theosophy and, on
the other hand, the possibilities of disorderly female rule.[69]

Even more than Madame Blavatsky or Annie Besant, the notorious
American femme fatale Victoria Woodhull incarnated both these revolutionary possibilities. Beginning her career, together with her equally
notorious sister Tennessee Claflin, as a magnetic healer and spiritualist,
Woodhull soon ascended the lecture platform to speak for the twin
causes of free love and women's suffrage.[70] In addition, again together
with "Tennie C." (as she liked to be called), she founded both a radical
newspaper—*Woodhull & Claflin's Weekly*—and, with the backing of
Cornelius Vanderbilt, a Wall Street brokerage firm. Beautiful, seductive, and frequently married, she and her sister were known (and even

caricatured) as the "Bewitching Brokers" or the "Fascinating Financiers," and their paper was read by a range of dissident groups (figure, below).[71]

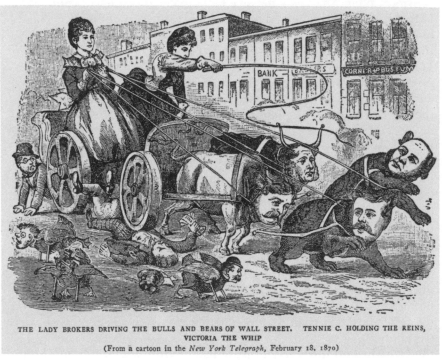

THE LADY BROKERS DRIVING THE BULLS AND BEARS OF WALL STREET.   TENNIE C. HOLDING THE REINS,
VICTORIA THE WHIP
(From a cartoon in the *New York Telegraph*, February 18, 1870)

Cartoon from the *New York Telegraph*, February 18, 1870

But it was as president of the National Society of Spiritualists, as the author of the "Woodhull Memorial" to Congress (calling for votes for women), as a fiery advocate of free love, as an implacable opponent of what she considered the sexual hypocrisy of the renowned clergyman Henry Ward Beecher, and as—repeatedly and quixotically—a candidate for the presidency of the United States that Woodhull became most famous and posed the most unnerving threats to established nineteenth-century values. In her capacity as a spiritualist leader, for instance, she proclaimed that her creed "demonstrates the fallacy of the existence of the orthodox heaven and hell. . . . The churches and the politicians may sneer at the intentions of the spirit world, but they may do well to remember that it is in arms and impatiently waits the signal to move upon their threshold."[72] Just as rebelliously, in her capacity as suffragist, Woodhull spoke before the Judiciary Committee of the House of Representatives—becoming the first woman to appear before that august body—"praying Congress to enact such laws as were necessary to enable women to exercise the right to vote already vested in them by the Fourteenth Amendment."[73]

As for Woodhull's most widely publicized role, that of free love advocate, her impassioned speeches on the subject, made to overflow crowds in huge auditoriums, were marked by a rhetoric that theatrically mingled the language of purity with the vocabulary of desire. "I deem it false and perverse modesty that shuts off discussion" of the erotic, she asserted during a famous appearance at New York's Steinway Hall, adding, "So long as [women] knew nothing but a blind and servile obedience . . . to the will and wish of men, they did not rebel; but the time has arrived . . . wherein they rebel, demanding . . . freedom to hold their own lives and bodies from the demoralizing influence of sexual relations that are not founded in and maintained by love."[74] Such a rhetoric, combining a redefined feminine purity with a rousing feminist frankness, also characterized Woodhull's stance throughout what became known as the "Beecher-Tilton scandal," a case in which she was sued at the behest of the Puritanical Anthony Comstock for having revealed in her *Weekly* details of Henry Ward Beecher's clandestine affair with the wife of his disciple Theodore Tilton.[75] As public sympathy for her cause mounted, she herself, like some American Ayesha, triumphantly repeated to the *New York Evening Post* a statement that she attributed to the poet William Cullen Bryant: "The terrible syren has defeated you and charmed your cohorts and battalions to silence and inaction."[76]

But perhaps it was in her repeated campaigns for the presidency that Woodhull most bizarrely prefigured Ayesha's plan to "assume absolute rule" and "to change the order of the world." When the "Victoria League" first nominated her for the office in 1872, the "terrible syren" frankly vaunted her ambitions, making the extent of her program quite explicit in an article in the *Weekly:*

> It is true that a Victoria rules the great rival nation . . . on the other shore of the Atlantic, and it might grace the amity just sealed between the two nations, and be a new security of peace, if a twin sisterhood of Victorias were to preside over the two nations. . . . I have sometimes thought . . . that there is . . . something providential and prophetic in the fact that my parents were prompted to confer on me a name which forbids the very thought of failure; and as the great Napoleon believed in the star of his destiny, you will at least excuse me, and charge it to the credulity of the woman, if I believe also in fatality of triumph as somehow inhering in my name.[77]

And indeed, though Woodhull's candidacy was hopeless and her campaigns often farcical, by the 1880s she had invaded England, where she married a wealthy banker and where, in preparation for the election of 1884, she "issued a manifesto to the English newspapers" calling for "the people of all Europe, America, and the world" to "rally round her standard."[78]

Whether or not Haggard followed the activities of this "other Victoria," then, the third contemporary phenomenon that concerned him and his readers would in a sense have integrated the first two, for like both the ideology and the image of rebellious women spiritualists, the figure of the New Woman, strengthened by new visions of the power of Everywoman, vividly suggested an ultimate triumph of otherness. Although most were more decorous than Woodhull, feminist thinkers from Elizabeth Barrett Browning to Maud Gonne had long identified their work for women's rights with such related challenges to patriarchal authority as spiritualism, abolitionism, and the Home Rule movement in Ireland. Moreover, even without overt articulation of the links between feminism and other antipatriarchal movements, the very idea of the New Woman was, as the sexual battle she precipitated suggests, so threatening that her aspirations might indeed tend to evoke all the other subversive aspirations that were suddenly, or so it seemed, being voiced throughout the empire and in the New World, with some even being conveyed from the invisible realm of the dead. But beyond the anxieties aroused by suffrage militancy, men of Haggard's generation would have had cause to worry about the principle Goethe had decades earlier termed the "Ewig-Weibliche." For during the nineteenth century the very nature and history of the "feminine" were being radically defined by both biologists and anthropologists, redefined in such a way that Goethe's eternally angelic "Loving-holy penitent women," as well as his forever welcoming *Mater Gloriosa,* could no longer be said to function, the way they had in *Faust,* as little more than nobly passive handmaidens to men.[79]

From classical Greece onward, woman's womb—her *hyster*—had usually been imaged as an empty and inert vessel (or, if not appropriately "filled," as a troublesome animal whose importunate appetites fostered *hysteria*). Similarly, the female "seed" was generally seen as no seed at all, but simply "matter" *(mater)* to be shaped by the spirit or essence carried in the *male* seed. Apollo's famous judgment at the end of the *Oresteia*—"The true parent is he who mounts, the mother is not the parent at all"—was therefore frequently associated, until at least the eighteenth century, with "the highly influential concept of the relative roles of male and female in development" which Aristotle postulated in his *Generation of Animals:* males were believed to provide "the form, at once formal, efficient, and final cause" and females no more than "the substance, the material cause, for the new organism."[80]

Thus when, in 1845, the American gynecologist Marion Sims first inserted a rudimentary speculum into a human vagina, he was astounded by the intricacy of the organs he viewed, a kind of internal landscape about which he spoke in terms that seem almost to prefigure the amazement recorded by Haggard's male travelers into Her queendom. "Introducing the bent handle of a spoon," confided Sims, "I saw everything as no man had ever seen before. . . . I felt like an explorer in medicine who first views a new and important territory."[81] To be sure, Sims imagined himself as a colonizing and conquering hero; indeed, as G. J. Barker-Benfield observes, he depicted himself as "Columbus," the vagina as his "New World."[82] But his astonishment at the terrain he surveyed also suggests a new awe at the complexity of female anatomy and therefore at the creative potential of female destiny.

Just as disturbing to male self-assurance must have been some of the discoveries of embryologists which counterpointed Sims's work: by the end of the eighteenth century, Caspar Friedrich Wolff's theory of ovular epigenesis (emphasizing the activity rather than the passivity of the woman's part in reproduction) had been widely accepted, and by the end of the nineteenth century, in just the years when Haggard fictionalized Her powers, experimental embryologists had established the nature of the cleavage by which the egg-embryo manifests its developmental potency.[83] Equally—or perhaps even more—disturbing, however, would have been some of the anthropological speculations which gave further resonance to these biological discoveries, specifically speculations about the possibility of a matriarchal prehistory.

Again, from classical Greece (or indeed biblical Palestine) onward, prehistory had usually been imagined in the west as patriarchal, with (in the Bible) founding fathers begetting famous sons and (in Greek myth) Titanic males struggling to fashion inert mother earth into meaningful shapes. But in 1861 the Swiss jurist J. J. Bachofen proposed in his massive *Mother Right* a startling new argument: the earliest form of social organization, he declared, was *matriarchal,* and though his notion appeared shocking, it was soon widely disseminated.[84] By 1903, in her ambitious *Prolegomena to the Study of Greek Religion,* the British classicist Jane Ellen Harrison had censoriously noted that "the modern mind, obsessed and limited by a canonical Olympus, an Olympus which is 'all for the Father,' has forgotten the Great Mother," but, she added jubilantly, as she commented on the Cretan excavations of the archaeologist Sir Arthur Evans, "in Crete most happily the ancient figure of the mother has returned after long burial to the upper air."[85]

Within several decades after Harrison wrote, her vision of the resurrected (matriarchal) mother was being elaborated by such diverse figures as Sigmund Freud, D. H. Lawrence, and H. D., each of whom responded with (usually male) anxiety or (usually female) exuberance to the newly powerful idea of the Great Mother. Confessed Freud nervously in *Totem and Taboo* (1913), "I cannot suggest at what point . . . a place is to be found for the great mother-goddesses who may perhaps in general have preceded the father gods."[86] As if explaining the reason for Freud's unusual bafflement, Lawrence grimly insisted in a 1929 essay on "Matriarchy" that the "modern young man is afraid of being swamped, turned into a mere accessory of bare-limbed swooping women. . . . He knows perfectly well that [man] will never be master again."[87] But H. D. (who had quarreled with Freud over precisely the issue of the mother goddess) exclaimed ecstatically, in a draft of *The Gift* (1941–43), that "Beneath every temple to Zeus . . . there was found on excavation without exception, some old cell or cellar or the rough groundwork of some primitive temple to the Early Goddess . . . the first deity, the primitive impulse, the primitive desire, the first love."[88]

In addressing himself to a fantasy of Ayesha and Her land, Haggard was surely meditating on many of these same issues. Not only does the dreamlike landscape of his romance recall the extraordinary "territory" discovered by Sims, but that landscape, with its glamorous intricacy, functioned as a kind of "objective correlative" for ideas about female power that were increasingly popularized throughout the nineteenth century. In 1875, the Christian Scientist Mary Baker Eddy had defined "MOTHER" as "God; divine and eternal Principle; Life, Truth, and Love," while in 1885 Haggard had one of the three heroes of *King Solomon's Mines* meditate on "Asthoreth of the Hebrews . . . the Astarte of the Phoenicians . . . who afterwards was the Aphrodite of the Greeks."[89] Thus, though Ayesha is not herself a mother, she has quasi-maternal powers over life and death, and when the American writer Mary Austin, visiting London in the 1920s, asked Haggard "whether he hadn't figured 'She' as the matriarch, he admitted that he had."[90] Indeed, in *Ayesha, the Return of She* (1905), Haggard had himself made this point explicit by portraying his reborn heroine as "the head priestess of a cult whose central symbol is an idealized representation of Universal Motherhood."[91]

At the same time, besides confronting the mythic and psychological meanings of female power, Haggard was also, consciously or not, examining the frightening yet fascinating possibility of female political and literary power. The son of one of the many nineteenth-century "scribbling women" who not only read romances to their children but actually wrote such works themselves—his mother's epic poem *Myra, or the Rose of the East* appeared in 1857, a year after he was born—he had special personal reasons to be absorbed by "the woman question."[92] But as a citizen of a community that was becoming increasingly absorbed by that "question," Haggard had equally pressing reasons to be concerned by the matter, even though (or perhaps because) he was a professed antifeminist.[93] In just the year when he dated the arrival in his imaginary Cambridge of the palimpsestic sherd that was Her emissary, the real Cambridge was also being invaded by women: for the first time, in 1881, female students were allowed to matriculate at the university and to be examined for degrees along with their male peers.[94] In addition, his adult reading as well as his childhood listening was, at least at one point, focused on the product of a female imagination: the first bestselling novel ever written about Africa was, after all, a book by a woman, and a feminist woman at that—Olive Schreiner's *The Story of an African Farm* (1883).

Like Englishmen from Gladstone to Rhodes, Haggard read *African Farm* with fascination. In fact, he always identified it as one of the two books that had meant the most to him (the other, interestingly, was Robert Louis Stevenson's *Dr. Jekyll and Mr. Hyde*).[95] At his first opportunity, he sought out Schreiner to express his admiration, although some of his comments about *African Farm* suggest that he felt toward its author exactly the kind of ambivalence that (as we argued in *The War of the Words*) many modernist men felt toward particularly successful female precursors and contemporaries. Nevertheless, Haggard's magnetic Ayesha may have been half-consciously modeled on Schreiner's equally magnetic Lyndall, a femme fatale whose passionate self-possession enthralls her male admirers just as surely as Ayesha's captivates hers.

But Schreiner's feminine realism—perhaps, indeed, her feminist pessimism—dooms her heroine to a life far shorter, drabber, and less triumphant than Ayesha's: with bleak irony, Schreiner argues, as we shall show, that it is fatal to be a femme fatale, while Haggard fantasizes, on the contrary, that such a femme must be punished with "devolution" precisely because she is fatale. His revision of Schreiner's Lyndall suggests, then, that *She* is haunted not only by overt anxieties about "the matriarch" but also by covert worries about both the feminist Schreiner and the femme fatale Lyndall, as well as about the meaning of the society such an author and such a heroine might imagine for themselves.[96]

Finally, therefore, what might have been Schreiner's utopia—a "world elsewhere" in which Lyndall could survive and thrive—became Haggard's dystopia, a dystopia that dramatically integrates nineteenth-century male fears about the rise, and the redefinition, of female power with imperialist worries about the claims of colonized peoples and

Christian fears about the challenges posed by alternative theologies. Following thinkers like Levi-Strauss and Simone de Beauvoir, the French feminist theorist Hélène Cixous has argued that patriarchal culture is founded on equivalent sets of "hierarchical oppositions"—"Culture/ Nature . . . Father/Mother . . . Man/Woman . . . Superior/Inferior"—that analogically relate woman with the other, the inferior, the earth, nature.[97] But when we consider the European imperialist consciousness in the context of these equations, it becomes clear that (as a number of other thinkers have also observed), women = "outlanders"/ "barbarians" = colonized peoples, and hence colonized peoples = women, a point that Freud emphasized when he defined female sexuality as a "dark continent" and to which Ashley Montagu implicitly addresses himself when he reminds us of the "Victorian saying that the last thing man would civilize would be woman."[98] That both women and "natives" simultaneously began to manifest frightening drives toward independence just as England's great century of empire drew to its uneasy close would, of course, have sealed the fin-de-siècle connection between these two previously silent and disenfranchised groups.

As Lewis Wurgaft has pointed out in his useful study *The Imperial Imagination,* such a connection had long been implicit in, say, the psychohistory of the British Raj. Analyzing "Myth and Magic in Kipling's India," Wurgaft argues that the colonized peoples of India, particularly the Hindus of Bengal, were associated in the minds of their Victorian rulers with "fantasies of destructive female sexuality." From the point of view of administrative Englishmen, a "highly charged female sensuality" marked "native India's plains and cities."[99] More specifically, "the mercurial mother goddess Kali," who ruled the plains, "seemed to fascinate the British," and the harem, or *zenana,* struck them not as a place of female subordination or imprisonment but rather as a kind of Kôr, a separate female realm ruled by " 'a shrill-tongued virago, a tyrant unassailable in her own domain.' "[100]

In many of the Indian stories and sketches by Haggard's longtime friend Rudyard Kipling, Wurgaft observes, these concerns are quite openly explored.[101] But perhaps Kipling's most explicit text on the subject is a poem he published in 1888, a poem which seems almost like a kind of addendum to Haggard's novel. Entitled "An Interesting Condition," this sardonic *vers libre* piece—which has something of the stylistic flavor of Yeats's odd redaction of Pater—portrays an "Ewig-Weibliche" whose politicized sexuality reflects just the sexual politics on which so many fin-de-siècle thinkers were brooding:

> Above all, reposes the East.
> She is old, but she is beautiful.
> A beautiful woman is always old. As old as Beauty.

She is of moral reputation indifferent. . . .
With the Tourkh.
It was an affaire militaire only. . . .
With the Rajput; with the Hindou.
It was to pass the time. . . .
With the Frenchman.
It was an affair of the heart. . . .
It is now the Englishman who is kicking her children
to school. She has a menage of the Britannic ideal—
solid, sumptuous, and wearying above all. . . .
The Englishman has taken her by the arm. He
promenades with her upon Sundays. He laughs.
He exhibits his teeth. She slaps his leg. He
also pats her upon the back.
These things are the marks of the husband.
English. But . . . ask her.
She has seen many lovers.
A woman who has seen many lovers will see more.
This woman will exist for ever, and she will
always be beautiful.[102]

Simultaneously subordinated (a wife to the imperial "husband") and insubordinate (she will see many more "lovers" and no doubt rebelliously welcome them), this feminized colony endures as beautifully and alarmingly as Haggard's Ayesha or Yeats's and Pater's Gioconda have for two thousand years, suggesting that Kipling himself might have liked to invent an extended fiction like Haggard's romance of the seductress of Kôr. Certainly, as Wurgaft notes, he tried to do so: throughout his years in India, "he was at work on a manuscript entitled *Mother Maturin,*" a book he was never able to bring to completion but which evidently articulated his obsession with the "castrating female" side of India, and which must have colored his admiration for both *She* and Haggard.[103]

But of course, even before Kipling and his imperialist contemporaries sexualized colonized India in this way, the western imagination had, in America, connected racial otherness with sexual pollution, and, in England, associated the orient with feminization, with a blurring of gender boundaries, and more generally, with sexual perversity of all kinds. In the United States, as Barker-Benfield points out, the eugenics movement and the attempt by gynecologists to sanitize female sexuality had much in common. Many nineteenth-century

social leaders and molders—doctors, clergymen, popular novelists, and politicians—saw America as a beleaguered island of WASP righteousness, surrounded by an encroaching flood of dirty, prolific immigrants, and sapped from within by the subversive practices of women. . . . These males saw society as a body invaded by foreign germs, its native blood corrupted and used up from outside and within. . . . The separation and subordination of blacks was formalized at a national level in 1896, and their segregation, castration, and lynching coincided with the growing nativism, the lynching of immigrants, the extirpation of resistant Filipinos and Indians, and the peak of the castration of women.[104]

Indeed, with almost allegorical appropriateness, many of Marion Sims's earliest (and most excruciating) gynecological experiments—some thirty in a four-year period—were performed on a black slave named *Anarcha*.[105] It must have been more than a little unnerving, then, that Victoria Woodhull's running mate in her first (1872) bid for the presidency was a black reformer—Frederick Douglass. To the melody of "Comin' Thro' the Rye,' " her supporters chanted

> Yes! Victoria we've selected
> For our chosen head:
> With Fred Douglass on the ticket
> We will raise the dead.
>
> Then around them let us rally
> Without fear or dread,
> And next March, we'll put the Grundys
> In their little bed.[106]

If conditions in England did not imply such radical threats from within the 'scepter'd isle," they were nevertheless just as alarming, since what was inside, or at the edge of, the empire was also, in a sense, inside England. Most notably, perhaps, in the mid-century, Sir Richard Burton, traveling through the east, became fascinated by the homoeroticism practiced in what he called the "Sotadic Zone," an area which was "bounded westwards by the northern shores of the Mediterranean (N. Lat 43)" and "by the southern (N. Lat 30)" and which also "embrac[ed] Asia Minor, Mesopotamia and Chaldaea, Afghanistan, Sind, the Punjab and Kashmir" besides "enfolding China, Japan and Turkistan" along with most of the New World. In this huge geographical sector, "there is a blending of the masculine and feminine temperaments," declared Burton, "a crasis which elsewhere occurs only sporadically. Hence the male *feminisme* whereby the man becomes *patiens* as well as *agens,* and the woman a tribade, a votary of mascula Sappho, Queen of Frictrices or Rubbers." [107]

More specifically, Burton associated Egypt, which—following Herodotus—he defined in any case as "that classical region of all abominations," with a celebration of hermaphroditism or "androgynic human-ity": explaining that the "Phoenicians spread this androgynic worship over Greece," he brooded on "the castrated votar[ies] of Rhea or Bona mater, in Phrygia called Cybele" as well as on the "bearded Aphrodite" of Cyprus, "with feminine body and costume, sceptered and mitred like a man." More generally, as if to emphasize the female unruliness fostered by such gender fluidity, he reported the "formal outburst of the Harems" during "the unhappy campaign of 1856–57" and re-marked, "In the Empire of Dahomey I noted a corps of prostitutes kept for the use of the Amazon-soldieresses."[108] Although, as Said insists, such writings were no doubt "meant to be testimony to [Burton's] vic-tory over the sometimes scandalous system of Oriental knowledge," they bear witness, at the same time, to a kind of representatively anxious western awe at the sexual otherness of the east.[109]

Burton's *The Sotadic Zone* first appeared as a "Terminal Essay" to the original edition of *The Arabian Nights*, which was brought out in this form by the Kama Shastra Society of London in 1885–86, just the years when Haggard was contemplating the composition of *She*. Although the startling epilogue was quickly suppressed, its original publication, in the words of one commentator, "shook the foundations of literary England, then at the crest of Victorian prudery"[110] even while it must have implicitly confirmed not only the concept of what Said calls "Ori-ental sex" but also the connection between the (mysterious) "native" and the (perverse) "female." Whether or not Haggard ever read Bur-ton's "Terminal Essay"—and it is hard to imagine that he was not, at the very least, aware of the furor it created—in 1885 he himself pro-duced a sensationally successful adventure story, *King Solomon's Mines*, that linked the "female" and the "native" in its depiction of the trials and tribulations, as well as the opportunities for triumph, that colo-nized peoples offered to white men.

The explorers who journey into the wilds of Africa in this novel—three Englishmen and a native, prefiguring the group that is captured by the Amahagger in *She*—encounter an evil but mortal native king instead of an apparently immortal queen who must be obeyed. But the terrain through which they travel is explicitly female, even more so than the *paysage moralisé* in *She*. To reach Solomon's "treasure cave," the men must follow an ancient map which leads them to two moun-tains called "Sheba's breasts," and then "follow the map, and climb the snow of Sheba's left breast till he comes to the nipple, on the north side of which is the great road Solomon made, from whence three days journey to the King's Place" (34).[111] And the "King's Place" is, of course, the queen's womb, a treasure chamber filled with diamonds which promises to make the invaders "the richest men in the whole world"

(191) but which also, when they are trapped behind its five-foot-thick
rock walls, threatens them with the terrible destiny of a living burial in
female anatomy.

Equally to the point, the white men's guide during the final stages
of their expedition is the bad black king's witchlike right-hand woman,
Gagool, an ancient and bestial creature who is described throughout
the novel much as Ayesha is depicted after her "devolution." Gagool is
a bald and "wizened monkey-like figure" with "a most extraordinary
and weird countenance" because she is "a woman of great age, so
shrunken that in size [she is] no larger than . . . a year-old child" (109).
Defining her fatal relationship to history (as Ayesha does), she crows,
"I am old! I am old! I have seen much blood; ha, ha! but I shall see
more ere I die, and be merry. How old am I, think ye? Your fathers
knew me, and their fathers knew me, and their fathers' fathers" (110).
And indeed, before the tribe she rules is released from her awful hegemony, Gagool has not only decimated their numbers but also forced
the supposedly dominant English explorers, who define themselves as
"white men from the stars," to confront their own absurdity. Leading
them into Solomon's "treasure chamber," she taunts the imperialists
with the monstrosity of their own greed, functioning, until the moment
when they manage to crush her beneath one of the rocky walls within
which she seeks to confine them, as a paradoxical *id* and *superego* in
one: " 'Hee! hee! hee!' went old Gagool behind us, as she flitted about
like a vampire bat. 'There are the bright stones that ye love, white men,
as many as ye will; take them, run them through your fingers, *eat* them,
hee! hee! *drink* them, ha! ha!' " (191).

Even before he wrote *She,* then, Haggard implied with anxious xenophobia that what Joseph Conrad's Kurtz was to call "the horror, the
horror" of Africa, or of any of the "dark" colonized places on the globe,
inhered in what seemed to be a subliminal conspiracy between "strange"
races and the (eternal) feminine. Such racial/sexual otherness could un-
man western marauders, he hinted, precisely because it might ironically call into question the very nature and culture of the imperialist
project, but at the same time, in a more Darwinian sense, it might be
disturbing to supposedly "civilized" westerners because it forced them
to confront what they feared was the primordial "barbarism" of the
human. Certainly at least a few of Haggard's descendants dramatized
this last point. As late as 1911, for instance, Stoker thickened the plot
of *The White Worm* by imagining an unholy affinity between the serpentine Lady Arabella March and a kind of descendant of Gagool, a male
witch-hunter named Oolanga who was "a lost, devil-ridden child of the
forest and the swamp" (31). And only a few years later, T. S. Eliot,
despite his public decorum and his "suit of clerical cut," was sending
Conrad Aiken and Ezra Pound a series of bawdy verses about the ob-

scene, indeed "barbaric," activities of one King Bolo and his big black Queen.[112]

But ultimately the genius of *She* consisted in Haggard's less grotesque and more detailed dramatization of the notion that women and colonized peoples were analogically a single group, and that that group, from a masculinist point of view, was affiliated with a power of darkness like the voice that spoke in "language strange" through Madame Blavatsky, Lady Caithness, and Victoria Woodhull, a power that, as Bachofen and Harrison argued, had always been there, abiding and biding its time under the hill of patriarchal reality. As he explored this intuition, moreover, Haggard not only anticipated the connections that Kipling and others tentatively outlined and that Cixous and Montagu would later make explicit but went beyond them in examining the possibility that the female and the "barbarian" may be other *without* being inferior, passive, or part of nature, a possibility that may have, finally, constituted the most unnerving aspect of "the white man's burden." In a sense, too, he presented, albeit in crude outline, just the complex of male imperialist and postimperialist anxieties that such figures as E. M. Forster and Lawrence Durrell were later to explore with greater subtlety in *A Passage to India* (1924) and *The Alexandria Quartet* (1957–60) as well as the configuration of racial and sexual tensions that would preoccupy, say, William Faulkner in *Light in August* (1932) and numerous other texts.

That such worries were, even in Haggard's time, both representative and well founded is clear. In 1897, Kipling—England's principal editorialist of "the white man's burden"—surprised a number of his admirers with a celebration of Victoria's jubilee which took the form of a somber "Recessional," a hymn that might have been written by one of the explorers of Kôr. The British Empire seemed at the height of its hegemony that year, holding unquestioned "Dominion over palm and pine." Yet in verses warning against the arrogance of "lesser breeds without the Law" and haunted by the unruliness of "heathen heart that puts *her* trust / In reeking tube and iron shard," Kipling wrote bleakly about the decay of patriarchal / imperial rule: "The Captains and the Kings depart . . . Far-called, our navies melt away— / On dune and headland sinks the fire— / Lo, all our pomp of yesterday / Is one with Ninevah and Tyre!"[113] Like Haggard—no doubt in part through Haggard—he seemed to have looked into the "heathen heart" of a darkness that threatened his country's empire from without *and* within.

"Ordinary" readers from "provincial lads" to newspaper critics were not the only contemporaries to find Haggard's exploration of what we might call "separate-but-equal otherness" compelling. Within a decade of *She*'s publication, just in the years when *Lilith, Salome,* and *Dracula* were appearing, two writers who were both considerably more sophisticated than Haggard himself recorded dreams and recounted adventures which clearly drew upon the elaborate configuration of anxieties that *She* and other texts expressed.

First, a decade before he commented on the difficulty of "placing" mother goddesses but within a year or so of the composition of Kipling's "Recessional," Sigmund Freud had a dream that, as his self-analysis revealed, depended heavily on details borrowed from *She* and from another Haggard novel with the resonant title *The Heart of the World.* In this dream, Freud wrote, he had been given a strange task which

> related to a dissection of the lower part of my own body, my pelvis and legs, which I saw before me as though in the dissecting-room, but without noticing their absence in myself and also without a trace of any gruesome feeling. Louise N. was standing beside me and doing the work with me. The pelvis had been eviscerated, and it was visible now in its superior, now in its inferior, aspect, the two being mixed together. Thick flesh-coloured protruberances . . . could be seen. . . . I was then once more in possession of my legs and was making my way through the town. . . . Finally I was making a journey through a changing landscape with an Alpine guide who was carrying my belongings. Part of the way he carried me too, out of consideration for my tired legs. The ground was boggy; we went round the edge; people were sitting on the ground like Red Indians or gipsies—among them a girl. Before this I had been making my own way forward over the slippery ground with a constant feeling of surprise that I was able to do so well after the dissection. At last we reached a small wooden house at the end of which was an open window. There the guide set me down and laid two wooden boards, which were standing ready, upon the window-sill, so as to bridge the chasm which had to be crossed over from the window. At that point I really became frightened about my legs, but instead of the expected crossing, I saw two grown-up men lying on wooden benches that were along the walls of the hut, and what seemed to be two children sleeping beside them. It was as though what was going to make the crossing possible was not the boards but the children. I awoke in a mental fright.[114]

As Freud himself rather dryly remarks, "a full analysis of this dream" would take up quite a number of pages, but he does undertake a partial explanation, which, significantly, emphasizes the influence of imagery drawn from *She,* a work he explains he had recently offered to lend to the Louise N. who "assists" him in the dream. " 'A *strange* book,' " he tells us he had observed to her, "but full of hidden meaning . . . The eternal feminine, the immortality of our emotions" (490). But his tentative words had merely elicited the scornful response, "I know it already. Have you nothing of your own?" to which he had nervously replied, "No, my own immortal works have not yet been written." Later in his comments he had added that in both *She* and *The Heart of the World* "the guide is a woman; both are concerned with perilous journeys; while *She* describes an adventurous road that had scarcely ever been trodden before, leading into an undiscovered region"—all points, especially the last one, suggesting ways in which Haggard's novels might have seemed to Freud to provide appropriate metaphors for the pioneering trips on the "royal road to the unconscious" along which his own female patients were guiding him. It is certainly likely, therefore, that, as Norman Etherington has argued, the very topography as well as the motion and direction of Haggard's quest-plots helped Freud conceptualize the psychic geography that was to be so crucial to his theory of "layered personality."[115]

What are we to make, though, of the fact that Freud's Haggardesque adventure begins with a pelvic dissection that implies a desexing and that his journey ends in feelings of impotence and terror? Like Leo and Holly, who have to be carried on litters into the womb/tomb that is Her land, Freud seems to have been castrated and infantilized early in this dream, so that when he is borne inward over slippery, boggy ground it is hard, given his own hermeneutics, to avoid seeing his journey not as a classic trip into the self but as a voyage into an other who is horrifyingly female. His final despairing vision of "the chasm which had to be crossed" and of the sleeping, immobilized men and children would inevitably, then, lead to a sense of failure and "mental fright," not because (as he suggests) he wonders how much longer his legs will carry him toward the end of his self-analysis, the composition of his "own immortal works" but for precisely the opposite reason. Freud fears that he *will* reach an end that must include an impotent confrontation with— even an engulfment in—the "barbarous" but autonomous female.[116]

It is telling, however, that Freud's dream broods so insistently on "the chasm that had to be crossed" by means of narrow planks, for this frightening image derives from what is essentially the turning point of Haggard's tale. Holly, Leo, and Ayesha can only bridge the gulf they must cross in order to reach the "place of Life" when, "like a great sword of flame, a beam from the setting sun [pierces] the Stygian gloom." Then, as "right through the heart of the darkness that flaming sword [is] stabbed," they and their readers are given a symbolic preview of the fate in store for Ayesha. It is possible, therefore, that in his dream-allusion to this moment, Freud was not only enacting crucial male anxieties but offering himself a paradigmatically patriarchal hope, the hope of renewal through a reiteration of the Law of the Father.

The second of the more sophisticated fin-de-siècle works that we can directly associate with *She* also pays tribute to this crucial moment when, symbolically speaking, the "flaming sword" of phallic enlightenment pierces the female "heart of the darkness." But Conrad's *Heart of Darkness* (1899), written not long after Freud dreamed his dream and Kipling composed his hymn, penetrates more ironically and thus more inquiringly into the dark core of otherness that had so disturbed the patriarchal, the imperialist, and the psychoanalytic imaginations. Through the ambiguities and ellipses of Marlow's narrative, after all, the Polish exile was able to pose questions that neither Haggard nor Holly (nor, for that matter, Stoker, Macdonald, Wilde, Kipling or Freud) allowed themselves to consider. At the same time, though, Conrad designs for Marlow a pilgrimage whose guides and goal are as eerily female as those Holly and Leo must confront and conquer.

Like Haggard's characters, for instance, Conrad's protagonist begins his quest under female patronage; Leo has received a message from a dead Egyptian ancestress, while "I, Charlie Marlow, set the women to work—to get a job" on a steamboat in Africa.[117] Again, just as Leo and Holly must ritually pass through the matriarchal territory of the Amahaggar in order to reach Her deadly land of Kôr, Marlow must pass through an antechamber ruled by two "uncanny and fateful" women who are "guarding the door of Darkness, knitting black wool as for a warm pall" (11). When he reaches a key way station on his African journey, moreover, he is "arrested" by "a small sketch in oils" done by the mysterious Kurtz, a totemic-seeming image of "a woman, draped and blindfolded, carrying a lighted torch. The background was somber—almost black. The movement of the woman was stately, and the effect of the torchlight on her face was sinister" (25). Evoking an image of Justice, the picture also disturbingly suggests the contradictions between power (the torch) and powerlessness (the blindfold), and thus it introduces the idea of the other who has been excluded and dispossessed—symbolically blindfolded even—but who, despite such subordination, exercises a kind of indomitable torchlike power.

Finally, Marlow's discovery of the dying Kurtz in the center of the "dark continent" and at the end of the serpentine river definitively establishes the meaning of such a female totem. For when Marlow and his "pilgrim" companions try to rescue the sick man from the spell of his black Venus and Her people, they fail as abjectly as Wagner's pilgrims fail in *Tannhäuser*. Muttering of his "immense plans" (67), Kurtz crawls, like Haggard's Billali, back into the jungle, back toward the African queen of night into whose power he has fallen. Destroyed by his greed for the ivory bones of Her country as well as by his enthrallment to the alien passions She represents, he has become, himself, "an animated image of death carved out of old ivory" (60), like the "pale Kings and Princes" who haunted Keats's knight-at-arms or the dead bodies that litter Ayesha's terrible realm. Even his name, *Kurtz,* with its incorporation of *Kôr,* suggests not only, as the German implies, that he has been cut off or curtailed, but also that he is ultimately meant to signify the nightmare corpse at the core of the anxious patriarchal/imperialist mind, the dead father who has been "blasted" into impotence by "the horror, the horror" of otherness.[118] There is nothing now for Marlow and the "pilgrims" to do but prepare to sail away, bearing the alive-in-death body of this ruined ruler like a sacred relic back to the illusory, often sinister (and female) world of the "Intended," a world that Kurtz had "intended" to master but whose own secretly ambitious (female) intentions have now been clarified.[119]

As the Europeans prepare to sail away, however, *She-who-must-be-obeyed* actually makes a brief but dramatic appearance at the edge of the night wood she inhabits, as if she were a silent hieroglyph in the language strange that articulates both her mysterious history and her threatening hystery. Shadowing the marble-pale "Intended" the way Ayesha shadows the matriarchal Victoria, she walks

> with measured steps, draped in striped and fringed cloths, treading the earth proudly, with a slight jingle and flash of barbarous ornaments. She carried her head high; her hair was done in the shape of a helmet; she had brass leggings to the knees, brass wire gauntlets to the elbow, a crimson spot on her tawny cheek, innumerable necklaces of glass beads on her neck; bizarre things, charms, gifts of witch-men, that hung about her, glittered and trembled at every step. She must have had the value of several elephant tusks upon her. She was savage and superb, wild-eyed and magnificent; there was something ominous and stately in her deliberate progress. And in the hush that had fallen suddenly . . . the colossal body of the fecund and mysterious life [of the land] seemed to look at her as though it had been looking at the image of its own tenebrous and passionate soul. [62]

Like Haggard's Ayesha, She is "wild and gorgeous," "tragic and fierce"; like Haggard's Ayesha, She is guarded by powerful but mute and subjugated male figures. And like Haggard's Ayesha, She generates quite reasonable terror and quite understandable plans for revenge in the hearts of most male European onlookers. "If she had offered to come aboard I really think I would have tried to shoot her," remarks the Russian "man of patches" (62), a fellow traveler who has been as certainly (if not as strikingly) destroyed by Her land as Kurtz was.

There *is*, after all, "something ominous and stately in Her deliberate progress" through the nineteenth century. Perhaps inevitably, then, by the first decade of the twentieth century, Kipling was meditating far more explicitly on "the matriarch" than he had either in "An Interesting Condition" or in "Recessional." In Her matriarchal power and Her powerful sexuality, he mused resignedly in 1911, "The female of the species must be deadlier than the male," for "She the Other Law we live by, is that Law and nothing else."[120] Despite his friend Haggard's willed destruction of Ayesha by a phallic pillar of fire, Kipling nervously implies that the Law of the Mother—the newly defined Law of the "Ewig-Weibliche"—must always take precedence over the fragile and belated Law of the Father.

Perhaps inevitably, too, Yeats felt impelled to link the idea of the "modern" with an image of the femme fatale, and in particular with a representation of Her mysterious energies that emphasizes their historicity. What, the author of "Leda and the Swan" implies, if the "eternal feminine" really *did* "put on [the father god's] knowledge with his power"? Does (male-defined) modernism—with its severe experimentation, its struggle to reconstitute a shattered *patrius sermo*, its anxieties about the past—originate in a recognition that, as Yeats puts it in an elliptical prose meditation on the "Mona Lisa," "Somewhere . . . da Vinci's sitter had private reality like that of the Dark Lady among the women Shakespeare had imagined, but because that private soul is always behind our knowledge, though always hidden it must be the sole source of pain, stupefaction, evil . . ."?[121]

If so, many men of letters—second- as well as first-generation modernists, poets as well as fiction writers—had reasons to deploy recuperative strategies not unlike those Haggard dramatized in *She*. Yeats's anthology of *Modern Verse*, for instance, ended with a selection of poems by the then twenty-three-year-old George Barker, a member of the Auden circle, who specifically sought a renewal of masculine authority in a piece entitled "The Leaping Laughers":

> When will men again
> Lift irresistible fists
> Not bend from ends
> But each man lift men
> Nearer again. . . .
>
> When will men again
> Lift irresistible fists
> Impede impediments
> Leap mountains laugh at walls?[122]

2 Home Rule: The Colonies of the New Woman

No Votes for Women—No Home Rule!

—Suffragist slogan

Where dwell the lovely, wild white women folk,
  Mortal to man?
They never bowed their necks beneath the yoke,
They dwelt alone when the first morning broke
  And Time began.

—Mary Elizabeth Coleridge

The theory of a male supreme God in the interests of force and authority, wars, family discord, the sacrifice of children to appease the wrath of an offended (male) deity are all due to the Patriarchate. These were practices entirely out of consonance with woman's thought and life.

—Matilda Joslyn Gage

Thus far women have been the mere echoes of men. Our laws and constitutions, our credo and codes, and the customs of social life are all of masculine origin. The true woman is as yet a dream of the future.

—Elizabeth Cady Stanton

One year after the publication of Rider Haggard's best-selling *She,* Jack the Ripper became virtually a media hero. Like a parodic Haggard protagonist questing to "Seek out the woman" in order to "slay her," Jack the Ripper murdered five women in a slum district of East London during the autumn of 1888. More freakishly still, he seemed even more determined than Haggard's heroes to "learn the secret of Life" through such murders, for—after strangling his victims and slashing their throats—he removed their intestines and their uteruses. As Colin Wilson has observed, "It was the womb itself that fascinated him."[1]

But it also fascinated the policemen, detectives, journalists, and moral crusaders whose speculations about the Ripper's eviscerated women— all of whom had been prostitutes—established what Judith R. Walkowitz has called a "Ripper myth" of a sinister but titillating battle between predatory men and fallen (but not fatal) women.[2]

Almost like a grotesque elaboration of male artists' rebellion against the femme fatale, the Ripper myth implicitly presented male hostility toward women as a necessary retaliation against female erotic power. At the same time, however, as Walkowitz has demonstrated, it "offer[ed] women no strategy for resistance; on the contrary, it [was] about female passivity in the face of male violence." Although midwives and female medical students were considered possible candidates in speculations about a female Ripper and although newspapers occasionally portrayed women "secretly armed" against "the Whitechapel fiend," the overwhelming message of Ripper-pursuers consisted of a warning to "good" women that "bad" women could not protect themselves against a punishment they really deserved, and that no woman was safe outside the security of her home.[3]

That, for the most part, feminists did not rally around the prostitutes of Whitechapel indicates exactly how effective the myth was in convincing women that there was no defense imaginable against an assault that was sure to destroy them. The myth was convincing because it paradoxically promulgated values also implicit in a major strand of feminist thinking during this period. In England the protests led by Josephine Butler against the Contagious Diseases Acts of 1864, 1866, and 1869—which forced accused prostitutes to submit to physical examinations but let their customers go unbothered by the police—had emphasized exactly what Victorian feminists underscored in America, namely "the lustful domination of man" and the "fearful strain" such domination placed on women.[4] Coming, as the murders did, only two years after the successful campaign against these acts, they focused sensational attention on the relationship between the sexes in a way that shared with the polemics of many feminists a sense of men as sexual predators and of women as their victims. And though the femme fatale represented male anxiety about the enigmatic language, consciousness, and history of female potency, even New Women continued to find the old problem of female power perplexing.

No Jill the Ripper would emerge to retaliate for her sex either in fact or fiction during the fin de siècle.[5] Instead, the extreme vulnerability of women—emblematized through the figure of the helpless prostitute by both the police searching for the Ripper murderer and by the activists fighting the Contagious Diseases Acts—stands in stark contrast to the mythology of female otherness inscribed in Haggard's

She, Stoker's *Dracula,* Macdonald's *Lilith,* and Wilde's *Salome,* as well as in the sinister sensuality of Aubrey Beardsley's Venus, Dante Gabriel Rossetti's Astarte, and Edward Burne-Jones's Vivien. Clearly, many men reacted with dread to the legal and social reforms that provided women a modicum of property and custodial rights at the beginning of the modernist period. The *Times,* for example, deplored the 1891 decision of *Queen v. Jackson* (which declared that a man could no longer imprison his wife in his house so as to enforce conjugal rights) by sorrowfully exclaiming that "one fine morning last month marriage in England was suddenly abolished."[6]

And in the year before the first major Married Women's Property Act was passed, Walter Besant, who was to read *She* in one night, had himself composed *The Revolt of Man* (1882), a nightmare vision of misrule in which men are confined to the domestic sphere by autocratic female authorities until an enterprising hero luckily manages to conquer all and right the wrongs of men.[7] Readers of the September 26, 1894, issue of *Woman* received this definition of the New Woman who was causing such havoc:

> She flouts Love's caresses
> Reforms ladies' dresses
> And scorns the Man-Monster's tirade;
> She seems scarcely human
> This mannish New Woman
> This Queen of the Blushless Brigade

while readers of the November 10, 1894, issue of *Punch* were treated to a parody of Whitman's "Pioneers! O Pioneers!" chanted by "Literary dames," who proclaim:

> We primeval fetters loosing,
> We our husbands taming, vexing we and worrying Mrs. GRUNDY
> We our own lives freely living, we as batchelor-girls residing,
> Pioneers! O Pioneers![8]

But many of the female contemporaries of the *Time*'s editorial staff and of Walker Besant might have believed that the "Queen of the Blushless Brigade" had cause to fear "the Man-Monster's tirade" or that the "primeval fetters" imposed by "husbands" and "Mrs. GRUNDY" were not so easily loosed. Indeed, a number of them would have agreed with Frances Swiney, President of the Chiltenham branch of the National Union of Women's Suffrage Societies, that "the only being in civilised life from whom the human female has to be protected is the male of her own species."[9] As we suggested in *The War of the Words,* men's literary reactions against even the most tentative developments in women's liberation do not match the sense of vulnerability that permeates the writings of women of letters. This modern literary asymmetry—which, given the ambivalent responses to the visibility of women in our own largest professional organization, we would call the MLA syndrome—means that masculinist revenge scenarios at the end of the nineteenth century are not offset by comparable feminist ones. However, a number of women of letters did fantasize about a different world in which an aggressive male species miraculously self-destructs and in which women gain the fruits of victory in the sex struggle without directly engaging in combat.

Specifically, although both of the major feminist-polemicists of the turn-of-the-century—Olive Schreiner in South Africa and Charlotte Perkins Gilman in America—confronted women's fear that they had been constructed in such a way as to ensure their defeat in the battle of the sexes, both sought to imagine a female primacy that transcended debilitating sex roles, and both therefore investigated the image of the New Woman Rider Haggard paradoxically incarnated as the 2,000-year-old She. Schreiner described the psychosocial conditions which gave rise to Her birth while Gilman depicted the new world She would establish. Just as Haggard's novel revealed the connections that the male imagination made between the "recessional" of the British Empire, spiritualism, and the rise of New Women, Schreiner's *The Story of an African Farm* (1883) and Gilman's *Herland* (1915) illuminate the significance of those issues in the female literary tradition. First, locating their fictions on the outskirts of civilization, Schreiner and Gilman went in search of the heart of female darkness not to recolonize it but to confront their own colonization. Second, although neither Schreiner nor Gilman had Haggard's passionate interest in spiritualism, both criticized traditional Christianity and examined alternative theological possibilities that might lend women spiritual centrality. Finally, illustrating the dialectic between politics and poetics at the turn of the century, Schreiner and Gilman variously strove to redefine female power in works which imply that woman's fantasies have frequently been feminist in nature and that, concomitantly, feminism imagines an alternative reality which is truly fantastic.

In direct opposition to those male artists who mythologized the sinister potency of the female, Schreiner and Gilman implied that the vision of woman as an omniscient, omnipotent ruler of a matriarchal society was not merely a mythic configuration but, quite simply, a fiction. For them, indeed, women—less troubled by a sense of exotic priority than by signs of their all too familiar secondariness—find the feminist movement and the entrance into modernity a perilous challenge. The murderous seductiveness of the femme fatale, who inspired so many literary men with a dread that bred retaliatory stories, hardly matches their female contemporaries' portrayal of the fragile singleness or singularity of the New Woman. Men and women of letters, however, did seem to agree that theirs was an age marked by a decline in male domination. While *The Story of an African Farm* associates the breakdown of patriarchal culture with the tormented but subversive desires of a heroine whose tragic fate is identified with her feminism, *Herland* links the emergence of matriarchal culture with the futility and fatality of masculinism. Both Schreiner and Gilman, moreover, defined the woman as the secret source of life by seeking—even in the face of personal difficulties which severely qualified their writings—to affirm the power of the womb, and both countered the paternal curse with a maternal blessing by striving to imagine Her in Her own land.

In 1881, when Olive Schreiner had traveled to England in part to find a publisher for *The Story of an African Farm,* H. Rider Haggard was cutting hay and raising ostriches with his pregnant wife on an African farm at the Transvaal border. Although he left Natal following a series of Boer victories, Haggard did not relinquish his ownership of the farm until 1883, the year that *The Story of an African Farm* was published under the pseudonym Ralph Iron. Two years after its extremely successful reception, Haggard wrote a friend, "I am very anxious to make the acquaintance of the woman who wrote the S. A. Farm so I . . . sent her a copy of 'Dawn' addressing of course 'Ralph Iron.' "[10] There were at least two and possibly more meetings between Schreiner and Haggard, at one of which he apparently suggested that "she should write something more cheerful, advice which she considered to come ill from one who had 'a murder or a suicide on every other page.' " Perhaps, however, the man whom Andrew Lang would call "King Romance" had glimpsed more than Schreiner's portrayal of "inward personal suffering," for she had remarkably managed to capture the quality of life on a farm not unlike his own.[11]

The contrast between Schreiner's domestic farm and Haggard's exotic Kôr is, of course, striking. While he describes the high adventure of Englishmen entering darkness to conquer it, she portrays displaced men and women who die on the karroo where they were raised. While he focuses on male exploration, she depicts the customs of Boer culture and the spiritual perplexities of characters exiled from western civilization. Most importantly, while Haggard describes the passions of a woman who waits 2,000 years for the reunion she craves with her lover, Schreiner creates a heroine who rejects not only her lover but the marriage with him that she is supposed to desire. As Haggard's friend and sometime collaborator Andrew Lang remarked, Schreiner wrote about "people . . . always tackling religious problems, or falling in love on new and heterodox lines, instead of shooting deer, and finding diamonds, or hunting up the archeological remains of the Transvaal."[12] In the preface to the second edition of *The Story of an African Farm*, moreover, Schreiner seems to be responding to precisely such descriptions of her work:

> It has been suggested by a kind critic that he would better have liked the little book if it had been a history of wild adventure; of cattle driven into inaccessible "kranzes" by Bushmen; "of encounters with ravening lions, and hair-breadth escapes." This could not be. Such works are best written in Piccadilly or in the Strand. . . .[13]

Given this criticism of "wild adventure" and specifically of the romance associated with Bushmen, lions, and hairbreadth escapes, Schreiner would probably have agreed with the later judgment of Gertrude Stein that a "white hunter is nearly crazy."[14]

Schreiner's refusal to provide the sort of adventure story Haggard and Lang would go on to sell so successfully is related to her belief that, unlike them, she wrote inside Africa. More specifically, for Haggard, the threat of native power is encoded through the disturbing magnetism of his heroine, *She-who-must-be-obeyed*, and his imperialist script dramatizes how She must be sought, silenced, and destroyed. But for Schreiner the colonies are situated on the margins of patriarchal culture in a space where history might be reconstituted so as to let women rebel against the power of Him-who-had-been-obeyed in the past. Writing four years before the publication of *She*, a twenty-one-year-old governess on the Cape succeeded in suggesting—through her charismatic heroine Lyndall—that the enigmatic language and alien longings of the New Woman must inevitably question the spiritual and familial structures governed by what Schreiner presents as a morally bankrupt male species.

Lyndall's subversive vision in *The Story of an African Farm* is not articulated, however, until those structures have been notably weakened. In fact, the central problems of this often incoherent work arise from its author's inability to find a plot commensurate with her own and her heroine's desires. Thus *The Story of an African Farm* is a story of contradictions precisely because, even while Schreiner argues for female freedom, she cannot seem to represent such freedom effectively in the life of her heroine. Not only do Lyndall's pleas for women's independence appear after many chapters devoted to seemingly unrelated issues but also, like several other characters, Lyndall almost inexplicably disappears and reappears from the world of the farm throughout the novel, and in the final half of the book her angry protests against female dependence on men seem oddly unsubstantiated, given the absence of any masterful patriarchs and the presence of the female owner of the farm, Tant' Sannie. Just as important, far from celebrating this last character or her land, Schreiner continually emphasizes the selfishness, stupidity, and voracious appetites that are symbolized by Tant' Sannie's obesity. Perhaps, as Rachel Blau DuPlessis has argued, the incongruities of Schreiner's plot testify to the disparity between feminist yearning for a new age and female despair at the difficulty of evading the old world's imperatives, exactly the discrepancy that Lyndall so passionately mourns.[15] Schreiner's narrative difficulties, though, as well as her heroine's tortured decline into death, also reinforce the idea that some literary women's perspectives were very different from those of literary men, for while men like Haggard viewed the New Woman as a *femme* fatal to men, Schreiner presents the New Woman's feminism as a fatality that will eventually kill *her*.

On the one hand, with its omniscient narrator and its essayistic meditations, *The Story of an African Farm* evokes Victorian literary conventions; on the other hand, in its use of generically incongruous chapters (composed of farce, polemic, parable) and a fractured plot, it adumbrates modernist experimental techniques. By means of this odd formal juxtaposition, Schreiner's novel depicts the diminution of masculine authority along with a vision of female power through characters who are situated between two worlds, one dead, the other striving to be born. Set on the isolated farm of the huge Tant' Sannie, the novel traces the fates of her overseer, Otto, and three children: Otto's son Waldo, Tant' Sannie's stepdaughter Em, and Em's cousin Lyndall. Specifically, inside the female-dominated farm, all of Schreiner's characters confront the breakdown of both patriarchal theology and the patriarchal family in order to come to terms with the sexchanges that both men and women faced in the last quarter of the nineteenth century.

The first book of *The Story of an African Farm* documents not only the death of God but also the demise of any meaningful patrilineage. In the first chapter, therefore, Schreiner focuses on the young boy, Waldo, who discovers the impossibility of achieving redemption through, or communication with, transcendent being. Gazing one night at his father's watch. Waldo hears each tick as a man's death and each death means damnation: *"For wide is the gate, and broad is the way, that leadeth to destruction and many there be which go in thereat"* (23). The ticking watch, "like God's will," tortures the boy, who weeps over his inability to move God to save a multitude of damned souls. In the day that follows this nightmare repetition of ideas about death and damnation, Waldo plays the part of a "priest" as he places a mutton chop on an altar of stones. When the sun melts the fat on the chop which the ants have come to eat, he decides that, like Cain's, his sacrifice is a failure, a sign that divine presence had departed. Converted to hatred of God, he declares: "I love Jesus Christ, but I hate God" (28). However, Waldo's effort to disentangle good from evil, cruel from loving authority, will be thwarted by a series of uncanny events that revolve around the appearance of a malevolent stranger whom Waldo's godly father welcomes as the embodiment of Jesus Christ: "He saw not . . . the evil face of the man; but . . . the form that long years of dreaming had made very real to him. 'Jesus, lover, and it is given to us . . . to take *Thee* in!' " (42).

The curious entrance of the wandering Irishman Boneparte Blenkins into the African farm—signaled by the only date in the novel, 1862—signifies the entrance of history into the tale, albeit history in a debased form. For this impostor, who claims to trace his ancestry back to Napoleon and the Duke of Wellington, represents the imperialist project. Named after the rags-to-riches hero who was associated with ambitious efforts to conquer the world, Schreiner's Boneparte has come to Africa, a "struggling country," where "they want capital; they want men of talents, they want men of ability to open up that land" (47). But the talents and abilities of this man, who comes out of nowhere with nothing, issue only in a series of glib lies and sadistic punishments that threaten not only Tant' Sannie and her overseer, Otto, but also the three children who live on the farm. To be sure, as the embodiment of the history made by great men, Boneparte Blenkins is a rather ludicrous con-man whom Waldo, Lyndall, and Em can immediately discount as a fraud. Yet old Otto, the epitome of Christian charity, is so taken in that he literally takes the wandering "son" in. Indeed, by illustrating how Waldo's naive father is actually responsible for the hypocrite's success, Schreiner dramatizes not only the moral inefficacy of Waldo's effort to disentangle good from evil authority but also the destructive reciprocity of the imperialist ideology Boneparte spouts and the Christian theology Otto preaches.

At first glance, of course, no two characters could seem more dissimilar than the saintly fool and the upstart infidel. While Otto provides Waldo, Lyndall, and Em with the shelter and affection they need, Boneparte punishes the children physically and mentally. While Otto benevolently welcomes "the stranger" he associates with Christ, Boneparte demonically traps Otto in a network of lies that precipitates the old man's expulsion from the farm and his subsequent death. Yet, paradoxically, there are a number of indications that the violent betrayals of the newcomer are made possible by the gullible piety of the overseer.

After Boneparte arrives, for example, Otto outfits him from top to toe with his own shoes, coat, and hat. Since the only thing Tant' Sannie worships is the respectability endowed by good clothes, Otto turns Boneparte into a "man of God" in her eyes (56). Looking like a seamy imitation of the overseer, "Bon"—as he likes to call himself—effectively demonstrates the bankruptcy of Otto's biblical language in a grotesque sermon against love. Besides dressing like Otto and acting in his stead, moreover, Boneparte owes his incredible presence on the farm to his credulous friend, or so Tant' Sannie implies when, after agreeing to let Boneparte stay, she exclaims to Otto, "all the sin he does I lay at your door" (39).

In a sense she is right, for the old German seems to create Boneparte or at least to make his existence possible. Supposing the interloper to be a scholar, for instance, Otto ignores all the evidence that testifies to Boneparte's ignorance and sets the younger man up as the children's schoolmaster. When Boneparte puts soap on his eyelids so as to weep over the fabricated "news" of his fictional wife's death, he is enacting the part of the grieving old Otto, a widower who still treasures his dead wife's ring. Although Boneparte himself is trying to woo Tant' Sannie in order to get her farm, he tells her that Otto expects to exploit her by marrying her, thereby causing the old man's expulsion from the farm. When the German dies on the day he is forced to leave, the Irishman actually inherits Otto's house and goods, even becoming the overseer of the farm. When he discovers the German's wedding ring, moreover, he plans to do what he has claimed Otto wanted to do, namely to put it on Tant' Sannie's finger. After virtually destroying the old man, this interloper goes on—while paying court to Tant' Sannie—to usurp Otto's role as father of the family on the farm. Whether he locks Lyndall and Em in their rooms or beats Waldo bloody, Boneparte makes good on his promise to the boy that "I shall act as a father to you" (111). Finally, however, Boneparte is himself cast out of the African Farm because Tant' Sannie discovers that he is considering giving the ring he stole from Otto to her wealthier niece. Although Otto was replaced because he mistook this "stranger" for Jesus Christ, Waldo—who had looked to Christ as an alternative to a cruel Jehovah—does not need to witness Boneparte's parodic imitation of Otto, for he had immediately responded to the news of his father's death with the painful decision that "There is no God . . . not anywhere!" (89).

Whether Otto and Boneparte are weirdly extravagant characters because they are monsters of the psyche representing split halves of one self or whether they are allegorical figures embodying, say, the reciprocity of an effete God and a powerful devil or the complementarity of Christianity and imperialism (two missionary projects), their contest catapults us into a realm of fantasy that dramatizes the psychosexual crisis of the novel's younger generation. For Waldo, Lyndall, and Em, the problem of growing up in the world of the African Farm is a consequence of their adoption by parodic parents. If Tant' Sannie is the only mother figure on the farm, we can understand the dilemma she poses by crystallizing it into the sentence, There is no mother and she is huge. Like Schreiner, who admitted, "My mother has never been a mother to me,"[16] the three children are literally motherless, although they are oppressed by the presence of a huge, foreign woman whose search for a third husband seems to hint at a terrible female voracity. After Tant' Sannie has observed Boneparte's courtship of her niece and flung the contents of a pickle barrel over his head, she expels him from the farm and retains control over her land. But her monstrous appetites and her ignorance of even the children's language bespeak a grotesque egotism that transforms her and her land into a horrifying image of female misrule.

If, out of revulsion at this figure, Waldo, Lyndall, and Em turn to male figures, they become victims of the proposition, There are two fathers and he cannot be killed.[17] Certainly the splitting of the fathers into the good Otto and the evil Boneparte represents a weakening of patriarchal authority, for their very doubleness is a sign of a splintering that signals their death and disappearance by the end of book one. In spite of the patricidal outcome of this contest, however, neither father can be killed or replaced by the children: Otto because, like Schreiner's own father, who was both saintly and incompetent, he has himself exchanged "being killed by" with "dying for"; Boneparte because he is so much a force of gratuitous evil that his disappearance promises the repetition compulsion of his return. To add to the children's dilemma, moreover, the entire kinship system has broken down, for maternal and paternal figures are not married. As if to emphasize the children's hopeless situation, their youth, presented in the first book, is completely discontinuous with the adulthood they have mysteriously managed to attain in the second.

The alliance Waldo and Lyndall form in response to their perplexing family situation can be compared to Heathcliff and Catherine's intimacy in *Wuthering Heights* (1847), just as Schreiner's eerie karroo evokes Brontë's windswept Yorkshire. Even Lyndall's cousin Em(ily) speaks of Schreiner's affiliation with her foreign-born precursor. As in *Wuthering Heights*, moreover, where the passionate quasi siblings are abused by surrogate parents, Lyndall and Waldo are tormented by Boneparte and Tant' Sannie. But the differences between *Wuthering Heights* and *The*

Story of an African Farm are as notable as the similarities, for they hint at a startling decline in masculine potency.

First, as complex as it is, there is a patrilineal genealogy in *Wuthering Heights,* while the familial structure has entirely broken down in *The Story of an African Farm.* Second, in spite of the cleavage they experience during their lives, Heathcliff and Catherine do seem to attain the consummation they desire after their death, just as their successors do in the next generation. The tenderness Lyndall and Waldo feel for each other, however, is not commensurate with their sense of their fates. Specifically, it does not speak to the feeling of impotence that haunts Waldo or to the ferocity of Lyndall's desires. While Heathcliff, who kicks "'T' Brooad Way to Destruction" into the dog kennel, functions as Catherine's "whip," Waldo, who suffers over the broad way to destruction, watches Boneparte crush his first invention, a sheep-shearing "machine," and passively resigns himself to injustice. Indeed, his response—"Why hate, and struggle, and fight? Let it be as it would" (107)— seems to accept the inevitable castration of no-manhood. Only Lyndall imagines retribution for their childhood suffering: "we will not be children always; we shall have the power too, someday" (114). Though, as we argued in *The Madwoman in the Attic,* together Catherine and Heathcliff embody an ideal of androgynous wholeness, here Lyndall alone emerges as the prophet of a time when women will be, in Brontë's words, "half savage and hardy, and free." [18]

Like Waldo in the first part of Schreiner's novel, all the men in the second part who enter the farm owned by Tant' Sannie and entailed to Em are secondary, belated, insubstantial, or impotent. Four strangers enter and leave Tant' Sannie's land, as if to illustrate Schreiner's description of her own fictional technique: "There is a strange coming and going of feet . . . and what the name of the play is no one knows" (v). Waldo's, Em's, Tant' Sannie's, and Lyndall's strangers, who trigger the plot in Schreiner's subsequent theater of cruelty, are examples of what Doris Lessing has called Schreiner's "nothing-men." [19] Not only are their inexplicable appearances and disappearances an index of the discontinuity of colonial culture,[20] but together they continue to exemplify the weakening of patriarchal authority which seems to call forth the passion play Lyndall will enact in the concluding chapters of the novel.

Waldo's mysterious stranger, who "believes nothing, hopes nothing, fears nothing, feels nothing" (145), appears on the karroo to teach the boy (through a parable about the bird of Truth) that "salvation is in work" (153). But, as Rachel Blau DuPlessis has shown, the Victorian work ethic quickly becomes ironic when, toward the end of the novel, Waldo leaves the African farm to labor in the world, where he finds the same sadism he had witnessed in Boneparte and the same "impotent anguish" he had himself suffered.[21] In Waldo's initial glimpse of his stranger, he had mistaken him for the "new man" due to arrive on the farm, and certainly the pseudo-refinement of the "new man" Gregory Rose is almost a parodic version of Waldo's stranger's gentility. "[A] noodle and a milksop" (162), Em's stranger is a fawning but vacillating suitor who is despised as "a true woman" by Lyndall (184), a view born out by Gregory's subsequent masochistic thralldom to Lyndall.

When two more strange horsemen arrive at the farm, they further demonstrate the impotence of men on the karoo. The widower Little Piet Vander Walt appears like a sacrifical lamb led to the slaughter, as well he might because he is being delivered at the express wishes of his dead wife to his wife-to-be, Tant' Sannie, who has prophetically dreamed of killing a sheep and who explains that "my killing him meant marriage" (188). While Little Piet prepares for the murder that marriage means, the stately aristocrat who visits Lyndall prepares for the disappearance that a rejected marriage proposal means. This nameless stranger is clearly the father of her child, the "little stranger" (196) within her. But although Lyndall's suitor is, she says, "the first man I ever was afraid of" (225), his unsuccessful efforts to woo her turn him into a cardboard Byronic hero, a curiously ineffectual master who is no less insubstantial than the other three men who enter the African farm.

Only in this context of male impotence can a female fantasy of potency be articulated, or so Schreiner implies as Lyndall's furious speeches take over the second half of the book. As a vision of a no man's land, then, *The Story of an African Farm* recalls Schreiner's more starkly autobiographical novel *Undine* (1929), in which her heroine takes the sheet off a dead lover and presses her living cheek next to his cold face:

> In his ear [Undine] whispered the wild words of love that to the living she would never utter—wild passionate words, the outpourings of a life's crushed-out love, . . . And the dead man lies so still; he does not send her from him; he does not silence her; he understands her now; he loves her now.[22]

The silence of the dead man releases the speech of the living woman here, as in *The Story of an African Farm* where Lyndall rails against the social construction of a debilitating femininity after her return from an England associated with an education that inducts women into the sex roles she despises.

Speaking to the foppish Gregory Rose, who seems like "a fine baby" (170), and to the passive Waldo, who acts "Like an old hen that sits on its eggs month after month" (175), Lyndall sardonically argues that even these enervated men would not exchange their lot for hers: "every

man thanks the Lord devoutly that he isn't [a woman]" (172). Unlike
those men of letters who sought to ward off the femme fatale, Schreiner
claims through Lyndall that the fatality of femininity and of feminist
efforts to resist femininity is enforced by what we would today call sex
role socialization. For, although the sexes "were equals once when we
lay new-born babes on our nurse's knees" (177), although "We all enter
the world little plastic beings," women are "cursed from the time our
mothers bring us into the world till the shrouds are put on us" (175)
because they "shape us to our cursed end" (176). But this curse dooms
men as well as women.

Even though the plot does not substantiate Lyndall's claims, Schreiner seems to endorse her heroine's belief that men are drained of energy by women, who have been socially constructed to sustain themselves through men. Female Napoleons, according to Lyndall, could
only "rule in the dark, covertly, and by stealth, through the men whose
passions they feed on, and by whom they climb" (179). While men can
attempt to make their own way in the world, Lyndall speculates, women
have been virtually finished in schools that are "nicely adapted machines for experimenting on the question 'Into how little space a human soul can be crushed?' " (172–73). Such enforced female subjugation means that women, who "are not to study law, nor science, nor
art," must seek to study and use men: "You are our goods, our merchandise, our material for operating on; we buy you, we sell you, we
make fools of you, we act the wily old Jew with you, we keep six of you
crawling to our little feet, and praying only for a touch of our little
hand" (179).

Idleness produces this sexual exploitation, which is also the central
subject of Schreiner's feminist tract *Woman and Labour* (1911): the drop
in infant mortality and the rise of industrialization have robbed women
of their past functions, Schreiner argues, and therefore "for the first
time sex-parasitism has become a danger . . . to the mass of civilized
women, perhaps ultimately to all."[23] No longer obliged to fill her life
with incessant childbearing or to produce the necessities for the home,
the woman is turned into a lady, who is "the human female parasite—
the most deadly microbe which can make its appearance on the surface
of any social organism" (*WL* 82). Women who are bred to believe that
they can only sustain themselves through men are forced to resort to
subterfuge, for society constructs the two sexes differently: "To you it
says—*Work!* and to us it says—*Seem!*" (175).

The image of the woman as a deadly but seductive dissembler evokes
again the popular image of the insatiably desirous and destructive femme
fatale. Lyndall, like the femme fatale, is a "queen" with "no conscience"
(222) who can assert her magnetic beauty and imperious will over

everyone on the farm, even ruling Tant' Sannie with a touch of her hand or the raising of an eyebrow. Like the femme fatale, Lyndall knows that (but not what) she wants, and she is filled with a dissatisfaction that imbues her with a restless energy which underscores the passivity of those with whom she comes into contact. Self-divided, Lyndall admits that she uses her charms to gain her ends (with "this little chin, I can win money . . . I can win love" [176]), but she also bitterly resents a socialization process she associates with Chinese footbinding ("The parts we are not to use have been quite atrophied, and have even dropped off" [176]). Stalking apart "in joyless reverie," Lyndall becomes a Byronic figure and the fitting prototype of such characters as Haggard's Ayesha when her cryptic but passionately rebellious speeches are punctuated by rage that causes her to gnash her teeth until her lips bleed. Desirous of a love that will liberate her from what she experiences as the prisonhouse of her solipsism, Lyndall nevertheless seems fated to wound everyone who seeks to serve her. For all these reasons, then, she is afflicted, like the femme fatale, with a tormented and tormenting consciousness.

Yet Lyndall's speeches demonstrate her knowledge that the source of her power is contaminated, that the carnal knowledge attributed by Haggard to the femme fatale is actually the sexual symbiosis of the sex parasite. For, according to Schreiner, the parasite drains life from the independent organisms upon which she feeds and thereby reduces men to instrumentality while simultaneously diminishing her own chance of autonomous survival. Unlike Ayesha, moreover, Lyndall demonstrates her awareness of the source of her priority when she analyzes the humiliating discrepancy between the social construction of female parasitism and women's biological primacy. "*We* bear the world, and *we* make it" (180), Lyndall defiantly exclaims, foreshadowing Schreiner's later proclamation that "No man ever yet entered life farther than the length of one navel-cord from the body of the woman who bore him. It is the woman who is the final standard of the race" (*WL* 109).

But the decline in masculine dominance dramatized throughout *The Story of an African Farm* implies that women can no longer exploit a male race that has already been effectively exhausted. The monetary figure of Tant' Sannie, moreover, discredits traditional forms of female survival as monstrous and vampiric. As the Old Woman Tant' Sannie grows larger at the end of the novel, then, the New Womanly Lyndall declines not—like Ayesha—into an animal but instead into a frail shadow of herself. Her anorexic devolution proves the truth of her assertion that the female parasite is incapable of an independent existence.[24] Protesting women's acceptance of degrading dependence,

Lyndall demonstrates that the role of the femme fatale is fatal even to those women who struggle against it.

Disease, weakness, confinement, paralysis, thwarted ambition: these are the fate of the female parasite that Lyndall first outlines and then typifies as she journeys alone "out of the world" (226), across the Free State of the Transvaal, to give birth to a baby that dies. Later, haunted by her dead baby, lying on a couch, wasting away, unable to eat, and furnished with a lap dog, a mirror, and a wardrobe of lovely dresses, she is an image of the "curse" of femininity, of the woman crucified on the cross of gender. Through the interpolated portrait of Lyndall provided by Gregory Rose (when he disguises himself as a woman in order to nurse her and later recounts her story to Em), Schreiner's passion play encapsulates the sacrificial plot that haunted many of the authors and heroines of nineteenth-century literature: Mary Wollstonecraft, who was subjected to a primitive treatment meant to cure the puerperal fever that would kill her, a treatment that included puppies brought in to draw the milk from her breasts; Emily Dickinson, who imagined herself as the "Empress of Calvary" (J. 1072); George Eliot's Hetty Sorel, who is tormented by a feeling that she has herself died after she commits infanticide; Charlotte Brontë's Jane Eyre, who is burdened with dream-children; and Charlotte Brontë herself, whose death during pregnancy has been attributed by some biographers to starvation induced by a terrible case of "morning sickness."[25]

Most strikingly, of course, Lyndall resembles Emily Brontë's Catherine Earnshaw Linton, who feels split in two just before childbirth. Schreiner seems to ask, "What would have happened to Brontë's Catherine if she had refused to marry Edgar Linton or to join with Heathcliff?" Her answer implies that such a Catherine would have lost everything, even her child. Through Lyndall, Schreiner examines what she sees as the martyrdom women have suffered in maternity, even as she invokes spiritual language to consecrate this sacrifice. A "little ewe lamb" (260), Lyndall has her feet annointed as she travels in her pilgrimage toward the Blue Mountain to find "something to worship" (266), convinced that "till I have been delivered I will deliver no one" (183).

To be sure, despite the religious rhetoric that informs Gregory Rose's description of Lyndall's pilgrimage, she seems almost narcissistic about her bondage, self-pitying about her confinement. But what makes her childish petulance and her furious diatribes more than just pathetic or insane is her rebellious determination to be independent even when she herself realizes that independence spells death for the parasite. Lyndall, who will either take a man without his name (her lover) or a name without the man (Gregory Rose), drives a wedge between language and male presence that subverts masculine authority. Refusing marriage during her pregnancy, she attacks wedlock as a protection bought at the expense of integrity: "A little weeping, a little wheedling, a little self-degradation, a little careful use of our advantages, and then some man will say—'Come, be my wife!' " (177). Marriage is associated with prostitution, for the "Professional duties" of looking "perfectly exquisite" (186) mean that "a woman who has sold herself, even for a new ring and a new name, need hold her skirt aside for no creature in the street. They both earn their bread in one way" (177).

Rejecting *the* profession of women, therefore, Lyndall reclaims singleness as an honorable choice in the face of ridicule. Even more importantly, by electing single motherhood she rejects chastity as a masculine ideal established to insure male ownership of children, and she thereby threatens the patrilineage at the heart of patriarchy. Choosing illegitimacy for herself and her child, she disentangles reproduction from marriage while rejecting heterosexual desire as an unacceptable form of sadomasochism. To her nameless suitor, Lyndall claims that men love women who can be "mastered" or "broken" while women love men "because they are strong" (225), and she refuses to "be bound to one whom I love as I love you" (266). An exercise in denial, her suicidal anorexia constitutes a radical refusal to continue bearing the race, for, unlike Schreiner's mother—Rebekkah Lyndall Schreiner, who was wearied by birth after birth—this new Lyndall will not submit to incessant childbearing. Neither madonna nor madwoman, Lyndall is the New Woman, and, both in the world of the novel and the world of women, she had a number of converts. Just as Waldo, Gregory Rose, and Em respectfully serve and celebrate her, such eminent late Victorians as Hugh Walpole, W. E. Lecky, Charles Dilke, William Gladstone, Havelock Ellis, Eleanor Marx, and Vera Brittain viewed the novel in which she appeared as marking an epoch, in Walpole's words, "as scarcely any other book can do."[26]

It is significant, therefore, that Elaine Showalter's identification of Schreiner's ambivalence with "the distress signals of a transitional generation"[27] is substantiated by the suffering inflicted on all of Lyndall's fictional converts. Her two male apostles within *The Story of an African Farm* are destroyed by their adherence to her creed. Gregory Rose, who "for[gets] that it is a man's right to rule" (232), obliterates his identity when he dons women's clothes to accompany Lyndall during her pilgrimage in the Transvaal. After this "new man" is given in marriage by Lyndall to Em, he is no less controlled by the dying "angel" (259) than her other convert, Waldo, who can only solace himself at her death by constructing a compensatory story of the African farm as a divine mother. But in the final scene of the novel, when "Nature enfolds you" and "It is as though our mother smoothed our hair, and we are comforted" (285), Waldo either dozes or dies into oblivion. If, as a number of critics have speculated, Waldo represents Schreiner's tribute to Ralph Waldo Emerson, the dreaminess and passivity she identifies with her character's philosophic meditations qualify that tribute, as does her affixing the last name "Iron" to the "Ralph" she used as her pseudonymous first name.[28] Not a hero of "self-reliance," Waldo never gains the strength that his namesake prescribes.

At the same time, both Tant' Sannie and Em survive at least in part because they do not rebel against the conventionality of their lives. Weighing 260 pounds, Tant' Sannie accepts her marriage on the assumption that "it's very much the same who one has . . . A man's a man, you know" (280), while Em, who "fills up the gaps in other people's lives, and is always number two" (218), resigns herself to longing for what she will never receive in her lifetime; Lyndall's fate teaches Em that she is destined to pray for what is bound to come too late. But if Lyndall's effect is fatal within the world of the African farm, in the world outside the novel a number of women readers would have agreed with a Lancashire worker's belief about Lyndall that "*she* could speak what we feel."[29] For, through its prototypical portrait of the New Woman, *The Story of an African Farm* helped to establish both the intellectual basis and the rhetorical tropes of turn-of-the-century feminism, specifically that movement's identification of women with the colonized, its use of revisionary religious metaphors, and its utopian impulses.

As the first influential novel written in English about South Africa, *The Story of an African Farm* presents the wilderness of the karroo as a liminal zone in which characters freed from the normative restraints of western civilization can act out their desires and thereby dramatize the meaning of those restraints. By situating Lyndall as prophetess in an alien African landscape, moreover, Schreiner implies that the New Woman has no place in the old world, and she therefore establishes a precedent for the identification of women with the colonized.[30] Just as important, Schreiner's concept of sexual parasitism is directly linked to imperialism in two ways. First, female idleness is only possible "when, owing to the extensive employment of the labour of slaves, or of subject races or classes, the dominant race or class has become so liberally supplied with the material goods of life, that mere physical toil on the part of its own female members has become unnecessary" (*WL* 80). Only "advanced" or industrialized nations produce a sexual parasitism that inevitably heralds their decline and fall. Second, besides being a by-product of imperialism, sexual parasitism is a metaphor for it because the interdependence of the parasite and the host is parallel to the interdependence of the colony and its imperial "parent": while the colony is dependent on the "parent" society for its laws, institutions, rulers, currency, and language (as the female is legally and economically reduced to a childlike dependence on the male), the imperial country needs the labor and materials of the colony for its very subsistence (as the male is biologically dependent on the female).

As we speculated in chapter one, throughout the late Victorian period the geopolitical and racial otherness of the colonies was analogically connected in the western, male imagination to the sexual otherness of women. An avid reader, Schreiner would probably have been familiar with meditations on this theme by such thinkers as Charles Darwin, Carl Vogt, and John Stuart Mill. In *The Descent of Man* (1871), Darwin identified even women's strongest traits of intuition and perception as "characteristics of the lower races, and therefore of a past and lower state of civilization."[31] Similarly, in his *Lectures on Man* (1864) the cranologist Vogt argued that "the female skull is smaller" than the male and therefore "approaches, in many respects, that of the infant, and in a still greater degree that of the lower races."[32] In other words, as Brian Harrison has argued, "There was . . . a partial correlation between anti-suffragist and imperialist feeling," and what Harrison calls the "clubland" of all-male colleges and professional institutions, of pubs and clubs, set itself in opposition to the dreams of Herland that energized the women's movement.[33] In his *Subjection of Women* (1869) Mill was simultaneously reacting against just such charges and extending the imperialist analogy to the American institution of slavery when he declared that the British wife is "the actual bond-servant of her husband: no less so, as far as legal obligation goes, than slaves commonly so called."[34]

Of course, for feminists like Elizabeth Cady Stanton and Sojourner Truth, abolition had early served as an impetus for feminist activism. Before and after 1866, when the Fourteenth Amendment to the U.S. Constitution granted freed *male* slaves the vote, both Truth and Stanton identified women's subordination in patriarchy with the dispossession of blacks under slavery. Sojourner Truth's famous speech "Ain't I a Woman?" begins by prophesying that " 'twixt the negroes of the South and the women at the North, all talking about rights, the white men will be in a fix pretty soon"; and Stanton's "Address to the New York State Legislature, 1860" points to "the similarity" between the slave's condition and that of wives, who have no name of their own, no right to their earnings, no ownership of their children, and no legal existence.[35] Both were participating in a tradition established by, among other works, Elizabeth Barrett Browning's poems protesting the effects of slavery on women, verse based on Barrett Browning's belief that any woman who thinks she "has no business with questions like the question of slavery" should "subside into slavery and concubinage herself."[36]

In England, where the abolitionist cause was widely discussed, activists for women's rights used the racial analogy to emphasize their own grievances. When the suffragists in England carried placards proclaiming "No Votes for Women—No Home Rule,"[37] they meant to express their hostility toward a parliament that considered the grievances of the Irish before confronting the problems of women. Yet, in spite of such overt rivalry (if there are no votes for women, let there be no home rule), such posters implicitly identified women with the colonized, indeed, with the urgent necessity of attaining home rule (if there were votes for women, there would be home rule). More, the punning phrase implies that women who rule at home, and only at home, represent a model for the colonial independence struggle. As Nancy F. Cott has recently pointed out, moreover, the Pankhursts (and their admirers in America) "had learned their most extreme militance—destruction of property, arson, and physical assault—from Irish nationalists."[38]

The colonies, Schreiner knew, had long been dumping grounds not only for second sons, but for so-called "redundant" (that is, single) women as well as for prostitutes.[39] Often, too, fictional madwomen like Bertha Mason Rochester and Hetty Sorel either come from or are relegated to what we now call the third world. Yet, as Nina Auerbach has shown, Victorian spinsters shared a "vision of salvation through exile" that was perhaps best expressed by Charlotte Brontë's friend Mary Taylor, who welcomed the work available in the colonies as a release from the idleness usually imposed on middle-class women: "The new world will be no Paradise," she explained to another prospective traveler, "but still much better than the nightmare [of England]."[40] That, for a number of reasons, women first received the vote in outposts far removed from the centers of European culture —in Wyoming, for example, in 1890; in Colorado and New Zealand in 1893; in South Australia in 1894—tends to corroborate Taylor's judgment.[41]

Many turn-of-the-century and early twentieth-century women, whether they worked for or against the empire, seem to have associated the colonies with the physical, economic, and social freedom denied them at home. As late as 1928, for example, the African-born heroine of Winifred Holtby's *The Land of Green Ginger* feels stifled in England and hears a voice urging her to escape:

Why were you not in your own country? Your marble towers lie
awaiting you. Your unseen islands blossom from the sea. . . . Here
are trees withholding their beauty of leaves and flowers until your
cry of pleasure summons them. Here are roads built for the welcome of your feet. You are lost, lost, lost, unless you seek your
country.[42]

While Holtby toured Africa, returning to England in order to plead the
cause of natives in 1926, the suffragist heroine of Elizabeth Robins's
novel *The Convert* (1907) speculates on the inevitable destruction of
"successive clutches at civilization": "What if the meaning of history is
that an Empire maintained by brute force shall perish by brute force!"[43]

As if explaining why Mary Taylor, Mary Kingsley, the Pankhursts,
Annie Besant, and Gertrude Bell traveled to the colonies as a release
from the constraints of Victorian culture, Florence Nightengale celebrated the "One [who] discovers the new world" in *Cassandra,* part of a
book that was privately printed in the 1850s (right before Nightingale
determined to escape domestic confinement by journeying to the Cri-
mea) but that in its excerpted form was first publicly available in Ray
Strachey's history of the suffrage movement, *The Cause* (1928).[44] When
Nightingale exclaimed, "Give us back our suffering," she might have
been writing about Lyndall's struggle against the material comforts that
reward female idleness and feminine dissembling, a struggle through
which Schreiner established what would become a fertile tradition of
literature by women that speculates on the feminization of the colonies,
the colonization of the female, or the nature of the relationship between colonization and feminization.

Extending from texts by Rudyard Kipling's sister, Beatrice Kipling, and Nightingale's biographer Elspeth Huxley to works by Jean
Rhys, Christina Stead, Margaret Laurence, Margaret Atwood, Nadine
Gordimer, and Doris Lessing, this tradition typically enables the writer
to negotiate between a colonial outpost (often experienced as a place
of exile) and imperial centers of culture (also often experienced as places
of exile). As Judith Kegan Gardiner has recently demonstrated, marginalization both in the colony and in the cultural center makes the idea
of home problematic and causes women writers to resist "the sentimental claims of the home canon, country, and culture."[45] Significantly,
then, while Rudyard Kipling's poem "An Interesting Condition" portrays "the East" as "A beautiful woman [who] is always old," Beatrice
Kipling's story "The Little Pink House" records the homesickness and
exhaustion of a young wife who finds in "The gorgeous East . . .
neither glamour nor glory."[46] As if commenting on the psychology of
Beatrice Kipling's heroine, who "lived in India, save for the wide dif-

ference of heat, discomfort, and loneliness, exactly as she would have lived in England" and whose death reveals the deadliness of a transplanted (British) domesticity, Doris Lessing once explained that her mother "hated" the veld which "trapped" her, although Africa became for the daughter residing in England "quite simply, the luckiest thing that ever happened."[47]

But the literary woman who most ecstatically invoked Africa as "the luckiest thing that ever happened" was Isak Dinesen, whose *Out of Africa* (1937) elaborated on the idea that the "relation between the white and the black race in Africa in many ways resembles the relation between the two sexes."[48] Because the stories of women, "when they sit amongst themselves and know that no man can hear them, [go] to prove [this point]," Dinesen describes the natives' "enclosed women's world" within whose "walls and fortifications" she feels "the presence of . . . the idea of a Millennium when women were to reign supreme in the world": one "old mother at such times would take on a new shape, and sit enthroned as a massive dark symbol for that mighty female deity who had existed in old ages, before the time of the Prophet's God." Dinesen's own friendship with another female farmowner also gains in symbolic resonance, for together "we were in reality a pair of mythical women, . . . a unity, the Genii of the farmer's life in Africa."[49] Dinesen, who acknowledged her indebtedness to Schreiner by producing an introduction to *The Story of an African Farm*, and through her preference for the Danish title of *Out of Africa—Den afrikanske Farm (The African Farm)*—clearly identified Africa with what she prized "above everything else that I possess," namely "my freedom."[50]

Understandably, then, in 1926, when Dinesen was operating her farm by herself, she considered "feminism . . . the most significant movement of the nineteenth century," a movement whose "upheavals" were "far from *'done with'* at the present moment."[51] But Dinesen's frequent admission that she had gained her powerful persona of "Baroness" by paying for it through the syphilis she had contracted from her husband reminds us, as does Nightingale's "Give us back our suffering," that *The Story of an African Farm* helped to establish a link between self-sacrifice and feminism that also infiltrated turn-of-the-century suffragist activity. To be sure, Lyndall's attacks on what she defines as the sadomachism of heterosexual desire, on marriage as prostitution, and on the economic and social degradation of single women contributed to the emergence of a new generation of feminist scholars, including historians like Alice Clark, who documented her indebtedness to Schreiner in her *Working Life of Women in the 17th Century* (1919) because Schreiner was the first to recognize the link between capitalism and sexual parasitism. But the militant suffragists at the turn of the century often seemed to want to replicate Lyndall's martyrdom. Just as Lyndall tries to smash the windows and burn down the house when she is imprisoned by Boneparte, the suffragists smashed windows and set fire to symbols of "clubland." Just as Lyndall starves herself at the end of the novel, the suffragists fasted in prison. Just as Lyndall presents herself as a "little ewe lamb," the militants were accepted, according to Teresa Billington, "not as rebels, but as innocent victims, and as innocent victims we were led to pose."[52]

The idea of a female Christ had, of course, fascinated Protestant mystics from Joanna Southcott and Ann Lee to Florence Nightingale, who believed that "The next Christ will perhaps be a female Christ."[53] But many militants, too, extolled what Christabel Pankhurst acclaimed as "the martyr-spirit [which] . . . shines out again in a blaze of glory," for as Emily Wilding Davison proclaimed before she killed herself in 1913 by running onto the racing track of the King's Derby, "to re-enact the tragedy of Calvary . . . is the last consummate sacrifice of the Militant!"[54] Not only did Christabel Pankhurst compare the suffragists with "the saints and martyrs of the past," but Frances Swiney viewed female martyrdom as a direct result of sex antagonism. "No female animal has been so ruthlessly, so brutally, so generally mercilessly exploited by the man, as woman," Swiney announced. "She stands the martyr of organised and systematic sexual wrong-doing on the part of the man who should be her mate."[55]

Despite her famous friendships with male intellectuals, Schreiner herself seemed to agree with Swiney that "Woman's cruelest and most relentless foe is her brother, Man," for on more than one occasion the novelist expressed the view recorded in a letter to Havelock Ellis that "in that you are a man I am afraid of you and shrink from you," and she believed, too, that when anyone "breaks away from all old mooring and shapes a higher path of morality for oneself, and perhaps for others who shall follow one, it cannot be done without suffering."[56] Even feminist contemporaries who protested against the female martyrdom Schreiner sometimes fetishized sought to save women from what they viewed as an historical sacrifice that had not led to female redemption. As early as 1871, Elizabeth Stuart Phelps argued that "It is no figure of speech to say that the 'woman question' is the most tremendous question God has ever asked the world since he asked, 'What think ye of Christ?' on Calvary."[57] In a utopian dream vision entitled *A Sex Revolution* (1894), moreover, Lois Nichols Waisbrooker's heroine explains that "Man may be nailed to a wooden cross with spikes of iron, but woman groans from the torture inflicted by a cross of flesh and blood."[58] Precisely this sense of female crucifixion is decried in some of the turn-of-the century stories we discussed in *The War of the Words*, specifically in George Egerton's "Virgin Soil" (1894) and Charlotte Mew's "A White Night" (1903).

Whether women embraced or rejected such martyrdom, the link between self-sacrifice and feminism established the same point Schreiner made in *Woman in Labour,* namely that the women's movement had to be understood as a "religious" (*WL*125) development. When Margaret Fuller asked women to "retire within themselves" in order to "come forth again, renovated and baptized" so that "their sweet singing shall not be from passionate impulse, but the lyrical overflow of a divine rapture,"[59] her religious language raised the spiritual questions that issued in Elizabeth Cady Stanton's 1895 *The Woman's Bible,* a highly controversial book aimed at dismantling any "religion [which] teaches woman's subjection and man's right of domination."[60] Condemning Abraham's "conduct" as "reprehensible," viewing "the Jewish Lord" as "a very contradictory character, unworthy [of] our love and admiration," and indicating that the "chief point of interest in [the] parable of Balaam and his ass, is that the latter"—who sees the angel of God and is beaten by the unseeing Balaam—"belonged to the female sex," the authors of *The Woman's Bible* fervently believed that "The antagonism which the Christian church has built up between the male and the female must entirely vanish."[61] With their processions, hymns, and martyrs, many "converts" to the "cause" clearly agreed with Elizabeth Robins that "the ideal for which woman suffrage stands has come, through suffering, to be a religion,"[62] albeit a religion very much at odds with traditional Judeo-Christianity.

To be sure, there were, as we have seen, female spiritualists and theologians—for instance, Madame Blavatsky and Mary Baker Eddy—who used female symbols of divinity without endorsing explicitly feminist goals. But many mystically-inclined women of letters looked either backward or forward to what Dinesen had found in the natives' "women's world"—the "idea of a Millennium when women were to reign supreme." Published in a 1913 American edition, Rosa Mayreder's *A Survey of the Woman Problem* claimed that "it is the women who are the first burden-bearers, the first tillers of the soil, the first builders and the first potters—if, indeed, the whole industrial part of primitive life, together with the first inventions belonging thereto, may not be said to be the work of the female sex."[63] Precisely such a vision of "the reins of power in the shape of a Matriarchate" animated Mary Austin's portraits of visionary Indian women, for this Southwest regionalist, who had interpreted Haggard's " 'She' as the matriarch,' " encountered the mythic and mystic meanings of female primacy in the figure of the basket maker: "Every Indian woman is an artist,—sees, feels, creates, but does not philosophize about her processes."[64] Matilda Joslyn Gage, who had worked with Stanton on *The Woman's Bible,* summarized both the critique of Christian doctrine and the effort to transform feminism itself into an alternative religion when she argued not only against any "belief in a trinity of masculine gods," but also for the "religious revolution" of a women's movement that would "undermine the whole fabric of christendom."[65] Gage's claim that the Christian church has "shown cruelty and contempt for women" was grounded in her belief that "During the Matriarchate all life was regarded as holy."[66]

Yet all of these thinkers' prophecies about the transformative nature of feminism also illustrate how *The Story of an African Farm* is typical in its insistence that the New Woman ushers in an entirely new age in history. Lyndall's search for "something to worship" may end, like all striving in the novel, in nothing, but she has always acknowledged her entrapment in historical time. "[I]f I might but be one of those to be born in the future," Lyndall speculates, "then, perhaps, to be born a woman will not be to be born branded" (175). From Waldo's revulsion with his father's watch, which ticks out men's death and damnation, to Lyndall's glimpse of "that new time" when "love is no more bought or sold" (182), *The Story of an African Farm* is informed by the same futuristic fantasies that issued in Schreiner's subsequent dreams and allegories and in the conclusion of *Woman and Labour,* where she looks toward a new "dream of a Garden" which lies in a distant future when men and women "shall together raise about them an Eden nobler than any the Chaldean dreams of; an Eden created by their own labour and made beautiful by their own fellowship" (*WL* 282).

Such utopian visions were, of course, glimpsed by the heroines of a number of earlier novels by female authors. In *The Mill on the Floss* (1860), for example, Maggie Tulliver wishes that she "could make myself a world outside [of loving], as men do."[67] A world outside of loving proved to be a world elsewhere for feminists like Elizabeth Cady Stanton and Geraldine Jewsbury: while Stanton explained that the "true woman is as yet a dream of the future," Jewsbury viewed herself as "a mere faint indication" of "certain higher qualities and possibilities that lie in women."[68] With its portrayal of men wearing the suffragist colors to further the women's cause, Cicely Hamilton's 1909 play *How the Vote Was Won* best represents the wishful fantasies of turn-of-the-century feminists, while Rebecca West's sardonic comment—"The worst of being a feminist is that one has no evidence"—serves as a model for the anxiety that attends such leaps of faith.[69] In its deployment of utopian strategies, Mary Elizabeth Coleridge's poem "The White Women" (1908) summarizes this tradition through a reworking of a Malaysian legend about the power achieved by a primordial community of women.[70] Coleridge's "lovely, wild white women folk . . . never bowed their necks

beneath the yoke, / They dwelt alone when the first morning broke /
And Time began."[71]

Yet, judging from Lyndall's hunger strike, even the most passionate
New Women found passive resistance an easier strategy than active
rebellion. Indeed, like Rider Haggard, Schreiner explores the idea that
a sacrifice of the alien New Woman is inevitable in the context of patriarchal history. While Haggard dramatizes this sacrifice as, at least
implicitly, a triumph of patriarchal law, Schreiner mourns it as a tragedy of femininity. But what if the entropy that characterizes patriarchal
culture in *The Story of an African Farm* and the energy that motivates its
heroine lead to "that new time" Lyndall so eagerly anticipates? In *Herland,* Charlotte Perkins Gilman provides an answer to this question,
and her New Women's new world—representing a radical break with
the patriarchal past—is as wounding to men as the old order had been
to women. Like Schreiner, Gilman cannot imagine women successfully
fighting to bring that new world into being. Yet the utopian strategies
in Gilman's work play an important part in feminist intellectual history
because they solve precisely this problem of female uncertainty. Rather
than attacking what women have been, the utopian writer celebrates
what women can yet become; instead of implying that the political and
economic steps necessary for creating a different world are unclear,
she imagines those steps already having taken place in a different di-
mension.

Working within the intellectual framework constructed by Schreiner—whose novels and allegories the American recommended and
quoted to friends and took on her lecture tours[72]—Gilman in *Herland*
revises the imperialist romance made popular by Rider Haggard. That
she shared Schreiner's perspective on the situation of women is clear
from her essay "Parasitism and Civilised Vice" (1931), which reads like
a meditation on Schreiner's *Woman and Labour.* Contrasting "sex parasitism, in which the female is dependent upon the economic activities
of the male," with what she identifies as male parasitism in lower life
forms, the American feminist emphasizes how the sexual parasitism of
women directly contradicts any known biological model.[73] In *Herland,*
written more than a decade and a half earlier, Gilman created an all-
female society whose culture suggests that the figure Haggard portrayed as a femme fatale needs to be understood, in the terms supplied
by Schreiner, as a sex parasite. By approaching Haggard's *She* from
Schreiner's feminist perspective, Gilman links male anxieties about biological secondariness with masculine exploration and exploitation. Yet
although her text illustrates the ways in which the ideology of feminist

self-determination, spirituality, and fantasy might subvert itself, the tale nevertheless comically implies that men who experience themselves as secondary will exhibit all of the psychological foibles generally ascribed to the second sex. Masculinist dystopias, *Herland* demonstrates, fuel feminist utopias, for if woman is dispossessed, a nobody, in the somewhere of patriarchy, it may be that she can only become somebody in the nowhere of utopia.

Gilman specified her critique of *She* by situating Herland on a "spur" of land "up where the maps had to be made," even in an extinct volcano.[74] In fact, it was a volcanic blast that destroyed all the men of this society who were fighting in a war, and sealed the women into a community of their own. As in *She*, where the native Amahaggars trace descent from the mother's line, the society in *Herland* is matrilineal. As in Haggard's novel, moreover, this isolated community ruled by women worships a woman who has solved the riddle of life and death, but while Haggard's Ayesha seeks personal immortality, the female inhabitants of Herland value the immortality of the species, and each woman is capable of parthenogenetically reproducing herself. They gained this power, Gilman explains, 2,000 years ago, 2,000 being the approximate age of She. The men who enter Herland initially discount stories of an all female land; they "knew the stuff that savage dreams are made of" (3). Yet, just as three virile men, one a self-proclaimed misogynist, penetrate the caves of Kôr, *Herland* is explored by a three-man team of adventurers whose misogyny is astutely analyzed by Gilman.

To be sure, Gilman also seems to be revising the plots of Tennyson's *The Princess* and Gilbert and Sullivan's *Princess Ida,* for she is satirizing male stereotypes about female communities.[75] Her intrepid explorers—Terry O. Nicholson (Old Nick), Jeff Margrave, and the narrator, Vandyck Jennings—therefore represent three faintly ludicrous specimens of masculinity, each with his own all too predictable fantasy of what to expect in a country ruled by women. Terry, whose passion is exploration and mechanics, is a prototypical sexist with a vision of "a sort of sublimated summer resort—just Girls and Girls and Girls" (7) where he can rule as the "king of Ladyland" (10). Chivalric and sentimental Jeff, a poetic geologist turned doctor, expects a world "just blossoming with roses and babies and canaries and tidies." Van, a sociologist, may be reclaimable—he neither subordinates nor elevates the other sex—so his vision of a society "built on a sort of matriarchal principle" in which women visit men in an annual wedding call (7) comes closest to anticipating what he will encounter.

But, when they actually enter the no man's land of Herland, all three find their stereotypes of women disabused. Lo and behold, women do not bicker; they are well organized; they are not jealous for male attention; they are physically agile and spiritually cooperative. As each of the sexist stereotypes of the men is discarded, we see the "diametrical reconfigurations" that Eric Rabkin considers so central to fantastic literature:[76]

> We had expected a dull submissive monotony, and found a daring social inventiveness far beyond our own, . . .
> We had expected pettiness, and found a social consciousness besides which our nations looked like quarreling children. . . .
> We had expected jealousy, and found a broad sisterly affection [81]

The satiric critique here means that the better Herland looks as an all-woman culture, the worse patriarchal America seems by contrast.

Especially in the introductory chapters of Gilman's utopia, the tables are turned, and the men suffer from culture shock when they are treated like the minority they, in fact, are. Secondary creatures, they are pushed around like cattle, drugged like criminals, bedded down like babies, soothed like invalids, instructed like schoolboys, and put on display as anatomical curiosities marketable only for matrimony. Considered inferior for their gender-related secondary sexual characteristics, such as combativeness and competitiveness, they become petulant, irritable, jealous, vain of their physical appearance, and rivalrous for approval, as Gilman humorously diagnoses the faults ascribed to her own sex as symptoms of a disease called marginalization. In one of their more extreme situations, frightened by the "quiet potency" of a mass of women, the men find themselves "much in the position of the suffragette trying to get to the Parliament buildings through a triple cordon of London police" (23). While the three heroes of *She* valiantly hold on to their masculine grace under pressure even as they penetrate the womblike tomb that Ayesha rules, the quarreling men who are cooped up in a fortress in Herland try, like fairy-tale princesses, to escape at night by tying together bedsheets and lowering themselves to a ledge so as to reach their airplane, only to find what they call "our machine" (39) "swaddled," literally sewed up in a bag (42).

Part of what these men must discover is that there is no central, secret interior place to penetrate, for there are no tombs or caves in *Herland*. Bold and brave, the three men of Haggard's romance penetrate not only to the womb/tomb but also to the single source, She, who is everywoman, the essentially feminine. They will either possess her or be possessed by her, the plot implies. But the men in Gilman's utopia are "tamed" and "trained" (72, 73) into the realization that there is no She, but instead there are many Hers, some of whom are cautiously willing to welcome them as an experimental opportunity to restore "bisexuality." What Gilman seeks to call into question is the idea that there is or should be a single definition of what constitutes the female. There is no Kôr or core in *Herland*. Historically such a core definition has fixated on eroticism, and therefore Gilman gives us women with no sexual desire at all.

Gilman's project to decenter definitions of the real woman requires an imaginative leap beyond empirical data to postulate the possibility of female primacy. In such influential texts as *Women and Economics* (1898), *The Home* (1903), *Human Work* (1904), and *Man-Made World* (1911), after all, she had repeatedly documented the historical subordination of women. For Gilman, the economic dependence of women means that female sexual arts became crucial for attracting and keeping a man: woman therefore identified herself with the sexual function completely, while man was considered the human prototype. As if writing about the femme fatale from Lyndall's perspective, Gilman claims that economic dependence causes sexuality to become highly exaggerated in women, making "a race with one sex a million years behind the other": "in her position of arrested development, she has maintained the virtues and the vices of the period of human evolution at which she was imprisoned."[77] Not only is the seemingly socialized woman a savage, she is a parasite who consumes what the male produces: "He is her food supply" (*WE* 22).

Haggard's denizen of the darkness with her massive lengths of hair, her gauzy veils, her turbulent desires, her looks that kill, contrasts strikingly with the short-haired citizens of Herland, who wear tunics quilted with functional pockets for greater freedom of movement in their work. Not merely a reflection of the dress reform movement, the desexualized costumes of women in *Herland* also emphasize the multiple lives open to the female of the species in a society that no longer opposes reproduction to production. Although Gilman could point to no matriarchal, or even egalitarian, culture in recorded history, she had been influenced by the sociologist Lester Ward, who argued that the female is the original "race-type," while the male is only the "sex-type,"[78] and in *Herland* her feminism consists in a vision of society in which the word "woman" conjures up the whole world of exploring, herding, reaping, and toiling that have made a two-thousand-year-old civilization, while the word "man" means only male, the sex (137). In doing this, she deploys a strategy of role reversal that is central to the feminist rhetorical tradition from Anna Denton Cridge's *Man's Rights; or, How Would You Like It?* (1870) to the witty essay by Bette-Jane Raphael entitled "The Myth of the Male Orgasm" (1980).[79]

Not content to reverse gender hierarchies, however, Gilman would replace the parasite-siren with the fruitful mother, for she believed that

"Maternal energy is the force through which have come into the world both love and industry" (*WE* 126). The middle chapters of *Herland* portray motherhood completely transformed, divorced from heterosexuality, the private family, and economic dependence. Maternal feeling is shown to flow "out in a strong, wide current, unbroken through the generations, deepening and widening through the years, including every child in all the land" (95). Motherhood therefore becomes a paradigm of service so that childbearing and nursing are models for labor. Similarly, what Gilman saw as all the evils of the private home—the isolation of women, the unhealthy amateur cooking, the waste of labor and products, the improper upbringing of children, the lack of individual privacy—are avoided not by destroying the idea of home but by extending it so the race is viewed as a family and the world as its home. Redefinitions of work, of the home, and of motherhood itself confuse the male visitors who had initially insisted that in any *"civilized"* country there "must be men" (11). Eventually they are forced to renounce not only this assumption but the definition of "civilization" that makes it possible.

"Civilized and still arboreal—peculiar people" (17): Van first glimpses the society of Herland when he sees its inhabitants playing, like wood nymphs, in the branches of a huge tree. With its forests that are cultivated like farms and gardens that look like parks, Gilman's earthly paradise banishes wilderness, replacing it with cultivation. In fact, the crucial difference between Herland and our land is the feeling Gilman strives to give us that culture in her feminist utopia is no longer opposed to nature, in part because of the intercession of the female. If women can be considered closer to nature because of the their role in perpetuating the species, Gilman implies, then they can break down the dichotomy between mind and matter, man and nature.[80] Because the all-female Herlanders define the human as female, mother earth is no longer an antagonist. The implications of the mother as landscape, the landscape as mother, suggests the author of *Herland*, are quite different for the two sexes.

Symbolically, then, parthenogenesis functions to represent the creativity and autonomy of women as well as the interplay of nature and human nature. At the same time, it releases women from the female Oedipus complex as defined by Freud: the daughter's rejection of the mother, her resulting sense of self-hatred, the extension of her desire for a phallus to desire for the man who possesses the penis. Whereas Haggard celebrates the phallic pillar of fire that strikes Ayesha down, Gilman valarizes the creativity of the womb. But her radical rejection of Freud's identification of the penis with power is probably made clearest in her emphasis on the erotics of motherhood in *Herland:* "before a child comes," we are told, "there is a period of utter exaltation—the whole being is uplifted and filled with a concentrated desire" (70). As the three male visitors admit the greater power of the "overmothers," the superwomen of this superland, two of them are converted to what they call "loving up," a phrase that evokes the "stirring" within them "of some ancient dim prehistoric consciousness . . . like—coming home to mother" (142).

Yet another consequence of Gilman's refusal of the phallic law of the fathers is her substitution of a reverential "prehistoric conscious-ness" of the mother for the idea of God the father. Criticizing the idea that the Word of God is a closed revelation confined to a single set of sacred texts, one of Gilman's characters contrasts it to the "Indwelling Spirit" of service the Herlanders worship as the accumulated mother-love of the race. Haggard's Ayesha is obsessed with obtaining eternal life for herself and her lover Vincey. But while Haggard implicitly crit-icizes the barbaric vanity of this desire of every woman for personal physical immortality, Gilman claims that the Christian doctrine of per-sonal spiritual immortality is no less egocentric, "a singularly foolish idea . . . And if true, most disagreeable" (116). Instead of desiring to go on forever, Gilman's spokeswoman wants her descendants to go on forever. Identification with the species replaces personal identity, as Gilman insists on the importance of accepting death as an aspect of life and of placing life, not death, at the center of religion. Therefore, in contrast to Ayesha, who reigns over a realm of perfectly embalmed bodies, Gilman's Herlanders practice cremation. By replacing a tran-scendent God the father with "Maternal Pantheism" (59), moreover, Gilman attributes to traditional Christianity the faults ascribed by Hag-gard to Ayesha. As in her theological book *His Religion and Hers* (1923), Gilman argues, "Had the religions of the world developed through her mind, they would have shown one deep, essential difference, the dif-ference between birth and death."[81]

Gilman's garden of parthenogenesis replaces the Judeo-Christian garden of Genesis, and, specifically, her pastoral implies that the au-thority of the father—biological or spiritual—is a myth fast degenerat-ing to the status of a fiction. Writing at the turn of the century, she agrees with Schreiner that the disappearance of God reflects and per-petuates a weakening in patriarchal domination. But besides symboliz-ing the autonomous creativity of women, the insignificance of the male, and the disappearance of God, parthenogenesis also effectively solves the problems produced by motherhood's status as a political institution in patriarchal society. Just at the time Gilman was imagining the free mothers of Herland, thinkers from Annie Besant and Margaret Sanger to Emma Goldman were advocating contraception in an effort to liberate the female body from male sexual and medical control and to end what Goldman called "the traffic in women."[82]

In her own life, Gilman had been profoundly afflicted by the problematics of maternity in a male-dominated culture. The painful experiences she describes in *The Living of Charlotte Perkins Gilman* (1935)—of being abandoned by her father at an early age, of being brought up by an economically and psychologically impoverished mother who denied her physical affection, of severe postpartum depression following marriage and the birth of her daughter—led to the mental breakdown her physician, S. Weir Mitchell, attempted to alleviate with his rest cure. In *Herland,* she gives us this experience transmuted into an enabling fantasy celebrating mother-daughter reciprocity and hinting at Gilman's own dream of deserting the father who, in fact, deserted her. Gilman's inability to nurture her daughter, as well as her difficulty concentrating on her work, are dramatized in "The Yellow Wallpaper" (1892), where a nameless woman, denied pen and paper by her physician-husband during a severe postpartum depression, can neither care for her baby nor herself as she becomes obsessed with the yellowing wallpaper in the upstairs bedroom to which she is confined. Even in the midst of her despair at her entrapment in the bedroom with the intricately patterned wallpaper in which she reads the terrible script of women's lives in patriarchy, however, the narrator glimpses through her window a horde of women moving freely through a garden where everything is green rather than yellow. Journeying toward "mysterious deep-shaded arbors, . . . riotous old-fashioned flowers, and bushes and gnarly trees,"[83] where can these women be fleeing if not toward the queens' gardens of Herland?[84]

Yet the contrast between fantasy women escaping into the greenly growing country and a narrator horrified by the patterns in the yellow book of her wallpaper reminds us that the visions of "The Yellow Wallpaper" and *Herland* are not easily reconciled. More, the tension between Gilman's life and her utopian fiction recalls the equally severe ironies of Olive Schreiner's life and art, for though Schreiner attained the intellectual and economic authority that Lyndall sought, even at the height of her fame she continued to suffer from asthma, eating disorders, headaches, and restlessness, ailments comparable to those that destroy Lyndall. Torn between her love for the physical beauty of Africa and her desire for the intellectual stimulation of England, Schreiner was also divided about her sexual identity, and she therefore explained to the intellectual men with whom she corresponded that, although she considered herself a "man-friend," she knew her "sex must

always divide" her from them.[85] In pursuit of the autonomy Lyndall
seeks, Schreiner married a man who took her last name and supported
her efforts to write; however, like her heroine, she witnessed the mysterious death of her newborn baby; she found it impossible to live with
the baby's father; and she never completed her most ambitious projects.[86] Not only the lives but the works of Schreiner and Gilman reveal
the contradictions that shape turn-of-the-century feminist thinking and
call into question early feminist forecasts of a brave new world of New
Women.

The ideological tensions within Gilman's utopia are particularly useful for illuminating how women's use of the colonial metaphor threatens to invalidate itself by replacing or effacing those who are literally
colonized. In *Herland,* "negative eugenics" (69)—women controlling the
population by denying themselves motherhood—turns parthenogenesis into voluntary motherhood, an ideal form of birth control. But Gilman also describes how "the lowest types" of girls (including those with
sexual drives) are "bred out" (82) of the species. While eugenics em-
powers woman, it entraps her in the maternal role: she is important
not for herself but as the Mother of a Race that is judged in terms of
the purity of an Aryan stock. Gilman's belief, as stated in *With Her in
Ourland* (1916), that "only some [of] the races—or some individuals in
a given race—have reached the democratic stage"[87] is not far removed
from the attitude toward blacks emphasized in *The Story of an African
Farm.* Although Schreiner resigned from the Cape Women's Enfran-
chisement League when it agitated for votes only for white women, the
Hottentot and Kaffir servants in her novel are typically characterized
as "sullen, ill-looking . . . , with lips hideously protruding" (73) or as
cruel in their vindictive feeling that "It was so nice to see the white man
who had been master hunted down" (76).[88]

For many other feminists, too, the metaphorical identification of
women and the colonized threatened to displace blacks in precisely the
way they are marginalized in *The Story of an African Farm.* Even in the
nineteenth century, women schooled in the abolitionist movement found
themselves competing (often with racist arguments) against the claims
of black men and generally insensitive to (or even hostile toward) the
double jeopardy of black women. The most extreme consequence of
Elizabeth Cady Stanton's tendency to place women and blacks in a competition of victimization is reflected by her response to the lynching of
a black man accused of raping a white woman: Stanton wrote that "The
Republican cry of 'Manhood Suffrage' creates an antagonism between
black men and all women that will culminate in fearful outrages on
womanhood," a response which reveals her belief that, as Paula Giddings has put it, "giving Black men the vote was virtually a license to

rape"; and Stanton's logic, as well as Susan B. Anthony's and Alice Paul's accommodations to southern suffrage groups that refused to accept black women, helps explain Nadine Gordimer's comment about Olive Schreiner that "the women issue" which animated "her wronged sense of self . . . withers in comparison with the issue of the voteless, powerless state of South African blacks, irrespective of sex."[89] From Mary Elizabeth Coleridge's wild *"white"* women to Isak Dinesen's playing the role of "The Baroness" for the natives dependent on her largesse, white women writers who used the colonial metaphor to confront their own struggle against subordination may have reinforced the even greater victimization of native women who were oppressed both by their own cultures and by an imperial one.[90]

But Gilman's *Herland* also calls into question both her own alternative theology and that proposed by feminists like Schreiner, for the spirituality advocated by these two thinkers often ended up, like Schreiner's, either fetishizing sacrifice, or, like Gilman's, denying it altogether. Even more than in her novel, Schreiner's fascination with self-sacrifice is apparent in her shorter meditations. While in "A Little African Story" an indentured girl willingly martyrs herself to save a family that had always beaten and abused her, in a religious parable Schreiner formulated in a letter to Havelock Ellis the correlation between crucifixion and feminization is so fundamental as to be inescapable:

> Once God Almighty said: "I will produce a self-working automatic machine for enduring suffering, . . . capable of the largest amount of suffering in a given space"; and he made woman. But he wasn't satisfied that he [had] reached the highest point of perfection; so he made a man of genius. He was [not] satisfied yet. So he combined the two—and made a woman of genius—and he was satisfied![91]

If Schreiner's Lyndall masochistically embraces martyrdom as evidence of her genius, however, Gilman's Herlanders are exempted from all suffering. In *Herland*, evil is projected onto the male race with the result that, for example, all such negative traits as violence, hostility, and competitiveness are viewed as male problems. Presented as inherently nurturing and pacifist—hardy survivors of a war between men[92]—Gilman's idealized women are also consistently healthy. The physician who represents an oppressive medical establishment in "The Yellow Wallpaper" is notably absent from *Herland*, as if Gilman were endorsing the influential view of Dr. T. L. Nichol that "the so-called Diseases of Women" were due "directly or collaterally to one form or another of *masculine* excess or abuse."[93] Finally, and most importantly, Gilman's women are strikingly free of the kinds of sexual drives that lead to what Rachel Blau DuPlessis calls "romantic thralldom."[94] Thus, with women characterized not only as peace-loving and naturally healthy but also as virginal and maternal, every woman in Herland is—in the words of Sheila Delany—"the Blessed Virgin Mary."[95]

In this regard, though, how new is the New Woman? If Schreiner's Lyndall rejects sexuality to present herself as a female Christ, Gilman's Herlanders reject sexuality to view themselves as modern madonnas. Does Schreiner's and Gilman's draining away of the erotic unconsciously perpetuate the Victorian ideal of the chaste angel in the house? While the heroine of "The Yellow Wallpaper" gnaws at a double bed she cannot seem to move out of the room she is made to inhabit, the men of *Herland* are banished from the bedroom in a fantasy that goes so far as to eliminate both desire and difference. Paradoxically, then, although Gilman viewed herself as a critic of the medical establishment, she shared many doctors' views about the nonexistence of female sexuality, theories more representative of (male) "wishes and anxieties" than (female) "biological or physiological facts."[96] Indeed, after both Schreiner and Gilman were attacked by Ellen Key, the Swedish mentor of Margaret Sanger, Gilman responded by admitting that, unlike Key—who believed that "woman needs . . . an even fuller exercise, development and recognition of her sex"—she herself saw "sex [as] a minor department of life."[97]

Although Schreiner was influenced by Havelock Ellis, Edward Carpenter, and Karl Pearson in her attitude toward the significance of female desire, she believed that "for natures more highly developed" any union based on "physical attraction, affection and fidelity" is "wrong."[98] In addition, both the diatribes of her heroine Lyndall and the fractured shape of the plot of *The Story of an African Farm* testify to the problem female eroticism posed for some feminist imaginations in this period. Just as sibling compassion unites Lyndall and Waldo, tenderness and friendship characterize the relationships between women in *Herland,* as they did in Gilman's life, and there is no sexuality in her single-sex community, for sexuality is closely identified with an unacceptable heterosexuality, as it is in "The Yellow Wallpaper." Even as the climax of Gilman's utopia moves toward "bi-sexuality," a word that implies optimistically that heterosexuality is as singular a choice as any other form of sexuality, the plot works to reduce the three male visitors to women's tools or to banish them altogether.

In the final chapters of *Herland,* Terry, Jeff, and Van must accept marriage on radically new terms: without a home, without a wife, without sex. For unregenerate Terry, who attempts what constitutes marital rape, there can be nothing but anaesthesia, confinement, and expulsion. Weir Mitchell's rest-cure treatment, which had caused Gilman the pain documented in "The Yellow Wallpaper," is turned against the oppressor. The Herlanders' reaction to Terry is, moreover, similar to their response to all aberrant behavior: they use "preventive measures" instead of punishment, and sometimes they "send the patient to bed" as part of the "treatment" (112). The sinister ring to their rest cures reminds us that Gilman's strategy of reversal threatens to invalidate her feminism by defining it in precisely the terms set up by the misogyny it would repudiate.

To the extent that Schreiner and Gilman seem to have sought an emancipation not only from the double standard that had, for example, put in place the Contagious Disease Acts, but also from sexuality itself, their works illuminate writings by such novelists of the New Woman as George Gissing (*The Odd Women* [1893]), Mona Caird (*The Daughters of Danaus* [1894]), Emma Frances Brooke (*A Superfluous Woman* [1894]), Grant Allen (*The Woman Who Did* [1895]), Menie Muriel Dowie (*Gallia* [1895]), Sarah Grand (*The Heavenly Twins* [1895]), and Thomas Hardy (*Jude the Obscure* [1896]).[99] For although, as one reviewer asked about *Gallia*, "what male novelist would have treated with similar boldness the sexual problem, that unveiling and exposure of the deformed image of Priapus in the innermost recesses of the Temple of Marriage?,"[100] in fact both men and women of letters expressed the view propounded by Gissing's significantly named Rhoda Nunn:

> before the female sex can be raised from its low level there will have to be a widespread revolt against sexual instinct. Christianity couldn't spread over the world without help of the ascetic ideal, and this great movement for woman's emancipation must also have its ascetics.[101]

At their most optimistic, New Women—as described by the admiring Randolph Bourne—responded to "the ascetic ideal" by "talk[ing] much about the 'Human Sex,' which they claim to have invented, and which is simply a generic name for those whose masculine brutalities and egotisms and feminine pettinesses and stupidities have been purged away so that there is left stuff for a genuine comradeship and healthy frank regard and understanding."[102] At their most despairing, though, such women saw themselves as, in Schreiner's words to Ellis, "self-working automatic machine[s] for enduring suffering."

The daughters of *Herland* are thus fittingly called "New Women" (56) not only because they embody Gilman's vision of a female coming of age at the beginning of the twentieth century; not only because they represent Gilman's version of herself, now adequately nurtured and nurturing; but also because the tensions of turn-of-the-century feminism are reflected so clearly in the world she imagines. To be sure, the very radicalism of Gilman's mythology of parthenogenesis reveals the difficulty of altering patriarchy in a way that Schreiner's work also documents. In *Woman and Labour* the metaphor Schreiner uses to define the importance of women to the development of the race involves her in a bizarre meditation that seeks to valorize the uterus but does so by analysing the ways in which the *os cervix* of the female limits the size of the human brain, "a size which could only increase if in the course of ages the *os cervix* of women should itself slowly expand" (130). The original subtitle of Schreiner's novel—*A Series of Abortions*—also illustrates her conflicted metaphorizing of the womb.

Whether the womb is a source of female suffering, as in *The Story of an African Farm,* or the origin of female superiority, as in *Herland,* it is linked to a profoundly pessimistic belief that only by changing women's anatomy could one redefine women's destiny. There were, antithetically, a number of turn-of-the-century thinkers who argued that a change in women's social destiny would alter female anatomy. Elizabeth Wolstenholme Elmy and Ben Elmy, writing under the pseudonym "Ellis Ethelmer," even argued that menstruation was "an acquired and inherited bodily result of ages of corporal subjugation," a disease that could be cured by recognizing women's right to regulate intercourse.[103] But all these participants in the women's movement who sought, in the words of Rosa Mayreder, "to adapt existing social conditions to their nature and needs, and to transform the prevailing idea of what women should be in the interests of those women who vary from the norm—the accepted type"[104] indicate the problem of feminism for the female imagination and specifically the difficulty of conceptualizing precisely those sexchanges the authors of *The Story of an African Farm* and *Herland* desired.

Although both Schreiner and Gilman speculated on the social, spiritual, and even biological primacy of women, then, they forged a tradition that, by identifying the woman primarily with the womb, continued to deny women either tactical strategies for resistance to male domination or psychological strategies for coming to terms with female eroticism. To those women artists who were no more at home with the expanding *os cervix* of Schreiner or the parthenogenetic maternity of Gilman than they had been with Haggard's African queen, feminist fantasy bequeathed the problem of reimagining female rebellion and sexuality beyond the confines of the colonies of the New Woman.

3

The Second Coming of Aphrodite: Kate Chopin's Fantasy of Desire

The radiant Venus of antiquity, the foam-born Aphrodite, has not passed unscathed through the dreadful shades of the Middle Ages. Her dwelling is no longer Olympus, nor the shores of a perfumed archipelago. She has retired into the depths of a cavern, magnificent, it is true, but illumined by fires very different from those of benign Apollo.
—Charles Baudelaire, 1861

Then to me so lying awake a vision
Came without sleep over the seas and touched me,
Softly touched mine eyelids and lips; and I too,
   Full of the vision,
Saw the white implacable Aphrodite,
Saw the hair unbound and the feet unsandalled
Shine as fire of sunset on western waters.
—A. C. Swinburne, 1865

I was born under the star of Aphrodite, Aphrodite who was also born on the sea, and when her star is in the ascendant, events are always propitious to me.
—Isadora Duncan, 1927

Swiftly re-light the flame,
Aphrodite, holy name . . .
return, O holiest one,
Venus whose name is kin
to venerate,
venerator.
—H. D., 1945

Although the New Women imagined by Olive Schreiner and Charlotte Perkins Gilman either suffer from or repudiate the erotic, the relationship between late nineteenth-century feminism and female desire was by no means clear cut. To be sure, many suffragists recoiled from the free-love advocate Victoria Woodhull because of her unsavory reputation, but both Elizabeth Cady Stanton and Susan B. Anthony emphatically endorsed her work for the vote in the early 1870s. Exclaimed Stanton, using the occasion to attack the prevailing double standard, "When the men who make laws for us in Washington can . . . declare themselves . . . unspotted from all the sins mentioned in the Decalogue, then we will demand that every woman who makes a constitutional argument on our platform shall be as chaste as Diana," while Anthony wrote to Woodhull enthusiastically urging her to "Go ahead doing, bright, glorious, young and strong spirit, and believe in the best love and hope and faith of S. B. Anthony."[1] Even more radically than Stanton and Anthony, however, some women in this period began not only to excuse or justify but to celebrate the transgressive sexuality of the "fallen woman." For Kate Chopin, in fact, such a woman paradoxically became a resonant symbol of the same need for drastic social change that impelled Schreiner and Gilman in various ways to renounce erotic desire. Ultimately, Aphrodite, the goddess of love—not Mary, the mother of God—became Chopin's ideal.

In February 1899, while *The Awakening* was still in press, Kate Chopin wrote a poem called "The Haunted Chamber," in which a male speaker tells the tale "Of a fair, frail, passionate woman who fell." Narrated in neat couplets, the story seems at first merely an item for masculine delectation, an after-dinner diversion:

> It may have been false, it may have been true.
> That was nothing to me—it was less to you.
> But with bottle between us, and clouds of smoke
> From your last cigar, 'twas more of a joke
> Than a matter of sin or a matter of shame
> That a woman had fallen, and nothing to blame,
> So far as you or I could discover,
> But her beauty, her blood and an ardent lover.

But surprisingly, as the night wears on, the speaker, left alone with his thoughts, finds himself haunted by this fallen woman's fate. When "the lights were low," he confesses,

> And the breeze came in with the moon's pale glow
> The fair, faint voice of a woman, I heard.
> 'Twas but a wail, and it spoke no word.
> It rose from the depths of some infinite gloom
> And its tremulous anguish filled the room.[2]

Unspoken and unspeakable, the destiny of one lost lady symbolizes the wordless wail of every woman whose passion for self-fulfillment had been forbidden or forgotten.

That such forbidden passion was a major theme for Kate Chopin became clear to American readers two months later, when *The Awakening*—a novel that might be seen as a book-length vindication of the rights of women like the "fair, frail" heroine of "The Haunted Chamber"—was published. But the irony and urbanity of Chopin's poem suggest that she was hardly prepared for the outrage that greeted her novel on the same subject. The novel "leaves one sick of human nature," complained one critic; "the purport of the story can hardly be described in language fit for publication," asserted another. Even Willa Cather, who admired Chopin's art and was eventually to produce her own tales of lost ladies, deplored the fact that the author had "devoted so exquisite and sensitive . . . a style to so trite and sordid a theme."[3] Within a few months, the libraries of St. Louis, Missouri, Chopin's native city, had banned the book; Chopin was shunned by a number of acquaintances; and, according to her biographer, Per Seyersted, she was refused membership in the St. Louis Fine Arts Club.[4]

At first the novelist attempted an insouciant self-defense:

> Having a group of people at my disposal, I thought it might be entertaining (to myself) to throw them together and see what would happen. I never dreamed of Mrs. Pontellier making such a mess of things and working out her own damnation as she did. If I had had the slightest intimation of such a thing I would have excluded her from the company. But when I found out what she was up to, the play was half over and it was then too late.[5]

But as time passed, the wound to Chopin's aesthetic morale became ever more painful. Her royalties from the book were minimal, and her third collection of short stories was rejected by *The Awakening*'s publisher. The "moving procession of human energy," the writer confided in a sorrowful essay entitled "A Reflection," "has left me by the roadside!"[6]

Ironically, this daughter of a distinguished and pious Catholic family found herself in a position where her own authorial "torment" reflected the pain experienced by the heroine of "The Haunted Chamber." At first a "conscientious mother" of six—indeed, according to her daughter, a model "Lady Bountiful" of the Louisiana neighborhood where she had settled for a while after her marriage—and later an "inconsolable" widow, Chopin had ventured into chambers haunted by the erotic, the illicit, the "sordid".[7] Yet though censorious reviewers and confused readers were shocked by what seemed to be her unprecedented boldness, this artist had been, from early in her career, a very different person from the decorous "Lady Bountiful" that the world believed her to be. Indeed, even as a feminist she had swerved significantly from the essentially puritanical creed that was espoused by many New Women and that would eventually become a central tenet of Gilman's *Herland*.[8]

On her honeymoon, Chopin had quite fortuitously encountered one "Miss Clafflin" *(sic)*. A sister of Victoria Woodhull, this "fussy, pretty, talkative little woman," wrote Chopin in her diary, "entreated me not to fall into the useless degrading life of most married ladies—but to elevate my mind [and] I assured her I would do so."[9] Living in New Orleans, she had followed "Miss Clafflin's" advice in her own way, adventurously exploring the city and taking notes on scenes that impressed her, attending the theater and the opera, and continuing her compendious reading during long summers at Grand Isle, the resort where *The Awakening* is set. By the time that, as a young widow, Chopin seriously embarked on literary projects, she had abandoned the Catholicism of her girlhood and become an acolyte of the "direct and simple" stories of Maupassant, whom she defined as "a man who had escaped from tradition and authority, who had entered into himself and looked out upon life through his own being and with his own eyes."[10]

Though such "escapes" also fascinated Olive Schreiner and Charlotte Perkins Gilman, the ones envisioned by Chopin were in some ways more controversial. Despite its radical polemics, after all, Schreiner's *African Farm* was morally acceptable enough to become a bestseller, and, though they were notably revolutionary, Gilman's critical and creative works were not greeted with significant opprobrium. But *The Awakening* was almost universally excoriated or deprecated for more than three decades. Perhaps, however, that was because, unlike many of her female contemporaries, Chopin was aligned with a particularly sensational, largely male-dominated fin-de-siècle rhetoric, a rhetoric which explored, and often defended, what society defined as "damnation."

Kate Chopin was born in St. Louis in 1851, three years after the publication of *Jane Eyre* and *Wuthering Heights*, two years before the appearance of *Uncle Tom's Cabin*, and six years before the publication of *Aurora Leigh*. In that year, Emily Dickinson was twenty-one, just returned from Mary Lyon's Ladies Seminary at Mount Holyoke, where, already a rebel, she had refused to "accept Christ" during an evangelical revival, while Marian Evans, not yet George Eliot, had produced her translation of Strauss's theologically revisionary *Lebens Jesu* (1846). As for male artists, just four years after Chopin's birth, Walt Whitman was to bring out the first version of *Leaves of Grass,* a work whose sensual frankness and stylistic freedom made it at least as daring in 1855 as *The Awakening* was in 1899. By 1851, moreover Richard Wagner's epochal *Tannhäuser,* with its shocking depiction of a fiery Venusberg, had already had its premiere in Germany, and within little more than a decade it was to be performed in Paris, where it would be defended by Charles Baudelaire, whose own controversial masterwork, *Les Fleurs du mal,* had appeared in 1857.

It is relevant to review this history because Kate Chopin has often, especially in recent years, been detached from the rich intellectual fabric of the age that nurtured her. Originally seen by her most sympathetic critics as a "local colorist," a purely American phenomenon like George Washington Cable or Mary E. Wilkins Freeman, she has lately been upgraded by even keener enthusiasts to a sort of feminist sociologist but still defined as an artist whose principal sources of energy were empirical observation and political theorizing. Paradoxically, however, in their dislike of the novel's erotic boldness and their willful refusal to sympathize with Edna's "unfocused yearning," some of *The Awakening*'s earliest reviewers came closer to understanding its content and origins.

The novel "is like one of Aubrey Beardsley's hideous but haunting pictures with their disfiguring leer of sensuality," declared a reviewer for the *Los Angeles Sunday Times,* for instance.[11] Three decades later, the writer of the first full-length study of Kate Chopin elaborated upon this position. "*The Awakening* follows the current of erotic morbidity that flowed strongly through the literature of the last two decades of the nineteenth century," observed Daniel Rankin, adding that Kate Chopin, in an attack "of the prevailing artistic vertigo," had absorbed such diverse influences as Schopenhauer, Wagner, "the Russian novel," and Maeterlinck, while sharing in "the mania for the exotic" that turned so many fin-de-siècle imaginations toward femmes fatales like Haggard's Ayesha, Wilde's Salome, and Flaubert's Salammbô.[12] Rankin was thinking in terms that were just being explored in Mario Praz's *The Romantic Agony,* though his descriptive phrases, like those of the *Los Angeles Times* reviewer, had an emphatically negative moral cast. Beneath the judgmental surface, however, we can discern an accurate definition of who and what Kate Chopin was: a woman of the nineties, a writer of the fin de siècle.

What did it mean, though, to be a *woman* of letters during the fin de siècle, that era whose French label gives it a faintly sinister, voluptuously apocalyptic air?[13] Superficially, at least, the phrase *fin de siècle* meant, for some literary women as for many literary men, a kind of drawing-room sophistication—smoking Turkish cigarettes, subscribing to *The Yellow Book*, reading (and translating) French fiction, all of which Chopin did, especially during the St. Louis years of her widowhood, which were also the years of her major literary activity. More integrally, the fin de siècle was associated with the artistic and intellectual rebels mentioned by Rankin and by Chopin's early reviewers, with, that is, such figures as Beardsley and Wilde, and with their most significant precursors: Swinburne, Pater, Whitman, Wagner, Baudelaire. To such women as Chopin (along with Victoria Woodhull, Emma Goldman, and others), however, the second half of the nineteenth century had also offered the revolutionary concept of "free love," an idea which in some ways qualified, and was sometimes at odds with, the even newer persona of the New Woman. In addition, as we have seen, to be a woman of the nineties meant to have come of age in a new kind of literary age, an era whose spirit was shared and shaped by significant female imaginations.

Like many of her contemporaries, Kate Chopin began quite early to read the works of such ancestresses as Austen, the Brontës, and Eliot. Early and late, moreover, she admired the writings of the iconoclastic George Sand, in honor of whom she evidently named her only daughter "Lélia." In addition, she knew the works of American writers from Stowe to Jewett as well as those of British women from Barrett Browning to Schreiner, for she belonged to a circle in St. Louis where the writings of such figures were actively discussed.[14] Like the fictions of so many women, however, her earliest full-length narrative—the 1890 novel *At Fault*—dramatizes its author's ambivalent affiliation with the female literary tradition through a complex engagement with that most inescapable of women's novels, *Jane Eyre*. Indeed, like Barrett Browning's *Aurora Leigh*, Eliot's "The Lifted Veil," and other female fictions, *At Fault* depends on crucial elements of the *Jane Eyre* plot: specifically, a husband helplessly shackled to a mentally "incompetent" wife (in this case an alcoholic rather than a madwoman), a "pure" woman who insists on the holiness of wedlock, a fire that destroys much of the husband's property, and a providential death that happily resolves the unhappy triangle.[15]

Unfortunately, though, what had worked so well in 1847 for Charlotte Brontë, almost as well in 1856 for Barrett Browning, and comparatively well in 1859 for Eliot, helped the apprentice Chopin not at all. The splitting of her female protagonist into a sober and noble heroine, on the one hand, and a drunken ignoble double, on the other, seemed for Chopin actually to block the sort of feminist speculation such a strategy had energized in Brontë's novel. Equally hampering were the Gothic elements of fire, murder, and providential death, which had given metaphorical intensity to *Aurora Leigh* and "The Lifted Veil" as well as to *Jane Eyre*. In the forties, Brontë had pioneeringly used such properties of mystery and melodrama to vitalize the theater of desire in which her heroine was a central actor. By the nineties, however, with femmes fatales and New Women making both social and literary history, it seemed specious to fracture the female protagonist.

Whether the heroine was Haggard's Ayesha or Schreiner's Lyndall, events that seemed as "sad and mad and bad" as one of Chopin's reviewers called Edna Pontellier's fate occurred precisely because the mad rebellious woman and the sane submissive woman were now really inhabitants of the same body, and their life-and-death struggle took place not in an attic or a parlor but in the troubled female consciousness.[16] Yet that struggle, often an essential subject of literature by women, must be not only analyzed but rendered, as Chopin had learned from Brontë and other literary foremothers. After the failure of *At Fault*, therefore, she evidently realized that her most pressing task was to learn how to narrate a modern female psychomachia without actually dividing the female personality into two warring selves.

In their different ways, of course, writers like Haggard and Schreiner confronted the same problem, as they set out to record the adventures of the femme fatale or of the New Woman. On the one hand, despite her Medusan powers, the sweetly beautiful but fatal Ayesha has been angelically loyal to her Kallikrates for a millennium, and though she is shown from the first to be belligerent in her relations with other women, she is only gradually revealed to be mad, monstrous, murderous in her relations with all of male culture, and only at the very end of the novel, when she "devolves" into a creature "no larger than a monkey," is her ontological identity revealed. On the other hand, though Schreiner's New Womanly Lyndall is a more complex figure than many late nineteenth-century femmes fatales, she is characterized through a reversal of the dramatic denouement that reveals Ayesha's "true" self. At first, she is seen as strange and rebellious, but later, especially in her angelic death scenes, she becomes a noble victim. Moreover, whether or not New Women consistently used this dramatic pattern to explore their heroines' psychic development, they tended to resort to discursive debates among their characters, a major strategy of Schreiner's; they tended, that is, to tell rather than show the meaning of the conflicts their heroines experienced.[17]

To Chopin, however, such solutions were plainly unacceptable. Inheriting Charlotte Brontë's feminist passion, she also inherited a sense of dramatic coherence comparable to Brontë's, an equally intense poetic energy, and a similar commitment to narrative urgency. At the same time, Chopin preferred a disinterested Flaubertian voice to an impassioned Brontë-esque or Dickensian one. Her version of the feminist psychomachia, therefore, would have to have both the fierce vitality of *Jane Eyre* and the scrupulous restraint of *Madame Bovary*. But how could she negotiate the passage from the clumsily derivative *At Fault* to such a paradoxical romance? To put the question another way, how could she move, as a woman writer, from the often melodramatic or sentimental conventions that shaped even the most "realistic" nineteenth-century novels to the more elliptical structures of twentieth-century fiction?

At first, for Chopin, "local color" writing offered both a mode and a manner that could mediate between the literary forms she had inherited and those she had begun to envision. Like such American contemporaries as Grace King and Constance Woolson, Sarah Orne Jewett and Mary E. Wilkins Freeman—the last two of whom she particularly admired—she could work in what seemed to be a minor, understated (and therefore "ladylike") mode which nevertheless allowed her to explore a number of subversive themes.[18] Because the "local color" writer is in a sense a sort of ethnologist or cultural anthropologist, the recounting of tales based on idiosyncratic customs, folk character, and regional behavior could help her to narrate fictions with the almost scientific detachment of Chekhov, Maupassant, and Flaubert. More important, by reporting odd practices that were part of a region's "local color," she could even tell what would ordinarily be shocking stories without fear of the moral outrage that a more "mainstream" work like *The Awakening* would evoke. Finally, by detaching herself from a specific set of customs she could learn to detach herself from all customs. Like so many other regionalists—among male authors, for instance, Twain, Yeats, and Joyce, and, among women, especially Freeman and, as we shall later show, Edith Wharton and Willa Cather—she could move from theorizing about a particular subcultural group to theorizing about culture itself.

Modest as they may seem, some of Chopin's stories suggest the ways in which large issues had always been implicit in what conservative critics approvingly called her "delightful sketches."[19] With its triangle of upper-class heroine, lower-class heroine, and upper-class lover, for instance, "At the 'Cadian Ball" (1892) dramatizes the hierarchies that structure even so apparently simple a society as that of *"La Côte Joyeuse,"* for the local farm girl—Calixta—has ultimately to watch her well-born sweetheart—Alcée—pledge his allegiance to Clarisse, his aristocratic fiancée (*CW* 1:219–27). Recounting a man's repudiation of a young wife whom he believes to have black origins, "Desirée's Baby" (1893) goes further and interrogates the arbitrary race distinctions that could divide man from wife, child from parent, in such a culture (*CW* 1:240–45). "At Chênière Caminada" (1894), set at the summer resort that was to play so crucial a part in *The Awakening,* and "Nég Creol" (1897), set in a very different New Orleans from the *quartier* inhabited by either Edna Pontellier or Kate Chopin herself, offer poignant portraits of southern ladies from the sympathetically delineated point of view of working-class men—one white, one black—into whose consciousness a decorous lady like Chopin herself might not have been expected to enter (*CW* 1:309–18 and 505–10).

Perhaps even more radically, "The Story of an Hour" (1894), "Athenaïse" (1896), and "The Storm" (comp. 1899) question the very institution of marriage. "The Story of an Hour" records a wife's sense of liberation and ecstasy on hearing a false report of her husband's death (*CW* 1:352–54); "Athenaïse" explores the rebellious feelings of a runaway bride (*CW* 1:426–54); and "The Storm" dramatizes a brief but volcanic—indeed, proto-Lawrentian—sexual encounter between Calixta and Alcée, the lovers who were separated by class lines in "At the 'Cadian Ball" (*CW* 2:596–96). Similarly, "Lilacs" (1896) movingly delineates the love between two strikingly dissimilar women—a nun and a kind of courtesan—and protests the social rules which would condemn such a relationship (*CW* 1:355–65). In all these pieces, although Chopin appears to begin by setting herself a comparatively limited narrative task, she ultimately confronts large, even (as in "Desireeé"s Baby," "The Storm," and "Lilacs") deeply "improper" social questions to which many fin-de-siècle artists were coming from other directions.

In an important essay on "The Decadent and the New Woman," Linda Dowling has suggested that both these turn-of-the-century intellectual "types" shared the "fundamental desire of the *fin de siècle avant garde:* the dream of living beyond culture, the dream of pastoral."[20] To say this, however, is to say that artists like Beardsley and Wilde, with literary goals quite distinct from Chopin's, had also begun to speculate on the nature of culture as well as on the nature of nature itself—on the nature, that is, of what is beyond or beneath culture. As Holbrook Jackson put it in 1913, "the intellectual, imaginative and spiritual activities of the Eighteen Nineties [were] concerned mainly with the idea of social life or, if you will, of culture. . . . it was a time when people went about frankly and cheerfully endeavoring to solve the question 'How to Live.' "[21] Confronting such questions through her quasi-anthropological work as a local colorist, Chopin must also have been influenced by the kinds of related speculations she would have encountered in French literature and in *The Yellow Book* as well as in the New Woman fictions of Schreiner or, indeed, of such other contemporaries as George Egerton and Sarah Grand.

Of course, however, as they fantasized "living beyond culture," two such different beings as the decadent and the New Woman yearned toward drastically different versions of the revitalized natural world that Dowling calls "pastoral." The New Woman, for instance, frequently dreamed of a transfigured society where both "sex distinction" and the "sex-passion" had dissolved away.[22] As Schreiner put it in one of her "allegories," in the highest heaven sex "does not exist," and as Gilman sought to demonstrate in *Herland,* the most intense sexual pleasure derives, at least for women, from an erotics of the maternal.[23] In the words of one British suffragist, "How can we [women] possibly be Freewomen if, like the majority of men, we become the slaves of our lower appetites?"[24] Such male artists as Beardsley and Wilde, however, envisioned a society transfigured not beyond but through homosexual or heterosexual eroticism. What Lord Henry Wotton in Wilde's *The Picture of Dorian Gray* (1891) called "the new Hedonism," wrote the critic and author Grant Allen in 1894, would repudiate "the asceticism that deadens the senses," and do so specifically through a revitalizing of the erotic which would return men and women to the Eden of polymorphous perversity from which Protestant morality, with its threats of "damnation," had cast them out.[25]

Because Chopin had come to cultural theory through a figurative as well as a literal subscription to *The Yellow Book,* and through both the antipuritanical traditions of French literature and the scrupulously empirical observations of literary anthropology, she was disinclined even to try to imagine a de-eroticized pastoral Eden. Rather, she dreamed of a specifically sexual culture beyond culture, a sensual Eden whose heroine's motto might be defined by a passage from one of Victoria Woodhull's most famous speeches of the mid-century: "I will love whom I may . . . I will love as long or as short a period as I can. . . . I will change this love when [conditions] indicate that it ought to be changed; and . . . neither you nor any law you can make shall deter me."[26]

At the same time, Chopin must have seen that the erotic pastoralism which both she and Woodhull were inclined to espouse usually involved either a misogynistic exploitation of the female, as in the brilliant pornographic text which Aubrey Beardsley first published with the title *Under the Hill* and which later appeared as *Venus and Tannhäuser,* or in a misogynistic revulsion against the female, as in Haggard's *She* or Wilde's *Salome.*[27] From the sardonic extreme unction Flaubert as narrator intones over the corpse of Emma Bovary to the pornographic Black Masses of Aleister Crowley and his prurient celebrations of Venus as "Daughter of Lust" and "Sister of shame," the French and decadent writers alike used the erotic image of woman to annihilate culture through blasphemy and to picture a world whose sexual energy arose specifically from its sacrilegious concentration on the female, its self-nauseating worship of Venus's hellish and adorable flesh.[28] Without denying or deriding the erotic, as so many New Women tended to do, Chopin strove to purify it of such decadent misogyny.

But in formulating her feminist dream of a sexual culture beyond culture, Chopin—like Woodhull before her and Gilman after her—was aligning herself with a strain of nineteenth-century thinking about eroticism that, although historians have tended to ignore or repress its existence, was real and vivid in its time. As Peter Gay has recently argued, the now notorious views of the British doctor William Acton have been mistakenly taken to represent a monolithic Victorian notion of female sexuality. "The majority of women (happily for them) are not much troubled with sexual feelings of any kind," wrote Acton in 1857, adding that the "married woman has no wish to be treated on the footing of a mistress."[29] But in fact, as Gay demonstrates throughout *The Education of the Senses,* a female capacity for sexual desire and pleasure—a capacity assumed by both the theories of Woodhull and the fiction of Chopin—was, if not taken for granted, at least affirmed by many of these women's contemporaries.

"I have come to the conclusion," wrote Elizabeth Cady Stanton in 1881, "that the first great work to be accomplished for women is to revolutionize the dogma that sex is a crime, marriage a defilement and maternity a bane," and in 1883 she complained that "Walt Whitman seems to understand everything in nature but woman. . . . he speaks as if the female must be forced to the creative act, apparently ignorant of the great natural fact that a healthy woman has as much passion as a man."[30] In the same vein, the medical pioneer Elizabeth Blackwell declared in 1884 that the "physical pleasure which attends the caresses of love is a rich endowment of humanity, granted by a beneficent Creative power."[31] More empirically, in 1892 one Dr. Clelia Mosher undertook to survey some four dozen American women about their sexual reactions, and, as Gay reports her results, "More than a third of [her] respondents claimed that they reached orgasm 'always' or 'usually.' "[32]

But, as we have seen, even in the seventies Victoria Woodhull had become both mystical and explicit about erotic pleasure. "In a perfected sexuality shall continuous life be found," she exclaimed at a Spiritualists' Camp Meeting in Vineland, New Jersey, adding that "I never had sexual intercourse with any man of whom I am ashamed to stand side by side before the world with the act. . . . if I want sexual intercourse with one hundred men I shall have it. . . . And this sexual intercourse business may as well be discussed now, and discussed until you are so familiar with your sexual organs that a reference to them will no longer make the blush mount to your face any more than a reference to any other part of your body."[33]

As if elaborating on Woodhull's assertions, the British sexologist Edward Carpenter insisted in the first edition of his widely read *Love's Coming of Age* that "Sex is the allegory of love in the physical world." In fact, he remarked, "the state of enforced celibacy in which vast numbers of women live to-day [should] be looked upon as a national wrong, almost as grievous as that of prostitution." And, anticipating—perhaps, indeed, influencing—Kate Chopin's celebration of Edna Pontellier's "splendid body," he fulminated that the Victorian prudery which kept nakedness "religiously covered, smothered away from the rush of the great purifying life of Nature" was itself a cause of prurience, for "Sexual embraces [should] receive the benison of Dame Nature, in whose presence alone, under the burning sun or the high canopy of the stars . . . their meaning can be fully understood."[34] Following Carpenter's lead, moreover, his friend and disciple Havelock Ellis was soon to develop a theory of female sexuality which defined woman's eroticism (in terms that strikingly prefigure the recent arguments of such French feminists as Hélène Cixous and Luce Irigaray) as "more massive and more diffuse than male sexuality."[35]

Sharing the views of all these thinkers, Chopin dreamed of yet a third version of pastoral, a sacramental rather than sacrilegious garden of earthly delights, a culture beyond culture whose energy would arise from the liberation and celebration of female desire. And she insisted that this Eden should be ruled by a Venus who would be as free and regal as Beardsley's (or Crowley's) was degraded and whimsical. But her vision of such a goddess surely gained its strength from the same movement toward theological revision that not only fostered the theories of J. J. Bachofen and Jane Ellen Harrison but also inspired *The Woman's Bible* produced by Elizabeth Cady Stanton and others, along with Florence Nightingale's hope for a "female Christ" and Mary Baker Eddy's argument that because "the ideal woman corresponds to Life and to Love . . . we have not as much authority for considering God masculine as we have for considering Him feminine."[36] Even more specifically, Chopin's visionary eroticism was energized by the same impulse that led Victoria Woodhull to speculate "that the long-lost Garden of Eden is the human body" and Woodhull's acolyte Laura Cuppy Smith to characterize the free love advocate, during her appearance at Vineland, as "The Redeemer," and "virtue and respectability as the two thieves on the cross."[37] Finally, Chopin's sense of the goddess's sacramental sensuality may have been fortified not just by the fervent radicalism of Woodhull and her disciples but also by the radical eroticism of Walt Whitman, an eroticism that Chopin and others clearly saw as transcending the tendency toward misogyny to which Stanton objected.[38]

Equally important, however, was the revisionary female aesthetic that Chopin constructed as, in striving to imagine the healthy eroticism of a culture beyond culture, she searched through the myths she had inherited from patriarchal civilization itself. For in reexamining such myths she began, if only half-consciously and tentatively, to create a narrative structure in which she might coherently dramatize the female psychomachia that was her central subject, a structure that would prove more viable than the unwieldy literary frameworks upon which so many other New Women depended. As her son sketched it in 1899, not long after the publication of *The Awakening,* the room in which Chopin worked was emblematic of her philosophical as well as literary goals. "There were hardly any ornamentations in it," her biographer tells us, "apart from a few paintings on the wall and a candle and a naked Venus on the bookshelf."[39] Abandoning both the religion in which she had been raised and the nineteenth-century literary conventions she had learned, Chopin evidently understood her own desire to revitalize and vindicate the pagan presence of the goddess of love.

Toward the end of *The Awakening* there is a dinner party scene which has been ignored by many critics though it has fascinated and puzzled a few. On the verge of leaving her husband's house for a nearby cottage that she hopes will become both a spiritual and material room of her own, Edna Pontellier has invited a "select" group of friends to join her at a birthday dinner which will also be a celebration of her departure from one household and her entrance into another. Splendid in gold satin and lace "the color of her skin," she presides over an equally splendid table, which is similarly decked in "pale yellow satin," lit by "wax candles in massive brass candelabra," and heaped with "full, fragrant roses."[40] More strikingly still, "the ordinary stiff dining chairs" have been "discarded for the occasion and replaced by the most commodious and luxurious which could be collected throughout the house" while "before each guest [stands] a tiny glass that [sparkles] like a garnet gem," containing a magical-looking cocktail.

Enthroned at the head of the table, Edna herself appears equally magical, for there is "something in her attitude, in her whole appearance, which [suggests] the regal woman, the one who rules, who looks on, who stands alone." At the same time, however—even in the midst of triumphant merrymaking which climaxes in one of the women guests weaving a pagan garland of roses to crown the dark curls of the handsome young man beside her—we are told that Edna feels an "old ennui overtaking her . . . a chill breath that seemed to issue from some vast cavern wherein discords wailed" (chap. 30). Ranging as it does from sumptuous feasting to secret sadness, from gorgeousness to gloom, the dinner party chapter is, as Cynthia Griffin Wolff observes, "one of the longest sustained episodes in the novel."[41]

Perhaps it is because so many contemporary critics would agree with Lawrence Thornton's description of *The Awakening* as a "political romance"[42] that so few have paid close attention to this scene. Though in the past few decades *The Awakening* has become one of the most frequently analyzed American novels, writers about the book commonly describe Edna's party as just one more occasion on which Chopin's half-mad housewife experiences "unfocused yearning" for romantic transfiguration or social liberation.[43] Yet, besides occupying an exceptionally long and elaborate chapter in a novel of economical, obliquely rendered episodes, Edna's dinner party constitutes an extraordinarily complex literary structure. What does it mean, after all, when the narrator of this apparently "realistic" work suddenly calls her heroine "the regal woman, the one who rules, who looks on, who stands alone"? The vocabulary of such a description seems more appropriate to a fantasy or a fairy tale, and yet this mysterious definition seems also to evoke the narrator's next perception of the "chill breath" her queenly heroine feels, together with Edna's equally mysterious sense of "acute longing which always summoned into her spiritual vision the presence of the beloved one." Who or what, indeed, is the oddly vague "beloved one"? And why, finally, does the enigmatically wise Mademoiselle Reisz take her leave of Edna with a French sentence—*"Bonne nuit, ma reine, soyez sage"*—that seems to confirm our feeling that this magical hostess is clothed in a paradoxical veil of power and vulnerability?

As a speculative explanation of these puzzles, we will argue that *The Awakening* is a female fiction which both draws upon and revises fin-de-siècle hedonism to propose a feminist myth of Aphrodite/Venus as an alternative to the patriarchal western myth of Jesus. In the novel's unfolding of this implicit myth, the dinner party scene is of crucial importance, for here, as she presides over a Swinburnian Last Supper, Edna Pontellier (if only for a moment) "becomes" the powerful goddess of love and art into whose shape she was first "born" in the gulf near Grand Isle and in whose image she will be suicidally borne back into the sea at the novel's end. Thus when Victor, the darkhaired young man who was ritually garlanded at the climax of the feast, tells his friend Mariequita that "Venus rising from the foam could have presented no more entrancing a spectacle than Mrs. Pontellier, blazing with beauty and diamonds at the head of the board," he is speaking what is in some sense the truth about Kate Chopin's heroine.

To see *The Awakening* in these terms is not, of course, to deny that it is also the work most critics have thought it is: a "Creole Bovary," a feminist "critique of the identity of 'mother-women,' " "a New Orleans version of the familiar transcendentalist fable of the soul's emergence, or 'lapse' into life," "a eulogy on sex and a muted elegy on the female condition," a turn-of-the-century "existentialist" epiphany, and "a tough-minded critique of the Victorian myths of love."[44] Taken together, all these definitions of the novel suggest the range of political, moral, and philosophical concerns on which Chopin meditates throughout this brief but sophisticated work. What unifies these often divergent matters, however, is the way in which, for all its surface realism, *The Awakening* is allusively organized by Kate Chopin's half-secret fantasy of the second coming of Aphrodite.

To be sure, Chopin's "Creole Bovary" has always been understood to be, like its French precursor, a novel that both uses fantasy and comments upon that genre in order to establish the character of its heroine and the nature of her character. But many critics see such fantasies as, like Emma Bovary's, symptoms of inadequacy, of an "over-idealization of love" and a "susceptibility to romantic codes." People like Edna Pontellier and Emma Bovary, wrote Willa Cather in 1899, "are the spoil of the poets, the Iphigenias of sentiment." Edna's commitment to fantasy, concludes Cynthia Griffin Wolff in a somewhat extreme summary of this position, is the ultimate mark of the "schizoid" personality which causes her "disintegration."[45] We will show, however, that the details of desire which the text of *The Awakening* records ultimately shape themselves into a tale of romantic transfiguration that not only uses and comments upon fantasy but actually becomes a fantasy, albeit a shadowy one. Both seriously and ironically, this work of Kate Chopin's demonstrates, from a female point of view, just what would "really" happen to a mortal, turn-of-the-century woman who tried to claim for herself the erotic freedom owned by the classical queen of love.

We will argue, moreover, that to see this novel as such a shadowy fantasy or fantasy *manqúe* is to begin to explain a number of qualities that have puzzled its detractors as well as its admirers: its odd short chapters, its ambiguous lyricism (what Cather called its "flexible iridescent style"), its editorial restraint, its use of recurrent images and refrains, its implicit or explicit allusions to writers like Whitman, Swinburne, and Flaubert, and its air of moral indeterminacy. In addition, we will suggest that to see *The Awakening* as such a fantasy is to begin to grasp the purpose of some of the scenes in the book that have always appeared problematic. Finally, we will show that, in creating this generically equivocal fantasy, Kate Chopin was working in a mode of mingled naturalism and symbolism analogous to the one explored by her near contemporary George Moore and his younger countryman James Joyce. Learned from such varied continental precursors as Turgenev and Maupassant, this artful combination of surface and symbol evolved through Moore's *The Untilled Field* (1903) and Joyce's *Dubliners* (1914) to a culmination in *Ulysses* (1922). But Kate Chopin in America, inheriting the same tradition and similar techniques, also began to explore the mythic radiance which might at any moment flash through ordinary reality. As a woman writer, however, she saw such epiphanies from a feminine point of view and in what we would call feminist terms. Indeed, the next literary women to employ comparable modes would be such modernists as May Sinclair, Virginia Woolf, Katherine Mansfield, and even at times Willa Cather herself—and they too, in particular Woolf, would often use these techniques to articulate new visions of the feminine.

Appropriately enough, Kate Chopin's portrait of Aphrodite as a "Creole Bovary" begins and ends at a seaside resort, on the margin between nature and culture, where a leisured or, anyway, a lucky few may be given the chance to witness the birth of erotic power in the foam. But to start with, despite the nearness of the sea and the incessant sound of its "seductive" voice, Chopin offers scenes that are determinedly realistic, low-key, landbound. In addition, as if briefly acknowledging Flaubert's influence, she opens her novel about a woman's fateful transformation by examining her heroine from a stolid male perspective. *Madame Bovary,* of course, begins with a brief summary of Charles Bovary's history, including a description of the way Emma Roualt appears to the bovine but passionate young physician whom she will soon marry. Similarly, the author-omniscient of the first chapter of *The Awakening* emphasizes the point of view of Edna Pontellier's conventional husband, Léonce.

Like Madame Bovary's husband-to-be, who at one point gazes at Emma as she stands beneath a parasol which colors "the white skin of her face with shifting reflections" (13), Mr. Pontellier watches from a porch of the main building of Madame Lebrun's Grand Isle summer colony as "a white sunshade [advances] at a snail's pace from the beach" 20th his wife Edna and her friend Robert Lebrun strolling "beneath its pink-lined shelter" (chap. 1). In both cases, the woman appears first as an object, and Edna, whether she "is" herself or the walking sunshade that contains her, is presented as she seems to Léonce: valuable, even treasured, but nevertheless, a *thing* to be guarded rather than a person to be heard or heeded. Even this early in her novel, however, and even while acknowledging her debt to Flaubert, Chopin swerves from him by emphasizing this last point. For where the French novelist creates sympathy for Charles with his devastating portrait of the first Madame

Bovary, a skinny, pimpled Jocasta who is not only old enough to be the young doctor's mother but had been chosen for him by his mother, Chopin immediately characterizes Léonce as an impatient businessman who scrutinizes his wife for sunburn "as one looks at a valuable piece of personal property which has suffered some damage" (chap. 1).

Most of *The Awakening* is told from Edna's perspective, with occasional editorial interpolations from the narrator, but despite its unrepresentative point of view and its air of almost impressionistic improvisation, this opening chapter constitutes a surprisingly complete introduction to the problems and personae of the novel. As an overture, in fact, it includes many of the major leitmotifs of the work to follow: symbolic objects (houses, clothing, jewelry, food); symbolic activities (piano playing, swimming, housecleaning, gambling); symbolic figures, both human and inhuman (the birds, the lady in black, the twins, Edna and Robert, Mr. Pontellier, Madame Lebrun); symbolic places (the Gulf, the beach, the city, the summer colony on Grand Isle), and crucial relationships (husbands and wives, mothers and children).

First encountered here, most of these ultimately extraordinary elements appear as vividly physical as objects in a painting by Renoir or Seurat. It is only as one scene dissolves into another, as the narrative point of view gradually enters Edna's strengthening consciousness, and as objects and activities insistently recur, like parts of a protracted dream, that they gain what eventually becomes an almost uncanny significance. Porches and pianos, mothers and children, skirts and sunshades—these are the props of domesticity, the key properties of what in the nineteenth century was called "woman's sphere," and it is in this sphere, on the edge of a blue gulf, that Edna Pontellier is securely caged when she first appears in the novel that will tell her story. In a larger sense, however, she is confined in what is not only literally a "woman's sphere" but also, symbolically speaking, a Woman's House, a place to which, in civilized as in primitive cultures, women are ritually consigned at crucial times in their lives.[46] Here, therefore, every object and figure has both a practical domestic function and a female symbolic significance.

The self-abnegating "mother-women" who seem "to prevail that summer at Grand Isle" (chap. 4), the mutually absorbed young lovers who always appear in the neighborhood of the sepulchrally religious lady in black, Edna's own children trailed by their omnipresent quadroon nurse with her "faraway meditative air," imperious Mademoiselle Reisz in her "rusty black lace" (chap. 9), the Farival twins "always clad in the virgin's colors" (chap. 9), the skirt-dancing little girl in black tulle, even Edna herself sharing out her husband's gift of *friandises*—all seem like faintly grotesque variations on the figures from *La Vie d'une femme* who appear in Charlotte Brontë's *Villette* (1853): the young girl, the bride, the mother, the widow. That the *pension* in which all these women have gathered is ruled by the pretty widow Madame Lebrun, who sews and oversees in a light airy room with a view at the top of the house, seems quite appropriate. At the same time, however, it seems equally appropriate that the novel opens with the comical curse of the caged parrot—"*Allez vous-en! Allez vous-en! Sapristi!*"—and with the information that this bird also speaks "a language which nobody understood, unless it was the mocking bird that hung on the other side of the door" (chap. 1). For these birds together prefigure both Edna's restlessness and her irony, her awakening desire for freedom and her sardonic sense that freedom may ultimately be meaningless, as well as what the world sees as the incomprehensibility of the language in which she struggles to tell the tale of her desire.

Before these problems are fully stated, however, Chopin begins to explore her heroine's summer of discontent through a series of "realistic" interactions between Edna and her husband. Indeed, though the technique of these exchanges may be derived in part from French writers like Flaubert and Maupassant, the scenes themselves are most thematically indebted to the female literary tradition in English of which Kate Chopin was also an ambivalent heiress. Thus, depicting Léonce's casual self-absorption and Edna's mild rebelliousness, the narrator of *The Awakening* at first seems primarily concerned to represent with Austenian delicacy a marriage on the edge of (George) Eliotian fissures. Pontellier is not, of course, either a Casaubon or a Grandcourt, but that seems to be Chopin's revisionary point. As she depicts his imperiousness in swift understated domestic episodes—the scene in chapter three when he wakes Edna and the children, for instance, or his offhand gifts of money and friandises—Chopin shows that he, too, is possessed by the possessive male will which speaks differently but equally in the tyrannical husbands of *Middlemarch* (1871–72) and *Daniel Deronda* (1876).

At the novel's start, therefore, Edna's "awakening" is both domestic and prosaic. Like Dorothea Brooke and Gwendolyn Harleth, she awakens from the romantic dreams of girlhood first to find herself a married woman and then to find that the meaning of marriage is quite different from what she had supposed. Like another nineteenth-century heroine, Emily Brontë's Catherine Earnshaw Linton, she experiences what Chopin calls "an indescribable oppression" which seems to come at least in part from her sense of herself as, in Brontë's words, "the wife of a stranger; an exile, and outcast . . . from what had been [her] world." For when, like the subject of one of Emily Dickinson's poems, she rose to "His Requirements" and took on "the honorable work of Woman and of Wife," she seems to have accepted a confinement that excludes all visions of "Amplitude and Awe."[47]

For George Eliot's comparatively docile Dorothea and her chastened Gwendolyn, even for Emily Brontë's more satanically ambitious Catherine, such a recognition of domestic entrapment, along with its corollary spiritual diminution, is the product of a long process of social reconciliation that must ultimately end in these heroines accepting their own comparative powerlessness. For Edna, however, whose author is struggling both to reinscribe and to revise the insights of her precursors, this maritally induced recognition of "her position in the universe as a human being, and . . . her relations as an individual to the world within and about her" (chap. 6) presages a more complicated, more metaphysical awakening to the visionary intimations both of her own selfhood and her own sexuality.

To be sure, once she has left her husband's bed to sit on the porch and listen to "the everlasting voice of the sea," Edna has already, like Eliot's and Brontë's heroines, acquired what her author ironically calls "more wisdom than the Holy Ghost is usually pleased to vouchsafe to any woman" (chap. 6). But, like Emily Dickinson, Chopin seeks to record not only the body's rebellion at confinement but the soul's "moments of Escape" (J.512), along with the visions of power that empower such escapes. In addition, because she is a fiction writer, she wants to create a narrative that will enact those visions. After Edna's first prosaic discoveries of spiritual uneasiness, therefore, her "awakenings" become increasingly fantastic and poetic, stirrings of the imagination's desire for "Amplitude" and "Awe" rather than protests of the reason against unreasonable constraint.

Paradoxically, it is just Edna's realistic awakenings to domestic confinement and her domestic confinement itself which make possible these later, more visionary awakenings. Specifically, Edna awakens to the possibilities as well as the problems of "her position in the universe" because she has come to spend the summer in what is both literally and figuratively a female colony, a sort of Herland. For Madame Lebrun's *pension* on Grand Isle is very much a woman's place, not only because it is owned by a woman and dominated by "mother-women" but also because, as in many summer colonies, its principal inhabitants are actually women and children whose husbands and fathers visit only on weekends. It is no doubt for this reason that, as Chopin observes, "that summer at Grand Isle [Edna] had begun to loosen a little the mantle of reserve that had always enveloped her" (chap. 7) and had begun to do so under "the influence," first, of the sensual Adèle Ratignolle and, later, of the more severe Mademoiselle Reisz.

From the eighteenth century on, middle-class women's culture has often been fragmented by the relegation of each wife to a separate household, by the scattering of such households to genteel suburbs, and by the rituals of politeness that codified interchanges between the ladies of these separate households.[48] While husbands joined together in a public community of men, women were isolated in private parlors or used, as Thorstein Veblen observed, in stylized public appearances, as conspicuous consumers to signify their husbands' wealth.[49] Only a few situations, most notably the girls' school and the summer hotel, offered the isolated lady any real chance to participate in a community of women. And, as *The Awakening* shows, for married women of Edna Pontellier's age and class, the communal household of the vacation hotel provided a unique opportunity to live closely with other women and to learn from them.[50] Our use of the word "colony" is, therefore, deliberately ambiguous. For if a summer colony like Madame Lebrun's *pension* is a place where women have been colonized—that is, confined by the men who possess them—it is also a place where women have established an encampment of their own, an outpost of the dream queendom that Charlotte Perkins Gilman was eventually to imagine in *Herland*.

Finally, then, Nancy Cott's punning use of the phrase "the Bonds of Womanhood" is also useful here.[51] For in the close-knit summer colony locks become links: bonds in the negative sense of "fetters" gradually give way to bonds in the positive sense of "ties." This transformation of bondage into bonding makes it possible for both Adèle Ratignolle, the "mother-woman," and her antithesis, Mademoiselle Reisz, the spinster-artist, to facilitate Edna's passage into the metaphorically divine sexuality that is *her* fated and unique identity. Responding to Adèle's questions and caresses in chapter seven, for instance, Edna begins to comprehend the quest for significant desire that has shaped her life. Similarly, responding in chapter nine to the implicit challenge posed by Mademoiselle Reisz's music, Edna becomes conscious that "the very passions themselves were aroused within her soul, swaying it, lashing it, as the waves daily beat upon her . . . body."

The oceanic imagery embedded in Chopin's description of Edna's response to Mademoiselle Reisz's music is neither casual nor coincidental; rather, it suggests yet another agency through which Madame Lebrun's predominately female summer colony on Grand Isle awakens this Creole Bovary. For Chopin's Aphrodite, like Hesiod's, is born from the sea, and born because the colony where she comes to consciousness is situated, like so many places that are significant for women, outside culture, beyond the limits and limitations of the cities where men make history, on one of those magical shores that mark the margin where nature and culture intersect. Here power can flow from outside, from the timelessness or from, in Mircea Eliade's phrase, the "Great Time" that is free of historical constraints,[52] and here, therefore, the sea can speak in a seductive voice, "never ceasing, whispering, clamoring, murmuring, inviting the soul to wander for a spell in abysses of solitude; to lose itself in mazes of inward contemplation" (chap. 6).

It is important, then, that not only Edna's silent dialogues with Mademoiselle Reisz but also her confessional conversations with Adèle Ratignolle incorporate sea imagery. Reconstructing her first childhood sense of selfhood for Adèle, Edna remembers "a meadow that seemed as big as the ocean" in which as a little girl she "threw out her arms as if swimming when she walked, beating the tall grass as one strikes out in the water" (chap. 7). Just as significantly, she speculates that, as she journeyed through this seemingly endless, uncontained and uncontainable grass, she was most likely "running away from prayers, from the Presbyterian service, read in a spirit of gloom by my father that chills me yet to think of." She was fleeing, that is, the interdictions of patriarchal culture, especially of patriarchal theology, and running into the wild openness of nature. Even so early, the story implies, her search for an alternative theology, or at least for an alternative mythology, had begun. In the summer of her awakening on Grand Isle that quest is extended into the more formalized process of learning to swim.

Edna's education in swimming is, of course, symbolic, representing both a positive political lesson in staying afloat and an ambiguously valuable sentimental education in the consequences of getting in over your head. More important, however, is the fact that swimming immerses Edna in an *other* element—an element, indeed, of otherness—in whose baptismal embrace she is renewed, reborn. That Chopin wants to emphasize this aspect of Edna's learning process is made clear by the magical occasion on which her heroine's first independent swim takes place. Following Mademoiselle Reisz's evocative concert, "someone, perhaps it was Robert [Edna's lover-to-be], thought of a bath at that mystic hour and under that mystic moon." Appropriately, then, on this night which sits "lightly upon the sea and land," this night when "the white light of the moon [has] fallen upon the world like the mystery and softness of sleep" (chap. 10), the previously timid Edna begins for the first time to swim, feeling "as if some power of significant import had been given her" and aspiring "to swim far out, where no woman had swum before." Her new strength and her new ambition are fostered by the traditionally female mythic associations of moonlight and water, as well as by the romantic attendance of Robert Lebrun and the erotically "heavy perfume of a field of white blossoms somewhere near."

At the same time, Chopin's description of the waves breaking on the beach "in little foamy crests . . . like slow white serpents" suggests that

Edna is swimming not only with new powers but into a kind of alternative paradise, one that depends upon deliberate inversions of conventional theological images, while the author's frequent reminders that this sea is a *Gulf* reinforce our sense that its waters are at least as metaphysical as those of, say, the Golfo Placido in Conrad's *Nostromo* (1904). Thus, even more important than Edna's swim are both its narrative and its aesthetic consequences, twin textual transformations that energize the rest of Chopin's novel. In swimming away from the beach where her prosaic husband watches and waits, Edna drifts away from the shore of her old life, where she had lingered for twenty-eight years, powerless and reticent. As she swims, she struggles not only toward a female paradise but out of one kind of novel—the work of nineteenth-century "realism" she had previously inhabited—and into a new kind of work, a mythic/metaphysical romance that elaborates her female fantasy of paradisal fulfillment.

In a sense these textual transformations can be seen as merely playful fantasies expressed by Robert and Edna as part of a "realistically" rendered flirtation. When closely analyzed, though, they must be understood to have a metaphorical intensity far keener than what would appear to be their mimetic function, and through such intensity they create a ghostly subtextual narrative which persists with imagistic insistence from Edna's baptismal swimming scene in chapter ten through her last, suicidal swim in chapter thirty-nine. For when Edna says "I wonder if any night on earth will ever again be like this one," she is beginning to place herself in a tale that comes poetically "true." Her dialogue with Robert, as the two return from the moonlit Gulf, outlines the first premises of this story. "It is like a night in a dream," she says. "The people about me are like some uncanny, half-human beings. There must be spirits abroad tonight" (chap. 10). Robert's reply elaborates upon this idea. "It is the twenty-eighth of August," he observes, and then explains:

> On the twenty-eighth of August, at the hour of midnight, and if the moon is shining—the moon must be shining—a spirit that has haunted these shores for ages rises up from the Gulf. With its own penetrating vision the spirit seeks some one mortal worthy to hold him company, worthy of being exalted for a few hours into realms of the semicelestials. His search has always hitherto been fruitless, and he has sunk back, disheartened, into the sea. But tonight he found Mrs. Pontellier. Perhaps he will never wholly release her from the spell. Perhaps she will never again suffer a poor, unworthy earthling to walk in the shadow of her divine presence. [chap. 10]

Fanciful as it seems, this mutual fantasy of Edna's and Robert's is associated both with a change in their relationship and with a change in Edna. Sitting on the porch in the moonlight, the two fall into an erotic silence that seems to be a consequence of the fiction they have jointly created: "No multitude of words could have been more significant than those moments of silence, or more pregnant with the first-felt throbbings of desire" (chap. 10). And the next day, when Edna awakens from her night of transformative dreaming, she finds herself "blindly following whatever impulse moved her, as if she had placed herself in alien hands for direction, and freed her soul of responsibility" (chap. 12).

The scenes that follow—Edna's awakening of Robert (chap. 12), their voyage (again, chap. 12) to the Chênìere Caminada, their attendance at church (chap 13), Edna's nap at Madame Antoine's cottage (again, chap. 13), and their return to Grand Isle (chap. 14)—constitute a miniature fable of further transformation, a sort of wistful adult fairy tale that lies at the heart of this desirous but ultimately sardonic fantasy for adult women. Journeying across the gulf to Mass on the nearby island called Chênìere Caminada—the island of live oaks—Edna and Robert find themselves in the surreal company of the lovers, the lady in black, and a barefooted Spanish girl, Robert's sometime girlfriend, with the allegorically theological name of *Mariequita*.[53]

Yet, despite this society, Edna feels as if she were being borne away from some anchorage which had held her fast, whose chains had been loosening" (chap. 12), and together with Robert she meditates on "pirate gold" and on yet another voyage, this one to the legendary island of "Grande Terre," where they will "climb up the hill to the old fort and look at the little wriggling gold snakes and watch the lizards sun themselves." When she finally arrives at the "quaint little Gothic church of Our Lady of Lourdes," therefore, she is overcome by "a feeling of oppression and drowsiness." Like Mariequita, the Church of Our Lady of Lourdes is named for the wrong goddess; and Edna struggles, as she did when "running away from prayers" through the Kentucky meadow, to escape its "stifling atmosphere . . . and reach the open air."

Everything that happens after Edna leaves the church further implies that she has abandoned the suffocation of traditional Christian (that is, patriarchal) theology for the rituals of an alternative (female and feminist) religion. Attended by Robert, she strolls across the "low, drowsy island," stopping once, almost ceremonially, to drink water that a "mild-faced Acadian" is drawing from a well. At "Madame Antoine's cot," again almost ceremonially, she undresses, bathes, and lies down "in the very center of [a] high, white bed," where, like a revisionary Sleeping Beauty, she sleeps for almost a whole day. When she awakens, for perhaps the most crucial time in this novel of perpetual "awakening," she wonders, as if she were a female Rip Van Winkle. "How many years have I slept? . . . The whole island seems changed. A new race of beings must have sprung up . . . and when did our people from Grand Isle disappear from the earth?" (chap. 13).

Again, almost ritually, Edna bathes, and then she eats what appear to be two sacramental meals. First, she enters a room where she finds that though "no one was there . . . there was a cloth spread upon the table that stood against the wall, and a cover was laid for one, with a crusty brown loaf and a bottle of wine beside the plate." She bites "a piece from the brown loaf, tearing it with strong, white teeth," and drinks some of the wine. Then, after this solitary communion, she dines à deux with Robert, who serves her "no mean repast." Finally, as the sun sets, she and Robert sit reverently at the feet of fat matriarchal Madame Antoine, who tells them "legends of the Baratarians and the sea," so that, as the moon rises, Edna imagines she can hear "the whispering voices of dead men and the click of muffled gold" (chap. 13).

Having bathed, slept, feasted, communed, and received quasi-religious instruction, Edna seems to have entered a fictive world, a realm of gold where extraordinary myths are real and ordinary reality is merely mythical. Yet of course the pagan paradise into which she has been initiated is quite incompatible with the postulates of gentility and Christianity by which her "real" world lives. Metaphorically speaking, Edna has become Aphrodite, or at least an ephebe of that goddess. But what can be—must be—her fate? Shadowing her earlier "realism" with the subtextual romance she has developed in these chapters of swimming and boating, sleeping and eating, Chopin devotes the rest of her novel to examining with alternate sadness and sardonic verve the sequence of oppressions and exaltations that she imagines would have befallen any late-nineteenth-century woman who experienced such a fantastic transformation. If Aphrodite, or at least Phaedra, were reborn as a fin-de-siècle New Orleans housewife, says Chopin, Edna Pontellier's fate would be her fate.[54]

The rest of The Awakening is primarily a logical elaboration of the consequences of Edna's mythic metamorphosis. Having awakened to her "true" self—that is, to an apparently more authentic way of formulating her identity—Edna begins "daily casting aside that fictitious self which we assume like a garment with which to appear before the world" (chap. 19). Yet as the episodes on the Chênière Caminada reveal, neither she nor her author are eschewing fictions and fantasies altogether. Rather, Chopin has allowed the moon, the sea, the female summer colony, and Madame Antoine to recreate Edna Pontellier as a quasi-mythic character in search of a story that can accommodate her and her power. That such a tale will be both hard to find and hard to tell, however, is revealed almost at once by Robert Lebrun's abrupt departure from Grand Isle. Though he is the would-be lover of a newly incarnated goddess, he experiences himself as Hippolytus to Edna's Phaedra, Tristan to her Isolde, even Léon to her Emma, and thus he conscientiously strives to do what is both morally and fictionally "right," assuming that because he is a "good" man and not a seducer, the traditional plot in which he imagines himself enmeshed now calls for renunciation.

By the end of the novel, Edna will have created a different story, one in which she would have Robert play Adonis to her Aphrodite: "no longer one of Mr. Pontellier's possessions to dispose of or not," she will declare that, like the Queen of Love, "I give myself where I choose" (chap. 36), as if dramatizing Victoria Woodhull's assertion that "I will love whom I may [and] neither you nor any law you can make shall deter me." But in chapter fifteen, as Chopin's heroine struggles toward such a new project, she finds herself incapable of proposing any serious plot alternatives. She does notice, though, that Robert has announced his plans "in a high voice and with a lofty air [like] some gentlemen on the stage." Perhaps for this reason, she retires to her cottage to tell her children a story which she does not—evidently cannot—end, so that "instead of soothing, it excited them . . . [and] she left them in heated argument, speculating about the conclusion of the tale" (chap. 15).

The tale of Edna's own life moves just as haltingly to its strange conclusion. As she gradually becomes aware that she is "seeking herself and finding herself," she attempts with increasing intensity to discard, deny, and even destroy the social conventions by which she has lived: her wedding ring, her "reception day," even her "charming home" that has been so well-stocked with Mr. Pontellier's "household gods." Yet though she stamps on her ring, "striving to crush it, . . . her small boot heel [does] not make an indenture, not a mark upon the little glittering circlet" (chap. 14). And though she plots to move out of her big house on Esplanade Street into a smaller cottage nearby, a home of her own which she fictionalizes as the "Pigeon House," her husband counters with a fiction of his own "concerning the remodeling of his home, changes which he had long contemplated, and which he desired carried forward during his temporary absence" (chap 32).

Edna's painting, her gambling, and her visits to the races, as well as her relationships with Mademoiselle Reisz and Adèle Ratignolle, with the Flaubertian Alcée Arobin (clearly a sort of Rodolphe) and his friends Mr. and Mrs. Highcamp, constitute similar efforts at revisionary self-definition. Painting, for instance, lets her try to recreate both her present and her past in more satisfactory forms. Mademoiselle Reisz brings her closer to Robert, and to the oceanic passions and poetic ideas that had inspired her feelings for him from the first. Adèle Ratignolle reinforces her sense of the "blind contentment" implicit in the sequestered domesticity she has rejected (chap. 18). Her trips to the racetrack remind her of the freedom of her Kentucky childhood, when the "racehorse was a friend and intimate associate" (chap. 25), a spirit like herself, let loose in illimitable fields. And her rapidly developing sexual relationship with Arobin acts "like a narcotic upon her," offering her a "cup of life" (chap. 28) that drugs and drains her awakening egotism even while her choice to drink it manifests the new freedom she is trying to taste.

Yet none of these activities or relationships succeeds in yielding an open space in the plot where Edna finds herself. In fact, precisely because her entanglements have a social reality that gives them plausibility as therapeutic possibilities, none is equal to the intensity of what is by now quite clearly Edna's metaphysical desire, the desire that has transformed her and torn her away from her ordinary life into an extraordinary state where she has become, as Chopin's original title for the novel put it, "a solitary soul." Stranded in this state, having been visited by the Holy Ghost of the allegorically resonant "Gulf," who rarely vouchsafes so much "ponderous" wisdom "to any woman," she can only struggle to make her own persuasive fictions, like the story she tells at a party about "a woman who paddled away with her lover one night in a pirogue and never came back. They were lost amid the Baratarian Islands, and no one ever heard of them or found trace of them from that day to this" (chap. 23).

As Edna eventually realizes, even such a fiction betrays desire into the banalities of conventional romance, so that ultimately her dinner party in chapter thirty is the best, the most authentically self-defining, "story" she can tell. Here she actually enacts the part of the person she has metaphorically become: "the regal woman, the one who rules, who looks on, who stands alone." Yet, as the sadness which shadows this scene implies, in the context of the alternative theology through which Chopin mythologizes this "solitary" heroine's life, the story of Edna's dinner party is the tale of a Last Supper, a final transformation of will and desire into bread and wine, flesh and blood, before the "regal woman's" inevitable crucifixion by a culture in which a regenerated Aphrodite has no viable role. More specifically, it is a Last Supper that precedes Edna's betrayal by a plot that sets both Adèle Ratignolle, the "mother-woman," and Robert Lebrun, the stereotypical lover, against her. In one way or another, each of these characters will remind her of her instrumentality—Adèle, exhausted by childbirth, whispering that she must "think of the children," and Robert passionately envisioning a transaction in which Mr. Pontellier might "set" Edna "free" to belong to *him* (chap. 36).

Finally, therefore, Chopin's heroine can think of only one way "to elude them," to become absolutely herself, and that is through her much-debated last swim. Once again, however, our interpretation of this denouement depends on our understanding of the mythic subtextual narrative that enriches it. Certainly if we see Edna's decision to swim into the sea's "abysses of solitude" as simply a "realistic" action, we are likely to disapprove of it, to consider it, as a number of critics have, "a defeat and a regression, rooted in a self-annihilating instinct, in a romantic incapacity to accommodate . . . to the limitations of reality."[55] But, if we attend to the metaphoric patterns of Chopin's novel, Edna's last swim may not seem to be a suicide—that is, a death—at all, or, if it is a death, it is a death associated with a resurrection, a sort of pagan female Good Friday that promises an Aphroditean Easter. In fact, because of the way it is presented, Edna's supposed suicide enacts not a refusal to accept the limitations of reality but a subversive questioning of the limitations of both reality and "realism." For, swimming away from the white beach of Grand Isle, from the empty summer colony and the oppressive imperatives of marriage and maternity, Edna swims, as the novel's last sentences tell us, not into death but back into her own life, back into the imaginative openness of her childhood.

It is notable, in this regard, that in depicting Edna's last swim Chopin swerved from precursors like Flaubert and Pierre Louÿs and also charted a very different path from the ones chosen by such contemporaries as Haggard and Schreiner or such a descendant as Edith Wharton. All these writers not only show the desirous Aphroditean woman dead but actually linger over the details of her mortification. Flaubert, for instance, follows his censorious extreme unction with horrifying visions of Emma's dead mouth "like a black hole at the bottom of her face," pouring forth "black liquid . . . as if she were vomiting" (241–42). In *Aphrodite,* Louÿs undercuts his Chrysis's triumphant epiphany as Aphrodite with a ghastly picture of her corpse, a "thread of blood" flowing from one "diaphanous nostril" and "some emerald-colored spots . . . softly [tinting] the relaxed belly."[56] And as we have seen, Haggard emphasizes the bestial horror into which his Venus/Persephone "devolves" as she dies.

Similarly, even though Schreiner and Wharton are far gentler with their heroines, both linger with a certain necrophiliac interest over their protagonists' lovely remains. After Lyndall expires—narcissistically studying herself in a mirror—Schreiner comments that the "dead face that the glass reflected was a thing of marvellous beauty and tranquillity," while in *The House of Mirth,* brooding on the dead "semblance of Lily Bart" (who is in any case, as we shall later show, a less Aphroditean woman than any of these other heroines), Wharton imagines Lily's "estranged and tranquil face" definitively motionless and thereby, through that motionlessness, offering her watching lover "the word which made all clear."[57] By contrast, Chopin never allows Edna Pontellier to become fixed, immobilized. Neither perfected nor corrupted, she is swimming when we last see her; nor does she ever, in Dickinson's words, "Stop for Death." To be sure, we are told that "her arms and legs were growing tired," that "exhaustion was pressing upon and overpowering her" (chap. 39). It is clear enough that both reality and "realism" will contain her by fatiguing and drowning her. Yet Chopin seems determined to redeem Edna through a regeneration of myth.

Thus, as she enters the water for her last swim, this transformed heroine finally divests herself of "the unpleasant, pricking garments" of her old life as a "real" woman—a wife, mother, and mistress—and stands "naked under the sky . . . like some new-born creature, opening its eyes in a familiar world that it had never known." Together, her ceremonial nakedness, the paradoxically unknown familiarity of the world she is entering, and the "foamy wavelets [that curl and coil] like serpents about her ankles" (chap. 39) tell us that she is journeying not just toward rebirth but toward a genre that intends to propose new realities for women by providing new mythic paradigms through which women's lives can be understood. Even in the last sentences of Chopin's novel, Edna Pontellier is still moving. *And how, after all, do we know that she ever dies?* What critics have called her "suicide" is simply our interpretation of her motion, our "realistic" idea about the direction in which she is swimming. Yet as Chopin's last words—incorporating a memory from Edna's childhood—tell us, that direction is toward the mythic, the pagan, the aphrodisiac. "There was the hum of bees, and the musky odor of pinks filled the air." Defeated, even crucified by the "reality" of nineteenth-century New Orleans, Chopin's resurrected Venus may be returning to Cyprus or Cythera.[58]

This reading of *The Awakening* is, of course, hyperbolic, so that it is certainly not intended to displace those interpretations which honor the text's more obvious aims. Rather, it is meant to suggest the tension between realistic and mythic aesthetic strategies that complicates Chopin's brilliant novel. More, it is meant to underscore the literary history as well as the poetical significance of the goddess Aphrodite in the nineteenth and twentieth centuries. Finally, it is intended to clarify the dialectical relationship into which Chopin, as an innovative feminist mythmaker, entered not only with ancestresses like the Brontës, Dickinson, and Eliot but also with such crucial male precursors as Flaubert, Whitman, and Swinburne.

If we once again compare Chopin's novel to Flaubert's *Madame Bovary*, we can see that where the French writer censures what he considers the destructive, even nihilistic power of the female imagination, Chopin honors what is positive in that power, never copying Flaubert (the way Cather and others thought she did) but always responding to him. For Flaubert, water is, as D. L. Demorest noted in 1931, the "symbol of Venus the delectable" (as it is for Chopin), but this means in Flaubert's case that throughout *Madame Bovary* "images of fluidity" dissolve and resolve to "evoke all that is disastrous in love." Emma's girlish sentimentality, for example, is represented in what the writer himself called "milky oceans of books about castles and troubadours" while the final horror of her imagination pours as black liquid, a sort of morbid ink, from her dead mouth, as if she were vomiting the essential fluid which had inscribed the romantic fictions that killed her and would eventually destroy her uxorious husband.[59]

Such Flaubertian images slowly filter the idea of the fluid female imagination—the idea, that is, of female fluency—through what Jean-Paul Sartre called "a realism more spiteful than detached," and it is possible to speculate that they are general defensive strategies against the developing cultural power of women as well as specific defenses by which Flaubert armored himself against Louise Colet, a woman of letters on whom he felt helplessly dependent, strategies, to quote Sartre again, "in the diplomacy of Flaubert with regard to this pertinacious poetess."[60] Whatever the source of Flaubert's anxieties, however, Chopin defends herself and other literary women vigorously against such Flaubertian defenses, for she consistently revises his negative images of female "fluency" to present not a spitefully "realistic" but a metaphysically lyric version of the seductive mazes of the sea from which her Aphrodite is born, substituting the valorizations of myth and fantasy for the devaluations of "realism."

In this revisionary struggle, Chopin was aided by aesthetic strategies learned from other male precursors. From Whitman and Swinburne, for instance, she learned to imagine the sea the way she did—as, implicitly, "a great sweet mother" uttering "the low and delicious word 'death' " even while rocking her heroine in life-giving "billowy drowse."[61] In a sense, in fact, her Edna Pontellier is as much a cousin of the twenty-eight-year-old "twenty-ninth bather" in Whitman's "Song of Myself" as she is a niece of Flaubert's Emma Bovary. "Handsome and richly dressed," like Whitman's woman, Edna has had "twenty-eight years of womanly life, and all so lonesome," hiding "aft the blinds of the window," and now, "dancing and laughing," she comes along the beach to bathe in the waters of life. Yet again, much as she had learned from Whitman, Chopin departs from him to create a woman who does not enter the sea to "seize fast" to twenty-eight young men but rather to seize and hold fast to herself. Similarly, she revises Swinburne to create an ocean that is not simply an other—a "fair, green-girdled mother"—but also a version of self, intricately veined with "mazes of inward contemplation" and sacramental precisely because emblematic of such subjectivity.[62]

Because of this last gesture, the sea of Chopin's *Awakening* has much in common with the mystically voluptuous ocean Emily Dickinson imagines in the love poem "Wild Nights—Wild Nights!" (J.249). For when Dickinson exclaims "Rowing in Eden, / Ah! the Sea! / Might I but moor / Tonight in thee!" she is imagining an ocean of erotic energy that will transform and transport *her,* an ocean that exists *for* her and in some sense *is* her. More, in identifying this sea with Eden, she is revising the vocabulary of traditional Christian theology so as to force it to accommodate the urgency of female desire. Such a revision is exactly the one that Chopin performed throughout *The Awakening.* Thus where the extreme unction that Flaubert intones over the corpse of Emma Bovary functions as a final exorcism of the ferocity of the imagining and desirous woman, Chopin's redefined sacraments of bread and wine or crimson cocktails function, like Dickinson's, to vindicate female desire in yet another way. For in creating a heroine as free as Aphrodite, a "regal woman" who "stands alone" and gives herself where she "pleases," Chopin was taking an important step in the historical female struggle both to imagine an independently desirous female self and to envision a deity who would rule and represent a strong female community, a woman's colony transformed into a woman's country.

To be sure, as we suggested in the discussion of *She,* men from Wagner (in *Tannhäuser*) to Baudelaire (writing on Wagner), Swinburne (in "Laus Veneris," "Sapphics," and by implication his version of "Phaedra"), William Morris (in "The Hill of Venus"), Beardsley (in *Venus and Tannhäuser*), and Pierre Louÿs (in *Aphrodite* and *Songs of Bilitis*) had begun, almost obsessively, to dramatize encounters with the goddess of love, who in the past, as Paul Friedrich notes in his study of *The Meaning of Aphrodite,* had often been "avoided" by poets and scholars because they found her female erotic autonomy both "alarming" and "alluring."[63] But for the most part these aesthetically revolutionary nineteenth-century artists used Aphrodite in the same way Haggard used Ayesha and Flaubert used Emma Bovary—to objectify new fears about female power.

Wagner's Tannhäuser, for instance, only escapes damnation—after he has sung of his "unquenchable" longing for the "honeyed fascination" of Venus—when the saintly Elizabeth sacrifices herself to save his soul; Swinburne's Tannhäuser, imprisoned in the Venusberg, feels himself to be confined in "the sea's panting mouth of dry desire" and knows that "sudden serpents hiss across [his Venus's] hair"; Morris's hero sees his Venus as "a curse unto the sons of men" and falls from her embrace into "a night whereof no tongue can tell"; Beardsley's Tannhäuser is first attired, at the Venusberg, in a "dear little coat of pigeon rose silk that hung loosely about his hips, and showed off the jut of his behind to perfection" and then "as a woman," in a costume in which, with humiliating irony, he "looked like a Goddess."[64] For Chopin, however, as for such feminist descendants as Isadora Duncan and H. D., Aphrodite/Venus became a radiant symbol of the liberation of desire that turn-of-the-century women had begun to allow themselves to desire.

The source of Aphrodite's significance for this revisionary company of women is not hard to discern. Neither primarily wife (like Hera), mother (like Demeter), nor daughter (like Athena), Aphrodite is, and has her erotic energy, for herself. As Friedrich observes, moreover, all her essential characteristics—her connections with birds and water, her affinity for young mortal men, her nakedness, her goldenness, and even her liminality, as well as her erotic sophistication—empower her in one way or another.[65] Her dove- or swan-drawn chariot enables her to travel between earth and sky, while her sea-birth places her between earth and sea. Naked yet immortal, she moves with ease between natural and supernatural, human and inhuman, nature and culture. Golden and decked in gold, she is associated with sunset and sunrise, the liminal hours of awakening or drowsing that mediate between night and day, dream and reality.

Appropriately, then, Aphrodite is the patron goddess of Sappho, whom Virginia Woolf called "the supreme head of song" and whose lyric imagination was fostered by unique erotic freedom.[66] And because this goddess became a crucial image of female divinity during the fin de siècle, Kate Chopin made her a model for a "regal," sea-born, gold-clad, bird-haunted woman whose desire for freedom, and for a younger man, edged her (first) out of a large patriarchal mansion into a small female cottage and (then) across the shadowline that separates the clothing of culture from the nakedness of nature. Violent though it was, after all, the origin of the queen of love might have seemed compelling to a protofeminist like Chopin. According to Hesiod, Aphrodite was born when the father god Ouranos was castratred by his son Kronos at the behest of the mother goddess Gaia: after his torn-

off genitals were cast into the sea, "shining white *aphros*, / 'foam' arose
from the flesh of the god, and in this a girl / came into being . . . a
revered and beautiful goddess."[67]

It is no coincidence that Kate Chopin imagined her Venus rising
from the foam of a ceremonial dinner party in 1899, the same year
that another American artist, Isadora Duncan, was beginning to dance
the dances of Aphrodite in London salons while the classicist Jane Ellen
Harrison, who would soon recover the matriarchal origins of ancient
Greek religion, chanted Greek lyrics in the background. The daughter
of a "bold-minded St. Louis Irish girl about the same age as . . . Kate
Chopin," Duncan had always been affected by her own birth "under
the star of Aphrodite," and later she was to sit "for days before the
Primavera, the famous painting of Botticelli" and create a dance

> in which I endeavored to realise the soft and marvelous move-
> ments emanating from it; the soft undulation of the flower-cov-
> ered earth, the circle of nymphs and the flight of the Zephyrs, all
> assembling about the central figure, half Aphrodite, half ma-
> donna, who indicates the procreation of spring in one significant
> gesture.

Musing on the "sweet, half-seen pagan life, where Aphrodite gleamed
through the form of the gracious but more tender Mother of Christ,"
this prophetess of the beauty of female nakedness was struggling, as
Chopin had, to see the power of the pagan through the constraints of
the Christian and the triumph of the female through the power of the
pagan.[68] She was striving, as H. D. later would, to "relight the flame"
of "Aphrodite, holy name," and of "Venus, whose name is kin / / to
venerate, / venerator."[69] And she was laboring, as Chopin had, to define the indefinable mythic essence of "a familiar world that [she] had
never known."

Like Chopin's and H. D.'s, too, Duncan's revisionary program marked
an apex of feminist confidence in the erotic authority of Aphrodite.
But even as these artists sought to reimagine the ancient powers of the
queen of love, some women who were their contemporaries or descendants had begun to reiterate the old feminine (and feminist) mistrust
of female sensuality. By the nineties, for instance, that once "terrible
syren" Victoria Woodhull was righteously denying that she had ever
advocated free love, and by 1920 a dark and bitter vision of Venus
appeared at the center of Willa Cather's "Coming Aphrodite!"[70] In
part a retelling of Louÿ's *Aphrodite*, this brilliantly ironic tale also so
intensively subverts the allusive terms of *The Awakening* that it might

almost be considered an extension of Cather's earlier censorious review of Chopin's novel.[71] Specifically, Cather's story portrays an ambitious Illinois farm girl named *Edna* Bowers who, along with studying "Sapho" [sic] and "Mademoiselle de Maupin" (30), has resolved to become a great actress-singer called "Eden Bower"—a name drawn from Christina Rossetti's equally censorious Victorian poem about Eve's sinfulness and from Dante Gabriel Rossetti's frightening vision of Lilith and the serpent dominating "Eden Bower" in a poem of that title.[72]

Willful and wily, Edna/Eden has casually stepped outside ordinary social confinement and made herself erotically independent. When Cather's story begins, she is being kept (entirely for her own convenience and in the furtherance of her career) by a handily absent Chicago millionaire in a New York apartment next door to a studio occupied by Don Hedger, a struggling painter. Tracing the stages of their romance, Cather splits Chopin's erotic and artistic Edna into two characters: the metaphysically awakened painter, who falls in love with Eden by peering at her through a hole in the wall of his closet, and the physically awakened Eden, whom he watches while, like a latterday Isadora, she exercises naked before a mirror until, like both Edna and Isadora, she takes on a mythic radiance. Thus, at the tale's intensest, Hedger thinks of her body "as never having been clad, or as having worn the stuffs and dyes of all the centuries but his own." And "for him [Eden has] no geographical associations unless with Crete, or Alexandria, or Veronese's Venice. She [is] the immortal conception, the perennial theme" (22).

Throughout the tale, however, Cather hints that when this unclothed Aphrodite ceases to be paradigmatic and becomes personal, or, to put it differently, when she refuses to be merely an artwork—a "conception" or a "theme"—and asserts herself as an autonomous being, she becomes not an embodiment of Eden but a troublesome and anti-Edenic Eve. Early on, for instance, she threatens Hedger's masculinity by scorning his allegorically phallic bulldog "Caesar" (who does, in fact, "seize her" and is in return seized and silenced by his master, who is himself seized by desire). Later, when Hedger tells an extravagant story about a sexually voracious Aztec princess who gelds a captive prince and destroys a series of lovers, we understand the fable to be a monitory one: the power of female desire may be castrating, even murderous. Finally, therefore, Cather separates Hedger and Eden with the suggestion that Eden's desirousness also implies a greed that would ruin the career of Hedger, the "true" artist. And indeed, by the end of the tale this anti-Edenic Eve's ambition has led to a death of the soul even more terrible than the dissolution Cather associated with Edna Pontellier's erotic dreams.

Now a major international star, scheduled to sing in an operative version of Louÿs's *Aphrodite,* Eden has learned that Hedger, whom she hasn't seen in twenty years, has become an originatory figure, "decidedly an influence in art," and it is plain that he has become this by freeing himself from her influence. As she drives off in her luxurious car, her face turns

> hard and settled, like a plaster cast; so a sail, that has been filled by a strong breeze, behaves when the wind suddenly dies. Tomorrow night the wind would blow again, and this mask would be the golden face of Aphrodite. But a "big" career takes its toll, even with the best of luck. [63]

Cather's point seems clear enough: as in Louÿs's novel and as in Hedger's fable of "The Forty Lovers of the Queen," female erotic autonomy, symbolized by the golden nakedness of Aphrodite, is doomed to rigidify, not only repelling any lover unlucky enough to remain captive but also reifying the shining queen of love herself. As D. G. Rossetti said of Lilith in his "Eden Bower," it might be said of *this* Eden Bower that "Not a drop of her blood was human, / But she was made like a soft sweet woman."[73]

There is no doubt that Willa Cather had a number of personal motives for imagining a story like "Coming, Aphrodite!" which reinterprets Aphrodite so bitterly, motives that probably included both a deep distrust of heterosexual desire and a covert identification with the closeted (male) artist who admires and desires the naked girl next door.[74] If we look at the tale as a revisionary critique of *The Awakening,* however, we can see that the creator of Edna/Eden Bower(s) is withdrawing unsympathetically from Chopin's Edna at least in part because that earlier Aphrodite had to swim away from the solid ground of patriarchal reality and die into what was no more than a myth of erotic power. As Mademoiselle Reisz tells Edna, the artist "must possess the courageous soul. . . . The brave soul. The soul that dares and defies" (chap. 21), but Edna, naked and defeated on the beach, is haunted by a bird with a broken wing, "reeling, fluttering, circling disabled down, down to the water" (chap. 38).

Given her own anxieties, Cather must have needed to clarify this problem for herself; and, after all, her ambivalence toward female eroticism was representatively female even while it had personal origins. More, hers were worries that accurately, if paradoxically, summarized Chopin's own wounded reaction to the hostile reviews *The Awakening* received. Thus Cather implicitly decides in "Coming, Aphrodite!" that Edna Pontellier cannot be an artist *because* she is desirous. Art, which requires courage and demands survival, must be left to the (male) Hedgers of this world, who hedge their bets by renouncing desire and protecting themselves against women with a snarling canine Caesar. Yet, as Chopin understood, it is precisely because she is desirous that Edna becomes an artist in the first place, and her art, as at her dinner party, is as much an art of eroticism as it is a "pure" aesthetic activity.

Despite Woodhull's recantation and Cather's skepticism, however, Chopin was not the last feminist to revise patriarchal visions of Aphrodite/ Venus. Just two decades after the publication of *The Awakening,* Amy Lowell produced in "Venus Transiens" a love poem to her companion, Ada Russell, which reinvented the image of the goddess of love as an homage to her beloved:

> Tell me,
> Was Venus more beautiful
> Than you are,
> When she topped
> The crinkled waves,
> Drifting shoreward
> On her plaited shell? [75]

And more than a half century after Chopin's controversial novel appeared, Muriel Rukeyser clarified at least one strand of the feminist rebelliousness that impelled the fin-de-siècle writer's vision of the second coming of Aphrodite, drawing explicitly upon Hesiod's account of the inception of the goddess to write in "The Birth of Venus" that the queen of love was "born in a / tidal wave of the father's overthrow, / the old rule killed and its mutilated sex." [76]

Yet these feminist visions of Aphroditean empowerment were by no means universal. So recent a writer as Anne Sexton, for instance, could see no way to free herself from the problems that Cather had outlined. In a posthumous volume, *Words for Dr. Y.,* her daughter Linda Gray Sexton printed a piece called "To Like, To Love" in which the poet addresses "Aphrodite, / my Cape Town lady / my mother, my daughter" and admits that, though "I dream you Nordic and six foot tall, / I dream you masked and blood-mouthed," and in the end "you start to cry, / you fall down into a huddle, / you are sick. . . . // because you are no one." [77] For women, striving to liberate desire, there was evidently a key moment of Aphroditean rebirth—the neo-Swinburnian moment when Edna enthroned herself in gold satin at the head of a fictive dinner table and Isadora Duncan theatrically brooded before Botticelli's *Primavera*—and then, as Virginia Woolf wrote of the erotic in a slightly different context, "the close withdrew; the hard softened. It was over—the moment."[78] "Realism," implies Cather, may be more than a fictional mode; it may in fact reflect a social reality in which the golden Aphrodite is no more than a metal mask.

A number of male writers, too, became increasingly contemptuous of the ancient goddess of love in these years. Most notably—where such precursors as Wagner, Swinburne, Baudelaire, and even the satiric Beardsley had at least expressed a kind of anxious respect for what they saw as Venus's horrific powers—D. H. Lawrence had his hero, Rupert Birkin, scornfully declare in *Women in Love* (1920) that "Aphrodite is born in the first spasm of universal dissolution" (chap. 14); and Lawrence's persistent portrayals of the "seething electric female ecstasy" of desire that intermittently afflicts characters from Ursula (in *The Rainbow* [1915]) and Gudrun (in *Women in Love*) to Kate (in *The Plumed Serpent* [1926]) embody references to the "shining white *aphros*," or "foam" out of which the erotic goddess arose.[79] By the end of his life, moreover, Lawrence had transformed the classical deity into a figure of fun. Railing in *Pansies* (1929) against "The modern Circe-dom," he asked

> What does she want, volcanic Venus? as she goes fuming round?
> What does she want?
> She says she wants a lover, but don't you believe her. . . .

and he added sardonically

> How are we going to appease her, maiden and mother
> now a volcano of rage?
> I tell you, the penis won't do it.[80]

At the same time, however, it is significant that among recent poets it was a male artist, Wallace Stevens, who produced one of the most celebratory lyrics about the desire implicit in *The Awakening*'s allusive structure. Stevens's vision may have been facilitated by his freedom from the anxieties that serious identification with a mythic female entails for a woman (as both Chopin and Cather, in their different ways, discovered), and it may also have been fostered by his espousal of a philosophy of existential hedonism which neither Wagner nor Swinburne nor Lawrence would ever have shared. In any case, whatever the reason, when, in "The Paltry Nude Starts on a Spring Voyage" (1919), Stevens's "discontent" goddess, "Tired of the salty harbors," embarks, like Edna Pontellier, on her first voyage out, the twentieth-century poet imagines the kind of second coming of Aphrodite for which Chopin's novel had earlier implicitly yearned. The paltry nude's journey, Stevens insists,

> . . . is meagre play
> In the scurry and water-shine
> As her heels foam—
> Not as when the goldener nude
> Of a later day
>
> Will go, like the centre of sea-green pomp,
> In an intenser calm,
> Scullion of fate,
> Across the spick torrent, ceaselessly,
> Upon her irretrievable way.[81]

Still, because Chopin was a woman writer, her fantasized Aphrodite was at least as different from Stevens's "goldener nude" as Stevens's goddess was from, say, Lawrence's "Volcanic Venus." Chopin, after all, painfully dreamed a surrogate self into the ancient divinity's sacred nakedness. Imagining (even if failing to achieve) transformation, the erotically awakened author of *The Awakening* was haunted in the chamber of the realism she had inherited by her longing for a redemptive Aphrodite, who would go "like the centre of sea-green pomp" into a future of different myths and mythic difference.

II
Feminization and Its Discontents

Illustrations on preceding page:
E. F. Cooper. *Edith Wharton.* c. 1889. Courtesy of the Collection of American Literature, The Beinecke Rare Book and Manuscript Library, Yale University.

Edward Steichen. *Willa Cather.* 1926. Gelatin-silver print, 16¾″ × 13⅜″. Collection of The Museum of Modern Art, New York. Gift of the photographer. Reprinted with the permission of Joanna T. Steichen.

4

Angel of Devastation:
Edith Wharton on the
Arts of the Enslaved

She a writer, a novelist, a colleague of the great old craft?—She was a dazzling intruder, *la femme fatale,* the golden pheasant invading the barn-yard.
> —Percy Lubbock on Edith Wharton

She rode the whirlwind, she played with the storm, she laid waste what-ever of the land the other raging elements had spared, she consumed in 15 days what would serve to support an ordinary Christian community (I mean to regulate and occupy and excite them) for about 10 years. Her powers of devastation are ineffable, her repudiation of repose absolutely tragic and she was never more brilliant and able and interesting.
> —Henry James on Edith Wharton

It was once said of Edith Wharton, and she liked and repeated the remark, that she was a "self-made man."
> —Perry Lubbock

Alas, I should like to get up on the house-tops and cry to all who come after us: "Take your own life, every one of you."
> —Edith Wharton

Judging from her photographs, one would not expect the stereotypi-cally decorous Edith Wharton, society matron and popular novelist, to have been a fierce critic of the discontents fostered by the process of feminization through which American "ladies" were constructed. Yet such a contradiction between her manner and her matter is hinted at in the hyperbolic verbal portraits promulgated by Henry James and perpetuated by Percy Lubbock, among them the two we have used as epigraphs here. "The Angel of Devastation," James remarked, "was the mildest name we knew her by," and he supported his point with allu-

123

sions to the "General eagle-pounces and eagle-flights of her deranging
and desolating, ravaging, burning and destroying energy," with references to the "Reign of Terror" he associated with her visits, and with
anxious complaints that she might at any moment sweep him away
"struggling in her talons."[1] Reign of terror? Angel of devastation?
Despite James's plainly comic intent, it is hard to reconcile such phrases
with the elaborately gowned, furred, and bejeweled lady who poses for
the camera with such propriety—and often with a lapdog or two.
Nevertheless, like so many of his insights into matters social and psychological, James's apparently exaggerated claims about Wharton represent both her life and her work with notable accuracy, with, indeed,
considerably greater accuracy than what was until recently the more
widely prevalent view of her as an intellectual grande dame who merely
"gives us correct pictures" of the manors to which she was born and
who suffers from "a limitation of heart."[2]

Perhaps most obviously, James's comments illuminate, as he meant
them to, the virtual ferocity with which Wharton pursued her hectic,
sometimes even frantic travels. Besides being seen as a model of propriety, Wharton was long defined as primarily a sometimes satiric,
sometimes nostalgic *raconteur* of "old New York." If she was related to
any other milieux, she was set against the harsh New England of *Ethan
Frome* (1911)—which many critics thought she misunderstood—or the
elegant, faintly superannuated Faubourg Saint-Germain of early twentieth-century Paris. But as the author of *The Ambassadors* (1903) knew
almost better than anyone else except the hapless Teddy Wharton, this
American abroad was an indefatigable explorer of faraway places with
strange-sounding names, a modern Lady Mary Wortley Montagu who
assaulted the world as if she were indeed what Lubbock called "the
golden pheasant invading the barnyard." In the course of her career,
Wharton produced no less than seven expertly researched and richly
detailed travel books, and even her first full-length work, *The Decoration
of Houses* (1897), is as much a kind of Baedeker as it is a domestic manual, for she chose to document her precepts of interior design with, as
she dryly put it, "illustrations . . . chiefly taken from houses of some
importance" (such as the "Palace of Versailles," the "Chateau of Chan-
tilly," the "Ducal Palace, Urbino," and the "Palace of Fontainebleu")
since she believed that her examples of good taste should be "accessible
to the traveler."[3]

Sometimes by chartered yacht, sometimes by train or ocean liner,
but most often in a chauffeured automobile, Wharton invaded countless major and minor corners of Europe—chateaus and cathedrals, vil-
las and villages, gardens and galleries—whose histories she assimilated
and, as we shall see, appropriated for her own ends. Indeed, what she

called her "motor-flights" through France and Italy became as James and Lubbock implied, not so much pilgrimages to the past as American acts of counter-colonization, a point made by the rhetoric of her own remark that the automobile facilitated "the delight of taking a town unaware, stealing on it by back ways and unchronicled paths, and surprising in it some intimate aspect of past time."[4] Accordingly, Lubbock reported James as feeling that "Here was America, brilliantly flashing upon Europe . . . flashing across to meet this Europe on the highest terms, any terms she pleased—she had only to make her own."[5]

As James would also have known, however, the "ravaging, burning and destroying energy" which fueled the "eagle flights" taken by his angel of devastation arose not just from a passion to possess Europe's highways and byways, its past and present, but also, even more intensely, from a revulsion against America, for what Elizabeth Ammons has called "Edith Wharton's argument with America" was, if possible, even more passionate than his own.[6] On one level, of course, this quarrel was motivated by a disgust with the crude commercialism, the culture of anarchy, that in the view of both artists characterized the new world's "Gilded Age." As early as 1897, Wharton fulminated about "the vulgarity of current decoration," inveighed against the "exquisite discomfort" of the "dreary" American drawing room (*Dec.* 20) and scornfully dismissed contemporary American "knick-knacks" as "useless trifles" (*Dec.* 185). By the time she produced such masterworks as *The House of Mirth* (1905) and *The Custom of the Country* (1913), it was clear that the vulgar yet pretentiously genteel houses she had attacked in her first book were objective correlatives for the national character, while Europe's beautifully proportioned chateaus and palazzi were highlights of a *paysage moralisé* which she felt should instruct and delight her countrymen. She must reconnoiter and even, if necessary, reinvent Europe, Wharton seems to have felt, in order to tell herself and her readers not just how to decorate their houses but how to live their lives.

Indeed, for Wharton, Europe, especially France, was more than a monitory terrain; it was the only imaginable heaven and America an all too present hell. "It used to be said," she once wrote, "that good Americans went to Paris when they died," and, less whimsically, Percy Lubbock testified that if in the United States she had had to scour the country to find a "chosen band" of companions, "a houseful that could give her what she wanted, in Paris the house became a city, a kindgom. . . . with Europe around her she had room, liberty, encouragement, to be what she was."[7] The French, she herself averred, "are the most human"—the least beastly—of the human race."[8] Correspondingly, however, she appears to have felt that the Americans were the least human, the most beastly. Mourning a flood that devastated Paris in 1910, she exclaimed, "If it could only have happened to Omaha!" and in 1913, on one of her last trips to New York, she openly described "this appalling city" as "exactly like a Mercator's projection of hell—with the river of pitch, and the iron bridges, and the 'elevated' marking of the bogie, and Blackwell's Island opposite for the City of Dis."[9]

But the more covert—and more powerful—source of Wharton's attraction to Europe and contempt for America is in a sense camouflaged by the Dantesque geographical hierarchy that, on the surface, chiefly governed her expatriation as much as it largely determined the self-exile of Henry James. Rather, the wellspring of Wharton's role as traveling angel of devastation is revealed by her meditations on European women as compared to their American cousins: on, for instance, her heroine George Sand and on "the continual stream of greatness that Paris poured out upon" the legendary writer's chateau at Nohant, which "gives the measure of what Nohant had to offer in return" (*M-F* 39); on the nature of the typical Frenchwoman, who is "as different as possible from the average American woman" because she is "*grown up*" (*FW* 100); and on the rebellious charms of the early nineteenth-century French novelist Hortense Allart, who was the mistress of (among others) Chateaubriand and Bulwer-Lytton and, in Wharton's words, "an extraordinary woman . . . a George Sand without hypocrisy."[10]

Most strikingly, perhaps, the significance of these women in Wharton's mental landscape is revealed by the name she gave one of the cars in which she took those "motor-flights" which so terrorized Henry James: *Hortense,* after the independent, adventurous, and erotic Mlle. Allart.[11] For it was the de facto liberation of women—the partnership of the sexes and perhaps more particularly the female power—that she sought and felt she had found in Paris and on her frantic motor-flights through France which really underlay Wharton's impassioned critique of America. What Henry James saw as a hellish country because it was in the grip of a "feminine, a nervous, hysterical, chattering, canting age" Wharton saw as specifically a hell for women, a hell whose discontents arose directly from a debilitating feminization.[12]

As her own memoirs and those of others make clear, Wharton was emphatically not a feminist in the ordinary sense of the word. On the contrary, she seems often to have gone out of her way to present herself as an old-fashioned "man's woman" who felt nothing but contempt for New Womanly strivings. In *A Backward Glance* (1937), for instance, the autobiography she published almost a decade after Virginia Woolf had celebrated women's colleges in *A Room of One's Own,* Wharton dismisses female learning and upholds traditional domestic virtues. It is deeply regrettable, she declares, that the "ancient curriculum of house-keeping . . . at least in Anglo-Saxon countries, was . . . swept aside by the 'monstrous regiment' of the emancipated; young women taught by their elders to despise the kitchen, and the linen room, and to substitute the acquiring of university degrees for the more complex art of civilized living. . . . Cold storage, deplorable as it is," she adds sardonically, "has done far less harm to the home than the Higher Education." [13] More specifically, when Mary Berenson sent her a copy of *The Cause* (1928), her daughter Ray Strachey's history of the suffrage movement, Wharton thanked her but commented that in her view "women were made for pleasure and procreation." [14]

As a woman writer, moreover, Wharton made remarks which continually emphasized the ambivalence of her affiliation with the female literary tradition. Though she admired Jane Austen as well as George Sand and Hortense Allart, and though Percy Lubbock reported that she was willing to "be blind" to the faults of George Eliot, Lubbock also noted her "curt dismissal of Charlotte Brontë," [15] and she herself complained of "the rose-colored spectacles" through which "my predecessors, Mary Wilkins and Sarah Orne Jewett" looked at the world while priding herself on being "exasperated by the laxities of the great Louisa" May Alcott (*BG* 293, 51). Toward her female contemporaries she was equally scornful. Though she knew and liked Vernon Lee, Alice Meynell, and Mrs. Humphry Ward, for example, and though she especially admired the French poet Anna de Noailles, she was notably hostile to Virginia Woolf, the woman writer who was arguably her most significant peer, commenting when the same Mary Berenson who had urged her to read *The Cause* suggested she read *Orlando* (1928), that "the photographs of the author in the advertisements 'made me quite ill. I can't believe that where there is exhibitionism of that order there can be any real creative gift. " [16] Just as censoriously, about the lesbian writer Natalie Barney, her fellow expatriate *salonnière*, she told one friend that whatever else she did, "You never must go near Mrs. Barney," for that noted hostess of the Rue Jacob was "something—appalling," while even more contemptuously, she dismissed Radclyffe Hall's controversial novel about homosexuality, *The Well of Loneliness* (1928), as "dull twaddle." [17]

Furthermore, from the juvenile novel *Fast and Loose*, composed, using the pseudonym "David Olivieri," when she was about fifteen, to such mature tales as "Xingu" (1911) and "Writing a War Story" (1919), Wharton dramatized her hostility to women of letters with gleeful wit. *Fast and Loose* parodically plays fast and loose with such precursor texts as *Jane Eyre* and *Villette*: its heroine, Georgina *Rivers*, rides a horse named *Rochester* and marries a bad baronet called Lord *Bretton* of *Lowood*, while its hero marries angelic Madeleine *Graham*.[18] "Xingu" deflates the pretentions of a best-selling, sepulchrally self-important woman novelist whose pseudonym is "Osric Dane" and whose chef d'oeuvre is *The Wings of Death*, a brilliant exploration of "the dark hopelessness of it all."[19] And "Writing a War Story" recounts the absurd efforts of pretty but brainless Ivy Spang to produce an inspiring tale for *The Man-at-Arms*, a soldiers' magazine (*S* II 359–70). In all these works and in a number of others, Wharton generally defines the scribbling woman in much the way she characterized her pseudonymous "David Olivieri" in one of the hilarious mock reviews that she appended to *Fast and Loose*: "a sick-sentimental school-girl who has begun her work with a fierce & bloody resolve to make it as bad as Wilhelm Meister, Consuelo, & 'Goodbye Sweetheart' together, & has ended with a blush, & a general erasure of all the naughty words which her modest vocabulary could furnish" (*FL* 121).[20]

Given such stories and such statements, then, it is not surprising to find Percy Lubbock observing that Wharton "preferred the company of men" to that of women and supporting his point with the following testimony from the novelist's friend Mrs. Gordon Bell: " 'Being a very normal person she preferred men to women, and often terrified the latter with a cold stare. . . . many women who only knew her slightly have said to me, "She looks at me as if I were a worm." ' "[21] It is not surprising, either, to find Wharton taking pleasure in the remark that she was a "self-made man," and one might expect, too, that she took some private delight in one journalist's quip that she was a "masculine Henry James."[22]

Nevertheless, despite all this evidence that Edith Wharton was neither in theory nor in practice a feminist, her major fictions, taken together, constitute perhaps the most searching—and searing—feminist analysis of the construction of "femininity" produced by any novelist in this century. For in fact there is little reason to suppose that Wharton misogynistically scorned woman per se. Rather, as recent critics from R. W. B. Lewis and Cynthia Griffin Wolff to Elizabeth Ammons have observed, what she loathed was what woman had been made to become. Mrs. Bell's remark is again apropos here: "Being a very normal person, she preferred men to women." In Wharton's view, the "custom of the country" had in America created women, especially women of the type that Virginia Woolf was to define in *Three Guineas* as "the daughters of educated men"—that is, "ladies"—in such a way that any "normal person" of taste and discrimination would look at most as if they were "worms," or at best creatures useful only "for pleasure and procreation."[23]

Wharton's rage at this state of things cannot be overestimated. Indeed, starting with the early parable "The Valley of Childish Things" (1896), most of her fiction is focused with cold fury on the limits and liabilities of "the feminine" in a culture that fashions women to be ornamental, exploitative, and inarticulate. "A woman's standard of truthfulness [is] tacitly held to be lower than her husband's," muses Newland Archer toward the end of *The Age of Innocence* (1920), because "she [is] the subject creature, and versed in the arts of the enslaved."[24] *The subject creature. The arts of the enslaved.* These two phrases summarize issues that Wharton examined in book after book, story after story. What Schreiner's Lyndall (and Schreiner herself) inveighed against yet did not really document, what Gilman's Herlanders and Chopin's Edna in their different ways fled from into realms of fantasy, became the subject of Edith Wharton's unflinching and unremitting exploration: the precise details as well as the cruder contours of the process by which women are socialized as prisoners of sex, and more specifically the horror (to the "lady" herself and others) of the cultural techniques of feminization that created the female "sex parasite."

But where Schreiner, Gilman, and Chopin had each struggled to find ways out of the Hisland that so degraded and diminished women—"*sorties,*" to use Hélène Cixous's phrase, into a utopian Herland—Wharton mostly saw signs that said NO EXIT. An intransigent realist and a self-defined "priestess of reason," she frankly declared that "Life is the saddest thing there is, next to death" (*BG* 379) and never openly elaborated full-scale fantasies about the liberation and gratification of female desire or about the unleashing of female power in the ways that more optimistic feminists did. In fact, the two major kinds of feminist possibilities celebrated by so many of her precursors and contemporaries seemed to Wharton to be nonexistent or delusive. On the one hand, she repudiated the notion that bonds of sisterhood might be formed in what Carroll Smith-Rosenberg has called the "female world of love and ritual" that was woman's separate sphere, and on the other hand, she did not believe in the "shoulder to shoulder" feminist solidarity that supposedly marked the colonies of the New Woman.

Writing to a friend in 1904 about the sort of summer hotel which, as we have seen, had functioned for Chopin's Edna Pontellier as a Woman's House of self-discovery, Wharton confided, "I have been spending my first night in an American 'summer hotel,' and I despair of the Republic! Such dreariness, such whining callow women, such utter absence of the amenities, such crass food, crass manners, crass landscape!"[25] The next year, in *The House of Mirth*, she brought the desperate Lily Bart into a tearoom which was clearly an outpost of the colonies of the New Woman. But there is no sisterly sympathy for Lily to find there. Explained Wharton:

> The room was full of women and girls, all too much engaged in
> the rapid absorption of tea and pie to remark her entrance. . . .
> [Lily's] eyes sought the faces about her, craving a responsive glance.
> . . . But the sallow preoccupied women, with their bags and note-
> books and rolls of music, were all engrossed in their own affairs,
> and even those who sat by themselves were busy running over
> proof-sheets or devouring magazines between their hurried gulps
> of tea.[26]

If the "Old" Woman was, in her own sphere, a "whining callow" parasite, the New Woman, invading a man's world, was just another wage
slave.

Even Wharton's depictions of Europe, which we have called her only
imaginable heaven, were consistently constrained by what she saw as
the limits of the probable, and in patriarchal culture, as constituted
throughout the west, all that was probable for women seemed to her
to be the chance of developing their minds (as she thought French-
women did) through "contact with the stronger masculine individual-
ity" (*FW* 102–03). Indeed, such chances were in her view inevitably
qualified by the intransigence of the social institutions that mediate between the sexes. When Newland Archer begs Ellen Olenska to flee with
him from such traditional "categories" as "mistress" and "wife" to a
place "where we shall be simply two human beings who love each other,"
Ellen's bleakly skeptical reply speaks for Wharton too:

> "Oh, my dear—where is that country? Have you ever been there?
> . . . I know so many who've tried to find it; and, believe me, they
> all got out by mistake at wayside stations: at places like Boulogne,
> or Pisa, or Monte Carlo—and it wasn't at all different from the
> old world they'd left, but only rather smaller and dingier and more
> promiscuous." [*AI*, 290]

Finally, then, primarily because of such skepticism but no doubt also
in part because she was an indefatigable reader of the physical and
social sciences, Wharton was, as a novelist, a cultural determinist and a
sociologist in the mode of Thorstein Veblen, whose widely read and
radical *The Theory of the Leisure Class* her entire oeuvre may be said to
gloss.[27] Published in 1899, Veblen's treatise explored the social laws
through which, in a capitalist economy, bourgeois and upper-class wives
were constructed to function as apparently autonomous but really servile creatures whose "conspicuous consumption" signified their husbands' wealth and power. As "the latter-day outcome" of the evolution
of the "archaic institution" of marriage, Veblen explained, the modern
wife, "who was at the outset the drudge and chattel of the man, both in

fact and in theory—the producer of goods for him to consume,—has become the ceremonial consumer of goods which he produces. But she still quite unmistakably remains his chattel in theory; for the habitual rendering of vicarious leisure and consumption is the abiding mark of the unfree servant."[28]

Veblen's book was fierce in its critique of woman's place in what he called "pecuniary culture." But in tracing the diverse destinies of such figures as Lily Bart (in *The House of Mirth*), Undine Spragg and Ralph Marvell (in *The Custom of the Country*), May Welland and Newland Archer (in *The Age of Innocence*), Wharton even more devastatingly dramatized the dynamics by which the laws of that culture made themselves felt, while in studying the fates of Ethan Frome and Mattie Silver (in *Ethan Frome*) or Charity Royall (in *Summer* [1917]), she turned her attention from the urban class to the rural poor, in order to investigate the anti-romantic family romances that may have ultimately determined those laws. Indeed, as she hints in *A Backward Glance,* she seems to have taken a kind of sadomasochistic pleasure in tracing the forces that inexorably shape the needs of her characters. "It is always a necessity to me," she confides, "that the note of inevitableness should be sounded at the very opening of my tale, and that my characters should go forward to their ineluctable doom like the 'murdered man' in 'The Pot of Basil.' From the first I know exactly what is going to happen to every one of them; their fate is settled beyond rescue, and I have but to watch and record" (*BG* 204). Her rhetoric here—murder, ineluctable doom, beyond rescue—is telling. The quality that unfriendly critics defined as her "limitation of heart"—her apparent lack of sympathy for her characters, her coldness, her *hauteur*—may simply have been their misperception of the grim delight with which she forced herself, and her readers, to face the social facts that made her women (and their men) what they were.

The parts of stories that Schreiner repressed (Lyndall's sojourn in England and the lessons she learned there), that Gilman glossed over (the lives of Herlanders before the lucky strike that killed all their men), and that Chopin perhaps could not bear to tell (the nature of Edna's life in the Pigeon House after a separation or divorce from Pontellier): these were precisely the narratives on which Wharton concentrated with what feels at times like sickening ferocity.[29] For this reason, James's definition of her as an angel of devastation applies even more strikingly, if less obviously, to her work as a novelist than it does to her life as a traveler. After a Wharton visit to Rye in 1909, her theatrically exhausted mentor told a mutual friend, "I feel even as one of those infants of literary allusion whom their mothers hush to terror by pronouncing the name of the great historical ravager of *their* country, Bonaparte, Attila, or Tamerlaine." But as Wharton's biographer,

R. W. B. Lewis, observes in a mild understatement, the master's "language seems unduly strong to describe a visit of less than three days and a drive to Chichester and back."[30] Consciously or not, James must have understood that the force which transformed Edith Wharton into an apocalyptic angel of devastation was not just a passion for whirlwind travel but an impassioned disgust with the laws governing the world that Veblen described, along with mingled pity and contempt for their victims.

More, as James's extravagant comparison of Wharton to such "great historical ravagers" as Bonaparte, Attila, and Tamerlaine implies, he may have intuited this society matron's secret desire to destroy and despoil the country in which most men and women lived, the happy valley of childish things whose economy turned on the infantilization and commodification of women as much as it did on the subordination and exploitation of workers. And as we shall see, though Wharton never allowed herself to imagine utopian alternatives to that country, she did seek to circumvent its laws in a number of devious ways: in life, through the energetic decoration of (her own) houses; in art, through the impassioned "making up"—to use her own childhood term for literary creation's furtive pleasures—of uncannily vengeful ghost stories; through intermittent, hesitant, flickering, but persistent visions of female triumph in the "secret garden" of heterosexual eroticism; and through hints at an untellable tale of female power and guarded allusions to the alien language in which it would have to be told.

"She was herself a novel of [James's], no doubt in his earlier manner," wrote Percy Lubbock of Edith Wharton.[31] Among other things, he may have meant to emphasize the fact that, like James's Isabel Archer, Wharton seemed born and bred to be the heroine of a novel of manners. Indeed, to put the point rather crudely, far more than the heroine of *Portrait of a Lady* (1881)—and, for that matter, far more than Olive Schreiner, Charlotte Perkins Gilman, Kate Chopin, or any of their various heroines—Edith Wharton, née Jones, was born and bred to be what Schreiner called a "sex parasite." Among the earliest memories that she recorded in *A Backward Glance* were two episodes having to do with the crucial significance of women's costume, and having to do in particular with her precocious understanding of what Veblen called "Dress as an Expression of the Pecuniary Culture"[32] and of Lyndall's insight that to men the world says *"Work"* while to women it commands *"Seem."* On a walk with her father that is "the first thing I can remember" and therefore the day from which she dates "the birth of her identity," Wharton confides, the very little girl that she was "woke to the

importance of dress, and of herself as a subject for adornment" (*BG* 2).
Not too much later, when she was still "a small child," she recalls, she
had a conversation with a favorite aunt in which the question "What
would you like to be when you grow up?" elicited the solemn response
"the best-dressed woman in New York" (*BG* 20). In fact, her mother,
Lucretia Rhinelander Jones, was at least *one* of the best-dressed women
in the city as well as a woman who administered the curriculum of
decorum to her daughter with the kind of severity that, for instance,
marked Aurora Leigh's education in gentility at the hands of her English aunt.

Keeping up with the Jones's, therefore, would have been difficult
for all but the most elite families in Wharton's "old New York," and the
eminence of the parents must have been certified not just by their own
hauteur but by the correct elegance of their daughter, by the idealized
image of her in miniatures and oil paintings that adorned their drawing room, and by her appearance—"slender, graceful and icy cold," in
the words of one observer, "with an exceedingly aristocratic bearing"—
at New York balls and Newport teas.[33] And that the girl's reification as
a charming and ornamental commodity was also signified by two nicknames, "Pussy" and "Lily," which emphasized her likeness to a domestic pet or a hothouse flower was certainly not unusual in her society.
Nor, on the surface, was the equanimity with which "Pussy/Lily" Jones
accepted such a status.

As Wharton reports her youth, she drifted passively into a debut—

> I was . . . put into a low-necked bodice of pale green brocade,
> above a white muslin skirt ruffled with rows and rows of Valen-
> ciennes, my hair was piled up on top of my head, some friend of
> the family sent me a large bouquet of lilies-of-the-valley, and thus
> adorned I was taken by my parents to a ball [*BG* 77]

—and then into marriage with the sportsman and socialite Edward
Wharton, a kindly nonentity who must have seemed a good catch in
her set because he always kept a thousand-dollar bill in his wallet "in
case Pussy wanted something."[34] Thus, even when she had in all prob-
ability already begun to write, Wharton, according to her own bemused
report, could think of no better way to prepare for her first meeting
with Henry James than "to put on my newest Doucet dress, and try to
look my prettiest," for "those were the principles in which I had been
brought up." And though this meeting had not, despite Doucet, been
successful, she confesses that the following year she sought (still unsuccessfully) to attract the master with *"a beautiful new hat!"* (*BG* 172).

But that this fashionable young matron actually aspired to interest
so rarefied an intellectual as Henry James is, of course, a sign that she

was from the start something quite other than a "sex parasite" or a conspicuous consumer. As Wharton almost spitefully emphasizes throughout the early chapters of *A Backward Glance*, her parents and their circle were vehemently antiliterary, as if authorship were morally opprobrious. "I cannot hope," she declares, "to render the tone in which my mother pronounced the names of such unfortunates [as Poe and Melville], or on the other hand, that of Mrs. Beecher Stowe, who was so 'common' yet so successful" (*BG* 68–69).[35] Even after she had become a successful novelist, she writes, "none of my relations ever spoke to me of my books, either to praise or blame—they simply ignored them; and among the immense tribe of my New York cousins . . . the subject was avoided as though it were a kind of family disgrace" (*BG* 144). But despite the efforts that members of this quite powerful clan may have made to repress, or at least resist, her aesthetic aspirations, from childhood on, with an almost demonic intensity, Wharton indulged in what she called "making up," and the reading which fueled her creative fires was evidently as omniverous as her storytelling was impassioned.[36]

Such energies apparently seemed not only socially scandalous but stereotypically unfeminine, yet family and friends did covertly or overtly acknowledge their existence. R. W. B. Lewis points out that Wharton's brother Harry—and later sometimes her husband, Teddy—called her "John" and suggests that this was because both detected "the streak of virile toughness that lay behind her enjoyment of pretty dresses," a toughness associated with unfeminine intellectual ambition.[37] When her first, abortive engagement (to one Harry Stevens) was broken, the *Newport Daily News* explained that "the only reason assigned . . . is an alleged preponderance of intellectuality on the part of the intended bride. Miss Jones is an ambitious authoress, and it is said that, in the eyes of Mr. Stevens, ambition is a grievous fault."[38] And some years later, after this aspiring "authoress" had married Teddy and become a fashionable Newport hostess, one of her guests—the French novelist Paul Bourget, later to become a close friend—savagely caricatured her as a typical American "intellectual tomboy": "though . . . she gets her gowns from the best houses of the Rue de la Paix, there is not a book of Darwin, Huxley, Spencer, Renan, Taine, which she has not studied. . . . [But] one would say that she has ordered her intellect somewhere, as we would order a piece of furniture. . . . One longs to cry—'Oh, for one ignorance, one error, just a single one.' "[39]

But if Wharton sought to circumvent the appellation "tomboy" and presented herself as a "feminine" writer, she risked another kind of censoriousness from friends and associates, who dismissed her as a mere "popular" novelist, a creature not unlike the "sick-sentimental school girl" authoress she herself had caricatured in the mock review of *Fast and Loose* that we quoted earlier. As late as 1910, indeed, Henry James subtly satirized her aesthetic aspirations in "The Velvet Glove," a tale of a successful man of letters who must struggle to resist the importunities of a high-born scribbling woman. James's "Princess"—whose title evokes the phrase *"la princesse lointane,"* one of his many epithets for Wharton—swoops up the bemused playwright John Berridge for a ride in her costly motorcar and begs him to write a "lovely, friendly, irresistable log-rolling Preface" for her latest romance, *The Velvet Glove,* one of the crassly and trashily commercial novels she produces under the pseudonym "Amy Evans." When he refuses, she seems "all divinely indulgent but all humanly defeated," as if even James had to qualify his characterizations of Wharton as a supernally powerful angel of devastation by attributing to her in fiction a human vulnerability he did not always recognize in life.[40]

Such portraits of the (woman) artist as, on the one hand, a monstrous and unfeminine "thinking machine" and, on the other hand, a presumptuous and untalented scribbling woman reflect the extremity of the situation in which the young Wharton found herself. Inevitably, her selves were at war: the "sex parasite"—beautifully gowned "Pussy/Lily" Jones—could hardly be reconciled with "John," the "intellectual tomboy" and "self-made man." And at first the inner warfare was so brutal that it literally immobilized Edith Wharton, who suffered in 1898 a nervous breakdown not unlike the one Charlotte Perkins Gilman recorded in "The Yellow Wallpaper." Debilitated by extreme fatigue, weight loss, "inability to read or write," headaches, nausea, and "profound melancholy,"[41] Wharton was sent to Philadelphia for the "rest cure" that had been perfected by the neurologist S. Weir Mitchell, also Gilman's physician. But Wharton was not "all humanly defeated" by the notorious cure: unlike Gilman or "The Yellow Wallpaper"'s mad protagonist, the New York novelist got well after three months of Mitchell's treatment, which seems (also unlike the treatment of Gilman and her heroine) to have included the encouragement of literary ambitions.

Tellingly, this historian-to-be of the arts of the enslaved signaled her recovery by purchasing "an expensive black fur ensemble" and sending to Scribner's for galleys of her first collection of short stories. Though—until the years of her affair with Morton Fullerton—she would continue, at least privately, to define her marriage as a prison, intermittently comparing her life to that of Emma Bovary and her husband to the doltish Charles, the radical estrangement from society that was a crucial tenet of Mitchell's treatment had allowed her to pull her two selves together into a third creature. Distanced from the conflicts of her situation, she was empowered to become an observer who dissected what had been her own dilemma—the struggle of the captive lady against the bars of her gilded cage—with steely accuracy. For out of the battle between "Pussy" and "John" was born the angel of devastation, *"la femme fatale,* the golden pheasant invading the barnyard" of letters: a woman who was more than what one provisional title of *The House of Mirth* called "a moment's ornament," more than that because she dressed to kill. And kill Wharton now did, in murderous analyses of "sex parasitism" and its discontents, as well as in symbolic vendettas against, or at least exposés of, the men whom her theory of the leisure class held in various ways accountable for the status of her artificially feminized heroines as mostly damaged but sometimes damaging goods.

At a key point in *Summer,* Wharton's youthful protagonist, Charity Royall, haunted by a failed love affair and trapped by an illegitimate pregnancy, broods on what Wharton would call her "ineluctable doom": "In the established order of things as she knew them," comments the novelist, "she saw no place for her individual adventure."[42] The girl is reviewing several of the unsatisfactory alternatives through which she might solve her problem—on the one hand, abortion, on the other hand, prostitution—when she comes to this conclusion, and, as we later discover, even more apparently viable possibilities offer little hope of freedom or fulfillment for Charity. Yet though her story seems on the surface melodramatic, Charity's situation is not idiosyncratic but representative in the Wharton canon, for from the start this writer's critique of her culture appears to have been designed to reveal the hopeless incompatibility between "the established order of things" and the "individual [female] adventure."

A first formulation of this conflict appears in "The Valley of Childish Things" (1896), a now comparatively well-known parable whose style strikingly echoes that of the feminist allegories collected in Olive Schreiner's *Dreams* (1890) and *Dream Life and Real Life* (1893). But where the South African writer's visionary mode is frequently ecstatic, Wharton's is already bleak, sardonic. Schreiner's "Three Dreams in a Desert," for instance, charts the journey of a captive woman toward a future utopia, a "Land of Freedom": "I dreamed I saw a land. And on the hills walked brave women and brave men, hand in hand. And they looked into each other's eyes, and they were not afraid."[43] As if in response, Wharton's tale describes the defeat of a little girl who, also in search of a "Land of Freedom," leaves "the Valley of Childish Things" in order to learn "many useful arts, and in so doing [grows] to be a woman" (*S* I 58). After resolving to return to her valley to work with her former comrades, the heroine encounters an old playmate who has himself grown to be a man and who is also journeying back to the valley. She assumes that the two will labor together there, among other "splendid men and women"; indeed, she seems to think that, like Schreiner's men and women, they will gaze fearlessly "into each other's eyes."

But when they reach their homeland Wharton's heroine discovers that the other children have remained infantile, and her "fellow traveler . . . the only grown man in the valley [falls]

> on his knees before a dear little girl with blue eyes and a coral necklace. . . . and when she who had grown to be a woman laid her hand on the man's shoulder, and asked him if he did not want to set to work with her building bridges, draining swamps, and cutting roads through the jungle, he replied that at that particular moment he was too busy.
>
> And as she turned away, he added in the kindest possible way, "Really, my dear, you ought to have taken better care of your complexion." [*S* I 58–59]

As a number of critics have observed, "The Valley of Childish Things" points to problems that would preoccupy Wharton throughout most of her literary career, and its bitterness illuminates the deliberately anti-utopian cast of her feminism.[44] But precisely because it is a Schreiner-esque allegory, it barely hints at the wealth of empirical detail with which, from *The House of Mirth* (1905) on, this writer would justify her rage at "the established order of things" in a society dedicated not only to Ve-blen's "conspicuous consumption" but also to what he called "conspic-uous waste."[45] As we shall see, for Wharton, who stubbornly main-tained—in the face of what she saw as wrongheaded modernist experimentation—that "verisimilitude is the truth of art," a central goal of the novel was the excavation and organization of such detail, an activity that was apparently dispassionate though often really polemi-cal.[46]

Reflecting in *A Backward Glance* on *The House of Mirth,* her first major novel of contemporary life, Wharton remembered the moment when she realized that leisure-class New York was her true subject: "There it was before me, in all its flatness and futility, asking to be dealt with as the theme most available to my hand since I had been steeped in it from infancy" (*BG* 207). On the surface, the rhetoric of her condem-nation is conventionally moral. Besides being flat and futile, she de-clares, rich New York was frivolous, and she intended her novel to show that "a frivolous society can acquire dramatic significance only through what its frivolity destroys" (*BG* 207)—in this case, the beautiful

and scrupulous hothouse flower Lily Bart. With their biblical overtones, both Lily's name and the novel's title reinforce this monitory
point. "The heart of the wise is in the house of mourning; the heart of
the fool is in the house of mirth," Ecclesiastes preaches, and "Consider
the lilies of the field; they toil not, neither do they spin," proclaims the
Sermon on the Mount, "Yet . . . even Solomon in all his glory was not
arrayed like one of these."[47] Wharton's heroine, these statements and
allusions seem to imply, might have redeemed herself by making right
choices—for wisdom, sobriety, and mourning; against futility, frivolity,
and showy artificial glory.

But Wharton's novel is no morality play; instead, like Veblen's *Theory
of the Leisure Class,* it is determinedly and deterministically sociological.
Thus "in the established order of things" there is no more place for
Lily's "individual adventure"—no more chance for her redemption—
than there is for Charity's. In fact, trapped in "the great gilt cage" of
her culture (*HM* 59), Lily, as Wharton delineates her, is constructed
in such a way that she is torn between the horror of self-gratification
and the "emptiness of renunciation" (*HM* 332), between the wasteful-
ness of leisure and the waste land of labor. For Wharton, then, the
biblical adage about the house of mourning does not mean something
comparatively hopeful, like "be wise and renounce pointless mirth,"
but rather, more nihilistically, it means that in a flat and futile society
"the only thing sadder than life is death," while the name "Lily," beyond an ambiguous reference to the uses of raiment, immediately suggests both young "Pussy/Lily" Wharton herself and one of the characteristically voluptuous art nouveau flowers that decorated drawing rooms
and lamp shades, mirrors and Metro entrances, at the turn of the century—suggests, that is, a fashionable commodity.[48] More, the "ineluctable doom" to which Lily is led as she stumbles down the social ladder
proves, not that this flower of society should have chosen to be wise
and let who will be merry, should have chosen morality over materialism, but rather that, in Veblen's icily dispassionate formulation, "The
canons of decent life are an elaboration of the principle of invidious
comparison, and they accordingly act consistently to inhibit all non-
invidious effort and to inculcate the self-regarding attitude."[49] In other
words, in what Veblen, like Wharton, sees as a "predatory" and "pecuniary" culture, "good" society rewards selfishness and sacrifices self-
sacrifice.

Because of the rich detail with which Wharton documents it, the
story of Lily Bart is not easily told, but its rough outline can be summarized. Educated to be decorative and luxury-loving, exquisite Lily is,
when we first encounter her at twenty-nine, "like some rare flower grown
for exhibition" (*HM* 329), or "some superfine human merchandise"

(265) displayed on the marriage market. But though she tries diligently to practice "the arts of the enslaved" as she searches for a man to buy her body and soul, in every instance a failure of will causes her to lose the sale. From Percy Gryce, a dull millionaire collector of Americana (who she hopes will collect *her*), to a wealthy Italian prince, to Sim Rosedale, a *nouveau riche* Jewish entrepreneur, Lily accumulates, then just misses ensnaring, eligible suitors, partly because of her attraction to the detached and uncatchable Lawrence Selden, partly because of her inability to use the sort of "self-regarding" survival tactics deployed by her rivals (for instance, she will not blackmail the hostile and profligate society matron Bertha Dorset, whose love letters to Selden have come into her possession), and partly because of a fatal revulsion against self-marketing.[50] Lily "works like a slave preparing the ground and sowing her seeds," remarks one observer about her labors in the nuptial marketplace, "but the day she ought to be reaping the harvest, she oversleeps herself or goes off on a picnic" (196). By the novel's end, therefore, Lily has been reduced from a classy *objet d'art* to a lower-class maker of beautiful objects, a hired milliner sewing hats for the ladies who can still afford the conspicuous consumption she is now denied. And her death from an overdose of chloral makes literal the social death inflicted on her when leisure-class society, no longer having any use for her, threw her "out into the rubbish heap" of wage-labor.

In its literary context, Wharton's tale of the decline and fall of Lily Bart may be said to respond with vengeful sarcasm to a number of late nineteenth-century fictions about belles dames and femme fatales, including three we have discussed at length in this volume: *She, The Story of an African Farm,* and *The Awakening.*[51] Like Haggard's seductive Ayesha, Lily at a crucial moment in her career exhibits her lightly veiled body to an awed audience of men, who sense that the "touch of poetry in her beauty" (*HM* 142) arises from the tension between nature and culture, between flesh and art, that she incarnates. As she poses in a parody of Reynolds's *Mrs. Lloyd* for one of the *tableaux vivants* at a society ball, her "pale draperies and the background of foliage against which she [stands] serv[e] only to relieve the long dryad-like curves that [sweep] upward from her poised foot to her lifted arm" (142).

Unlike Ayesha, however, Lily is only dryad-*like;* she is no near-immortal, no sorceress. She may, like Ayesha, find "nothing in life . . . as sweet as the sense of her power over" a man she desires (*HM* 147), but she exhibits herself with conscious narcissism—"self-intoxication" is Wharton's phrase—as part of a mercantile project, a point well understood by the male voyeurs who gaze at and appraise her body. "Deuced

bold thing to show herself in that get-up; but gad, there isn't a break in
the lines anywhere, and I suppose she wanted us to know it!" (142)
comments one, while another later remarks that she was "standing there
as if she was up at auction" (166). Where Haggard's Ayesha is a terrifying fantasy figure who embodies the deadly power men attribute to
insubordinate women, Wharton's Lily dramatizes the unremitting care
with which the enslaved must practice their arts, as well as the limitations of those arts, limitations made clear by her failure at self-marketing.

Moreover, if Haggard pictures Ayesha as a darkly unique femme
fatale, Wharton, going "behind the social tapestry" to "the side where
the threads [are] knotted and the loose ends [hang]" (*HM* 285), demonstrates that her hothouse Lily is just another face in the crowd, or,
more accurately, just another product on a kind of aesthetic assembly
line. A dozen other women at the ball have been "subdued to plastic
harmony" in tableaux vivants by the "organizing hand" of a well-known,
male portrait painter; like Lily, who is reified as a Reynolds, they are
re-produced as Goyas, Titians, Van Dycks, and Veroneses, expensive
and fashionable objets d'art. And if Ayesha's armory of weapons includes looks that kill, ancient wisdom, and volcanic passion, Lily has no
weapon but what is shown to be her fragile beauty,[52] so that she is "an
organism as helpless out of its narrow range as the sea-anemone torn
from the rock" (311). Like Schreiner's Lyndall, then, Wharton's Lily
proves that, at least for a sensitive plant, it is fatal to be a femme fatale.

Yet though Schreiner and Wharton plainly agree on this fundamental precept, the knots and nots that Wharton discovers behind the social
tapestry are far denser and more tangled than any Schreiner uncovers.
As we noted earlier, Wharton relentlessly examines an aspect of Lyndall's story that Schreiner represses: the South African girl's "feminine" education in England. But the American novelist also implicitly
critiques several key points in the plot that Schreiner does explore, as
if arguing that *The Story of an African Farm* is in its way as fantastic as
Haggard's *She* or as any of Schreiner's utopian *Dreams*. To begin with,
by exposing the futility of Lily's toils on the marriage market, Wharton
shows in grim detail just how hard a job it is to be a "sex parasite."
Lyndall's Byronic "stranger" seems to have miraculously fallen at the
girl's feet, despite all her feminist tirades and all her female scorn. Indeed, as we have seen, Lyndall—ostensibly speaking for all women—
boasts that men "are our goods, our merchandise . . . we buy you, we
sell you." But Lily, more realistically in Wharton's view, sees herself as
merchandise and broods that to attract a husband a woman must continually "be ready with fresh compliances and adaptabilities, and all on

the bare chance that [a man like Percy Gryce] might ultimately do her the honor of boring her for life" (29).[53]

More humiliating still, Lily is never allowed the theatrical luxury of rejecting either a wanted or an unwanted suitor. Where Lyndall spurns a proposal from her handsome "stranger" and is devotedly nursed by another prospective suitor, Lily, far from being a *belle dame sans merci*, is twice reduced to broaching the subject of marriage to a man who responds by rejecting her. Comparatively early in the novel, she asks Selden, "Do you want to marry me?" (77) and hears him reply, laughingly, "No, I don't want to—but perhaps I should if you did." And toward the end of the book, when in despair she confesses to her one-time suitor Sim Rosedale that "I am ready to marry you whenever you wish" (263), she hears him give "a short laugh" and reply apologetically, "My dear Miss Lily, I'm sorry if there's been any little misapprehension between us—but you made me feel my suit was so hopeless that I had really no intention of renewing it." Where Schreiner's Lyndall might have been acting out the observation made by Jane Austen's Henry Tilney that a woman's only power is "the power of refusal," Wharton's Lily demonstrates that, no matter how carefully their beauty has been constructed, some women do not have even that option.[54]

Perhaps most tellingly, where, in a decline that recalls the demise of Emily Brontë's Catherine Earnshaw Linton, Lyndall slays herself on the cross of gender through self-starvation and a sheer death wish, Lily struggles to live, resolves not "to pamper herself any longer" by going "without food because her surroundings made it unpalatable" (329), and dies by accident from a sleeping draught she has taken to give her "strength to meet" the next day (335). Furthermore, where Lyndall sickens after giving birth to a premature baby who dies two hours later and whose wet grave effectively kills her (after she visited it, "she had gone to bed, and had not risen again from it; never would, the doctor said" [*AF* 256]), Lily dies hallucinating the body of a living infant, the child of the young working-class wife Nettie Struther, whom she had encountered a few hours earlier. Lyndall's dead baby is a polemical symbol that reinforces the righteousness of her self-immolation: as we have seen, the dystopia she inhabits can only be cured by the utopia she heralds. But Lily's imaginary baby is a more complex and (Wharton would probably argue), paradoxically enough, a more "realistic" symbol of the fleshly continuity—specifically, the mother-child bond—from which a "predatory" society has inexorably alienated the artifically constructed femme fatale.[55]

Finally, even in comparison to Chopin's Edna Pontellier, Wharton's Lily Bart is not only constrained but in effect created by circumstances which seem to have left the earlier heroine relatively untouched. For though the author of *The Awakening* examines in detail the dynamics by which Léonce Pontellier controls his wife, and though Chopin is both accurate and bitter about the socially determined sexual ethos that shapes the behaviors of such other characters as Robert Lebrun, Alcée Arobin and Adèle Ratignolle, she does leave her heroine an inner space in which she can be at least spiritually free. No matter how imprisoned she is in her culture, Edna has, as Chopin's first title put it, a "solitary soul,'" while Lily has been educated to be no more than a "moment's ornament." Thus where Edna is allowed to listen to "the everlasting voice of the sea" and thereby offered "more wisdom than the Holy Ghost is usually pleased to vouchsafe to any woman" (chap. 6), Lily's "whole being dilate[s] in an atmosphere of luxury" which is "the only climate she [can] breathe in" (29), for "Inherited tendencies [have] combined with early training to make her the highly specialised product she [is]" (311). Thus, too, where Edna is brought to metaphysical consciousness and encouraged to swim beyond the limitations of the "real" by her illicit love for Robert, Lily is merely brought to material ruin by her impractical attraction to Selden, for the "siren" must not love her "prey,"[56] and there is no place for female desire in the network of "pecuniary" transactions that constitutes the House of Mirth.

Ultimately, then, as Elaine Showalter has observed, Lily's awakening—specifically, the terrifying insomnia, the "glare of thought" (334) from which she suffers at the end of the novel and which leads to her death—involves a "gradual and agonizing" awareness of virtually "unendurable" truths about her society next to which Edna's more erotic and spiritual awakenings seem "easy."[57] Compared to Edna's suicide, moreover, Lily's death is itself as horrifying as her insomnia is in relation to Edna's awakenings. As we pointed out earlier, Chopin never allows Edna to stop for death, to become fixed, immobilized; her suicide is a willed voyage out from the shores of a culture whose constraints she deliberately repudiates. But Lily's accidental suicide results from a desire for the cessation of consciousness, leaves her definitively motionless, and exposes her "estranged" and helpless body, like the corpses of Flaubert's dead Emma and Louÿs's dead Chrysis, to a male gaze (in this case the gaze of Lawrence Selden) which alone seeks to possess and interpret her meaning. Thus where Chopin depicts Edna's death as an escape from social imprisonment ("She knew a way to elude them!" the author comments), Wharton characterizes Lily's death as a final sign of the Veblenesque reification that is her "ineluctable doom."

But if Wharton's divergences from Chopin's and Schreiner's feminist texts as well as from Haggard's masculinist romance reveal a dark, even dyspeptic vision of the belle dame, whether that figure is defined as a "sex parasite" or a femme fatale, the novelist's implicit responses to social theory, even what we have called her gloss of Veblen, are equally pessimistic. As Elizabeth Ammons suggests, Wharton's view of the "excessive 'sex-distinction' " that cripples women like Lily has much in common with the fundamental argument of Charlotte Perkins Gilman's *Women and Economics: A Study of the Economic Relation between Men and Women as a Factor in Social Evolution* (1898) as well as with Veblen's concept of female conspicuous consumption in *The Theory of the Leisure Class*.[58] And indeed, it is hard to believe that the young matron whom Bourget caricatured as an "intellectual tomboy" did not read (or at least know of) both these works, and it is difficult to imagine, too, that she did not also encounter Schreiner's "The Woman Question," which, like Veblen's influential book, was published in New York in 1899.[59] Elaborating on Lyndall's complaints about female subjugation, Schreiner here further developed the notion of the sex parasite—"the effete wife, concubine or prostitute, clad in fine raiment, the work of others' fingers; fed on luxurious viands, the result of others' toil; waited on and tended by the labour of others"—which was later to be the central image of *Woman and Labour*. "The parasitism of the female heralds the decay of a nation," she warned, and she claimed, significantly, that such a woman inevitably creates no-men, for "only an effete and inactive male can ultimately be produced by an effete and inactive womanhood."[60]

To arrive at some of the basic hypotheses on which Wharton built her *House of Mirth* and other novels, we can conflate these ideas with Gilman's concept of "excessive 'sex-distinction.' " In addition, we can put them together with Veblen's theories of (female) consumption as well as with his social Darwinism ("The life of men in society, just like the life of other species, is a struggle for existence"), and with his belief, no doubt derived from Engels, that "the earliest form of ownership is an ownership of the women by the able-bodied men of the community."[61] Certainly Lily's reification, her commodification, and her specialization all illustrate these points. Wharton's heroine has "cost a great deal to make" (*HM* 7), she is "superfine human merchandise" (265), she is "highly specialised" (7), and it would seem that in leisure-class New York, as Selden comments, "there must be plenty of capital on the lookout for such an investment" (14).

Crucial as these matters are to *The House of Mirth,* however, they are only part of the novel's theoretical argument. For James's angel of devastation demonstrated the incompatability between Lily Bart's individual adventure and the established order of things not just by criticizing other portraits of the femme fatale and not just by fictionalizing key tenets of contemporary sociological thought but also by exploring aspects of such theory that the theorists themselves virtually ignored. Her novel, for example, takes as its starting point a proposition to which Veblen devotes only one sentence: "Wherever the canon of conspicuous leisure has a chance undisturbed to work out its tendency, there will therefore emerge a secondary, and in a sense spurious, leisure class— abjectly poor and living a life of want and discomfort, but morally unable to stoop to gainful pursuits."[62] What, Wharton wants to ask, will become of a conspicuous consumer who has nothing to consume? What will happen to a sex parasite with no one to feed on? Worse still, if in "pecuniary culture" a leisure-class lady is not just a consumer but also a commodity—in Veblen's phrase, a "unit of value"—who represents her owner's (her father's or her husband's) wealth, what must become of a woman who represents no one and nothing?

Clearly, as *The House of Mirth* proves, the laws of predation determine that nothing can come of nothing except, as Lily discovers, a negative social and financial balance. Indeed, as Wai-Chee Dimock has observed in a fine analysis of this novel's economy, Lily is the only character in *The House of Mirth* who both figuratively and literally "pays routinely and scrupulously" for her errors as well as her pleasures, since "nonpayment . . . is a privilege of the powerful, those who fix the rate of exchange."[63] To put the problem in the best light, Lily is in this position because she has no means, therefore no credit rating, and thus must pay rapidly for everything. But to formulate the issue more bleakly (as Lily's death implies it should be formulated), Lily is, in current parlance, a signifier with no signified, a kind of counterfeit bill with nothing to back her up, so that in the end only her flesh—her purely material, nonsymbolic body—is left to signify her self. In death, says Wharton, Lily enigmatically utters a "word which made all clear," yet this word is arguably relevant precisely because it seems to be unspeakable, nonreferential, the ultimate statement made by the "unit of value" when it is detached from that which is valued.[64]

What reinforces the bleakness of Lily's individual adventure is the fact that, as Wharton tells the tale, this heroine encounters virtually no redemptive alternatives. Who or what would it be better for Lily Bart to become in the deterministic, flat and futile universe of *The House of Mirth* except the hopelessly specialized and doomed creation that she is? Certainly none of the other women of her own class would seem to provide what we now call "positive role models." Among those society ladies who do successfully function as conspicuously consuming signifiers of male power, for instance, Lily's implacable enemy Bertha Dorset may be seen as most representative, if only because she is most ex-aggeratedly villainous. In fact, the book's other commodified wives and widows—among them, Judy Trenor, Mrs. Peniston, Mrs. Welly Bry, and Norma Hatch—are in effect all shadows of the type of which Bertha constitutes, as it were, the Platonic form. For, pleasant as some of them may intermittently seem, all are ultimately shown to live by the code that consistently motivates Bertha's behavior—*Destroy or be destroyed*—since in the predatory House of Mirth the "self-regarding attitude" always wins out over "non-invidious effort."

As an interesting revision of Bertha Mason Rochester in *Jane Eyre,* moreover, Bertha Dorset functions like another nihilistic NO EXIT sign, to show that Wharton's social analysis diverges as grimly from that of a major nineteenth-century precursor as it does from that of near contemporaries like Haggard, Schreiner, and Chopin. Sexually voracious, dissipated, profligate, and duplicitous, this Bertha permits herself all the self-indulgent excesses—the affairs, the temper-tantrums, the lies—that, we are told in *Jane Eyre,* led to the madness and confinement of Bertha Mason Rochester. In the course of *The House of Mirth,* in fact, she begins "behaving more than ever like a madwoman" (247), as if Wharton were mapping the only path that desire can take for the com-modified creature.

But unlike her predecessor, Bertha Dorset is uncontainable. Her dark energy can be neither repressed nor (as Bertha Rochester's arguably is in *Jane Eyre*)[65] redirected into saner channels, and her almost allegori-cal destructiveness is revealed by her likeness to "a disembodied spirit who [takes] up a great deal of room" (27). More, her own indestructa-bility is manifested by the ironic persistence of her compromising let-ters to Selden, which Lily never loses though she can never bring her-self to use them for survival, while her perversity is implied by "the large disjointed hand, with a flourish of masculinity which but slightly disguised its rambling weakness" (109) in which the letters are written. In "frivolous" twentieth-century American society, Wharton shows, the liberation of the once illicit libido is as deadly as was the Victorian im-prisonment of such desire.

To be sure, some critics have suggested—and Wharton's text may seem at times to hint—that Lawrence Selden's cousin, the New Wom-anly Gerty Farish, is a figure who stands outside the *Destroy or be destroyed* laws of predation that govern most of the characters in this novel. Like Selden himself, after all, Gerty has a room of her own, one that, small though it is, would very likely have satisfied Virginia Woolf's Mary Carmichael, and she also has a profession of sorts, social work, which has taught her a "disciplined sympathy" (172) that seems to transcend the more humiliating arts of the enslaved. That from Lily's perspective

Gerty's room seems a "poor slit" (177) while Gerty herself appears "fatally poor and dingy" (94), and that even the more tolerant Selden faintly scorns "the dowdy animation of his cousin's tea-hour" (278) are points which simply indicate, after all, the limitations of Lily and Selden.

Nevertheless, by depicting Gerty throughout the book as, on the one hand, naively loving and, on the other hand, inexorably marginalized, Wharton implies that even if this New Woman's obscure existence in a shabby corner of her culture may be somehow "right," it is so tenuous, so tentative, that it can hardly be said to foreshadow the coming of a utopia. On the contrary, because, in the words of Wharton-the-narrator, Gerty is "accustomed, in the way of happiness to such scant light as shone through the cracks of other people's lives," she is a paradoxical counterpart of Lily, for where Lily has been trained to be a "sex parasite," Gerty is, as Wharton puts it, a "parasite in the moral order, living on the crumbs of other tables and content to look through the window at the banquet spread for her friends" (158). And if, for Lily, sex parasitism proves impracticable even in a flat and futile society, for Gerty moral parasitism is equally impractical, even self-destructive.

It may be objected, of course, that *The House of Mirth* does not adequately represent Wharton's "argument with America" since it is so relentlessly deterministic in the Hardyesque or Howellsesque mode. Either a victim of Hardy's "Crass Casualty" or of Howells's crass capitalism, Lily may be not only a specialized creature of her culture but a specialized creation of her author. Yet if we turn to what are generally considered the other major Wharton novels about leisure-class New York, *The Custom of the Country* and *The Age of Innocence*, we find that, because their analyses of "pecuniary" society are just as devastating as those proposed by *The House of Mirth*, they offer no more "positive role models" for a Lily Bart than does the earlier book. Indeed, Undine Spragg, the ambitiously "self-regarding" protagonist of *The Custom of the Country*, is a kind of vicious caricature of villainous Bertha Dorset, while May Welland, the apparently dutiful and innocent young matron who stars, along with her cousin Ellen Olenska, in *The Age of Innocence*, is in her way as implacable and duplicitous as Bertha. As for Ellen, she would at least on the surface seem, like Gerty Farish or Lily Bart herself, to be an emblem of the self-determined and "non-invidious" femininity that has no place in a world whose parasitic women can only make their wishes known by practicing what Veblen calls "the tactics of subservience."

Like Lily—or Lyndall—Undine functions in a literary context as a commentary on the stock figure of the femme fatale. But if Lily's vulnerability demonstrates that it is fatal to be such a woman, Undine reinforces conventional notions of her fatality. A cynical serial polygamist, she is presented as responsible for the suicide of her second husband, Ralph Marvell, a sensitive and literary scion of "old New York"; for decimating the home of her third husband, Raymond de Chelles, a French aristocrat whose heirloom tapestries she ruthlessly appropriates with the help of her first (and later her fourth) husband, Elmer Moffatt, a vulgar Wall Street wheeler-dealer and (ironically enough) an indefatigable art collector; and for inflicting desolation on Paul Marvell, the son (from her second marriage) to whom she is utterly indifferent.[66]

Yet, like Lily, Undine is no stereotypical belle dame. Though, as Wharton emphasized and a number of critics have observed, her name links her with the supernatural—with water nymphs, with ocean goddesses, with *"divers et ondoyant"* forces beneath the sea—her upstart parents, her mother explains, " 'called her after a hair-waver father put on the market the week she was born. . . . It's from *Un*doolay, you know, the French for crimping.' "[67] Showily beautiful as she is, moreover— like "some fabled creature whose home was in a beam of light" (21)— Undine has a sensibility as unpoetic as the origin of her name. When she first goes into New York society, she has "read no new book but 'When the Kissing Had to Stop,' " while her favorite plays are " 'Oolaloo' " and " 'The Soda-Water Fountain' " (37). And even after she has become the toast of the town, "Her mind [is] as destitute of beauty and mystery as the prairie school-house in which she had been educated" (147). Unlike the learned and tormented Ayesha, or the countless thought-worn Lamias, Giocondas, and Monetas who haunt nineteenth-century literature, Undine is not only a femme fatale but also a *femme banale*.[68]

Precisely for this reason, however, Wharton demonstrates that, like Bertha Dorset, Undine is both the ultimate survivor and the destined victress in the pecuniary society that destroys Lily Bart while marginalizing Gerty Farish. Undine's "invidious" and "self-regarding" instincts, together with her culturally constructed exhibitionist impulses, are so keen that she wonders, "What could be more delightful than to feel that, while all the women envied her dress, the men did not so much as look at it? Their admiration was all for herself" (228). At the same time, where Bertha, like her nineteenty-century namesake, does risk madness in the pursuit of illicit sexual desires, albeit perverse and predatory ones, Undine is the perfect commodity, untroubled by any passion other than the one for self-marketing: "her physical reactions were never very acute," Wharton remarks sarcastically, so that "she always vaguely wondered why people made 'such a fuss' " about sexuality

(294). As an alternative to Lily Bart, then, Undine reemphasizes, in broadly satiric terms, the devastating double-bind of feminization that Wharton had already examined in *The House of Mirth:* as "goods," women in a "frivolous society" are either damaged or damaging, and they must destroy or be destroyed. The depth of the novelist's own emotional investment in this problem, moreover, can be inferred from the fact that, while *Lily* bears one of Wharton's own girlhood nicknames, Undine's husband Elmer Moffatt at one point calls her by another of them— *"Puss"* (115).

By comparison to Undine or Bertha Dorset, May Welland, the blameless ingenue of *The Age of Innocence,* seems virtually angelic. Indeed, even in relation to Lily Bart, May appears noble and pure. Lily, after all, shares Undine's proclivities for narcissism and exhibitionism, but, lovely as she is, May, as Newland Archer reflects after their marriage, is "incapable of tying a ribbon in her hair to charm him" (198).[69] Yet May is one of Wharton's subtlest and bitterest portraits of ladies who are manufactured, like "superfine merchandise," by leisure-class society. For in her artificially nurtured, hothouse "innocence," May is both damaged and damaging.

As a young unmarried girl, May appears to her fiancé to be a "terrifying product of the social system," a "creation of factitious purity" who has been rendered metaphorically blind to reality like "the Kentucky cave-fish, which had ceased to develop eyes because they had no use for them" (40, 43, 81). With a face that wears "the vacant serenity of a young marble athlete" (141), May suffers, or so Archer fears, from the "invincible innocence" that "seals the mind against imagination and the heart against experience!" (145). Though she is not intellectually crude like Undine, in her mental blankness, Wharton proposes, she is just as damaged. And looking back on her life after she has died, her husband reiterates his sense of his dead wife's failings: though she had been a conventional "good" woman, May had been "so lacking in imagination, so incapable of growth, that the world of her youth had fallen into pieces and rebuilt itself without her ever being conscious of the change. This hard bright blindness had kept her immediate horizon apparently unaltered" (351).

But if May's innocence is a sign that the culture which constructed her also disfigured her, it is at the same time a force that hurts others, specifically Newland Archer and the woman he really loves, May's cousin Ellen Olenska. For in pursuit of her goal, the marriage that she has been bred to achieve, May is in her own "pure" way as ruthless and duplicitous as Bertha Dorset or Undine Spragg. Specifically, on two occasions she takes steps to separate Newland and Ellen. First, sensing that her fiancé is drifting into a serious relationship with her sophisticated cousin, she advances the date of their wedding just at the moment when he has begun to think of breaking the engagement. Second, after their marriage, when Newland's relationship with Ellen has reached such a crisis that he has resolved to leave his young wife for her, the "innocent" May persuades her cousin to leave the country (and Archer) by confiding to her that she, May, is going to have a baby, though in fact she is not yet sure of her pregnancy. Genteel as she is, May is not only invincibly innocent, she is invincible, and Newland's marriage to her, which leaves him missing "the flower of life" (350), is in its way almost as deadly as Ralph Marvell's match with Undine Spragg. Indeed, about May and Newland as much as about Undine and Ralph, Wharton implies that "they were fellow-victims in the *noyade* of marriage" (*CC* 224–25), a notion she at one point unconsciously emphasized by a notable Freudian slip: in the first printing of *The Age of Innocence,* the Archers' wedding ceremony began with the opening line of the Anglican funeral service.[70]

Comments made by observer-figures in two Wharton novels, both clearly speaking for the writer, illuminate the feminist rage which made this artist so relentless in her depiction of the moral and social options available to young American women who were, like Lily Bart, falling out of (or, like Undine Spragg, rising into) the leisure class. American girls, charges a character in *The Fruit of the Tree* (1907), are brought up "in the double bondage of expediency and unreality, corrupting their bodies with luxury and their brains with sentiment, and leaving them to reconcile the two as best they can, or lose their souls in the attempt."[71] Perhaps even more bitterly, a character in *The Custom of the Country* remarks that in America women are trivialized and infantilized because men "don't take enough interest in *them.*" It is the "custom of the country" to "slave for women" while being absolutely indifferent to them: "the American man lavishes his fortune on his wife because he doesn't know what else to do with it" (207). In Europe, however, the wife is "not a parenthesis, as she is here—she's in the very middle of the picture" (206–07).

Logically enough, then, the only woman in these Wharton novels who seems to have learned arts that are not the arts of the enslaved is, in effect, a foreign lady: the Europeanized Ellen Olenska, once Ellen Mingott of "old New York" but, by the time Newland Archer encounters her, a woman of the world who is neither a fatal belle dame sans merci nor a commodified objet d'art. But of course it is Ellen Olenska who must inevitably be exorcised from "good" New York society by what Veblen would see as the necessary conservatism of its moral and economic laws.[72] Consistently referred to as "poor Ellen Olenska" from the first moment of her return to her childhood home, she seems at first to prove that her compatriots are right to shudder at Europe's wicked ways. Her marriage to a Polish count was an unhappy one— after her nuptials, Wharton comments dryly, she disappeared "in a kind of sulphurous apotheosis" (61)—and, legally at least, she appears to be hopelessly doomed to a marital *"noyade"* far more sinister than Newland Archer's could ever be.

Yet Ellen, and only Ellen in Wharton's major urban novels of manners, can stand apart from the customs of her country and appraise them objectively. Neither destructive nor destroyed, she forces Archer to scrutinize "his native city objectively" and, "viewed thus, as though through the wrong end of a telescope, it looked disconcertingly small and distant; but then from Samarkand it would" (77). Given both her moral clarity and her social alienation, therefore, Ellen represents—to use the anthropological rhetoric that permeates *The Age of Innocence*— that autonomy which is taboo, that objectivity which the tribe must ritually expel.[73] In a sense, like the women of France, her adopted country, she has become from Wharton's point of view a *"grown up"* who can no longer find a home in the happy valley of a childishly mercantile leisure class. For her individual adventure, then, no less than for Lily Bart's, there is no place in America's established order of things.

———

Devastating as Wharton's critique of American womanhood is, however, there is one character in *The House of Mirth* whose life adventure has a denouement which suggests a way out of the double binds that fetter Lily Bart, Undine Spragg, May Welland, and even Gerty Farish: the "fallen woman" Nettie Struther. Nettie is not, to be sure, of the class of any of these ladies; on the contrary, she may be one of the "many dull and ugly people" who were "sacrificed to produce" such hothouse flowers (7). Yet it is in Nettie's "extraordinarily small" but "miraculously clean" kitchen that Lily has "her first glimpse of the continuity of life," and it is Nettie's baby, emblem of that continuity, whom she wearily and wistfully hallucinates as she is dying. Neither a sex parasite like victorious Bertha Dorset nor a moral parasite like marginalized Gerty Farish, Nettie has "found strength to gather up the fragments of her life and build herself a shelter with them" that reaches "the central truth of existence" and that has "the frail, audacious permanence of a bird's nest built on the edge of a cliff" (332). Lily, it would seem, ought to be able to learn something from her.

But what Lily learns is disturbing. Nettie's tenuous but remarkable achievement has been made possible not just by her own energy and integrity, but by her relationship with the man she has married, a husband who is as much his wife's equal partner as are the spouses of the

French women whom Wharton celebrated in *French Ways and Their Meaning*. Though she had been contaminated (and perhaps, we are meant to understand, impregnated) by the sexual advances of a "gentleman [who] was too stylish for me," Nettie explains to Lily, "George cared for me enough to have me as I was . . ." (326). Thus, Lily sees, "it had taken two to build the nest; the man's faith as well as the woman's courage" (332), and in one of the bitterest epiphanies of *The House of Mirth* she realizes that this chance of redemption, too, is not available to her, for the trials Selden's belief in her has undergone have been "too severe" for this man she loves, though he presumably reciprocates her feeling.

Ironically, of course, Lily is far more "innocent" than Nettie. George really knows (and forgives) what Nettie has done, while Selden only thinks he knows (and does not forgive) what Lily has done. In fact, many of Lily's most compromising actions have been in his behalf: she has consistently guarded Bertha's incriminating letters so as to protect him, and her reward is her perception, on the night before her death, of "the emptiness of renunciation" (332). As the cynical Sim Rosedale puts it, "I'll be damned if I see what thanks you've got from him!" (269) For Selden's name, like Lily's, has allegorical overtones. Because Wharton deliberately defined him as, in her own words, "a negative hero,"[74] he is a *slender* reed indeed on which to lean, and in any case he is *seldom* around to lean on.

But just as Lily could not have encountered any "positive role models" among the women in Wharton's other novels, she could not have discovered many men in the other books who are better—stronger, wiser, "manlier"—than Selden, because Wharton's critique of femininity also involves a critique of masculinity. Ralph Marvell, the sensitive suicide in *The Custom of the Country;* Raymond de Chelles, the victimized aristocrat, and Elmer Moffatt, the vulgar entrepreneur, in the same novel; Newland Archer, the cheated protagonist of *The Age of Innocence*—all are no-men because they are either fools or knaves. Ralph deludes himself into believing that Undine is what she is not; Raymond loses his tapestries, symbolic of his family history, to her; Elmer collects her but is scorned by her; and Wharton implies that it is because of the weakness incarnated in all these men that Undine's voracity can survive and triumph even on the supposedly civilized soil of France.

As for Newland, he misses "the flower of life" (*AI,* 347) because he realizes too late the hollowness of the "conventions on which his life [is] moulded: such as using two silver-backed brushes with his monogram in blue enamel to part his hair . . ." (3), and ultimately he becomes "a man to whom nothing was ever to happen" (228), a man "who married one woman because another one told him to" (243); he too, like Selden, is a "negative hero." And that Wharton at one point has an iconoclastic journalist tell Archer that "you're in a pitiful little minority: you've got no centre, no competition, no audience. You're like the pictures on the walls of a deserted house: 'The Portrait of a Gentleman' " (12) reinforces this point while suggesting that she understands herself to be engaged here in a dialogue with the James of *Portrait of a Lady*. Certainly, too, Newland *Archer*'s name echoes that of Isabel *Archer* at least as much as it evokes the name of Christopher *Newman*, the hero of *The American* (1876).[75] But in Wharton's "Portrait of a Gentleman" it is the male, not the female, protagonist who is entombed in marriage, and, unlike Christopher Newman, her American hero is imprisoned while his Europeanized *inamorata*, in direct opposition to *The American*'s Claire Cintré, goes free in Paris.[76]

From Percy Lubbock to Louis Auchincloss, male critics have complained about Wharton's delineations of such men as Newland Archer or Lawrence Selden. The typical Wharton hero, alleged Lubbock in 1947, is a hollow man: "he is reported [to be] a man of powerful passions [but] a tap from a man of real bone beside him, any of a score in the jostle of the crowd, and this admirable figure, this gracious mould of a man, is dead upon our hands, a shell, a simulacrum with nothing inside it to match the flesh and blood of its vulgar neighbour. That is what this novelist in all good faith has taken for a man . . ."[77] Almost two decades later, writing specifically about *The House of Mirth*, Auchinchloss called Lawrence Selden a "tepid lover" and a "seeming hypocrite," deplored the fact that Lily could not find "a man to love her instead of a prosy prig," and concluded that "poor Mr. Selden" was "a victim of plot requirements."[78] And more recently, even one of Wharton's major feminist critics—Elizabeth Ammons—has reproached the novelist for a tendency toward "misandry."[79]

All three readers were observing a significant aspect of Wharton's writing, but only Auchincloss, in mentioning "plot requirements," offered the germ of an insight which might explain the phenomenon. The sociological and political "requirements" of the plots that dramatized Wharton's analyses of the early twentieth-century "woman question" were necessarily as (if not more) angry in their characterizations of men as they were in their depictions of women. For though this writer was never consciously to align herself with the female camp in the battle of the sexes, her secret feelings toward men, even toward men she loved, were often, and not surprisingly, at least subtly hostile.

In her life, as well as in her art, Wharton both perceived the varieties of male diminution in her culture and found ways of articulating ostensibly sympathetic but often destructive feelings toward the "negative heroes" she encountered. By the time she had begun to become famous, Louis Auchincloss remarks, her husband, Teddy, appeared to at least one observer "as a kind of cipher in Edith's life . . . 'more of an equerry than an equal, walking behind her and carrying whatever paraphernalia she happened to discard,' "[80] and ultimately it was Teddy himself, whom, continuing to compare him to Charles Bovary, she discarded. But at various times even Wharton's once beloved Morton Fullerton and her long-cherished Henry James became objects of her patronage, if not of her scorn.

Both Fullerton and James, for instance, were beneficiaries of covert financial aid from their angel of devastation; in both cases, Wharton engineered situations in which these men of letters received ersatz royalties or advances that she had provided, gifts that, despite their generosity, emphasized her power and her male friends' powerlessness.[81] To be sure, James vigorously rebuffed at least one of Wharton's more public attempts to be his benefactress,[82] but in any case (as "The Velvet Glove" hints) he knew all too early and all too well the competitive ferocity that he was up against in a mercantile society of which his ostensible protegée was not only a critic but also an exemplar. When she told him that she had purchased an expensive motorcar with some of the money she had earned from her first long novel, *The Valley of Decision* (1902), James commented comically that "With the proceeds of my last novel [*The Wings of the Dove* (1902)], I purchased a small go-cart or hand-barrow on which my guests' luggage is wheeled from the station to my house. It needs a coat of paint. With the proceeds of my next novel I shall have it painted."[83]

Moreover, although, with the possible exception of George Eliot, Wharton's major literary idols were male, she could be surprisingly acrimonious about the aesthetic "fathers" who had influenced her the most. About "the egregious Nathaniel" Hawthorne, for instance, the author of the Hawthornean novella *Ethan Frome* maliciously remarked that his prose "seems to me about as classic as a bare hotel parlor furnished only with bentwood chairs,"[84] while even about the writings of Henry James, she permitted herself a series of caustic comments, including the really quite belligerent claim that James "tended to sacrifice to [his technical theories and experiments] that spontaneity which is the life of fiction" (*BG* 190).

Perhaps inevitably, therefore, such rivalry and hostility toward men (most of which could be only indirectly expressed in life) spilled over into, and intensified in, Wharton's art. In fact, in the major deterministic fictions of "old New York" that are usually defined as her "novels of manners," she seems to have set out to depict male characters who would document the point that Schreiner made in 1899 in "The Woman Question": "only an effete and inactive male can ultimately be produced by an effete and inactive womanhood."[85] In other words, damaged women can only create damaged men; a society that reifies a Lily Bart will offer her (if not a predatory Gus Trenor) only a highly specialized, slender, and seldom-there Selden.

But Wharton's analyses of the destructive effects that custom had on men as well as women went even farther than the theories of the leisure class that she incorporated into her urban novels. In *Ethan Frome* and *Summer,* the two "regional" works ostensibly designed to shatter the "rose-colored spectacles" through which she thought Sarah Orne Jewett and Mary Wilkins Freeman looked at the world, she moved beyond the economic speculations of *The House of Mirth* to quasi-psychoanalytic dissections of the family. Through these, this woman who seemed to one friend "to look on all family life as more or less of a calamity" implicitly sought to define the deep structures that shaped the network of social and economic transactions in which Lily Bart is caught.[86]

Both of Wharton's regional books were written in France—*Ethan Frome,* in fact, was originally a French language exercise—as if their author could only bear to look from a safe distance at the stripped-down lives that she knew were lived within a few miles of her palatial Berkshire home, The Mount. But even more than Kate Chopin's "local color" stories, both these books, though composed from afar, are essays in empirical, cultural anthropology as well as psychoanalytic projects. As such, they argue that the incompatability between the established order of things and the individual adventures of figures like Lily Bart (or Ethan Frome or Charity Royall) is not merely a function of Gilded Age capitalism and its Veblenesque economy. Rather, they show that such an economy, with its roots in the ownership of women as well as its consequent exploitation and infantilization of the female, is itself a product of the patriarchal family in which, as Freud's theories of asymmetrical male and female Oedipus complexes explain, desire for the maternal image must be repressed or annihilated so that the son may achieve proper manhood (in which women belong to him as owner-"father") and the daughter may attain proper womanhood (in which she gives herself to the owner-"father").

Documenting these points, *Ethan Frome* and *Summer* are complementary counterparts: in fact, the French version of *Ethan Frome* is called *Hiver,* while Wharton herself jokingly called *Summer* "the Hot Ethan."[87] In the first book, Wharton examines the triangle formed by the taciturn Ethan, the nagging mother-figure Zenobia (seven years his elder) to whom he is married, and their servant, Zeena's charming cousin Mattie Silver (seven years his junior).[88] And because Zeena (whom Ethan married to fill the vacancy left after his mother died) dominates this bleak novella—because, no matter how Ethan and Mattie, like ineffectual children, struggle to escape her, her will prevails—*Ethan Frome* might be called the book of the mother.[89]

As such, the tale reveals the horror that must inexorably come from maternal domination in a society where, at least from Wharton's point of view, what we would now call the Lacanian Law of the Father associates the feminine with regression and chaos. In patriarchal culture, Wharton shows, the woman who does not relinquish herself to a "father"-husband but instead retains perverse power over a "son"-husband is physically and psychically deadly. In this case, she has reduced her husband, Ethan, to a no-man who can only imagine fleeing her by taking the girl who should be his "daughter"-bride on a suicidal (and parodically adolescent) sledride into a tree. But Ethan and Mattie cannot even succeed in escaping Zeena through death. Grimly, the tormented trio live on—Mattie paralyzed, Ethan wounded, Zeena hideously "mothering" them—to prove by their example that if women are not owned by men, if women do not signify *male* power, both sexes are doomed to "distress and oppression" in what one description of the Frome farmstead depicts as a "forlorn and stunted" house.[90]

If, however, as happens in *Summer,* the man does claim his "daughter"-bride, her life, too, must inevitably be "forlorn and stunted." Charity Royall, the teenage heroine of this novel, seeks (but cannot find) a place for her individual adventure in the established order of things by struggling to escape from the sexual advances of her adoptive father, Lawyer Royall, a middle-aged alcoholic who is nevertheless a "magnificent monument of a man" (27). But her passionate affair with the young architect Lucius Harney, a summer visitor from the city, leaves her illegitimately pregnant and ultimately with no option but a loveless marriage to Royall, the man who has always owned her as a daughter and will now possess her as a wife.[91]

To be sure, like Ethan and Mattie, Charity does try to flee her fate. Indeed, her attempt at escape is on the face of it far more practical and purposeful than Ethan's and Mattie's nihilistic downhill flight: it is an uphill search for her lost mother, who supposedly lives on a wild "Mountain" that shadows the girl's town. (Curiously, this mountain is always named with a capital *M*, a point which paradoxically evokes the name—The Mount—that Wharton gave to her own, very different home in the Berkshires.) But on the Mountain Charity discovers only the dead body of her dissolute mother along with an undifferentiated horde of nameless relatives, so that when Lawyer Royall comes to rescue her she is only too glad to be borne back into the established order of things. If it was Ethan's calamity that he ought to have dominated Zeena (or

Mattie) yet was not "man" enough to do so, it is Charity's catastrophe that she can only redeem her individual adventure by giving herself into the possession of Mr. Royall, who formulates the connection between this psychoanalytic book of the father and Veblen's concept of (female) conspicuous consumption when his first gesture, on the morning after their marriage, is to give Charity two twenty-dollar bills and tell her to "buy yourself whatever you need. . . . You know I always wanted you to beat all the other girls. . . . If it ain't enough there's more where that come from—I want you to beat 'em all hollow" (284–85).

In a sense, then, though *Ethan Frome* and *Summer* focus on people and places that are strikingly different from those of the leisure-class world Wharton studies in *The House of Mirth, The Custom of the Country,* and *The Age of Innocence,* this pair of regional tales dramatizes, with a kind of mythic resonance, precisely the double bind that the writer also analyzes in her "society" novels. A woman is "goods," either damaged (Lily, Charity), or damaging (Undine, Zeena). Whatever James's angel of devastation may have intended to argue in *Ethan Frome* and *Summer*—or indeed in the three novels of manners we have discussed here— it becomes clear when one conflates the five books that her work documented what, at least from a feminist perspective, are the most painful theories of Freud as well as the bleakest claims of Veblen. No wonder James saw her as "threatening" and analogous to a "great historical ravager." Genteel as this lady of letters may have seemed, there were, from her point of view, few *sorties* out of the locked room of the culture in which she imprisoned her characters.

———————

Where in Wharton's canon, then, is there a place for the new, for even a minimal vision of the redemptive sexchanges—the metamorphoses of rules and roles—that alarmed Rider Haggard while energizing Schreiner, Gilman, and Chopin? Although this novelist saw little room for openly utopian transformation in the social institutions on which her fictions obsessively focused, the force of her desire was (as James knew) strong; there were few checks on the "ravaging, burning, and destroying energy"[92] with which she sought at least her own emotional and intellectual emancipation from the custom of the country. "I should like to get up on the house-tops, and cry to all who come after us: 'Take your own life, every one of you,' " she wrote to a friend in a passage we have used as an epigraph here, and though R. W. B. Lewis insists that the "exclamation was not a summons to suicide,"[93] both the ambiguity and the intensity of the statement are notable. The phrase "Take your own life, every one of you" does inevitably suggest a "summons to suicide"—indeed, to mass suicide—no matter what its author's conscious intention may have been. But the phrase can also be construed as, and may well have been meant as, what Lewis takes it for: "an urgent appeal to others—and most particularly to self-sacrificing women—to lead *their* individual and personal lives." [94] In a single sentence, then, this quotation summarizes the oscillation between despair and desire—or, perhaps more accurately, the simultaneity of despair and desire—that marks this writer's work.

Perhaps because these two feelings were so closely linked, Wharton's imaginings of change or at least of (momentary) freedom from institutions that may be changeless, are almost always mediated through allusions to what is literally or figuratively *unsayable:* through evocations of what is illicit, what is secret, what is silent; through representations of what does not "fit" into ordinary language or conventional systems of signification; and through fantasies of what can only be spoken from beyond the grave, from, that is, a position beyond the boundaries of the humanly possible. In keeping with her ambivalence, moreover, Wharton's narratives of the change or difference (and in particular of the empowering metamorphosis of woman) that is normally unsayable are frequently stories of vengeful anger which can only utter itself outside the ordinary world and of forbidden eroticism which functions, if only temporarily, to annihilate the ordinary world.

The representations of unsayable transformation that Wharton's fictions offer as the only possible glimpses of liberation from the prison-house of culture are complemented, and in some cases even predicted, by strategies the writer adopted in her own life. As we noted earlier, for instance, the decoration of houses was far more than a ladylike hobby for Edith Wharton: it was an aesthetic strategy through which she symbolically demolished and redecorated the House of Mirth, stripping away its vulgar excrescences and replacing them with the images of an alternative history that she desired to possess. Both in the treatise on interior design that she wrote with Ogden Codman and in her work on The Mount, the young Wharton began her "argument with America" not just through words but in stones and gardens, rooms and furnishings. Modeled after a Lincolnshire country house designed by Christopher Wren, The Mount was also influenced, especially in the plan of its formal gardens, by Wharton's extensive and impassioned travels on the continent, and the "statement" she made through its construction was clearly grasped by many of her visitors, one of whom is reported to have remarked that "when I look about me I don't know if I am in England or Italy." [95]

Subsequent Wharton residences had equally important symbolic functions. Her winter villa at Hyères on the French Riviera was historically a kind of Herland: it had once, R. W. B. Lewis records, "been a convent for 'Clarisses'—nuns of the order of Ste. Claire—built within the walls of an old chateau."[96] As for Pavillon Colombe, her summer estate near Paris, it was historically female in a different sense, for, Lewis tells us, it had been named after "two sisters who had been installed there by their lovers around the middle of the eighteenth century"; a "high-ranking French officer was said to have died as the result of excesses committed with" one of them, a young woman to whom the word *"cocotte . . .* was first applied in its modern meaning of courtesan."[97] Edith Wharton, Lewis continues, was charmed by this last history in particular. If the nuns of Ste.-Claire constituted a female community located slightly outside the structures of patriarchy, the cocottes of the Pavillon Colombe seem in her view to have incarnated a disruption within the patriarchal economy itself. Indeed, the same impulses that attracted Wharton to the "energetic" adulteress Hortense Allart drew her also to the eighteenth- and nineteenth-century French institution of the courtesan, which she seems to have seen as a kind of gap in culture through which metamorphic libidinous energies might flow. Though when she purchased this estate it had long (no doubt in an attempt to erase its shadily erotic past) been decorously called "Jean-Marie," "one of the first things" she did as its new owner "was to change the name back to Pavillon Colombe."[98]

That Wharton made her subversive gestures consciously, even if covertly, is indicated by a number of her own furtive communications to the future, texts that (in the manner of some of her characters) she herself in effect "sent" or "spoke" from beyond the grave. These include the records she carefully preserved of the events leading up to her divorce and, interestingly, of a secret financial transaction having to do with herself and Henry James, as well as the love diary she wrote to Morton Fullerton and also carefully preserved. In the first case, she made claims after death that she was either too personally or too professionally discreet to make in her own lifetime: most dramatically, in a "note 'for my biographer' " she confided that "I gave Mr. Scribner this $8,000 from the earnings of *The House of Mirth* to encourage H. J. to go on writing, as he was so despondent about his work. The result was successful and no one ever knew."[99]

In the second case, she produced a journal for Morton Fullerton, her lover from 1908 to 1910, that was clearly labeled to emphasize its disruption of the ordinary. "The Life Apart" (subtitled *"L'Ame Close"*) was written in several languages besides English—mostly German but also Italian and French—and "conceived . . . as a narrative, with a definite theme."[100] And the illicit passion it recorded was compelling, so much so that Fullerton, too, spoke passionately to his onetime mistress's biographers from, as it were, beyond *her* grave. After Wharton's death and "many years after" their affair, Fullerton remarked "to Elisina Tyler, who was proposing to write a biography of Edith Wharton, 'Pleases seize the event, however delicate the problem, to dispel the myth of your heroine's frigidity,' " adding, according to R. W. B. Lewis, a number of explicit details about the sexual adventurousness of the supposedly staid Edith Wharton.[101] Again, Wharton had communicated after death what she felt to be culturally unsayable, to be, in fact, unspeakably revolutionary in life.

Obviously the paradox of saying the unsayable, of speaking the unspeakable, infuses and energizes the very genre of the ghost story, a genre of which Wharton, like James, was one of America's most brilliant practitioners. Because both were novelists of manners and psychological "realists," neither would seem to have been a major candidate for such a role. Yet James arguably turned to the genre in an effort to examine the inchoate wellsprings of character, while Wharton was driven to it by precisely the bleak skepticism that kept her from fantasizing, as so many of her feminist contemporaries did, about changes in sex roles and social rules. Like the "Life Apart" that she had with Morton Fullerton, the ghost story offered her a literature apart in which, for once, she could allow herself to imagine transcending the limits of the possible and liberating desires for which there was no appropriate place in her culture.[102]

The importance of this genre to the writer who felt that "Life is the saddest thing there is, next to death" should not be underestimated. For Wharton, ghost stories were not only frequently about the powers of unsayable words. They themselves, more than any other kind of writing, incarnated the power of the *forbidden* word, the word that refuses to be limited by the "laws" of nature and culture. " 'Till I was twenty-seven or eight," she confessed in an extraordinary canceled passage from *A Backward Glance*, "I could not sleep in a room with a book containing a ghost-story; and . . . I have frequently had to burn books of this kind, because it frightened me to know that they were downstairs in the library!"[103] Some of her own best ghost stories illuminate one source of her terror: the unleashing of female rage as well as the release of female desire. Others document another source of fear: the expression of female pain at the repression of rage and the killing of desire. Most, in one way or another, indicate that what may have been especially terrifying to Wharton about the ghost story was the fact that it consistently made possible just the transgressive protest against "reality" that she secretly longed to mount.

"Kerfol" (1916), one of Wharton's most famous supernatural tales, focuses, like a number of her other works in this genre, on what she saw as the mortal, or indeed even immortal, "knots" of "the marriage tie."[104] Visiting "the most romantic house in Brittany" (*S* II 282) which also seems to him like "the loneliest place in the whole world," the narrator encounters a pack of eerily silent dogs, about whom he later learns that, according to the local peasantry, they appear once a year and "are the ghosts of Kerfol" (287). When he investigates, he is given the transcript of the seventeenth-century murder trial of a certain Anne de Cornault. As he reads through it, he discovers the bizarre story of the marriage between the wealthy, middle-aged lord of Kerfol and a young woman who came from a family that was "much less great and powerful" than his but whom he locked up like a rare treasure in his great mansion, where her only companions were a series of dogs that he strangled one by one after deciding she had been unfaithful to him. When the husband died under mysterious circumstances—"He had been dreadfully scratched and gashed about the face and throat, as if with curious pointed weapons; and one of his legs had a deep tear in it which had cut an artery" (291)—his wife had been arraigned for murder, but she had insisted (rightly, the story suggests) that the true killers were "my dead dogs" (299). Yet of course, as Wharton surely meant to imply, the animals were themselves agents of their mistress's unspeakable and deadly desire, a fury that erupts at the center of the tale when the courtroom transcript has the young wife describing what she heard during the murder: "dogs snarling and panting . . . once or twice he cried out. I think he moaned once. . . . then I heard a sound like the noise of a pack when the wolf is thrown to them—gulping and lapping" (298).

What gives this tale its weird authority is its odd blending of the superhuman (ghosts) and the subhuman (dogs), a juxtaposition that enables "Kerfol" to dramatize with special intensity the importance to Wharton of a genre in which she could say the unsayable. For just as she associated ghost stories with fearful and unspeakable transgression, this writer who was all her life an impassioned dog lover connected animals with the fear and fascination of that which could not speak or be spoken. In one of the earliest passages in *A Backward Glance* she remembered how her first dog awoke in her "that long ache of pity for animals, and for all inarticulate beings, which nothing has ever stilled" (*BG* 4). To be sure, the fantasy of supernatural or quasi-supernatural vengeance that is played out in "Kerfol" recurs in a number of Wharton stories. "Miss Mary Pask" (1926), for example, records a punitive encounter between a self-satisfied bachelor and a "dowdy old mai[d]"— a kind of Gerty Farish—whom he has always patronized in the past but who now terrifies him because he mistakenly thinks she is dead. Similarly, "The Eyes" (1910) documents the haunting (by a pair of sinister red-rimmed eyes) that devastates another smug bachelor after he has twice, in different ways, betrayed a young woman who is in love with him. But "Kerfol" brings together the elements of the vengeful tale—in particular the elements of unspeakable oppression and unsayable rage—with singular force.

At the same time, "Kerfol" does allow the dead Anne de Cornault, who after her husband's demise had spent the rest of her life imprisoned in "the keep of Kerfol . . . a harmless madwoman" (*S* II 300), to speak from beyond the grave. Testifying in the transcript that the narrator then transcribes and that Wharton ultimately publishes, Anne reveals the secret history of subordination and insubordination that still haunts "the most romantic house in Brittany" and that may, by implication, haunt romance itself. Because of this, her story represents not only one of Wharton's central strategies for fantasizing that moment in which the worm/woman turns on her master but also one of the writer's major devices for simultaneously saying the unsayable and enacting its unsayability.

Far more than "Kerfol" does, two other brilliant Wharton ghost stories—"Mr. Jones" (1930) and "Pomegranate Seed" (1936)—depend on portrayals of women who speak from beyond the grave, in one case to articulate pain at a life that is like a death and in another to exact tribute that is due from a living man. The main action of "Mr. Jones" is a piece of collaborative detective work by Lady Jane Lynke, a travel writer, and an older friend named Edward Stamer, a Jamesian-sounding novelist who likes "to settle down somewhere in the country where he could be sure of not being disturbed" when he is finishing a novel (*S* II 604). Together, these surrogates of Wharton and her mentor learn that Bells, a beautiful Sussex estate that Lady Jane has inherited, is ruled by the ghost of one "Mr. Jones," an old family retainer—indeed, the amanuensis of a Regency aristocrat who was one of the last heirs of Bells actually to use the estate. This historical personage is introduced in a parodic passage that provides a key to the story's theme. Strolling among the family monuments, Lady Jane comes upon a

> plain sarcophagus . . . surmounted by the bust of a young man with a fine arrogant head, a Byronic throat and tossed-back curls.
>
> "Peregrine Vincent Theobald Lyncke, Baron Clouds, fifteenth Viscount Thudeney of Bells, Lord of the Manors of Thudeney, Thudeney-Blazes, Upper Lynke, Lynke-Linnet—" so it ran, with the usual tedious enumeration of honors, titles, court and country offices, ending with: "Born on May 1st, 1790, perished of the plague

at Aleppo in 1828." And underneath in small cramped characters, as if crowded as an afterthought into an insufficient space:
"Also His Wife."

That was all. No names, dates, honors, epithets, for the Viscountess Thudeney.[105]

The oppressive silencing and dehumanizing of "Also His Wife" is,
of course, the real subject of this chilling tale, in which Wharton ultimately gives a name and a voice to an anonymous, speechless woman.
Exploring the house despite the spectral interdictions of Mr. Jones (who
manifests his will through the present-day servants, all of whom are his
descendants), Lady Jane and Stramer discover, first, a portrait of "Juliana, Viscountess Thudeney, 1818"—"Also His Wife"—whose "long
fair oval" face looks "dumbly" out at them "in a stare of frozen beauty"
(606), and then a pile of papers that the dead Mr. Jones had hidden,
including a poignant letter from "Also His Wife" in which, though her
text reveals that she was literally deaf and dumb, the "frozen" Juliana
is at last granted the release of speech, if only speech to the future.
Complaining to a husband who is perpetually absent that "Mr. Jones
persists—and by your express orders, so he declares—in confining me,"
she protests that "to sit in this great house alone, day after day, month
after month . . . is a fate more cruel than I deserve and more painful
than I can bear" and begs to be allowed to make "the acquaintance of
a few of your friends and neighbors" (613).

As the story makes plain, the unfortunate Juliana was never granted
her wish in life, and, as it also reveals, she was imprisoned in this way
because she was an object of exchange: the daughter of a rich East
India merchant who apparently sought a connection with the aristocracy, she brought a vast dowry to her husband, who was ashamed of
her speech impediment (and therefore imprisoned her) but needed
her money to carry on a career of gambling and womanizing. The secret that is at the center both of the story and of the patriarchal estate
of Bells is thus a horrifying one, a secret of the silencing of woman and
of the traffic in women. And the relentlessly analytic author of *The
House of Mirth* insists, with her usual pessimism, that the revelation of
such social ills will not necessarily cure them; at the end of the tale, the
spirit of Mr. Jones, the faithful servant of patriarchal authority, still
tenaciously inhabits Bells. Yet that the estate has come into the hands
of a literary woman who has purloined the letters that record its inequities and who has at last liberated the words of "Also His Wife" suggests some hope of a transformation which, though unsayable here,
might be speakable in the future.[106]

Despite such guarded optimism, however, "Mr. Jones" mainly uses the convention of speech from beyond the grave to examine the same reification of woman that Wharton studied in so many novels. By contrast, "Pomegranate Seed" turns to this convention in order to explore the enigma associated with the inscription of female desire. Charlotte Ashby, the second wife of the "heartbroken widower" Kenneth Ashby, notices immediately after her honeymoon that her husband has begun to receive a series of mysterious letters, which are "always the same—a square grayish envelope with 'Kenneth Ashby, Esquire' written on it in bold but faint characters" (*S* II 764). After reading these, he behaves oddly, complains of headaches, and has "the look of a man who [has] been so far away from ordinary events that when he returns to familiar things they seem strange" (765). Finally, when he has received nine letters, he disappears, leaving Charlotte and his mother—who, on being shown the latest missive, recognizes the handwriting of her former daughter-in-law—with the dreadful realization that all the communications have come from his dead wife, whom he has now gone to join.

In the story's wonderful final scene, the two living women struggle to interpret the script from beyond the grave which has exerted such triumphant control over Kenneth Ashby, though it seems to them to be "only a few faint strokes, so faint and faltering as to be nearly undecipherable" (785). Cries the mother-in-law: "we're going mad—we're both going mad. We both know such things are impossible." But her daughter-in-law replies: "I've known for a long time now that everything was possible." If not in life, Wharton here implies, then in death, beyond the boundaries of logic and the logic of boundaries, a kind of female victory becomes possible, albeit a cryptic and problematic one.[107] And, not insignificantly, though she examined such cryptic victories in the greatest detail in her ghost stories, this otherwise skeptical writer also alluded to them in her more "realistic" fictions, notably in the early novella *The Touchstone* (1897) and in *The House of Mirth*.

As we argued in *The War of the Words*, *The Touchstone* explores a number of issues relating to the female affiliation complex,[108] but the central *donnée* of the story is the unearthly triumph of Margaret Aubyn, whose posthumously published letters ultimately convince their one-time recipient, the weak-spirited Glennard, that he must change his life because her dead "presence"—morally instructive, powerfully maternal—is now "the one reality in a world of shadows."[109] (Indeed, the affinity of *The Touchstone* with the supernatural tale was recognized by its English publisher, who renamed the work *A Gift from the Grave*, a title whose sensationalism Wharton disliked but whose accuracy she did not seriously dispute [*BG* 125–26].) Similarly, in *The House of Mirth*, the dead "semblance of Lily Bart" (*HM* 338) speaks the unsayable to Lawrence Selden, uttering the enigmatic "word which made all clear." Although Lily's world has reduced her to a kind of dead letter, a signifier who signifies nothing in the society she inhabits, after death—and only after death—she does manage cryptically to rebuke the novel's "negative hero" for his unmanliness. In her depiction of Lily's death, and of the body language through which this heroine speaks from beyond the grave, Wharton may be covertly alluding to Tennyson's "Elaine," the episode in *The Idylls of the King* that recounts the fate of the *"lily* maid of Astolot," who, rejected by Sir Lancelot, died and floated downstream on a barge, in one lifeless hand a lily, in the other a reproachful letter confessing "I loved you, and my love had no return. / And therefore my true love has been my death."[110] But also, precisely because Lily's dead "semblance" speaks of a love that can *have* "no return" in the Veblenesque economy of *The House of Mirth,* her author may be incorporating this dead heroine into an extended "ghost story" of female desire, a tale that Edith Wharton would continue telling all her life.

Besides being what is materially "impossible," the unsayable is, of course, what is erotically illicit—and for Wharton that clearly meant what represents, like Hortense Allart and the courtesans of the Pavillon Colombe, a fissure in the "laws" of female chastity and male-dominant marriage that govern heterosexual relations in patriarchal culture, or even, like the unrequited loves of Margaret Aubyn and Lily Bart, what constitutes an excess of (female) desire that has no place in the marriage market's system of exchange. Thus, despite her consistent rejection of utopian feminism, Wharton had a concealed commitment to the subversive credo of erotic self-possession that moved both Kate Chopin's Edna Pontellier and the feminist free-love advocate Victoria Woodhull: with Chopin's heroine, she would boast (but in private) that "I give myself where I choose," and with Woodhull she would declare (but in secrecy) that "I will love whom I may [and] neither you nor any law you can make shall deter me."[111] As both R. W. B. Lewis and Cynthia Griffin Wolff have shown, the unsayable but redemptive secret at the heart of this writer's own history was her affair with the journalist Morton Fullerton, for which reason she no doubt intended the love diary of her "Life Apart" to speak from beyond her own grave. But in addition, though at one point she hinted that she would need an "alien language" to narrate her erotic tale,[112] Wharton celebrated her illicit romance in an interesting group of published and unpublished poems.

The sonnet sequence "The Mortal Lease" (1909), for instance, included a poem in which Wharton defined the kind of woman she wanted to be in her relationship with her lover: an unconquerable woman, located outside the conventions of culture, or at least placed at that

archaic, originatory point in history where convention has not yet
solidified.

> . . . I would meet your passion as the first
> Wild woodland woman met her captor's craft,
> Or as the Greek whose fearless beauty laughed
> And doffed her raiment by the Attic flood.[113]

More strikingly, the Whitmanesque poem "Terminus" describes a night
of adulterous passion at the Charing Cross Hotel, emphasizing not only
the blisses of the illicit—of the secret life that disrupts and temporarily
annihilates the ordinary world—but also the pleasure of perceiving the
ubiquitousness of the illicit behind society's facade of decorum.[114]

Beginning "Wonderful was the long secret night you gave me, my
Lover," "Terminus" goes on to describe "The bed with its soot-sodden
chintz" and to speculate "perchance it has also thrilled / With the pressure of [other] bodies ecstatic, bodies like ours." "I was glad," the poet
adds, "as I thought of those others, the nameless, the many, / Who perhaps thus had lain and loved for an hour on the brink of the world, /
Secret and fast in the heart of the whirlwind of travel," and she singles
out for special fantasy "some woman like me waking alone before dawn, /
While her lover slept, as I woke and heard the calm stir of your breath-
ing." The ambiguous title of the piece—which could refer to a railroad
terminal (Charing Cross), to the termination of an experience or relationship, or to a final *goal* or culmination—emphasizes the unsayable
significance of "the long secret night" the poem describes.[115] And certainly, although Wharton never published the work in her lifetime, she
preserved it as carefully as she saved her love diary, and preserved it,
we might suppose, because it gives a local habitation, if not a name,
both to her own illicit doings and to those of the "nameless, the many"
whom she honored for their similar erotic defiance.

Rarely, though, did Wharton allow such celebrations of illicit sexuality to erupt into her fiction. As we have seen, this angel of devastation was too skeptical in her cultural analyses to permit herself fully
elaborated radical imaginings. She did, however, secretly plan and preserve one extraordinarily enigmatic erotic fantasy: the only partly written tale of "Beatrice Palmato." The now notorious manuscript of this
work consists of an outline of a story about father-daughter incest, which
was accompanied, when it was found among the novelist's papers, by a
fragmentary pornographic scene that has no obvious place in the outline. The outline relates a catastrophic story of incest in which the
daughter ultimately kills herself as a result of her relationship with her
predatory father; the pornographic scene brilliantly and seductively
dramatizes the sexual relationship between father and daughter, em-

phasizing the illicit delight experienced by both partners in the erotic encounter.[116]

Significantly, the daughter has just married, and evidently been "deflowered" by her husband a week before the scene takes place, and in a brief conversational exchange the father contrasts the pains of the wedding night (and, by implication, the oppression of the marriage bed) with the pleasures of forbidden sexuality: "That experience [the wedding night] is a cruel one—but it has to come once in all women's lives. Now we shall reap its fruit."[117] And though the outline of "Beatrice Palmato" implies that such fruit is bitter, even deadly, the scene dramatizes its sweetness. For, unlike the patriarchal *Lawyer* Royall in *Summer,* also arguably a work about father-daughter incest, Mr. Palmato appears to function in Wharton's imagination as a paradigm of the *illicit* father, the father who refuses to surrender his daughter to the socioeconomic system represented by the institution of marriage but instead releases her back into the polymorphous eroticism of childhood, eliciting from her an "old swooning sensation" that causes her to feel "lightnings of heat" shooting from the "palpitating centre all over her surrendered body" and plunging her into "new abysses of bliss."[118]

To be sure, the outline of the story punishes both father and daughter for this illicit activity: the realistic Wharton of *The House of Mirth, Summer,* and *The Custom of the Country* would have had to document the destructiveness of the chain of causation in which she had entangled her characters. But the Wharton of "Terminus" and of some of the ghost stories was driven to say the unsayable, in this case by using the pornographic scene to reimagine the patriarchal father-daughter paradigm so that it becomes, not a model for the sexual inequities of marriage, but a fantasy about the *jouissance* that denies and defies social law. And that the scene has absolutely no place in the outline—indeed, as Lewis observes, "the outline . . . planned to *conceal* the incest until the last page"[119]—further emphasizes the unsayability of its argument, an argument which can only be transcribed and inscribed in "faint and faltering" letters, that is, in a logically "undecipherable" set of notes "sent" by Edith Wharton from beyond the grave.[120]

Nevertheless, just as the unspeakability that is dramatized in Wharton's ghost stories also, more tenuously and marginally, infuses such "mainstream" works as *The Touchstone* and *The House of Mirth,* so the visions of the illicit memorialized in idiosyncratic texts like "Terminus" and "Beatrice Palmato" secretly seep into the writer's "realistic" fictions. Perhaps the most notable case in point is the extraordinary epiphany that concludes *The Age of Innocence.* After she has gone to live in France, outside the customs of her own country, Ellen Olenska seems to represent for author and characters alike an illicit, indeed taboo, force that has been in effect exorcised from the decorous society of "old New York."[121] But like Wharton herself—and unlike the variously imprisoned heroines of the two James novels *(The American* and *Portrait of a Lady)* that Wharton here revises—Ellen lives insouciantly on, in a glamorous expatriation. Claire de Cintré, the beloved of *The American*'s Christopher Newman, is theatrically immured in a convent, while Isabel Archer, in *Portrait of a Lady,* is locked in "the house of darkness, the house of dumbness, the house of suffocation" that is her marriage.[122] Ellen, however, escaping both virginal confinement and marital *couverture,* has become the mistress, rather than the victim, of "French ways and their meaning."

Along with Newland Archer, we discover this in the novel's poignant coda, when, more than a quarter century after their parting, Archer stands below Ellen's window in exactly the Paris *quartier*—perhaps, in fact, the very street[123]—where Wharton herself lived for many years, and meditates on the complex and, to him, alien existence that she has had there:

> her life—of which he knew so strangely little—had been spent in this rich atmosphere that he already felt to be too dense and yet too stimulating for his lungs. . . . More than half a lifetime divided them, and she had spent the long interval among people he did not know, in a society he but faintly guessed at, in conditions he would never wholly understand. During that time he had been living with his youthful memory of her; but she had doubtless had other and more tangible companionship. [362]

In granting Archer an intuition of the *difference* that Ellen has experienced, Wharton also forces him to recognize that he himself has been only an episode in the intricate narrative of this cosmopolitan exile's life, a one time lover replaced by "other . . . more tangible" (and, in his society's terms, illicit) companionship. Thus, because he is at best no more than "a relic in a small dim chapel, where there was not time to pray every day," Archer can neither understand nor analyze the larger architecture that dwarfs him.

At the same time, the novelist herself cannot (or will not) describe that architecture, will not narrate Ellen's life, will not stipulate the details of its radiant difference. With Newland Archer, she imagines but does not enter the foreign room inhabited by "a dark lady, pale and dark, who would look up quickly, half rise, and hold out a long thin hand with three rings on it" (361): a dark lady who incarnates just the metamorphoses that this writer herself underwent in her passage from a provincial origin as "Pussy/Lily" Jones, New York debutante, to a brilliant career as Edith Wharton, expatriate novelist. Like her hero,

Wharton has no language for such changes, even though they are, in her case, the transformations that made her into Henry James's angel of devastation. " 'It's more real to me here than if I went up,' " she has Newland say—and for the experienced author of *The Age of Innocence*, too, the changes of rules and roles implicitly demanded by her murderous assaults on the economy of sexuality and the arts of the enslaved were evidently "more real" if they remained unsaid, unsayable.

5 Lighting Out for the Territories: Willa Cather's Lost Horizons

Such was that happy Garden-state,
While Man there walk'd without a Mate:
After a Place so pure, and sweet,
What other Help could yet be meet!
But 'twas beyond a Mortal's share
To wander solitary there:
Two Paradises 'twere in one
To live in Paradise alone.

—Andrew Marvell

A Woman here, leads fainting Israel on,
She fights, she wins, she tryumphs with a song,
Devout, Majestick, for the subject fitt,
And far above her arms, exalts her witt,
Then, to the peacefull, shady Palm withdraws,
And rules the rescu'd Nation, with her Laws.
How are we fal'n, fal'n by mistaken rules?
And Education's, more than Nature's fools,
Debarr'd from all improve-ments of the mind,
And to be dull, expected and dessigned.

—Anne Finch

Looking backward toward the horizon of dawning society, what do we see standing clearly against the sky? Woman—assuming chief responsibility for the continuance and care of life. We are in the presence of a force so vital and so powerful that anthropologists can devise no meter to register it and the legislator no rein strong enough to defeat it.

—Mary Beard

What was unsayable to Edith Wharton was equally unsayable to Willa Cather, perhaps because both of these notably popular women writers were similarly horrified by feminization and its discontents. Nevertheless, no subject better highlights the different sensibilities of Edith Wharton and Willa Cather than that of illicit eroticism. Judging from her first novel, *Alexander's Bridge* (1912), Cather viewed the sort of affair Wharton experienced in life and hinted at in art as more of a reflection of the problems posed by sexuality than a solution to them, for the eponymous Bartley Alexander's adultery dramatizes his psychological inability to commit himself either to his wife or his mistress as well as the aesthetic failure that ultimately results in the collapse of his most ambitious engineering project. But Cather's rejection of illicit heterosexuality was more profound and enduring than Bartley's individual situation might suggest. Indeed, it could be said to thread its way as a theme throughout her fiction.

From *O Pioneers!* (1913), in which an unhappily married woman and her lover are shot and killed by her aggrieved husband, to *Sapphira and the Slave Girl* (1940), in which a wife jealous of a potential rival for her spouse's affections plots to have the younger woman raped by her husband's nephew, Cather meditated on the Gothic repercussions of extramarital desire. After she rejected *Alexander's Bridge* as "conventional" apprentice work,[1] however, she radically extended the basis of her critique of the erotic desire. Whether Cather's extraordinary attack on heterosexuality was motivated by what Blanche Gelfant identifies as regressive anxieties or by what Sharon O'Brien and Judith Fetterley consider covert lesbian allegiances,[2] it issued in a series of works that reverse societally normative assumptions about gender in order to suggest that sexuality is itself a betrayal of the deepest desire of men and women.

It was, as we have seen, Cather's dislike of the "trite and sordid" subject of adultery that informed both her explicit criticism of Kate Chopin's *The Awakening* in an 1899 review and her implicit criticism of Aphrodite in her 1920 story "Coming, Aphrodite!" Nor was this critique unrelated to a more all-embracing rejection of romance. According to Cather's diagnosis of the case of Edna Pontellier, "the over-idealization of love" is a "disease" that "attacks only women of brains," turning them into "Iphigenias of sentiment" who "pay with their blood for the fine ideals of the poets."[3] In Cather's story, moreover, Eden Bower is associated with financial success (as opposed to avant-garde aesthetic originality) that can only be attained by pandering to popular taste and therefore through a debased and debasing commercialism that virtually prostitutes the woman artist.[4] Significantly, then, in the retrospective essay that contrasts the artifice of *Alexander's Bridge* with the spontaneity of *O Pioneers!,* a novel not about an adulterous Alexander but about an autonomous Alexandra, Cather juxtaposes the novelty of her Nebraskan setting (before the "novel of the soil" became fashionable) with "drawing-room" fiction that focuses on the manners of "smart or clever people," adding that "Henry James and Mrs. Wharton were our most interesting novelists, and most of the younger writers followed their manner, without having their qualification" (*OW* 93).

When Cather stopped following the example of James and Wharton and instead rebelled against the view that "Nebraska is distinctly declassé as a literary background," she distinguished herself in yet another and, of course, more obvious way from Edith Wharton. Indeed, her quotation of a "New York critic" who " 'simply don't care a damn what happens in Nebraska' " (*OW* 94) accurately represents the view of Wharton, who, as we have noted, responded to the 1910 flood of Paris by exclaiming, "If it could only have happened to Omaha!" Unlike Wharton, Cather believed by the age of twenty-two that the "difference between French and American society" was that a woman in France met men "only as a woman," while a woman in America met them "in school, in business, in a hundred prosaic relations that wear off that sex consciousness so prevalent in France" (*WP* 1 149–50). Clearly if for Wharton "in Paris the house became a city, a kingdom," Cather—following Sarah Orne Jewett's famous advice—found her world in the parish.[5]

During travels that took her repeatedly back to Nebraska, to Arizona in 1912, Mesa Verde and Taos in 1915, and New Mexico in 1925 and 1926—as well as during a number of stimulating journeys through Europe—Cather revived memories of probably the single most crucial event in her life, namely her transplantation at nine years of age from the cultivated farms of Virginia to the sense of "the end of everything" she encountered in the wilderness of Nebraska.[6] Declaring later, with cosmopolitan verve, that "I go everywhere, I admire all kinds of country. I tried to live in France," Cather explained about the west that "when I strike the open plains, something happens. I'm home. I breathe differently. That love of great spaces, of rolling open country like the sea,—it's the grand passion of my life."[7] No wonder, then, that while Wharton scorned the "rose-colored spectacles" of her regionalist predecessors, Cather celebrated Jewett, for "She early learned to love her country for what it was. What is quite as important, she saw it as it was" (*OW* 56).

If Wharton and Cather seem dramatically opposed in their attitudes toward, say, Paris and Omaha or the New England local color artists, their childhood and adolescent self-definitions also seem to set them at odds. While the young Wharton dreamed of becoming "the best-dressed woman in New York," the young Willa Cather responded to the petting of an avuncular visitor by warning "I'se a dang'ous nigger, I is!," posed a few years later for the camera with bow and arrow as Hiawatha, and at the age of fifteen defined "the greatest folly of the Nineteenth Century" as "Dresses and Skirts."[8] While Wharton geared up for her literary encounters by donning her most fashionable gowns, Willa Cather prepared for her university education by cutting her hair and putting on man-tailored suits with boyish ties and caps. While some of Wharton's nicknames were extravagantly feminine, Cather—baptized "Wilella"—called herself "Willie," "William Cather, Jr.," "Wm. Cather, M.D.," or just plain "Billy," thereby virtually transforming herself into what Sharon O'Brien calls "her own twin brother."[9]

Even more to the point, while Wharton "preferred the company of men," Cather located the emotional center of her life in a series of passionate relationships with women: Louise Pound was her intimate during the years at the University of Nebraska and Edith Lewis her companion from 1908 until her death. But, as James Woodress has demonstrated, her friendship with Isabelle McClung "grew into a great love that lasted a lifetime,"[10] although the two only lived together for the five years during which Cather earned her living in Pittsburgh doing journalism and teaching high school English and Latin. This last episode, of course, emphasizes the greatest contrast between the early lives of Wharton and Cather, for the younger author had to support herself and, rather than disdaining writing as socially disreputable the way that Wharton's family did, Cather's relatives and friends viewed the drama reviews she wrote in college, her travel essays, and her editorships of *Home Monthly* and *McClure's* as crucial sources of income.

Paradoxically, however, despite all these differences between Wharton's and Cather's backgrounds, the two shared projects that relate to their sense of themselves both as American and as women writers. Just as Wharton gained a fresh perspective on America in France, Cather escaped to New York to describe the prairie of her childhood. Moreover, though she was troubled by her linguistic inadequacy in France, Cather—like Wharton—responded with a special intensity to a country that produced such favorite authors of hers as Dumas père, Flaubert, and George Sand, and she had France represent youth and freedom to fictional surrogates, including Claude Wheeler in *One of Ours* (1922) and Professor St. Peter in *The Professor's House* (1925).[11] To be sure, when in "The Novel Démeublé" (1922) Cather used French literary models to define her fictional technique by claiming "We have had too much of the interior decorator," she sounds as if she would be antagonistic to a contemporary who began her career as the co-author of *The Decoration of Houses*. Yet what we have described as Wharton's revulsion at "knick-knacks" and "useless trifles" is reiterated in Cather's exclamation, "How wonderful it would be if we could throw all the furniture

out of the window." [12] For although Cather was differentiating her craft
from the literalness of literary realism as it had developed in the nineteenth century, she was also rebelling against the overcrowded, stuffy
furnishings she associated not only with tasteless consumerism but also
with the conventionality of sex roles that turn women into either consumers or commodities.

Similarly unconventional, both Wharton and Cather lived lives of
extraordinary independence, pursuing professional careers with a sin-
gle-mindedness that resulted in public acclaim, financial success, and a
remarkable number of publications and prizes. Inhabiting domestic
spaces outside the constraints imposed by men—Wharton in her man-
sions and Cather in her Greenwich Village apartment, in the Gros-
venor Hotel, and eventually in a house in Jaffrey, New Hampshire, and
a cottage on Grand Manan Island—both escaped the confinement experienced by so many of their female precursors. In other words, both
exemplified the experimental lives of New Women. Indeed, each typi-
fied the sexchanges that marked the early decades of the twentieth century. Just as the seemingly feminine Wharton was called "John" by her
husband and characterized as an "intellectual tomboy," the apparently
tomboyish Cather posed not only for a famous Edward Steichen photograph (in which she wears a sailor's middy blouse) but also for a
succession of portraits that parade ornately flowered and feathered
hats. [13] Yet in their fiction Wharton and Cather ignored their own freedom from traditional gender arrangements in order to demonstrate
precisely how limited contemporary women were. In other words, both
expressed skepticism not only about conventional sex roles but also about
the possibility of changing them.

Like Wharton, then, Cather quarreled with contemporary America
in general and with the "laws" that govern heterosexual relations in
particular. Indeed, despite the contrast between their characteristic
tones—Wharton's ferocious irony and Cather's elegiac nostalgia—Cather
discovered on the frontier what Wharton found in Europe, namely a
landscape in which women were, as Wharton put it, "in the very middle
of the picture." Suspicious, as Wharton was, about the suffrage movement, the New Woman, and the female literary tradition, Cather memorialized a time in history when women were economically produc-
tive and socially central. Just as Wharton eventually sought the
extravagant, if not downright lurid, subjects of ghosts, dead dogs, and
incest to voice what was virtually unsayable in her culture, Cather created Edens which receded further and further into a prehistory recalcitrant to the excavations of the anthropological novelist. Disturbed, as
Wharton was, by the feminization and commodification of women in
contemporary America, Cather was sometimes no more successful than

Newland Archer and Ellen Olenska in her efforts to find an age of innocence before the sex antagonism produced by the categories of "mistress" and "wife." Yet in two of the earliest of her prairie fictions she constructed a myth of personal and national origins that redefines America itself as a Herland even while it illuminates a fall into gender from the sexual frontier that her gardens of earthly and early delight represent.

"Miss Cather is a poet in her intensity and Mrs. Wharton is not," Burton Rascoe claimed in a 1922 review that contrasts the "correct pictures" of Wharton with "the poetry and beauty" of Cather's depictions of "emotions" (*KA* 51). Yet Cather resembled Wharton in finding it necessary to separate herself from the didacticism of the feminist movement and from what she viewed as a fatally feminized literary matrilineage. Although readers of her novels do not generally consider Willa Cather a satirist, her scathing comments on suffrage and on her female precursors sound very much like Wharton's. Indeed, in their distanced perspective on the feminism of figures like Olive Schreiner and Charlotte Perkins Gilman and on the feminization evident in what Nina Baym calls "woman's fiction,"[14] Cather's critical statements raise interesting questions about the concept of female misogyny, for the intensity of her hostility implies that—as the old saying goes—it takes one to know one.

Besides protesting the fanaticism she associated with feminism, Cather objected to the ignorance and the sentimentality that led suffragists to idealize women. An early review of the *Woman's Bible*, for instance, criticizes Elizabeth Cady Stanton and her editorial committee, marveling "at the temerity of these estimable ladies, who, without scholarship, without linguistic attainments, without theological training, not even able to read the Bible in the original tongues, set themselves upon a task which has baffled the ripest scholarship" as well as at their turning each biblical female character into "a ministering angel unjustly and cruelly misplaced upon a sphere peopled with shocking men": "Ruth, Deborah, Bath-sheba and Esther are each taken up and idealized and romanced about and fondled and wept over, much as Juliet and Rosalind are in Mrs. Jamison's book on the *Girlhood of Shakespeare's Heroines*" (*WP* 2 539). Similarly, Cather identifies Margaret Fuller with William Wetmore Strong's sculpture *Cleopatra*, "a lady capable only of frenzies of the intellect, who would have held long conversations on the destiny of the soul in the famous library of Alexandria" (*WP* 2 579). Even a laudatory review of a lecture by Jane Addams begins with Cather's admission that "I have an absolute aversion for women who lecture," continues by distinguishing Addams from women who believe in "the abolishing of saloons, or the prohibition of cigarettes," and concludes by viewing Addams as "strangely unlike the well-known woman with a hobby, or woman with a theory, or woman with a wrong" (*WP 2* 742–43).

Nor do Cather's novels deviate from her disdain for suffragist activism. In *My Ántonia* (1918), for example, a quarrelsome female character is associated with feminism. Though she is neither a New Woman nor a feminist, Mrs. Cutter is imprisoned in a barren marriage with a man who enjoys nothing more than disputing with her over the question of inheritance, arguments that have helped endow this "giantess" with "hysterical eyes" and a face "the very colour and shape of anger."[15] Yet the narrator of *My Ántonia* goes on to remark, "I have found Mrs. Cutters all over the world; sometimes founding new religions, *sometimes being forcibly fed*—easily recognizable, even when superficially tamed" (213–14; emphasis ours). And if the early *My Ántonia* implies that the suffragist is a fanatic or a madwoman, the middle period *One of Ours* presents the temperance activist Enid Royce as a sexually repressed and relentless lecturer.[16] Marriage to her means a living death for Claude Wheeler, and specifically it means "Platitudes, littleness, falseness" (220). Finally, a posthumously published story "The Old Beauty" (1948) sustains Cather's critique of "liberated" womanhood by contrasting the elegance of an aging socialite with the vulgarity of two New Women: complete with "bobbed" hair and "dirty white knickers," the women known as "Marge" and "Jim" are presented as "swaggering" creatures whose "sharp voices" seem shockingly "impertinent."[17] In some mysterious way, too, the appearance of these New Women seems to cause the death of "the old beauty," for the automobile accident their own driving precipitates leads ultimately to her demise.

Cather's distrust of New Women was matched by her ambivalence toward her female literary inheritance, an ambivalence as marked as Wharton's, for the two writers shared an appreciation of such male masters as Henry James as well as a revulsion against the sort of commercially successful novelists that George Eliot has earlier called "Silly Lady Novelists" and that Nathaniel Hawthorne had labeled a "damned mob of scribbling women."[18] In the opening story of Cather's first collection of fiction, a female culture-vulture who constructs a salon—actually a grotesquely mediocre "House of Song"—represents the link between the New Woman and the debasement of art.[19] "Flavia and Her Artists" (1905) presents the genuine author of "twelve great novels" as a Frenchman who satirizes his hostess in an essay on "The Advanced American Woman as He Sees Her; Aggressive, Superficial and Insincere" (167). In this portrait of a lady to whom aesthetic achievement means "exactly as much . . . as a symphony means to an oyster" (164), Cather—who "began by imitating Henry James"[20]—sees the modern American woman as a creature who vampirically "absorbs rather than produces" (159). How ironic, then, that when mailed a copy of *The Troll Garden*, James expressed his abhorrence of "promiscuous fiction" especially when it came "from the innocent hands of young females, young American females perhaps above all."[21]

Even before taking James as a model, however, Cather had praised male masters as well as genres written specifically by men and about men or boys. Her first European tour included a stop at Highgate to meet A. E. Housman, whose *A Shropshire Lad* (1896) she much admired, as well as a pilgrimage through France where she paid her respects to the memories of Flaubert, de Musset, Balzac, and Daudet.[22] As Sharon O'Brien has demonstrated, the youthful author's preference for such classical writers as Virgil and Ovid and for such modern authors as Rudyard Kipling, Robert Louis Stevenson, Walt Whitman, Ralph Waldo Emerson, and Thomas Carlyle "reveal[s] her equation of creativity both with paternity and with an aggressive, phallic masculinity."[23] Given Cather's assumption that creativity and femininity are contradictory terms, she suffered from precisely the anxiety of authorship that marked the works of so many of her female precursors. And like those foremothers who adopted male pseudonyms, Cather attempted to ease that anxiety by erasing or camouflaging her own gender.

Noting that "Haggard's *She* was universally read because the world has not yet outgrown the liking for fairy tales" (*KA* 363), Cather clearly counted herself among those not yet grown up, for she cherished books like *Treasure Island* that "gratif[y] the eternal boy in us" (*KA* 323) by presenting "wild adventures on land and on water, of buried treasure and encounters on the high seas" (*WP* 1 136). Implicitly, for Cather, "all the weird suggestions of unknown lands and peoples, of mystery and awful age, of reckless daring, and of careless love" do "lend Mr. Haggard's book its charms." Only a particularly bad dramatization of *She* makes Cather long for the time "When the Rudyards cease to Kipling, / And the Haggards Ride no more" (*KA* 268). Indeed, admonishing Kipling not to let his wife circumscribe his travels, Cather urged him to return to Asia so as to "Tell us of love and war and action that thrills us because we know it not, of boundless freedom that delights us because we have it not" (*WP* 1 138).

Like Stevenson and Kipling, Mark Twain was another favorite who gratifies "the eternal boy in us": "What a red-letter day it is to a boy, the day he first opens *Tom Sawyer*," Cather exclaims, adding "I would rather sail on the raft down the Missouri again with Huck Finn and Jim than go down the Nile in December" (*WP* 1 347). Given her attraction to this kind of reading, it is hardly surprising that by the time Cather was editing *McClure's Magazine,* her friend Elizabeth Sergeant saw "No trace of the reforming feminist" in the "boyish, enthusiastic manner" of "this vital being."[24] Precisely this reading also allowed Cather later to explain that the "fact that I was a girl never damaged my ambitions to be a pope or an emperor" (*WP* 1 368) and to compose tales with tomboy heroines (like "Tommy, the Unsentimental" [1896]) or with boyish heroes (like those in "The Enchanted Bluff" [1909]).[25]

Masculine adventure, not feminine romance, was Cather's youthful literary ideal, as her comments on the "trite and sordid" theme of *The Awakening* illustrate:

> I have not much faith in women in fiction. They have a sort of sex consciousness that is abominable. They are so limited to one string and they lie so about that . . . When a woman writes a story of adventure, a stout sea tale, a manly battle yarn, anything without wine, women and love, then I will begin to hope for something great from them, not before. [*KA* 409]

Clearly Cather's admiration for stout sea tales and manly battle yarns was proportionate to her dislike of female "sex consciousness." Yet elsewhere Cather constructed a double bind for the woman writer by implying that women poets are only effective when they confine themselves to "reverence or love." Not endowed with man's powers of rationalism, the "woman has only one gift," namely "the power of loving." A classical education will therefore cause a woman poet like Elizabeth Barrett Browning to "blunder" because it will divert her from the talent that issues in her only great verse, that is, *Sonnets from the Portuguese* (*WP* 1 146).

Whether she was writing about women's poetry, women's traditional roles, or even women's influence on creativity, Cather repeatedly admitted that she "wonder[s] why God ever trusts talent in the hands of women" (*WP* 1 275). "It is a very grave question whether women have any place in poetry at all," she declared in one review, asking in another, "Has any woman ever really had the art instinct, the art necessity?" (*KA* 348, 158) Cather's belief in the austere dedication demanded by the "art necessity" also caused her to question the possibility of combining artistry with female social roles, creativity with marriage: "Married nightingales seldom sing" (*KA* 176). As for the wives of men of genius, they "are not generally helpful" (*KA* 170). Metaphorically allergic throughout her life to polemical literature, Cather was convinced only that the "mind that can follow a 'mission' is not an artistic one" (a fact that caused her to condemn *Uncle Tom's Cabin* as "exaggerated, overdrawn," [*KA* 269]) but also that the "feminine mind has a hankering for hobbies and missions, consequently there have been but two real creators among women authors, George Sand and George Eliot" (*KA* 406). But unfortunately, of course, "the great Georges . . . were anything but women" (*KA* 409).

Like Wharton, then, the youthful Cather responded to the complex problem of affiliation by eschewing contaminated bloodlines and by distancing herself from scribbling women writers. When Cather began publishing her stories at the end of the nineteenth century, what we are calling the feminization of women and their work had already been identified as a pernicious influence on American culture in general and literature in particular. "[T]he monthly [magazines] are getting so lady-like," Gilman's and Wharton's physician Dr. S. Weir Mitchell declared, "that naturally they will soon menstruate."[26] Reading the writing of other women, Cather (herself the onetime editor of a *Monthly Magazine* for women) plainly inherited a literary tradition of her own. But remarks like Mitchell's may well have contributed to her anxiety—shared with contemporaries like Wharton—that femininity (defined as either grossly biological in its menstruation or ludicrously refined in its gentility) precluded creativity. Like Virginia Woolf, Cather reserves her most scornful remarks for such writers as Ella Wheeler Wilcox, Ouida, and Marie Corelli, whose works she repeatedly attacks as "more maudlin, more sensational, more trashy" and "more lucrative" that anything written by, say, "George Meredith, or the late Mr. Stevenson" (KA, 194). Satirizing "That organ of exquisite literary culture, the *Ladies' Home Journal*," Cather is hilariously irreverent about women's culture in general and in particular on the subject of Ruth Ashmore's piece on "Girls," Margaret Simmons's on "New Designs in Knitting," Emma M. Hopper's on "Holiday Gowns," and Patty Thumb's on "Marking Initials," asking only, "in the name of the venal vampire and the great primeval mystery, who, who is Patty Thumb?" (*KA* 189)

How could Cather use the "one gift" of feeling with which women writers were endowed without accepting the limitations of "sex consciousness"? Could she compose "a story of adventure, a stout sea tale," or was she destined to align herself with Patty Thumb? One escape route from the problem of affiliation was provided by those female precursors she did revere. Although, in some of her early critical statements, Cather's contempt for women writers qualified even her grudging praise of her most celebrated ancestresses,[27] she did suggest that a number of important exceptions prove the rule of female mediocrity in letters, specifically such foremothers as Charlotte Brontë, George Eliot, and Christina Rossetti. In every case, what Cather relishes are passages in which the author reaches back to represent not women in love, not "Iphigenias of sentiment," but those Wordsworthian spots of time that turn childhood into what Edna St. Vincent Millay once called a "kingdom where nobody dies,"[28] the most evocative subject in the kingdom of art.

About *Jane Eyre,* for example, Cather admits that the "maniac's laughter" and "the consciously theatrical" Mr. Rochester failed to thrill, but she finds that the portrait of Jane's education at Lowood "will never grow old" because "it was painted with heart's blood" (*KA* 371–72). Not the "sensational" passages but those about Miss Scatcherd, Miss Temple, Helen Burns, and their "cowed, half-starved" students guarantee *Jane Eyre* its stature as a "masterpiece." Like Brontë, moreover, Eliot, in Cather's view, returns us to "the places and memories of our childhood." Recounting Eliot's descriptions of generous uncles and proper aunts, of a pretty prim cousin and a mother secretly sorrowing over her tomboy daughter (*KA* 362), Cather praises *The Mill on the Floss* because she "feels like a child again in reading those pages" (*WP* 1 262). Finally, the explicitly nonerotic passages Cather singles out in the fiction of Brontë and Eliot illuminate her tribute to Rossetti's "gift of song" in *Goblin Market,* a poem which demonstrates how "the purchase of pleasure" is associated with "its loss in its own taking" and which is "so melodious that it does not depend on its significance for its beauty" (*WP* 1 145).

Female contemporaries of Cather's like Louise Imogen Guiney, Sarah Orne Jewett, and Katherine Mansfield also remained noteworthy to her for creating works whose seeming simplicity redirects the reader's desire away from the "over-valuation" of romantic thralldom and back toward the kingdom of childhood. Just as important, she lauded all three writers as modest but accomplished singers whose compositions, like *Goblin Market,* are "so melodious" that they do "not depend" on "significance for [their] beauty." According to Cather, Guiney's refrain in "Hylas"—" 'Keep—young!' but who knows how?"—reflects the ways in which her verse adapts "her meters to her subject, so that the mere melody of her verse often takes the color of the sentiment," a sentiment approaching "a sort of gentle, tolerant asceticism" (*WP* 2 885).

Similarly, Jewett's stories eschew "Othellos and Iagos and Don Juans," replacing them with "everyday people who grew out of the soil" (*NUF* 82). Praising Jewett's "individual voice" (NUF 95), Cather honors the sense of decorum that caused the regionalist writer to encourage her neighbors to regard her "sketches" as "a ladylike accomplishment" (*NUF* 86). Similarly, in her essay on Mansfield, Cather contrasts the "unpleasantly hysterical" story "Je ne parle pas français"—a Parisian tale about the perversity of (male) homosexuality—with the "luminous" effects

Mansfield achieved when she chose the "small reflector" of familial interactions (*NUF* 135). Cather clearly identifies with the bohemian, Lon-
don-based author's homesickness for her childhood in New Zealand
and attributes the "magic" of such New Zealand stories as "Prelude"
and "At the Bay" to an "overtone, which is too fine for the printing
press" (*NUF* 137), a unique "timbre" that "cannot be defined or explained any more than the quality of a beautiful speaking voice can be"
(*NUF* 135).

Cather's tributes to her female precursors and contemporaries emphasize the ability of women of letters to capture those moments of
being before the emergence of an eroticism predicated upon the social
construction of gender. But her essays also attribute such visions to a
style characterized as exceptional in its melody or tone. In other words,
balanced against her admiration for the *patrius sermo* or "father speech"
of male authors from Virgil to Emerson and Carlyle stands a tradition
defined through "timbre," "cadence," and "voice" as a kind of mother
tongue. From Cather's adolescent interest in pioneer women's storytelling to her college reviews of actresses, her *kunstlerroman The Song of
the Lark* (1915), and her theory of fiction in "The Novel Démeublé,"
moreover, her definition of female creativity emphasizes the primacy
of the voice and the mouth over against the secondariness of the pen,
as if she were meditating on the competing claims of maternal and
paternal metaphors of authority.[29]

As Cather once recalled, during her youth on the Divide immigrant
women "who used to tell me of their home country" furnished "the
initial impulse" for a would-be writer who "didn't know any writing
people."[30] Later, during Cather's literary apprenticeship as a journalist, Sarah Bernhardt, even at sixty years of age, evinced "that mighty
force that seemed to go back and awaken the primitive elements in man
and analyze things into their first and simplest constituent" (*KA* 118).
Then, as many critics have noted, Cather's portrait of the artist as a
young girl in *The Song of the Lark* drew many of its circumstances from
her own early life as well as from that of the prima donna Olive Frem-
stad, suggesting that Thea Kronborg's discovery of her aesthetic potential in a "cleft in the world" called Panther Canyon empowered not only
the successful career of the singer-character but also that of the singer's
author, a fact that helps explain why Cather wanted the novel adver-
tised in women's colleges.[31]

As we mentioned in our first volume, *The Song of the Lark* records
Thea's discovery that ancient pottery offered her an analogy between
water in the Indian women's jars and breath in the "vessel of one's
throat" so that "any art" could be reimagined as "an effort to make a

sheath, a mold in which to imprison for a moment the shining, elusive element which is life itself" (304). Only after Thea's reconstruction of this myth of creative origins is she free to reinvent the operative role of, say, Wagner's Fricka so as to reclaim the goddess from the shrew or to sing in her hometown at the funeral of a girl significantly named Maggie Evans. Thea, a goddess of song herself, embodies Cather's belief that "Whatever is felt upon the page without being specifically named there" represents true creation, for this writer seeks "the inexplicable presence of the thing not named, of the overtone divined by the ear but not heard by it, the verbal mood," in her own mature fiction (*NUF* 50). For Cather, indeed, literary women—especially those who "have such an unfortunate tendency to instruct the world"—must learn to catch "the verbal mood" from the "women of the stage [who] know that to feel greatly is genius and to make others feel is art" (*KA* 348).

This artist would remain divided between her paternal and her maternal inheritances throughout her career, and her major novels record not only a competition between written and oral modes of creativity but also a tension between male- and female-dominated genres, a predictable pattern for an author whose apprenticeship included writing *The Life of Mary Baker G. Eddy and the History of Christian Science* ("by" Georgine Milmine) and *My Autobiography* ("by" the editor S. S. Mc-Clure).[32] In particular, though, Cather—who identified *Huckleberry Finn* and *The Country of the Pointed Firs,* along with *The Scarlet Letter,* as "the three American books which have the possibility of a long, long life" (*NUF* 58)—evokes two quite different versions of pastoral: the adventure literature of, for example, Kipling, Stevenson, and Twain and the regionalist impulse she admired in the productions of Eliot, Jewett, and Mansfield. In her prairie novels, *O Pioneers!* and *My Ántonia,* Cather lights out for the territory she found so thrilling in books like *Treasure Island* and *Huckleberry Finn,* but she brings the muse of her foremothers to her own country. The frontier, a place with hardly any furniture at all, enables her to write "a stout sea tale" because the "rolling open country" surrounding her little houses on the prairie is "like the sea."

First implicitly and then explicitly setting an originatory culture against contemporary society, Cather could be said to be wondering, along with Anne Finch, "How are we fal'n, fal'n by mistaken rules?" For, as she explores a time when sex roles were blurred or indeterminate, the note of sorrowful lament which characterizes Finch's "Introduction" displaces Cather's cynicism about a contemporary femininity constructed so as to be trivial, sentimental, self-indulgent, or missionary. Ultimately, indeed, Cather's backward glance at the childhood of the individual and the childhood of civilization radically revises legends of the west to mythologize the birth of the nation by representing women not yet entrapped in the "sex consciousness" and the "over-idealization of love" that their own efforts at cultivation will later, paradoxically enough, establish.

The woods of Arcady were to come alive for Willa Cather when she excavated a past and produced a pastoral which could provide an adventure story for women. In doing so, she had to come to terms with scholarly and literary myths of the frontier that presented an image of women's misery in the wilderness. For writers from Alexis de Tocqueville to D. H. Lawrence, after all, the frontier woman was a tired wife and wretched mother. Tocqueville's frontier woman is "prematurely pale" with "shrunken limbs," a "frail creature" who has "already found herself exposed to unbelievable miseries." Although a "profound sadness" marks her features, although she has "exhausted herself" giving birth to her children, "she does not regret what they have cost her."[33] In a similar vein, as G. J. Barker-Benfield has pointed out, Hamlin Garlin claimed that "the wives of the American farmers fill our insane asylums," while Lawrence imagined the homesteader's mate as a "poor haggard drudge, like a ghost walking in the wilderness."[34] But perhaps the privations of the pioneer women were most brilliantly described by the critic Thomas Beer. Considering "women stately as great cows, and grammarless, before whose eyes the legend of the West had been erected," Beer recognized how their experiences had been erased and hoped that "the forgotten kindness of their hands may raise them up a chronicler, else they are lost who were not ladies."[35]

Both *O Pioneers!* and *My Ántonia* question the view that pioneer women were shrunken, frail, maddened, or—for that matter—"stately as great cows, and grammarless." Yet both novels do provide a chronicle to reclaim those "who were not ladies" from historical and imaginative oblivion. For even while Cather revised myths of pioneer women's misery, she also implicitly rejected legends of the west that denied women's existence. As R. W. B. Lewis's analysis of the American Adam "poised at the start of a new history" and "undefiled by . . . family" suggests, and as Leslie Fiedler's account of "the pure marriage of males" with each other and "their union with the wilderness itself" documents, the literary tradition of the frontier from Cooper to Twain uses both male bonding and masculine escape from civilization to characterize a quest that provides what Fiedler terms "an innocent substitute for adulterous passion and marriage alike."[36] Lewis and Fiedler show that the heroes of frontier novels exert "strenuous efforts to stay outside" society—to remain inside "a lost childhood and a vanished Eden"—an effort inextricably related to their authors' protests against the feminization of American culture and those same authors' creation, in Fiedler's words, of a "mythic America [which] is boyhood."[37] But, of course, for such writers as Stevenson and Kipling in works like *Treasure Island* and *Kim,* the adventure story, with its setting in unexplored territory and its celebration of male bonding, also functions to mythologize boyhood.

As Henry Nash Smith and Marcus Cunliffe have observed, moreover, diction quite similar to that of the literature of adventure informs the arguments of the foremost turn-of-the-century historian of the American frontier, Frederick Jackson Turner. In his famous 1893 essay "The Significance of the Frontier in American History" and in a number of other influential articles, Turner claimed that the settlement of successive areas of free land fostered economic, political, and social equality in American society. Like the novelists, Turner identified the virgin land as a female: "this great American West took [European man] to her bosom," and "she opened new provinces, and dowered new democracies."[38] Turner's ideal of rugged individualism was not unrelated to his admiration for Tennyson's "Ulysses," who aspires "To sail beyond the sunset and the baths / Of all the western stars," and for Kipling's "Explorer," who seeks to "blaze a nation's way, with hatchet and with brand, / Till on his last-won wilderness an empire's bulwarks stand."[39] Praising the heroic ideals—"grim energy and self-reliance"— of the pioneer who is always assumed to be male,[40] Turner's essay functions as a gloss on the imaginative vision established in The Leatherstocking Tales and *Huckleberry Finn* and in the Whitman poem whose title Cather uses in *O Pioneers!,* as well as by the figure of Robinson Crusoe that Carl Linstrum draws at the beginning of *O Pioneers!* and the pages of *The Life of Jessie James* that Jim Burden brings with him to Nebraska at the beginning of *My Ántonia.*[41]

Cather's first two versions of pastoral invoke the adventure tales "the boy in us" loved but reject their masculinist ideology by drawing upon a regionalist perspective even while they resist the limitations imposed by that perspective. As Richard Brodhead has recently argued, regionalism functioned "to open up isolated native regions to public knowledge and to figure a new population of foreigners; to dramatize the pluralism of contemporary American culture and to put such pluralism under the sway of a culture more concerned than ever to maintain its rule."[42] Cather, who praised the local color writings of Eliot, Jewett, and Mansfield, struggled to use and yet extend a genre whose apparent modesty had been particularly congenial for women like Mary E. Wilkins Freeman, Rose Terry Cooke, Constance Woolson, Grace King, and Kate Chopin.

Not merely recording "sketches" about backwater customs in remote countries and counties, Cather nevertheless brought the muse of the regionalists to the frontier in order to undermine the identification of assertive strength (the west) with masculinity and of effete gentility (the east) with women. The injunction "Go West, young man" becomes ironic in her works because when male characters like Carl Linstrum and Jim Burden go west, they encounter not male freedom but female primacy. In other words, for Cather, the American frontier functions in a manner similar to that of the colonized country or remote outpost in the works of Olive Schreiner and Charlotte Perkins Gilman. Specifically, in both *O Pioneers!* and *My Ántonia,* Cather creates a mythic America which is girlhood, for she tells the story of the gender dislocation fostered by immigration into the wilderness, a dislocation that results in the death of the father, the diminution of the son, and the empowerment of the daughter with the concomitant centrality of female work. That shades of the prisonhouse of culture inevitably threaten to obscure this centrality serves only to emphasize Cather's darkening vision of the "boundless freedom" she celebrated in Kipling's books, a "freedom that delights because we have it not" (*WP* 1, 138).

"The wilderness masters the colonist," Turner wrote, going on to declare, as Cooper did in a different way, that "It strips off the garments of civilization and arrays him in the hunting shirt and moccasins"; but Cather is haunted by the realization that initially the frontier environment is, as Turner mentions, "too strong for the man."[43] At the beginning of *O Pioneers!,* "The great fact [of] the land itself, which seemed to overwhelm the little beginnings of human society that struggled on its sombre wastes," makes the wild land a waste land for the boys and men who believe "that men were too weak to make any mark here, that the land wanted to be let alone, to preserve its own fierce strength, its peculiar, savage kind of beauty, its uninterrupted mournfulness."[44] Even the plow only leaves imprints likened to "feeble scratches on stone left by prehistoric races, so indeterminate" that they seem more like glacial "markings" than a human "record" (19–20).

Precisely this indeterminacy convinces John Bergson that the "Genius" of the Divide is "unfriendly to man" (20). On his deathbed, Mr. Bergson commands his sons Otto and Lou to "be guided" by their older sister, Alexandra (27). Because these young men "were meant to follow in paths already marked out for them, not to break trails in a new country" (48), they submit to their sister's directions (albeit with petulance) after trying unsuccessfully to convince her to sell the farm. Otto works "like an insect, always doing the same thing over in the same way" (55), and such mindlessness is also evident in Lou, who is "fussy and flighty," often getting "only the least important things done" (56). Though the third son, Emil, is sent by Alexandra to the university, Otto and Lou are ruled by her determination to keep and enlarge their farm, but all three recognize that "the struggle in which [their] sister was destined to succeed while so many men broke their hearts and died" (78) somehow excludes or belittles them.

The frontier is therefore a virtual no man's land, as two other male characters demonstrate. First, Alexandra's childhood companion Carl—whose family has "depended so" on her (52)—leaves the land because his sensitivity and artistic aspirations make him "a fool" (53) there, and when he briefly returns looking "stooped" and "pale," he explains to Alexandra that he is "a failure," with no ties, no family, and no property: "It is your fate," he tells her, "to be always surrounded by little men" (181). Second, Ivar—a religious recluse and a self-taught veterinarian who forbids the killing of wild creatures—is presented as "a man [who] is different" (93), a kind of misfit: subject to spells, unable or unwilling to speak English, he is "a queerly shaped old man, with a thick, powerful body set on short bow-legs" (36–37). Although he begins in a "wild homestead" where "his Bible seemed truer to him" (38), this 'little man" is a no-man who brings his knowledge of nature to Alexandra, whom he calls "Mistress" and to whom he devotes his services. By the end of the novel, moreover, both Carl and Ivar have become inhabitants of Alexandra's house and instruments of her pioneering idealism.

If anything, the portrait of the frontier as a no man's land is extended in *My Ántonia,* for this more complex novel begins with a meditation on the land's resistance to men's strivings and on the father whose death and burial mark the sacrifice exacted by the wild. When the young Jim Burden arrives at the place where "the world ended" (16), he feels himself to be "outside man's jurisdiction" (7). Not only "erased" (8) by a landscape which is "not a country at all, but the material out of which countries are made" (7), he is all but dissolved by the "rough, shaggy, red grass" which "was the country, as the water is the sea" (14–15). No wonder, then, that the resonant scene in which Jim kills a snake in the garden and thereby supposedly saves Ántonia, the damsel-in-distress, while proving himself the "equal" to the "great land," turns out to be "in reality . . . a mock adventure" (49). Although Ántonia claims Jim is "a big fellow" (46), she has in fact constructed a fiction of Jim's masculinity, for the rattler was old, torpid, with "not much fight in him" (49). In addition, as a number of critics have noted, what is probably most clearly revealed in this fall in the garden is Jim's nausea at the phallic snake's "abominable muscularity, his loathsome, fluid motion" (45).[45]

But the first in a succession of figures who will become Jim's male mentors is an even more crucial sign that the frontier is a no man's land. Mr. Shimerda, "the old man [who] had come to believe that peace and order had vanished from the earth" (86), cannot endure the dislocation and homesickness of immigration. Having lost his trade as a weaver, his art as a fiddler, and his youthful friendship with another musician, Mr. Shimerda retains only remnants of his old world culture, specifically the gun and fiddle which he wants to bequeath to Jim and Ántonia respectively. Unable to provide for his family during the harsh frontier winter, he shaves, washes, dons clean clothes, then lies down on the bunk bed next to the ox stall, puts the end of his gun barrel in his mouth, and pulls the trigger with his big toe. Coming during the Christmas festivities of the Burden household, the tragedy at the Shimerdas' is described in devastating detail: the farmhand who relates the story to Jim and his grandmother explains, " 'When we found him, everything was decent except'—Fuchs wrinkled his brow and hesitated—'except what he couldn't nowise foresee' " (96).

Frozen in a pool of blood and excrement, this dead father—who is strikingly similar to the central character in Cather's first published story, "Peter" (1892)—is literally buried at the crossroads. Many years later, his grave, dug by axes chopping out the frozen earth, becomes an unmowed "little island" of tall red grass, a relic of the frontier saved by the curve of two roads around it, for Mr. Shimerda's buried life almost seems to represent the paternal absence—the sacrifice—that becomes a signifier of the wilderness. In any case, the suicidal father represents the settlers' bewilderment at the impermanence of human signification on the frontier. His refinement makes him unfit to tame a land that here, as in *O Pioneers!*, seems to "overwhelm the little beginnings of human society that struggled in its sombre wastes" (15). As in the earlier novel, the surviving sons are inadequate to the world in which they find themselves: like Otto and Lou, Ambrosch, although the favorite of Mrs. Shimerda, is described as almost stupidly surly, while Marek, like Ivar, seems a strangely primitive creature, for he has webbed fingers and barks like a dog or crows like a rooster. As in *O Pioneers!*, then, the death of the father means the end of the old world's patrilineage. John Bergson sees in his daughter "the strength of will" that comes from his father and that he "would much rather, of course, have seen . . . in one of his sons" (24), and Mr. Shimerda recognizes in Ántonia the survivor who inherits his father's strength so it is she who literally steps into the dead man's shoes.

Cather was as fascinated as other mythologists of the American west by the idea that originatory moments—the beginning of culture itself—recurred over and over again on the frontier. An Italian economist quoted by Turner argues that "America has the key to the historical enigma which England has sought for centuries in vain, and the land which has no history reveals luminously the course of universal history."[46] As Eudora Welty has shown, Cather was inspired by "the absence of history as far as she could see around her," a blank that "only made her look further, gave her the clues to discover a deeper past."[47] But in particular Cather can be said to be uncovering the "universal history" of gender in those works that examine the primacy of the female in the context of the "historical enigma" of the development of patriarchy. For her, the west is a place in which women at least briefly experienced an exhilarating autonomy. According to one contemporary historian, this freedom, which meant that " 'women's work' soon came to mean whatever had to be done," helps explain why the first suffrage laws in America were passed by western states.[48] Far from being a waste land to the inheriting daughters of *O Pioneers!* and *My Ántonia*, the frontier is a blank page on which Cather inscribes "women's work." Indeed, the wild land is a kind of wild zone between what Turner called "savagery and civilization,"[49] a liminal space in which Alexandra Bergson and Ántonia Shimerda can exercise their powers.

Wearing "a man's long ulster," which she carries as if it "belonged" to her and as if she were "a young soldier" (6), Alexandra exhibits an "Amazonian fierceness" (8) that from the very beginning of *O Pioneers!* extends far beyond her physical vitality, for she reads the papers, follows the markets, and learns the agricultural innovations that allow her to make the family's fortunes. Although Cather explains that the "history of every country begins in the heart of a man or a woman," it is the face of Alexandra which, "For the first time, perhaps, since that land emerged from the waters of geologic ages," is "set toward it with love and yearning" (65). Not a particularly "clever" person, Alexandra discovers that her chief source of joy comes from contemplating "the great operations of nature" and "the law that lay behind them" (70–71).

The orchards, fields, and beehives of her farm, soon the richest on the Divide, therefore contrast oddly with her "curiously unfinished" and oddly furnished house because her real home is "the big out-of-doors" (83–84). The "fiery ends" of curls escaping from her braids "make her head look like one of the big double sunflowers" in her vegetable garden, and, although her face is tanned, the rest of her skin has the smoothness, whiteness, and freshness "of the snow itself" (88). To Carl, remembering her in "the milky light" of dawn (126), Alexandra looks "as if she had walked straight out of the morning itself" (126). With her soul reflected in the cultivation of the soil, Alexandra has no trouble defending herself against Otto's and Lou's later efforts to assert their claim that "the property of a family really belongs to the men of the family" (196). Indeed, when she invokes the laws of culture to state her faith in her own entitlement—"Go to the county clerk and ask him who owns my land" (168)—her farm becomes a luminous image, although quite different from Charlotte Perkins Gilman's, of Herland. For unlike that of Gilman's Herlanders, Alexandra's inheritance is not merely the result of a lucky strike, but, like theirs, it recalls the "morn by men unseen"—the "different dawn"—that Emily Dickinson envisioned in her poem about a "mystic green" (J. 24).

Besides the patrilineal "strength of will" Alexandra has inherited, at least part of her resilience comes from exactly the sort of gardening that Annette Kolodny identifies with women's mythologizing of the wilderness. Rejecting male metaphors of "either erotic mastery or infantile regression," women writers, according to Kolodny, replace the forest with rolling fields and log cabins, the woodsman or the hunter with the gardener.[50] But, of course, Cather could also have drawn upon the domestic artistry celebrated in *The Country of the Pointed Firs,* as her dedication to Jewett makes clear.[51] Just as in that book Mrs. Todd's herbal concoctions produce comforting medicines, Mrs. Bergson's "unremitting efforts to repeat the routine of her old life among new surroundings" (28) result (when the family first moves to the Divide) in the construction of a log—instead of a sod—house, and in a garden that allows her to preserve and pickle to her heart's content. Similarly, as in Jewett's Dunnett Landing, where gardening and gossiping knit together the community, in *O Pioneers!* preserving—which "was almost a mania with Mrs. Bergson" (29)—is a metaphor for the preservation of life women accomplish through their work.

Although in its depiction of the extremity of the daughter's situation and in its disparaging of the maternal inheritance, *My Ántonia* offers a more qualified vision, it nonetheless still hints at the "Amazonian fierceness" of its heroine. Terence Martin, who finds Ántonia "a bit too muscular for conventional romantic purposes,"[52] inadvertently points to the physical vitality of this heroine who, four years older than Jim, refuses to submit to his sentimental impulses. Initially, to be sure, Jim's childhood companion experiences even greater deprivation than he does on their entrance into the wilderness. As a foreigner who is considered contaminating, as a Bohemian with no knowledge of English, Ántonia lives in a house "no better than a badger hole" (20) which is far more primitive than Jim's home: a cave made out of earth, her sod house in the significantly named Squaw Creek resembles the tunneled nests in the "prairie dog town" where the earth-owls live a "degraded" life (30). Underdressed in cotton, sharing a single overcoat with her siblings, Ántonia knows that "Things will be easy for [Jim]. but they will be hard for us" (140). As if contrasting Jim's and Ántonia's situations so as to meditate on the historic poverty of daughters, Cather nevertheless attributes her heroine's resiliency at least in part to her youthful dispossession.

Soon after arriving on the Divide, Ántonia manages to escape with her sister and Jim for a series of adventures in the "great fresh open" that "made them behave like wild things" (64). But even in the context of her family, Ántonia is immediately singled out as the Shimerda interpreter, the one who is to learn English. Quick to name the new country with the new words Jim supplies, she is "the only one of his family who could rouse the old man from the torpor" of his misery (41). At least in part, this is because Ántonia is the repository of the family's communicable past. She tells Jim stories about the Old World, but she also translates Mr.Shimerda's stories about his sense of loss in the New World, even as she relates the "mock adventure" of Jim's induction into masculinity. Just as significantly, she recounts in English a story told by yet another man dying in the wilderness. Pavel's tale about the sleigh ride of a Russian wedding party pursued by hundreds of hungry wolves culminates in his confession that he decided to lighten the load by throwing the bride overboard. That Ántonia's retelling of this legend gives her and Jim "a painful and peculiar pleasure" (61) testifies to their freedom as children in the New World, for this story of brutality seems to suggest that in the world of the past all brides were on their wedding night at least metaphorically thrown to the wolves they married.

After the deaths of both Pavel and her father, Ántonia—now "Tony"—appears to acquire the physical freedom of a man. Working the land and aged beyond her fifteen years by her labor, she displays "arms and throat [that] were burned as brown as a sailor's" (122). Because she cannot be spared from the farm, she condescends with seeming bravado to Jim when he begins his education: although she "always wanted to go to school" (230), she declares, " 'I ain't got time to learn. I can work like mans now. . . . School is all right for little boys. I help make this land one good farm" (123). Eating "noisily now, like a man" (125), she disgusts Jim, who feels that there are "some chores a girl ought not to do" (126). Indeed, after he sees her "come up the furrow, shouting to her beasts, sunburned, sweaty, her dress open at the neck, and her throat and chest dust-plastered" (126), Jim snobbishly thinks of her as a peasant. But she defends herself and defies his censorious notion that "work out-of-doors" is indecorous: "I like to be like a man" (138). That Ántonia's sexchange has less to do with biology than it does with farm work becomes clear when she returns to both ploughing and male clothing during her first pregnancy.

At the same time, however, Ántonia also excels in the kitchen, for she learns all of the arts of her own mother and of Jim's grandmother:

cooking, baking, preserving, and pickling.[53] Empowered by both their paternal and their maternal inheritances and pictured amid "the feathered stalks [which] stood so juicy and green" in the "world's cornfields" (137), both Alexandra and Ántonia recall popular pictures of Columbia, imagined as a sort of Demeter figure offering cornsheaves or a cornucopia. Like the woman Mary Beard sees on "the horizon of dawning society" in a passage we have used as an epigraph here, both illuminate Margaret Mead's more recent characterization of the girls "willing to come to America": "they weren't afraid of facing new conditions; they weren't afraid of hardship; they weren't afraid that they might be left alone."[54] Given Cather's success at imagining what Fiedler calls "an innocent substitute for adulterous passion and marriage alike," these figures might seem (at least from their author's point of view) significantly different from, say, Lyndall, petulantly railing against her lover's strength, or Edna Pontellier, pursuing an affair with one man when she desires another, or Lily Bart, languishing on the marriage market.

Because Cather's heroines are older, wiser, and stronger than the male characters—brothers and brother surrogates—to whom they are implicitly compared, this writer sets her analyses of sex roles against any biological explanation of gender asymmetries within a patriarchal culture. If anything, those traits that distinguish the girls of *O Pioneers!* and *My Ántonia* demonstrate their superiority to boys. But actually, Carl and Alexandra, like Jim and Ántonia, have "always felt alike about things . . . we've liked the same things and we've liked them together" (52), for the fluid boundaries between male and female roles on the frontier resemble those on the sexual "frontier" Havelock Ellis identified with modern society. Yet both of Cather's novels go on to document the social construction of rigid gender demarcations at the turn of the century, not as a result of biological essentialism but as a consequence of surplus value and, ironically, a surplus value that women's work helps to produce. Inevitably, then, first in *O Pioneers!* and then even more definitively in *My Ántonia*, the emergence of a mercantile economy leads to a sexual division of labor. Like Anne Finch, who saw women as "Education's, more than Nature's fools," Cather views sex roles as the result of an education "dessigned" to alienate her characters from the Divide of Nebraska, which becomes symbolic of a widening divide that separates men from women.

In the world of *O Pioneers!*, the very different desires Lyndall, Edna, and Lily express for male lovers or protectors reappear as an index of a process of feminization that would be inconceivable in an agrarian economy. To begin with, the contrast between the first two parts of this

novel—"The Wild Land" of 1883 and the "Neighboring Fields" of 1899—
highlights a process of cultivation that has brought the Bergsons the
comforts of new riches as well as the crudities of the nouveau riche.
Even Alexandra is "willing to be governed by the general conviction
that the more useless and utterly unusable objects were, the greater
their virtue as ornament" (97). And Cather's satire against Lou's family
comes close to Wharton's attack on the female as ornament and on
conspicuous leisure because the "reassuring emblems of prosperity"
Alexandra only produces for her guests' approbation have totally com-
promised her brother's wife.

Wearing "her yellow hair in a high pompadour," Annie Lee—Lou's
spouse—"is bedecked with rings and chains and 'beauty pins' " (99).
Preoccupied not only with her own "high-heeled shoes [which] give her
an awkward walk" (99) but also with a hat that "look[s] like the model
of a battleship" (113), she plans to "move into town as soon as [her]
girls are old enough to go out into company" (111) so that instead of
running about the country as she herself used to do, they will—like her
oldest daughter—attain such ladylike accomplishments as piano playing and, of all things, pyrography ("That's burnt wood, you know" [110]).
Despite her blustering husband's warning that the "West is going to
make itself heard" (112), he and his wife have assimilated eastern values, and they therefore make Annie's mother feel humiliated about her
immigrant ways.[55]

As the youngest brother, Emil, realizes, "Lou and Oscar would be
better off if they were poor," for "it gets worse as it goes on" (238–39).
But Emil is another example of the destructiveness of surplus value. "I
want you to be independent," Alexandra confides to Otto and Lou at
the beginning of the novel, "and Emil to go to school" (68). Although
Emil's adventures in the world outside the farm reconcile Alexandra to
the hardness of her fate, his upward mobility—his college education,
traveling, and plans to attend law school—may, in fact, have "ruined
him," as Lou and Oscar suppose (302), for, having become a person
"fit to cope with the world" (213), Emil "scarcely remember[s]" (78) the
wild country of his childhood when, at twenty-one years of age, he
returns to the farm after college.

Many critics have noted the way in which Alexandra's story is yoked
by violence to the tale of the far more conventional triangle that joins
Alexandra's neighbor Marie Shabata and Marie's husband, Frank, to
Emil.[56] When Emil realizes that he is too old to "play" with Marie "like
a little boy" (156) and when he goes off to Mexico because of his scru-
ples about desiring a married woman, the familiarity of Cather's plot
appears to be almost deliberately uncovered, for the story of this doomed
romance echoes the plot of Kate Chopin's *The Awakening.* Just as Rob-

ert Lebrun flees from Edna Pontellier, Emil hopes to find a vocation in Mexico that will save him from adultery. Like Edna, Marie reads the letters her lover has purportedly written to another person, letters really meant for her eyes. Like Edna, who is jealous of the women with whom Robert might have flirted, Marie wonders if Emil brought his guitar to serenade "all those Spanish girls" (193). And evoking Chopin's major metaphor, the narrator of *O Pioneers!* likens the lovers' first embrace to a sigh, "as if each were afraid of *wakening* something in the other" (225; emphasis ours). But, of course, Marie does not decide to leave her husband. Instead, when Emil and Marie finally consummate their desire, they are accidentally discovered by her husband and murdered. Cather's swerve from Chopin's plot demonstrates her belief that the "overvaluation of love" which fuels her precursor's tale must precipitate an expulsion from paradise that can only elicit the mournful verdict of the wise healer Ivar when he discovers the dead bodies of the lovers in the Shabatas' orchard: "it has fallen! Sin and death for the young ones!" (271).

The unhappy marriage of the Shabatas that at least partially contributes to the love and death of Emil and Marie is itself a reflection of a fatal fall into gender. Even as a "city child" (11) visiting the Divide, Marie Tovesky was an exceptionally "pretty and carefully nurtured" (12) coquette who was offered "bribes" of candy by her uncle's friends, men who wanted to become her "sweetheart" (12). Her later elopement with Frank Shabata is presented not only in terms of the construction of her ornamental femininity, but also in relation to Frank's almost parodic masculine posturing. For, according to Cather, the femme fatale meets her match in the figure of the *homme fatal*. "[T]all and fair, with splendid teeth and close-cropped yellow curls" (143), Frank exhibits an expression of discontent as well as a cambric handkerchief and a yellow cane, all of which endow him with a "melancholy and romantic" charm (144). But the narcissism that leads him to give his fiancée photographs of himself, "taken in a dozen different love-lorn attitudes" (146), eventually causes him to resent in his wife what attracted him during his courtship, namely Marie's vivacity and friendliness. Like a working-class version of the speaker in Browning's "My Last Duchess," Frank becomes a jealous braggart who bullies Marie, and, although she begins as "his slave," she eventually experiences what Browning's duchess must have endured: "always the same yearning, the same pulling at the chain—until the instinct to live had torn itself and bled and weakened for the last time, until the chain secured a dead woman, who might cautiously be released" (248).

That Marie's analysis of her incompatability with Frank is superficial, however, is clarified by uncanny similarities which connect the man she dislikes to the man she desires. Like Frank, Emil becomes jealous of Marie's high spirits on more than one occasion.[57] In addition, if Marie fell in love with the almost comically Byronic posturings of Frank (whom her father recognized immediately as a "stuffed shirt" [144]), she grants her first kiss to Emil when he is costumed in a black velvet coat with real silver buttons, a silk sash, and a tall Mexican hat. At a church fair where young women sell their embroidery to their suitors, Marie becomes angry that Emil offered his shirt studs to the highest bidder and so she is delighted when he enters her fortune-telling tent to bestow a handful of uncut turquoises, an event that recalls the "bribes" of candy she had received as a child. In addition, the fair held at the Church of Sainte-Agnes—besides evoking the romanticism of Keats's "Eve of St. Agnes" in the context of a sexual auction[58]—takes on an ominous centrality because of the fate of a couple married there.

From the moment one of Emil's friends becomes a bridegroom, he is inexplicably doomed, as if Cather wanted to italicize not her indictment of adultery but her sense of the fatality of heterosexuality. At first, the death and funeral of this "good boy" (252) teach Emil a way to convert his destructive erotic desire into "a kind of rapture in which he could love forever without faltering and without sin" (255). But the "equivocal revelation" (256) that leads both Emil and Marie to believe that they can relinquish each other and yet still "live a new life of perfect love" (249) fails to disentangle love from desire. Paradoxically, at the very moment when they meet to renounce each other and dedicate themselves to an ideal that transcends sexuality, Emil and Marie embrace, and both are made "to pay with their blood for the fine ideals of the poets" (*WP* 2 689).

Toward the realm of gold that is the moonlit orchard of romance in which Marie dreams, Emil is driven "wild with joy," like "an arrow shot from the bow" (258). The embracing lovers lying next to the resplendently white mulberry tree, the suspicious husband parting the leaves to peer in on shadowy figures, the gun that springs to his shoulder, the moaning of a mutilated woman who leaves a trail of blood on the orchard grass and on the white mulberries in her effort to drag herself back to her lover's corpse: Cather's primal scene of sex is a version of sex war. But, as Sharon O'Brien has noted, this scene also brings together all the images in *O Pioneers!* that draw upon Sarah Orne Jewett's now classic story "A White Heron" (1886).[59]

A tale about the young girl Sylvia's attraction to a handsome hunter who is searching for a rare white bird, "The White Heron" records the sylvan girl's decision not to give away the secret of a heron's nest. Her silent refusal implicitly rejects an alliance with the hunter and explicitly protests against birds "dropping silently to the ground, their songs

hushed and their pretty feathers stained and wet with blood."[60] Cather
links the scene in the orchard to Jewett's story through an earlier episode in *O Pioneers!* during which Emil shoots down five birds and Marie
lifts one of them out of her apron, "a rumpled ball of feathers with the
blood dripping slowly from its mouth" (128). Although Marie goes on
to prohibit the killing of "wild things" (128), as a result of the secret
logic that has connected husband to lover, a gun—which Jewett associated with the hunter and Cather originally identifies with Emil—appears in Frank's hands, and the blood of Jewett's heron transforms
itself into the blood of Cather's heroine. For while Jewett seems to acquiesce in the necessity of the renunciation of (female) desire, Cather
questions the possibility of such renunciation.

Far from being tacked on, in Cather's "two-part pastoral" Marie's
story tells us what Alexandra's fate would be, if she had been constructed as a feminine ornament. Like Marie, Alexandra agrees with
Ivar that "wild things" must not be killed. Ivar makes this point initially
about a "big white bird. . . . she was in trouble of some sort, but I could
not understand her" (40). And Alexandra soon feels "as if her heart
were hiding down" in the long grass of the Divide, "somewhere, with
the quail and the plover and all the little wild things . . ." (71). Stirred
for a bird, Alexandra also treasures an image of a wild duck—"a kind
of enchanted bird that did not know age or change" (205)— as one of
her happiest recollections. Through the death of Marie, however, Cather
questions the efficacy of Alexandra's identification with nature, for *O
Pioneers!* swerves from what Louis A. Renza sees as Jewett's faith that
"women can reclaim a gender-exclusive relation to the origins of life or
the Edenic Garden."[61] With far deeper pessimism than Jewett, who
presents the bond between women and nature as a viable alternative to
the culture of death represented by a man and his gun—a hunter-tax-
onomist who threatens to kill the heron/heroine into art—Cather envisions female centrality in the natural realm as an empowerment qualified by the inescapable advent of a culture that depends on private
property and that links ownership to the possession of women.

For this reason, even Alexandra's potency is interrogated as the Nebraskan Divide moves from savagery to civilization. Besides serving as
a patron to Emil, Alexandra is inexplicably insensitive to the affair
brewing between him and her closest friend. More malevolently, the
Swedish girls whom she has "broken in" as domestic servants and whom
she marries off (often to "men they were afraid of" [228]) testify to "the
impervious calm of [this] fatalist," a calm that is "disconcerting" (226).
After the death of the lovers, moreover, Alexandra's final assertion
that "the people who love [the land] and understand it are the people
who own it" (308) illustrates her massive repression, for it ignores the

fate not only of Marie but also of two no-men. Frank Shabata—turned into the number 1037 in prison—is "not altogether human" (294) so he wants to go back home to enlist his mother's protection; Carl—back on the farm that is Alexandra's home—disregards the evidence of Frank's and Emil's guilt and instead echoes her blaming of Marie for the tragedy in the orchard: "There are women who spread ruin around them through no fault of theirs, just by being too beautiful, too full of life and love" (304).[62]

Because her own personal life is "almost a subconscious existence" (203), Alexandra exhibits a lack of imagination that reflects the limits of her capacity for experiencing "in her own body the joyous germination in the soil" (204):

> Her mind was a white book, with clear writing about weather and beasts and growing things. Not many people would have cared to read it; only a happy few. She had never been in love, she had never indulged in sentimental reveries. Even as a girl she had looked upon men as work-fellows. She had grown up in serious times. [205]

Of course, there seems to be one crucial exception to the "white book" of Alexandra's blankness, namely her recurrent fantasy of union with the Genius of the Divide. "It was a man, certainly, who carried her, but he was like no man she knew." Large, strong, and swift, he bears her "as easily as if she were a sheaf of wheat," although it is he who—"yellow like the sunlight"—emanates the smell of cornfields. That Alexandra "prosecutes her bath with vigor" after this dream and that later in life the "old sensation of being lifted" (206–07) occurs when she is fatigued suggest that this is a compensatory sexual fantasy appropriately imagined as a kind of union with the fertile wilderness incarnate. Later, when grief over Emil's death causes her to long "to be free from her own body," she again receives "the old illusion of her girlhood, of being lifted and carried lightly by some one very strong." But this time she sees her Genius clearly and realizes that his arm was "of the mightiest of all lovers" (282–83). Finally, after Alexandra's emotional crisis manages to convince Carl to overcome his anxieties that union with her would turn him into an exploitative dependent, she sees her impending marriage as an alternative to the obliteration her phantom suitor offered.

Yet this dream sequence, mentioned first directly after the description of Alexandra's mental "white book," is introduced not as an exception to but as an instance of the "clear writing about weather and beasts and growing things": "There was one fancy indeed, which persisted through her girlhood" (205). Neither a love story nor a sentimental reverie, the fantasy about the Genius of the Divide is associated with the price exacted by Alexandra's renunciation of desire. Therefore, if Marie's story demonstrates that love leads to death, Alexandra's recurrent dream hints that thanatos is the only alternative to eros. Half in love with an easeful death that would release her from the gravity of her autonomy, Alexandra represents all those characters in Cather's later novels who seek an earlier, lighter, childhood self—stripped of social baggage—that will carry them back to an impersonality which is both unsayable and unlivable. In this context, Carl's view that on the Divide "the old story has begun to write itself over" takes on an ominous ring: "there are only two or three human stories," Carl had told Alexandra earlier in the book in a passage that now fatalistically hints at the deadliness of romance and the romance of death, "and they go on repeating themselves as fiercely as if they had never happened before" (119).

The old stories of love and death may be written—as Alexandra insists at the end of *O Pioneers!*—"with the best we have" (307), but Carl is not wrong to recall the grandeur of "this country when it was a wild old beast" (118), for the "safe" marriage between mature friends (308), and even the milk and honey of their farm are not due recompense for earlier splendors in the grass. "Wo bist du, wo bist du, mein geliebtest Land' " (118) is the old German song that haunts not only Carl but also Cather, who wrote about the "fierce necessity" and "sharp desire" at the beginning of life in her introductory poem to the novel, a poem in which both necessity and desire are "Singing and singing, / Out of the lips of silence, / Out of the earthy dusk." Although Cather dedicated *O Pioneers!* to Sarah Orne Jewett because "in this book I tried to tell the story of the people as truthfully and simply as if I were telling it to her by word of mouth" (*KA* 448), the evocative phrase "the lips of silence" intimates that this novel about a heroine "who could not write much" or "very freely" (286) would give way as inevitably as would the mother tongue to a kind of paternal or patriarchal speech.

Alexandra's mental "white book" helps explain why every story Cather wrote about exciting adventures on the frontier can be matched by another sort of tale about the ways in which the prairie kills or stunts the artist. Typical are "A Wagner Matinee" (1904, 1920), in which a frontier woman responds to a Boston concert with dismay at the beauty she has forgotten during a life of drudgery, and "The Sculptor's Funeral" (1905, 1920), in which the provinces are a perpetual funeral from which the aspiring creator must escape, plots dramatizing a competition between art and nature that is related to Cather's identification of artistry with masculinity. Although Jewett had advised Cather early in her career that "a woman writ[ing] in the man's character . . . must always be something of a masquerade,"[63] precisely that "masquerade" enabled the younger author to question her precursor's more utopian association of women and nature.

As an analysis of this issue, *My Ántonia* devotes itself, after the opening section about the arrival of Jim and Ántonia on the Divide, to an examination of the social construction of gender, and the novel specifically identifies the ways in which conventionally masculine prerogatives need to be understood in terms of what Turner called "a recurrence of the process of evolution" in the west. As James E. Miller, Jr., has noted, "The books of *My Ántonia* reflect the varying stages of this evolutionary process of cultural development."[64] But Jim Burden's progress from the prairie town of Black Hawk, to the university town of Lincoln, and finally to Harvard and New York does not illuminate what Miller calls the "greater cultural riches farther East" as much as it records what Gerda Lerner, writing about *The Creation of Patriarchy*, describes as "[t]he contradiction between women's centrality and active role in creating society and their marginality in the meaning-giving process of interpretation and explanation."[65]

As in the earlier novel, in *My Ántonia* education functions as the central symbol of childhood's end and of the beginning of social roles that are as Finch put it, "dessigned." When Jim and Ántonia move to the town of Black Hawk, he begins his course of study while she becomes a "hired girl." Although both evolve into a seemingly "higher" stage of cultural development, Cather emphasizes the "lost freedom of the farming country" (145). While Jim learns how to "fight, play 'keeps,' tease the little girls, and use forbidden words" (145), Ántonia sews "pretty clothes for herself" (175) or wears party dresses and high-heeled shoes on her trips downtown. Through Jim's portraits of two unhappy, middle-class marriages and of the vitality of a number of immigrant, working-class girls, moreover, Black Hawk itself becomes a symbol of the effects of gender and class divisions.

Both the Harling and the Cutter families exhibit a tension at least partially produced by a mercantile economy that reduces married women to private property. Energetic and jolly, Mrs. Harling must stop all the activities of her household so as to devote herself entirely to her husband, a grain merchant and cattle buyer, when he returns home to demand "a quiet house" and "all his wife's attention" (156). The "arrogant" and "commanding figure" of Christian Harling, with "a glittering diamond upon [his] little finger" (157), seems antithetical to the "peculiar combination of old-maidishness and licentiousness" (211) in Wick Cutter. But Cutter—a moneylender, whose almost parodic name evokes castration anxieties that suit his hectic philandering—is just as imperious as the entrepreneur. Engaging himself in "perpetual war-fare" (210) with a wife who confines her domestic activity to china painting, Cutter escalates a sex war in order to gain ultimate control over his property and his wife by murdering her and going on to commit suicide only after he has established that his survival beyond her death invalidates her will.

Just as the couples in Black Hawk illustrate the debilitating consequences of marriage for the wife whose personal or legal will must be negated, the "hired girls" represent Cather's idiosyncratic version of New Women who are producers rather than products. Although the phrase "hired girls" suggests that girls are hired and fired (until, as women, they are taken off the market), the immigrant girls who are helping make their mothers' lives more comfortable evade being owned, and they do so by being hired, thereby resisting both their mothers' sacrifices and the dependence of the middle-class wives for whom they work. Obtaining rooms of their own in town, girls like Lena Lingard and Tiny Soderball, who were "wild" on the farm (165), continue to be "considered as dangerous as high explosives" (203) by the respectable townfolk. Indeed, they exhibit a subversive eroticism that is attributable in part to the "out-of-door work" that transforms them into "almost a race apart" (198). While the refined daughters of the bourgeoisie seem to Jim "cut off below the shoulders, like cherubs" (199), the resourcefulness of the regiment of working young women makes them "a menace to the social order" (201).

Of course, when Jim writes with pride about "my country girls" (201), he is endowing them with "a kind of glamour" (229) that springs not only from his romantic imagination but also from a financial security which distances him from the arduous reality of their labors. Indeed, three major episodes in the second section of the novel establish how the engendering of Jim and Ántonia further widens the gap between their situations. First, at the popular dances in Black Hawk Ántonia performs the schottisch with the adventurous audacity of a boy, and Jim moons after the hired girls with the sentimentality of a stereotypical girl; however, when both are prohibited from attending these festivities (Ántonia by her employers the Harlings, Jim by his grandparents) Ántonia defiantly leaves the Harling household to work for the Cutters so she can continue a flirtation with the "professional ladies' man" (223) Larry Donovan, but Jim decides to spend his time dutifully studying Latin so as to prepare himself for the university. In other words, following the scripts Freud considered normative for girls and boys, Ántonia devotes herself to romance while Jim pursues his ambitions.[66]

Second, both Ántonia and Jim come to terms with the death of Mr. Shimerda in a way that reflects, on the one hand, her puzzled entrapment in her parents' tragedy and, on the other hand, his induction into the *parius sermo* of the classical education he will pursue at college. Ántonia's story about a tramp who "jumped head-first" into a threshing machine and got "all beat and cut to pieces" by the belt (178) leads her to wonder "What would anybody want to kill themselves in summer for?" (179) Because she implicitly attributes her father's suicide to the hardships of winter and because she later accepts a story of her parents' marriage that suggests her father lowered himself by marrying her illegitimately pregnant mother, Ántonia seems destined to repeat their fates. Thus, after her romance with the railroad conductor Larry Donovan—a hired man who is fired and a no-man whose superficial sophistication impresses her—she goes through an illegitimate pregnancy and eventually marries a "crumpled little man" from the city who "often [grows] discouraged" (356, 342) on the farm they manage.

But for Jim, Mr. Shimerda provides a crucial "positional identification" with a male figure through whom he certifies his masculinity. According to Nancy Chodorow, the construction of masculine identity—based as it is on difference from the mother—depends on the boy's displacing his earliest identification with the mother onto the (secondary) figure of the father, and Jim's development illuminates both the fragility and the empowerment produced by this process. Not only does Mr. Shimerda seem to return after death to Jim, who receives such "vivid pictures" of the old man's past that he believes "they might have been Mr. Shimerda's memories, not yet faded out from the air in which they had haunted him" (102), but the immigrant also becomes a kind of ghostly instructor, for eventually Jim dedicates his high school commencement oration to the dead man. Commenting on an elegiac convention from "Lycidas" to "Thyrsis," Cather examines not only the limits but also the necessity of the male bonding that shapes the pastoral tradition in which she wants to place her own artistic accomplishments.[67]

Although Jim and Ántonia take a holiday in "a sort of No Man's Land" (233) by the river, then, a third episode seals their quite different educations into masculinity and feminity. When Jim goes over to the Cutters' house so Ántonia need not stay there alone to guard "their silver and old usury notes" in the couple's absence (247), he becomes the prey of Wick Cutter's surprise sexual attack. Like Lena Lingard, who had hidden in Ántonia's bed to flee from the attacks of a jealous wife, Jim is made to understand his vulnerability when he sleeps in Ántonia's stead. A "battered object" (249), he is so humiliated by the would-be rapist and by his powerlessness to punish the man that he turns his rage against Ántonia: "I hated her almost as much as I hated Cutter. She had let me in for all this disgustingness" (250). Besides illustrating the symbiotic emotional system in which the Cutters collaborate ("Perhaps he got the feeling of being a rake more from his wife's rage and amazement than from any experiences of his own" [253]), the scene of Jim's humiliation is a spur to the subsequent construction of a gendered identity that will establish his difference from the woman he now despises, for to be like a woman or in the place of a woman is to be subjected to rape.

In his quest to avoid a feminization associated with violent penetration, Jim seeks another mentor like Mr. Shimerda, and he finds a literary precursor who illuminates Cather's views on the "positional identification" boys need to become men (and women writers need to adopt to exploit what we have called, following Freud, the "masculinity complex").[68] The black plough magnified against the circular disk of the sun—an image "heroic in size, a picture writing on the sun" (245) that Jim sees just before leaving for the university—evokes the destiny of a son who seeks to inherit a "pen [which] was fitted to the matter as the plough is to the furrow" (264). According to Jim, that phallic pen produced "the perfect utterance" of Virgil in the *Georgics,* and it is conveyed to him by his college teacher Gaston Cleric, whose name implies that he is the celibate cleric who will confirm the initiation Jim requires. That this head of the Latin department is "enfeebled by a long illness in Italy" (257) qualifies the monastic fellowship pursued under a map of ancient Rome which Jim has hung on his walls. Yet, reiterating the veneration Dante had for his "sweet teacher" Virgil, Jim is to Cleric as Dante was to Virgil, and so the acolyte assents to the redefinition of his origins Cleric provides when he recites Statius: " 'I speak of the "Aeneid," mother to me and nurse to me in poetry' " (262).

Jim himself, then, experiences what Walter Ong identifies as the puberty rite of a classical education that defines men of letters as the inheritors of a patrilineal literary history.[69] Now the images of his past life are endowed with a "new appeal" (262), although he "scarcely stopped to wonder whether they were alive anywhere else, or how" (262). It is, of course, Virgil's "Georgics" which supplies not only the epigraph for Cather's novel but the epitaph for the nostalgic strain of Jim's reflection that, "in the lives of mortals, the best days are the first to flee" (263). The primacy of the "first days" is directly transmuted by Cleric and Jim into the primacy of the author: "for I shall be the first, if I live, to bring the Muse into my country" (*"Primus ego in patriam mecum . . . deducam Musas"* [264]). But, as Blanche Gelfant has observed, Jim's selective memory erases probably the most imperative phrase for Jim in Virgil's verse on "the best days," a line set in the context of cattle breeding:

"Release the males."[70] Released through Cleric from his first days, Jim consolidates the hired girls into a monolithic "muse" in order to claim his "patria" as his own, or so the possessive *My* in his title suggests. Such a heritage ensures the fact that Ántonia in particular and women in general will be of the utmost importance imaginatively, even though they are practically either insignificant or absent.

But Ántonia's name implies that this heroine who is christened in honor of the patron saint of lost things can never be fully recaptured in Jim's paternal language. And the centrality of the "Georgics"—not a "high" genre like the epic or ode but a farming handbook that might be said to resemble Alexandra Bergson's "white book" with its "clear writing about weather and beasts and growing things" (205)—constitutes precisely the compromise with the *patrius sermo* which Cather was seeking. In addition, Jim recognizes the priority of his muses—"If there were no girls like them in the world, there would be no poetry" (270)—even while he seems to sense that their image, floating *"like* the memory of an actual experience" (271; emphasis ours), displaces their reality, that the words meant to celebrate them in some sense replace them.

On the one hand, through her identification with Jim, Cather illuminates the linguistic potency she herself attained by exploiting male narrators and thereby establishing her distance from (and, as we argued in *The War of the Words*, thralldom to) a female muse; on the other hand, the disappearance of Ántonia from the novel as well as the emergence of Lena Lingard modifies an imaginative posture that draws inspiration from a fictionalized femininity which—for all its power—is itself denied aesthetic outlet. For this reason, Jim's stereotypes of the threateningly erotic Lena (who appears in his dreams with a reaping hook to seduce him) and of the maternally supportive Ántonia (who refuses his kisses and treats him "like a kid" [224]) are at least in part refuted by the subsequent lives of these women. Lena's staunch rejection of any relationship with men and Ántonia's unmarried pregnancy allow Cather to interrogate two crucial incarnations of the muse, specifically the femme fatale and the earth goddess.

When Jim falls under Lena's seductive influence during his college days, the lure of the femme fatale is presented as a diversion from his serious studies, an entrance into a community of other men enthralled by her, and a kind of slumming, for Jim hovers between his attraction to Lena's fleshy pliancy and ironic diversion at her use of such "flat commonplaces" as naming "a leg a 'limb' or a house a 'home' " (281). As a seamstress who creates the clothes that make the man, however, Lena is clear that "as soon as you marry," men "turn into cranky old fathers," and she therefore rejects domesticity, defining it as "always too many children, a cross man and work piling up around a sick woman"

(291). But the sickness of the woman who is kept and the crossness of the man who is, or plays the role of, a father are also dramatized even in romantic settings through the longest digression in this section of the novel, the description of a performance of *Camille* that Lena and Jim attend.

If artistry in Black Hawk finds suitable expression in the primitive music of the black pianist Blind d'Arnault, Dumas's play appears to represent the more refined culture of Lincoln. Yet, in spite of Jim's racist description of his character, Blind d'Arnault draws forth an intense voice from the "mouth" of the piano that belies "the note of docile subservience" in a performer who "would never consent to be led" (184, 183), while Dumas's play records a heterosexual thralldom shown to be literally sickening, for Marguerite, over whom Jim and Lena weep, is a quite different "hired girl" than those in Black Hawk. The scenes of *Camille*—Armand's love of the consumptive courtesan, his father's intervention, his jealousy of her other lovers, and his remorse at her death—cause Jim to congratulate himself on his and Lena's maturity: "Lena was at least a woman, and I was a man" (275). But Marguerite's consumption nevertheless reinforces Cather's argument that the woman who functions like currency will be consumed in the exchange between men. Predictably, therefore, Jim heeds his tutor's advice about the disease of desire ("You won't recover yourself while you are playing about with this handsome Norwegian" [289]) and extricates himself from Lena by going with Gaston Cleric to the same bastion of male solidarity that fascinated Henry James in *The Bostonians,* Harvard University. Understandably, too, Lena, refusing the part of the in-valid invalid, eventually settles down in San Francisco with Tiny Soderball, who lost three toes in the Alaskan wilderness but emerged with a fortune from a gold mine deeded to her by a man who lost his life.

If Jim's portrait of the femme fatale is curiously at odds with Lena's fate, his celebration of Ántonia as an earth goddess is just as qualified by the personal repercussions of her destiny. But at first Jim's education at Harvard has made him so priggish that he is "bitterly disappointed" (298) in Ántonia, whom he tries to shut out of his mind. Lost to Jim, she is nevertheless found by the Widow Steavens, who relates the details of Ántonia's seduction, betrayal, pregnancy, and lonely childbearing. "The Pioneer Woman's Story" is simultaneously the tale of Ántonia's single motherhood and of the Widow Steavens' pioneering nursing, stories Jim can hear but not tell. When those tales do propel Jim toward a meeting with Ántonia, his declaration of plans to study law in New York City contrasts with her determination to "live and die" on the prairie (320).

Yet in a mystical moment Jim glimpses on the horizon the sun setting "like a great golden globe in the low west" and the moon rising "in the east, as big as a cart-wheel," and he interprets this primal scene as a natural hieroglyph. Not merely solipsistic, Jim's statement "You really are a part of me" (321) needs to be understood in the context of these "two luminaries confront[ing] each other across the level land, resting on opposite edges of the world" (322). For Ántonia, setting in the west, and Jim, rising in the east, represent precisely the polarities—allegiances divided between female imaginative primacy and male aesthetic ambition—that energized Cather's own artistry as well as her belief that "at the very bottom of . . . memory" most people resemble Jim in believing that even during maturity "a boy and girl ran along beside me, as our shadows used to do, laughing and whispering to each other in the grass" (321–22).

Through her ambivalent identification with Jim, Cather can mythologize America as Herland even while she presents such a mythology as compensatory and belated. After a twenty-year absence, Jim returns to the Divide to discover a matriarchal land ruled by an Ántonia who has become a kind of fertility goddess. It is, of course, the fruit cave—from which her children emerge in "a veritable explosion of life" (339)—that best symbolizes "the miracle" (331) through which Ántonia fires the imagination by revealing "the goodness of planting and tending and harvesting at last." Because she is "a rich mine of life, like the founders of early races" (353), Jim can feel "like a boy" again (345) in her presence, as can her husband. Referring to his wife's leniency—"She ain't always so strict with me" (365)—Cuzak sounds like a child who has "been made the instrument of Ántonia's special mission" (367). That mission—enacted through childbearing, storytelling, farming, and housekeeping—turns Ántonia into an oral historian of the lives of the obscure, for she "had always been one to leave images in the mind that did not fade—that grew stronger with time." These images, fixed in Jim's memory "like the old woodcuts of one's first primer" are supplemented by Ántonia, herself an image who evokes "immemorial human attitudes which we recognize by instinct as universal and true" (353).

The "universal history" that Cather records in the "land with no history" pays tribute to the traditions of creativity that Ántonia's domestic artistry preserves, for Turner's emphasis on the frontier as a "gate of escape from the bondage of the past" (38) modulates into Cather's celebration of the frontier as a gate of escape from the bondage of the present. Delivered at a session of the American Historical Association held at the Chicago World's Columbian Exposition, Turner's thesis mourned the closing of the frontier and sounded the death knell to a central myth of virility. That the exposition also contained the Woman's Building, with its exhibition honoring female accomplishments, indicates how this moment of masculine enervation is linked to female exhilaration, and certainly in both *O Pioneers!* and *My Ántonia* Cather imaginatively opens the frontier to women.

Yet Jim's mythologizing of Ántonia as the creatrix of America allows him firmly to associate the female with reproductive forces that presumably legitimize women's exclusion from the privileges that make possible not only his life story but also the writing of her story. Furthermore, by identifying Ántonia so closely with the frontier, he confines her influence to the past, to the best days which are the first to flee. By focusing exclusively on Ántonia's power as a mother, moreover, Jim implies that the biological function provides the only proper role for women who are supposed to produce boys, or so the last section's title—"Cuzak's Boys"—implies. The frame of *My Ántonia* brings these points home. Jim is said to be married to an "executive" woman—someone like the superficial salon hostess Flavia—who "play[s] the patroness" to a group of eastern painters and poets of "advanced ideas and mediocre ability" (intro.). Economically independent, intellectually arrogant, Mrs. Burden is one of Jim's adult burdens.

Having produced no children, moreover, his wife is described in the first version of the frame as a woman who "gave one of her town houses for a Suffrage headquarters, produced one of her own plays at the Princess Theater, was arrested for picketing during a garment-makers' strike, etc.,"[71] and even in the revised version of the "Introduction" her "energetic" temperament recalls the assiduous intensity of Mrs. Cutter, whose murder—recounted in the final pages of *My Ántonia*—demonstrates that such barren, burdensome, modern wives are still destined to be fed to the wolves. Traveling in a railroad car crossing Iowa, always on the verge of reaching his mythic Nebraska but never entering it, Jim refers to his wife with a disgust that undercuts his efforts to unburden himself by eulogizing the "country, the conditions, the whole adventure of our childhood" (intro.) and by celebrating the fecundity of Ántonia—a prematurely aging, toothless, "battered" woman (332).

As Cather's writing progressed and she left the midwestern frontier—whose strangeness was at least in part (as was the uncanniness of Kôr for Haggard) a result of a reversal of the normative relations between men and women—her effort to recover female potency became more hidden. "The world broke in two in 1922 or thereabouts" (NUF, Prefatory Note), Cather remarked. In work composed directly before and after that moment of such landmark publications as *The Waste Land, Jacob's Room,* and *Ulysses,* her fiction described the inescapable commodification of modern women and the escalation of sex wars, both of which help to explain her attraction to male narrators and to all-male communities as well as her implicit admission that both functioned as a camouflage which virtually made women's most profound experiences unsayable. But perhaps her greatest literary problem—broached in both *O Pioneers!* and *My Ántonia* through her characters' various efforts to disentangle love from erotic desire and erotic desire from aesthetic ambition—resulted from her fatal attraction to a renunciation of passion.

Cather came closest to expressing Edith Wharton's revulsion at the commodification of women in the period between her two prairie novels when she returned to the figure of the prima donna at the center of *The Song of the Lark*. Two stories in particular—"The Diamond Mine" (1916, 1920) and "Scandal" (1919, 1920)—deal with female singers who suffer because they "appealed to the acquisitive instinct in men."[72] For her rapacious husbands, her coach, and her sisters, Cressida Garnet in the first story functions like "a natural source of wealth; a copper vein, a diamond mine": "It seemed never to occur to them that this golden stream, whether it rushed or whether it trickled, came out of the industry, out of the mortal body of a woman" (*YBM*, 119). Similarly, although in the second story Kitty Ayrshire is "the sort of person who makes myths" (*YBM* 159), gossip about her has been generated by a public that finds her not a "rich mine of life" (like Ántonia) but a "natural source of wealth" (like Cressida) and specifically by one Siegmund Stein, who creates a counterfeit companion to impersonate the prima donna. As a worker in a shirtwaist factory, the impostor Ruby Mohr is at the opposite end of the economic ladder from Kitty. But when the singer herself is exploited through the media manipulations of Stein, the genuine Kitty knows about the fake Kitty that "She and I are in the same boat" (*YBM* 177), for they are both "immured within a harem" (*YBM* 176) by "a patron of the arts" (*YBM* 168) who uses them to certify his social climbing. While indefensible, the anti-Semitism that issues in portraits of Cressida's parasitic coach and Kitty's exploitative businessman is related to Cather's view that women are victimized by a cash nexus that reduces them to their market value.[73]

"You are all the same," Kitty explains to a male companion; "You never see our real faces" (*YBM* 164). In several texts that also display her sense of escalating sex antagonism, Cather went on to analyze what Kitty calls the "cheap conception" (*YBM* 165) of women that men construct. Marian Forrester, the central character of *A Lost Lady* (1923), has "the power of suggesting things much lovelier than herself" to the men she attracts.[74] And because she is "not willing to immolate herself . . . and die with the pioneer period to which she belonged" (169), her destiny reflects the fate of frontier women confronted by an emerging "generation of shrewd young men, trained to petty economies" (107). When, after Marian's husband's death, the avaricious Ivy Peters "unconcernedly put both arms around her, his hands meeting over her breast" (169), his possessiveness is ominous, for earlier in the novel he is shown capturing a woodpecker whom he addresses as "Miss Female" and whose eyes he slits with a knife (24). That the "Old West . . . settled by dreamers, great-hearted adventurers," is now "at the mercy of men like Ivy Peters, who had never dared anything, never risked anything" (106), explains the desperation of a lady as lost as the "wild and desperate" creature that blindly beats its wings in the branches of a tree (925).

Just as symbolic to the narrator of her story as Marian Forrester is to hers, Myra Henshawe of *My Mortal Enemy* (1926) exhibits "something in her nature that one rarely saw, but nearly always felt; a compelling, passionate, overmastering something for which I had no name."[75] If Marian Forrester gains social security from her husband in *A Lost Lady,* Myra loses her wealth when she marries for love. But like Marian Forrester, Myra Henshawe, who is "not at all modern in her make-up" (111), ends up "crippled" and "broken" (80), in her case because she and her husband have been "lovers and enemies at the same time" (105). Cather viewed a *Chicago Tribune* review—describing "the steady rhythm of the fundamental hatred of the sexes one for the other and their irresistible attraction one for the other"—as the most accurate assessment of the theme of *My Mortal Enemy.*[76] And certainly, although Oswald believes that throughout his marriage he "nurs[ed] the mother of the girl who ran away with me. Nothing ever took that girl from me" (121), the ferocity of his wife's dying whisper—"Why must I die like this, alone with my mortal enemy?" (113)—represents an intensification of Cather's identification of sex and war, an identification that explains not only Myra Henshawe's but also Cather's attraction to an ascetic Catholicism in which *"seeking is finding . . .* desire was fulfillment" (112).[77]

But it is in *The Professor's House* (1925) that Cather most brilliantly explores the nausea instilled by erotic desire, a nausea that threatens to lead to the repression of all aesthetic ambition. When she wrote that book, Cather explained,

> I tried to make Professor St. Peter's house rather overcrowded and stuffy with new things; American proprieties, clothes, furs, petty ambitions, quivering jealousies—until one got rather stifled. Then I wanted to open the square window and let in the fresh air that blew off the Blue Mesa, and the fine disregard of trivialities which was in Tom Outland's face and in his behaviour. [*OW* 31–32]

Cather compared her formal experiment to a Dutch painting in which living rooms full of furniture contrast with the view glimpsed through windows where "one saw the masts of ships, or a stretch of grey sea" (*OW* 31–32). Through this technique of interpolation, she dramatized, on the one hand, her withdrawal from the trivial proprieties of "overcrowded and stuffy" interiors that epitomize the feminization of modern society and, on the other hand, her attraction to the freedom she previously associated with manly battle yarns or stout sea tales. In other words, she could juxtapose an adventure story the "boy in us" loved with the novel of manners, creating a hybrid genre that captures her impulse to throw out all the furniture of femininity as well as masculinity.

That St. Peter's household is not only overfurnished but also fatally feminized is signaled through the figures of his wife and his two daughters, all of whom exhibit a voracious materialism. The new house purchased with the prize money won by Professor St. Peter's eight-volume *Spanish Adventurers* seems so alien to him that he refuses to relinquish the dilapidated study he had shared with the seamstress, Augusta, in his old, rented home. Although his wife Lillian grows "severe" when her husband opposes her will, with her two sons-in-law "she had begun the game of being a woman all over again," a game that involves dressing up for, and flirting with, them.[78] Lillian's older daughter Rosamond and her husband, who are building a "Norwegian manor house" (39) on the funds deeded by her dead fiancée Tom Outland, compete in ostentation with her younger sister Kathleen and her husband, a struggling journalist who remembers Tom Outland and sneers at the ersatz mansion to which his inheritors are applying the young scientist's name: "Outland, outlandish!" (42). While Professor St. Peters' sons-in-law are at least partially redeemed from crudity by acts of generosity, his daughters have entered into a catty competition that makes one "singularly haughty" (82) over her "org[ies] of acquisition" (154), while the other turns "green with envy" (86).

"Your bond with him was social, and it follows the laws of society, and they are based on property," St. Peter explains; "Mine wasn't" (63). In opposition to his relatives, who are cashing in on Outland's inventions, St. Peter understands that his relationship with his student Tom Outland might liberate him from the laws of society, of property, and of heterosexuality, for through Tom Outland's tale of his boyish adventure on the Mesa the Professor reaches back to "another boy . . . the boy the Professor had long ago left behind him . . . the original, unmodified Godfrey St. Peter" (263). "After he met Lillian Ormsley, St. Peter forgot that boy had ever lived" (264), but through Tom Outland's story he recovers "his original ego" and discovers that "he was solitary and must always be so; he had never married, never been a father" (265). As she had before, Cather contrasts an authentic, original self—before it was "modified by sex" (267)—with the falsities of sex roles.

Like D. H. Lawrence in such works as "The Woman Who Rode Away" and *The Plumed Serpent* (both about Mexico), Cather uses the southwest to reconstruct prehistoric native culture in order to analyze the interaction between civilized and primitive societies. Yet unlike Lawrence, whom she met and admired but who mythologized and mystified masculinity,[79] Cather seeks in "Tom Outland's Story" to excavate a land beyond gender, not a Herland so much as an Outland that stands in direct contrast to "our" land. To be sure, when Tom and his buddy Rodney Blake light out for the territory around the mesa, riding the range with cattle for the summer, their adventures are similar to those of the books they take with them, *Robinson Crusoe* in particular. Ten years younger than his "pal," Tom knows that Rodney "liked to be an older brother" (185). When they set up housekeeping with a castaway Englishman, they recapture a mythic American boyhood so that their cabin shines "like a playhouse" (197), and they are thrilled by the prospect of climbing "the naked blue rock set down alone in the plain" and becoming "the first men up there" (186–87). Like the three explorers in Haggard's *She,* in other words, Cather's threesome view their confrontation with an *Ur*-culture as a kind of initiation.

At the same time, however, Tom comes neither to conquer nor to appropriate but to excavate and preserve a lost civilization. Indeed, in the myth-haunted territory of Cow Canyon, Tom Outland first feels "I had found everything instead of having lost everything" (250). Tracing his way through a deep canyon, Tom follows runaway cattle onto an idyllic mesa where he and Rodney find intact the ruins of an ancient cliff city. Cataloguing the relics left in a terrain inhabited hundreds of years ago by Pueblo Indians who lived "facing an ocean of clear air" (213), Tom speculates they "they were probably wiped out . . . by some roving Indian tribe without . . . domestic virtues" (221). The beautifully proportioned, harmonious city of stone seems "to mark a difference" (203) to Tom, to represent an aesthetic and spiritual community not only among its individual members but also between humanity and nature, a peaceful world whose relics—pots and utensils like those found by Thea in Panther Canyon—will be either ignored or exploited by the corrupt politicians with whom he attempts to negotiate in Washington, D.C.

Discovered on Christmas eve, the cliff city becomes a "sacred spot" toward which Tom feels "reverence" (221). Here, then, "in a little group of houses stuck up in a high arch we called the Eagle's Nest," Tom and Rodney discover a murdered woman whom they name Mother Eve:

wounded in her side, she has decomposed into "dried flesh," and "Her mouth was open as if she were screaming," while "her face, through all those years, had kept a look of terrible agony." After Tom returns to the mesa from his doomed trip to Washington, he is outraged at Rodney's selling the results of their excavation and in particular at the sale of the dried mummy who is worth more to him than "any living woman" (244). But, as the spirit of the place, Mother Eve proved recalcitrant to Rodney's efforts to transport her by mule into the modern world. Indeed, she "refused to leave. She went to the bottom of Black Canyon and carried [the] . . . mule along with her" (244). Angered by the profit Rodney has sought to gain for them both, Tom realizes that what they had found "wasn't mine or his" (245). But perhaps the murder of Mother Eve marked a devolution into "mine or his," a decline into property and the murderous appropriation of the woman as wife. Certainly one visitor suggests that she might have been "an unfaithful wife" punished with death (223). Certainly, too, Mother Eve's demise defines the fall of a culture that was different, and, as her name suggests, a paradise lost.

For Cather's Tom Outland and for her professorial protagonist, that death poses, too, the problem of a paradise which cannot be regained. Tom is himself killed in World War I and thereby saved, according to at least some of his survivors, from the fallen materialism of the older man's new household, while the aging professor with the patriarchal name of Napoleon Godfrey St. Peter reconstructs Tom Outland's narrative about the ancient cliffs and glyphs of Cow Canyon in order to learn how to die. More specifically, the professor remembers his own prepatriarchal self, the boy he was before he became a man and a father, in order to confront death. Renouncing the Law of the Father that tied him to his family, this disillusioned scholar retreats to an attic furnished with female forms—the dressmaker's dummies used by Augusta—and in the end it is the fateful and august figure of the spinning spinster who guides him on his spiritual passage out of both life and patriarchy. "Like the taste of bitter herbs," Augusta hasn't "any of the sentimentality that comes from a fear of dying" and "her manner of speaking about it [makes] death seem less uncomfortable" (281).

Rigorous in her dedication to the Virgin Mary, Augusta represents not the mastery of men but the mystery of women. Fitting dummies with intricate female costumes, Augusta, as the professor concludes, "makes those terrible women"—dummies and mummies alike—"entirely plausible!" (101). Her disquieting muses consist of a headless, armless female torso called "the bust," a figure that looks billowy enough to provide "deep-breathing softness and rest safe" but that actually presents a painfully hard, "unsympathetic surface," and a full-length figure in a wire skirt with a bosom resembling "a strong wire bird-cage" (18). In their mechanical fakery as they are tricked up in new party dresses, they are suitable emblems of the feminine for an intellectual who identifies with Euripides, a man who "lived in a cave by the sea" because "he had observed women so closely all his life" (156). But Augusta herself—a solitary and spiritual creator of contemporary patterns—seems to represent an earlier and almost mystical female wisdom, all that is left from the self-reliance of her predecessors, Alexandra and Ántonia. At last, then, when the professor, once the master who propounded the secrets of history to his race, is sacrificed to Augusta's bitter herbs, he heeds the muses of the attic room and seeks suicide. That Augusta drags him back to the living and that he accepts with resignation the "bloomless" end she has promised him only heighten his sense that his remaining life is a living death. Whether Cather identifies with the authorial professor or the authoritative Augusta, therefore, *The Professor's House* demonstrates how preoccupied this writer had become with the renunciation of both erotic and aesthetic desire.

"Desire under all desires": St. Peter eventually realizes that his quest has led him to relinquish desire altogether, "to live without delight" (282), and through him Cather examines her own attempts to reach back to the "root of the matter" beyond all the "conjugating [of] the verb 'to love' " (264–65), beyond the "painful" bond of "the paternal relation" (281). Both in her final works and in her final acts, moreover, she implicitly recognized the problems of just such renunciation, problems that speak of her own painful and potentially self-destructive efforts to find an eros uncontaminated by eroticism. Perhaps the two figures who emblematize that effort best are the young girl Cecile and the recluse Jeanne Le Ber in Cather's historical novel about seventeenth-century Quebec, *Shadows on the Rock* (1931), for Cecile—a ten-year-old who dutifully takes her dead mother's place in perpetuating the domestic rituals of her father's household—represents a blessed and virginal girlhood destined to pass away, while Jeanne Le Ber—the cloistered solitary who rejects marriage to conserve the most rigorous spiritual rituals of the Roman Catholic Church—only attains a room of her own in a walled-up isolation that testifies to the anguish of her asceticism.[80]

That Cather grew ever more dependent in her fiction on historical sources, that she composed a number of tales about the fatality of the kind of talent that she had celebrated in her earlier fiction, and that she found it increasingly difficult to integrate nostalgic portraits of childhood into the plots of her novels reinforce our point that *The Professor's House* had brought together tensions whose resolution would weaken her last works.[81] Biographical explanations for Cather's retreat into pessimism can certainly be found. After 1927, when she was forced to leave her Bank Street apartment, she suffered through the death of her father, the prolonged illness and death of her mother, the impoverishment of farming friends during the Depression, the fatal disease of Isabelle (McClung) Hambourg, and the demise of her brothers. But at least one factor relating to her late conservatism may be attributed to the radical struggle in which she had continually engaged throughout her oeuvre, an effort to recapture an oneiric vision of ontological freedom before or beyond the disastrous divisiveness of sex roles and sex antagonism, an effort that was defeated by the culturally prescribed feminization that generated her (and many other women's) ineradicable discontents.

Finally, Cather confronted not only her alienation from contemporary femininity but also the ways in which the "masculinity complex" that shaped her writing career might modulate into a renunciation of aesthetic desire, or so the late story "Before Breakfast" implies. Here an aging businessman fulfills St. Peter's dream of escaping his clever, cultivated, and cold family, for Henry Grenfell feels "like a whole man" when he vacations alone every year in a cabin on Grand Manan Island. After arising early, just as he is about to use his eye drops, Grenfell witnesses Venus—"Serene, impersonal splendour. Merciless perfection, ageless sovereignty" (*OB* 144)—shining in the morning sky, and he goes out into the "new-born light, yellow as gold" (*OB* 160), in which he glimpses on the ancient rock of the coast a woman bathing in the sea, a young woman who seems to fulfill the promise of the title "Coming, Aphrodite!": "Her bathing-suit was pink. If a clam stood upright and graciously opened its shell, it would look like that" (*OB* 164). Half exasperated by the silliness of her swimming in "the death-chill" (*OB* 165) of the Atlantic, he nevertheless understands in "the light . . . just waking up" (*OB* 160) how Aphrodite can fleetingly appear between the eyedrops of his early toilet and the taking of toast and tea at breakfast.[82]

Before the dawning of culture and presumably after its demise stands the vision of desire that had haunted Kate Chopin but that can never spring Grenfell from the "jail" of his business associates, his wife, or his children (*OB* 150), to whom he is destined to return without communicating his mystical sense of momentary release. Like Grenfell, whose name evokes a fall from the green world that Marvell eulogizes in "The Garden," Cather herself found it impossible to speak of some of the most intense revelations she herself had had of Aphrodite. In contrast to Edith Wharton, who wrote a "note 'for my biographer' " so as to communicate from beyond the grave, Cather dedicated herself to "the thing not named" by destroying all of her letters to Isabelle McClung, the woman who provided the attic workroom that served as a model for the home of the muses in *The Professor's House*.[83] In addition, Cather's will stipulated that "neither my Executors nor my Trustee shall consent to, or permit, the publication in any form whatsoever, of the whole, or any part of any letter or letters written by me in my lifetime, nor the use, exploitation or disposal of any other right therein."[84] But what Cather felt to be culturally unsayable nevertheless spoke through her characters' "lips of silence" most luminously in the "happy Garden-state" of her early fiction and most somberly when her "green thought in a green shade" led to the recognition that only by "Annihilating all that's made" could she "wander solitary . . . in Paradise alone."

III
Reinventing Gender

"She Meant What I Said": Lesbian Double Talk

If ever—come now! Relieve
this intolerable pain!

What my heart most hopes will
happen, make happen; you yourself join forces on my side!

—Sappho

From the depths of my past, I return to you,
Mytilene, crossing the disparate centuries,
Bringing you my passion, my youth and my faith,
And my love, like a present of aromatics . . .

—Renée Vivien

She is the island of artistic perfection where the lover of ancient beauty
(shipwrecked in the modern world) may yet find foothold and take breath
and gain courage for new adventures and dream of yet unexplored
continents and realms of future artistic achievement. She is the wise
Sappho.

—H. D.

I have often thought that she meant what I said.

—Gertrude Stein

If such mainstream artists as Edith Wharton and Willa Cather analyzed
not just the discontents of feminization but, more fundamentally, the
pains of gender, in what ways did more marginalized writers reinvent
or reimagine sex roles in this period? As we have noted, many fin-de-
siècle sexologists sought to engender the new in markedly different
ways. In 1896, for example, a year after the sensational prosecution of
Oscar Wilde for indulging in "the love that dare not speak its name,"

215

Edward Carpenter placed a vindication of the rights of the "intermediate sex" at the center of his *Love's Coming of Age,* a treatise on the
erotic that was to become one of the most widely read and influential
works in the new field of sexology that was just beginning to evolve at
the turn of the century. Describing people "born . . . as it were on the
dividing line between the sexes," he drew on K. H. Ulrichs's definition
of "Urnings" as beings "belonging distinctly to one sex as far as their
bodies are concerned [but] belong[ing] *mentally* and *emotionally* to the
other" so as to insist that "beneath the surface of society" there was "a
large class" of such "homogenic" types.[1]

Carpenter was popularizing a view of sexual deviance that was also
pioneered by Havelock Ellis in England as well as Magnus Hirschfeld,
Richard von Krafft-Ebing, and Ulrichs himself in Germany. By 1914,
when Carpenter became the first president of the newly formed British
Society for the Study of Sex Psychology, the group of scientists for
whom he spoke had begun to provide a vocabulary for experiences that
had been virtually unsayable. To be sure, as historians of lesbianism
from Lillian Faderman to Carroll Smith-Rosenberg have shown, the
entrance into language of such concepts as "inversion" and "perversion" was usually associated with a kind of essentialism (as in Ulrichs's
concept of a *"male soul* in a female body" [emphasis ours]) or frequently
involved a morbidification of what had earlier seemed innocent because unlabeled (as in the claim that same-sex love was anomalous or
even freakish).[2]

Yet certainly such scientists of sexuality as Ellis and Carpenter saw
themselves as libertarians, questioning the moral censure and censor-
ship with which their society surrounded homosexuality. As Michel
Foucault has argued about the appearance of late nineteenth-century
psychiatry and jurisprudence, discourse on homosexuality "made possible a strong advance of social controls into this area of 'perversity,' "
but it also enabled "homosexuality . . . to speak on its own behalf, to
demand that its legitimacy or 'naturality' be acknowledged."[3] Ellis declared, for example, that "inversion [is] not a disease or a 'degeneration,' " and Carpenter claimed that "men and women of the exclusive
Uranian type are by no means necessarily morbid in any way," while
both advocated the decriminalization of homosexuality, with Carpenter actually insisting that the "homogenic affection is a valuable social
force, and in some cases a necessary element of noble human character."[4]

In fact, Carpenter was a prophet of the new who specifically linked
social change with sexchange, feminism with lesbianism. "It is notice-
able," he commented,

that the movement among women towards their own liberation and emancipation, which is taking place all over the civilised world, has been accompanied by a marked development of the homogenic passion among the female sex. It may be said that a certain strain in the relations between the opposite sexes which has come about owing to a growing consciousness among women that they have been oppressed and unfairly treated by men, and a growing unwillingness to ally themselves unequally in marriage—that this strain has caused the womenkind to draw more closely together and to cement alliances of their own. But whatever the cause may be it is pretty certain that such comrade-alliances—and of quite devoted kind—are becoming increasingly common, and especially perhaps among the more cultured classes of women, who are working out the great cause of their sex's liberation; nor is it difficult to see the importance of such alliances in such a campaign. In the United States where the battle of women's independence is also being fought, the tendency mentioned is as strongly marked.[5]

Whether late nineteenth-century and early twentieth-century lesbians defined themselves as feminists or not, then, they had been given and could now produce new words, even while they themselves were identified by the most extravagant thinkers with linguistic innovation: "Urning men and women," wrote Otto de Joux in a passage Carpenter repeatedly cited, are people "on whose book of life Nature has written her new word which sounds so strange to us."[6]

That the "new word" sounded "strange" meant, of course, that despite Carpenter's optimism it was a problem for many of the women who bore it or spoke it. Indeed, as in the case of Willa Cather, the naming of "the thing not named" probably became less possible precisely because the new language could be, and often was, used as a weapon against autonomous women. It was no doubt the new concept of "the lesbian" that impelled Edith Wharton to dismiss Natalie Barney as "something—appalling." But even those literary women who sought, in the face of such disapproval, to construct a grammar of their own out of the new words about lesbian eroticism suffered the inhibitions that accompany speech after long silence. For a new vocabulary does not constitute an enabling tradition, and what literary tradition was there, after all, for the woman artist who felt her erotic destiny to be alien from the scripts culturally identified with her anatomy? What community could she find in which she could commune with others who, like her, felt other than their bodies? Could there be a way of

expressing difference through the discovery of an other whose difference constituted a kind of likeness? Just as important, what aesthetic
strategies could she devise to represent her alienation from her literary
inheritance?

These questions, implicitly answered by many lesbian modernists,
are explicitly posed by Radclyffe Hall in *The Well of Loneliness* (1928), a
novel influenced and defended by Havelock Ellis. Stephen Gordon,
Radclyffe Hall's famous heroine, learns early in life "that the loneliest
place in this world is the no-man's-land of sex," and in analyzing Stephen Gordon's feeling that she is "nothing but a freak abandoned on a
kind of no-man's-land" Hall's book delineates the isolation that modernist lesbian writing seeks to ease.[7] Indeed, *The Well of Loneliness* demonstrates that in the early twentieth century the loneliness of lesbian
artists led not only to their concern with the lesbian community and the
lesbian couple, but also to their construction of aesthetic strategies which
alleviated the anxiety that their alienation from an overwhelmingly heterosexual literary history had instilled.

Described in an enigmatic phrase as "not like" (118) by her dying
father, Stephen is haunted by the sense that she is destined to be disliked as a singular and solitary anomaly, indeed as what Ulrichs called
"a male soul in a female body." When she decides to live in Paris after
the war, however, she is searching for a sense of commonality, a quest
that her governess describes in language which suggests that it is a solution to the father's sentence: "Like to like! Like to like! Like to like!"
(248), Stephen's mentor muses. And Stephen does at first manage to
gain some validation from the growing expatriate community she finds
in postwar Paris, as Hall pays tribute to the support generated in salons
and bars where "Like to like" could congregate. Consolidated as a "battalion" during the Great War, a historical confluence that, as we shall
see in our next chapter, Hall describes with real insight, the lesbian
community "would never again be completely disbanded" (272). It is
from this perspective that *The Well of Loneliness* eulogizes Natalie Barney in the fictional character of Valerie Seymour.

In contrast to Stephen's gloomy assumption that the invert is a lonely
freak stands Seymour-Barney's cheerful confidence that "Nature was
trying to do her bit; inverts were being born in increasing numbers"
(406). Just as important is the atmosphere Seymour-Barney creates,
namely "the freedom of her salon, the protection of her friendship"
(352). While Britons and Americans have always defined France as the
country of illicit love, by 1918 when Stephen Gordon and her lover
Mary Llewellyn were living in Paris, that city had become the site of
both the overtly feminist salon established by Natalie Barney and the
more heterogeneous salon founded by Gertrude Stein and her famous

brother Leo. Indeed, certain neighborhoods in Paris may have seemed—at least to sophisticated visitors—like the eroticized quarters of a city of ladies in which lesbian artists could evolve exclusive coteries based on their defiance of conventional codes of behavior and their pursuit of an artistry linked to their love affairs.

Yet when Stephen and Mary try to escape their isolation by socializing within the network established by Seymour-Barney, they find themselves inexorably "gliding" not out of but "into" a "no-man's-land—the most desolate country in all creation" (356). The homesickness, self-hatred, poverty, illness, and alcoholism of the "miserable army" (387) they encounter imply that no separatist dream of an eroticized Herland could come true within a dominant culture so saturated in fear and hatred of homosexuality. The only social milieu within which Stephen and Mary can shed the secrecy of their lives is depicted as ghettoized and therefore sadly limited and self-destructive. Hall implies, then, that even those lesbians who were sustained by the communities that Barney and others had established continued to experience themselves as exiles, for to be ex-*patria,* outside one's father's land, is not necessarily to be inside either the mother country or Herland.

As a voluntary gesture expatriation represents the transformation of an ignored or despised outcast into a visibly free outsider. Neither an emigrant nor an immigrant, the expatriate defines herself in resistance to both the first country in which she was born and the second country in which she resides. As Shari Benstock has demonstrated, the women who left England and America to live in France "were not affected by French mores and prejudices," and, in fact, the "need for separateness" was what "brought them to Paris."[8] The residence of lesbian modernists in foreign countries thus symbolized their alienation from all countries, their realization that, as lesbians, they had been banished from or had had to withdraw from the ground of their origins, the supposedly native land that is heterosexuality. Although they were less likely to be commented upon, ostracized, or attacked for being lesbians in Paris than in the cities where they were born, few lesbian expatriates made the mistake of thinking that the streets of Paris—or any streets in the other cities they inhabited—would be completely safe. Rather, by many of the women who lived mainly in Paris but who traveled throughout the Continent, lesbianism itself was imagined as a perpetual, ontological expatriation.

If the lesbian expatriates find not so much community as commiseration in *The Well of Loneliness,* is the individual female couple a more effective social unit? By bestowing the address of "rue Jacob" upon the street where Stephen and Mary live, Hall intimates that perhaps the lesbian couple could create an autonomous world of its own, for the rue Jacob was the actual location of Barney's salon. And, as Mary begins sorting Stephen's socks, answering her letters, planting a garden, supervising the housekeeping, and typing Stephen's novels, the older woman does feel that "she was all things to Mary; father, mother, friend and lover, all things; and Mary all things to her—the child, the friend, the beloved, all things" (314). Yet sometimes the "limitless" nature of their relationship causes Stephen to believe that, "With the terrible bonds of her dual nature, she could bind Mary fast, and the pain would be sweetness, so that the girl would cry out for that sweetness, hugging her chains always closer to her" (300). When their lovemaking becomes an effort to retaliate against the ignorance or ostracism they continually encounter in so-called polite society, Stephen embraces Mary "cruelly so that her kisses were pain," as she "striv[es] to obliterate, not only herself, but the whole hostile world through some strange and agonized merging with Mary" (371).

Stephen and Mary fall into cruel lovemaking, Hall hints, precisely because they are all-in-all to each other. The pressure on the lesbian couple to set itself up in defiance of the world isolates the lovers so that they lose a separate sense of identity, and this occurs in two very different sorts of homosexual relationships. In *The Well of Loneliness*, as in Paris during the first two decades of the twentieth century, the sexual escapades of what we might call the libertine lesbian contrast with the monogamy espoused by couples who live—like Stephen and Mary—as if they were married. Yet both "libertine" and "monogamous" lesbians suffer in *The Well*, where eroticism is inevitably described as disruptive. While, as Hall depicts it, the promiscuity of the "libertine" might destabilize women's relationships by estranging the lover from a beloved who feels herself to be exchangeable, she also shows that the "monogamous" lesbian threatens to replicate heterosexual roles even though she is unable to provide marital security to her partner.

How could the lesbian writer express herself in a hostile world where the lesbian community and even the lesbian couple failed to provide adequate nurturance? Although Hall was struggling with a sense of lesbianism as a tragic transsexuality, at the end of her portrait of the artist as a lesbian she proposes a strategy of aesthetic survival. Stephen Gordon—having voluntarily relinquished Mary to a male suitor—is described as a city under siege. But her fall may be fortunate, for it might issue in a new kind of art, an art based on ventriloquism. Specifically, Stephen sees throngs of people invading her room and herself; she feels "rockets of pain" as countless voices, in "their madness to become articulate through her," cut off her retreat. Realizing that neither bolts nor bars can save her, Stephen experiences the walls of her self crumbling, hears voices declaring, "We are coming, Stephen—we are still coming on, and our name is legion—you dare not disown us!," and hears as "her own" a "voice into which those millions had entered" (437). In this respect, as in its dedication to "Our Three Selves,"[9] *The Well of Loneliness* defends the lesbian writer against the fragility of the homosexual community and the homosexual couple by invoking a rhetoric of literary collectivity that also characterizes the work of the lesbian expatriates who were Hall's contemporaries.

To be sure, in a number of ways the lesbian expatriates about whom Hall was writing need to be and have been read in the context of work produced by their male contemporaries, for many of them helped shape the environment that fostered the achievements of such modernists as Ernest Hemingway and James Joyce, a fact that is perhaps best illustrated by the wide influence of Sylvia Beach's bookstore, Shakespeare and Co. Certainly, too, the real-life counterparts of Stephen Gordon shared with their male contemporaries the economic and social benefits—the profitable exchange rates, for example, or the alcohol unavailable in Prohibition America—of life on the Continent. Like Malcolm Cowley, a number of lesbian expatriates believed themselves to be "exiles" in a Paris which was at least symbolically their "mistress." Like Henry Miller and Robert McAlmon, others hoped that "being geniuses together" abroad would liberate them from a puritanical American culture.[10] In addition, many of the English and American literary women who sought such liberation came from and depended upon economically and socially privileged families.

However, the urgency of their need to create a mythology upon which their artistry could be based can be understood as a response to the images of lesbians produced by many of their male contemporaries. As late as 1921, the very effort to define lesbianism was publicly decried in England as socially detrimental. An attempt to introduce legal provisions against lesbianism failed to obtain parliamentary approval because, as one official put it, "You are going to tell the whole world that there is such an offence, to bring it to the notice of women who have never heard of it, never thought of it, never dreamt of it."[11] While to legislators lesbianism was presumed to be unimaginable in the context of assumptions about the "naturalness" of women's heterosexuality or their maternal instinct, the word "offence" here links homosexuality not only to a conspiracy of silence but also to a sinfulness that writers had attributed to the lesbian throughout the fin de siècle.

Certainly from Balzac's *The Girl with the Golden Eyes* (1835) to Sheridan Le Fanu's *Carmilla* (1871–72) and Henry James's *The Bostonians* (1886), men of letters had claimed that lesbian desire is morbid and destructive or that, as George Moore argued, "Every woman knows deep down in her heart that all her existence is comprised in man's love of her."[12] This idea meant that the lesbian was often considered either pathetic and ludicrous (bereft of "man's love") or titillating and perverse (rebelling against her "heart's" desire for "man's love"). By turn-of-the-century painters, according to Bram Dijkstra, "a woman kiss[ing] another woman" was often presented "as if she were kissing her own image in the glass" so as to define "lesbianism as a sort of extension of [women's] supposed autoerotic fixation," a fixation that was seen as both narcissistic and nonthreatening to the voyeuristic male spectator.[13] From Swinburne's "Anactoria" to Lawrence's *The Rainbow,* however, the female homosexual was imagined by literary men as threatening or deserving of punishment. As he so often did, indeed, Lawrence boiled down this stock to clarify its essence: explaining that "Ego-bound women are often lesbian, / perhaps always," he exclaims, "of all passions / the lesbian passion is the most appalling, / a frenzy of tortured possession / and a million frenzies of tortured jealousy."[14]

Estranged not only from the art produced by such men but also from a female literary tradition that could be just as biased against the female homosexual,[15] lesbian writers evolved a collaborative aesthetic out of their common sense of an extreme cultural expatriation. The need for such an aesthetic arose not only from their rejection of their native and adopted lands, not only from their repudiation of stereotypes of masculinity, femininity, and homosexuality, but also from their resistance to their patrilineal and matrilineal literary inheritance. At home neither in any geographic place nor in any literary-historical space, lesbian modernists attempted to forge a literary tradition out of what they had: each other. Mythologizing their erotic relationships through a number of quite different linguistic strategies, they shared a collaborative rhetoric that offered a solution to the problem of the exile's vulnerability and a vision of a Herland more erotic than the ones Charlotte Perkins Gilman and Willa Cather had been able to imagine.

In their attempts to write new and strange words that evade the territorial battles between literary men and women, the lesbian expatriates looked back to an ancient, almost mythic literary history or forward to the total annihilation of literary history. In terms of what we have called the female affiliation complex, turn-of-the-century and modernist women of letters managed to create a self-consciously lesbian literary tradition for the first time and to do so by resurrecting an antique foremother of lesbian artistry or by rejecting virtually all literary foremothers and forefathers as proponents of "Patriarchal Poetry."[16] Whether lesbian authors wrote "as" an ancient precursor associated with lesbian love or "for" a lesbian lover, they demonstrated both the advantages and the disadvantages of such strategies. If we take the salons on the rue Jacob and the rue de Fleurus as prototypical of lesbian culture, their foremost writers—Renée Vivien and Gertrude Stein—can be seen as representative. For, while Renée Vivien forged a collaboration with Sappho by celebrating a Mytilene that had faded from literary history, Gertrude Stein, through a private collaboration with her lover, turned herself into a "man of genius" capable of obliterating literary history altogether.

As the daughter of a mythic lesbian foremother or as a rivalrous "son" usurping the place of the literary father, the lesbian modernist grappled with what Hall delineates as the loneliness of the lesbian in heterosexual society and the loneliness of the lesbian artist in literary history. For those writers who harked back to Sappho in an effort to recover a foremother, the project was endangered by nostalgia. For those who anticipated an apocalyptic post-patriarchal future, the project paradoxically risked recycling the patriarchal past. In either case, however, such artists as Renée Vivien and Gertrude Stein established the lesbian literary tradition as a form of double talk based on an aesthetic of mutuality that simultaneously attracted and disturbed contemporaries like H. D., Amy Lowell, and Djuna Barnes. Finally, even though most of these writers intimated that the principle of pain associated with sexual difference persisted in lesbian relationships, they did question any monolithic definition of homosexuality, and because they were confronting—albeit in different ways—a common problem, their artistic strategies established a separate place for them in the literature composed before, during, and after the Great War.

In *The Book of the City of Ladies* (written 1405), Christine de Pizan praised Sappho's invention of lyrical forms and meditated on Horace's report that "when Plato, the great philosopher who was Aristotle's teacher, died, a book of Sappho's poems was found under his pillow."[17] She was drawing on a vision of Sappho's power that had become eroticized by the time Virginia Woolf wondered whether Vita Sackville-West was like other "sapphists [who] *love* women; friendship is never untinged with amorosity."[18] Of course, from poems by the seventeenth-century woman of letters Katherine Philips ("The English Sappho") celebrating female friendship to the provocative blank page under the entry for "Sappho" in Monique Wittig's and Sande Zeig's lexicon for *Lesbian Peoples* (trans. 1979), from Christina Rossetti's meditations on the poet's life story to recent publications like *Sappho Was A Right-On Woman* (1972) and *Sapphistry* (1980), the person and poetics of Sappho have haunted the female imagination.[19]

Since the late nineteenth century, however, the words we use to describe female homosexuality derive from the poet of Lesbos, although

the 1971 edition of the *Oxford English Dictionary* actually defines
"Sapphism" as "unnatural sexual relations between women" and "Lesbian" as "a mason's rule made of lead." In a manner that might have
surprised the lexicographers, Sappho fascinated a number of women
writing in the early decades of the twentieth century, and no doubt she
did so because of a flood of male-authored classical scholarship and
poetry at the turn of the century. Just when translators of Sappho were
beginning to honor her choice of a female pronoun for her beloved [20]
and classicists were struggling to investigate the legends and facts about
her life, Sappho's status as a female precursor became especially significant for a number of women poets.

Like the collaborative couple who wrote under the name "Michael
Field" (Katherine Bradley and Edith Cooper), whose volume of sapphics was entitled *Long Ago* (1889), Isadora Duncan viewed Sappho as a
legendary figure from a paradise lost long ago, while Sara Teasdale
idealized Sappho as a mother-poet crooning to her daughter Cleis, Edna
St. Vincent Millay identified Sappho first as a love-lost suicide and later
as a singer refusing to die for a man, Elizabeth Robins meditated on a
Sappho who is "the nursing mother of intellectually free women," and
Isak Dinesen wore a costume she called "Sappho." [21] In spite of their
differences, all evinced the same desire to recover Sappho that impels
Virginia Woolf's proto-women's studies collective in her 1921 short story
"A Society." When the members of this Society of Outsiders evaluate
the world of culture created by men, they discover one "Professor Hobkin's" edition of Sappho, which is primarily devoted to a defense of
Sappho's chastity. As Jane Marcus has shown, Professor Hobkin's gynecological obsession with—in Woolf's words—"some implement which
looked . . . for all the world like a hairpin" dramatizes the novelist's
recognition that exceptional women like Sappho have frequently been
used not to valorize but to trivialize a female literary tradition. [22]

One year before writing "A Society," moreover, Woolf discerned in
Desmond MacCarthy's newspaper article on the paucity of women's
poetry precisely the sentence her Society would read in the newspaper:
" 'Since Sappho there has been no female of first rate—.' " In a letter
of rebuttal, Woolf claimed that "external restraint[s]" have inhibited
the growth of women's literary history after Sappho, for Sappho lived
in a time that, in J. A. Symond's phrase, accorded "social and domestic
freedom" to women who were "highly educated and accustomed to
express their sentiments." According to Woolf, the conditions that make
possible the birth of a Sappho are, first, artistic predecessors; second,
membership in a group where art is freely discussed and practiced; and
third, freedom of action and experience: "Perhaps in Lesbos but never
since, have these conditions been the lot of women." [23]

Some of Woolf's contemporaries, however, were in the process of recovering the artistic freedom they, too, associated with this classical literary foremother. Because a number of lesbian expatriates agreed with Edith Sitwell that—with the exception of Sappho and a "few poems" of Dickinson and Rossetti—"Women's poetry . . . is *simply awful*,"[24] they resembled Woolf and Sitwell, both of whom brooded on the inadequacy of their classical education, which made it difficult for them to be what Woolf called Sappho, "an inheritor as well as an originator."[25] Nevertheless, such artists certainly would have agreed with Willa Cather that, "If of all the lost riches we could have one master restored to us, . . . the choice of the world would be for the lost nine books of Sappho," for "Those broken fragments have burned themselves into the consciousness of the world like fire."[26] Of course, as Lawrence Lipking has demonstrated, male writers from Catullus to William Carlos Williams also turned to Sappho.[27] But the male artist's recovery of Sappho—which was especially noteworthy in the publications of Swinburne in England and Bliss Carman in America—was sometimes experienced by the woman writer as an appropriation to be met by poetic counter assaults, sometimes as an opportunity to view and claim her only classical precursor. And, as Louise Bogan explained, women readers searched for the lost fragments of Sappho "less with the care and eagerness of the scholar looking for bits of shattered human art, than with the hungry eyes of the treasure hunter, looking for some last grain of a destroyed jewel."[28]

Bogan's point is even more pertinent for lesbian artists, to whom Sappho represented all the women of genius in literary history whose voices were censored or silenced because they were deemed aberrant.[29] At the same time, the effort to recover Sappho illustrates how twentieth-century lesbian poets tried to solve the problem of poetic isolation. For the woman poet who experienced herself as inadequately nurtured by a problematic literary matrilineage, but especially for the bisexual or lesbian poet who looked in vain for a poetic tradition of her own, Sappho was a special precursor. Precisely because so many of this poet's original texts were destroyed, the modern woman could write "for" and "as" Sappho and thereby invent a classical inheritance of her own. Such a writer was not infected by Sappho's stature with a Bloomian "anxiety of influence" because her ancient precursor was paradoxically in need of a contemporary collaborator, or so the poetry of Renée Vivien and H. D. seems to suggest.

What we would call a "fantasy precursor" or a "fantastic collaboration" simultaneously healed the anxiety of authorship and linked Renée Vivien and H. D. to a literary history they could create in their own image. Certainly, Sappho's preeminence provided them evidence that the woman who achieves the lyricism of Sappho will take her place beside (but apart from) a poet like Homer. Through the dynamics of their collaboration with Sappho, Renée Vivien and H. D. created myths of the primacy of women's literary language, even as they offered divergent interpretations of what lesbianism means as an imaginative force. Whether the recovery of Sappho resulted in a decadent aesthetic, as it did for Vivien, or a chiselled classicism, as for H. D., it held out the promise of excavating a lyricism that inscribes female desire as the ancient source of song.

Like Cather, who especially admired Sappho's creation of "the most wonderfully emotional meter in literature," Renée Vivien was fascinated with Sappho's lines that, in Cather's words, "come in like a gasp when feeling flows too swift for speech." But, unlike Cather, who composed only one poem—"The Star Dial" (1907)—in which she identifies with Sappho,[30] Vivien repeatedly attempted to regain Sappho's erotic language specifically for lesbians. In 1900, Vivien met the woman she would desire and resist all her life: at a theater, Natalie Barney was reading a letter from Liane de Pougy that would be published the next year in her *Idyll saphique*. And, as Elyse Blankley has shown, Sappho continued to provide a background for the stormy relationship Vivien and Barney pursued, as well as a central symbol of their respective arts.[31]

Motivated at least in part by her friendship with Pierre Louÿs, the author of *Chansons de Bilitis* (1894) as well as *Aphrodite* (1896), Natalie Barney published *Cinq petits dialogues grecs* in 1902. Four years later she produced her *Acts d' entr'actes* with Marguerite Moreno playing the leading role of a Sappho who dies not from love of the boatman Phaon, as the followers of Ovid claimed, but because of her desire for a girl promised in marriage. During this same period, after teaching herself Greek, Vivien published *Sapho* (1903), a collection of translations and imitations of Greek fragments that the Anglo-American Vivien composed in French. In 1904, she and Natalie Barney traveled to Mytilene where Vivien eventually purchased a house of her own. In that same year, she published *Une femme m'apparut (A Woman Appeared to Me)*, a roman à clef that focuses on an androgynous avatar and disciple of the poet of Mytilene who argues not only that Phaon is the vulgar invention of low humorists but also that Sappho is the only woman poet of distinction because she did not deign to notice masculine existence, which is the "Unaesthetic par excellence."[32]

In both her poetry and her novel, Vivien appropriated the tormenting and tormented Sappho so prevalent in the nineteenth-century work

of Baudelaire and Swinburne.[33] In a setting of voluptuous, "evil" flowers and narcissistic mirrors like those associated with Swinburne's vampiric and suicidal heroine Lesbia Brandon, Vivien's Sappho morbidly
sings, "I believe I take from you a bit of your fleeting life when I embrace you"; like Baudelaire, who portrays the sinful delights of Lesbos,
Vivien identifies Sappho with Satan, the antagonist of both God and
his poet, Homer.[34] Waging war against men ("What I hold against them
is the great wrong they have done to women"), Vivien's sapphic surrogate in *A Woman Appeared to Me* wants "to injure" her "political adver-
saries . . . for the good of the cause"; specifically she wants to triumph
over what she views as a predatory male (hetero)sexuality ("I began to
hate the male for the base cruelty of his laws and the impurity of his
morals," this same character explains). But her victories are as qualified
as Vivien's poems describing a sapphic desire characterized by self-division about "the delicate art of vice" which nevertheless "quench[es]"
the lover's "thirst."[35] This satanic Sappho is, of course, the same haunted
figure Colette perceived in Vivien herself, wasting away at the end of
her life in a twilight of anorexic self-incarceration.[36] But while in reality
Vivien suffered the consequences of such an internalization of the image of the lesbian femme fatale, in her art she tapped the energy of the
decadents' alienated lesbian. Indeed, Vivien suggests that the "unnatural" longing of the decadents' Sappho turns the lesbian into a prototypical artist, for her obsession with a beauty that does not exist in nature is part of a satanically ambitious effort against nature to attain the
aesthetic "par excellence."

As if meditating on the iconography of Georges de Feure's *The Voice
of Evil*, a painting about female fantasy and lesbianism which we reproduced in *The War of the Words*, Vivien evokes the centrality of the lesbian in decadent art to claim this image for herself. Like Proust, who
had noted that "Femmes damnées" was considered the "most beautiful
[long poem] that Baudelaire had written," Vivien must have been struck
by what Proust called the "strange privilege" Baudelaire assigned himself in "Lesbos":

> Car Lesbos entre tous m'a choisi sur la terre
> Pour chanter le secrèt de ses vièrges en fleurs
> Et je fus dès l'enfance admis au noir mystère.
>
> For Lesbos of all on this earth elected me
> To sing the secret of its flowering virgins
> And as a child I was admitted to the dark mystery.[37]

Swinburne, with less presumption, responded to a friend's critique of
his Sappho-persona by explaining, "It is as near as I can come; and no
man can come close to her."[38] As if diagnosing his and Baudelaire's

efforts to "come close," the Sapphic androgyne of Vivien's novel explains the limits of such voyeuristic visions of lesbianism: "Men see in the love of woman for woman only a spice that sharpens the flatness of their regular performance. But when they realize that this cult of grace and delicacy will permit no sharing, no ambiguity, they revolt against the purity of a passion which excludes and scorns them" (36).

Vivien implies that Baudelaire, who originally gave the title *Les Lesbiennes* to *Les Fleurs du mal,* and Swinburne, who spoke to "Anactoria" in the accents of a passionately depraved Sappho, were themselves excluded from what she is elected to sing, the secrets, the dark mysteries of Mytilene. She subversively insinuates, moreover, that the lesbian is the epitome of the decadent and that decadence is fundamentally a lesbian literary tradition. No wonder, then, that this Anglo-American girl, who was christened Pauline Tarn, renamed herself after the crafty seductress Vivien of Arthurian legend: by modeling herself on the enchantress Vivien who steals Merlin's magical book of charms in Tennyson's *Idylls of the King* and Burne-Jones's *The Beguiling of Merlin,* a reborn (re-née) Vivien appropriates the male book of power to usurp masculine authority and to break what Gayle Rubin calls the male monopoly over women.[39]

In a number of poems, therefore, Vivien flouts heterosexual definitions of her desire: "You will never know how to tarnish the devotion / Of my passion for the beauty of women." In others, she praises female virginity as a protection against "the cruelty of [men's] laws and the impurity of [men's] morals": "I shall flee imprint and soiling stain. / The grasp that strangles, the kiss that infects / And wounds I shall shun."[40] For Vivien, Sapphism, precisely because it is what the decadents called "barren," provides access not to the future of the human species but to the present of the female of the species. "Our love is greater than all loves," Vivien declares, for "we can, when the belt comes undone, / Be at once both lovers and sisters."[41] Similarly, in "Union," Vivien begins, "Our heart is the same in our woman's breast," and she explains, "Our body is made the same"; "we are of the same race"; "I know exactly what pleases you"; "I am you."[42] Because the beloved feels so much like oneself, however, the realization of her separateness is tormenting. Vivien's feelings about Barney's promiscuity, to which Sappho's poems on the loss of Atthis could serve as utterance, underscore this sense of aloneness, allowing Vivien to valorize lesbianism as the preferred eroticism because it raises crucial issues of fusion and identity.[43]

For, of course, by opening up the relationship between women to eroticism, Vivien admits an influx of jealousy and self-abasement as well as of consolation and pleasure. Sapphic desire implicates the lover in the beloved's abandonment and the rival's competition, both of which complicate the monolithic ideal of sisterhood that informed so much feminist rhetoric at the turn of the century: "For Andromeda," Vivien laments in one Sapphic meditation, "the lightning of your kiss," while she herself is left with only "the grave cadences" of Atthis's voice.[44] Even when the beloved is present to the lover, their lovemaking is an intimation of the impossibility of obliterating their separateness: in "Chanson," for example, Vivien sees in her beloved a "form . . . that leaves me clutching emptiness."[45] The need to "evoke the fear, the pain and the torment" of such love repeatedly turns Vivien toward the "Priestess" of Lesbos who can "Teach us the secret of divine sorrow."[46]

While several of Vivien's verse dramas mourn the death of the poet of fugitive desire,[47] a number of her lyrics suggest that "Sappho Lives Again," reborn as Vivien: "Some of us have preserved the rites / Of burning Lesbos gilded like an altar."[48] Prefaced with fragmentary quotations from Sappho, Vivien's French becomes an aspect of the other muted languages of langour in the poetry: the lexicon of scents, the syntax of flowers, the sign language of fingers on flesh, the intonation of swooning voices sighing in broken phrases. While Vivien's French aligns her poetry with continental eroticism in the *belle époque* and thereby frees her to speak the unspoken, her most fragmentary translations seem to attest to a form of aphasia, for her French is as foreign to her native English as her homosexuality is to the hegemonic heterosexual idiom. Thus, at a loss for words, she signals her exile from Lesbos, her expatriation from a native language of desire.

Yet two of the finest of Vivien's original poems that equate the recovery of Sappho with the rediscovery of a distant but distinct female country and the translation of the poet carried across the seas and the centuries to this country are "While Landing at Mytilene" ("En débarquant à Mytilene") and "Toward Lesbos" ("Vers Lesbos"). Both represent a utopian response to the alienation evident in Vivien's feeling that "Everywhere I go I repeat: *I do not belong here.*"[49] In the first, the poet begins with an effort at return: "From the depths of my past, I turn back to you / Mytilene, crossing the disparate centuries" ("Du fond de mon passé, je retourne vers toi, / Mytilene, à travers les siècles disparates"). Similarly, in "Toward Lesbos," she speaks to a beloved on board a ship headed for Mytilene: "You will come," she tells her lover, "your eyes filled with evening and with yesterday" ("Tu viendras, les yeux pleins du soir et de l'hier"). In both poems, fine fragrances fill the air: in the first, the poet brings her love "like a present of aromatics" ("ainsi qu'un présent d'aromates") and in the second "Our boat will be laden with amber and spices" ("Nôtre barque sera pleine d'ambre et d'épices"). In both poems the trip to Greece involves dying into a new life so that the speaker discovers a place to "melt and dissolve" ("où je me fonds et me dissous"), or the boat is "Frail like a cradle" ("Frêle comme un berceau") as the lovers, sleeping through the risks and rites of passage, wonder if they will be able to move to where "we will live tomorrow" ("quel est ce pays où nous vivrons demain?"). Most importantly, in both poems the Greek island is a place of the female erotic imagination: in the first, Mytilene is quite simply a woman's body rising out of the sea, "Golden flanked Lesbos" ("Lesbos aux flancs dorés"); in the second, the lovers on board hear "mysterious songs," the intimation of "supreme music," as they approach "the island of magic" ("l'île chimèrique").

Vivien's utopian yearning for a visionary land and language of female primacy was also expressed by the American-born poet H. D., who shuttled between Switzerland, London, Paris, Greece, and Egypt throughout most of her career. The Englishwoman Bryher saved H. D.'s life in 1919 by caring for her through influenza and a difficult childbirth when she had been abandoned both by her husband and by the father of her child; and in 1920 Bryher took H. D. to the Greek islands to recuperate.[50] Before and after that trip, the expatriate H. D. evoked the spirit of Greece to mark her commitment to what J. A. Symonds identified as Sappho's "fire of the soul . . . crystallized," the "yearnings of an intense soul after beauty, which has never on earth existed."[51]

H. D. described the events that led to her recovery in the first section of her novel *Palimpsest* (1926): her heroine, Hipparchia, is a translator of Moero, an ancient women poet whose imagery resembles Sappho's, although Hipparchia has renounced the struggle to recapture Sappho "as savouring of sacrilege."[52] After she is visited by a girl who has memorized all her translations, Hipparchia embarks on the regenerative voyage which taught H. D. that "Greece is not lost" because "Greece is a spirit."[53] Yet, in spite of her and Vivien's similar meditations on Greece, they excavate two quite different Sapphos: while Vivien's Sappho is languorous and tormented, H. D.'s is stark and fierce in her commitment to artistic perfection, a shift that doubtless reflects the translation history of Sappho's texts in this period as well as the pedagogic influence of Ezra Pound and Richard Aldington, both of whom guided H. D. through the *Greek Anthology*. Also, unlike Vivien, who consistently defines Sappho as a satanic lesbian, H. D. uses Sappho's verse to deal with the relationship between poetic ambition and heterosexual desire. Placing Sappho in a Greek context that extends from Homer to Euripides, H. D. adopted Sappho's texts as part of what Louis Martz calls her "masks of Greece,"[54] and in the process she implicitly demonstrated that lesbianism furnished her with a refuge from the pain of heterosexuality and with the courage necessary to articulate that pain.

H. D.'s first use of Sappho, "Fragment 113," is an original poem that presents itself as an exploration of Sappho's fragment "Neither honey nor bee for me."[55] Organized around a series of negatives, this poem refrains from assenting to an old desire. "Not honey," the poet reiterates three times in the first stanza, refusing thereby "the sweet / stain on the lips and teeth" as well as "the deep / plunge of soft belly." The voluptuous flight of the plundering bee is related to sweetness and softness. "Not so" would the poet desire, "though rapture blind my eyes, / and hunger crisp / dark and inert my mouth." Refusing "old desire— old passion— / old forgetfulness— old pain— ," H. D. speculates on a different desire:

> but if you turn again,
> seek strength of arm and throat
> touch as the god;
> neglect the lyre-note;
> knowing that you shall feel,
> about the frame,
> no trembling of the string,
> but heat, more passionate
> of bone and the white shell
> and fiery tempered steel.

Bone, not belly; fiery tempered steel instead of the stealings of the plundering bee: as in her essay on Sappho, H. D. finds in Sappho's poems "not heat in the ordinary sense, diffused and comforting," but intensity "as if the brittle crescent-moon gave heat to us, or some splendid scintillating star turned warm suddenly in our hand like a jewel."[56]

Sappho's imagery infiltrates H. D.'s early poetry, and the lyricism of both poets is characterized by a yearning intensity expressed through direct address and situated in a liminal landscape.[57] In the note on Sappho (1920), which we used as one of our epigraphs, H. D. imagines Sappho as "the island of artistic perfection" that inspires the contemporary poet to "gain courage for new adventures" in "artistic achievement," and certainly, from H.D.'s earliest Imagist verse to her later epics, the Greek island is a place of female artistry. Specifically, from her dramatization of Odysseus fleeing Calypso's island in "Calypso" (1938) to her paradisiacal vision in *Trilogy* (1944–46) of "the circles and circles of islands / about the lost centre-island, Atlantis," to the central section of *Helen in Egypt* (1961) which is situated on Leuké, *L'isle blanche,*

H. D. affirms what she proclaims in her last volume, *Hermetic Definition* (1972), that "the island is herself, is her."[58]

Susan Friedman has explained that "Sappho's influence on imagists no doubt helped to validate H. D.'s leadership role in the development of the modern lyric."[59] Just as important, Sappho's Greek fragments furnished H. D. with a linguistic model for the poems that would define the Imagist aesthetic. "Fragment 113" presents itself as a numbered remnant, a belated version of a mutilated vision, a translation of a lost original. As H. D. knew, Sappho's texts, some of which were excavated in 1898 from Egyptian debris, often survived as narrow strips torn from mummy wrappings. Her own poems, narrow columns of print with not a few phrases broken off with dashes, meditate on a loss they mediate: the speaker's series of negatives, presumably a response to a prior sentence omitted from the poem, seems to imply that the text has been torn out of an unrecoverable narrative context. H. D.'s life-long effort to recreate what has been "scattered in the shards / men tread upon"[60] is reflected in her early fascination with Sappho's poetry, as is her recurrent presentation of herself as a translator of ancient, foreign phrases.

"Fragment 113" was published in the volume *Hymen* (1921). In the title piece of this volume, H. D. began to extend her short lyrics in the direction of narrative. A cluster of poems describes the bride's impending fate, the loss of her virginity, in terms of the plundering bee who "slips / Between the purple flower-lips."[61] In the context of "Neither honey nor bee for me," Love's song of the bee's penetration foregrounds the silence and isolation of the veiled, white figure of the bride. In addition, as Alicia Ostriker has pointed out, the very title, "Hymen," with its evocation of female anatomy and a male god, turns this celebratory sequence into a somber meditation on the predatory pattern of heterosexuality,[62] a pattern explicitly associated with the simultaneity of the bride's marriage to Love and her divorce from the female community. H. D. transforms several epithalamia attributed to Sappho into the choruses of girls, maidens, matrons, and priestesses accompanying the silent bride. The stage directions between the lyrics consist of descriptions of musical interludes and of costumes, as well as of the spatial arrangement of figures in their processionals before the temple of Hera. Linking the lyrics into a liturgy, these italicized prose passages solve the poetic problem H. D. faced as she struggled to extend a minimalist form without losing the intensity she associated with the image.

Unlike her husband, Richard Aldington, who published a book of voluptuous Sapphic lyrics, *The Love of Myrrhine and Konallis* (1916, 1926), and unlike Ezra Pound, whose elegiac point in *Lustra* (1917) was that Sappho's fragments could not be reconstituted, H. D. uses the other

five meditations on Sapphic fragments that she wrote early in her career to address the contradiction between artistic vocation and female
socialization.[63] But the contradictory need for the autonomy of lyricism
and the dependency of desire is heightened in the two poems that directly confront her sense of fragility and frigidity. In "Fragment Forty-
one" (". . . thou flittest to Andromeda"), H. D. describes her beloved's
betrayal while defending herself against his charges: "I was not asleep,"
she declares; or "I was not dull and dead." In "Fragment Forty" ("Love
. . . bitter-sweet"), Sappho's bitter-sweet love becomes H. D.'s honey
and salt, an unnerving blend of tastes that epitomizes the grief of love's
abandonment.[64] In these two poems, H. D. is "deserted," "outcast,"
"shattered," "sacrificed," "scorched," "rent," "cut apart," and "slashed
open" by her love for a man who is absent or unfaithful. Paradoxically,
however, it is precisely the torment of rupture that sparks the poetry
of rapture H. D. associates with Sappho's ecstasy, her ex-stasis, her
breaking out of the self into lyric song.[65] In "Fragment Forty-one," the
poet discovers her strength in a supremely generous gift, namely "the
love of my lover / for his mistress." Similarly, at the close of "Fragment
Forty," she admits that "to sing love, / love must first shatter us."

That Eros is "he" in "Fragment Forty" and that the poet's lover is in
love with "his mistress" in "Fragment Forty-one" unmistakably and, in
the Sapphic context, surprisingly mark desire as heterosexual. Why
would H. D. invoke the celebrated poet of lesbianism to articulate what
Rachel Blau DuPlessis has called her "romantic thralldom" to a series
of male mentors?[66] While it is certainly true that H. D. writes obsessively about her desire for the mastery of such men as Ezra Pound,
Richard Aldington, and D. H. Lawrence, her poetry was motivated less
by their presence than by their absence. Like her autobiographical prose,
which frequently records her frigidity when she is with such mentors,[67]
H. D.'s revisions of Sapphic fragments articulate her ambivalence toward
the intensity of desire that, transcending the beloved and his inevitable
desertion, compels the poet to translate erotic abandonment into poetic
abandon. The very number of Sappho's beloveds—Atthis, Anactoria,
Gyrinno, Erinna, Gorgo—implies that Sappho's verse is an occasion for
expressing "a world of emotion" which H. D. considers the "spirit of
song."[68] For H. D., then, inspiration and abandonment were inextricably intertwined.

Just as Sappho's lyrical evocation of the goddess Aphrodite triumphs
over the loss of mortal love, H. D.'s lyrical invocation of Sappho testifies
to her own artistic survival, which was in large measure due to the companion who took her to the Hellas she associated with Helen, her mother.
Indeed, just as H. D. was empowered to find the strength and integrity
to create poetry out of the pain of abandonment by turning to the

passion she associates with Sappho, in her life she survived male rejection by returning to Bryher, a woman who paid many of this poet's bills, adopted her daughter, and shared her visions. Despite their numerous disagreements, throughout her autobiographical prose H. D. reveals not only how Bryher encouraged her to maintain the heretical concentration necessary to sustain the mystical experiences that would shape her poetic development but also how Bryher occasionally saw such visions "for" her.[69] The prophetic wisdom H. D. associated with her mother country (Hellas, Helen) was made possible, therefore, by both Sappho and Bryher, both of whom functioned as refuges for the modern poet, protective respites from what she saw as the inexorable grief inflicted by heterosexual passion. By using Sappho's verse to describe her dreaded longing for a male lover and by maintaining intense relationships not only with Bryher but also with Bryher's male companions, moreover, H. D. dramatized the bisexuality that, as we shall show in volume three of this study, would lead her early in her career to present herself as a seductively sensuous but chaste Greek nymph and that would eventually result in her efforts to formulate a spiritual solution to the problem posed by her ambivalent desires.

———————————◆———————————

While the dynamic of collaboration shaped the verse of both Renée Vivien and H. D., it was analyzed most consciously by Amy Lowell, a poet who used Sappho's images to celebrate her passionate response to her companion, Ada Russell.[70] Living in the ancestral mansion Sevenels, representing her famous family in Boston's most prominent social and cultural circles, Lowell was as identified with America as Vivien and H. D. were estranged from it, and in the meditation on literary matrilineage we discussed in our analysis of the female affiliation complex—"The Sisters" (1926)—she specifically explored the limitations of precisely the collaboration with Sappho that Vivien and H. D. undertook. Sappho is first "remembered" by Lowell, as she is by Vivien and H. D., at the moment when she is wondering why there are so few women poets: "There's Sapho, now I wonder what was Sapho."[71] Imagining a conversation with Sappho, Lowell supposes that she could surprise Sappho's reticence by flinging her own to the wind in order to learn how this irrepressibly sensuous "sister" came at the "loveliness of [her] words."

For Lowell, as for Vivien and H. D., Sappho embodies the elemental grandeur of a "leaping fire" and of "sea cliffs," in direct opposition to a poet like Mrs. Browning, who seems to write "close-shuttered" and "squeezed in stiff conventions." Unlike the Victorian poetess, shut up in the parlor of propriety, Sappho represents a physical release into wind, sea, and sun as well as the mental relief from reticence associated with the "tossing off of garments" and with female conversation. Yet, despite her attraction to Sappho, Lowell also implies that the gulf between the ancient tenth muse and the modern woman poet may not be negotiable: Lowell does not actually talk with Sappho; she wishes that she could. Imagining what "one might accomplish" in a conversation with Sappho, speculating on Mrs. Browning speculating on Sappho, Lowell describes the first sister of her "strange, isolated little family" as "a burning birch-tree" who wrote like a "frozen blaze before it broke and fell."

Although both Vivien and H. D. rejected Ovid's influential story of Sappho leaping suicidally from the Leucadian cliff because of her unrequited love for Phaon, both appear to have agreed with Lowell that the intensity of Sappho's passion presages a fall: Vivien literally starved and poisoned herself, and H. D. wrote about how she experienced *eros* as *eris,* love as strife. But just as potentially destructive, Lowell implies, is the strangely isolated situation of a classical poet defined not as a powerful foremother but as a vulnerable sister. From this point of view, the central position of Sappho in female poetic history defines personal sincerity and passionate ecstasy as appropriately "feminine" sources of lyricism. In terms of lesbian literature, moreover, Sappho's preeminence as a model sets up a single standard for writers defining themselves in terms of their sexual difference, a standard that further personalizes experiences already made painfully private. Writing colloquially and conversationally, Lowell concludes "The Sisters" by admitting to Sappho and her descendants, "I cannot write like you." Indeed, all of her older "sisters" leave her feeling "sad and self-distrustful."

Lowell's swerve from Sappho seems motivated less by a fear of being obliterated by the Greek poet's originatory power, as it would be if she were suffering from a Bloomian "anxiety of influence," than by a fear that Sappho was herself enmeshed in contradictions that threaten to stunt the modern woman writer's creative development, a point also made by Marguerite Yourcenar, whose prose poem about Sappho was written four years before the French novelist departed for America with her companion, Grace Frick.[72] Indeed, Yourcenar's title, "Sappho, or Suicide" (1935)—with its ambiguous "or"—implies, on the one hand, that the woman writer must choose either suicide or a lifeline to Sappho, her personal "sky companion," or, on the other hand, that Sappho's second name may be suicide, for the writer who invokes Sappho's fame might be destined to associate her art with the anguish of a fated, if not fatal, eroticism. Just as Yourcenar and Lowell hint that the dream of recovering Mytilene may not be powerful enough to allow the female poet to redefine what these writers see as the barren grounds

of heterosexual culture, Djuna Barnes in the *Ladies Almanack* (1928)
implicitly demonstrates that such a dream must be vigorously transformed by the modern lesbian writer who seeks to celebrate homosexual culture in an anatomy not of melancholy but of gaiety.

Introducing her *Almanack* as "Neap-tide to the Proustian chronicle,
gleanings from the shores of Mytilene," Barnes replaces Proust's *Sod-
ome et Gomorrhe* with her own vision of a city of lesbian ladies.[73] But only
"a peep of No-Doubting-Sappho, blinked from the Stews of Secret Greek
Broth, and some Rennet of Lesbos" (71–72) are added to the recipe
she concocts for a love potion because Barnes seeks to substitute for
Sappho, who was "given to singing over the limp Bodies of Girls" (32),
Dame Evangeline Musset (Natalie Barney) and her numerous followers, who include not only frigid Patience Scalpel (Mina Loy), ethical
Lady Buck-and-Balk (Una, Lady Troubridge) and her friend Tilly-
Tweed-in-Blood (Radclyffe Hall), the coachman-costumed Cynic Sal
(Romaine Brooks), vain Senorita Fly-About (Mimi Franchetti), Doll Furious (Dolly Wilde), and the journalists Nip and Tuck (Janet Flanner
and Solita Solano) but also "Women who had not told their Husbands
everything" (83–84).

Barnes used the formation of the female coterie around Saint Musset to explore the differences among lesbians, just as she adopted Renaissance diction and orthography, as well as the chapbook-calendar
framework, to present the lesbian "Crusade" (34) as a genuine Renaissance for women. Loving without the "trifle" that men possess, the followers of Dame Musset engage in "Slips of the Tongue" and "bringing
up by Hand" (9) while they "ride," "Tamper," "come down," or "thaw"
together, as Barnes documents what is "nowhere" described, namely
"how a Maid goes at a Maid" (43). Although, with its rhythmic archa-
isms, its encyclopedic catalogues, its astrological, alchemical charts, and
its riddling, punning prognostications, Barnes's English sounds and looks
like a foreign language, it is Renaissance English—not ancient Greek—
that she exploits to express the expatriation of lesbian culture from
contemporary literary history as well as the lure of lesbian lore. Threatening to begin a whole new literary history for a coming age that lib-
erates female coming, Barnes's *Almanack* implicitly confirms Dame
Musset's view that "Love of Woman for Woman should increase Terror" (20).[74]

In the *Ladies Almanack,* as in *Nightwood* (1936), Barnes managed to
delineate the unique problems and passions of both the lesbian community and the lesbian couple. In part she suggests, as Hall does, that
the lesbian-expatriate coterie is a menagerie of eccentrics, some of whom
are wealthy voyeurs seeking to buy or steal the love they cannot otherwise attain. Like the lesbian community, moreover, the female couple

suffers the same consequences of promiscuity detailed in *The Well of Loneliness*. *Nightwood* records Nora Flood's anguished reaction to her lover Robin Vote's sexual flings, an anguish explained by Nora's claim that if "A man is another person—a woman is yourself."[75] Thus, the loss of the beloved is experienced as a loss of self, a point in *Nightwood* which reflects Barnes's own tortured erotic relationship with the sculptor Thelma Wood. Yet to the extent that Barnes attributes wisdom and creativity to Natalie Barney's circle and to the lesbian couple, she challenges assumptions about the autonomy of the author and the singularity of the subject.

Throughout *Nightwood*, in particular, lesbian desire educates the soul through a visionary breakdown of the self that illuminates the imperatives of the collaborative stance we have been tracing here: "She is myself," the lover exclaims about her beloved, the character modeled on Thelma Wood; "What am I to do?" (127). Indeed, *Nightwood* can be read as an anxious meditation on the problem of identity in a lesbian relationship. When, early in their life together, Nora realizes that she cannot keep Robin from wandering to other lovers, her pain feels like self-division: "As an amputated hand cannot be disowned . . . so Robin was an amputation that Nora could not renounce" (59). For all of her altruistic devotion to the other, Nora's unnerving dependency on her beloved sometimes feels like selfishness: "I thought I loved her for her sake, and I found it was for my own" (151). The question Barnes poses is thus the query Nora puts to her spiritual adviser, the transvestite Dr. O'Connor: "have you ever loved someone and it became yourself?" (152). Viewing the lesbian couple as a modern equivalent of Emily Brontë's passionately bonded Catherine Earnshaw and Heathcliff— "I can't live without my heart" (156), Nora exclaims—Barnes delineates lesbianism as offering an almost mythic plenitude of being from which her characters, destined to fall, discover the knowledge of their perpetual exile.

Finally, then, Barnes suggests that lesbian creativity cannot be said to originate from the single self, as Lowell does, too, when she entitles her sequence of love poems to her companion Ada Russell "Two Speak Together." Indeed, in her own way Lowell was as indebted to the woman she called "Peter" as Vivien was to Barney, as H. D. was to Bryher, and as Barnes was to the woman she called "Simon," for Ada Russell scrupulously guarded Lowell's privacy and served not only as the source of her poetic inspiration but also as a secretary and a nurse. No wonder that Lowell wanted to put up a sign above the doorway at Sevenels— "Lowell & Russell, Makers of Fine Poems."[76] A comparable gesture may have been contemplated by Radclyffe Hall, who had provisionally entitled her novel *Stephen* but quickly exchanged it for Una Troubridge's more evocative title, *The Well of Loneliness*.[77] Barney's effort to establish an Academie des Femmes, like Bryher's participation in H. D.'s visions, is yet another (quite different but fitting) symbol of the aesthetic of mutuality that informs the sapphistries of Renée Vivien and H. D. and that would furnish one of the most confounding problems Gertrude Stein confronted.

Both Lowell and Barnes uncovered the reason why Gertrude Stein, one of the creators of what Lillian Faderman calls "Lesbos in Paris,"[78] rejected the confessional lyricism, the wounded eroticism, and the foreign exoticism linked to her classical Greek precursor. Certainly, too, Stein's atelier, with its collection of famous male painters, contrasted strikingly with the Temple of Friendship behind the rue Jacob in which Natalie Barney at times established a virtual no man's land. Significantly, the only time Stein attended Barney's salon was for an evening arranged by Barney in Stein's honor.[79] Djuna Barnes captures the revulsion that Barney's other friends may have felt about Stein's solipsism: "I couldn't stand her. She had to be the centre of everything. A monstrous ego."[80] Yet, it was precisely because Stein "had to be the centre" that she analyzed the problems implicit in the same collaborative enterprises that fueled Vivien's relationship to Barney, H. D.'s to Bryher, Lowell's to Ada Russell, Barnes's to Thelma Wood, and Hall's to Una Troubridge. In particular, Stein asks, what does it mean to "have" Natalie Barney, Bryher, Ada Russell, Thelma Wood, or Una Troubridge? And what does it mean to "be" Natalie Barney, Bryher, Ada Russell, Thelma Wood, or Una Troubridge? In terms of her contemporaries' use of Sappho, moreover, Stein asks, what does it mean to write "as," "for," or "with" another?

Stein came to this question, which animates her finest work, through the problem poetry poses for the lesbian writer. Although a number of her contemporaries forged a language to express their desire for women by excavating a fantastic lesbian precursor, Stein refused all predecessors: "If you write the way it has already been written . . . then you are serving mammon, because you are living by something some one has already been earning or has earned." Determined, instead, to "write as you are to be writing," even if that means "not earning anything," Stein placed herself in opposition to everything that "has already been written."[81] She would express her desire not by reclaiming a pre-patriarchal past through Sappho but by claiming a post-patriarchal future. Significantly, then, in Otto Weininger's *Sex and Character* (1904), which influenced her early literary development, she would have learned that "Sappho was *only* the forerunner of a long line of famous women who were either homo-sexually or bisexually inclined . . . . homo-sex-uality in a woman is the outcome of her masculinity and presupposes a higher degree of development" (emphasis ours).[82]

How does the twentieth-century woman poet resolve the contradic-tion between creativity and femininity, if she wishes to express her de-sire not for a master but for a mistress? How can the younger sister of an ambitious, artistic brother go about proving her own priority, as Stein later did when, claiming superiority to her brother Leo, she as-serted that "it was I who was the genius, there was no reason for it but I was, and he was not"?[83] What do, say, such different geniuses as Shakespeare, Tolstoi, William James, Whitehead, Einstein, Picasso, and Matisse have in common? To certify the authority identified with both maleness and genius, these men had what Stein needed: a wife. Ex-ploiting a strategy of male impersonation—the "masculinity complex" we discussed in *The War of the Words*—to appropriate male authority and to reclaim the muse for herself, Stein evolved some of her most innovative aesthetic strategies after she "married" Alice B. Toklas, and their partnership resulted in what D. H. Lawrence called most mar-riages, an *"egoïsme à deux."*[84]

With the help of her "wife," Stein sought to stand the nineteenth-century poetic tradition of her foremothers on its head. Replacing their humility with her hubris, she decided to tell the truth not "slant" but in a language that consists of "the exact word and the words that should be used."[85] Indeed, she placed in opposition to what we called in *The Madwoman in the Attic* the nineteenth-century "aesthetic of renuncia-tion" a twentieth-century aesthetic of solipsism. Paradoxically, though, she shaped this aesthetic out of her collaboration with Alice B. Toklas, who served as muse, model, lover, alter ego, audience, secretary, pub-lisher, cook, and travel agent rolled into one. Together, the two were one self-sufficient unit, and their self-sufficiency served not only as the source but as the subject of Stein's explorations of the psychological and ethical repercussions of lesbian collaboration.

Many readers of Stein's early works—*Q.E.D.* (composed 1903), *Three Lives* (1909), and *The Making of Americans* (1906–11)—would agree with Catharine R. Stimpson that in them "lesbian experiences become, if possible, sadder and sadder"[86] However, in the last of these novels, written just during the period when Stein invited Alice B. Toklas to replace Leo in the apartment on the rue de Fleurus, she explains why her loneliness and frustration would disappear when she found the acceptance she craved:

> you are ashamed for every one must think you are a silly or a
> crazy one and yet you write it and you are ashamed, you know

you will be laughed at or pitied by every one and *you have a queer feeling* and you are not very certain and you go on writing. Then *someone says yes to it,* to something you are liking, or doing or making and then *never again can you have completely such a feeling of being afraid and ashamed* that you had then when you were writing or liking the thing and not any one had said yes about the thing.[87] [emphasis ours]

Whether it is writing or lovemaking, the "something you are liking or doing or making" is no longer "silly" or "crazy" or "queer" when "someone says yes to it," and Alice B. Toklas, who helped type this manuscript, remained the yes-sayer throughout Stein's career.

The word "queer" appears in another important passage in *The Making of Americans,* where Stein explains why she differs from the Hersland family she is describing. Of German-Jewish stock, her characters are assimilating themselves into American culture: "The old people in a new world, the new people made out of the old, that is the story that I mean to tell, for that is what really is and what I really know" (*MOA* 3). As a new person in the old world, Stein reverses the progress of her family, explaining that "queer people" or "Brother Singulars" escape "the disapproval of our cousins, the courageous condescension of our friends" by fleeing "to the kindly comfort of an older world accustomed to take all manner of strange forms into its bosom" (*MOA* 20). Avoiding the disapproval "queer people" face through her expatriation and the discomfort of a "queer feeling" through her relationship with "someone [who] says yes," Stein evades the fate of the Herslands to establish herself in her own land. Later she would explain even more explicitly that, precisely because Paris did not shape her identity, it was a perfect home: "I am an American and I have lived half my life in Paris, not the half that made me but the half in which I made what I made."[88] Surrounding herself with French speakers so as to be "all alone with english and myself,"[89] Stein sought an autonomy which she was destined to attain by being "alone" with English and with Alice B. Toklas.

Stein's first, brief portrait, "Ada" (1922), reveals that her singularity in literary history was indebted to the complementarity she attained with her lifelong companion. The portrait begins with Barnes Colhard, a man who is stymied in all aspects of his life by passivity and negativism: "Barnes Colhard did not say he would not do it but he did not do it."[90] Antithetically, his older sister tells him to marry and tells her mother "pretty stories," some of which her mother does not appreciate. But when her mother dies, Ada is inhibited in a house inhabited by dying generations of male ancestors, and she must struggle for independence from her father even after she leaves, sending him "tender letters" until she wins his reluctant acquiescence in her departure. Just as Ada's living is contrasted with her brother's denying, her ecstatic union is contrasted with his passionless marriage. "She came to be happier than anybody else who was living then," for "She was telling someone, who was loving every story that was charming." Although before "she was always trembling" amidst the dying of her father's house, now "Trembling was all living, living was all loving, some one was then the other one." As if writing about the intensity Lowell felt about *her* Ada, Stein brilliantly captures the ecstasy of finding "one" whose reality is as substantial (or more so) than one's self.[91]

Composed in 1909, "Ada" is in many respects remarkably accurate about Alice B. Toklas's relationship with her younger brother, her remote father, and the mother who died from cancer when Alice was twenty years old.[92] Revising Clarence and Ferdinand Toklas into the cold, hard Barnes and Abram Colhard, transforming Alice into Ada, Stein presents Alice as the beginning—the Aleph or the Adam—of what would "aid her" to escape patriarchal constraints, as she does, too, in a later celebration of her "wedding": "Aid and added, to aid to be added. I am sure that she has been added to me."[93] But Ada's history also resembles Stein's own life, namely her efforts to extricate herself from Leo. In *Two*, which in the Yale edition has as its subtitle *Gertrude Stein and Her Brother* (composed 1910–12), Stein juxtaposes two characters in a vocabulary that echoes that of "Ada": while he is "The one [who] is one hearing himself," she is "The other one [who] is one hearing some one."[94] That it was Ada and Ada's story which made Stein a genius is clarified in "Portraits and Repetition," where Stein explains that "the essence of genius, of being most intensely alive," consists in "being one who is at the same time talking and listening" (*LIA* 170). Again, in her American lectures, Stein claimed that "being a genius, I am most entirely and completely listening and talking, the two in one and the one in two" (*LIA* 180).

Whether Ada is Alice or Gertrude, she is undoubtedly an artist, telling "pretty stories" to her mother, exchanging "tender letters" with her father, and, finally, recuperating her oral intimacy with her mother through a relationship with "one" who was "almost always listening." Because they exchange roles as author and audience, attaining the intersubjectivity of "the two in one and the one in two," the subjects of "Ada" experience their erotic union as an aesthetic liberation, as do Stein's "Miss Furr and Miss Skeene," a couple who live together in order to be "regular in being gay" and who simultaneously "cultivat[e] their voices."[95] By the end of "Ada," as the listening "one" becomes the telling "one," the creature Stein sometimes calls "Lilly and Tilly," sometimes "Baby and jew," sometimes "Lovey and Pussy," sometimes

"Gertrice and Altrude," is born, and it therefore seems appropriate that, according to Richard Bridgman, this manuscript appears to be written in two hands.[96]

As Carolyn Burke has demonstrated, "Ada" solved the mathematical problem of how two can be one by imagining "loving sisters" no longer "trapped in the frustrating emotional structures of family life,"[97] although "Ada" also presents the lesbian couple as an alternative family. As early as 1909, when she wrote *Q.E.D.*, moreover, Stein had created a fictional surrogate who espouses the middle-class "ideal of affectionate family life" even as she exclaims (like a parodic orthodox Jew in his daily morning prayer), "I always did thank God I wasn't born a woman."[98] Stein thought, too, that it was precisely her identity as sister to Leo that she had to exchange to become not only the husband of Alice but a man of genius. Indeed, it may have been precisely that transformation from little sister to man of genius which drew Stein to the one woman author who influenced her early development, George Eliot,[99] for Marian Evans had anguished over her elopement with a married man, a socially disreputable decision that divorced her from both her brother and polite society even as it turned her into a "man of letters." Just as Eliot avoided the woman question, a youthful Stein, when advised to "remember the cause of women," had responded, "you don't know what it is to be bored" (*AABT* 77). *The Autobiography of Alice B. Toklas* further explains, moreover, that, while Stein does not "[mind] the cause of women or any other cause," it "does not happen to be her business" (*AABT* 78).

One way to make sense of Stein's belief that the woman's cause is not her business may be to place it in the context of the two major roles—those of "husband" and "baby"—that she played with Alice B. Toklas, roles which paradoxically freed Stein to love both her "wife-mother" and herself even as they empowered her to continue writing and shaped the way she wrote. In such pieces as "If You Had Three Husbands" and "Farragut or a Husband's Recompense," Stein announces that "A husband's recompense is to have his wife."[100] In "A Sonatina Followed by Another" (composed 1921), "Little Alice B. is the wife for me," Stein explains, adding that "she can be born along by a husband strong who has not his hair shorn" [sic] (*YGS* 295). Similarly, in "Didn't Nelly and Lilly Love You" (1922), Stein boasts, "I am a husband who is very very good I have a character that covers me like a hood and must be understood which it is by my wife whom I love with all my life" (*AFAM* 245). Here the decision to live with Alice is quite explicitly sexual: "How can you control weddings. When all is said one is wedded to bed. She came and saw and seeing cried I am your bride. And I said. I understand the language" (*AFAM* 223). Although at times her relationship with Alice

B. Toklas is described as "so wifely" (*AFAM* 226), more frequently Stein's "language of the self" exploits the diction of marriage to present the writer as, in Stimpson's words, "male and masculine."[101]

But Toklas and Stein are not just a husband and wife writing team. "Mutter to me" (*AFAM* 227), Stein puns as Toklas's "baby," an infant who frequently asks to eat or be eaten, to please or be pleased. In "A Sonatina Followed by Another," several refrains—"I see the moon and the moon sees me god bless the moon and god bless me which is she" (*YGS* 298)—reflect the same pleasure in babytalk that Stein associates with her private conversations with Alice B. Toklas: "little baby sweet can always be a treat," Stein rhymes about why "I play for baby I play she is baby and I play that baby" (*YGS* 307, 311). As Marianne DeKoven has demonstrated, "the fact that [Stein] was Baby needn't undermine her power as long as Mama was also subservient wife rather than dominant father or brother."[102] The interdependency of Stein and Toklas as husband-wife and as parent-baby—"She and I say we" (*AFAM* 226)—means that together "We find that there was really no need of men and women" (*AFAM* 234).

One of the most ambitious of Stein's love poems, "Lifting Belly" (1915–17), presents one lover's request—"Please be the man"—with the other lover's ready compliance: "I am the man" (*YGS* 51). Even as it celebrates the stability of affectionate family life and portrays lesbianism as the epitome of any loving relationship, Stein's verse dramatically depicts the lesbian couple taking or relinquishing the roles provided by heterosexuality. Far from being a deviation from the norm, as it is in *The Well of Loneliness,* or a form of damnation, as it is in Renée Vivien's verse, or a refuge from the pain of heterosexuality, as it was in H. D.'s life, or a transcendental wisdom, as it is in *Nightwood,* lesbianism here involves the playfulness of improvisational role playing between "Darling wife" and "Little husband" (*YGS* 49), both of whom are devoted to a "Baby love" (*YGS* 8) that allows them to savour the pleasures of "Come eat it" (*YGS* 35).

As Stein repeatedly asks to be babied as a husband, she slyly jokes that husbands *are* babies. Some of the patter between husband-baby and wife sounds vaudevillian: "Call me semblances. / I call you a cab sir" (*YGS* 29). Some of the chatter is baby-talk: "Here is a bun for my bunny. / Every little bun is of honey. / On the little bun is my oney. / My little bun is so funny" (*YGS* 41). Some of the dialogue illustrates the pleasure of both erotic and linguistic repetition:

> Kiss my lips. She did.
> Kiss my lips again she did.
> Kiss my lips over and over and over again she did. [*YGS* 19]

Breaking down the distinction between life and art, "Lifting Belly" proposes that the language of love and love of language become indistinguishable and inextinguishable: "I can rhyme. / In English. / In loving"
(*YGS* 43).

For a writer who could name her dogs "Basket" and "Byron" and
her Ford "Aunt Pauline," even the imposed secretiveness of lesbian
encoding seems to have provided an exhilarating opportunity to display the arbitrariness of naming, to demonstrate the gratuitous relationship between things and names, between, for example, orgasms
and "cows" or "Caesars."[103] Who is in a better position to prove that
"Any and every one is an authority" (*YGS* 4) than the two characters
called—in the only work Stein wrote in French—*"Deux Soeurs qui ne sont
pas soeurs."*[104] The interchangeability of the speakers in "Lifting Belly"
sometimes merges Toklas and Stein into one antiphonal self, although
elsewhere Stein emerges as, say, a "Mount Fatty," who is in a splendid
position to lift her belly in a belly laugh or a belly dance. The phrase
"Lifting Belly" reappears countless times in the poem: it is "a language," "so strong," "so erroneous," "no joke," "a terminus," "so kind
to me," "so able to be praised," "not noisy," "so dear," and "here." Not
a specifically genital term, Stein's "belly" refers us to the location of the
Stein-Toklas country house outside of Belley, to the womb, to the stom-
ach, to the appetites that are fed without being sated.

A fitting tribute to the woman who would later compose a famous
cookbook, "Lifting Belly" also illuminates Stein's chant in "Patriarchal
Poetry" (1927):

> I double you, of course you do. You double me, very likely to
> be. You double I double I double you double. I double you dou-
> ble me I double you you double me. [*YGS* 115]

The speaker's decision here "To be we to be to be we" is made possible
by "the wife of my bosom" who "makes of her husband / A proud and
happy man" (*YGS* 124). Like a character in her late novel *Ida* (1941),
Stein was clearly "tired of being just one."[105] In her poetry, then, she
joyously recorded her sense that "In the midst of writing there is merriment" (*YGS* 54) and celebrated her intuition that the affiliative stance
we identify with the "masculinity complex" involved her in a creative,
collaborative enterprise with Toklas.

———————

But what Stein defines as "merriment" sometimes reads like a dreary
experiment, for the private role of husband-baby-genius often functioned as a kind of trap in the construction of a public oeuvre. Certainly
the personal allusions and repetitions of "Lifting Belly" and "Patriar-

chal Poetry," like the obscurity of many of the portraits, plays, and poems Stein composed in this period, pose problems to her readers that critics have attempted to solve with diverse theories. Steinese has variously been understood as an incantatory form of chanting, as automatic writing, as a poetic equivalent to Cubist painting, as a literary analogue to atonal music, and as a linguistic form of either scientific relativism or philosophic nominalism. Most recently, the incomprehensibility of this writing has been explained in terms of two, quite different strategies. Some critics suggest that Stein's obfuscation is a camouflage to hide and simultaneously express her lesbianism in a hostile, heterosexual culture while others argue that it is a subversive strategy of deconstruction which critiques the phallogocentrism of language.[106]

Most tempting of all is a combination of these last two theories, Neil Schmitz's brilliant reading of Stein's linguistic exuberance as a struggle with "the power of classification, and the consequence of gender," an effort to "move back and forth between different symbolic orders, different discursive systems, in language, between a figurative identification with the Father and a figurative identification with the Mother, between scientific discourse and chatter."[107] Schmitz considers Stein's "program" a comic form of *"jouissance"* which seeks "to deconstruct an entire system of patriarchal identification."[108] As exhilarating as it is to imagine Stein as a composite of the Marx brothers, Hélène Cixous, and Jacques Derrida, however, both the works she attempted to publish throughout the twenties and the theories she evolved to explain her development seem less comic than persistently, tenaciously, even boringly incomprehensible and self-serving. Draining significance from what has historically signified, Stein's oeuvre in the middle of her career is easier and more fun to theorize about than it is to read.

For the most part, the literature Stein produced throughout the twenties—even the lesbian poetry we considered earlier—can only be "interpreted" through a selective process of decontextualization because it is so completely devoted to divorcing language from meaning. As Natalie Barney put it, speaking of Stein, "It's hard to get something to mean nothing and nothing to mean something."[109] Indeed, in spite of the heroic efforts of Stein's critics and biographers, it is also hard to get something that is meant to mean nothing to mean something. Just a glance at the beginnings of some of this writer's texts from the twenties illustrates the dilemma she poses to her readers. "A History of Having a Great Many Times Not Continued to Be Friends" (1924) begins: "It was merely that after having been for what might be said unified and not forbidden it might be said of it that this follows in order that more are to be seen" (*AFAM* 287). The first sentence of "Colored as Colors, a Gift" (1924) is "She gave, he gave he gave she gave, he gave it as he gave it she said she would consider it as her gift" (*AFAM* 381). Written in simple English words that are at least sometimes presented in grammatically "correct" constructions, Stein's texts can nevertheless only function as Rorschach tests in which readers discover their own theories corroborated, for Steinese constitutes an attack on the very idea of literature.

Precisely because so many of Stein's sentences cannot be interpreted, the reader is thrown back on the need to contextualize them as speech acts coming from *someone,* namely the Stein who then gets reconstructed by the critic in any number of different guises. What is important here, regardless of those guises, is that Stein herself remains the central focus of interpretation at least in part by creating what appears to be either supra- or substandard English. Whether they are produced by the artist-genius or the artist-baby, a number of Stein's linguistic experiments can be viewed as meditations on or enactments of literary incompetence or illiteracy. Early in her career, Stein's language had captured American immigrants' diction so well that a publisher was once led to suppose that she herself had not mastered the English language (*AABT* 63). Later—in the two examples above, for instance—Stein's speaker could be imagined as an illiterate freshman trying out formal, self-certifying phrases ("It was merely that," "it might be said of it that," "this follows in order that"); or her speaker could be parsing English verbs or using the words as a kind of rhythmic accompaniment to, say, bouncing a ball against the pavement ("She gave, he gave he gave she gave, he gave").

Stein's most ingenious successful linguistic experiments are closely connected to the role of baby she played to the mother of her invention. Some of her most famous *bon mots* are notable for rhymes—"Pigeons on the grass. Alas."—that explain why she earned the title "Mother Goose of Montparnasse." In the poetry, we find take-offs on popular songs ("I see the luck / and the luck sees me I see the lucky one be lucky" ["Sonnets That Please"]), joke definitions ("What is a nail. A nail is unison" ["Susie Asado"]), and nonsensical sing-songs ("I like a motto. / Lotto. / Pearls by girls. / Logs by dogs. / Pens by hens. / And suits by fruits" ["Brim Beauvais"]).[110] In her verse conversations with Alice, the interchangeability of the lovers might explain the reason why the speaker's identity cannot be established; however, the same strategy is used in a portrait of "Mrs. Whitehead," where it is not clear who is saying, "I cannot say to stay," and who is answering, "No please don't get up."[111] In addition, the arbitrariness of gender categories established by the lesbian relationship may seem related to the arbitrariness of generic conventions in the plays, which sometimes have as many as one hundred acts.

If we acquiesce in the theories of Julia Kristeva, as Schmitz and DeKoven have, this sort of baby-talk would read like a pre-Oedipal, pre-symbolic mode of playful, anarchic signification which calls into question the order, hierarchy, linearity, and mastery of patriarchal discourse.[112] Certainly, by using nonsense Stein defamiliarizes sense; by composing illiterate lines, she questions literacy; by exploiting baby-talk, she deconstructs adult talk; by unmaking meaning, she lays bare the conventionality of all naming. In other words, Stein's efforts to take to its absurd limits the autonomy of the genius allow her to satirize the tradition of authority: the author—like the husband—*is* a narcissistic baby, she implies, an egotistical maniac creating over and over again a world of words that means something only to himself. "Joyce and I are at opposite poles,"[113] Stein quite rightly explained, for his efforts to pack each sentence with more and more arcane allusions were directly at odds with her attempts to put literary history behind herself by unraveling meaning, by making it impossible to mean.

Yet, after announcing that "Joyce and I are at opposite poles," Stein added, "but our work comes to the same thing, the creation of something new." One could further speculate that, like Joyce, Stein takes to its absurd limits the autonomy of the genius. The only meaning the sentences we just quoted really establish is the point that, in Stein's words, "Grammar is in our power."[114] Unmaking is a form of composition that confers masculinity even more inexorably than making does, as Stein implies in *A Novel of Thank You* (1925–26), where what she claims about fiction—"A novel makes a man"[115]—applies to her own anti-novel as well. If writing guarantees masculinity, what is written is female: "She is my wife. That is what a paragraph is."[116] "Finally George A Vocabulary of Thinking" and "Arthur A Grammar," two sections of *How To Write*, epitomize Stein's identification of anti-grammar with male names. Benstock therefore argues that Stein—associating the signified with the male and the signifier with the female—tried to disrupt "the referential notion of meaning implied by the equation *signifier* + *signified* = *sign*."[117] But surely by subtracting the signifier from the signified, Stein could refuse to reveal meaning, and she thereby exerts her control over language just as her most obscurely experimental contemporaries did by multiplying the significance of the signifier. Indeed, what Schmitz's theories and most other readings of Stein's development evade is how the unmaking of language, even more than the making of language, remains for her a mode of mastery and of masculinity. From this perspective, the child-Stein is no less imperious than the husband-Stein, for both resemble the character Freud called "His Majesty the baby."[118]

As if to emphasize her control over meaning-(un)making and her audience's impotence or irrelevance, Stein outlined in her lectures on composition and literature a self-authorizing aesthetics of solipsism. First, she announces that all of literary history is somehow her own: "it is a pleasure to know that there is so much English literature and that any any moment in one's life it is all inside you. At any rate it is all inside me" (*LIA* 12). Second, by committing herself to "making what I know come out as I know it, come out not as remembering," Stein refuses to write what she calls "soothing" or representational works (*LIA* 181). Instead she analyzes only one subject, namely the dynamics of her own consciousness while she is in the act of creating. Third, because this process of writing is "very exciting" (*LIA* 181), it is intrinsically worthwhile, and Stein therefore refuses either to revise or reject any of her work: "I have never understood how people could labor over a manuscript, write and rewrite it many times, for to me, if you have something to say, the words are always there."[119] Fourth, insulated from her American readers, Stein creates only for herself: "In a created thing it means more to the writer than it means to the reader. It can only mean something to one person and that person the one who wrote it."[120]

While a number of readers have felt victimized by Stein's impenetrable sentences or resentful about their failure to make sense of her nonsense,[121] even the responses of her admirers identify her authorial audacity with male mastery. In a review of *The Making of Americans,* for example, its publisher Robert McAlmon captured precisely the magisterial quality of Stein's childlike pose:

> One feels that Miss Stein triumphs within herself to think that she can put words together, and, having done so, feels charmed enough to repeat them again and again, as a three-year-old child who is playing with clay might say to a nurse, "Shall I make a man? Shall I make a man?"[122]

Similarly, Virgil Thomson's view that Stein became "a Founding Father of her century" because she "dominated . . . language"[123] illuminates both the coerciveness and the male mimicry of the linguistic experiments she undertook until the moment when the stress of the Second World War propelled her into an effort to communicate. Although Sherwood Anderson imagined Stein cooking up new words in a linguistic kitchen, Thornton Wilder claimed that her writing does not imagine a reader but instead "refreshes" the writer, for "the writer is all alone, alone with *his* thoughts and *his* struggle and even with *his* relation to the outside world that lies about *him*" (emphasis ours), and Katherine Anne Porter—who sometimes thought of Stein as one of the "Amazons," beings "not-men, not-women, answerable to no function in either sex"—elsewhere called Stein "a handsome *old Jewish patriarch*" (emphasis ours).[124]

Exploiting both the use of a private language and the role of husband-baby that she had learned through her partnership with Alice B. Toklas, but also certifying the genius and the self-sufficiency she attained through her "wife," Stein presented herself as a demonic anti-God who unmakes significance in her non-literature and thereby reduces all of literary history to a history of naive signification. In fact, the very autonomy Stein achieved in her marriage with Alice helped her turn her words into weapons which rob her readers of their ability to comprehend. As Alice's phallus, Stein saw herself as "a roman and Julius Caesar and a bridge and a column and a pillar and pure how singularly refreshing" ("A Sonatina Followed by Another" [*YGS* 296]), and it took the judicial calm of a roman, a Julius Caesar, a bridge, a column, and a pillar to extrapolate a public discourse from her private life. As His Majesty the baby, moreover, Stein believed that "I can be as stupid as I like because my wife is always right."[125]

But just as His Majesty the baby oscillates between flaunting his omnipotence and suffering the anxiety of his radical dependency on the mother, the private role of husband-baby-genius continued to remain a problem for Stein precisely because the authority it conferred continuously dramatized her dependence on Alice B. Toklas. During this time, when she was—for the most part—unpublished and unread, Stein was especially touchy about the rights and rites of her own writing. "Subject-cases: The Background of a Detective Story" (1923) explicitly meditates on "collaboration, collaboration and collusion, collusion and carefulness," declaring that "there is collaboration that in collusion that there has been collusion" (*AFAM* 11).

At the end of the twenties, moreover, Stein did participate in a collaboration that became a collusion. Translating George Hugnet's "Enfances," she wanted her name on the title page of what she described to him as "our book," but the announcements "said it was his book and . . . did not say it was my book."[126] Bridgman explains that "pique" caused Stein to change the title first to "Poem Pritten on the Pfances of Georges Hugnet" and then, erasing Hugnet altogether, "Before The Flowers of Friendship Faded Friendship Faded." Significantly, the final work includes the lines:

> I love myself with a b
> Because I am beside that
> A king[127]

Beside Alice B., Stein managed to maintain a magisterial confidence: "Nobody knows what I am trying to do but I do and I know when I

succeed" (*YGS* 244). Finally, however, the fact that she could only accomplish her task by creating pages of virtually unreadable and (for
many years) unpublishable words involved her in an imitative fallacy
she would only escape when she published *The Autobiography of Alice B.
Toklas,* a book which brilliantly analyzes both the liabilities and the benefits of being a female man.

Throughout *The Autobiography,* where Stein "writes in" Alice's voice
to tell the story of their lives together, Stein presents Alice as a creator,
not only as the author of her own autobiography but also as a crafty
needlepoint artist, an ironic aphorist, the historian of Cubism, the biographer of the genius Stein, and a literary critic of Stein's linguistic practices. Alice also emerges as the person who understands and facilitates
Stein's creation of literary modernism: "I always say that you cannot
see what a picture really is or what an object really is until you dust it
every day and you cannot tell what a book is until you type it or proof-
read it" (*AABT* 106). Providing tea and sympathy when Stein's depression mounts over her unpublished manuscripts, Alice also gossips, particularly about the wives and housekeepers of geniuses, to define not
only the domestic arts of typing and dusting, of cooking and needlepoint as well as the domestic economy informing the artistic production
of masterpieces. Calling attention to Madame Matisse, who models for
and sells her husband's paintings, Alice shapes art history as the subject
of art, the source of its inspiration, the creator of those social meetings
that produce the exchange of ideas, and the economic facilitator of a
career. Besides extolling the wives of geniuses, through the figure of
Marie Laurencin *The Autobiography* justifies the atelier's division of labor between the genius and the wife. As Marjorie Perloff has recently
observed, Marie Laurencin, who functions in the text as both an artist
and the muse of Apollinaire, is often presented as drunk.[128]
    One of the few explorations we have of the wives of geniuses and
their impact on the production of culture, *The Autobiography* is a rare
tribute to the "little women" behind all the great men. Much of the
humor of the book derives from Alice's malice as she contrasts the Pro-
methean tasks of these "little women" with the Lilliputian stature of
their so-called great men. From Alice's perspective, even before the
Great War the painters reflect the housekeeper Hélène's later point
that, "worn by the war," "all men are fragile" (*AABT* 205). Living off
his wife's hat business and freezing in the apartment he must keep cold
so as to save expensive fruit for a still life, Matisse weeps when he is too
moved to speak of a sale to his wife, while even the admittedly great
Picasso combs his hair in order to heighten what he takes to be his

resemblance to President Lincoln. Understandably, then, Alice is drawn to Stein, the powerful force who arranges not only the paintings on the atelier wall but also the painters, cleverly seated at dinner parties so that they will face their own canvases.

Alice's judgment of the literary scene is even more sardonic than her view of the Impressionists and Cubists. The first time Stein took her to see Apollinaire, Alice recalls, "The room was crowded with a great many small young gentlemen." After she is told that "these little men" are poets, she is overcome: "I had never seen poets before, one poet yes but not poets" (59). Later, viewing the masters of modernist poetics, Alice portrays a series of "little men" or no-men: Wyndham Lewis ("measuring" the paintings on the atelier wall [115]), Ezra Pound ("a village explainer" [189]), Ernest Hemingway (a "yellow" "Rotarian" [204, 207]), and T. S. Eliot (who says he will only print the "very latest thing" [189] by Stein but does not). Taken in the aggregate, "everybody came and no one made any difference" (*AABT* 116).

Through the gossipy, feminine mode of Alice's voice, we are made to understand that one genius in *The Autobiography* does make a difference, the one whose presence strikes a Pavlovian "bell" in Alice's mind. Yet, although Stein implies that the effaced efforts of hostesses and mistresses need to be articulated, although she satirizes great men by demonstrating their dependence on "little women," her collaboration becomes an appropriation that further effaces such women. Most critics assume that, by impersonating her "wife" Alice to tell Ada's "pretty stories," Stein frees herself in *The Autobiography* from the isolation of her linguistic experimentation.[129] But in the context of the mystique of genius that infiltrates Alice's adulation of Stein, Picasso, and Whitehead, creativity is imagined as solitary and individualistic, a fact that explains why the narrator goes to such pains to distinguish between Picasso and his followers and why she argues that it was Whitehead who was truly responsible for the books he published jointly with Bertrand Russell. Usurping Alice's persona, appropriating Alice's voice, Stein presents herself as an unappreciated, isolated pioneer, and she thereby turns collaboration into collusion: living, listening, and telling do transform one into the other, but the result is a kind of cannibalism, as Stein makes Alice into a character of her own devising who, in turn, certifies Stein as the genius who will usher in the twentieth century.

To "have" Alice is to be a genius; but to "be" Alice is to be fictionalized as a creature who functions like a rubber stamp. The placement of "Ada" within *The Autobiography,* which clearly establishes the earlier portrait as a lesbian fairy tale, further demonstrates how lesbian collaboration can degenerate into collusion. The episode in *The Autobiography* that describes the composition of "Ada" places it in the context of

Alice's and Gertrude's conflicting needs to feed and be fed: Alice, "an extremely good five-minute cook" who wants to eat her food hot, resists reading the portrait while the food is cooling. Although she is eventually "terribly pleased with it," her initial response is one of the first clues we have about the "actual" author of *The Autobiography:* "I thought she was making fun of me and I protested, she says I protest now about my autobiography" (107). The cooking and eating of Alice are interrupted by a telling that is a forced feeding which Stein's Alice can only feebly protest.

If the manuscript written in two hands at Yale is the original "Ada," then Stein's Alice—who writes that she "can still see the little tiny pages of the note-book written forward and back"—is lying, robbing Toklas of her part in the creation of "Ada." According to W. G. Rogers, Toklas herself disliked being asked if she had a "touch in the Stein genius,"[130] and perhaps it was she who shaped this portrait of herself as a deferential helpmate. Indeed, Bridgman's meticulous account of Toklas's revisions of the manuscript of Stein's most famous book hints that the title of *The Autobiography of Alice B. Toklas* may be more accurate than we have been led to suppose by the conclusion of the text, as does his discussion of the "puzzling ailment" Stein suffered after its reception, a disturbance in her identity which "is not easy to account for."[131] By emphasizing the importance of Stein's "Stanzas in Meditation," composed during the same year that *The Autobiography* was written, Bridgman has provided all the clues without explicitly making the case.[132] Is it possible that Alice B. Toklas actually wrote *The Autobiography of Alice B. Toklas?*

A long poem that functions like an extended analysis of collaboration, "Stanzas in Meditation" is a typically obscure but atypically troubled Steinese reflection on what "he" (Stein) can claim as "mine," on what "he" has with "her" (Toklas), and on what "they" (the public or the couple) like, remember, praise, and recognize. The speaker of the poem, who is exceptionally insecure ("I cannot often be without my name" [*YGS* 365]), is obsessed with the issue of authorial ownership. With reception and reputation at stake, the speaker declares that "What I have is made to be me for mine / I should not please to share oh no of course" (*YGS* 420). Should the speaker "share" what is "mine," the art object itself might be flawed, for collaboration could produce a divided or unintegrated product. In other words, "They could however collaborate" (*YGS* 364), but such a collaboration might mean that "A poem is torn in two" (*YGS* 376). Earlier in her career, Stein had rejoiced, "How can I tell you that she wrote, that I did not write, that we quote, I quote everybody" (*AFAM* 224). But now the anxieties of collaboration revolve around betraying the other who is the beloved or being obliterated by her: "I refuse to hear her" (*YGS* 444), the speaker admits; or "I would have liked to be the only one" (*YGS* 459).

For this reason, problems of identity and integrity seem to haunt the speaker, who is ambitious to establish her own reputation, but who dreads being left alone without the support of the other. Obsessed by some sort of subterfuge ("Now how could you disguise joins," she asks, adding "After all I am known / Alone / And she calls it their pair" [*YGS* 373]), the speaker seems to fear that, because collaboration robs her of her identity as a single subject, she is collaborating with an enemy. Although Stein has "begun by thinking that it is mine," she becomes convinced that "This is an autobiography in two instances" (*YGS* 389):

> This is her autobiography one of two
> But which it is no one which it is can know [*YGS* 390]

In "Lifting Belly" Stein's motto—"When this you see, remember me"—appears in several variations, including "When this you see believe me" (*YGS* 28) and "When this you see you will kiss me" (*YGS* 48), but it surfaces in this later poem in a new, ominous form: *"She will be me when this you see"* (*YGS* 291; emphasis ours), a hint that Toklas may have written *The Autobiography* for Gertrude, who now suffers the guilt associated with the crime of false attribution or of plagiarism.

Although most readers feel that Stein created Alice B. Toklas, then, it is possible to speculate that Alice B. Toklas actually authored Gertrude Stein, or so several details in *The Autobiography* suggest. Alice, for example, did manage one impersonation through writing, a sign that she could imagine others. While corresponding with T. S. Eliot's secretary, Alice signed herself A. B. Toklas, just as his secretary used initials, and both addressed the other as "Sir": "It was only considerably afterwards that I found out that his secretary was not a young man. I don't know whether she ever found out that I was not" (*AABT*, 190). In addition, at least some suspicion is thrown on Stein's autonomous creativity through the story about her early inability to draw: during her student days, when she could not sketch a still life, one of her brothers "drew it for her," and she won the class prize (*AABT* 72). As an adult, Stein's handwriting is so "illegible" that Alice is "very often able to read it when she is not" (*AABT* 71), another indication that Alice may not be merely "copying" Stein's manuscripts. Stimpson points out, moreover, that lines attributed in Stein's work to Toklas—"This must not be put into a book" or "Husband obey your wife"—prove that Toklas used the role of subordinate to sustain her own power and serve her own ends.[133]

Toklas's authorship of other texts raises comparable doubts about the creator of *The Autobiography of Alice B. Toklas*, a work which is completely idiosyncratic in Stein's oeuvre, but which very much resembles

Toklas's cookbook and her late memoir, *What Is Remembered* (1963). *The Alice B. Toklas Cook Book* (1954), with its hilarious admission that "before any story of cooking begins, crime is inevitable,"[134] includes not only imaginative, "bloodthirsty" recipes in the section entitled "Murder in the Kitchen" but also numerous instances of domestic artistry (the *soufflé* served to Picasso surrounded by tricolored sauces [31]), inventive namings of such new creations ("Mutton Chops in Dressing-Gowns," "Giant Squab in Pyjamas," "Nameless Cookies"), and episodes that illustrate Toklas's superior insight (her realization that a particularly wonderful servant was illiterate, although "Gertrude Stein was unable to interpret Jeanne's mystery" [185]).

Ostensibly deferential even in her amused declaimer at the very end of the book ("As if a cook-book had anything to do with writing" [298]), Toklas nevertheless went on to produce in *What Is Remembered* a memoir that resembles *The Autobiography of Alice B. Toklas*. With the help of her friend Max White, who quit the project because, according to Linda Simon, he could not accept Toklas's idea of "the book as a novel," Stein's survivor created a work that, a *Times* reviewer maintained, "reads like Gertrude Stein," a view borne out by its malicious details (the "visibly large teeth" of Sarah Bernhardt),[135] its transmission of gossip ("Fernande said Marie [Laurencin] made low wild cries like small animals" [35]), its anecdotes about both wars (the Resistance fighters acknowledging Toklas's possession of a Picasso painting as a kind of badge of her Allied allegiances [167]), and its scenes from the life of the genius Stein (inquiring on her deathbed "What is the answer?" and responding to Toklas's ensuing silence by asking "what is the question?" [173]. If, given the evidence of Toklas's skill as a writer, we can consider the authorial attribution at the end of *The Autobiography* one of the most successful hoaxes in literary history, the book is less an ego trip on the part of Stein then a subversive gift from Alice B. Toklas: a gift, because it bestowed upon Stein authorship of the only book attributed to her that was and is read outside the academy; a subversive one, because its wit and clarity contrast shockingly with the dull repetitiveness of so much of Stein's other writing.

In any case, ironically, the success of *The Autobiography* would in some sense always be Toklas's, for Stein continued to be troubled by the fact that her most serious efforts remained neglected: "It always did bother me that the American public were more interested in me than in my work" (*EA* 50). To be sure, *The Autobiography* itself implies that, while Stein can write "as" Alice, Toklas is not allowed successfully to impersonate Gertrude. At one point in the narrative, when Alice carries Stein's papers to interview an officer during the war in order to get some gas for their car, she has to explain almost immediately, "I am not Mademoiselle Stein" (*AABT* 166). Yet in the cookbook account of this episode, Toklas does "replace" Stein long enough to establish a friendship with the major who is quite "alarmed" by the eventual appearance of the "real" Stein (*ABTCB* 65). Ellery Sedgwick, the editor at the *Atlantic Monthly* who had repeatedly rejected Stein's work, welcomed in *The Autobiography* "the real Miss Stein" who now "would pierce the smokescreen with which she has always so mischievously surrounded herself." [136] Almost sixty years old at the time of its publication, Stein may have been forced to recognize that this "real" writer was a character who had been created by Toklas or to recognize that, in any case, this character had certainly been presented through Alice's voice.

At the same time, however, Stein courageously confronted precisely these problems throughout her life with Toklas. Just as she had struggled in "Lifting Belly" with the idea that "Any and every one is an authority. / Does it make any difference who comes first" (*YGS*, 4), in "Stanzas in Meditation" she repeatedly acknowledges that "In union there is strength" (*YGS* 343) and meditates on whether it makes a "difference" that "one" is "two." Although competition for public recognition and anxiety about private dependency are inevitable, the poet admits, "It does not make any difference / That which they like they knew / Nor could it make any difference to use two" (*YGS* 415). Eventually, then, "our equality can indubitably spell well" (*YGS* 398), for "They like alike" (*YGS* 443). "Stanzas in Meditation" closes with the speaker asserting, "I wish once more to say that I know the difference between two" (*YGS* 463), even as she "call[s] carelessly that the door is open" (*YGS* 464), presumably to admit the other who may have been there in the writing process all along. As if to pay tribute to Stein's knowledge of "the difference between two," many years after her death Toklas attributed her initial attraction to Stein not only to the latter's "golden brown presence" but also to a voice "unlike anyone else's voice—deep, full, velvety like a great contralto's, like two voices" (*WIR* 23).

Whether the voices of *The Autobiography* were "authored" by Stein or by Toklas, their long partnership managed to dramatize both the triumphs and the tribulations of the collaborative rhetoric which shaped the achievements of so many members of the lesbian expatriate community. When Stein explains to Alice in the last sentences of *The Autobiography* that "I am going to write it for you. I am going to write it as simply as Defoe did the autobiography of Robinson Crusoe" (237), she suggests—as Neil Schmitz explains—that, just as Defoe *is* Crusoe, she *is* Alice and that, isolated together like Crusoe and Friday, they inhabit, even in the midst of Paris, a desolate desert island. [137] Defoe's hymn to entrepreneurial individualism seems like an appropriate framework for Stein's pride in herself as a self-made man and for her indebt-

edness as a self-made man to what she elsewhere called her "solitude
à *deux*."[138] Published without an author's name on the title page but
with a frontispiece photograph of Stein and Toklas which makes it
impossible to tell which is the subject and which the author, *The Autobiography of Alice B. Toklas* functions not only as a fascinating biography of
Gertrude Stein but also as an "autobiography one of two" (*YGS* 390)
that meditates on whether "it make[s] any difference to use two"
(*YGS* 415).

To return to our last epigraph and our title for this chapter, Stein's
conviction that Alice "meant" what she herself "said" (or that Alice "said"
what she [Stein] "meant") takes to its logical extreme the dynamic of
collaboration that shaped the art of even those lesbian modernists whose
works are notably different from her own. That this first, fully self-
conscious generation of lesbian writers was followed by poets and novelists who no longer needed recourse to such a strategy only underlines
the function of literary and literal forms of double talk at the beginning
of the twentieth century. Whether lesbian modernists wrote for and as
Sappho, their fantasy precursor, or for and as a lover, they derived
protection from singing, in Stein's word, "A great many songs [which]
are plural" (*AFAM* 199).

In the case of the plural songs sung with Sappho, Amy Lowell's ob-
jections to Sappho as a fantasy precursor have been reiterated by a
number of contemporary women writers. For every Rita Mae Brown,
writing "Sappho's Reply" to protect those "who have wept in direct
sunlight" with Sappho's voice which "rings down through thousands of
years," there is a Muriel Rukeyser who, rejecting "Sappho, with her
drowned hair trailing along Greek waters," calls out, "Not Sappho,
Sacco"; or an Ann Shockley who uncovers the implicit racism of elitist
Sapphic cults in "A Meeting of the Sapphic Daughters."[139] Indeed, in
recent years both heterosexual and homosexual poets seem suspicious
of the preeminence of Sappho. Carolyn Kizer begins "Pro Femina" by
considering the poetic line "From Sappho to myself," only to remind
herself that it is still "unwomanly" to discuss this subject; Susan Griffin
writes marginalia to her poems that condemn them as "Too much an
imitation of Sappho"; and Robin Morgan exclaims defiantly, "get off
my back, Sappho. / I never liked that position, / anyway."[140] But perhaps May Sarton explains Lowell's resistance to Sappho best when,
placing Sappho in the company of Emily Dickinson and Christina Rossetti, she claims that "Only in the extremity of spirit and the flesh / And
in renouncing passion did Sappho come to bless."[141]

As for the literal collaboration Stein examined and exploited throughout her career, she and Toklas soon came under attack for their mimicry of heterosexual roles.[142] Yet, the continuing attraction of the double vision they attained is evident in a recently published volume of verse by Olga Broumas and Jane Miller, for *Black Holes, Black Stockings* celebrates "We the plural."[143] "One is odd and two is odd as each is separate," the poets declare, and they go on to pose precisely the sorts of questions Stein raised with Toklas: "There was no name for it, pair and odd, pair and odd, or did I dream you there, song of my region?" (25). Situated in Greek settings and punctuated by translations of Pierre Louÿs's *Les Chansons de Bilitis*, the poems of Broumas and Miller almost seem to ferry Stein and Toklas to Lesbos because the reader cannot tell about the authorship of any single poem "which [of the poets] it is no one which it is can know" (*YGS* 390). In "Making Love to Alice," M. F. Hershman—paying tribute to the tradition of the plural that relates back to Stephen Gordon's conviction that "our name is legion" and forward to *Black Holes, Black Stockings*—also envisions the odd couple who "must know each other, the two, the one." And the contemporary poet defiantly and lovingly flings pronouns back toward what her precursors did not inherit but had managed to establish, namely a native land of lesbian imaginings: "It is as with you and I. It is / with us as them. She then she and you then I / imagine."[144]

7

Soldier's Heart:
Literary Men,
Literary Women,
and the Great War

This great war . . . is Nature's vengeance—is God's vengeance upon the people who held women in subjection, and by doing that have destroyed the perfect, human balance.

—Christabel Pankhurst

The colossal evil of the united spirit of Woman. WOMAN, German woman or American woman, or every other sort of woman, in the last war was something frightening.

—D. H. Lawrence

What this war will come to is the thing the world has needed more than anything else, more than Religion, though it will help to bring religion back; more than Democracy, though it is in its way a democratic phase; more than Civilization, though there can be no civilization without it. It will come to sex emancipation.

—Mary Austin

[T]he symptoms of shell-shock were precisely the same as those of the most common hysterical disorders of peace-time, though they often acquired new and more dramatic names in war: 'the burial-alive neurosis,' 'gas neurosis,' 'soldier's heart,' 'hysterical sympathy with the enemy.' . . . what had been predominantly a disease of women before the war became a disease of men in combat.

—Eric Leed

"History has many cunning passages," wrote T. S. Eliot in "Gerontion" (1920), "deceives with whispering ambitions, / Guides us by vanities . . . gives with such supple confusions / That the giving famishes the craving."[1] In remarkable ways, these lines apply to the "supple confusions," especially the radical sexchanges, generated by the Great War of 1914 to 1918. For all the metamorphoses of sexuality and sex roles that we have so far discussed in this volume—the gender transformations connected with the decline of faith in a white male supremacist empire, with the rise of the New Woman, with the development of an ideology of free love, with the revolt against the discontents fueled by a widespread cultural "feminization" of women, and with the emergence of lesbian literary communities—seem to have issued in a crisis that set the "whispering ambitions" of embattled men and women against each other.

As we have all been told over and over again, World War I was not just the war to end wars, a holy crusade fought to make the world safe for democracy; it was also the war of wars, a paradigm of technological warfare that in some sense created all subsequent battles in its own bleak image. Indeed, with its trenches and zeppelins, its gases and mines, this conflict has become a diabolical summary of the idea of modern warfare—western science bent to the service of western imperialism, the murderous face of Galileo revealed at last. Even the name modern historians have given it, World War *I*, defines the event as merely the first in a series of global apocalypses, while the phrase by which it was known to contemporaries, the *Great* War, with its ambiguous muddling of size and value, seems also to describe a crucial (though slightly different) millennial occurrence.

That this apocalyptic Great War involved strikingly large numbers of men as well as shockingly powerful technological forces, moreover, has always been understood to intensify its historical significance. The first modern war to employ now familiar techniques of conscription and classification in order to create gigantic armies on both sides, World War I virtually completed the Industrial Revolution's construction of anonymous dehumanized man, that impotent cypher who is frequently thought to be the twentieth century's most characteristic citizen. Indifferent, ironic, alienated, this faceless being may or may not have gone off to the front with heroic aspirations, but the war, that dark satanic mill of death, soon taught him just what he and his aspirations were worth. Infinitely replaceable, he learned how little democracy meant. Helplessly entrenched on the edge of no man's land, he saw that the desert between him and his so-called enemy was not just a metaphor for the technology of death and the death dealt by technology, it was also a symbol for the state, whose nihilistic machinery he was powerless to control or protest. Whether he shot off his own hands in an attempt to escape the front or had his hands or feet or worse shot off by the enemy, his manhood was fearfully assaulted: by a deadly bureaucracy on the one side, and a deadly technocracy on the other. Either way, he was no man, an inhabitant of the inhumane new era and a citizen of the unpromising new land into which this war of wars had led him.[2]

Of course, these many dark implications of World War I had consequences for twentieth-century literature. As Malcolm Bradbury puts
it, "many critics have seen the war as . . . the apocalypse that leads the
way into Modernism. . . . It expressed itself, again and again, as violation, intrusion, wound, the source of psychic anxiety, generational
instability, and of the mechanistic inhumanity that prevails in, say, D.
H. Lawrence's *Lady Chatterley's Lover*—a novel dominated by the 'false,
inhuman bruise of the war.' "[3] From T. S. Eliot's mysteriously sterile
Fisher King and Ernest Hemingway's sadly emasculated Jake Barnes
to Ford Madox Ford's symbolically sacrificed O Nine Morgan and Lawrence's paralyzed Clifford Chatterley, moreover, the gloomily bruised
modernist antiheroes churned out by the war suffer specifically from
sexual wounds, as if, having traveled literally or figuratively through no
man's land, all have become not just no-men, nobodies, but *not* men,
*un*men. That twentieth-century Everyman, the faceless cypher, their
authors seem to suggest, is not just publicly powerless, he is privately
impotent.[4]

But such effects of the Great War were gender-specific problems
that only men could have. Still struggling to attain public power, women
could hardly worry about the loss of an authority they had not yet fully
achieved. As for private impotence, most late Victorian young girls were
trained (and some turn-of-the-century women writers were eager) to
see "passionlessness" as a virtue rather than a failure.[5] Yet women, too,
lived through these years, and many modernist writers suggest that
women played an unusually crucial part in the era. In poems by such
representative contemporary artists as Siegfried Sassoon, Wilfred Owen,
Isaac Rosenberg, and D. H. Lawrence the unmanning terrors of combat lead not just to a generalized sexual anxiety but also to an anger
directed specifically against the female, as if the Great War itself were
primarily a climactic episode in a battle of the sexes that had already
been raging for years.

Sassoon's "Glory of Women" (1917), for instance, sardonically as-
sures British mothers, wives, and sisters that "You love us when we're
heroes, home on leave, / Or wounded in a mentionable place," but almost snarlingly reproaches them because "You can't believe that British troops 'retire' / When hell's last horror breaks them, and they run, /
Trampling the terrible corpses—blind with blood."[6] Similarly, Wilfred
Owen's "Greater Love" (1917–18) bitterly parodies a conventional erotic
lyric, personifying "Love" as a young girl and telling her with scathing
hostility that "red lips" like hers "are not so red, / As the stained stones
kissed by the English dead." As if to suggest that in fighting for "Love"
the fallen English soldiers have been killed by "Love," skewed in a death

that looks like sex, the poet goes on to observe that "the fierce love they bear / Cramps them in death's extreme decrepitude," while in his "The Last Laugh" (1918) he makes this odd parallel between sexual "dying" and death-in-war even clearer, depicting a mortally wounded man whose "mood" seems "love-languid" while "his whole face kiss[es] the mud."[7] Still more explicitly, Isaac Rosenberg's "Daughters of War" (1917) presents a chilling image of scavenging Valkyries expressing a necrophiliac "sleepless passion for the sons of valour." Describing the war as a kind of ritual in honor of "these strong everliving Amazons," Rosenberg exclaims that

> I saw in prophetic gleams
> These mighty daughters in their dances
> Beckon each soul aghast from its crimson corpse
> To mix in their glittering dances. . . .

adding that "our corroding faces / . . . must be broken—broken for evermore / So the soul can leap out / Into their huge embraces."[8]

Most dramatically, D. H. Lawrence's "Eloi, Eloi Lama Sabachthani?" (1915) summarizes the complex hostilities enacted in Sassoon's, Owen's and Rosenberg's poems, drawing upon the words Christ cried out as he died on the cross to mourn the indifference of fathers, and presenting the war metaphorically as a perverse sexual relationship which becomes a blasphemous (homo)sexual crucifixion.[9] While battle rages and death attacks, the speaker assumes in turn the terrifying roles of rapist and victim, deadly groom and dying bride. Looking with a strange mixture of desire and dread across no man's land to the trenches, he sees his enemy as "A blanched face, fixed and agonized, / Waiting" for the hideously parodic consummation of the bayonet with which "I, the lover [will] so[w] him with the seed / And plan[t] and fertiliz[e] him." This perversely revisionary primal scene is made even more terrible, however, by the voyeuristic eyes of a woman who peers "through the rents / In the purple veil" and peeps "in the empty house like a pilferer." As in Owen's poem, indeed, the look of female "Love" is somehow responsible for male suffering: like the gaze of Medusa, any woman's casual glance makes things worse.

Can this be because the war, with its deathly parody of sexuality, somehow threatened a female conquest of men? Because women were safe on the home front, is it possible that the war seemed in some peculiar sense their fault, a ritual of sacrifice to their victorious femininity? At the center of his poem, Lawrence places a series of rhetorical questions which imply as much:

Why should we hate, then, with this hate incarnate?
Why am I bridegroom of War, war's paramour? . . .
And why do the women follow us, satisfied,
Feed on our wounds like bread, receive our blood
Like glittering seed upon them for fulfilment?

[emphasis ours]

Through a paradox that is at first almost incomprehensible, this war
which has traditionally been defined as an apocalypse of masculinism
seems here to have led to an apotheosis of femaleness, a triumph of
women who feed on wounds and are fertilized by blood. If we reflect
upon this point, however, we must inevitably ask a set of questions about
the relations between the sexes during this war of wars. What part,
after all, *did* women play in the Great War? How did men perceive that
role? More specifically, what connections might there be between the
wartime activities of women and the sense of sexual wounding that
haunts so many male modernist texts? Most importantly, did women
themselves experience the wound of the war in the same way that their
sons and lovers did?

If we meditate for a while on the sexual implications of the Great
War, we must certainly decide, to begin with, that it is a classic case of
the dissonance between official, male-centered history and unofficial
female history, a dissonance about which Joan Kelly has written tellingly and about which we have been speculating throughout these volumes.[10] For not only did the apocalyptic events of this war have very
different meanings for men and women, such events were in fact very
different for men and women, a point understood almost at once by
an involved contemporary like Vera Brittain, who noted about her relationship with her soldier fiancé that the war put "a barrier of indescribable experience between men and the women whom they loved.
. . . Quite early," she added, "I realised [the] possibility of a permanent impediment to understanding. 'Sometimes,' I wrote, 'I have feared
that even if he gets through, what he has experienced out there may
change his ideas and tastes utterly.' "[11]

The nature of the barrier thrust between Brittain and her fiancé,
however, may have been even more complex than she herself realized,
for the impediment preventing a marriage of their true minds was constituted, as we shall see, not only by *his* altered experience but by *hers*.
Specifically, we will argue here that as young men became increasingly
alienated from their prewar selves, increasingly immured in the muck
and blood of no man's land, increasingly abandoned by the civilization

of which they had ostensibly been heirs, women seemed to become, as if by some uncanny swing of history's pendulum, ever more powerful. As nurses, as mistresses, as munitions workers, bus drivers, or soldiers in the "land army," even as wives and mothers, these formerly subservient creatures began to loom malevolently larger, until it was possible for a visitor to London to observe in 1918 that "England was a world of women—women in uniforms." [12] A poem called "War Girls" (1916) by the propagandist Jessie Pope described the situation succinctly and somewhat smugly:

> There's the girl who clips your ticket for the train,
>   And the girl who speeds the lift from floor to floor,
> There's the girl who does a milk-round in the rain,
>   And the girl who calls for orders at your door. . . .
> There's the motor girl who drives a heavy van,
>   There's the butcher girl who brings your joint of meat,
> There's the girl who cries "All fares, please!" like a man,
>   And the girl who whistles taxis up the street.

For, in the words of another verse, this time by Nina Macdonald,

> Ev'ry body's doing
> Something for the War,
> Girls are doing things
> They've never done before, . . .
> All the world is topsy-turvy
> Since the War began. [13]

"*All the world is topsy-turvy / Since the War began*": that phrase is a crucial one, for as we shall more generally argue, the reverses and reversals of no man's land fostered the formation of a metaphorical country not unlike the queendom Charlotte Perkins Gilman called Herland. The ecstasy (along with the sometime agony) of that state is as dramatically rendered in wartime poems, stories, and memoirs by women as it is in usually better-known works by such men as Owen, Sassoon, Lawrence, Hemingway, and Eliot. Sometimes subtly, sometimes explicitly, writers from Alice Meynell and May Sinclair to Radclyffe Hall and Virginia Woolf explored the political and economic revolution by which the Great War at least temporarily dispossessed male citizens of the primacy that had always been their birthright, while permanently granting women access to both the votes and the professions that they had never before possessed. Similarly, a number of these artists covertly or overtly celebrated the release of female desires and powers which that revolution made possible, as well as the reunion (or even reunification) of women which was a consequence of such liberated energies.

In addition, many women writers recorded drastic re-visions of society that were also, directly or indirectly, inspired by the revolutionary state in which they were living. Their enthusiasm, which might otherwise seem like morbid gloating, was explained by Virginia Woolf in a crucial passage in *Three Guineas:*

> How . . . can we explain that amazing outburst in August 1914, when the daughters of educated men . . . rushed into hospitals . . . drove lorries, worked in fields and munitions factories, and used all their immense stores of charm . . . to persuade young men that to fight was heroic . . . ? So profound was [woman's] unconscious loathing for the education of the private house that she would undertake any task however menial, exercise any fascination however fatal that enabled her to escape. Thus consciously she desired 'our splendid Empire'; unconsciously she desired our splendid war.[14]

The words as well as the deeds of the women Woolf described inevitably reinforced their male contemporaries' sense that "All the world is topsy-turvy / Since the War began" and thus intensified the misogynistic resentment with which male writers defined this Great War as a major turning point in the battle of the sexes. Moreover, although historians of the conflict as a *literary* event have tended to overlook its gender implications, such dissonant definitions of the war as a sexual crux seeped into, and colored, even postwar classics of bereavement like *The Waste Land* and *Mrs. Dalloway,* both works which (as we shall show) meditate in very different ways on the figure of a dead "good soldier." But the sexual gloom expressed by many men as well as the sexual glee experienced by many women ultimately triggered profound feelings of guilt in a number of women: to the guilt of the female survivor, with her fear that "a barrier of indescribable experience" had been thrust between even living men and the women whom they once loved, there was often added a half-conscious fear that the woman survivor might be in an inexplicable way a perpetrator of some unspeakable crime. Thus, as we shall finally argue, the invigorating sense of revolution, release, reunion, and re-vision with which the war paradoxically imbued so many women eventually darkened into reactions of anxiety and self-doubt as Herland and no man's land merged to become the nobody's land T. S. Eliot was to call "death's dream kingdom" (*CP* 79).

Almost from the first, Paul Fussell has claimed, World War I fostered characteristically modernist irony in young men by revealing exactly how spurious were their visions of heroism, and—by extension—history's images of heroism.[15] In an attempt at least partly to counter this view of the conflict, Samuel Hynes has argued that "Students of modern literary history have [a] myth of the war, as a major *literary* event" which chiefly fostered a sense of what Wilfred Owen called "the irony and the pity" of war.[16] Such a concept, Hynes proposes, disregards the extent to which both male and female war propagandists acquiesced in what we might call the Rupert Brooke view of the conflict. "Now, God be thanked Who has matched us with His hour, / And caught our youth, and wakened us from sleeping," declared Brooke in one of the famously patriotic sonnets he produced at the outset of the war. With similar fervor, Alan Seeger proclaimed in another widely read poem that "I have a rendezvous with Death / At some disputed barricade," adding passionately, "I shall not fail that rendezvous."[17] But both Brooke and Seeger were writing in the early stages of the conflict, and both were killed before disillusionment could set in.

Judging from the testimony of most survivors (and from the letters and journals of dead combatants), the high spirits with which Brooke, Seeger, and so many others embarked for the front were soon dampened. Mobilized and marched off to "glory," many idealistic soldiers soon found themselves *im*mobilized, even buried alive, in trenches of death that seemed to have been dug along the remotest margins of civilization. Here, as Eric Leed has brilliantly observed, all the traditional categories of experience through which the rational cultured mind achieves its hegemony over the irrationality of nature were grotesquely mingled, polluting each other as if in some Swiftian fantasy.[18] The "God . . . Who matched us with His Hour" was offering not just a "rendezvous with death" but a rendezvous with decay and dissolution. Leed recounts the experience of a young officer, incurably shellshocked when he was flung down "on the distended abdomen of a German several days dead" and realized "before he lost consciousness 'that the substance which filled his mouth . . . was derived from the decomposed entrails of an enemy.' . . . It would be difficult," observes the historian, "to find a more complete violation of the distinctions which separate the dead from the living, friend from enemy, rotten from edible, than this experience which left a lasting mark of pollution upon the young officer."[19]

Such male novelists and memoirists of the war as Ford Madox Ford (in *Parade's End* [1924–28]), Richard Aldington (in *Death of a Hero* [1929]) and Robert Graves (in *Goodbye to All That* [1929]) remark almost casually on the same sort of experience, for it was a common one. Ford's

Christopher Tietjens sees a column of mud-covered German deserters
as

> moving slime . . . You could not see them: the leader of them
> . . . had his glasses so thick with mud that you could not see the
> colour of his eyes, and his half-dozen decorations were like the
> beginnings of swallows' nests, his beard like stalactites. . . . Those
> moving saurians compacted of slime kept on passing him. . . .

and Christopher's top sergeant shudderingly remembers a day when
"we trod on the frozen faces of dead Germans as we doubled."[20] Of
his "hero," George Winterbourne, Aldington tells us that "He lived
among smashed bodies and human remains in an infernal cemetery,"[21]
while Graves describes snatching his "fingers in horror from where I
had planted them on the slimy body of an old corpse."[22] Even Vera
Brittain, safe for a while at home, observes that when the filthy clothes
of her dead fiancé were returned from the front, "the mud of France
which covered them was not ordinary mud . . . it was as though it were
saturated with dead bodies" (*TY* 252–53). No wonder, then, that before
his death her Roland had written her bitterly about his spiritual metamorphosis and his radical alienation from the "normal" world she now

John Nash. *Over the Top*. Trustees of the Imperial War Museum

seemed to inhabit without him: "I feel a barbarian, a wild man of the woods [and] you seem to me rather like character in a book or someone one has dreamt of and never seen" (*TY* 216).

"I feel a barbarian, a wild man of the woods": entering the polluted realm of the trenches, young men like Roland understood themselves to have been exiled from the very culture they had been deputized to defend. From now on, their only land was no man's land, a land that was *not,* a country of the impossible. Here, Leed remarks, "the retirement of the combatant into the soil produced a landscape suffused with ambivalence . . . The battlefield was 'empty of men' and yet it was saturated with men."[23] Inevitably, such sinister invisibility combined with such deadly *being* created a sense of what Freud called the *unheimlich,* the uncanny. "In fifty years," wrote one veteran, Charles Carrington, "I have never been able to rid myself of [an] obsession with no-man's-land and the unknown world beyond it. On this side of our wire everything is familiar and every man is a friend, over there, beyond the wire, is the unknown, the uncanny."[24] As if to dramatize Carrington's point, Ford's Christopher Tietjens has an hallucinatory vision of Germans as "goblin pigs . . . emerging from shell-holes, from rifts in the

Paul Nash. *We Are Making a New World.* Trustees of the Imperial War Museum

torn earth, from old trenches" (551). Yet of course no man's land was real in its bizarre unreality, and to become a denizen of that Unreal Kingdom was to become, oneself, unreal (figures, pages 266–68).

Practically speaking, such a feeling of unreality or uncanniness was actually realistic. As Graves notes, "The average life expectancy of an infantry subaltern on the Western Front was, at some stages of the War, only about three months"[25] (*GAT* 59) so that a universal sense of doom, often manifesting itself as a *desire* for death, would seem to have been reasonable enough. Even a survivor, however, inexorably experienced the alienating metamorphosis Vera Brittain's Roland described, so that, lapsing away from his former life, the "wild man" soldier would ultimately ask, with the speaker of one of D. H. Lawrence's poems, "Am I lost? / Has death set me apart / Beforehand? / Have I crossed / That border? / Have I nothing in this dark land?" ("No Needs," *CP* 748–49). Finally, therefore, alive or dead, inhabitants of this sepulchral dream kingdom felt themselves to become—as in yet another Lawrence poem—ghosts even when they were still alive. Imagining the return of dead *and* living soldiers, Lawrence writes of "Victorious, grey, grisly ghosts in our streets, / Grey, unappeased ghosts seated in our music halls" ("Errinyes," *CP* 739–40). Forced over the borders of civilization into a country of paradox and pollution, the men of war were

Trustees of the Imperial War Museum

transformed into dead-alive beings whose fates could no longer be determined according to the rules that had governed western history from time immemorial.

Though less draconian—because less extended and less extensive— the experiences of American combatants were comparably unnerving, as, say, Hemingway's *The Sun Also Rises* (1926) and his *Farewell to Arms* (1929) as well as e. e. cummings's *The Enormous Room* (1922) testify. But perhaps the stories of black soldiers from the United States, as recounted by W. E. B. Du Bois and others, were most disturbing. As Du Bois put it in his "Essay Toward a History of the Black Man in the Great War" (1919), the conflict was a "Hell" which fostered utter "disillusion" for "Negro American troops" because "we gained the right to fight for civilization at the cost of being 'Jim-Crowed' and insulted," of having to submit to " 'nigger' drivers of the most offensive type," representatives of a "white Negro-hating oligarchy."[26]

To be sure, Du Bois (unlike his white male contemporaries) saw an advantage in the pain confronted by black troops for whom "this double experience of deliberate and devilish persecution from their own countrymen, coupled with a taste of real democracy and world-old culture [in France], was revolutionizing. They began to hate prejudice and discrimination as they had never hated it before. . . . A new, radical Negro spirit has been born in France" (*W* 895).[27] At the same time, however, Du Bois called attention to the ghastly slaughter of barely trained Senegalese soldiers—"great black fields of stark and crimson dead"—and to the assumption that "this [was] the kind of fighting that the French expected of the black Americans at first," even while noting that a "nation [the United States] with a great disease set out to rescue civilization; it took the disease with it in virulent form" (*W* 903, 921–22).

Ultimately, in other words, disease was as much Du Bois's theme as it was Lawrence's or Hemingway's or Graves's. And appropriately, therefore, the war is memorialized in Toni Morrison's *Sula* (1973)—a novel composed more than half a century after Du Bois produced his history—through the institution of National Suicide Day by the half-mad black veteran Shadrack. "Blasted and permanently astonished by the events of 1917," during which he "saw the face of a soldier near him fly off" while "the body of the headless [man] ran on," Shadrack has experienced just the disordering of categories, the "pollution" of reality, that Leed describes: "anything could be anywhere," Shadrack decides, and therefore, on January 3, 1920, he begins the annual celebration of self-immolation that will lead him and many of his fellow-citizens to apocalyptic death at the novel's end, in 1941.[28]

For the female counterparts of male combatants, however, the situation was very different. Where idealistic young men had learned at a terrible cost to deconstruct both their own aspirations to heroism and history's false images of the heroic, most young women had never needed to cope with any such illusions, either about themselves or about the official chronicle of male-dominated public events traditionally called "history." With little sense of inherited history to lose, therefore, they would seem to have had, if not everything, at least something to gain during the terrible war years of 1914 to 1918: a place in public history, a chance, even, to *make* history. Wrote one former suffragist,

> I knew nothing of European complications and cared less. The murder of an Archduke meant no more to me than some tale of an imaginary kingdom in Zenda. I asked myself if any horrors could be greater than the horrors of peace—the sweating, the daily lives of women on the streets, the cry of babes born to misery as the sparks fly upward.[29]

Ultimately, such revolutionary energy and resolute feminism as hers, together with such alienation from officially important events, was to lead to a phenomenon analyzed by Nina Auerbach in her *Communities of Women:* "Union among women . . . is one of the unacknowledged

Trustees of the Imperial War Museum

fruits of war," and particularly during World War I, "counterpointing the pacifist organizations that presented a frail, largely female bulwark against [the war] was a note of exaltation at the Amazonian countries created by the war, whose military elation spread from the suffrage battle to the nation at large."[30]

For as Jessie Pope's and Nina Macdonald's poems observe, when their menfolk went off to the trenches to be literally and figuratively shattered, the women on the home front literally and figuratively rose to the occasion and replaced them in farms and factories. Pope's "War Girls," moreover, records the exuberance with which these women settled into "the Amazonian countries created by the war." "Strong, sensible and fit, / They're out to show their grit," this writer exclaims approvingly, adding—as if in anticipation of Woolf—an important qualifier: "*No longer caged and penned up,* / They're going to keep their end up" (emphasis ours). Picture after picture from the Imperial War Museum's enormous collection of photos portraying "Women at War" illustrates her points. Liberated from parlors and petticoats alike, trousered "war girls" beam as they shovel coal, shoe horses, fight fires, drive buses, chop down trees, make shells, dig graves (figures, pages 270–76). Similarly, American women found that war, in the words of Harriot Stanton Blatch, "make[s] the blood course through the veins" be-

Trustees of the Imperial War Museum

cause, by compelling "women to work" it sends them "over the top . . . up the scaling-ladder, and out into 'All Man's Land.' " As one historian summarizes the situation, "the Great War . . . like a perverse, back-handed Santa Claus [gave countless women] the chance to infiltrate [a] man's world," or, perhaps more accurately, to transform "All Man's Land" into Herland.[31]

Although they wrote from different perspectives, a range of women who commented on the conflict nevertheless agreed on this point. The Englishwoman Iris Barry, for instance—later to become a major film critic and curator of the cinema archives at New York's Museum of Modern Art—produced in 1934 a candid and ironic memoir entitled "We Enjoyed the War," in which she noted that

> Girls older than myself were breaking away from home in the most alluringly novel manner, joining organizations called the Woman's Volunteer Reserve which had its own uniform, training as nurses, getting curiously well-paid government jobs. It was not merely that instead of staying at home they were allowed to take

Trustees of the Imperial War Museum

jobs, but that having work of this kind made them feel very important, patriotic, and highly meritorious.[32]

Indeed, Barry concluded, "We were all getting rich, or richer. . . . Wages were rising steadily" ("WEW" 280–81).

Similarly, the black American writer Alice Dunbar-Nelson declared in a brief history of "Negro Woman in War Work" (1919) that " 'Come out of the kitchen, Mary,' was the slogan of the colored woman in war time. She doffed her cap and apron and donned her overalls."[33] Although, like Du Bois, Dunbar-Nelson protested the asymmetrical wartime experiences of whites and blacks, observing, "Grim statistics prove" that black women's wages were not only lower than those of men who did the same work but also "sad to say a considerable fraction below [those] of white girls in the same service," she ultimately hailed "this marvellous influx of colored women into the industrial world" and rejoiced that "the colored women bore their changed status and higher economic independence with much more equanimity than white women on a corresponding scale of living ("NW" 396).

Trustees of the Imperial War Museum

At least as different as the backgrounds of Barry and Dunbar-Nelson were the philosophies of the British antisuffragist Mrs. Humphry
Ward and American (or for that matter British) militants who had been
struggling for years for the vote. Yet they too agreed that the war was
a kind of "backhanded Santa Claus" whose intervention in history might
create a Herland. Touring munitions factories throughout England,
Ward was struck by the "fresh . . . faces of the women, for whom
workshop life is new!"[34] "Often as I have now seen this sight, so new to
England, of a great engineering workshop filled with women," she enthused in *England's Effort: Letters to an American Friend* (1916), "it stirs
me at the twentieth time little less than it did at first," for "the 'eternal
feminine' has made one more startling incursion upon the normal web
of things!" (*EE* 42, 44).

And though in normal circumstances he was Mrs. Ward's political
antagonist, in 1915 the socialist Leonard Woolf saved in a special file
on the war a reprint of a piece from *The Maryland Suffrage News* which
observed that

> After having been told all their lives that nature has marked out
> woman's sphere and that it is wrong of her to overstep it or to
> intrude upon the sphere of men, woman is suddenly called upon
> to change herself and to fly in the face of this supposed nature.
> The result seems to show that after the war there will have to be
> a new delimitation of men's and women's work—a delimitation
> this time in which women will have a voice as well as men.

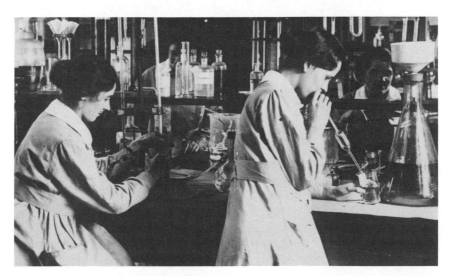

Trustees of the Imperial War Museum

In fact, this writer concluded dramatically, "if women are . . . liberated [by the war] from the old restrictions that forced them all into two or three forms of human activity—that gave them . . . the most wearisome and the most ill-paid employment, while all the better and more interesting forms of work were reserved for men—it may be that a future generation may decide that the war was worth all the stupendous cost." Three years later, such optimism was confirmed by, among other works, Mary Austin's "Sex Emancipation Through War" (1918). "Even before the war," observed Austin,

> we were beginning to suspect the footlessness of the old idea that Divine Providence had marked out women from the beginning for not more than two or three occupations. The war has come in time to save us endless agonies of doubt and discussion as to whether women have strength enough, or brains enough, for the four hundred and fifty-seven callings which war has added to those already open to women. ["SE" 611][35]

And with some jubilation she quoted "a Chicago manager with five hundred women employees" who believed that " 'Female labor, properly conditioned, is a benefit to the entire shop' " ("SE" 613).

Given the optimism of all these figures, it is very likely no coincidence that Charlotte Perkins Gilman's *Herland*, with its vision of a female utopia created by a cataclysm that wiped out all the men, was published in her feminist journal *The Forerunner* in 1915, and not surprising, either, that at least one feminist noted the accuracy of a cartoon in *Punch* depicting two women who "did not think the war would last long—it was too good to last."[36] As David Mitchell observes, "When the time came for demobilisation," many women "wept at the ending of what they now saw as the happiest and most purposeful days of their lives."[37] For despite the massive tragedy that the war constituted for an entire generation of young men—and for their grieving wives, mothers, daughters, and sisters—it also represented the first rupture with a socioeconomic history that had heretofore denied most women chances at first-class jobs—and first-class pay.

Trustees of the Imperial War Museum

To be sure, that denial persisted for a time. In June 1915, when some 78,000 women in England "had volunteered for war service in the fields of clerical and shop work, manufacture of armaments, agriculture and transport" and *The Maryland Suffrage News* was predicting a massive transformation of "woman's sphere," the "authorities" were still trying to stem the tide. And indeed, in that year, of those who had registered, only 1,800 were given employment, so that on July 17, Emmeline Pankhurst and the W.S.P.U. "organized in the centre of London a procession and demonstration of 30,000 women on behalf of women's 'right to serve.' "[38] But by 1918, the number of working women in England had risen to one-and-a-third million, with 700,000 directly replacing men, and similar figures could be given for the United States.[39] Replacing men, moreover, these women finally received the kind of pay only men had earned in the past, so that many a working-class girl could join in the ironic good cheer expressed by the speaker of Madeline Ida Bedford's "Munition Wages":

> Earning high wages? Yus,
>   Five quid a week.
> A woman, too, mind you,
>   I calls it dim sweet . . .

and boast with the same black humor that

> I drive out in taxis,
>   Do theatres in style.
> And this is mi verdict—
>   It is jolly worth while.
> Worth while, for tomorrow
>   If I'm blown to the sky,
> I'll have repaid mi wages
>   In death—and pass by.[40] [figures, pages 278–79]

Many a middle- or upper-class woman, too, could rejoice with Dr. Caroline Matthews, who asserted that because her medical services were needed at last, *"Life was worth living in those days.*[41] Such women could also triumph with the novelist Edith Wharton, who claimed "the honour of having founded the first paying work-room in Paris," an *"ouvroir"* for "wives, widows, and young girls without near relatives in the army"; who filed for safekeeping the program of a 1917 New York bazaar for war relief called "Heroland," which excitedly offered "the greatest spectacle the world has ever known" in response to "the greatest need the world has ever known"; and whose extraordinarily energetic labors for "fighting France" were rewarded with the highest prize the French government could bestow: in 1916, Wharton was made a Chevalier of the Legion of Honor.[42]

Inevitably, however, the enthusiasm and efficiency with which women of all ranks and ages filled in the vocational gaps their men had left behind reinforced the soldiers' sickened sense that the war had drastically abrogated most of the rules which had always organized western culture. Even noncombatant commentators, who conceded that their sisters "did splendid service during those days," were later to decide that "they were praised and petted out of all proportion to the value of their performances."[43] From the first, though, it had seemed to the man at the front not only that such female liberation was problematic but that his life and limbs were forfeit to the liberties and comforts of the *home* front. Thus, from Sassoon and Owen to Aldington and Graves, male war writers echoed the bitterness of Brittain's Roland, who imagined his fiancée as a citizen of a "dear, far, *forgetting* land" (*TY* 135;

Trustees of the Imperial War Museum

emphasis ours). Civilians, male and female, appeared to be fictive inhabitants of a world that had effectively insulated itself from the trenches'
city of dreadful night. Aldington's George Winterbourne goes to see
his wife, Elizabeth, and his mistress, Fanny, but "They were gesticulat-
ing across an abyss. The women were still human beings; he was merely
a . . . wisp of cannon-fodder" (*DS* 259). Graves tries to tell some London friends the story of a bombardment, which fascinates them when
they think the event took place in England, but when he explains that
it happened in France, he watches while "the look of interest faded
from their faces" (*GAT* 126). Seventeen-year-old John Kipling, dead at
the front by the time he was eighteen, writes to his father Rudyard
Kipling, who was at that time intensely involved in recruiting for the
so-called "New Army," that "You people at home don't realize how
spoilt you are."[44] And enraged at the smugness of civilians, Siegfried
Sassoon sits in a music hall and thinks "I'd like to see a Tank come
down the stalls / Lurching to rag-time tunes, or 'Home, sweet Home'"
("Blisters," *SP* 17).[45]

Ultimately, this barely veiled hostility between the front and the home
front, along with the exuberance of the women workers who had suc-

Trustees of the Imperial War Museum

ceeded to (and in) men's places, suggested that the most crucial rule the war had overturned was the rule of patrilineal succession, the founding law of patriarchal society itself. For as the early glamour of battle dissipated and late Victorian fantasies of heroism gave way to modernist visions of unreality, it became clear that this war to end all wars necessitated a sacrifice of the sons to the exigencies of the fathers—and the mothers, wives, and sisters. Even a patriotic bestseller like Ernest Raymond's *Tell England* (1922) implies, eerily, that in the new dispensation of war, sons are no longer the inheritors of their families' wealth, they *are* their families' wealth, a currency of blood that must be paid out indefinitely in order to keep the world safe, not for democracy, but for old men and for women of all ages. "Eighteen, by jove!" says a comfortable colonel to some schoolboys he is encouraging to enlist, "To be eighteen in 1914 is the best thing in England. England's wealth used to consist in other things. Nowadays you boys are the richest thing she's got. She's solvent with you and bankrupt without you."[46]

Similarly, in "The Parable of the Old Man and the Young" (1917), Wilfred Owen despairingly dramatized the generational conflict that, along with a sexual struggle, he and so many other soldiers like him saw as one of the darkest implications of the Great War. Retelling the tale of "Abram" and Isaac, he describes how the relentless father "builded parapets and trenches . . . And stretched forth the knife to slay his son," adding that even when an angel suggested that Abram "Offer the Ram of Pride instead of him . . . the old man would not so, but slew his son, / And half the seed of Europe, one by one" (*CP* 42). Finally, even Rudyard Kipling, long a spokesman for strengthening England's army, saw the ultimate tragedy of the war as a shattering of the father-son bond. Writing from a perspective diametrically opposed to Owen's essentially pacifist point of view, he blamed England's massive casualties on the failure of a militarily unprepared society to fulfill its obligation to its male heirs: "If any question why we died, / Tell them, because our fathers lied," he had a dead soldier lament in one of his bitterest "Epitaphs of the War."[47]

A comparably bleak vision of paternal failure, even culpability, is offered in a short story by Katherine Mansfield. "The Fly" (1922) focuses on a self-important older man, identified only as "the boss," who learns that a friend's daughters have seen the Belgian grave of his only son, killed in the war six years earlier. But though "the boss" tries to weep for "the boy"—to whom he had meant to pass on his business— he "wasn't feeling as he wanted to feel." Instead, he becomes preoccupied with a fly that "had fallen into his broad inkpot," and, in a perverse game, first fishes the insect out of the pot, then bombs "the little beggar" with great drops of ink, though "he felt a real admiration for the fly's courage." Mansfield's message is clear: as flies to wanton fathers are "the boys" to "the bosses" who have sacrificed their sons in the war and do not even know how to mourn them properly.[48] She and her friends, confessed Iris Barry, experienced "a feeling of rage against older people who had permitted and indeed encouraged these things to happen. . . . We had begun to blame them for the war. . . . When the war was over, the 'grown-ups' would find things changed. It would be the day for young people; we would rule then, not the old ones" ("WEW" 282).

That such a generational conflict was not just associated with but an integral part of the sexual struggle fostered by the war is made explicit in a poem by Alice Meynell which demonstrates that even while this woman artist was painfully conscious of the gloom felt by sons (and their mothers) in the years of the Great War, she was also quite capable of imagining a special glee experienced by daughters, a liberating delight energized by what Eric Leed calls "the abandonment of an old order and the actualization of a new one."[49] Specifically, Meynell, a longtime suffrage fighter, accurately foresaw that through one of the grimmer paradoxes of history the Great War might force recalcitrant men to grant women, the stereotypical peacemakers, not just a new sphere but a viable political inheritance in patriarchal society.

In fact, Meynell's "A Father of Women" (1917) seems almost to explain the sexual anxiety of D. H. Lawrence, who actually lived with her family during part of the war, for the speaker of this verse answers some of the questions Lawrence had asked in "Eloi, Eloi Lama Sabachthani?":

> Our father works in us,
> The daughters of his manhood. Not undone
> Is he, not wasted, though transmuted thus,
>   And though he left no son.
>
> Therefore on him I cry
> To arm me: "For my delicate mind a casque,
> A breastplate for my heart, courage to die,
>   Of thee, captain, I ask.

And she goes on to tell "The million living fathers of the War— / Mourning the crippled world, the bitter day" that they should finally "Approve, accept, know [us] daughters of men, / Now that your sons are dust."[50] Ostensibly calm and sympathetic, Meynell's last phrase— "Now that your sons are dust"—can be read almost as a taunt, though she very likely did not intend it that way. You have killed your sons, she seems to say, so now your daughters will inherit the world.

A devout Catholic and a "poet's poet," Meynell was plainly no war propagandist, yet some readers might well have felt that such a revolutionary vision of patriarchy "transmuted" by war aligned her with more frankly militaristic women writers. And of these there was a considerable number, a phenomenon which would also have reinforced male sexual anger by implying that women were eager to implore men to make mortal sacrifices by which they themselves stood to gain. For while their brothers groped though the rubble of no man's land, countless women manned the machines of state, urging more men to go off to battle. Robert Graves reprints a famous, indeed infamous piece of propaganda in the form of a letter from a "little mother" who argued that women should gladly "pass on the human ammunition" of sons to the nation and declared ambiguously that "we will emerge stronger women to carry on the glorious work [their] memories have handed down to us" (*GAT* 203–04).[51]

The opening lines of "The Recruit" (1917), a poem by Isabel Ecclestone MacKay, summarize the tensions Graves records:

> His mother bids him go without a tear;
>   His sweetheart walks beside him, proudly gay,
> "No coward have I loved," her clear eyes say—
> The band blares out and all the townsfolk cheer.
>
> Yet in his heart he thinks: "I am afraid!"[52]

More cynically, however, Iris Barry attributed such women's patriotic enthusiasm to a desire for literal profit. "There were widows who wore their mourning like a banner," she recalled, "and a little dressmaker who boasted proudly . . . that she had 'given three sons to England.' They were dead and she was getting compensation." "And how often," added Barry, "did I hear girls little older than myself, and their mothers, regret that they had not married poor so-and-so before he was killed! It was like throwing money out of the window!" ("WEW" 281, 282).

That one of the War Office's best-known posters proclaimed "Women of Britain say 'GO!'" (figure, opposite), therefore, and that a number of other conscription efforts harped on the same theme, would obviously have unnerved recruits and draftees. And that a kind of female censoriousness—or worse, a species of female greed—might be implicit in such a slogan seemed borne out by the fact that at times the vigorous, able-bodied "war girls," who had so often been found wanting by even the weakest of young men, became frighteningly judgmental about their male contemporaries (figure, page 284). Writing with some disgust about "the gratification that war gives to the instinct of pugnacity . . . that [is] so strong in women," Bernard Shaw described "civilized young women handing white feathers to all young men who are not in uniform."[53] Metaphorically speaking, moreover, popular women writers like Jessie Pope and Mrs. Humphry Ward (in England) as well as more serious artists like May Sinclair (in England) or Edith Wharton and Willa Cather (in the United States) distributed white feathers to large audiences of noncombatant readers.

"Who's for the trench— / Are you, my laddie?" asked Jessie Pope in her jingoistic "The Call" (1915), adding scornfully "Who's going out to win? / And who wants to save his skin— / Do you, my laddie?"[54] More mystically, May Sinclair described "the ecstasy" of battle in her *The Tree of Heaven* (1917) and Edith Wharton depicted the satisfactions of having "a son at the front" in her novel of that name. Even in correspondence with relatives and friends, indeed, Wharton saw chiefly glamour in combat: she congratulated a cousin on having given his son the "opportunity of seeing this great moment of history" and enthused to one mother that she "must be having thrilling times, with both the boys in the war already."[55]

As if in retaliation, Isaac Rosenberg included on a Christmas card that he drew for his Division in 1917 a poem that began "British women!

in your wombs you plotted / This monstrous girth of glory" and Wilfred Owen originally entitled his famous "Dulce et Decorum Est" (1917), with its violent imagery of gas-caused "vile, incurable sores on innocent tongues," "To Jessie Pope" and then "To A Certain Poetess" before deciding, instead, on a bleak allusion to Horace's "Dulce et decorum est / Pro patria mori."[56] Similarly, e. e. cummings, who spent six infuriating months in a *French* prison camp, wrote a comic poem which placed the greatest blame for male suffering on female enthusiasm. Declaring in "My Sweet Old Etcetera" (1926) that

> my sweet old etcetera
> aunt lucy during the recent
>
> war could and what
> is more did tell you just
> what everybody was fighting
> for,
> my sister
>
> isabel created hundreds
> (and
> hundreds) of socks not to
> mention shirts fleaproof earwarmers.

Trustees of the Imperial War Museum

cummings's speaker bitterly notes that "meanwhile my / self etcetera lay quietly / in the deep mud et / cetera."[57] For him, as for Rosenberg and Owen, the words of women propagandists as well as the deeds of feather-carrying girls had evidently transformed the classical Roman's noble *patria* into an indifferent or avaricious death-dealing *matria*.

Finally, then, Aldous Huxley's novella "The Farcical History of Richard Greenow" (1920)—which we discussed in *The War of the Words*— summarized the different meanings World War I had for at least some men and some women, including the fact that every feather given to a young man might mean another job, another position in society, for a young woman. Chronicling the unbrilliant career of a literary man nicknamed "Dick," Huxley tells in this satiric work the strange story of the sexual metamorphosis by which a young male intellectual's brain gives birth to a second self in the form of a popular woman novelist named "Pearl Bellairs." But, significantly, the crisis in "Dick-Pearl's" uneasily schizophrenic coexistence is reached when "Miss Bellairs, the well-known novelist" becomes a jingoistic propagandist, addressing "a series of inspiring patriotic articles" to "the Women of the Empire."[58] Worse still, the brilliant career of Dick's ambitious sister Millicent supplements and complements the life/work of "Pearl": while Dick's degraded (and degrading) female self writes "articles . . . short stories! . . . recruiting songs!" (71), Millicent first organizes a hospital supply depot, then becomes a leader in the "Ministry of Munitions . . . controlling three thousand female clerks with unsurpassed efficiency" (95). And when at last, rebelling against such alien feminine control, Dick declares himself a pacifist and goes on trial for draft evasion before the "Military Authorities," "Pearl's" vulgarly patriotic exhortations take over again, driving him irreversibly mad. Female patriotism crazes— and kills—men, says Huxley, and does so because, as Dick tells Millicent, "One sees now how the new world will be arranged after the war": the world will continue to be, in the words of Nina Macdonald's poem, "topsy turvy," and "you women will be . . . fiendishly and ruthlessly tyrannical in your administration" (96).

Putting aside such an exaggerated vision of "tyrannical" administration, it is worth considering that even the most conventionally angelic of women's wartime ministrations—jobs like rolling bandages, nursing the wounded or (as in Millicent's case) founding a hospital supply depot—may well have implied to many members of both sexes that while men were now unreal ghosts, wounded, invalid, and maybe in-valid, their sisters were triumphant survivors and apparently destined inheritors. Certainly both the rhetoric and the iconography of nursing would

seem to imply some such points. To be sure, the nurse presents herself
as a servant of her patient. "Every task," writes Vera Brittain of her
days as a v.a.d., "from the dressing of a dangerous wound to the scrub-
bing of a bed-mackintosh, had for us . . . a sacred glamour" (*TY* 210).
Yet in works by both male and female novelists the figure of the nurse
ultimately takes on a majesty which hints that she is mistress rather
than slave. After all, when men are immobilized and dehumanized, it
is only these potent women who can recall them to life, only these women
who possess the old (implicitly matriarchal) formulas for survival. Thus,
even when memoirists like Brittain express "gratitude" for the "sacred
glamour" of nursing, they seem to be pledging allegiance to a *secret*
glamour—the glamour of a knowledge which they will win from their
patients. "Towards the men," recalls Brittain, "I came to feel an almost
adoring gratitude for their . . . acceptance of my ministration. Short
of actually going to bed with them, there was hardly an intimate service
that I did not perform for one or another . . . and I [am] still thankful
for the knowledge of masculine functioning which the care of them
gave me" (*TY* 165–66; figure, below).

But of course this education in masculine functioning that the nurse

experienced as a kind of elevation was often felt by her male patient as
exploitation: her evolution into active, autonomous, transcendent subject was associated with his devolution into passive, dependent, imma-
nent medical object. In *A Farewell to Arms,* for example, Hemingway's
Frederic Henry clearly responds with a surface delight to being cared
for and about by Catherine Barkley. Yet there is, after all, something
faintly sinister in her claim that he *needs* her to make "unpleasant"
preparations for an operation on his wounded knee and something
frighteningly possessive in her assertion that "I don't want any one else
to touch you . . . I get furious if they touch you." Similarly, in *The Sun
Also Rises* Hemingway's Jake Barnes, consoled by the nymphomaniac
Brett Ashley as he lies limply on his bed, cannot forget that she "was a
V.A.D. in a hospital I was in during the war," and she fell in love with
him because "she only wanted what she couldn't have," a line that ambiguously implies a form of perverse penis envy as well as a species of
masochistic desire.[59]

More openly, Lawrence wrote in *The Ladybird* (1923) about a wounded
middle European prisoner, Count Dionys von Psanek, who tells a visiting English aristocrat with whom he is falling in love that she must
"Let me wrap your hair round my hands, like a bandage" because "I
feel I have lost my manhood for the time being," and who finally asks
her, in effect, to reconstruct him by sewing him some shirts with the
aid of an ancestral thimble that bears the emblem of his family.[60] At
the mercy of his aristocratic female nurse, this helpless alien parallels
wounded males who also appear in works by women—for example, the
amnesiac hero of Rebecca West's *The Return of the Soldier* (1918), whom
a former girlfriend restores by gathering his "soul" into "her soul . . .
and keeping it warm . . . so that his body can rest quiet for a little
time,"[61] and Lord Peter Wimsey, in Dorothy Sayers's *Busman's Honeymoon* (1937), who is so haunted by memories of the war that he can
only survive the execution of a murderer he has caught when he confesses to his bride that "you're my corner and I've come to hide."[62]

Where nurses imagined by men often do seem to have a disturbing
power, however, the nurses imagined by women appear, at least at first,
to be purely restorative; like West's Margaret and Sayers's Harriet, they
seem to want only to bring peace to their men; more important, they
seem positively (rather than negatively) maternal. The "grey nurse"
whom Virginia Woolf describes in a notoriously puzzling passage in
Mrs. Dalloway (1925) is thus a paradigm of her more realistically delineated sisters in other women's novels. Knitting steadily, "moving her
hands indefatigably yet quietly" while Peter Walsh dozes, she seems
"like the champion of the rights of sleepers" who responds to "a desire
for solace, for relief, for something outside . . . these craven men and

women." Yet even she is not an altogether positive figure. Like "The Greatest Mother in the World" depicted in Alonzo Earl Foringer's famous 1918 Red Cross War Relief poster—an enormous nurse cradling a tiny immobilized male on a doll-sized stretcher—Woolf's grey nurse evokes a parodic *pietà* in which the Virgin Mother threatens simultaneously to annoint and annihilate her long-suffering son, a point Woolf's imaginary male dreamer accurately grasps when he prays "let me walk straight on to this great figure, who will . . . mount me on her streamers and let me blow to nothingness with the rest" (below).[63]

Finally, Rudyard Kipling's "Mary Postgate" (1917) summarizes both secret male anxieties and secret female desires in a weirdly vindictive short story about a repressed nurse-governess who revenges herself for the wartime deaths of her former pupil and of a village child by watching with malevolent indifference as a dying German airman (whose plane has crashed in her garden) begs for "Le médecin! Toctor!" Brooding sadistically on death, "She hum[s]—Mary never had a voice—

Trustees of the Imperial War museum

RED CROSS OR IRON CROSS?

WOUNDED AND A PRISONER
OUR SOLDIER CRIES FOR WATER.
THE GERMAN "SISTER"
POURS IT ON THE GROUND BEFORE HIS EYES.
THERE IS NO WOMAN IN BRITAIN
WHO WOULD DO IT.
THERE IS NO WOMAN IN BRITAIN
WHO WILL FORGET IT.

Trustees of the Imperial War Museum

to herself," and later, after she has heard the unmistakable sound of the airman's last gasp, she goes upstairs to take a "luxurious hot bath before tea," from which she emerges looking "quite handsome!"[64] It is possible, of course, that her crime of omission (her failure to nurse the airman) together with her sin of commission (her delight in his death) express Kipling's own guilt at the death of young John, whose plaintive homesickness had dramatized the alienation of soldier sons from civilian fathers. At the same time, though, it is hard to overlook the writer's revulsion at his heroine's murderous sensuality—her "luxurious hot bath," her humming, her handsomeness. Does male death excite female nurses? (figure, above). Do figures like even the pious Red Cross mother experience bacchanalian satisfaction as, in Woolf's curiously ambiguous phrase, they watch their male patients, onetime oppressors, *"blow* [up] to nothingness with the rest?" (emphasis ours). A number of texts by men and women alike suggest that the revolutionary socioeconomic transformations wrought by the war's "topsy turvy" role reversals did bring about a release of female libidinal energies, as well as a liberation of female anger, which men usually found anxiety-inducing and women often found exhilarating.

On the subject of erotic release, a severely political writer like Vera Brittain is notably restrained. Yet even she implies, at least subtextually, that she experienced some such phenomenon, for while she expresses her "gratitude" to the wounded men from whom she learned as a v.a.d. about "masculine functioning," she goes on to thank the war that delivered their naked bodies into her hands for her own "early release from the sex-inhibitions that even today beset many of my female contemporaries" (*TY* 165–66). And, as if to confirm the possibility that Brittain did receive a wartime "sex education," Eric Leed notes that "Women in particular 'reacted to the war experience with a powerful increase in libido,' even though this libido attached itself to the very symbols signifying the uniformization of roles: stripes on officer's trousers . . . the sound of marching boots, batons, pistols, and so on.' " In fact, Leed quotes the psychiatrist Magnus Hirschfeld as declaring about "some of his women patients that their passion for their husbands was utterly quenched when they reappeared in civilian clothes [signaling] the resumption of domestic roles,"[65] and Hirschfeld's point is at least obliquely supported by Virginia Woolf, who discusses in *Three Guineas* "the connection between dress and war" (*TG* 21).

Was the war a festival of female sexual liberation in which the collapse of a traditional social structure "permitted," as Leed also puts it, "a range of personal contacts that had been impossible in [former lives] where hierarchies of status ruled?"[66] Certainly, as Arthur Marwick observes, one effect of the conflict seems to have been to "spread promiscuity upwards and birth-control downwards," besides fostering "nearly a threefold increase in the number of divorces."[67] "[T]he summer of 1918 was gay," confided Iris Barry. "Every one kept getting engaged to be married (often to several soldiers at once, since the chance of two of them turning up in London at the same time was remote). . . . Profitable widowhood was achieved by hundreds" ("WEW" 282). But more specifically, many male artists testify to a striking female libidinous release. In their different ways, for example, notorious heroines like Hemingway's Catherine Barkley and his Brett Ashley are set sexually free by the war, as are Lawrence's Connie Chatterley, Ivy Bolton, and Bertha Coutts, all of whom contribute to the impotence of his Clifford Chatterley and the anxiety of his Oliver Mellors.[68] In *Death of a Hero*, moreover, Richard Aldington is explicit about what he sees as the grotesque sexual permission the war has given such women. Speaking of George Winterbourne's mother, he remarks that "the effect of George's death on her temperament was . . . almost wholly erotic. The war did that to lots of women. [In] that eternity of 1914–1918 they [came] to feel that men alone were mortal, and they immortals." Similarly, George's wife and his mistress—based on Aldington's wife H. D. and his mistress

Dorothy Yorke—are "terribly at ease upon the Zion of sex, abounding in inhibitions, dream symbolism . . . masochism, Lesbianism, sodomy, etcetera" (*DH* 12, 19).

Comparable allegations against the deadliness of female desire were leveled in a number of Lawrence's stories, notably "Tickets, Please" (1918) and "Monkey Nuts" (1919). In the first, a bacchanalian group of girl tram conductors band together to enact a ritual scene of reverse rape on a tram inspector with the significant Lawrentian name of John Thomas, who they think has oppressed them by having "walked out" with too many women at once. In the second, a girl in the "land army" decides to seduce—that is, not to be chosen by but to choose—a passive young soldier. Manifesting the power of her perverse erotic will, she puts "a soft pressure" on his waist that makes "all his bones rotten," and draws him hypnotically away from his best (male) friend.[69] Finally, even when the war was over, the poet Wilfrid Gibson observed the chaos of the Armistice celebrations and, as if making even more explicit the thrust of Lawrence's and Aldington's fictions, he described the way the shrieking and prancing of "Girls who so long have tended death's machines" evoked "the frantic torches and the tambourines / Tumultuous on the midnight hills of Thrace."[70]

But the work which most explicitly associates the war with a battle between a corrosively erotic femme fatale, a kind of terrifying reincarnation of Haggard's Ayesha, and an increasingly unmanned hero is Ford's quartet *Parade's End*. This series of novels sets Sylvia Tietjens, an almost theatrically heartless socialite, against the long-suffering, indeed Christlike, Christopher Tietjens. A beauty who seems to one of her admirers like a picture "by Burne Jones . . . A cruel-looking woman with a distant smile . . . some vampire . . . La Belle Dame sans Merci" (ellipses Ford's; 386), Sylvia has already cuckolded her husband before the war, but during the war she determines to destroy him completely, if only because she has finally begun to desire him. After having spread devastating rumors about him both on the home front and at the front, Sylvia hums "Venusberg music" (442) as she sets out to seduce and betray Christopher, mentally comparing Valentine Wannop, the woman he really loves, to Wagner's pure (and, in her view, foolish) Elizabeth.

A woman who has long found "All men . . . repulsive" (30), whose marital endearments have always been "More like curses than kisses" (31), and who seems even to her own priest like a perverse worshipper of "Astarte Syriaca" (37), Sylvia has declared early in Ford's series that "I hate my husband . . . and I hate . . . I hate my child" (ellipsis Ford's; 38), a son whose legitimacy is in doubt throughout the book. But, as the same priest had predicted, "her hell on earth"—and Christopher's—really comes when her husband falls in love with another woman, at which point Sylvia immediately begins to feel "pure sexual passion" for him (400). For as Ford's searing transcriptions of her consciousness reveal, in the psyche of this vindictively liberated woman the erotic and the sadistic are inextricably entangled. Brooding on her sudden passion for her husband, Sylvia remembers

> the white bulldog I thrashed on the night before it died. . . . There's a pleasure in lashing into a naked white beast. . . . Obese and silent, like Christopher. . . . The last stud-white bulldog of that breed. . . . As Christopher is the last stud-white hope of [his] breed. [416–17]

That Christopher's struggle against Sylvia is shadowed by the story of O Nine Morgan—a Welsh miner who was senselessly killed at the front after Tietjens had refused to give him leave because the man's wife's prizefighter-lover would murder him if he went home—makes the author's point quite explicit. O Nine Morgan dies because he is not "over-sexed": he is "the other thing, that [his impotence] accounting for the prize fighter" (378). Thus, from the perspective of sexually as well as militarily embattled combatants, whether women are faithless or faithful, their eroticism is deadly.

But if male writers recounted primarily the horrors of unleashed female sexuality and recorded only secondarily the more generalized female excitement that energized such sexuality, women artists—novelists, poets, and memoirists alike—remembered, first, the excitement of the war and, second (but more diffusely), the sensuality to which such excitement led. Thus, where most male writers—at least after their earliest dreams of heroism had been deflated—associated the front with paralysis and pollution, many women imagined it as a place of freedom, ruefully comparing what they felt was their own genteel immobilization with the exhilaration of military mobility.

In her "Many Sisters to Many Brothers" (1919), Rose Macaulay articulated such women's envy of the soldier's liberation from the dreariness of the home and the impotence of the home front.

> Oh it's you that have the luck, out there in blood and muck;
>   You were born beneath a kindly star;
> All we dreamt, I and you, you can really go and do,
>   And I can't the way things are

adding (no doubt naively) that "In a trench you are sitting, while I am knitting" so "for me . . . a war is poor fun."[71] Similarly, Nora Bomford "damn[s] the shibboleth / Of sex" that leaves her "dreadfully safe," trapped "in bed / with ribbons in my nightie" while men "go to God-knows-where, with songs of Blighty," and in a poem called "Pierrot

Goes to War" (1917) Gabrielle Elliot hears "ghostly bugles, whispering down the wind—" wistfully concluding "Pierrot goes forward—but what of Pierrette?" Finally, even in an elegy for a fallen lover, Marian Allen wonders "what new kingdoms you explore" while she remains behind "beside the sluggish-moving, still canal."[72]

To women who managed to get to the front, moreover, the war did frequently offer the delight of (female) mobilization rather than the despair of (male) immobilization. For after all, to nurses and ambulance drivers, women doctors and v.a.d.s, women messengers and mechanics, the phenomenon of "modern" battle was very different from that experienced by entrenched combatants. Finally given a chance to take the wheel, these post-Victorian girls raced motorcars and motorbikes along foreign roads like adventurers exploring new lands, while their brothers dug deeper into the mud of France and Belgium. Retrieving the wounded and the dead from deadly positions, these once-decorous daughters and sisters had at last been allowed to prove their valor, and they swooped over the waste lands of the war with the energetic love of Valkyries far less sinister than Rosenberg's Amazonian

Trustees of the Imperial War Museum

"Daughters of War," their mobility alone transporting countless immobilized heroes to safe havens (figures, pages 293–98). "It is extraordinary how these women endure hardships; they refuse help, and carry the wounded themselves. They work like navvies," commented one observer.[73] And indeed, even the roar of the guns seems often to have sounded in the ears of some of these overseas volunteers like a glamorously dramatic rather than a gloomily dangerous counterpoint to adventure, and even combat's bloodier aspects sometimes appeared to them like what Lawrence called "glittering seed" instead of wounding shrapnel.

Thinking wistfully of an ambulance unit in Belgium that she had to leave, May Sinclair summarized such an ambiguously apocalyptic "joy of women in wartime" as a vision of high-speed travel through a world in process of violent transformation. "You go," she told her former mates in the Munro Corps,

> Under the thunder of the guns, the shrapnel's rain and the curved
>   lightning of the shells,
> And where the high towers are broken
> And houses crack like the staves of a thin crate filled with fire . . .
> And only my dream follows you. . . .[74]

Elsewhere, Sinclair confided, about the exhilaration of combat, that, at first, "It is only a little thrill" but it grows "steadily until it becomes ecstasy" and "[you think] 'What a fool I would have been if I hadn't come. I wouldn't have missed this run for the world."[75] Less mystically but just as enthusiastically, v.a.d.s, drivers, and nurses like Vera Brittain and Violetta Thurstan testifyied to "the exhilaration" of their departure from England, "the exciting diversion" of bombings, the "thrill in the knowledge that we were actually in a country invaded by the enemy," and the "great fun!" of life at the front (*TY* 292).[76] "Danger always adds a spice to every entertainment," confessed Thurstan, describing one retreat under heavy fire, "and as the wounded were all out and we had nobody but ourselves to think about, we could enjoy our thrilling departure . . . to the uttermost. And I must say I have rarely enjoyed anything more. It was simply glorious spinning along in that car."[77]

Even literary women who merely visited the front as observers often got caught up in the feeling that they were suddenly treading paths of glory. Recounting the places to which she had been "allowed to go" by a government that had enlisted her services as a war propagandist, Mrs. Humphry Ward exulted that she had been "to the far north" to "visit the Fleet," and

Trustees of the Imperial War Museum

been . . . within less than a mile of the fighting line itself . . . with a gas helmet close at hand! [and] been able to watch a German counter-attack, after a successful English advance, and have seen the guns flashing from the English lines, and the shell-bursts on the German trenches. . . . For a woman—a marvellous experience! (*EE* 8–9).

With equal enthusiasm, Edith Wharton declared in *Fighting France* (1915) that her "first sight" of French army headquarters at Chalons was "extraordinarily exhilarating . . . a vision of one of the central functions of a great war, in all its concentrated energy," and in *A Backward Glance* (1934) she associated her visits to the front with "jolly picnic lunches around boards resting on trestles." But even wartime Paris, far from actual combat, made her feel as though she were "reading a great poem on War" which inspired her with a sense of "exaltation."[78]

Perhaps inevitably, women writers of popular literature—including Wharton herself—exploited the excitement rather than the immobilization, the thrill rather than the filth, of the front. Troy Belknap, the young ambulance driver who is the hero of Wharton's propagandistic potboiler *The Marne* (1918) and thus a surrogate for Wharton and other women who worked for or with the ambulance corps, impulsively cries, "*Vive la France!*" and abandons his stalled vehicle to join a group of

Trustees of the Imperial War Museum

American soldiers going into battle because he feels "his greatest hour [has] struck."[79] And an even franker fantasy of patriotic excitement is played out in Alice B. Emerson's *Ruth Fielding at the War Front, or, The Hunt for the Lost Soldier* (1918). Here Ruth, the protagonist of a successful series of "books for girls," crosses no man's land to rescue a boyfriend who is being held behind the German lines. Though she only accomplishes her mission with the aid of a French spy who disguises her, first, as a German "Sub-Lieutnant" and, then, as a wealthy Bavarian lady, she never shows hesitation or fear but rather thinks boldly, as she embarks on her dangerous journey, "This was adventure, indeed!"[80]

"For a woman—a marvellous experience!" "This was adventure, indeed!" If such phrases sound inhumane or actually inhuman, it is worth remembering that most of their authors are in some sense recounting their feeling that the Great War was the first historical event to allow (indeed, to require) them to use their abilities and to be of use, to escape the private "staves" of houses as well as the patriarchal oppression of "high towers" and to enter the public realm of roads, records, maps, machines. Thus, even a pacifist like Virginia Woolf, who advised during the thirties that in the next war women should "refuse . . . to make munitions or nurse the wounded," was to cite a passage about the charisma of the Spanish civil war fighter Amalia Bonilla which observes that

"parliamentaries look at [this amazon who has killed five men] with the respectful and a bit restless admiration one feels for a 'fauve' of an unknown species" (*TG* 177–78). It is quite likely, moreover, that such a vision of "an unknown species" explains the apparently naive envy of male combatants expressed by women like Macaulay, Bomford, and Elliot; just as likely, it explains what seemed to some readers the equally naive and sentimental or even pernicious propaganda implicit not only in the writings of poetasters like Jessie Pope but also in the works of serious novelists like May Sinclair and Willa Cather.

Certainly Sinclair's account in *The Tree of Heaven* of the "ecstasy" experienced by her heroes Nicky and Michael Harrison, as well as her conviction that for these soldiers "the moment of extreme danger [is] always the 'exquisite' moment," reflects a transference to men of the liberation she herself experienced when she worked in Belgium with the Munro Corps (*IH* 346–47). Similarly, when in *One of Ours* (1923) Cather depicts the glorious luck of her hero Claude Wheeler's escape from rural Nebraska to wartime France—noting that "to be alive, to be conscious, to have one's faculties, was to be in the war" and associating

Trustees of the Imperial War Museum

the European cataclysm with the idea that now "the old dungeons and cages would be broken open for ever"—her vision of the doomed Claude's good fortune is surely a way of dreaming her own release from the deadening decorum of the provincial prairie town where she herself had always longed to be a sturdy "Willie" rather than a submissive Willa.[81]

For many women, moreover, but perhaps in particular for women like Cather, whose refusal to identify with conventional "femininity" had always made their gender an issue for them, the war facilitated not just a liberation from the constricting trivia of parlors and petticoats but an unprecedented transcendence of the profounder constraints imposed by traditional sex roles. Most dramatically, this transcendence is described in Radclyffe Hall's two crucial postwar fictions—her short story entitled "Miss Ogilvy Finds Herself" (1934) and her more famous *The Well of Loneliness*. In the first, which Hall herself saw as "the nucleus" of the early sections of *The Well* and of that novel's account of "the noble and selfless work done by hundreds of sexually inverted women during the Great War,"[82] the aging lesbian Miss Ogilvy remembers, as she is being demobilized, that her ambulance was "the merciful emblem that had set [her] free," and mourns the breaking up of the "glorious" all-female unit she has led. During her "turbulent years at the front, full of courage and hardship and high endeavour," she recalls, she had managed to forget "the bad joke that Nature seemed to have played her" in making her body a female one (*MD* 3, 4, 12).

Similarly, Stephen Gordon, the "invert" heroine of *The Well*, as we have seen, feels at the outset of the war like "a freak abandoned on a kind of *no-man's-land*" [emphasis ours] but finds herself paradoxically metamorphosed by "the terror that is war" into a member of a new woman's "battalion . . . that would never again be disbanded." For, explains Hall, "War and death" had finally, ironically, given "a right to life" to lesbians like Stephen, women who repudiated the traditions of femininity and the conventions of heterosexuality alike, and "never again would such women submit to being driven back to their holes and corners." Thus, Hall concludes, "the whirligig of war brings in its abrupt revenges."[83]

Rather than ascending what Aldington called a "Zion of Sex," then, many women saw that it was a sensuality of sisterhood which their new liberation made possible. To be sure, specifically erotic release was frequently associated with the unprecedented freedoms women were achieving, for Vera Brittain's "sex education" was complemented by the romantic permission given, in various degrees, to heterosexual characters like Miranda in Katherine Anne Porter's "Pale Horse, Pale Rider" (1936) and to lesbian heroines like Miss Ogilvy and Stephen

Gordon. Porter's protagonist, falling in love with a young soldier, meditates happily on "the simple and lovely miracle of being two persons named Adam and Miranda" who are "always in the mood for dancing."[84] As for Miss Ogilvy, mourning her shattered unit, she goes off on a vacation to Devon where Hall grants her a dream of unleashed desire in which, transformed into a powerful primitive man, she makes love to a beautiful young woman, enthralled by the "Ripe red berry sweet to the taste" of the female body (*MO* 34). Similarly, Stephen Gordon meets her lover, Mary Llewelyn, when they are sister drivers in the allegorically named "Breakspeare" ambulance unit, and after the war they too (if only temporarily) achieve a "new and ardent fulfillment" on a kind of honeymoon in Spain (*WL* 366).

A number of Hall's contemporaries—lesbian writers like Amy Lowell and Gertrude Stein—produced some of their most ecstatic erotica during the war years. Lowell's "Two Speak Together," for instance, a tribute to her companion Ada Russell, appeared in the same 1919 volume with her darkly elegiac "Dreams in War Time," while "Lifting Belly," one of Stein's most extended celebrations of lesbian sexuality, was composed, according to Richard Kostelanetz, between 1915 and 1917, the same years in which, as *The Autobiography of Alice B. Toklas* records with considerable relish, Stein and Alice B. Toklas bought their first car in order to travel around France as members of the American Fund for French Wounded.[85] Jolting from village to village in a tiny Ford with the nickname "Auntie" (whose successor was to be christened "Godiva"), the renowned lovers, according to *The Autobiography*, "did enjoy the life with these doughboys," and "It was during these long trips that [Stein] began writing a great deal again. The landscape, the strange life stimulated her" (*AABT* 172, 184, 185).

In a more explicit vein, Vita Sackville-West wrote in a postwar journal of how her love for Violet Trefusis was finally consummated in April 1918 when Violet came down to the Nicolson establishment at Long Barn because "the air-raids frightened her." With their men away on military business, the friends felt unexpectedly released from customary roles. As Vita tells the story, her "exuberance"—"I had just got clothes like the women-on-the-land were wearing, and in the unaccustomed freedom of breeches and gaiters I went into wild spirits"—finally made the "undercurrent" of sexuality between the two too strong to resist. Tellingly, after the war, when the pair eloped to Paris, Vita "dressed as a boy" with "a khaki bandage round [her] head" to impersonate a wounded soldier named "Julian," and despite the irony of having been liberated by such an equivocal costume, she later recalled that she had "never felt so free in [her] life" and "never been so happy since."[86]

Just as important as the female eroticism that the war energized, however, was the more diffusely sensual and emotional sense of sisterhood that the "Amazonian countries" created by the conflict inspired in nurses and v.a.d.s, land girls and tram conductors, ambulance drivers and armaments workers. As if to show the positive aspect of the bacchanalian bonding Lawrence deplores in "Tickets, Please," Vera Brittain, May Sinclair, and Violetta Thurstan remembered how their liberation into the public realm from the isolation of the private house allowed them to experience a female (re)union in which they felt "the joys of companionship to the full, the taking and giving, and helping and being helped in a way that would be impossible to conceive in an ordinary world."[87] For Radclyffe Hall, too, the battalion of sisters "formed in those terrible years" consisted of "splendidly courageous and great-hearted women . . . glad . . . to help one another to shoulder burdens" (*WL* 336). In a variation on this theme, Winifred Holtby told in *The Crowded Street* (1924) how her alienated heroine, Muriel Hammond, finally achieved a purposeful life through the friendship of Delia Vaughan, a feminist-activist (modeled in part on Vera Brittain, as Muriel is on Holtby herself) whose fiancé was killed in the war. Even as she incorporated a portrait of one of her close friends into the book, moreover, Holtby dedicated this novel, in which sisterly companionship replaced marriage as the happy ending of a heroine's quest for selfhood, to another of her close friends, Jean McWilliam, with whom she lived as a member of the waac in France in 1918.[88]

It is also of course true that, as Wilfred Owen's poems testify time and again, and as Paul Fussell has demonstrated, the Great War produced for many men a "front-line experience replete with what we can call the homoerotic."[89] From Robert Graves, who wrote what Fussell accurately calls a "sensuous little ode" in memory of his dead friend David Thomas, to Herbert Read, who wishes one of his dead soldiers to be kissed not by worms "but with the warm passionate lips / of his comrade here," to Wilfred Owen, who sends a poem and his "identity disc" to a "sweet friend," imploring "may thy heart-beat kiss it, night and day / Until the name grow blurred and fade away," male combatants frequently, in the words of one of Ford's characters, " 'get to love their pals, passing the love of women' " (436).[90] Indeed, as Eric Leed observes, "the comradeship of the front" was to create the crucial postwar phenomenon of veterans as "liminal" men who have nothing in common with anyone but each other.[91]

In Iris Barry's words, these soldiers "fresh from the front" seemed "ten years older, with a funny look around the eyes and too set a grin. They were hard and self-contained, difficult to talk to, shut up in themselves. . . . a band of brothers with little use for sisters ("WEW" 282).

Thus, where the liberating sisterhood experienced by women was mostly untainted by hostility to men—where it was in fact frequently associated with admiration for male soldiers (such as that expressed by Radclyffe Hall) or identification with male heroism (such as that articulated by Wharton and Cather)—the combatants' comradeship "passing the love of women" was as often energized by a disgust with the feminine as it was by a desire for the masculine. The war between the front and the home front, that is, issued in an inextricable tangle of (male) misogyny and (male) homosexuality, so that Owen, for example, reproaches female "Love" as a fatelike figure, an "imbecile with fair long hair" who "knoweth nothing of her wrong," while praising beautiful "lads."[92]

At the same time, too, the male comradeship fostered by the isolated communities of the trenches was continually countered and qualified by rifts between men that were not just accidental but essential consequences of the war. Most obviously, the "chaotic, crater-ridden, uninhabitable" barrier of no man's land that stretched between allies and enemies symbolized the fragmentation of the coherent civilization that Everyman—at least Everyman of a certain class—had formerly expected to inherit. As Sigmund Freud put it in "Reflections Upon War and Death" (1915),

> [Before the war] he who was not by stress of circumstance confined to one spot, could confer upon himself . . . a new a wider fatherland, wherein he moved unhindered. . . . [Now] that civilized cosmopolitan [stands] helpless in a world grown strange to him—his all-embracing patrimony disintegrated, the common estates in it laid waste, the fellow-citizens embroiled and debased![93]

"Strange Meeting" (1918), perhaps Owen's best known poem, stunningly dramatizes such a loss of patrimony—and specifically such a disintegration of prewar *blutbrüderschaft*—with its vision of brotherly doubles meeting in a "dull tunnel" where one tells the other, in a paradox that summarizes the perils of patriarchal bonding, "I am the enemy you killed, my friend" (*CP* 35–36). And as if to examine a slightly different consequence of the fragmentation of male community, the conclusion of *Parade's End* records the demise of a representative patrilineage and thus the destruction of a "fatherland" through the failure of Christopher's paralyzed brother to prevent Sylvia's felling of "Groby Great Tree," the giant cedar that had towered over the men's ancestral home and had been "the symbol of Tietjens" (733).

More comically, the heterogeneous crew of alleged spies and criminals who are absurdly imprisoned in "the enormous room" from which e. e. cummings's memoir takes its title continually act out both internecine hostilities and their rage at the authorities who have locked them up. Infuriated at the hypocrisies of *"La Gloire"* and *"Le Patriotisme"* preached by the "Almighty French Government" and scorning the no-manhood of the *plantons* who guard their jail, the prisoners also squabble and wrestle with each other, despite the bonding in oppression that, says the author, makes their concentration camp "the finest place I've ever been in my life." In fact, cummings reports being most impressed by the communal bravery of a group of whores who are sequestered in the wing of the prison reserved for *"les femmes."* "Up to the time of my little visit to La Ferté," he confesses, "I had innocently supposed that in referring to women as 'the weaker sex' a man was strictly within his rights. La Ferté, if it did nothing else for my intelligence, rid it of this overpowering error."[94]

But even Lawrence, that notorious celebrant of "blood brother-hood," balances his depiction in *Kangaroo* (1923) of the "half-mystical" homoerotic friendship between Richard Lovat Somers and the young Cornish farmer John Thomas with a portrayal of the horror Somers experiences when military doctors, as part of an army physical, "handl[e] his private parts." Even more theatrically alienated from military authority than cummings and his cohorts, Lawrence's protagonist vows that "Never would he be touched again. And because they had handled his private parts, and looked into them, their eyes should burst and their hands should wither and their hearts should rot." Yet so indelible is the trauma of the examination that, despite John Thomas's loyalty, by the end of *Kangaroo*'s chapter on "The Nightmare" of the war Somers feels "broken off from his fellow-men . . . loose like a single timber of some wrecked ship. . . . Without a people, without a land."[95]

———

But if the war forced men to qualify their dreams of brotherhood by confronting the reality of no man's land and imagining themselves as nightmare citizens "without a land," it liberated women not only to delight in the reality of the workaday Herland that was wartime England or America but also to imagine a revisionary worldwide Herland, a utopia arisen from the ashes of apocalypse and founded on the revelation of a new social order. Both the sisterhood and the sensuality celebrated by such diverse writers as Holtby, Hall, Brittain, and Sackville-West fostered this vision of a world revised, as did the release from Victorian constraints experienced by so many other women. For some women of letters, however—including Virginia Woolf and May Sinclair, Crystal Eastman and H. D., Olive Schreiner and Charlotte Perkins Gilman—the revisionary impulse went beyond the desire that a single battalion of sisters might persist into postwar patriarchy; it became a dream of global regeneration, a vision of patriarchy defied and denied. A perhaps unintentionally ironic headline in England's *Vogue* provides a miniature statement of the assumptions that underlay such a dream. "War Enlarges the Horizon for the Educated Girl and the Woman of Ideas and Modifies Man's Point of View," declared the editors of that fashionable journal.[96] Their claim about war's benefits was of course both comic ("enlarges the horizon") and timid ("modifies man's point of view"). Yet it summarizes the feeling shared by many feminists that the oppressive status quo could never be the same again.[97]

In a range of genres—poems and polemics, extravagant fantasies and realistic fictions—women writers expressed this feeling repeatedly throughout the war and postwar years. Gertrude Atherton's popular *The White Morning* (1918), for instance, told a utopian tale of the take-over of Germany by an army of women who rise violently against the Kaiser, threatening his general staff that "not one of you will live to eat rat sausage tomorrow morning" if you don't "disarm and march to the guard house." Amazonian as Woolf's Amalia Bonilla, their leader, Gisela, flies over Munich, a city now "packed with women from the Feldherrnhalle to the Siegesthor," noting with satisfaction that most are "armed to the teeth" and carrying "a white flag with a curious device sketched in crimson: a hen in successive stages of evolution" into an "eagle [whose] face, grim, leering, vengeful, pitiless, was unmistakeably that of a woman." " 'The hens are eagles—all over Germany,' " this heroine announces in the women's "full carrying voice," and while Atherton's account of her triumph over the German General Staff is at least partly patriotic propaganda for the Allies, the specific transformation of hen to eagle suggests that this novel is, more profoundly, a dream of the victory that might be won if "a solid mass of vindictive females" finally decided to change the course of that history from which they had previously been excluded.[98]

In less detail but just as dramatically, Dorothy Harrison, one of the protagonists of Sinclair's *The Tree of Heaven,* has a mysterious epiphany when she is imprisoned as part of the prewar suffrage battle, an epiphany that turns out to be a proleptic vision of how women will get the vote in "some big, tremendous way that'll make all this fighting and fussing seem the rottenest game." As part of her mystical experience, Dorothy sees "the redeemed of the Lord," noting that "They were men, as well as women . . . And they were all free . . . because they were redeemed" (*TH* 192–93). Similarly, Eleanor Pargiter in Woolf's *The Years* (1937) thinks in 1917 that, because of the war, things seemed "to be freed from some surface hardness" and "to radiate . . . some glamour," so that, as German planes raid London, she and her companions raise a toast "to the New World!"[99] Eleanor's (and Woolf's) intuition of an ecstatic apocalypse brought about by the war seems to explain an odd story that Iris Barry tells. "I had a friend who regretted the end of an air-raid," Barry relates. "When one began she used to take down her long hair, put on cloth slippers, and go out to the deserted embankment, where she ran madly up and down in a state of crazy exaltation" ("WEW" 282).

Did such exaltation signal the same yearning for the new explored in *The Years* and in such other texts as H. D.'s *Trilogy* (1944–46)? Later in Woolf's novel the postwar city is metamorphosed into a surreal landscape in which "the dawn—the new day" yields the enigmatic vision of an emblematic couple—a young man and "a girl in a tweed travelling suit" (*Y* 431, 434)—alighting from a taxi in a liberated *pas de deux* reminiscent of the one that symbolizes ideal androgyny in *A Room of One's Own*.[100] Finally, as we shall see in greater detail in our third volume, when, in *Trilogy*, H. D. looked back at World War I through the lens of World War II, the crucible of battle offered her and one of her characters an epiphany of reality transformed and transfigured by the resurrection of a female Atlantis.[101]

For many women, of course, such intimations of social change were channeled specifically through the politics of pacifism. From Schreiner, whose meditation on "Woman in War" (1911) had argued that the mothers of the race have a special responsibility as well as a special power to oppose combat, to Gilman, whose Herland was an Edenically peaceable garden because its author believed women to be naturally nonviolent, feminist activists had long claimed that, in the words of Crystal Eastman, "Woman suffrage and permanent peace will go together."[102] Thus, in 1915 Eastman defined Dr. Aletta Jacobs, the founder of the Woman's Peace Congress at The Hague, as "one of a group of 'international' women" whose "growing solidarity" showed that "when all Europe seems full of hatred they can remain united." Like the trade unionist Mrs. Raymond Robins, whose opinions were otherwise very different, Eastman had confidence that "it is the first hour in history for the women of the world. This is the woman's age!" And because this *was* such an unprecedented age, Eastman wrote, "Simplicity, directness, the glorious courage of children to whom everything is possible because it is untried,—these are the qualities [pacifist] women are bringing into the new world councils."[103] In his own way, even former American ambassador to Britain Joseph H. Choate, who introduced Mrs. Ward's militaristic *England's Effort*, agreed with Eastman's utopian speculation. "It is quite evident," he commented, "that this war is breaking down the barriers that have heretofore been impassable, not only between men and women, but between the various classes of society, and that it cannot possibly end without bringing these more closely together, all working to the same end in a more perfect harmony" (*EE* xvii).

Precisely because Schreiner, Gilman, Eastman, and Jacobs were uniformly convinced of woman's unique ability to encourage and enforce peace, however, there is sometimes an edge of contempt for men in their arguments, a misandry that expresses itself in the way Gilman's Herlanders "matronize" their male visitors or in the way Eastman and Jacobs rather smugly agree that "the neutral governments had hardly thought of using their good offices to stop the war, until the women came together and proposed it" (*CE* 240). But it is in Virginia Woolf's *Three Guineas,* the postwar era's great text of pacifist feminism, that such hostility to men comes most dramatically to the surface, in the form of violent antipatriarchal fantasies paradoxically embedded in an ostensibly nonviolent treatise on the subject of "how to prevent war."

Perhaps, Woolf even hints in an early, misspelled draft of this New Womanly book of revelation, the devastation wrought by war is a punishment (for men) exactly fitted not only to the crime of (masculine) warmaking but to other (masculine) crimes: "We should say let there be war. We should go on earning our livings. We should say its is a ridiculous and barbarous but perhaps necaary little popgun. The atwould be a help. Then we should live oursleves the sight of happiness is very make you envious" *[sic].*[104] Even in the final version of *Three Guineas,* moreover, Woolf seizes upon the imperative to prevent war as an excuse for imagining a conflagration that would burn down the old male-structured colleges of "Oxbridge," representative of all oppressive cultural institutions, and substitute instead an egalitarian and feminist "new college, [a] poor college" where "the arts of ruling, of killing, of acquiring land and capital" would not be taught (*TG* 34–36).

Later in *Three Guineas,* moreover, Woolf rebels even against the rhetoric of writers like Schreiner and Eastman, observing sardonically that "pacifism is enforced upon women" because they are not in any case allowed to offer their services to the army. Thus, most radically, she puts forward her famous proposal that "the daughters of educated men" should refuse to join with their brothers in working either for war *or* for peace, but should instead found a "Society of Outsiders" based on the principle that "As a woman, I have no country. As a woman I want no country. As a woman my country is the whole world" (*TG* 109). To be sure, Woolf recommends as part of this proposal a passive resistance to patriarchal militarism notably similar to that advocated by many other feminist pacifists: give "neither the white feather of cowardice nor the red feather of courage, but no feather at all" (*TG* 109). At the same time, though, with its calculated ex-patriotism and its revisionary vows of "indifference" to the uncivilized hierarchies of "our" civilization, her

Society of Outsiders constitutes perhaps the most fully elaborated feminist vision of a secret Herland existing simultaneously within and without England's "splendid Empire," a rightful and righteous woman's state founded on the antiwar passions the war produced in women. In some part of herself, therefore, Woolf may well have shared the delight that Hesione Hushabye bizarrely expresses when bombs begin falling at the end of Bernard Shaw's *Heartbreak House* (1919): "Did you hear the explosions? And the sound in the sky: it's splendid: it's like an orchestra: it's like Beethoven."[105]

Although they mourned the devastation wrought by the war, then, a number of women writers besides Woolf felt even at the height of the conflict that not only their society but also their art had been subtly strengthened, or at least strangely inspired, by the deaths and defeats of male contemporaries. Vera Brittain noted that when her fiancé, Roland, was killed, "his mother began to write, in semi-fictional form, a memoir of his life," and added that she herself was filled "with longing to write a book about Roland" (*TY* 251–52). And in *A Son at the Front,* the admiring tale of an artist-father whose art is mysteriously revitalized by the death of his soldier son, Edith Wharton offered an encoded description of a similar transformation of a dead man into an enlivening muse.[106]

More frankly, Katherine Mansfield confided to her journal after the death battle of her brother, "Chummie," that now "I want to write about my own country . . . Not only because it is 'a sacred debt' that I pay . . . because my brother and I were born there, but also because in my thoughts I range with him over all the remembered places." Through the memorable intervention of her dead brother/muse, moreover, she claimed she was vouchsafed a "mysterious" and "floating" vision of "our undiscovered country," a transfigured land not unlike the state imagined by feminists from Gilman to Woolf, in which the dead "Chummie" represented "the new man," so that Mansfield exclaimed, addressing her brother, "all must be told with a sense of mystery, a radiance, an afterglow, because you, my little *sun* of it, are set" [emphasis ours]. What issued from such ambivalent moments of inspiration, moreover, was her best set of stories—the New Zealand tales, "Prelude" (1917) and "At The Bay" (1921)—in which this grieving artist, herself dying, fulfilled the Whitemanesque desire she expressed when she told her dead "little boy brother" that "Now I will come quite close to you, take your hand, and we shall tell this story to each other."[107]

A comparable instance of female inspiration empowered by male desperation was embodied in H. D.'s *Bid Me to Live* (completed 1948;

published 1960), a novel which responded directly to the extraordinary
tangle of wartime anxieties expressed in *Death of a Hero* by her husband, Richard Aldington, and in *Kangaroo* by her friend D. H. Lawrence. The original of George Winterbourne's vicious wife, Elizabeth,
in the first of these books, and Richard Somer's patroness ("the American wife of an English friend") in the second, H. D. cast herself in her
own narrative as a poet named Julia, who is repelled by the deadliness
of her husband, Rafe (Aldington), and released by the Cornish landscape from which her muse-friend, Rico (Lawrence), has been expelled
for being a suspected spy, as D. H. Lawrence was during World War I.
Indeed, wandering among rocks and trees where Rico/Lawrence had
once strayed, Julia experiences such an access of prophetic energy that
it is as if the vanquished Rico's power had been victoriously transmitted
to *her* through the ruins of culture and the runes of nature. "Perfectly
at one with this land" that had rejected Rico, she implies that it has
become specifically Herland, meditating that its "subtle psychic rever-
berations" have changed her into "Medea of some blessed incarnation,
a witch with power. A wise woman . . . [a] seer, see-er."[108]

Tellingly, therefore, when H. D. later looked back on her experiences in two wars she reversed the imagery that her poetic double, "D.
H.", had used in his "Eloi, Eloi, Lama Sabachthani?" "Am I bridegroom
of War, war's paramour?" Lawrence's speaker had asked, and H. D.
seems almost to have wanted to answer him directly. Tracing her own
growth in an unpublished memoir called "The Thorn Thicket," which
also records her spiritualist relationship with Lord Hugh Dowding, the
famous R.A.F. Air Marshal, she declared with a curious and complicated satisfaction that "if my first husband [Aldington] was a non-com-
missioned officer, a 'private soldier' as he still calls himself, my second
. . . was the legendary Lord D. of fighter-command, who had turned
the tide in the Battle of Britain. . . . I had accepted the whole cosmic
bloody show. *The war was my husband*" [emphasis ours].[109] And at the
very least, if the war was not her husband, it was at certain points her
muse—as it was Mansfield's, Wharton's, and many other women's. Indeed, for many modernist women, the male muse whom nineteenth-
century writers from Charlotte Brontë and Margaret Fuller to Emily
Dickinson had defined as an almost preternaturally living Master metamorphosed into a literal or figurative dead good soldier.

———————

There is, of course, an emblematic good soldier buried (or sometimes drowned) at the heart of many modernist texts by male as well as
female survivors of the Great War. But the responses of male and female artists to the literal or figurative death of this symbolic good man

were different. For a number of crucial men of letters the apparently gratuitous sacrifice of the soldier not only reinforced the sense of cultural disruption represented by the war, it also ruptured or at least temporarily put in question certain key cultural forms through which death might have been confronted and conciliated. For many of the literary women who were the female counterparts of these men, however, the soldier's sacrifice at times seemed to signal a cultural wound or fissure through which radically new social modes might enter and often made possible the envisioning of new (implicitly female) ways of approaching and understanding death.

Mourning the lost male friend who functioned as a kind of surrogate self, the typical modernist man of letters grieved for the empowering sameness—the *blutbrüderschaft*, the homosocial bonding—that had reinforced his own identity. As the absence of the friend—the brother, son, companion—became a central presence in his life, he began to define himself as a debilitated inhabitant of a psychic no man's land comparable to the literal no man's land where the symbolic soldier was killed. And eulogizing the vanished companion, he found, with Wilfred Owen, that "these elegies are to this generation in no sense consolatory" (*CP* 31). But as *she* mourned the symbolic dead man who was friend, double, or brother yet always other to her, the representative modernist woman of letters frequently found her self—her identity—curiously strengthened. In the past, in a male-dominated society, the masculine other, however deeply loved, would have eclipsed, marginalized, or muted her. Now she felt, though at times quite guiltily, that she could speak because she *must* speak; there were not so many men left to do the verbal work of no man's land.

Although William Butler Yeats is not usually seen as a central commentator on the meanings of the Great War's madness, his "In Memory of Major Robert Gregory" (1919), with its eulogy of a perfect dead soldier, outlines the situation whose fundamental contours haunted both male and female artists.[110] Further, however, "In Memory" represents one mode of notably male response to the shock of cultural loss dramatized by the soldier's sacrifice. In "On Being Asked for a War Poem" (1916), Yeats had ironically declared "I think it better that in times like these / A poet's mouth be silent, for in truth / We have no gift to set a statesman right."[111] But despite its formal finesse, his lament for Augusta Gregory's exemplary son excavates the reasons for poetic silence even while it mythologizes the perfect man whose death has disrupted culture's patrilineage, thereby enjoining and enforcing silence.

Speaking to his young wife, the poet of "In Memory" reveals the lameness of his own generation as he catalogues "the friends that cannot sup with us" who are, through their absence, "All, all . . . in my thoughts tonight, being dead," adding that not a one can threaten the husband's attachment to his new bride—"can set us quarreling"—"For all that come into my mind are dead." But what seals the losses elaborated here is the fact that the symbolic scion of the writer's generation—"my dear friend's dear son"—shares "in that discourtesy of death" (*CP* 130, 131). "Our Sidney and our perfect man," Major Gregory is presented here and in the later "An Irish Airman Foresees His Death" (1919) as a paradigmatic good soldier who incarnates the Renaissance ideal of male perfection—"Soldier, scholar, horseman, he, / As 'twere all life's epitome"—by whom, from "Adam's Curse" (1904) to "Under Ben Bulben" (1938), Yeats imagined the "two eternities" of "race" and of "soul" should be carried forward in time. And, arguably, the mortal "discourtesy" that has swallowed up this manly paragon is associated with the historical "anarchy," the "blood-dimmed tide," that will drown the "ceremony of innocence" in "The Second Coming" (1921).

Yet though in the elegy's penultimate stanza Yeats struggles, through an homage to the metaphysicals, to formulate a time-honored courtesy—"Some burn damp faggots, others may consume / The entire combustible world in one small room"—which would at least rationalize death's ill-doing, he cannot really imagine even such a provisional but traditional triumph. As Major Gregory's death becomes the final sign of Yeats's own generation's unmanning, the poet openly unplans his poem, in a moving conclusion whose acquiescence in cultural and poetic defeat exemplifies one important mode of (male) modernist closure:

> I had thought, seeing how bitter is that wind
> That shakes the shutter, to have brought to mind
> All those that manhood tried, or childhood loved
> Or boyish intellect approved,
> With some appropriate commentary on each;
> Until imagination brought
> A fitter welcome; but a thought
> Of that late death took all my heart for speech.
>   [*CP* 133]

But if Major Gregory's drowning in the discourteous, blood-dimmed tide of the Great War evoked in Yeats a poignant (though temporary) withdrawal from one conventional aesthetic resolution, the death of T. S. Eliot's friend Jean Verdenal inspired a far more radical personal and poetic crisis. Understanding the young Frenchman to have been "(so far as I could find out) . . . mixed with the mud of Gallipoli," Eliot himself plunged into the dust of a waste land crisscrossed by the "rat's alley" of the trenches where "the dead men lost their bones," and a

waste land at whose center the absence of the dead good soldier is buried like a presence guaranteeing the no manhood of the poem's sexually equivocal protagonist.[112]

It was to Verdenal, as James E. Miller, Jr., reminds us, that Eliot's
Prufrock volume was dedicated from the start, with the words "mort
aux Dardanelles" and the Dante epigraph ("Now you are able to comprehend the quality of love that warms me toward you / When I forget
our emptiness / Treating shades as if they were solid") affixed from
1925 on. And it seems quite likely that it was of Verdenal as well as of
his own unhappy marriage that Eliot was thinking when he famously,
if ironically, remarked that the ostensibly "impersonal" cultural document he had produced in *The Waste Land* was "only the relief of a personal and wholly insignificant grouse against life . . . just a piece of
rhythmical grumbling."[113] Read as a dirge for Verdenal, therefore, *The
Waste Land* appears to be rather a different sort of cultural document
from what it has usually been considered. Instead of being a generalized meditation on civilization and its discontents, the poem becomes a
kind of fragmented and surrealistic pastoral elegy, a work that both
continues and, in response to drastic cultural change, disrupts the tradition of a man mourning for a man that extends from "Lycidas" to
"Adonais," *In Memoriam*, "Thyrsis," and "When Lilacs Last in the Door-
yard Bloom'd."

Interestingly, as Grover Smith reminds us, Eliot had "unquestiona-
bly" read "The Farcical History of Richard Greenow" that was included
in Huxley's *Limbo*, and the piece may well have inspired him not only
in his creation of the hermaphroditic "protagonist" Tiresias but also in
a subliminal association of Tiresias's problematic sexuality with the no-
manhood fostered by the Great War.[114] Having lost the friend whose
blutbrüderschaft guaranteed his own identity, Eliot-Tiresias becomes, like
Richard Greenow, a sacrifice to a feminized culture. At the same time,
however, he is also a mourner not unlike the speakers of "Lycidas,"
"Adonais," *In Memoriam*, "Thyrsis," and "Lilacs." As such, he deploys
many conventional features of the pastoral elegy: the ironic discrepancy between nature's endurance as manifested in the returning spring
and his own sense of mortal loss ("April is the cruelest month, breeding / Lilacs out of the dead land"); a consciousness that he speaks for,
even while he is somehow set apart from, a community of mourners
("crowds of people walking round in a ring"); a feeling that the world
which has survived his friend is itself debilitated by loss ("I had not
thought death had undone so many"); a vision of the dead man journeying deeper into death ("He passed the stages of his age and youth /
Entering the whirlpool"); a warning that such a fate is universal ("Consider Phlebas, who was once handsome and tall as you"); and an effort

to confront and confound death either by imagining resurrection ("a damp gust / Bringing rain") or by redefining the terror of mortality ("Shantih shantih shantih").

But because Eliot has lost his friend to an unprecedentedly calamitous war and finds himself in a postwar world where—in Freud's words—"his all-embracing patrimony [is] disintegrated," he has only fragments of the pastoral elegy to shore against his ruin. Thus the muses, nymphs, envoys of nature, and spectral visitors who appear in most elegies to guide the sufferer toward consolation are here distorted, fragmented, or disembodied. "Lycidas's" "sisters of the sacred well" and "Adonais's" or *In Memoriam*'s Urania become the parodic Madame Sosostris, the sinister Belladonna, and the vulgar Lil; Milton's and Shelley's nymphs and *In Memoriam*'s radiant bride metamorphose into the nymphs who have "now departed" with or without "the loitering heirs of city directors," into the bored typist, into the betrayed Thames daughters, and perhaps most horrifyingly into the intransigently common "Mrs. Porter and her daughter," antiheroines of a bawdy ballad that was sung by Australian troops at Gallipoli, where Verdenal died; Whitman's bird victoriously singing "death's outlet song" becomes the raped nightingale who only says "jug jug" (or jig jig) "to dirty ears," and his "Dark mother always gliding near with soft feet" becomes, first, the mysterious third "Gliding wrapt in a brown mantle, hooded / I do not know whether a man or a woman," and then the disembodied yet ubiquitous "Murmur of maternal lamentation," and the ghastly woman who "drew her long black hair out tight / And fiddled whisper music on those strings" while "bats with baby faces . . . Whistled, and beat their wings."

As for the dead friend himself, though he is tentatively assimilated into a scheme as neoclassical as that of "Lycidas," "Adonais," or "Thyrsis," his name—at least at one point *Phlebas*—has neither the Theocritan resonance of *Lycidas* or *Thyrsis* nor the deific, and thus transcendent, overtones of *Adonais*. Rather, as Grover Smith points out, it has in Greek not just the primary meaning of "vein" but the secondary and more crucial meaning of "phallus" or "phalluses," implying that the lost man not only makes the speaker feel as though he has lost his own phallus—his manhood—but also that the lost man *equals* the lost phallus.[115] That Smith, like other commentators, associates Phlebas the Phoenician with Near Eastern fertility cults which go back to the myth of dismembered Osiris is also important here. For when Osiris's sister-bride Isis sought to piece him together after he had been torn apart by his jealous brother Set, she was able to find every part of his body except his phallus, which she could restore only by constructing an artificial member—a virtual prosthesis.

Thus, unlike Lycidas, who is compared to the unequivocally dying and rising god-singer Orpheus, and Adonais, whose name echoes that of the dying and rising deity Adonis, Verdenal/Phlebas has problematic mythic as well as linguistic associations. As an avatar of the hyacinth girl who (in the view of some commentators, from John Peter Knight forward) masks a hyacinth *boy*,[116] the drowned Phoenician sailor is figured in terms of depersonalized and poignant vegetal, rather than divine, resurrection while evoking a vision of "sea-change" ("Those are pearls that were his eyes") which is merely, says the poem, a "Shakespeherian rag"—a meaningless scrap of cloth or, worse, a deceitful joke. And thus, as a drowned Phoenician, he is a Phoenix who will not rise again.

Finally, even the godlike voice of thunder which emerges from the text to instruct and presumably console the poet and his readers at the close of *The Waste Land* is problematic. Speaking from another culture, neither the classical nor the Christian west, this voice elicits the thought that "London bridge is falling down falling down falling down" even while it reminds the speaker of what has been (in the original manuscript, "we brother . . . my friend, my friend . . . / The awful daring of a moment's surrender"), that what has been will not be again (in the original manuscript, "friend, my friend I have heard the key / Turn in the door, once and once only"), and forces him to admit his present desolation (in the original manuscript, "You over on the shore [I left without you] [There I leave you / Clasping empty hands]") (*Facs* 79). That critics have emphatically divided into two schools on the issue of whether the poem's conclusion implies redemption either for the speaker or for the waste land that reflects his wounded virility stresses yet again the fragmentation and equivocation which mark Eliot's elegy. And that in discussing the poem's ending one finds it necessary to use the manuscript facsimile rather than the final text suggests again the stunning absence of Eliot's dead good soldier, who functions, in Miller's words, like "the primary term of a metaphor" which Pound and Eliot "succeeded in removing from the poem, or in carefully camouflaging."[117]

As Miller hints, they may have done this not only to generalize and depersonalize the work but also in order to allay Eliot's anxiety and embarrassment about his attachment to the lost "friend my brother." At the same time, however, they may have done this because for his male survivors the death of modernism's good soldier is a literally unspeakable event. In December 1917, Eliot wrote to his father about the Great War that "everyone's individual lives are so swallowed up in the one great tragedy that one almost ceases to have personal experiences or emotions, and such as one has seem so unimportant." But in 1916, just after Jean Verdenal's death and his own marriage to Vivien Haigh-Wood, Eliot wrote to Conrad Aiken that "I have *lived* through material for a score of long poems in the last six months" (*Facs* XIII, X). *The Waste Land,* with its oscillation between evasion and disclosure, may have been an attempt to mediate between these two statements, an effort to come to terms, in an elegy that was only tentatively "consolatory," with the public question formulated by Eliot's friend Herbert Read in a poem about his World War I companions—"O beautiful men, O men I loved, / O whither are you gone, my company?"[118] —while at the same time encoding a private and seemingly hopeless grief for the young French officer Jean Verdenal, who, "Scarcely recovered from pleurisy . . . did not hesitate to spend much of the night in the water up to his waist helping to evacuate the wounded by sea, thus giving a notable example of self-sacrifice."[119]

As we have seen, Virginia Woolf, to whom T. S. Eliot "sang" and "chanted" *The Waste Land* shortly after the work was completed, was also quite inevitably haunted by the Great War. Though she suffered no such grave personal loss as Eliot's of Verdenal, she persistently returned to the subject of the cataclysm not only in such works of social criticism as *A Room of One's Own* and *Three Guineas* but also in novels from *Jacob's Room* (1922) to *Mrs. Dalloway, To the Lighthouse* (1927), and *The Years.* Like Eliot, too, she had read Huxley's "Farcical History of Richard Greenow"; indeed, she had reviewed it.[120] But if what Woolf saw as Huxley's "stammerings" of faded faith were translated by Eliot into the halting, elliptical, and sexually anxious professions of *The Waste Land,* her critique of Huxley and of the society he found so debilitating metamorphosed into texts that seem to derive surprising strength from the collapse of the old order, from the sacrifice of the dead good soldier, and from the consequent empowerment of women, who must now, in the face of their brothers' absence or weakness, be recognized as, in Alice Meynell's words, "daughters of men."

Though both *A Room* and (especially) *Three Guineas* explore the possibility that a kind of feminist/pacifist Herland might be a product of the calamities of war, it is in the postwar novels *Jacob's Room* and, more crucially, *Mrs. Dalloway,* that Woolf dramatizes the idea, and dramatizes it specifically through an examination of the relationship between a female survivor and a dead good soldier which, on the one hand, fictionalizes the same transformation of dead soldier into male muse that was hinted at in works by Wharton, Mansfield and H. D. and, on the other hand, surfaces the differences between male and female experiences of postwar mourning and melancholia. Elegiac though it is, for instance, *Jacob's Room* broods on the final absence of a dead good soldier who had been, in his lifetime, the destined inheritor of a patrilineage toward which the novel's narrator has distinctly ambivalent feelings.

Loving the handsome Jacob, Woolf's speaker nevertheless makes it clear that she dislikes the culture which marginalizes his female counterparts while he walks through its corridors and streets with masterful certainty. Even before his wartime death, therefore, she uses oddly domestic imagery for the noise of battle as Jacob's mother in Yorkshire hears it across the channel: the guns sound like "nocturnal women . . . beating great carpets," as if the very notion of male combat had released some hidden fury for purification in the wives and mothers who knit and wait on the shore, or as if the battle itself were a kind of gigantic housecleaning. Then, on the sorrowful last page of the book—as Betty Flanders holds out her dead son's shoes, crying "What am I to do with these, Mr. Bonamy?"—it seems that, along with pain at this mother's loss, the novelist may have half-consciously wondered who, or what, might now step into those empty shoes of the doomed heir.[121]

In the war-haunted *Mrs. Dalloway,* however, as Woolf returns to the dyad of dead son and maternal survivor, she far more fully and inventively examines the asymmetrical gender meanings that the war had for its survivors, this time by deconstructing her central figure into a shellshocked war veteran and an upper-class middle-aged hostess who is peculiarly strengthened by the young man's death: "He made her feel the beauty, made her feel the fun" (*MD* 284). To be sure, one must not oversimplify any aspect of this complex novel, but from the start the book documents different male and female reactions to the European conflict, as it examines the ways in which women survive the catastrophe while even noncombatant men are killed by it. As if prefiguring Clarissa's triumphant survival and Septimus's defiant suicide, for instance, Woolf has Clarissa quite early on the day of her party think, first, of "Lady Bexborough who opened a bazaar, they said, with the telegram in her hand, John, her favourite, killed" (5) and, then, of "old Uncle William" who "turned on his bed one morning in the middle of the War" and, dying, said "I have had enough" (15).

Throughout the novel, too, Woolf seems at least intermittently to be responding to, and revising, key aspects of the Eliot poem she and her husband had published at the Hogarth Press in 1922. After a brief but bewildering meeting with the maddened Septimus and his wife Rezia, for instance, young Maisie Johnson thinks "Horror! horror!" (39), in an obvious allusion to the passage from *Heart of Darkness* that had been, as Woolf would very likely have known, Eliot's first epigraph for *The Waste Land*—the passage ending "The horror! The horror!" Later, "carrying guns . . . their arms stiff," the marching boys in uniform whom Peter Walsh foolishly admires reinforce our sense that in this book "the fingers of the European War" are "so prying and insidious" that Clarissa and Septimus inhabit a waste land where death has "undone" many (76, 129).

But it is through the figure of Septimus that Woolf most openly represents her vision of the war and most distinctly revises Eliot. In fact, though Septimus's story is significantly different from that of Eliot himself, two of its features may well have been derived from two of the facts of Eliot's life which precipitated the breakdown that led him to Lausanne and to *The Waste Land*. For, like the young poet Eliot, the young poet Septimus has been deeply shocked by the wartime death of a friend (Evans) and, like the young Eliot, Septimus has entered into a loveless marriage on "the rebound," as it were, from this loss: "he became engaged one evening when the panic was on him—that he did not feel" (131). Like Eliot, too, the neurasthenic Septimus reacts both to his grief and to his fortuitous marriage with sexual revulsion. Rereading the literary past, he decides that "Shakespeare loathed humanity—the putting on of clothes, the getting of children, the sordidity of the mouth and the belly! . . . Dante the same" (133–34), and as an artist himself he expresses his loathing "of these lustful animals, who have no lasting emotions but only whims and vanities," by "drawing pictures of them naked at their antics in his notebook" (135)—pictures which might be said to correspond to Eliot's misanthropic Sweeney poems, to his misogynistic Fresca passages, and to his obscene limericks about King Bolo and his big black Queen.[122]

At the same time, however, even while in some respects he resembles Eliot himself, Septimus is also crucially similar to Eliot's Phlebas, for as, in his own view, "the scapegoat, the eternal sufferer" (72) and "the drowned sailor on the shore of the world," he mentally reenacts Phlebas's fate. Indeed, because he sees himself as "the lord of men" (101) enduring "eternal suffering . . . eternal loneliness" (37), and because his sacrificial death in response to the viciousness of the doctors Holmes and Bradshaw leaves his body "horribly mangled" (227), Septimus might even be said to resemble the fertility god Osiris, to whom, as we saw, the figure of Phlebas at least partially alludes. But where Phlebas is a fertility figure whose sacrifice is problematic, Septimus is a scapegoat whose self-immolation somehow *works*, for Woolf revises Eliot's suggestion that Phlebas's death may be futile by implying that the waste land of England might be mysteriously revitalized through the mystical communion between this dead soldier who had always wanted to "tell the Prime Minister" (224) to "Change the world" (35) and the woman survivor who ultimately speaks to the Prime Minister "for" him. Moreover, where Eliot depicts a kingdom that has been laid waste not just by male impotence but by the poisonousness of women like the allegorically toxic "Belladonna," Woolf portrays a country where women are not just triumphant survivors but also potential redeemers and potent inheritors.

To be sure, not all the women in *Mrs. Dalloway* are redemptive or powerful. The resonantly named Miss Kilman, for instance, has been made by the war into an embittered creature, almost a madwoman, and Sir William Bradshaw's wife has been turned into a cipher by her husband's perverse passion for the bitch goddess Proportion, a passion that Woolf implicitly associates with the perversity of the male rulers who sent their sons to the trenches. Nevertheless, these problem characters finally function as foils for female figures who are shown to have extraordinary strength. Unlike Eliot's abandoned women, for instance, Lucrezia Warren Smith reacts to what might be seen as her seduction and betrayal by Septimus with self-renewing fertility: she is, her husband decides, "a flowering tree; and through her branches look[s] out the face of a lawgiver, who [has] reached a sanctuary where she fear[s] no one" (224). Similarly, unlike Eliot's lost and sexually ambiguous hyacinth girl/boy, Elizabeth Dalloway is "a hyacinth, sheathed in glossy green" who is destined to inherit the vitality of a powerful matrilineage, for her Dalloway ancestresses, the narrator observes, have been "Abbesses, principals, head mistresses, dignitaries, in the republic of women" (209).

Finally, unlike Eliot's frantic Belladonna, Clarissa herself is both a survivor and a ruler, even—figuratively speaking—a kind of queen of the sea-green world in which Phlebas, Septimus (and, earlier, J. Alfred Prufrock) have helplessly drowned. Even when she was a young girl, Peter Walsh remembers, she "was like iron, like flint, rigid up to the backbone" (97) in their battle of wills. Now, as she "escort[s] *her* Prime Minister down the room" (emphasis ours), Peter sees her as a magical divinity of water: in her "silver-green mermaid's dress," Clarissa seems to be "Lolloping on the waves and braiding her tresses . . . having that gift still; to be; to exist; to sum it all up in the moment as she passed" (264). In the end, therefore, as she empathetically imagines Septimus's death, reliving it in her mind as if she herself were a scapegoat who has survived and transcended catastrophe, her musings constitute a benediction very different from the incoherent "murmur of maternal lamentation" that permeates Eliot's waste land, for she gives purpose to what might otherwise have been pointless, order to chaos, as she decides that "A thing there was that mattered. . . . This he had preserved. Death was defiance. Death was an attempt to communicate" (280–81). The "terror" and "ecstasy" that she inspires in Peter Walsh thus constitute not just a tribute to her social grace but to a virtually divine grace through which—like the flowering Lucrezia and the hyacinth girl Elizabeth—she regenerates the postwar world that has "undone" Septimus, Phlebas, T. S. Eliot, and all too many others.

Given the fact that the war functioned in so many different ways to liberate women—offering a revolution in economic expectations, a release of passionate energies, a reunion of previously fragmented sisters, and a revision of social and aesthetic dreams—it seems clear that more than simple patriotism caused some leaders of the women's movement quite early to recognize a connection between feminist aspirations and military effects. In 1915, for instance, *The Suffragette,* the newspaper of the English Women's Social and Political Union, was renamed *Britannia,* with a new dedication: "For King, For Country, For Freedom." Even if a radical thinker like Woolf still preferred to pledge allegiance only to a Society of Outsiders, most women now began to see themselves as coextensive with the state, and with a female state at that, a Britannia, not a Union Jack. And as we know, the female intuition expressed in that renaming was quite accurate: in 1918, when World War I was over, there were eight-and-a-half-million European men dead, and there had been thirty-seven-and-a-half-million male casualities, while—with Prime Minister Asquith conceding that "women have aided in the most effective way in the prosecution of war" and President Wilson praising "the services of the women . . . upon the very skirts and edges of the battle itself"—all the women in England over the age of thirty were finally, after a sixty-two year struggle, given the vote, and less than a year later all the women in America over the age of twenty-one achieved the same privilege.[123]

For four years, moreover, a sizable percentage of the young men in England had been imprisoned in trenches and uniforms, while the young women of England had been at liberty in farm and factory. Paradoxically, the war to which so many men had gone in the hope of becoming heroes ended up emasculating them, confining them as closely as any Victorian women had been confined. As if to acknowledge this, doctors noted that (as we have seen in one of our epigraphs) "the symptoms of shell-shock were precisely the same as those of the most common hysterical disorders of peacetime, though they often acquired new and more dramatic names in war . . . what had been predominantly a disease of women before the war became a disease of men in combat."[124]

But while the Jake Barneses of the early twentieth century were helplessly imprisoned in the trenches of no man's land, their female counterparts were coming out of the closet as flappers like Lady Brett, barelegged, short-haired, corsetless. In fact, Mary Austin triumphantly cited "a report of the British Health Department, which demonstrates that with all their sorrow and strain, and in spite of their unaccustomed labors—perhaps because of them—the health of the English women has improved during the war" ("SE" 615). Because women developed a very different kind of "soldier's heart" in these years, "wearing pants" in the family or even "stepping into his shoes" had finally become a real possibility for them. For as one writer has put it, "if the first World War was a clear-cut victory for anything, it was a clear-cut victory for women's emancipation."[125] Yet that triumph was not without its darker consequences for feminism.

Ezra Pound was, after all, representative rather than idiosyncratic when, in "Hugh Selwyn Mauberley" (1920), he metaphorized the society for which the war had been fought as female. "There died a myriad," he wrote there, "For an old bitch gone in the teeth, / For a botched civilization."[126] And because many other male artists agreed that soldiers had been sacrificed so that some voracious woman could sleep surrounded by, in Wilfred Owen's words, a "wall of boys on boys and dooms on dooms" (*CP* 102); because they believed, with Hemingway, that a Lady Brett was a sort of monstrous antifertility goddess to whose powers the impotent bodies of men had ceaselessly to be offered up; because, finally, with Isaac Rosenberg they imagined "the Daughters of War" as "Amazons" yearning to "have their males / Clean of the dust" of life and power (*CP* 86), the literature of the postwar years was marked by an "anti-feminism" which, in the words of Rebecca West, was "strikingly the correct fashion . . . among . . . the intellectuals'" (figure, page 320).[127]

Inevitably, however, many women writers themselves internalized the misogyny that actuated such "anti-feminism." Heroines like Hall's Miss Ogilvy and her Stephen Gordon, for instance, who had been briefly freed by the war, ultimately succumb to the threat of a reconstituted status quo. Miss Ogilvy dies almost directly as a result of the sexual "dying" that climaxes her dream of erotic fulfillment, and Stephen Gordon is assaulted by "rockets of pain" which signal "l'heure de notre mort" as she surrenders Mary Llewelyn to the male lover who she decides is Mary's rightful spouse (*WL* 511, 507). Just as theatrically, Gisela in *The White Morning* realizes that she has murdered a man she loves when "all feeling ebbed . . . out of her" because she was merely "the chosen instrument" of woman's revolution (*WM* 133, 145), and Katherine Mansfield, even while she is inspired to art by her dead brother/ muse, speculates that she too is "just as much dead as he is" and wonders "why don't I commit suicide?" (*J* 38).

The guilt of the survivor implicit in such imaginings—a feeling very different from the feelings of "beauty" and "fun" that Woolf bestowed on Clarissa Dalloway—was articulated by one former nurse who defined what she saw as her culpable numbness in a dreadful confession:

> She [a nurse] is no longer a woman. She is dead already, just as I am—really dead, past resurrection. Her heart is dead. She killed it . . . Her ears are deaf; she deafened them . . . She is blind so that she cannot see the torn parts of men she must handle. Blind, deaf, dead—she is strong, efficient . . . a machine inhabited by a ghost of a woman—soulless, past redeeming.[128]

Describing comparable feelings of guilt and pain, Vera Brittain recounted the postwar nervous breakdown from which she suffered, an illness whose major symptom was her belief that her face revealed "the signs of some sinister and peculiar change. A dark shadow seemed to lie across my chin; was I beginning to grow a beard, like a witch? . . . 'Why couldn't I have died in the War with the others?' " Brittain remembered having "lamented" (*TY* 484, 490).

Trustees of the Imperial War Museum

As if to bring to the surface at least one secret assumption that triggered such misery, Katherine Anne Porter dramatized in "Pale Horse, Pale Rider" the fear of these former nurses (and what might have been a prevalent female anxiety) that if men were sick, they must have fallen ill because women were sickening. After her heroine, Miranda, down with influenza, has had a terrifying dream about her lover, Adam, in which "arrows struck her cleanly through the heart and through his body and he lay dead, and she still lived," Miranda learns that her disease has contaminated *him,* and indeed, he has died and she has lived, kept going by a "fiery motionless particle [which] set itself unaided to resist destruction, to survive and to be in its own madness of being" (*PH* 242, 253).

Even women who were not specifically recording anxieties about female survival seem sometimes to have been infected by the postwar misogyny that was so "strikingly the correct fashion." Certainly warwounded male artists—noncombatant survivors as well as those who had lived through combat—could, and frequently did, inflict severe pain on women of letters who were close to them. In the early twenties, for instance, T. S. Eliot's wife Vivien wrote a brilliant story entitled "The Paralysed Woman," in which she deftly depicted her marriage from Belladonna's rather than Tiresias's point of view. Calling her heroine *Sibylla,* as if alluding to the immobilized sibyl who ushered in the final version of *The Waste Land,* she made a paralysed woman who resembled a gigantic white doll into her protagonist's double—and a double who, unlike Woolf's Septimus, offers no empowerment. On the contrary, Sibylla finds little to do in life except to read *Holy Dying* and to indulge in hopeless dreams of becoming an exhibition dancer, because an exhibition dancer has neither to think nor act, just dance—and then collapse onto a sofa and forget everything until it is time to dance again.[129] As the story makes clear, Sibylla is at least in part responding to the problems created by her relationship with her gloomy husband André, a figure obviously based on the neurasthenic author of *The Waste Land.* Plainly, therefore, despite the female flowerings Woolf and others portrayed, some women *were* undone by the "rat's alley" of the war "where the dead men lost their bones."

Vivien Eliot was, of course, a special case, a woman who was within a decade to withdraw into madness, following her husband's desertion of her in the early thirties. But even a number of the sanest and most "ordinary" of women often appear to have been, first, anxious about the return to a peacetime status quo, and, then, traumatized by the antifeminist backlash of the twenties and thirties. On Armistice Day, Iris Barry reported, she thought: " 'What now?' I felt a distinct letdown. The future suddenly looked blank and a little alarming . . . I remember also thinking that now so many men would be coming back and the quite excellent jobs which any fairly proficient girl could get for the asking would be less plentiful. Indeed, most of the jobs would cease to exist" ("WEW" 283). Even more fatalistically, Alice Dunbar-Nelson predicted that "when pre-war conditions return" the "colored woman [would be] replaced by men and . . . forced to make her way back into domestic service"; her only hope was that "the latter will be placed on a strictly business basis and the vocation of housekeeping . . . raised to the dignity of a profession" ("NW" 396–97).[130]

Many women, however, blamed themselves for the loss of the ground they had gained between 1914 and 1918. Repressed by what was still, after all, a male-dominated community and reproached by their own consciences, a number retreated into self-doubt or guilt-stricken domesticity. "Generally speaking, we war women are a failure," confesses a character in Evadne Price's *Women of the Aftermath* (1931). "We had a chance to make ourselves solid in the working market . . . and came a hell of a cropper in most cases."[131] To be sure, as J. Stanley Lemons and others observe, their "peacetime levels [of employment] were [still] significantly higher than the pre-war situation."[132] Nothing would ever be the same again. But no war would ever function, either, the way this Great War had, as a battle of the sexes which initiated "the first hour in history for the women of the world." As we shall suggest in our third volume, World War II was to be as much a war against women civilians as it was against male combatants, with a battle front sometimes virtually indistinguishable from the home front.

In fact, as Virginia Woolf anticipated in *Three Guineas*, it was to be a war whose jackbooted Nazis, marching for the "Fatherland," enacted the ultimate consequences of patriarchal oppression, so that Sylvia Plath would imagine it as presenting her with "obstacles" that were emblems of almost ontological self-alienation: "The body of this woman / Charred skirts and death-mask, / Mourned by religious figures, by garlanded children."[133] In 1944, moreover, in her war-shadowed "Writing on the Wall," H. D. was to echo Radclyffe Hall's definition of "no-man's-land" as a "waste land" for "inverts" (Hall) and "hysterical women" (H. D.), while more recently, in a revision of the metaphor that Hall's Stephen Gordon temporarily transcended, Linda Pastan was to see her own body as a "no man's land" over which sons and husbands battle, and in 1981 Adrienne Rich was to publish a poem which despairingly declared that "there is no no man's land," by which she evidently meant that there is still no Herland.[134] With Rich, all of these women would understand themselves to be participants in an ongoing "war of the images" whose possibly apocalyptic denouement has not yet really been revealed.

Nevertheless, what Woolf called "that amazing outburst in August 1914" had at least—tragic though its origins were—accelerated sexchanges that threatened to shatter the "all-embracing" and often oppressive "patrimony" in which men like Freud had, until then, rejoiced.

8

Cross-Dressing and Re-Dressing: Transvestism as Metaphor

The gulf between . . . the most womanly man on earth, and the most manly woman, is just the same as ever: just the same old gulf between the sexes. The man is male, the woman is female. Only they are playing one another's parts, as they must at certain periods.

—D. H. Lawrence

What is the current that makes machinery that makes it crackle, what is the current that presents a long line and a necessary waist. What is this current.

—Gertrude Stein

Is me her was you dreamed before? Was then she him you us since knew? Am all them and the same now we?

—James Joyce

Unfunny uncles who insist
in trying on a lady's hat,
—oh, even if the joke falls flat,
we share your slight transvestite twist

in spite of our embarrassment.
Costume and custom are complex.
The headgear of the other sex
inspires us to experiment.

—Elizabeth Bishop

In 1920, when Vita Sackville-West looked back on her exuberant impersonation of the wounded soldier "Julian" during the height of her post–World War I love affair with Violet Trefusis, she was bemused. She had experienced herself, she remembered, as inhabited by several sexes: "I hold the conviction that as centuries go on . . . the sexes [will] become more nearly merged on account of their increasing resemblances," she noted, adding that "cases of dual personality do exist, in which the feminine and the masculine elements alternately preponderate."[1] Eight years later, in *Orlando* (1928), a "love letter" written at the height of *her* love affair with Sackville-West, Virginia Woolf addressed the same issue. "How many different people are there not—Heaven help us—all having lodgment at one time or another in the human spirit?" She exclaimed, "Some say two thousand and fifty-two. . . . [Orlando] had a great variety of selves to call upon, far more than we have been able to find room for, since a biography is considered complete if it merely accounts for six or seven selves, whereas a person may well have as many thousand."[2]

As a practical matter, Woolf put the problem in terms of the artificial impact of costume on identity: "There is much to support the view that it is clothes that wear us and not we them," she declared in *Orlando*, adding that "we may make them take the mould of arm or breast, but [clothes] mould our hearts, our brains, our tongues to their liking" (188). The publisher of the English translations of Freud's major works (indeed, Hogarth Press was eventually to print James and Alix Strachey's English translation of Freud's "Psychoanalytic Notes on an Autobiographical Account of a Case of Paranoia" [1911], the famous case study of the male transvestite/transsexual Dr. Schreber), Woolf was engaging precisely the question of bisexuality that had concerned Freud himself since his early friendship with Wilhelm Fliess. However, unlike Freud, who, as Jacqueline Rose and Juliet Mitchell have demonstrated, wavered throughout his career between, on the one hand, a kind of biological essentialism about gender and sexuality and, on the other hand, a commitment to the idea that sex roles are basically sociocultural constructs, Woolf forthrightly declared herself on the side of cultural determinism.[3] In this sense, she represented many twentieth-century women artists, whose persistent consciousness of the constraints of "femininity" led them to question gender categories altogether.

To be sure, from Shakespeare and Sidney on, men of letters had also tested gender categories through plots that turn on transvestism or even transsexuality. In such Renaissance works as Shakespeare's *Twelfth Night* and his *As You Like It* as well as Sidney's *Arcadia*, male and female characters interchange identities as they don and doff the garments of the opposite sex. The enduring charisma of the plot of sex-change suggests that male writers have long been fascinated with the artifice of sex roles. And as Peter Ackroyd has speculated, some transvestite performances may have traditionally had metaphysical as well as gender-testing functions: "The representation of life as it is implies the presence of death," observes Ackroyd, so that "transvestism implicitly defies the necessity of such natural laws by its explicit reversal of natural sexual characteristics."[4]

By the nineteenth century, the trope of transvestism and transsexualism—perhaps because of a Romantic interest in androgyny—had gained special prominence, with such works as Theophile Gautier's sensational *Mademoiselle de Maupin* (1834) and Honoré de Balzac's *Seraphita* (1835) celebrating radical role reversals. As Bram Dijkstra has argued (citing Mario Praz's assertion that by the second half of the century "the fascination of artists and writers with the concept of the androgyne began to assume 'alarming proportions' ") the dual-sexed figure may in this period have been a "central symbol of . . . revolt against the bourgeoisie, and against the society of exchange values and polar oppositions which the bourgeoisie had fostered."[5] Certainly Gautier's Théodore/Madelaine, who claims that "I belong to a third sex of its own," and Balzac's Seraphita/Seraphitus, who is alternately referred to as "she" or "he," depending on the sex of her/his interlocuter, are (though in different ways) radiant and revolutionary beings.[6] But such characters became even more crucial to both male and female artists of Woolf's generation, and, because of their differing experiences of both gender and modernity, the sexes used this distinctively sexual metaphor in distinctly different ways.

To begin with, it can be argued from a psychoanalytic perspective that because masculine identity is founded on the boy's recognition that he is not female—not, like the mother, "castrated," though he fears the calamity of castration—for the male artist/character female impersonation has always been both thrillingly transgressive and dangerously debilitating. From the same psychoanalytic perspective, moreover, male impersonation for the female artist/character is never so threatening, and this because of what Freud sees as the girl's greater bisexuality, a bisexuality he attributes to the pre-Oedipal time when the little girl is "really" a kind of "little boy."[7] But the transvestite plot thickened in the twentieth century, when male artists—still, of course, struggling with the imperatives of masculine identity-formation—had, in addition, particularly urgent sociocultural reasons for needing to insist that, as Freud put it, anatomy is destiny.

Confronting drastically changing sex roles as well as dramatically changing definitions of sexuality, and fearing the physical and metaphysical anomaly of no-manhood, modernist men of letters sought to excavate an ontological link between biological sexuality and the traditional sexual ideologies whose disintegration they found so disturbing. A number of their female contemporaries, however, no doubt drawing upon what Freud considered the girl's greater "bisexuality," sought to disengage anatomy from destiny, postulating an identity whose transcendence of biological sexuality either explicitly or implicitly questions the gender roles prescribed by the conventional sexual ideologies they sought to deconstruct. Whether, like Virginia Woolf, these women produced exuberant fantasies about gender fluidity; whether—more pragmatically—they experimented with male costume in order to usurp male privilege; or whether—more extravagantly and sometimes painfully—they actually believed themselves to have a gender identity at odds with their anatomy, all were defying the conflation of sex roles and sex organs that many of their male contemporaries sought to reinforce.

Thus, far more than their male contemporaries, female modernists frequently dramatized themselves through idiosyncratic costumes, as if to imply that, for women, there ought to be a whole wardrobe of selves. Of course, literary men did at times dress flamboyantly too. T. S. Eliot occasionally wore face power, and F. Scott Fitzgerald appeared as a simpering belle in a *New York Times* photograph advertising the annual Triangle Club show at Princeton. For the most part, though, men of letters tended to wear clothes that emphasized some version of masculinity, as if to suggest that the right garments reflect the right relationship not only between the sexes but between anatomy and destiny. Yet, as we shall show in our third volume, even such extravagantly feminine artists as Edna St. Vincent Millay, H. D., Elinor Wylie, Isak Dinesen, Zora Neale Hurston, and Edith Sitwell wore their glamorous garb so ironically that they could in some sense be considered female female impersonators. And from Renée Vivien to Radclyffe Hall and Djuna Barnes, from Vita Sackville-West to Willa Cather and Gertrude Stein, a number of other women transgressively appropriated male costumes or oscillated between parodically female and sardonically male outfits, as if to declare that, as Woolf said, we are what we wear, and therefore, since we can wear anything, we can be anyone.

———————◆———————

The modernist men and women who speculated on the significance of costume were all, of course, living in an era when the Industrial Revolution had produced a corresponding revolution in what we have come to call "fashion." Though there has always been a tradition of theatricality associated with the expensive clothing of aristocrats and wealthy merchants, until the middle or late nineteenth century most people wore what were essentially *uniforms*: garments denoting the one form to which each individual's life was confined by circumstance, by custom, by decree. Thus the widow's weeds, the governess's somber gown, the servant's apron, and the child's smock were signs of class, age, and occupation as fated and inescapable as the judge's robes, the sergeant's stripes, and the nun's habit. With the advent of the spinning jenny and the sewing machine, however, common men and women, following the lead of uncommon individuals from Bryon to Baudelaire, began to have a new vision of the kinds of costumes available to them and, as a corollary of that vision, a heightened awareness of the theatrical nature of clothing itself. By 1833, Thomas Carlyle was writing obsessively about the mystical significance of tailoring, and by the 1890s literary circles were dominated by writers who defined themselves at least in part as dandies, and whose art increasingly concerned itself with style in every sense of the word.[8]

As Ellen Moers has pointed out, Baudelaire's thought about dandyism "was transmitted to the *fin de siècle* through the feverish imagination of J.-K. Huysmans and the juvenile imagination of Algernon Swinburne."[9] But Oscar Wilde and Max Beerbohm were probably the most notable theorists of costume in turn-of-the-century England. Arguing in "More Radical Ideas Upon Dress Reform" (1884) that proper clothing is or should be "a realization of living laws," Wilde also asserted that "every right article of apparel belongs equally to both sexes, and there is absolutely no such thing as a definitely feminine garment."[10] And he notoriously practised what he preached, attiring himself in "knee breeches . . ., flowing green tie, velvet coat and wide, turned-down collar," with a "drooping lily" in his hand.[11] Beerbohm, however, preached a different practice. In his slyly satiric "Defense of Cosmetics" (1894), a piece which generated "a journalistic storm," Beerbohm opposed Wilde's unisex philosophy, declaring that

> If men are to lie among the rouge-pots, inevitably it will tend to promote that amalgamation of the sexes which is one of the chief planks in the decadent platform and to obtund that piquant contrast between him and her, which is one of the redeeming features of creation. . . . for if, in violation of unwritten sexual law, men take to trifling with the paints and brushes that are feminine heritage, it may be that our great ladies will don false imperials, and the little donner deck her pretty chin with a Newgate fringe![12]

In the same easy essay, in fact, Beerbohm claimed that the suffrage movement would be defeated by the fin-de-siècle fad for female makeup. "The horrific pioneers of womanhood . . . are doomed" he warned. "Though they spin their tricycle-treadles so amazingly fast, they are too late. . . . Artifice, that fair exile, has returned."[13] That some men did successfully "lie among the rouge-pots," though, was dramatically demonstrated by Julian Eltinge, an American female impersonator who became an internationally famous star in this period. So acclaimed was Eltinge that he actually published the *Julian Eltinge Magazine and Beauty*

Hints in which he displayed his metamorphoses from him to her (below), taught women readers how to wield "paints and brushes," and promoted his own brand of cold cream.[14] If Beerbohm felt that, as he once exclaimed, "Women are becoming nearly as rare as ladies,"[15] Eltinge proved that such a proposition did not matter because any man could become both a woman and a lady.

Inevitably, Beerbohm and Wilde noted that the late nineteenth-century "woman question" was increasingly couched in terms of costume. But the major figure who postulated a direct connection between female oppression and feminine garments was Amelia Bloomer, who invented the divided skirt—known as the "bloomer"— in the mid-nineteenth century and wore it "for some six or eight years," claiming that she was "amazed at the furor I had unwittingly caused."[16] Though her costume was ridiculed in the popular press and judged "sensible" but "ugly" by Wilde (who nevertheless did advocate some form of divided skirt),[17] it was enthusiastically espoused by such prominent feminists as

Julian Eltinge. Photograph from the *Julian Eltinge Magazine and Beauty Hints.* (Courtesy of Culver Pictures, New York)

Lucy Stone, Susan B. Anthony, and Elizabeth Cady Stanton, all of whom experimented with the daring new outfit, and all of whom shared Anthony's view that "I can see no business avocation, in which woman in her present dress *can possibly* earn *equal wages* with man."[18] "What incredible freedom I enjoyed for two years!" exclaimed Stanton, describing the time when she wore bloomers. "Like a captive set free from his ball and chain, I was always ready for a brisk walk through sleet and snow and rain . . . and, in fact, for any necessary locomotion."[19] Yet, she explained, she abandoned this costume because of such taunts and jeers as this "favorite doggerel that our tormentors chanted":

> Heigh! ho! in rain and snow,
> The bloomer now is all the go.
> Twenty tailors take the stitches,
> Twenty women wear the breeches.[20]

Still, despite Stanton's unpleasant experiences, Dr. Mary Walker, the founder of "The Mutual Dress Reform and Equal Rights Association," had achieved considerable fame by the turn of the century. Like Amelia Bloomer, Mary Walker fought not only for women's right to dress as they pleased, but also specifically for clothing that would allow freedom of movement. In *Hit* (1871) and *Unmasked; or the Science of Immorality* (1878), she argued on hygienic grounds against long skirts, tight lacing, crinolines, and dainty shoes. But she also reasoned from decency: on the one hand, she ridiculed hoop skirts as the cause of women's vulnerability to sexual attack and, on the other hand, she believed that women's clothes kept them "unnaturally excited, or in a condition to be easily excited sexually."[21] For this reason, she proclaimed that

> While bodies are caged in the petticoat badge of dependence and inferiority, minds and souls are subject to evil, psychologizing wills and cannot command themselves; whereas crowns of strength, joy and sufficiency, with choice of place in the exercise of power await the Unbound Woman.[22]

That Walker experienced what her biographer calls "one of the happiest epochs in her kaleidoscopic career" during the Civil War, when she was traded "man for man" for a Confederate officer, reminds us that war work has always had a potential for liberating women from the corsetlike constrictions of traditional sex roles.[23] In particular, though, World War I—as we have seen—brought countless post-Victorian girls out of the closet in trousers, overalls, even military uniforms. Indeed, by the time of the Great War, Walker herself ostentatiously appeared in masculine evening dress with a tall silk top hat and a prominently placed Medal of Honor (opposite).

Walker's strutting appropriation of masculine insignia underscores the difference between the ways female modernists defined literal or figurative costumes and the ways male modernists confronted such garments. Twentieth-century literary men, working variations upon the traditional dichotomy of appearance and reality, often opposed false costumes—which they saw as unsexed or wrongly sexed—to true, properly sexed, clothing and, by doing so, they elaborated a deeply conservative vision of what Beerbohm called an "unwrittten sexual law" governing society. The sociopolitical world, they implied, should be hierarchical, orderly, stylized. More specifically, they suggested that it should be founded upon gender distinctions, since the ultimate reality was in their view the truth of gender.

The feminist counterparts of these men, however, not only regarded all clothing as costume, they also defined all costume as prob-

Dr. Mary Walker Wearing the Medal
of Honor in 1912. Collection of the
Library of Congress

lematic. In fact, to most of these writers the supposedly fundamental sexual self was itself merely another costume. Thus where male modernist costume imagery is profoundly conservative, feminist modernist costume imagery is radically revisionary, for it implies that no one, male or female, can or should be confined to a uni-form, a single form or self. On the contrary, where so many twentieth-century men sought to outline the enduring, gender-connected myths behind history, many twentieth-century women struggled to define a gender-free reality behind or beneath myth, an ontological essence so pure, so free that "it" can "inhabit" any self, any costume.

———————◆———————

One of the most dramatic transvestite episodes in modern literature appears in the nighttown episode at the heart of Joyce's *Ulysses*. Here Leopold Bloom encounters a Circe named Bella Cohen, the whorehouse madam, who turns herself into a male named Bello and transforms Bloom first into a female, then into a pig, and finally into an elaborately costumed "charming soubrette."[24] It is the last of these transformations, the one depending upon costume, which is the seal of Bloom's humiliation, just as Bello's dreadful ascendancy is indicated by her/his clothing. "With bobbed hair, . . . fat moustache rings, . . . Alpine hat and breeches," Bello becomes a grotesque parody of masculinized female mastery, hunting and beating the tremblingly masochistic Bloom. Even more ludicrous clothing defines Bloom's disgrace. Pointing to the whores, Bello growls, "As they are now, so will you be, wigged, singed, perfumesprayed, ricepowdered, with smoothshaven armpits. Tape measurements will be taken next your skin. You will be laced with cruel force into vicelike corsets . . . to the diamond trimmed pelvis . . . while your figure, plumper than when at large, will be restrained in nettight frocks, pretty two ounce petticoats and fringes" (523).

Besides mocking fashion magazine descriptions of clothing, these sadomasochistic passages remind us that for the modernist both literary style *and* costume were often tools of ironic impersonation: Joyce is here specifically parodying Leopold Von Sacher-Masoch's famous *Venus in Furs* (1870). But in doing so, he is also satirizing a distinctively nineteenth-century pornographic genre, which Vern Bullough describes as follows:

> Closely allied to [erotic histories of] spanking and whipping were the underground Victorian epics about bondage that usually recount how recalcitrant and unmanageable boys were put into tight corsets and educated to be docile and feminine and lived more or less happily ever after as women. Two such works are *Miss High*

Heels and *Gynecocracy.* . . . In the first, Dennis Evelyn Beryl is transformed under the supervision of his step-sister Helen into a properly trained young woman. As part of his corset discipline he [is] sent to a girl's school, where he [is] punished with canes, riding whips, birch rods, and ever more restrictive corsets . . . In the second novel, Julian Robinson, Viscount Ladywood . . . had showed too much energy as a boy, and so his parents shipped him to a [similar] school. The novel concluded: "The petticoat . . . I consider extremely beneficial . . . I confess . . . that I love my bondage. . . . There is a wonderful luxuriousness and sensuality in being made to bow down before a woman. . . . My lady's stockings and drawers upon me give me . . . an electrifying thrill. . . . This world is woman's earth, and it is petticoated all over. Theirs is the dominion, turn and twist the matter as you will."[25]

In the dialogue between Bloom and Bella/Bello, Joyce almost literally echoes some of this language. ("Married, I see," says Bella to Bloom. "And the missus is master. Petticoat government." To which Bloom replies, "That is so," adding encomia to Bella as "Powerful being" and "Exuberant female" [515–16].) Does Joyce's parody suggest a serious if covert acceptance of the original pornography, a reinterpretation of the work in a spirit in which it was not intended? Might we decide, for instance, that, as several critics have claimed, the grotesque androgyny Joyce imagines for Bloom in nighttown (and elsewhere in *Ulysses*) hints at the possibility of a nobler and more vital androgyny? While some readers have presented such an optimistic (and implicitly feminist) interpretation of the nighttown episode, we believe it is largely mistaken.[26]

For one thing, Bloom's female costume is clearly a sign that he has wrongly succumbed to "petticoat government" and thus that he has become weak and womanish himself; his clothing tells, accordingly, not of his large androgynous soul but of his complete degradation. For Joyce's parodic narrative implies that to become a female or to be like a female is not only figuratively but literally to be de-graded, to lose one's place in the preordained hierarchy that patriarchal culture associates with gender. If this is so, however, Joyce is also hinting that to be a woman is inevitably to be degraded, to be "a thing under the yoke" (523). And certainly the language of the nighttown episode supports this notion, for as Joyce knew, it was not just Bella/Bello's whores who were "wigged, singed, perfumesprayed, ricepowdered," shaven, corseted, and "restrained in nettight frocks" (523). This reality of female costume is in fact at the heart of the pornography to which Joyce is alluding in *Ulysses*. The sadism associated with the male-female role reversal in transvestite Victorian pornography demonstrates, therefore, that the pornography itself is perversely reversing, exaggerating, and thereby parodying the male dominance-female submission that the authors of these works believe to be quite properly associated with male-female relationships.

In other words, just as Kate Millett extrapolated a true societal evaluation of femaleness from the posturings of Jean Gênet's male homosexual transvestites, we can extrapolate Joyce's vision of woman's place from Bloom's degraded androgyny.[27] It is significant, then, that after this episode the traveling salesman returns home and, instead of gaining an increased commitment to androgyny, he figuratively, if only temporarily, expels the suitors, gives the "viscous cream ordinarily reserved for the breakfast of his wife Marion" to his mystical son Stephen, and asserts his proper male mastery by ordering Molly to bring him eggs in bed for his own breakfast the next morning (661, 723). Casting off his false female costume, he has begun to recover his true male potency. "From infancy to maturity he had resembled his maternal procreatrix," but from now on he will "increasingly resemble his paternal creator" (692), for he has at last taken his place in a patrilineal order.

Bloom's dramatic recovery of power is, however, curiously associated not only with his repudiation of the feminine and the female costume but also with his wearing of that costume. For, oddly, his regained authority seems to have been energized by the sort of ritual sexual inversion that, as Natalie Davis has noted, traditionally accompanied festive misrule.[28] In sixteenth-century France, Davis has shown, the ceremonial functions of such sexual inversion were mostly performed by males disguised as grotesque cavorting females, and a primary purpose of their masquerades was arguably to reinforce the sexual/social hierarchy. Similarly, we would add, in post-World War I Britain and America, male fantasies of sexual inversion paradoxically served to counter the excesses of female misrule associated with women's liberation during the war years. Even an apparently alienated noncombatant like Joyce would have seen—as his extended Homeric simile implies—the need for righting wartime sexual wrongs by bringing the traditional (male) hero home to his proper manhood.[29] As in the France Davis has described, some male modernists believed that, through enacting gender disorder, men and women might learn the necessity for male dominant-female submissive sexual order. More specifically, through a paradoxical yielding to sexual disorder, the male, in particular, might gain the sexual energy he needed for ascendancy. Through parodic submission, he would learn dominance. Through misrule, he might learn rule. Through a brief ironic concession to "petticoat government," he would learn male mastery.

In Bloom's case, moreover, this revitalized male authority might not just derive from essentially conservative psychodramas of misrule. It might also be born from the creation of a transvestite enigma that has been studied by the psychoanalyst Robert Stoller. Discussing the phenomenon of "the phallic woman," Stoller has argued that the male transvestite uses the degrading apparatus of female costume to convert "humiliation" to "mastery" by showing himself (and the world) that he is not "just" like a woman, he is better than a woman because he is a woman with a penis. Unlike the transsexual, Stoller notes, the transvestite is excitedly "aware of the penis under his women's clothes and, when it is not dangerous to do so, gets great pleasure in revealing that he is a male-woman" and proving "that there is such a thing as a woman with a penis. . . . He therefore can tell himself that he is, or with practice will become, a better woman than a biological female if he chooses to do so."[30] Such a "phallic woman" does not merely gain female sexual power by impersonating a woman, he assimilates femaleness into his maleness—not his "androgyny"—so that he mysteriously owns the power of both sexes in a single, covertly but thrillingly male body.

In an analysis of transvestite masochism which is also obviously important for understanding Leopold-Von-Sacher-Masoch-Bloom's behavior, Stoller reviews the pornography "that repeatedly shows cruelly beautiful [women] . . . bullying the poor, pretty, defenseless transvestite." This image is associated, he claims, with the terrifying ascendancy of women (usually mothers or older sisters) in the lives of transvestites, Gea Tellus-women—like Molly Bloom—who have made their man-children as impotant as little girls: "they hang those bosom-bombs heavily over his head," says Stoller: "they are cruel and haughty: they are sure of themselves; their gigantically voluptuous bodies are strong, hard, slim, long, and smooth, i.e., phallic . . . [and] it takes little imagination," he remarks, "to recognize in the transvestite man's erotic daydream the little boy's impression of the woman or older girl, who, in her greater power, so damaged his masculinity." Yet, he adds,

> By a remarkable tour de force [the transvestite] takes the original humiliation and converts it into an active process of sexual mastery and pleasure . . . [For while the archetypal pornographic] illustration makes him appear like a poor cowering wretch, the fact is that the [transvestite] man who is excitedly masturbating while looking at such a picture is in fact filled with a sense of triumph as he is successful in producing an erection, excitement, and orgasm.[31]

The transvestism in Joyce's nighttown, like much of the costume play imagined by Victorian pornographers, almost exactly recapitulates the spirit of such sexually compensatory cross-dressing even while it depends upon the energy of the traditional ritual cross-dressing Davis discusses. Because it is the parodic product of an age of costumes rather than an era of uniforms, both its private/neurotic and its public/ritual functions are of course disguised, ironic, and oblique compared to those implicit in Stoller's case histories and Davis's social histories. Nevertheless, Leopold Bloom's imaginary escapade in the Dublin whorehouse is a kind of parodic feast of misrule from which this exiled husband regains the strength for true rule. Recovering himself in his proper male costume, he finds a spiritual son (Stephen), remembers a lost real son (Rudy), and returns from his wanderings to a moderately welcoming Penelope. Just as the ritual magic plant *Moly* saved Homer's Ulysses from the degradation threatened by Circe, Joyce's Bloom saves himself from the depradations of Bella/Bello Cohen by not only having but ironically pretending to *be* his own Molly, a covertly phallic version of the recumbent "Ewig-Weibliche," a "new womanly man" whose secret manliness may ultimately seduce and subdue insubordinate New Women.[32]

A number of other transvestite works by male modernists support these points, though in somewhat different ways. To begin with, in the same year that Joyce published *Ulysses,* his countryman George Moore produced, in a collection of tales entitled *Celibate Lives,* the story of one Albert Nobbs, a Dublin hotel waiter who is really a woman. Understated and scrupulously realistic, this poignant work offers, at least on the surface, a comparatively objective analysis of the poverty and sexual vulnerability that drove Albert Nobbs to adopt a male identity. Yet, though Moore's narrative stance is far more sympathetic to the transvestism he describes than Joyce's is, the story reveals that the consequences of such subterfuge are costly. An "outcast from both sexes," the pseudo-male Nobbs feels "her loneliness perhaps more keenly than before," and tearfully refers to herself as "an old perhapser . . . neither man nor woman!"[33]

Ironically, Nobbs makes this confession to Hubert Page, a young house painter who turns out also to be female, and who advises her to marry a woman as she—the painter—has done. Again, the introduction of this figure would seem at first to emphasize Moore's sympathy with transvestism, for he has Hubert explain that she posed as a man in order to leave her brutal husband. But the results of Hubert's advice are devastating to Albert, who is not only viciously exploited by a kitchen maid she tries to woo, but who is also forced during her unsuccessful courtship to confront the lack that Moore identifies with her femininity. Almost as if he were glossing Freud's notion of female "castration," the author delineates Albert's anxiety about erotic encounters, her inability to kiss the kitchen maid properly, her fear of the confession she would have to make on their wedding night, and the way she appears to other characters as "a capon" (97) and "a fool of a man" (104).

Even more dramatically, Moore embeds a definition of female sexuality at the center of the crucial scene where the eerie doubles, Albert and Hubert, reveal their common anatomical destiny to each other. When Albert refuses to believe that Hubert, too, is a woman, Hubert proposes to lift her nightshirt, exclaiming "Put your hand under my shirt; you'll find *nothing* there" (82; emphasis ours). This language is echoed at the tale's end when, after the doctor who examined Albert's dead body reveals that the waiter was female, the servants in the hotel begin to speculate on "What would have happened on the wedding night" of Albert and the kitchen maid. "Nothing, of course; but how would she have let on? The men giggled over their glasses, and the women pondered over their cups of tea; the men asked the women and the women asked the men" (117).

But if nothing has come to Albert of the "nothing" which is her sexuality, Hubert's ultimate fate is different, and different, Moore shows, because she has at least at one time been a proper woman—that is, a wife and mother. For this finally repentant transvestite, both the death of her mock "wife" and Albert's death function as monitory events, causing her to decide to doff her male apparel because the "rest of [her] life belongs" to her husband and daughters, and she "must return home as a woman, and none of them must know the life she had been living" (121). At the end of the tale—with the story of Hubert's male life repressed because its truth wouldn't "be believed" (121)—the misrule of transvestism has been exorcised, proper patriarchal rule has been reestablished, and "the Angelus [is] ringing" (122). The anomalous man-woman Albert Nobbs, whom the narrator had first met as a child, was "the ugliest thing I'd seen out of a fairy book. . . . a queer, hobgoblin sort of fellow" (65), the speaker remembers, but Moore's Dublin has now been even more effectively cleansed of the queerness this woman represents than Joyce's Dublin was purified by Bloom's recovery of his masculinity.

A similar but more violent process of purification is enacted in D. H. Lawrence's "The Fox," published a year after *Ulysses* and *Celibate Lives*. The tale of Banford and her transvestite companion, March, two New Women from the city who try to run a farm together, this story gloatingly shows how they fail when a literal fox attacks their chickens and a figurative fox, in the form of a young soldier, attacks them, first by making love to March and thus disrupting the women's relationship, and later by accidentally-on-purpose felling a tree in such a way that it kills Banford. Thus the foxy soldier, Henry, and his two vulnerable female opponents, Banford and March, form a love/hate triangle whose tension is only resolved when Henry manages to divest March of her male clothing, her female companion, and her independence.

In the beginning of the story, Lawrence tells us, March is dressed in "putties and breeches . . . belted coat and . . . loose cap," a costume in which "she looked almost like some graceful, loose-balanced young man." But he adds that "her face was not a man's face, ever," and it is not surprising that shrewd, foxily masculine Henry soon decides that he should marry her and take over the farm. A proud possessor of the phallus that Albert Nobbs lacks, he contemplates his courtship with profound self-confidence: "What if she was older then he? It didn't matter. When he thought of her dark, startled, vulnerable eyes he smiled subtly to himself. He was older than she, really. He was master of her."[34]

March's change of dress is the most dramatic sign that Henry's appraisal of her is correct. Coming in to tea one day, he finds her "in a dress of dull, green silk crape," and, as if to emphasize the sexual revelation this costume change represents, Lawrence comments that "If she had suddenly grown a mustache he could not have been more surprised" (156). Despite the surprise, however, March's dress confirms Henry's mastery and definitively transforms the two of them into the true male and true female each had been all along:

> Seeing her always in the hard-cloth breeches . . . strong as armour . . . it had never occurred to [Henry] that she had a woman's legs and feet. Now it came upon him. She had a woman's soft, skirted legs, and she was accessible. . . . He felt a man, quiet, with a little of the heaviness of male destiny upon him. [157]

But if March's dress emphasizes her true womanliness—indeed, just the accessibility to male penetration that Mary Walker had deplored—it also reveals, by comparison, the unwomanliness of Banford, who, with her "little iron breasts" (155) and her chiffon costumes, is a sort of absurd female impersonator. Thus Henry's murder of Banford is his most powerful assertion of his "destiny" as well as the final sign that he has achieved the virility he needs in order to dominate March. Seeming "to flash up enormously tall and fearful" (173), he fells Banford by felling "a weak, leaning tree" (172) which had appeared, in its attempt at upright assertiveness, to impersonate the phallic strength that must by rights belong to him, so that, more ferociously than in "Albert Nobbs," true rule has been reestablished, an order based upon male dominance-female submission recovered from transvestite disorder.

That order undergoes a similar process of testing and regeneration in *The Waste Land,* a poem that is, as we have seen, about sexuality but also about the horrors of transsexuality and, figuratively speaking, of transvestism. For though hermaphroditism of the sort Tiresias possesses is not the same as transvestism, metaphorically the two are close indeed. Certainly when Tiresias describes himself as an "Old man with wrinkled female breasts," he is defining his sexuality in much the way that Joyce defines Bloom's in nighttown. And "what Tiresias *sees*," according to Eliot, "is the substance of the poem," not only a world shattered by the absence of a dead good soldier but also, no doubt for this reason, a Dantesque inferno of sexual misrule, an unreal (and unroyal) city enthralled by the false prophetess Madame Sosostris and laid waste both by its emasculated king's infertility and by the disorderly ascendancy of Belladonna, the Lady of Situations (whose name, whether intentionally or not, echoes Bella Cohen's).[35]

Just as the perverse ceremonies of Joyce's female-dominated nighttown inevitably organized themselves into a Black Mass in celebration of the unholy "Dooooog!" who is God spelled backward, Eliot's infertile London is haunted by a sinister Dog, with first letter capitalized, who threatens to dig up corpses. For, like nighttown, this unreal city is a topsy-turvy kingdom where towers that should be upright hang "upside down in air" and baby faced bats crawl "head downward down a blackened wall."[36] And like nighttown, Circe's abode, it is haunted by a kind of sorceress, who fiddles sacrilegious "whisper music" on the "strings" of her hair (145). Even the central scene Tiresias "sees" in the upside-down world he describes—the seduction of the typist by the young man carbuncular—is merely a parody of the male dominance-female submission that should be associated with fertility and order, for the young man is "One of the *low* on whom assurance sits / As a silk hat on a Bradford millionaire," and the typist is not really submissive but simply ind*i*fferent (141; emphasis ours). Both, therefore, represent a society where everything and everyone are out of place, not just women on top but shopclerks unruly and carbuncular young men strutting in the false costume of the nouveau riche.

Some of the passages Pound and Eliot excised from the original manuscript of *The Waste Land* make it clear that both Tiresias's terrible vision and Eliot's vision of Tiresias's anomalous sexuality arise from anxiety about a blurring of those gender distinctions in which human beings ought properly to be clothed. The first draft of "The Burial of the Dead," for instance, begins with a description of a visit to a whorehouse called "Myrtle's place," a house not unlike Bella Cohen's establishment, for Madame Myrtle proves frighteningly independent, even masterful. Announcing that "I'm not in business here for guys like you," she explains that, as if anticipating Banford and March, she's going to "retire and live on a farm." And though she is ultimately kinder than

Bella—refusing to give the speaker a woman, she does give him "a bed, and a bath, and ham and eggs"—her kindness is disturbingly matriarchal. "[N]ow you go get a shave" (5), she tells her would-be customer, as she turns him out into the barren nighttime streets of the waste land. Her emasculating authority foreshadows the frightening dominance of sibylline Madame Sosostris, of enthroned Belladonna—that chess queen who can move in all directions, unlike her paralyzed king—and of the free-wheeling, unladylike ladies in the pub. It also adumbrates the perverse power of another character who was summarily cut from the final draft: "white-armed Fresca."

Appearing voluptuously "between the sheets," like insubordinate Molly Bloom, Fresca "dreams of love and pleasant rapes" in a series of antiheroic heroic couplets that echo Pope's often equally disturbing eighteenth-century parodies of the lives and aspirations of Blue Stockings. In addition, Fresca's dreams comment interestingly on those literal and figurative rapes (of Philomel, the Thames daughters, and the typist) which occur in Eliot's waste land. When she enters her "steaming bath," moreover, she does not purify herself; rather, costuming herself in deceptive "Odours, confected by the artful French," she willfully disguises what Eliot describes as her "good old hearty female stench" (23).

Worse still, although Eliot/Tiresias tells us that "in other time or other place" Fresca would have been her proper self, a creature devised by male poets, "A meek and lowly weeping Magdalene: / More sinned against than sinning, bruised and marred / The lazy laughing Jenny of the bard"[37] (and at the same time "A doorstep dunged by every dog in town"), in the upside-down realm Fresca now rules she is a woman poet, the inevitable product of an unnatural age of transvestite costumes, masks, disguises:

> Fresca was baptized in a soapy sea
> Of Symonds—Walter Pater—Vernon Lee . . .
> From such chaotic misch-masch potpourri
> What are we to expect but poetry?
> When restless nights distract her brain from sleep
> She may as well write poetry, as count sheep. [27]

Thus, "By fate misbred, by flattering friends beguiled, / Fresca's arrived (the Muses Nine declare) / To be a sort of can-can salonnière," and, significantly, the immediate consequence of her literary triumph for the speaker is that "at my back from time to time I hear / The rattle of the bones, and chuckle spread from ear to ear." For as this speaker had earlier reminded us, "Women [grown] intellectual grow dull, / And lose the mother wit of natural trull" (27). Losing nurturing mother wit, however, and artificially separating themselves from the natural trull in themselves, such antiheroines separate their men from the fertile order of nature, precipitating everyone, instead, into a chaotic no man's land of unnatural, transvestite women.

It is no coincidence, then, that the third in the series of nineteenth-century aesthetes who "baptized" Fresca into her unholy religion of art was, at least metaphorically, a female transvestite: Vernon Lee was the male pseudonym under which the writer Violet Paget achieved considerable literary success in the late nineteenth and early twentieth centuries.[38] Her fleeting appearance here is yet one more detail which suggests that *The Waste Land* is precisely the *Walpurgisnacht* of misplaced gender that a sexually anxious man of letters would define as the fever dream of the hermaphrodite. For ultimately Eliot yearns with Joyce and Lawrence for "the violet hour, the evening hour that strives / Homeward" (141), to bring a thoroughly male Ulysses home from the sea to his soft-skirted, definitively female Penelope. Because both time and Tiresias are out of joint, such a consummation does not happen in *The Waste Land*. But it is devoutly wished, and thus it represents a patriarchal sexual rule which is as implicit in the sorrowful misrule that haunts Eliot's poem as it is in the authoritative voice of thunder that tentatively concludes the work.

If *The Waste Land* objectifies gender disorder through the delineation of an infernal landscape haunted by Dantesque shadows, a more recent meditation on the subject is set, paradoxically enough, in an earthly paradise. Hemingway's *The Garden of Eden,* a work to which the author devoted himself on and off for the last fifteen years of his life but which he was never able to finish, is evidently much longer in manuscript than the volume Scribner's published in 1986, but the portion of the novel that has been edited and printed focuses on a fall into transsexuality which illuminates what Hemingway said was the theme of his book: "the happiness of the Garden that a man must lose."[39] Moreover, even more explicitly than *The Waste Land*, this novel associates female sexual misrule with a threat to male literary authority.

When we first encounter David and Catherine Bourne, the principal characters in this allusive allegory of seductive sexchanges and aesthetic anxieties, they are enjoying an Edenic honeymoon in the south of France, an interlude of bliss blessed by excellent food and fishing, as well as by the couple's erotic ecstasy and the success of David's recently published novel. Yet within a few weeks Catherine—whose name suggests she may be a demonic reincarnation of the charismatic Catherine Barkley in *A Farewell to Arms*—has conceived of a series of surprising changes which, she explains, will take "us further away from other peo-

ple" (30) because "Why do we have to go by everyone else's rules?" (15)
These transformations of rule into misrule—associated with Catherine's efforts to distract David from his writing—will ultimately include
the tanning of the pair's bodies so that each is "darker than an Indian"
(30), the cropping and lightening of their hair so that they look like
"brothers" as well as negative photographic images of "everyone else,"
and the metamorphoses of Catherine into a boy named Peter and of
David into a girl named Catherine.

But the last of these, which David calls "the dark magic of the change"
(20), is most crucial, representing a lapse from properly gendered innocence into improperly gendered experience that triggers the whole
of the novel's revisionary biblical plot. Returning to her husband with
her new boyish haircut, Catherine asks, "Dave, you don't mind if we've
gone to the devil, do you?" a question that takes on resonance when
she refuses to let him call her "girl" and instead sodomizes him, explaining "You are changing. . . . Oh you are, You are. Yes you are
and you're my girl Catherine" (17). Though he protests that "You're
Catherine," she insists that "I'm Peter," and "You're my wonderful
Catherine," and thus "At the end they were both dead and empty," and
David's "heart said goodbye Catherine goodbye Catherine goodbye my
lovely girl goodbye and good luck and goodbye" (18).

From this point on, David frequently calls Catherine "Devil," because she has plainly become a kind of Lilith or, at least, an Eve enthralled to satanic powers, and the rest of the book recounts this writer's struggle to retain his imperiled masculinity in the face of his wife's
increasingly mad sexual onslaughts. The fruit of the tree of knowledge
of good and evil, says Hemingway, is a disruption of "everyone else's
rules" which is purchased by women and fed to men. In this terrifying
script, therefore, the man is, like Leopold Bloom, degraded to no more
than an object of female aesthetic and erotic attention. In a scene at a
beauty parlor, David acquiesces in Catherine's accession to a role as
queen of cosmetology that uncannily echoes Bella/Bello's promise to
Leopold Bloom that "As they are now, so will you be": given "her haircut" but protesting against the bleach she desires, David finally submits
to Catherine's command to the coiffeur, "Go ahead and do it" (82).

Hemingway's fantasy of masculine degradation may, of course, reflect his long-standing ambivalence toward his mother, who, as Kenneth S. Lynn has recently documented, intermittently dressed him as a
girl for several years of his early childhood, fantasized that he was his
older sister Marcelline's same-sex twin, and labeled a photograph of
him at the age of twenty-three months "summer girl."[40] But ultimately
his manuscript agressively defines the young male writer's fall as a *felix
culpa,* as if more explicitly echoing the moves outlined by Joyce, Law-

rence, and Eliot, for Catherine's most extreme gestures boomerang. First, although she seduces a beautiful young woman named Marita and has a lesbian affair with her, the girl becomes David's muselike mistress, a "littly Mary" whom he calls "Heiress" because, in terms of the novel's allegorical structure, she must inevitably replace the "Devil" Catherine. Second, although Catherine, in a rage at David's commitment to his art, burns the manuscript he has written about his childhood relationship to his father and his own coming of age as a man, he is empowered by his love for Marita to reproduce his work so that it is better than it ever was before : "there was no sign that any of it would ever cease returning to him intact" (247).

If he has been borne out of Eden, David Bourne has also been born again, this time happily rid of the insubordinate woman who would penetrate him and appropriate his "Peter." Finally, therefore, though Hemingway appears in many ways to sympathize with Catherine's insistence that being "a girl [is] a god damned bore" because it involves "Scenes, hysteria, false accusations" (70), he demonstrates not only that these things are true (the masculinized Catherine continues to indulge in "Scenes, hysteria, false accusations") but also that his hero must extricate himself from the misrule she has inaugurated in order to regenerate a more appropriate gender hierarchy and, through his relationship with the Madonna-like Marita, more powerful literary texts.

That, two decades after he produced in *The Sun Also Rises* and *A Farewell to Arms* anxious meditations on sexuality which were associated with the unmanning trauma of the Great War, Hemingway was still brooding on the male "disease of modern life" that we have been tracing throughout this volume suggests just how pervasive and enduring this dis-ease was. Feeling themselves to be coerced by women, at the mercy of women, bedded down in the terrible house of women, male writers from Joyce and Moore to Lawrence, Eliot, and Hemingway must have felt that they had painfully to extract the truth of their gender's ancient dominance from an overwhelming chaos. Thus, the imagined vulnerability of these men of letters led them to an obsession with false and true costumes, deceptive history and true myth. For inevitably, in the aftermath of the emasculating terrors of the war, many men insisted that the ultimate reality underlying history is and must be the truth of gender.

Ulysses, "Albert Nobbs," *The Waste Land,* and "The Fox" were all published within a two-year period, and of course Virginia Woolf knew at least the most famous of these works—*Ulysses* and *The Waste Land*—so that her radical revisions of male costume dramas provide an extraordinarily useful paradigm of the skepticism with which feminist modernists questioned, subverted, and repudiated the conservative, hierarchical views of their male counterparts. When "Great Tom" Eliot came to Hogarth House and "rhythmed" *The Waste Land,* Woolf was so impressed by its "great beauty" that Hogarth Press published the poem in book form the following year. When Elliot defended *Ulysses* to her, however, her feelings about Joyce's novel were considerably less charitable. Though Eliot was eventually to praise Joyce not only for his literary abilities but for being "ethically orthodox," Woolf insisted in her diary that *Ulysses* was "brackish" and "underbred," adding within a few weeks that when "Tom said '[Joyce] is a purely literary writer,' " she had scornfully responded that he was "virile—a he-goat."[41] Five years later, when Woolf herself wrote a novel about transvestism—*Orlando*—she seems to have deliberately set out to shatter the "he-goat" vision of male mastery that she perceived in *Ulysses.*

Orlando, a work that is nominally about a transsexual, depicts transsexualism through witty costume changes rather than through actual physical transformations. In fact, as if to emphasize that costume, not anatomy, is destiny, Woolf comically eschews specific descriptions of the bodily alterations that mark Orland's gender metamorphosis. As "man become woman," Orlando stands naked before a mirror, but Woolf merely remarks that he/she looks "ravishing," then brings on three parodic "virtues" personified as ladies—Chastity, Purity, and Modesty—who throw a towel at the unclothed being. That the towel-bearers are ladies suggests at once the connection between self-definition, sexual definition, and costume, a connection that Woolf makes more clearly as her narrative unfolds. Her transsexual, she argues, is no more than a transvestite, for though Orlando has outwardly become a woman, "in every other respect [she] remains precisely as he had been" (138), and this not because sexually defining costumes are false and selves are true but because costumes are selves and thus easily, fluidly, interchangeable.

Unlike Leopold Bloom's humiliation, then, or the "corset discipline" imposed upon Dennis Evelyn Beryl and Viscount Ladywood, Orlando's sexchange is not a fall; it is simply a shift in fashion, so that Woolf associates it with shifts in literary style and shifts in historical styles, which remind us that, like Orlando, all is in flux, no fixed hierarchy endures or should endure. As a shift that is not a fall, moreover, Orlando's metamorphosis, and indeed the whole of her history, seem to comment on Bella/Bello Cohen's threat to Bloom that "As they are now, so shall you be"—wigged, powdered, corseted, de-graded. Although Orland's female costume discomfits her at times, it never degrades her, for, declares Woolf, "It was a change in Orlando herself that dictated her choice of woman's dress and of a woman's sex . . . [because] Different though the sexes are, they intermix" (188–89). Orlando, in other words, really is androgynous (as Tiresias, for instance, is not) in the sense that she has available to her a sort of wardrobe of male and female selves. Making herself up daily out of such costumes, Orlando rejoices in a society where there need be no uni-forms, for indeed (as if confusing nakedness and costume) Woolf remarks that Orlando's own "form combined in one the strength of a man and a woman's grace" (138).

Thus, unlike Tiresias, upon whom the worst of both sexes has been inflicted, Orlando has the best of both sexes in a happy multiform which she herself has chosen. And in accordance with this visionary multiplicity, she inhabits a world where almost anyone can change his or her sexual habits at any time. Yet this is not, like Tiresias's waste land, a kingdom of gender disorder but a realm of insouciant shiftings. After Orlando has become a woman, for instance, Archduchess Harriet becomes Archduke Harry; he/she and Orlando act "the parts of man and woman for ten minutes with great vigour and then [fall] into natural discourse" (179). Similarly, marriage for Orlando need not be the affair of pure masterful maleness embracing pure submissive femaleness that it was for Lawrence's foxy Henry. In fact, just the sort of dark change which left Hemingway's David feeling "dead and empty," gives joy to her and her mate. Wed to the magical sea captain Marmaduke Bonthrop Shelmerdine, Orlando comically accuses her *simpatico* husband of being a woman, and he happily accuses her of being a man, "for . . . it was to each . . . a revelation that a woman could be as tolerant and free-spoken as a man, and a man as strange and subtle as a woman" (258). A question with which Bella Cohen's Fan surrealistically initiated the phantasmagoria of sick horror that overtook Bloom in nighttown aptly summarizes, therefore, not the disease but the delight of *Orlando:* "Is me her was you dreamed before? Was then she him you us since knew? Am all them and the same now we?" (515).

Orlando is, of course, in one sense a utopia, a revisionary biography of society not as Woolf thinks it is but as she believes it ought to be; and in another sense *Orlando* is a kind of merry fairy tale, its protagonist an eternally living doll whose wardrobe of costume selves enables her to transcend the constraints of flesh and history. But though Woolf defined the book as a happy escapade, satiric and wild, *Orlando's* carefully plotted transvestism contrasts so strikingly with the transvestism we have seen in major works by male modernists that this fantasitic historical romance seems to be more than merely a lighthearted *jeu*. In fact, the book employs a technique that has, historically, been used by many female writers, a number of whom have always wished either to identify "selves" with costumes or to strip away all costumes (and selves) to reveal the pure, sexless (or, as we shall see, "third sexed") being behind gender and myth.

———————

The fantastically multiple creature called Orlando was born in response to a set of real problems that were being confronted—sometimes just as exuberantly, but sometimes more grimly—by a number of Woolf's most interesting contemporaries. Yet he/she also had important antecedents in the nineteenth century. Not only did many women employ male pseudonyms, not only did women artists from George Sand to Charlotte Mew costume themselves as men or as manly, but even Elizabeth Barrett Browning, who was later to be mythologized as the love-struck poetess of Wimpole Street, admitted to a friend that "through the whole course of my childhood, I had a steady indignation against Nature who made me a woman, & a determinate resolution to dress up in men's clothes as soon as ever I was free of the nursery," and she wrote a fragment of a story about a girl who wants to "be the feminine of Homer": "When she grew up she wd. wear men's clothes, & live on a Greek island."[42] In addition, as early as 1847 Charlotte Brontë's Rochester dresses himself as a female gypsy not to degrade himself but to try to "get at" the truth about Jane. In *Villette* (1853), moreover, Brontë's Lucy Snowe discovers ultimate truths about herself, first, when she impersonates a man for the school play and, later, when she perceives that the nun who has haunted her is really no more than a costume worn by a man. Just as the Brontës themselves became Currer, Acton, and Ellis Bell—names that they did not see as masculine but as free of sex markings—in order to transcend gender constraints, Rochester is trying to communicate with the "wild free thing" trapped in Jane, and Lucy is trying to uncover that purely powerful element in herself and her life.

Similarly, throughout the middle years of the century, Emily Dickinson defined herself variously as Emilie, Uncle Emily, Brother Emily, and Dickinson, as if attempting to name not what was fixed but what was fluid in herself, while in the same year Florence Nightingale continually called herself a "man of action" or a "man of business." Later in the century, one of Olive Schreiner's heroines in *From Man to Man* (1926) actually imagines herself turning into a "man of action," and her happy revery is notably different from the dark change Hemingway portrays:

> How nice it would be to be a man. She fancied she was one till she felt her very body grow strong and hard and shaped like a man's.

> She felt the great freedom opened *[sic]* to her, no place shut off
> from her, the long chain broken, all work possible for her, no law
> to say this and this is for woman, you are woman; she drew a long
> breath and smiled an expansive smile.[43]

Like latter-day gnostics, many of these women felt the transformation
or annihilation of gender to be theologically necessary. As we have seen,
Nightingale wrote in *Cassandra* (1852) that the "next Christ will perhaps be a female Christ," and in 1883 Schreiner created in *The Story of
an African Farm* a "new man," with the double-sexed name of Gregory
Rose, who dresses as a woman in order to become a ministering angel
to the woman he loves. In what amounts to a summary of all these
fantasies, Schreiner imagined a mystical encounter with "a lonely figure" standing on "a solitary peak," about whom she noted that "whether
it were man or woman I could not tell; for partly it seemed the figure
of a woman but its limbs were the mighty limbs of a man. I asked God
whether it was a man or woman. God said, 'In the least Heaven sex
reigns supreme, in the higher it is not noticed; but in the highest it
does not exist!' "[44]

The least heaven, of course, may be the most that can reasonably be
hoped for on earth. Consequently, for a number of late nineteenth-
and twentieth-century women artists, cross-dressing became a way of
addressing and redressing the inequities of gender categories. If "man
is defined as a human being and woman as a female," Simone de Beauvoir has argued, "whenever [woman] behaves as a human being she is
said to imitate the male."[45] But this means, conversely, that at least one
way woman could define herself as human and thereby function effectively in the world was by determining to imitate man. As Alfred Habegger has reminded us, such an implicitly feminist strategy plays a
crucial role in popular nineteenth-century women's fiction.[46] In a study
of E.D.E.N. Southworth's bestselling *The Hidden Hand* (1859), he points
out that this "widely-loved book" tells the story of a young woman who,
in an effort to "solve the problem of woman's vulnerability to man actually passes for a boy at the beginning of the novel." Thus he notes
that *The Hidden Hand* "offers a cross-dressing fantasy that represents a
major, mainstream response by author and readers to a felt female
weakness." More specifically, Habegger emphasizes the explanation that
Southworth's heroine proposes for her behavior: "While all the ragged
boys I knew could get little jobs to earn bread, I, because I was a girl,
was not allowed to . . . do *anything* that *I* could do just as well as *they*."[47]
Similarly, in Sarah Grand's *The Heavenly Twins* (1893), the young

Angelica dresses up as her twin brother, exclaiming "You often hear it said of a girl that she should have been a boy, which being interpreted means that she has superior abilities; but because she is a woman it is not thought necessary to give her a chance of making a career for herself."[48] In female costume, Angelica says, she found herself inhabiting a "groove" that was "deep and narrow, and gave me no room to move" (45), but in male attire she gains the latitude she associates with two idols—George Sand and James Barry (an "Inspector General of the Army Medical Department" [456] whose brother officers did not discover she was a woman until after her death). Equally important, disguised as a boy, she enjoys a free companionship with a male friend that (as if echoing Dr. Mary Walker) she believes she could not have had as a girl since "so unwholesomely is the imagination of a man affected by ideas of sex" (458).

But the kinds of issues raised by Southworth and Grand became increasingly important in the twentieth century. When, for example,

Willa Cather. Courtesy of the Nebraska State Historical Society

Willa Cather spent her youth dressed in masculine trousers, with her hair cut short, calling herself "Willie," and proudly displaying herself in a Civil War cap (opposite), she was presumably just a "tom boy," like the Harding girls in *My Ántonia* (1918). But, like her contemporary Dorothy Richardson, Willa Cather was attracted to male clothes for practical reasons that are succinctly articulated by several young women in Richardson's *The Tunnel* (1919). Exhilarated at the physical freedom conferred by knickers, they exclaim that "you could knock down a policeman"; delighted by the creative strength such garments seem to confer, they gloat that you feel "like a poet though you don't know it."[49] Several decades later, comparably specifying the way in which male garb solves what Habagger calls the "problem of woman's vulnerability to man," Anaïs Nin has a female character in *Ladders to Fire* (1946) explain that the first time a boy hurt her, she went home and dressed in her brother's suit. This "costume of strength" made her feel arrogant, she confesses, for "to be a boy meant one did not suffer." Later, this woman longs for the release and fulfillment of action that she continues to associate with male attire:

> All through the last war as a child I felt: if only they would let me be Joan of Arc. Joan of Arc wore a suit of armor, she sat on a horse, she fought side by side with the men. She must have gained their strength.[50]

An equally compelling vision of the woman warrior preoccupied the most important female science fiction writer of the interwar period. C. L. Moore published a series of stories from 1934 to 1939 about Jirel of Joiry, a "warrior lady" who is literally "mailed"—both armored and masculinized.[51] A version of *la fille soldat* of folk songs, the charismatic Jirel of Joiry reminds us that such a female bid for power has often been viewed with a considerable degree of tolerance in our culture. From Rosa Bonheur, who was authorized by the Paris police to wear male clothing in 1857, to Dorothy Arzner, who sometimes chose such feminine presences as Lucille Ball and Merle Oberon for her films in the 1930s, all the while herself looking directorial and masculine, women have assumed trousers and ties not only to authenticate their work but also to guard against literal and figurative masculine assaults.[52]

Of course such efforts sometimes expose the very contradiction between costume and gender that the transvestite woman may be striving to elide. Sexy theatrical cross-dressers like Sarah Bernhardt, Marlene Dietrich, Greta Garbo, and Katherine Hepburn would seem to testify to male (as well as female) fascination with female transvestism. Where in popular media, at least since the Restoration, the male cross-dresser is invariably either grotesquely comic *(Charley's Aunt, Some Like It Hot,*

La Cage aux Folles, Tootsie, and "the ballerinas" of *Les Ballets Trockadero);* or existentially tragic *(The Balcony, Psycho, Kiss of the Spider Woman, Performance, Dressed to Kill),* from Bernhardt's Hamlet and Garbo's Queen Christina to Barbra Streisand's Yentl and Julie Andrew's *Victor/Victoria,* actresses in male clothes appear to have delighted audiences by seeming to transcend gender asymmetries.[53] Yet in every case these asymmetries are paradoxically reinforced even by the glamorous image of the woman-as-man, for the masculinized actress is invariably marked either in her body or by the plot in which she is entangled as ultimately and rightly female.[54] Thus Bernhardt is always a femme fatale, even when she plays the tormented Hamlet; Dietrich wears a top hat and tuxedo jacket to show off her beautiful legs; Garbo as the transvestite Queen Christina is luminously lovely when she is a royal boy but even more so when she is finally obliged to wear women's clothes. No matter how inventively the woman armors herself with masculinity, these films imply, her armor itself calls attention to her vulnerability and to the inexorable fact that she is "no more than e'en a woman."

This last point has long been understood and mourned by women artists who either attempt or fantasize cross-dressing. One of Nin's heroines, for example, imagines that her armor lies broken around her and punningly grieves that the "mail had melted, and revealed the bruised feminine flesh."[55] Vita Sackville-West, moreover, impersonated a *wounded* soldier during her Parisian affair with Violet Trefusis, disguising her vulnerably female hair beneath a large bandage, while Radclyffe Hall's Miss Ogilvy dies when she reimagines herself as a hero of the stone-age, as if the tension between her fantasized masculinity and her "bruised feminine flesh" were a fatal one. Even when interrogating gender categories, then, these figures acknowledge the constraints that would keep them from being other than what they are supposed to be.

The portraits of transvestites by Romaine Brooks, the most important painter of female cross-dressers in the modernist period, illustrate just such a sense of contradiction. No longer either feisty tomboys or glamorous women warriors, Brooks's subjects—drawn from among her cosmopolitan circle of expatriate friends—are typically self-divided, brooding, Byronic figures who dominate the centers of their canvases yet in their Romantic gloom hint at joys diminished or lost. Satanic outsiders, they flaunt their perversity as if to assert their choice of a different destiny, even while they are wounded by the anatomy in which they feel trapped. Brooks's self-portrait (opposite), for example, affirms an ambiguous eroticism even as it hints at a mysterious source of anguish. Produced in 1923, primarily in a dark palette, the painting displays her wearing a black top hat, black jacket and gray gloves, with an open-necked white shirt. Only the title and a faint redness on the lips give away the gender of the subject, who stands in front of a waste land composed of crumbling, charred buildings that Brooks's biographer, Meryle Secrest, sees as "the aftermath of a holocaust."[56]

The painter's clenched fist and right arm, held tightly against her body, give the impression that she must keep herself together by an act of will. Her eyes have a piercing look, as if she is struggling not to turn away from what horrifies her or as if she is seeing through and beyond pain. Caught in a tension between costume and body that reflects some inner torment, she is marked by her shaded brow like Byron's Cain, but in her seductive glamour, too, she resembles Byron's wandering

Romaine Brooks. *Self-Portrait.* Courtesy of the National Museum of American Art, Smithsonian Institution, Gift of the Artist

outcast. Wan and world-weary, she is exotic and erotic, as dashing in her vaguely aristocratic evening clothes as are the other cross-dressers Brooks painted: the boyish "Peter" (1923–24; below); "Renata Borgatti" (1919), who sits tensely at the piano, a bent, black, hawk-like figure: and "Una, Lady Troubridge" (1924; opposite), whose evening clothes, monocle, and dachshunds make her look like a caricature of a model British gentleman.

Like Miss Ogilvy, all these subjects seem to proclaim that they have an ontological identity quite different from the one that the world would impose upon them, an identity signified by their costumes but subverted by their bodies. Thus they radiate a troubled grandeur which is illuminated by Radclyffe Hall's statement in *The Well of Loneliness* that the "invert" is "grotesque and splendid, like some primitive thing conceived in a turbulent age of transition," a martyr who is hideously maimed

Romaine Brooks. *Peter (A Young English Girl).*
Courtesy of the National Museum of American
Art, Smithsonian Institution, Gift of the Artist

but also a Romantic outlaw and rebel. When Stephen Gordon, Hall's transvestite heroine in *The Well of Loneliness*, realizes she is "flawed in the making," the product of a cruel God, her Bible falls open to "the Lord set a mark upon Cain,"[57] a line that refers not just to the biblical Cain but to Byron's outlaw heroes and, through Stephen's surname, Gordon, to George Gordon, Lord Byron himself. Feeling simultaneously victimized by biological fate and by parents who wanted male children, both Romaine Brooks and Radclyffe Hall identified cross-dressing with lesbianism and lesbianism with physiologically and psychologically masculine traits in women that caused society to set them apart as marked. But they may have also been drawn to the Byronic outcast who "stalks apart in joyless reverie" because, as several recent critics have observed, Byron's own homoerotic impulses were dramatized through some of the transvestite episodes in *Lara* and *Don Juan*.[58]

Romaine Brooks. *Una, Lady Troubridge.* Courtesy of the National Museum of American Art, Smithsonian Institution, Gift of the Artist

Known to her friends as John, wearing elegant men's jackets and ties, Radclyffe Hall wrote in *The Well* about the frustrations of a congenitally masculine girl born to a father who confirmed her inversion by treating her as the son he wanted. This myth of origins accords with the etiology of homosexuality Havelock Ellis had developed and therefore explains his defense of the novel in the famous court case brought against it. But since the story Hall tells about Stephen and her father represents only a slight exaggeration of one line of Freud-defined female psychosexual development in patriarchal culture, her analysis of her heroine's sense of freakishness repeats itself in the biographies of women whom Hall would have considered far more "normal" than herself: Dorothy Richardson, for example, who was called "son" by her father, or Carson McCullers, an inveterate cross-dresser, who considered herself an "invert" because she had been "born a man."[59] At the same time, however, Hall implies that a woman who feels the need to turn herself into a man is haunted by the feeling that, if judged as a man, she is inadequate. For, at its most didactic, *The Well of Loneliness* both records and protests the societally induced "stigmata of the abnormal—verily the wounds of One nailed to a cross" (246).

That Virginia Woolf protested the banning of the book, even while implicitly criticizing its title (which might have disturbed her by its equation of female anatomy with a tragic destiny) through her production of the more insouciant *Orlando* may at first seem odd.[60] Yet though Orlando's exuberance appears to controvert *The Well's* bleakness, the two works ultimately have in common a feminist modernist commitment to the subversion of gender categories, the disentangling of anatomy and destiny.[61] Indeed, while Woolf imagines a being who has many selves and several sexes, Hall is in a way just as radical. For the "fulfillment" Stephen Gordon and her female lover achieve on their honeymoon covertly questions Freud's notion that when little girls "notice the penis of a brother or playmate, strikingly visible and of large proportions, [they] at once recognize it as the superior counterpart of their own small and inconspicuous organ."[62] Thus, for both Woolf and Hall (one a part-time "Sapphist," the other a committed lesbian), gender became in some sense an artificial construct, as it also did for such a mythologizer of heterosexuality as Isak Dinesen.

Though Dinesen herself was quite consciously a fashion plate, she consistently distanced herself from her high style costumes by giving them such ironic names as "Sappho," "Sober Truth," "Beau Brummel," "Bohème," and even "Tate Gallery," implying that she literally commanded a wardrobe of identities. In addition, some of her stories are costume dramas which meditate on a dream of creating "a being of its own kind, an object of art which was neither boy nor girl."[63] Associating the mystique of such a being with the possibilities of modernity, Dinesen wrote that the women of the nineteenth century lived "in those tight corsets within which they could just manage to breathe," but implied that the women of the twentieth century have liberated themselves by learning how to manipulate costumes, even to play with them. As if to dramatize Dinesen's point, Susan Leonardi has reminded us of the pleasure Oxford women in the twenties took in literal theatrical transvestism. Focusing on Dorothy Sayers, Winifred Holtby, and their group, she reports that

> Sayers, in the Going-Down Play of her year, which she wrote and directed, took the part of the Oxford man she most admired, the director of the Bach choir; Holtby, one of her friends, Margaret Waley, later recalled, "often chose to take male parts" which preference Waley links to Holtby's "sexual ambivalence" . . . Even the proper Miss Emily Penrose enjoyed dressing as a man; she once represented, in some sort of tableau, Sir John Collier's portrait of T. H. Huxley, "holding a skull and wearing whiskers and her nephew's coat and trousers."[64]

Far more eccentrically than most of the women we have discussed so far, Gertrude Stein managed comparatively early in her career to look at costume, especially female costume, from what seems like a comically extraplanetary perspective. Specifically, in *Tender Buttons* (1914), one of her first major experimental works, she mocked the gender categories that obsessed so many of her male contemporaries. As the title hints, *Tender Buttons* is (are?) concerned with clothing, classification, sex, and language: are tender buttons tasty buttons? buttons meant to be tendered? sore buttons? belly buttons? nipple or clitoral buttons? Whatever they are, they point to Stein's obsession with the way in which clothing constitutes a sign system that can open or close off meaning, an obsession that, interestingly enough, predated that of Roland Barthes's *Système de la mode* (1967) by more than half a century.

More particularly, many of the definitions in the first section of the book, entitled "Objects," are of clothes, often women's clothes: "Mildred's Umbrella," "A Method of a Cloak," "A Long Dress," "A Red Hat," "A Blue Coat," "A Purse," "A Petticoat," "A Waist," "A Handkerchief," "Colored Hats," "A Feather," "Shoes," "A Shawl," and the concluding "This is This Dress, Aider." Most of these common female appurtenances are as mysterious as "A Cloth": "Enough cloth is plenty and more, more is almost enough for that and besides if there is no more spreading is there plenty of room for it. Any occasion shows the best way."[65] The rhetoric of clothing is reduced to nonsense here. But "any occasion shows the best way" also has the ring of some (admittedly mad) fashion magazine blurb. The subsequent sections on "Food" and "Rooms" strengthen the possibility that *Tender Buttons* is a demonic Mrs. Beeton's, a subversive conduct book that copes with traditionally female preoccupations—glamour tips, recipes, interior decorating—in a sibylline manner which ridicules social conventions even as it defies conventional interpretation. Furnishing her readers with a radically arbitrary set of new meanings for old words, Stein reminds us of the arbitrariness of conventional structures of signification.

Published at the beginning of World War I, *Tender Buttons* sets out to demolish the conventions of nineteenth-century literary realism as systematically as the first World War, in Stein's opinion, "tried to end the nineteenth century." And just as she characterized the 1914–1918 war as "a nice war,"[66] Stein shaped *Tender Buttons* to be "nice" in its optimistic certainty that the mimetic, representational function of language and literature could be annihilated. As she explained in her parodic rhetoric text *How to Write* (1931), a sentence "Pleases by its sense. This is a fashion in sentences."[67] But, if sense is merely fashion, it is also true that "A sentence is from this time I will make up my mind" (31). Therefore, Stein can be her own and only model, trying on "dress address name" (115) with studied abandon. Supplied with such a resplendently idiosyncratic wardrobe of words, she boasts, "Think how everybody follows me" (34).

But if everybody ought to follow Stein as a model of style who will lead them into the promised land of gender-free nonsense, she is really (in her own view) a holy prophet. "When this you see remember me," all of her writing insists by virtue of its very eccentricity. This early line, later reiterated in *Four Saints in Three Acts* (1928), implies that the artist is herself a kind of saint, and, if Stein sometimes used masculine clothing as a clown suit (figure, page 359), she always implied that the fool was divine. "Saints talk for me," Stein explained in an earlier piece, "Saints talk to me. / Saints talk with me. Saints talk with saints."[68] Accordingly, the sculptures of Stein by Jacques Lipchitz (1920) and Jo Davidson (1920), as well as the famous painting by Francis Picabia (1933), display her looking like a cross between Buddha and Julius Caesar (figure, page 358). Yet, tellingly, these icons of this woman artist allude to patriarchal figures whose powers she appropriates. Indeed, possibly the most expressive illustration of Stein's self-definition as a "being of its own kind" is Cecil Beaton's late photograph taken at Bilignin (opposite). Flanked by the seated Alice B. Toklas, on her right, the seated Bernard Fay, on her left, Stein stands as serenely as Joyce's "God of the creation . . . paring his fingernails"[69] in front of what looks like a pa-

Gertrude Stein. Photograph by Cecil Beaton. Courtesy of Sotheby's Belgravia

goda or miniature chapel, at a place where two paths cross, in robes that make her look priestly as she mediates horizontally between the human male and the human female, and vertically from the earth to the top of the spire and the sky.

But if Stein converted the image of the cross-dresser into an image of divinity, Djuna Barnes provided what might be considered an anatomy of the destiny of transvestism in *Nightwood* (1936), a novel that focuses on the way in which salvation is possible only through the subversion preached and practiced by the invert, for *Nightwood* introduces us to the third-sexed figures of Robin Vote and Dr. O'Connor, who star in a novel that was introduced by T. S. Eliot himself.[70] As James E. Miller, Jr., has argued, despite the Jacobean eloquence that must have appealed to the admirerer of Webster, Beaumont, and Fletcher, the sexually ambiguous Dr. O'Connor may have been the real reason why the creator of Tiresias was drawn to this book.[71] A kind of witch doctor

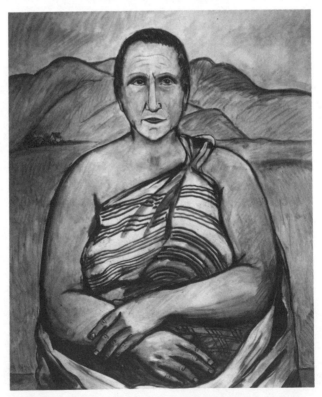

Francis Picabia. *Portrait of Gertrude Stein*, 1933. Courtesy of the Collection of American Literature, The Beinecke Rare Book and Manuscript Library, Yale University

or medicine man, half Circe, half Ulysses, Dr. O'Connor lies in bed
heavily painted with rouge and wearing a golden wig with long curls.
As for Robin Vote, a girl who habitually dresses as a boy, she too may
also have both unnerved and fascinated the creator of the hyacinth girl/
boy, for Robin's gender identity is deeply blurred. Indeed, she is described as "outside the 'human type'—a wild thing caught in a woman's
skin," whose first name connects her with nature and whose last name
associates her with the triumphs of the women's movement and the
votive powers of the sacred.[72]

From baptismal basins described as "loosing their skirts of water in
a ragged and flowing hem" (30), to rationalism which "dresses the un-
knowable in the garment of the known" (136), *Nightwood* is a clothing-
obsessed book which asks "what is this love we have for the invert, boy
or girl?" (136), as the male transvestite meditates on the passion the
female cross-dresser creates in all who meet her. A "tall girl with the
body of a boy" (46), Robin Vote initially wears men's clothes to gain a

Gertrude Stein and Alice B. Toklas. Courtesy of the Collection of American Literature, The Beinecke Rare Book and
Manuscript Library, Yale University

freedom from feminine constraints that allows her to wander through the streets at night like a libertine, a female Don Juan who enthralls all the women she meets. In addition, she rejects skirts because they allow women to be as easily violated as the "Tuppeny Uprights" Dr. O'Connor describes, prostitutes on London Bridge who for tuppence wait

> "Holding up their badgered flounces, or standing still, letting you do it, silent and as indifferent as the dead, as if they were thinking of better days, or waiting for something that they had been promised when they were little girls; their poor damned dresses hiked up and falling away over the rumps, all gathers and braid, like a Crusader's mount, with all the trappings gone sideways with misery." [130–31]

These "poor damned dresses" represent the femininity that Robin Vote repudiates, much as she renounces motherhood, wifedom, and domesticity.

But, like Romaine Brooks's subjects and Radclyffe Hall's Stephen, Robin often seems to be victimized by the contradiction between her female anatomy and her metaphorically transsexual destiny. One of a kind, appearing from the first in male garb, she is described as sickly, solitary, half child, half criminal. When we first encounter her, she is asleep "in a jungle trapped in a drawing room" (35) where, to Dr. O'Connor, she looks like "a beast turning human" (37). Throughout the novel, moreover, she is characterized as a somnambulistic sexual wanderer who can neither remember her past nor fully awaken herself to her present. But the terrible dissonance between her transsexual desire and her biological reality is most vividly dramatized by her experience with pregnancy and childbirth, which drives her to murderous rage and to increasing efforts at intense self-obliteration. Denied interiority by the text, which never records her consciousness, Robin appears even to her lovers to be subhuman, though she seems to signal her aspiration to full humanity at least in part by dressing as a man. But she also is doomed to fall because she and Dr. O'Connor are misfits, neither masculine nor feminine, belonging nowhere. Like the ironically named Felix, a Jew who longs to be assimilated, these transvestites are "alone, apart and single" (10), objects of derision and marked scapegoats, as well as appropriate symbols of a confused culture where everyone feels, in Dr. O'Connor's words, as if he or she "turned up this time as I shouldn't have been" (91).

Yet the artifice of O'Connor's parodic persona, like the level of the beast to which Robin sinks, paradoxically functions to gain both these odd creatures potency in this novel which ultimately associates the transsexual with the transcendent. An apostle of darkness, Dr. O'Connor wears a nightgown, the "natural raiment of extremity," one character explains, because "What nation, what religion, what ghost, what dream, has not worn it—infants, angels, priests, the dead: why should not the doctor, in the grave dilemma of his alchemy, wear his dress?" (80). As a man who would be a prophet, this vatic transvestite who inhabits a nightwood far more empowering than Joyce's nighttown identifies himself with feminine insight and with visionary intuition. A gynecologist of sorts, Dr. O'Connor resembles the witch doctors, shamans, and *berdaches* of primitive cultures who have traditionally used women's garb, women's medicinal crafts, and even self-castration as a sign of their dedication to female powers. Mourning the mark of (male) sexuality—the "Tiny O'Toole"—with which he has been afflicted, he questions, more explicitly than Hall's Stephen does, Freud's celebration of the penis as "strikingly visible and of large proportions" ("SPC" 132), and he calls God "She," identifying her with his mother because of the "way she made me" (*N* 150).

But if Dr. O'Connor is a perverse and parodic prophet, Robin Vote—to whom all the characters in *Nightwood* are devoted—incarnates the mystery he heralds, for, as they observe, her "flesh . . . will become myth" (37). Probably the most enigmatic scene in the book is the episode at the end in which Robin goes down on all fours either to play with her lover's dog or to mate with it, a scene curiously ritualized by its being performed in front of an altar laden with candles and Madonnas, inside a ruined chapel that evokes Eliot's chapel perilous, and oddly resonant in its implicit allusion to the perverse "Doooog" that haunts both Joyce's nighttown and Eliot's waste land. Crossing the boundaries between beast and human, between female and male, between night and day, Robin here enacts and sanctifies a myth of herself as an invert who recaptures the chaotic, chthonic energies that have been debased by culture.

She is "my heart," says Robin's lesbian lover Nora Flood, implying that Robin represents the wild reality beyond gender, the pure potency to be found in what Yeats called "the rag and bone shop of the heart." "I, who want power," says Nora, "chose a girl who resembles a boy," and Dr. O'Connor glosses this line as follows:

> The last doll, given to age, is the girl who should have been a boy, and the boy who should have been a girl! The love of that last doll was foreshadowed in that love of the first. The doll and the immature have something *right* about them, the doll because it resembles but does not contain life, and the *third sex* because it contains life but resembles the doll. [148; emphasis ours]

If we read *Nightwood* in the aftermath of this speech as a revisionary response to male modernists like Joyce and Eliot, Robin Vote can finally be viewed as a kind of sacred Dog, a reversed God (or Goddess) of the third sex. But unlike Joyce's and Eliot's grotesque transvestites, she embodies an intransigent savagery that can only be hidden, never obliterated, in the mystifying nightwood of sexuality.

Although in her bestiality Robin Vote spells God backwards, the theological rhetoric through which she is represented clearly extends a line of female thought about transvestism and transsexualism that goes back beyond Hall's image of the bleeding martyr and Stein's parodic sainthood to Nightingale's female Christ and Schreiner's asexual heaven. Both Renée Vivien and Natalie Barney, for instance, deployed such rhetoric in texts that drew on the nineteenth-century fascination with the celestial androgyne. Vivien's *A Woman Appeared to Me* celebrates the hard-won wisdom of its hero-heroine, San Giovanni, while Barney's *The One Who Is Legion* (1930), a dreamlike tale about the multiple sexual identities that haunt its protagonist—a mysteriously resurrected suicide—evokes Balzac's *Seraphita* in a dedicatory poem:

> A double being needs no other mate—
> So Seraphita-Seraphitus lives:
> Self-wedded angel, armed in self-delight,
> Hermaphrodite of heaven, looking down
> On the defeat of our divided love.[73]

Such a spiritualizing of the cross-dresser as "Hermaphrodite of heaven" appears also in the works of H. D., where it is seen as an end to the torment of sex roles. Meditating in her roman à clef *Bid Me To Live* on D. H. Lawrence's "sex-fixations, his man-is-man, woman-is-woman," H. D. protested that the imagination is "sexless, or all sex, it [is] child-consciousness, it [is] heaven. In heaven, there is neither marriage nor giving in marriage."[74]

Earlier, H. D. had recorded a dream which articulated her own confusion about gender identity, a confusion she associated with another of her male "initiators," Ezra Pound. In this dream about attending a dance with Pound, her onetime fiancé, she sees herself first dressed in a rose-colored ball gown and then in male evening garb, but in the latter outfit "I am not quite comfortable, not quite myself, my trouserband does not fit very well," she admits; "I realize that I have on, underneath the trousers, my ordinary underclothes, or rather I was wearing the long party-slip that apparently belonged to the ballgown."[75] Yet though this dream ended on a note of "frustration and bewilderment," H. D. went on to write a memoir of Ezra Pound, *End to Torment* (1979), in which she imagined a resolution to their relationship and of her own sexual confusion through spiritual rhetoric associated with "child-consciousness," for she fantasized giving birth to a magically transsexual being, Seraphitus-Seraphita, who (modeled, like Barney's protagonist, on Balzac's androgyne) is both her representative and Pound's and thus their androgynous Divine Child.[76]

In *Helen in Egypt* (1961), which she considered her *Cantos*, H. D. also sought to confront the problem represented by Lawrence's claim that "man-is-man," "woman-is-woman." Here she intimated that Helen and Achilles, the paradigmatic warrior male and the archetypal seductive female, should be redeemed as "New Mortals," a phrase that recalls and revises the phrase New Woman.[77] The salvation of the mythic couple begins in the sacred precincts of the Amen Temple and ends with a recollection of the androgyny they had as children. Helen remembers that when she was Helen of Sparta she spoke in a "heroic voice," praising war, "the rage of the sea, // the thunder of battle" and "the beauty of arrows" (176–77), while the narrator reminds us that Achilles' mother—the sea-nymph Thetis—dressed her heroic boy as a girl to hide him from the men who would make him into a warrior, and H. D. presents such transvestism not as humiliating but as redeeming. To be sure, throughout this enigmatic epic, H. D. oscillates between an attack on conventional male militarism and a surrender to its seductive potency. But at the end of the poem, she hints that the vulnerable New Mortal Achilles, freed from the iron ring of his Myrmidons through his mother's failure to dip his heel into the river Styx, may be reborn in Helen's arms as the potentially transvestite or "third-sexed" boy he once was, "the child in Chiron's cave" who cherished a wooden doll carved in his mother's image, a "Thetis-eidolon" (288–89).

When we consider this last, fetishistic doll in the context of the dolls, witch doctors, and magical third-sexed beings of *Nightwood* as well as in connection with the visionary multiplicity of the costumes depicted in *Orlando* and in Stein's *Tender Buttons*, it becomes plain that many feminist modernists were concerned not only with "wild free thing[s]" or "wild things caught in women's skins" or "third sexes," but also with a kind of utopian ceremonial androgyny whose purpose was very different from the ritual transvestism Joyce, Moore, Lawrence, Eliot, and Hemingway evoked to maintain or reassert a fixed social order. For in the view of such women as Woolf and Barnes, that social order was itself fallen. Thus the only escape that they could imagine from the disorder and disease of gender was an escape facilitated by the chaos of transvestism, a symbolic misrule related not to the narrow power of male mastery but to the wholeness and holiness of prehistory. For, as Mircea Eliade has noted in a passage that almost reiterates Hall's definition of the cross-dresser as "grotesque and splendid, like some primitive thing," the ceremonial transvestism practiced in many nonwestern societies is "a coming out of one's self, a transcending of one's own historically controlled situation . . . in order to restore, if only for a brief moment, the initial completeness, the intact source of holiness and power . . . the undifferentiated unity that preceded the Creation."[78]

Although the authors of *The Well of Loneliness* and *Orlando* would not have had access to most of the anthropological materials with which Eliade worked, they (and their contemporaries) would have been introduced to such ideas by Edward Carpenter, a thinker who links them not only with Olive Schreiner but also with, of all unlikely peers, D. H. Lawrence. Besides being a friend of Havelock Ellis, Carpenter influenced Bernard Shaw, Lowes Dickinson, and E. M. Forster as well as Schreiner, and in his two books on the so-called "third sexed" beings he named "Uranians" or "Urnings," meaning "children of heaven"—*The Intermediate Sex* (1908) and *Intermediate Types* (1914)—he postulated a connection between the "third sex" and what Eliade calls the ahistorical "Great Time" of the sacred, a link between the bisexual or "homosexual temperament and divinatory or unusual psychic powers."[79] His notions of the "man-womanliness" of such artists as Shelley, Shakespeare, and Michelangelo probably influenced Virginia Woolf (either through Forster or more directly), for they are exactly analogous to the ideas she defines in *A Room of One's Own*,[80] and they may have also shaped the thinking of Radclyffe Hall (either through Ellis or more directly). Even more to the point here, the vision of sacred transvestism that Carpenter offered in *Intermediate Types* is comparable to the magical transvestism depicted in *Orlando* and to the definition of the cross-dresser that Hall proposes in *The Well of Loneliness*.

As Emile Delavenay has pointed out, D.H. Lawrence was also affected by Carpenter's sermons on sexuality, even (in such works as *Women in Love* [1921] and *The Study of Thomas Hardy* [1936]) by that theorist's beliefs in the undifferentiated sexual energy that manifests itself as "femaleness" in males and "maleness" in females.[81] At the same time, however, Delavenay has demonstrated Lawrence's ambivalence toward Carpenter's ideas about androgyny, ceremonial transvestism, and sacred bisexuality. Ultimately, Delavenay shows, Lawrence withdrew as anxiously as Eliot or Joyce might have from a commitment to Carpenter's concept of an "Intermediate Sex"—leaving the theory to such feminist modernists as Woolf and Hall. It is, after all, only those who have been oppressed by history and society who want to shatter the paradigms of dominance and submission enforced by the hierarchies of gender, and restore a primordial, gender-free chaos. Such political devotees of "the third sex" obviously wish to say "I am not that fixed self you have restrained in those nettight garments; I am all selves—and no selves."

To be sure, though all of the female modernists we have discussed here may have felt oppressed by virtue of their gender, many were privileged because of their class, more so, indeed, than either Lawrence or Joyce. As historians of lesbian culture have noted, the sapphistries of artists from Woolf to Hall were perquisites of aristocracy, a point emphasized by the expensive evening clothes in which Brooks's brooding transvestite subjects generally pose. In fact, as Bertha Harris has argued, in this period "to be upper class was at its finest to be also gay."[82] Thus, when a nanny employed by Vita Sackville-West purloined one of Harold Nicolson's suits and took a stroll through the village near Long Barn accompanied by the Nicolson children, Sackville-West sacked her, commenting in a letter to her husband that such an escapade was *"un peu fort!"*[83] Though he knew of his wife's own masquerade as "Julian," Nicolson wondered whether it was "vice, drink, or foolishness" that made nanny do what she did, while Sackville-West herself dismissed the whole episode as "squalid." Obviously the transgressiveness of transvestism was not supposed to transcend class lines. At the same time, the very fact that this nanny could not only imagine but actually even enact such a presumptuous appropriation of her master's clothes and her mistress's pleasures re-emphasizes the increasing female fascination with sexchanges throughout this period of rapidly changing sex roles.

As the implications of such metamorphoses became ever clearer in the course of the century, literary men continued for the most part to express anxieties about or at the very least ambivalence toward sexchange in texts focusing on transvestism or transsexualism, while literary women generally persisted in seeking an ontological "wild free thing," a third sex beyond gender. Sherwood Anderson's "The Man Who Became a Woman" (1923), Nathanael West's *The Dream Life of Balso Snell* (1931) as well as his *Miss Lonelyhearts* (1933), and James T. Farrell's "Just Boys" (1937), all in various ways express a nausea associated with the blurring of gender boundaries.

The narrator of Anderson's story, for instance, experiences horror, first, when he glimpses his face in a barroom mirror and thinks it is "a girl's face, and a lonesome and scared girl too," and, then, when he is mistaken for a woman by two drunken black men why try to rape him.[84] As a number of critics have observed, Anderson's analyses of sex roles are complex and conflicted in this tale, but it is significant that his protagonist decides at a crucial moment that "the kind of up-and-coming women we have nowadays who are always saying, 'I'm as good as a man and will do what the men do,' are on the wrong trail if they really ever want to, what you might say, 'hog-tie' a fellow of their own" (221). Even more surrealistically than Anderson, West creates in Balso Snell a male character whose fantasy of sexchange is surrounded by violence, dread, and illness, while the literary sexchange undergone by the male reporter who becomes Miss Lonelyhearts is equally calamitous.[85] Yet more disturbing, if that is possible, are the events recorded by Farrell's tale, whose syphilitic, "artfully rouged" protagonist is hideously murdered at a drunken drag party by a black man whom he has seduced and polluted with his disease.[86]

Equally bleak depictions of sexchange and its discontents characterize such later works as Anthony Powell's *From a View to a Death* (1939), H. E. Bates's "The Triple Echo" (first published in 1970 but composed twenty-five years earlier), and John Rechy's *City of Night* (1963), each of which reflects an anxiety about cross-dressing comparable to the revulsion at female impersonation expressed by a transvestite prostitute in Jean Genet's *The Thief's Journal* (1949, trans. 1964)—" 'What bitches they are, those awful she-men!' "—as well as the author's own sympathy with such "Daughters of Shame": "From the memory of this cry is born a brief but profound meditation on their despair, which was mine."[87] As Ackroyd has observed, "In [such] imaginative accounts" as those of Powell, Bates, and Rechy, "transvestism is seen as a bizarre and threatening thing—an image which becomes so potent and pervasive that the narrative itself becomes a victim of its anarchy and disassociation."[88] The grim conclusion of Geoff Brown's *I Want What I Want* (1966) summarizes the nightmare of misrule that broods over so many male-written fictions which focus on this subject. Trying (as it turns out unsuccessfully) to kill himself, the cross-dressed protagonist imagines the verdict of the coroner at his inquest: " 'Suicide while of unsound sex.' "[89]

Only, or at least most notably, in Alan Friedman's *Hermaphrodeity* (1972), a fantasy which is not about transvestism but about a comic triumph of hermaphroditism, does nausea modulate into delight. Although the parents of the wonderfully named "M. W. Niemann," the poet who is heroine/hero of this extraordinary novel, respond to a gynecologist's discovery of her/his amazingly dual genitalia by insisting upon binary oppositions—"Either! Or!," exclaims her/his father; " 'Neither!' Mother winked"—she/he argues for "Both" and impregnates her/himself with a baby to prove just what can be done when " 'he' + 'she' = she."[90] In addition, she/he goes on to produce a slew of successful literary works, including a volume of poems entitled *Snatches,* a verse drama called *Hermes and Aphrodite,* and such archeological and ethnological treatises as *The Skirts of God* and *Climbing Mons*

Veneris (front matter). But as Leslie Fielder has complained, the exuberantly mystical *Hermaphrodeity,* which "seems the book the age [of the seventies] demanded," never caught on: "I tried in vain to persuade my fellow judges to give it the National Book Award," confides Fiedler, "or even to consider it a real contender in the year of its appearance."[91]

Nevertheless, despite Fiedler's feeling that *Hermaphrodeity* ought to have been more successful, M. W. Niemann's rejection of "Either! Or!" and "Neither!" in favor of "Both" represents a solution that was especially appealing to women writers in this period, many of whom, as the etymology of the word "transvestite" implies, sought to make a travesty of sexual signs in order to prove that, as Elizabeth Bishop put it in a passage we have used as an epigraph here, "Costume and custom are complex" so that "The headgear of the other sex / inspires us to experiment." To be sure, Carson McCullers in "The Ballad of the Sad Cafe" (1951) and Flannery O'Connor in "A Temple of the Holy Ghost" (1954) viewed the crossing of gender lines as potentially grotesque or dangerous,[92] for both of these writers appear to have dreaded either, in the first case, the punishment exacted for transvestism or, in the second, the monstrosity of hermaphroditism. But in her marvelously witty *The Left Hand of Darkness* (1969), the science fiction writer Ursula K. Le Guin (quite appropriately the daughter of anthropologists) created a gender-free planet whose inhabitants may be alternately described with the English pronouns *he* and *she*—as their author actually has described them in different versions of the same romance.[93]

Similarly, in Brigit Brophy's *In Transit: an heroic cyclic novel* (1969), the protagonist, Patricia/Patrick O'Rooly (later to be rechristened "Unruly"), cannot decide whether she/he is a woman or a man. Comically adducing the fad for unisex clothing, she/he remarks that "my costume constituted, through cogent causes, an impregnable enigma" and jots down "the paradigm of the possible truths of my own situation":

I am a man
I am a woman
I am a homosexual man
I am a homosexual woman.[94]

From Joanna Russ's *The Female Man* (1975), Lois Gould's *A Sea-Change* (1975), Maxine Hong Kingston's *The Woman Warrior* (1977), Erica Jong's *Fanny* (1980), and Joyce Carol Oates's *A Bloodsmoor Romance* (1982) in America to Simone Benmussa's *The Singular Life of Albert Nobbs* (1977) in France, a number of other contemporary works by women celebrate the transvestite or transsexual, as if to insist, with the speaker of Adrienne Rich's "Diving into the Wreck" (1973), that "I am she: I am he

. . . We are, I am, you are . . . the one who find our way back to this scene." [95] Russ's *The Female Man,* for instance, recounts the adventures of four differently costumed and customed selves while Kingston's *The Woman Warrior* records a fantasy of empowering transvestism; both works offer heroines who win battles in a sex war through figurative sex role changes.

More radically, Gould's *A Sea-Change* meditates on a literal sex-change, for Jessie, the central character of this disturbing and dream-like fantasy, is a blonde model who, in the course of the novel, turns into the black gunman—"B. G."—by whom she was raped and/or pistol fucked at the beginning of the book. Symbolically traumatized by the horror of a scene which emphasizes the equation pistol-penis, Jessie becomes a kind of incarnate phallus, entering the bedroom of Kate, her lesbian lover, in a travesty of sexual intercourse—"B.G. . . . made himself very straight tensing and pushing in head first. . . . That was how he wanted to get in, the hard way, head first, just twisting a little back and forth"—in order to rape Kate with a pistol. [96] And although Gould brilliantly dramatizes the torment generated by the violence at the heart of this novel—especially the near madness of Jessie's meta-morphosis into the terrifying B.G.—she also implies that such a sea-change/sexchange is the only way in which her heroine can come to terms with the crime committed against her, with her own oppression by her estranged husband Roy, with what she sees as Kate's potentially fatal attraction to men, and with a racist culture that turns some blacks into gunmen. By the end of the novel, Jessie has established herself as B.G. Kil*roy*, a peaceable painter and fisherman who is eking out a mar-ginal but, we are meant to understand, autonomous existence with two daughters on Reef Colony, an encampment at the edge of society where she is eventually joined by Kate.

If Gould's novel offers a grim analysis of the dynamics of sex roles and sex wars in patriarchal culture, Jong's *Fanny* constitutes a more comic treatment of the history of gender and costume. In particular, Jong explicitly questions Alexander Pope's belief that "Whatever is, is right" (including God's having "placed Women below men") by hav-ing her heroine decide, after she has been sexually assaulted by Pope, to cross-dress and run away, a decision she justifies in terms that recall Mary Walker's polemics and Sarah Grand's novel:

> To dress as a Boy gave one Privileges no Woman could e'er possess: first, the Privilege of being left in Peace . . . second, the very substantial Privilege of Dining where'er one wisht without being presum'd a Trollop; third, the Privilege of moving freely thro' the World, without the Restraints of Stays, Petticoats, Hoops,

and the like. For I had form'd the Theory that Women should ne'er be entirely free to possess their own Souls until they could ride about the World as unencumber'd as possible. The Hoop Skirt, I reason'd was an Instrument of Imprisonment.[97]

Just as *Fanny* critiques Pope, Oates's *A Bloodsmoor Romance* implicitly corrects Lawrence's "The Fox," for the most passionate and powerful of Oates's four heroines is Constance Philippa, who constantly whistles "A fox went out on a starlight night" as she turns into a man named Philippe Fox and returns to her ancestral home in order to abduct the woman whom she has always loved.[98] Similarly, Simone Benmussa's stage version of "Albert Nobbs" revises Moore's tale to expose "the genesis of the story" as a historical reality and swerves from Moore's ending by having Hubert Page decide *not* to turn herself back into a woman.[99]

Even contemporary women who do not produce transsexual or transvestite fantasies have figuratively played with costumes, as Stein did, in order to question gender categories. Although in one of the *Ariel* poems Sylvia Plath sees her world as a series of civilized suitcases "Out of which *the same self* unfolds like a suit / Bald and shiny, with pockets of wishes" (emphasis ours), in another poem she transcends the pain of her own life by imagining her "selves dissolving, [like] old whore petticoats"—the old whore petticoats, for instance, of the "tup-penny uprights" whose degradation Djuna Barnes describes with such nightmarish precision in *Nightwood*. And in the fierce monologue of reborn "Lady Lazarus," Plath's speaker boasts that she is a "big strip tease," a savagely naked shamanistic spirit who "eat[s] men like air."[100] In the end, Plath may have been killed by the fixity of her situation, her imprisonment in an identity the world refused to see as a costume. But she fought by trying to redefine herself as a wild free thing, sexless and "pure as a baby," rather than as "a thing under the yoke" like the masochistic female Leopold Bloom had impersonated. In *The Bell Jar* (1971), for instance, she had Esther Greenwood enact a utopian fantasy on the roof of the the Amazon Hotel in New York City. Biblically queenly in her first name, green with the chaotic power of forests and wishes in her last, this heroine renounces both true and false costumes as casually as Orlando adopts them. "Piece by piece, I fed my wardrobe to the night wind, and flutteringly, like a loved one's ashes, the gray scraps were ferried off."[101] To Bella Cohen's "As they are now, so will you be," she replies, like Orlando, *no I shall not.*

Curiously, Esther Greenwood's repudiation of costume anticipated comparable gestures that would be made by a range of structuralist, deconstructionist, and feminist theorists in the years after *The Bell Jar* appeared, gestures that were very likely responses to just the sociocultural sexchanges writers from Joyce to Plath were recording, protesting, or celebrating. Even more curiously, a number of these recent male and female thinkers have changed places, with some men (as well as some women) adopting the *Orlando*-like view that all gender is indeterminate, fluid, fictive, undecidable, and with other women (along with some men) declaring that, even if there is no ontologically essential gender in the Joycean or Eliotian sense, there are, in fact, "irreducable" differences between the sexes, if only culturally constructed ones.

About the first group, Naomi Schor has identified the move toward what Foucault called "desexualization" not only in the arguments of Roland Barthes's *S/Z* and *The Fashion System,* but also in Barthes's remark that the "opposition of the sexes must not be a law of Nature; therefore, the confrontations and paradigms must be solved, both the meanings and the sexes must be pluralized."[102] Moreover, about Foucault's edition of *Herculine Barbin,* a memoir of a nineteenth-century French hermaphrodite, Schor notes that the twentieth-century historian of sexuality celebrates here the "happy limbo of a non-identity."[103] In the same vein, Jacques Lacan, too, frequently proclaimed, in Stephen Heath's words, woman's "not-existence, her not-allness," once even boastfully identifying himself with the paradigmatic female patient: "When it comes down to it, I am a perfect hysteric, that is to say, without symptoms, except from time to time mistakes in gender."[104]

But the most influential statement of this "desexualizing" theory of gender fluidity came in Jacques Derrida's *Spurs* (1978, trans. 1979). "Although there is no truth in itself of the sexual difference in itself, of either man or woman in itself," Derrida asserted there, meditating on Nietzsche, "all of ontology, appropriation, identification and verification of identity, has resulted in concealing, even as it presupposes it, this undecidability."[105] Later in the same work, he added about such gender undecidability that "Man and woman change places. They exchange masks *ad infinitum*" (111). In a recent interview, moreover, Derrida has explained that "what I try to say particularly in *Spurs (Éperons)* is that woman has no essence of her very own, and that's the phallogocentric gesture."[106] And although Hélène Cixous can hardly be said to be a clone of Derrida, she has at times made claims comparable to his. Prescribing "the *other bisexuality*," she describes it as "the one with which every subject, who is not shut up inside the spurious Phallocentric Performing theater, acts up his or her erotic universe. Bisexuality—that is to say the location within oneself of the presence of both sexes."[107]

On at least one group of American feminist critics the impact of these notions of gender undecidability has been powerful, affecting concepts of author, character, text, and reader. Nelly Furman, Peggy Kamuf, and Mary Jacobus, among others, have all sought to disengage gender from the author and the author from the text. Furman, for example, insists that "literature is not a representation of experience" and that therefore "from a feminist viewpoint the question is not whether a literary work has been written by a woman and reflects her experiences of life," while Kamuf argues that "female writing" is not what some critics "quite banally understan[d]" as "works signed by biologically determined females of the species."[108] More generally, Mary Jacobus, drawing on the work of Shoshana Felman, declares that "Like words, gender identity can be travestied or exchanged; there is no 'proper' referent, male or female, only the masquerade of masculinity and femininity."[109] Going on to critique Elaine Showalter's essay "Critical Cross-Dressing," Jacobus adds that, because texts are not gender-marked but, rather, "disembodied, uncanny, and silent," "the very discontinuity of (female) body and (feminine) text is [a] scandal [for] experientially based theories of the woman reader."[110]

As Jacobus's need to attack "Critical Cross-Dressing" demonstrates, however, quite a few theorists see the fashionable new concept of gender fluidity as a shaky one, if only because, as even Barthes conceded, "reality itself requires" that we understand "the opposition between masculine and feminine."[111] Showalter has questioned the authenticity of men's claims to be able to read from a woman's perspective, declaring that the literary responses of (female) feminist readers have been "proved on our own pulses."[112] Similarly, Naomi Schor's analysis of "desexualization" in Barthes and Foucault uses as its epigraph Stephen Heath's comment that "the risk of essence may have to be taken."[113] As for Heath himself, even though he believes that "we have learned . . . not to confuse the sex of the author with the sexuality and sexual positioning inscribed in a text," he also flatly declares that "Male feminism . . . is a contradiction in terms" and that "There *is* a female impersonation in a man reading as a feminist."[114] Like Andrew Ross, he seems to feel that there is a distinction between *"theoretical men"* and *"men in practice,"* and, like Cary Nelson, he does not "identify with a gendered vantage point" but may not want to find himself "in the role of the 'wife' of the invited speaker."[115]

The positions taken by Cixous and Kamuf, on the one hand, and Ross and Nelson, on the other hand, are understandable because they extend the feminist fantasies of Woolf and the masculinist anxieties of Joyce. But how can we explain the departures of, say, Derrida and Showalter from what has been a fairly standard twentieth-century pattern? Why have a number of intellectual tables lately turned so that at least some men deny and decry gender categories while at least some women insist on their existence? One answer may have to do with the recent incursions of the women's movement, for male-authored philosophic and psychoanalytic attempts to "desexualize" the subject can be seen in this context as attempts to defuse feminist militancy. At one point in *Spurs,* for example, Derrida declares that

> Feminism is nothing but the operation of a woman who aspires to be like a man. And in order to resemble the masculine dogmatic philosopher this woman lays claim—just as much claim as he—to truth, science and objectivity in all their castrated delusions of virility. Feminism too seeks to castrate. It wants a castrated woman. [65]

Not surprisingly, the response of such feminists as Schor and Showalter is to insist on the validity of female experience as it has been socially shaped and on the urgent need to defend the woman-centered ideology known as feminism from definitions like Derrida's, which see it as castrated or castrating. Many women thinkers, moreover, even those who have never sprinkled themselves with the hypothetical perfume we might call "genderessence," would somewhat wryly assent to Henry Louis Gates's bemused observation that when "we [women and/or blacks] enter the academy, suddenly there is no more subject."[116] In any case, whatever the etiology and ideology of these different positions, the persistent concern of intellectuals with gender definitions illustrates the continuing centrality not only of "critical cross-dressing" but of sexchanges even as we approach our own fin de siècle.

———

Is it possible that some of the recent theorizing about gender has been triggered not just by (as most thinkers would claim) Freud's concept of bisexuality but also by the accelerated development of so-called unisex fashion and, more dramatically, by a medical technology that has made possible, among other wonders, transsexual surgery, artificial insemination, *in vitro* fertilization, surrogate motherhood, and genetic engineering (which may make possible prenatal choices of an infant's sex)? If, during and after World War I, women gained the freedom to don trousers and their hemlines rose as their hair got shorter, during and after the Vietnam war gender boundaries dramatically blurred as young women put on pantsuits and young men grew their hair long. By the seventies, participants in the women's and gay rights movements became icons of the sexual undecidability that Derrida propounds. Moreover, from Mick Jagger, Alice Cooper, and Patti Smith to David Bowie, Boy George, and Michael Jackson, rock 'n roll entertainers enacted or exploited a trend toward subversive "gender-fuck dressing."[117] In performance art, too, the model Veruschka (Vera Lehndorff) drew upon the anarchic impulses of transvestism by collaborating with the body-artist and photographer Holger Trülzsch. Her body painted and positioned in a series of landscapes (into some of which she blends), Veruschka also appears in a set of transsexual impersonations, including portraits in which she is made up to represent a cigar-smoking businessman, a coquette, a gunman, and so forth (below).

To be sure, Mick Jagger is a media star and Veruschka is a cult figure. Yet even "ordinary people" have lately had to confront the issues the self-dramatizations of these celebrities raise. "IGNORE MISTAKES ABOUT YOUR SEX," proclaims the headline of a recent Miss Manners column. Responding to a correspondent who complains that "I believe I have what could be considered a modern problem. It is that I am occasionally mistaken for a member of the opposite sex"—and mis-

Veruschka. Body-painting and photography by Holger Trülzsch. From *"Veruschka": Transfigurations.* Vera Lehndorff/Holger Trülzsch. Copyright © 1986, Little Brown.

taken because she wears "the uniform of youth: jeans, running shoes, oversized jacket"—the doyenne of eighties courtesy advises this sufferer either "to ignore a mistaken reference" or to say, "Actually, I'm not a young man."[118]

But gender mistakes may be more than skin- or cloth-deep, or so Jan Morris argued in her widely publicized *Conundrum* (1974), an elegant meditation on a literal sexchange from man to woman. Like Radclyffe Hall's Stephen Gordon, Morris evidently felt as a very young child "that I had been born into the wrong body," and like Virginia Woolf (whose "androgynous *Orlando* was already in the house" at that time), she sought to disentangle gender from genitalia by affirming that sex roles are in some sense a matter of choice: "To me gender is not physical at all, but is altogether insubstantial," she writes, adding that "sex was not a division but a continuum, and that almost nobody was altogether of one sex or another, and that the infinite subtlety of the shading from one extreme to the other was one of the most beautiful of nature's phenomena."[119]

Not everyone would agree about "the beauty" of such phenomena, however, at least when they are literalized in the transsexual body. Sharon Olds's poem "Outside the Operating Room of the Sex-Change Doctor" expresses a deep uneasiness with gender metamorphosis, even though its very existence as a text published in a feminist collection on the *Powers of Desire* acknowledges the increasingly routine nature of what was, even when Morris's book appeared, a shocking operation. Lying on a silver tray, the "chopped-off sexes" of the doctor's formerly male patients articulate Olds's sense of the various implications of sexchange surgery: "One says *I am a weapon thrown down*"; another says, *"I am a caul removed from his eyes. Now he can see"*; but the last "is unhappy. He lies there weeping in terrible grief, crying out, *Father, Father!*"[120]

Nevertheless, little grief of this kind has been recorded in popular culture, where sexual ambiguity, though commonly recounted, is regularly defined as a consequence of freakish but increasingly credible medical marvels. Some recent inventions that have drawn attention in the press: hollow, foam-rubber prosthetic breasts that can be filled with formula in order to allow fathers to "nurse" their babies, and tubes designed to let women urinate standing up. Some recent headlines in the supermarket paper *Sun:* "MAN PREGNANT" and "DOCS CHANGE BABY'S SEX IN MOM'S WOMB."[121] The first story explains that a Finnish woman was "unable to carry a child" so, through *in vitro* techniques, her eggs "were fertilized with [her husband's] sperm and implanted into his abdomen." Exclaimed the proud if mythic dad, "Imagine being both mother and father to your baby." The second story describes the case of a male fetus with damaged kidneys who was temporarily extracted from the uterus so that his "useless" penis could be amputated and female genitalia fashioned, after which "Robert—now Roberta—[was] safely tucked back inside the womb."

From Joyce, whose Leopold Bloom gives birth in nighttown to numerous children with "valuable golden faces," to Le Guin, whose hero has a baby in "Winter's King," such _Sun_ tales were anticipated by a range of modern fantasists, and such a strain of fantasizing by both men and women has endured into the seventies and eighties. The title poem of Robert Phillips's _The Pregnant Man_ (1978) recounts the labor of a man giving birth, like "a duck squeezing out / a Macy's Thanksgiving Day / parade balloon," to "an eight-pound blue / -eyed bouncing baby / poem."[122] But where Phillips metaphorizes the baby as a poem, Elizabeth A. Lynn describes a literal male childbirth. "Tall with a bushy brown beard," the hero of her "The Man Who Was Pregnant" (1981) is "an unlikely looking man to be a mother," but he nevertheless begins showing in the fourth month, watches his breasts growing in the eighth month, and in the ninth month delivers a healthy baby named "Kris," short for Krishna.[123] Yet significantly, Lynn's male mother does not feel emasculated. On the contrary, when his belly is swelling, he masturbates, finding it "dizzying to feel his cock stiffen in one palm, [while] pass[ing] his other palm over the soft stretched skin of his belly" (124); after the birth, he evades the doctor's diagnosis of the abnormality of his condition by pretending to be "his own (nonexistent) brother" (126); finally, he teaches his child "to call him Da not Ma" (126).

Da, ma, dada, mama: even these primordial definitions—the first words most babies speak—have now been put in question, though one wonders whether even Derrida would like to be a Derri-ma. In fact, precisely the parodic quality of such speculations energizes Caryl Churchill's recent _Cloud Nine_ (1979), a play whose cast of characters includes in Act I (set in Victorian Africa) "Clive; Betty, his wife, played by a man; Joshua, his black servant, played by a white; Edward, his son, played by a woman; [and] Victoria, his daughter, a dummy": all figures whose distorted identity calls attention to the absurdity of the Victorian sexual and racial ideology that shaped nineteenth-century imperialism.[124] But though in Act II the same characters reappear in contemporary London played by members of their own sex (with the exception of a five-year-old girl whose part is acted by a large man), most of them are now involved in same-sex love affairs which hilariously satirize heterosexual relationships.

At the same time, with equal hilarity, Churchill even mocks the search for spiritual origins undertaken by such writers as Barnes and H. D., as if to suggest that when the old roles dissolve the new ones are just as absurd and pathetic. Late in the play, her sexually equivocal shape-changing characters—trying to stage a polymorphously perverse orgy—drunkenly call to "Innin, Innana, Nana, Nut, Anat, Anahita, Istar, Isis," imploring this "Goddess of many names, oldest of the old, who walked in chaos and created life" to "give us back what we were, give us the history we haven't had, make us the women we can't be" (94). But the orgy keeps collapsing into a lecture, as the formerly transsexual characters, now supposedly liberated into their elected sexuality and spirituality, reveal themselves to be just as trapped in the new world of misrule as they had been in the old world of nineteenth-century rule.

As Churchill proves by the end of her play, the history we have had has continued—through shocking social change, costume change, and sex role change, through extravagant theoretical postulations and equally extreme technological possibilities—to require everyone to confront such arbitrary (if transformed) roles that on the doped and dopey "Cloud 9" of the modern world, from which there is of course no going back, everyone is bemused and everything is confused. In the words of one of the pop songs scattered through the play,

> The wife's lover's children and my lover's wife,
> Cooking in my kitchen, confusing my life.
> And it's upside down when you reach Cloud 9.
>
> Upside down when you reach Cloud 9. [100]

More comic than Eliot's, Churchill's wasted London is nevertheless an unreal city where the towers of the past hang problematically "upside down in air" and the bridges between anatomy and destiny are falling down not with an apocalyptic bang, not even with a whimper, but with a chuckle spread from ear to ear. For women, too, Joyce's "Is me her was you dreamed before?" may sometimes modulate into a cloudy question.

Notes

EPIGRAPHS ON PAGE VII: Ellis, *The Psychology of Sex* (New York: Ray Long and Richard R. Smith, 1933), p. 225; Porter, "Gertrude Stein: A Self-Portrait," *Harper's* 195 (Dec. 1947): 519–27; Lewis, *Men Without Art,* ed. Seamus Cooney (1934; Santa Rosa: Black Sparrow, 1987), p. 138; Sexton, "Consorting with Angels," *The Complete Poems of Anne Sexton,* with a foreword by Maxine Kumin (Boston: Houghton Mifflin, 1981), p. 111.

Preface

1 de Gourmont, *Natural Philosophy of Love,* trans. with a postscript by Ezra Pound (New York: Privately printed for Rarity Press, 1931), p. 169. Further references will be to this edition, and page numbers will appear in the text.
2 Ellis, *The Psychology of Sex,* p. 225.
3 Carpenter, *Love's Coming of Age* (New York: Mitchell Kennerley, 1911), pp. 120–21; Shaw, "Woman—Man in Petticoats," in Shaw, *Platform and Pulpit,* ed. Dan H. Laurence (New York: Hill and Wang, 1961), p. 174. We wish to thank J. Ellen Gainor for bringing this passage to our attention.
4 Arthur C. Young, ed., *The Letters of George Gissing to Eduard Bertz 1887–1903* (London: Constable, 1961), p. 171 (2 June 1893); this passage is discussed by Lloyd Fernando in *"New Women" in the Late Victorian Novel* (University Park: The Pennsylvania State University Press, 1977), p. 107.
5 Hardy, "The Tree of Knowledge," *National Review* 10 (1894): 681; discussed by Fernando p. 133.
6 Mencken, *In Defense of Women* (1918; New York: Octagon, 1977), p. 197.
7 See Linton, "The Wild Women as Politicians," and "The Wild Women as Social Insurgents," *Nineteenth Century* (1891), pp. 79–88 and 596–605; and Anthony M. Ludovici, *Woman: A Vindication* (New York: Alfred A. Knopf, 1923), p. 149. On Ludovici's connection with the Pound circle, see Iris Barry, "The Ezra Pound Period," *The Bookman* 74:2 (Oct. 1931): 166.
8 Mencken, p. 196.
9 Heape, *Sex Antagonism* (London: Constable, 1913), p. 23.
10 Praz, *The Romantic Agony,* trans. Angus Davidson, second ed. (1933; New York: Oxford University Press, 1970); Auerbach, *Woman and the Demon: The Life of a Victorian Myth* (Cambridge: Harvard University Press, 1982); Dijkstra, *Idols of Perversity: Fantasies of Feminine Evil in Fin-de-Siècle Culture* (New York: Oxford University Press, 1986).
11 See Moi, *Sexual/Textual Politics: Feminist Literary Theory* (London and New York: Me-

thuen, 1985), pp. 62–69; and Jacobus, *Women: Essays in Feminist Criticism* (New York: Columbia University Press, 1986), pp. 13–15.

12 Wittig, "One is not Born but Made a 'Woman,' " Paper delivered at the Simone de Beauvoir Conference, The Second Sex—Thirty Years After: A Commemorative Conference on Feminist Theory, New York, September 1979.

Chapter 1.

EPIGRAPHS: Swinburne, "Notes on Designs of the Old Masters in Florence," *Essays and Studies,* 5th ed. (London: Chatto & Windus, 1901), p. 319; Kipling, *Rudyard Kipling's Verse: Inclusive Edition, 1885–1926* (Garden City: Doubleday, Page & Co., 1927), pp. 421–24; Wylie, *Generation of Vipers* (New York: Farrar & Rinehart, 1942), p. 203; Jacques Lacan, *Seminar,* 11 February 1975.

1 Yeats, ed. *The Oxford Book of Modern Verse, 1892–1935* (New York: Oxford University Press, 1937), p. 1.

2 Pater, *The Renaissance: Studies in Art and Poetry,* with an intro. by Lawrence Evans (Chicago: Pandora, 1977), p. 125.

3 Wilde, "The Critic as Artist," in *The Writings of Oscar Wilde* (New York: Wm. H. Wise & Co., 1931; five vols. in one), 5:158–59. In *The Trembling of the Veil,* Yeats recalled Wilde discussing this work by Pater at the first meeting of the two literary men: "That first night he praised Walter Pater's *Studies in the History of the Renaissance:* 'It is my golden book; I never travel anywhere without it; but it is the very flower of decadence' " *(The Autobiography of William Butler Yeats* [New York: Macmillan, 1953], p. 80).

4 Longenbach, *Modernist Poetics of History: Pound, Eliot, and the Sense of the Past* (Princeton: Princeton University Press, 1987) p. 35. In making this point, Longenbach implicitly takes issue with Paul de Man's claim that "Among the various antonyms that come to mind as possible opposites for 'modernity'—a variety which is itself symptomatic of the complexity of the term—none is more fruitful than 'history' "; see de Man, "Literary History and Literary Modernity," in *Blindness and Insight* (New York: Oxford University Press, 1971), p. 144.

5 The Yeats poems that identify historical cruxes with moments of annunciation include, of course, "The Rose of the World," "The Second Coming," "Two Songs from a Play," "Leda and the Swan," and "Whence Had They Come?" (from "Supernatural Songs"); see Yeats, *The Collected Poems* (New York: Macmillan, 1955), pp. 36, 184, 210, 211, 286. Further references to Yeats's verse in this chapter will be to this edition, preceded by the citation *CP*.

6 Cited by Carolyn Burke in "The New Poetry and the New Woman," in *Coming to Light,* ed. Diane Middlebrook and Marilyn Yalom (Ann Arbor: University of Michigan Press, 1985), p. 37. We are grateful to Carolyn Burke for first bringing this remark to our attention.

7 Wylie, p. 184.

8 Praz, p. xv. For a more recent treatment of the femme fatale, from an art historian's perspective, see Virginia M. Allen, *The Femme Fatale: Erotic Icon* (Troy, N.Y.: Whitston, 1983), passim.

9 Tennyson, *The Princess,* IV. 480, in *The Poetical Works of Tennyson,* ed. G. Robert Stange, Cambridge ed. (Boston: Houghton Mifflin, 1974). Further references to part and line number will be included in the text. For an extended discussion of *The Princess,* see Gilbert and Gubar, *No Man's Land: The Place of the Woman Writer in the Twentieth Century, Vol. 1, The War of the Words* (New Haven: Yale University Press, 1988), pp. 6–11.

10 Quoted in Praz, p. 230.

11 For useful discussions of the connection between the rise of Romanticism and the revival of "matriarchal" imagery, see Leslie A. Fiedler, "The Politics of Realism: A Mythological Approach," *Salmagundi* 42 (Summer/Fall 1978): 31–43, and Northrop Frye, "The Revelation to Eve," in *Paradise Lost: A Tercentenary Tribute*, ed. Balachandra Rajan (Toronto: University of Toronto Press, 1969), pp. 18–47.

12 Walter Pater, *The Renaissance*, pp. 124–26; A. C. Swinburne, "Notes on Poems and Reviews," *Poems and Ballads and Atlanta in Calydon* (1866, 1865; Indianapolis and New York: Bobbs Merrill, 1970), p. 334 (all references in this chapter will be to this edition); Swinburne, "Laus Veneris," pp. 13–30; Swinburne, "Cleopatra," pp. 298–300; Harold Bloom, *Figures of Capable Imagination* (New York: Seabury, 1976), pp. 32–33.

13 Coleridge, "Christabel," 1.602; Swinburne, "Cleopatra," p. 299; George Macdonald, *Lilith*, in *Lilith and Phantastes* (1895; Grand Rapids: Erdmans, 1964); pp. 374–75.

14 See Byron, *Childe Harold's Pilgrimage*, canto I, 1.50.

15 Coleridge, "Christabel," 1.256, 258; Keats, "The Fall of Hyperion," 11.277–78; see Wilde, *Salome* (1894; New York: Dover, 1967, esp. pp. 66–67; "The Fall of Hyperion," 1.258. With their voluptuous juxtaposition of desire and cruelty, Salome's speeches to the bloody head of John the Baptist seem like morbid echoes of the most perilous lines of Swinburne's "Anactoria."

16 Praz, pp. 212, 238.

17 Coleridge, "Christabel," 1.250; Swinburne, p. 300 ("Cleopatra"), p. 109 ("Faustine"), p. 141 ("Dolores").

18 H. Rider Haggard, *She* (New York: Hart, 1976), p. 1. Further references will be to this edition, and page numbers will be included in the text.

19 For a discussion of the concept of the *patrius sermo*, see Walter Ong, *Fighting for Life* (Ithaca: Cornell University Press, 1981), passim, as well as *The War of the Words*, pp. 243ff.

20 Herodotus, *The Persian Wars*, trans. George Rawlinson (New York: Modern Library, 1942), p. 692.

21 Herodotus, pp. 133–34.

22 Since this is just the sort of vision that would haunt a misogynistic bachelor like Horace Holly, it is amusing that Holly momentarily saves the wretched Arab from the dreadful death for which he has been fated when, at the sight of the parodic seduction scene, he fires his revolver "by instinct straight at the diabolical woman who had been caressing Mahomed, and who was now gripping him in her arms" (106).

23 See Carl Jung, *The Integration of the Personality* (New York: Farrar & Rinehart, 1939), pp. 24, 78–80; Sigmund Freud, *The Interpretation of Dreams*, trans. and ed. James Strachey (New York: Avon, 1965), p. 490; Nandor Fodor, *The Search for the Beloved* (New York: Hermitage, 1949), p. 392, and *New Approaches to Dream Interpretation* (New York: Citadel, 1951), p. 27; Henry Miller, *The Books in My Life* (New York: New Directions, 1969), pp. 81–99; Morton Cohen, *Rider Haggard* (New York: Walker and Co., 1960); Norman Etherington, "Rider Haggard, Imperialism, and the Layered Personality," *Victorian Studies* 22:1 (Autumn 1978): 71–87; and Nina Auerbach, *Woman and the Demon*, pp. 36–38, 148–49.

24 Miller, p. 93. Etherington describes Ayesha more wittily as "a Diana in jack-boots who preaches materialism in philosophy and fascism in politics" (p. 47).

25 On the "Great Mother" as creator/destroyer/ preserver, see, for instance, Erich Neumann, *The Great Mother: An Analysis of the Archetype*, trans. Ralph Manheim (1955; Princeton: Princeton University Press, Bollingen Series 47, 1972): Robert Briffault, *The Mothers*, abridged with an intro. by Gordon Rattray Taylor (1927; New York: Atheneum, 1977): and Robert Bly, "I Came Out of the Mother Naked," in *Sleepers Joining Hands* (New York: Harper & Row, 1973), pp. 29–50.

26 For an examination of the mother-as-mummy, see Gilbert and Gubar, *The Madwoman*

in the Attic: The Woman Writer and the Nineteenth-Century Literary Imagination (New Haven and London: Yale University Press, 1979), pp. 244–46.

27 Unlike Ayesha, Noot refused to profit from the knowledge he had gained through "purity and abstinence, and the contemplations of his innocent mind"; indeed, he also forbade Her to make use of the fire. After this wise father-figure died, however, She disobeyed his command, so that now, twenty centuries later, nothing remains of him but "one little tooth," while She lives satanically on, threatening to humiliate all the men of England and regularly humiliating wise "fathers" like the Arab Billali.

28 Nina Auerbach argues that "no magic but [Ayesha's] own is sufficiently effective to annihilate her," and that "Her conquest of the world beyond her looking glass is prevented only by her lover's cowardice and her own metamorphic glory" (p. 37), but given the inexorability of the "Pillar of Life," this reading seems oddly ameliorative.

29 See Alexander Grinstein, *Sigmund Freud's Dreams* (New York: International Universities Press, 1980), pp. 392–422, for a discussion of the notion that She must die because Her "sexual relationship with a figure who clearly represents a son [i.e., Leo] is about to be consummated. . . . [Her] final unattainability . . . is an expression of the ultimate unattainability of an individual's Oedipal fantasies" (pp. 402–03), and her "death" scene is also, therefore, a version of a "primal scene." See also Fodor, *The Search for the Beloved*, p. 392, for an extended analysis of Ayesha's "death" scene in the "place of life" as a species of prenatal memory.

30 See George Meredith, "Lucifer in Starlight": "Around the ancient track marched, rank on rank, / The army of unalterable law."

31 See Exodus 13:21–22.

32 See Genesis 9:8–17.

33 Miller, *Sunday After the War* (New York: New Directions, 1944), p. 261.

34 Miller, *Books*, pp. 91–92. Miller identifies as "natural" a punishment that seems to be essentially cultural. Clearly he believes that Ayesha is punished for a sort of generalized *hubris*, whereas we are arguing that She is punished for a specifically female *hubris*. Her punishment is prefigured by the fact that, as we noted in *The War of the Words*, among the Amahaggar the men "worship" the women until "at last they grow unbearable," at which point "we rise and kill the old ones as an example to the young ones, and to show them that we are the strongest" (122; *War of the Words*, p. 23).

35 Bloom, *Figures*, pp. 32–33.

36 Miller, *Books*, p. 92. If we compare Ayesha's fate to the annunciation scenes that were to preoccupy Yeats not long after *She* appeared, we can see it as a sort of antiannunciation, an annunciation of death that definitively ends "twenty centuries of stony sleep" while sweeping away both Her knowledge and Her power.

37 Miller, *Books*, p. 93

38 As her reappearance in two sequels—*Ayesha, the Return of She* (1905) and *Allan and She* (1921)—indicates, Ayesha doesn't actually die, but certainly Leo and Holly experience Her as having been killed.

39 For a discussion of male-authored nineteenth- and twentieth-century texts which turn, more generally, on the punitive murder, defeat, or sacrifice of a New Woman or a femme fatale, see *War of the Words*, chap. 1, "The Battle of the Sexes"; for a discussion of female-authored texts which deal with comparable subjects, see *War of the Words*, chap. 2, "Fighting for Life."

40 Bram Stoker, *The Annotated Dracula* (New York: Potter, 1975), p. 194. For extended readings of *Dracula* which brilliantly surface the gender imperatives this work dramatizes, see Christopher Craft, " 'Kiss Me with Those Red Lips': Gender and Inversion in Bram Stoker's *Dracula*," *Representations* 8 (Fall 1984): 107–33; and Marjorie Howes, "The Mediation of the Feminine: Bisexuality, Homoerotic Desire and Self-Expres-

sion in Bram Stoker's *Dracula," Texas Studies in Literature and Language,* 30 (Spring 1988): 104–19. For a more general overview of *Dracula,* see Phyllis A. Roth, *Bram Stoker* (Boston: Twayne, 1982), chap. 5, "Dracula," pp. 87–126.

41 *Dracula,* p. 195.

42 Macdonald, *Lilith,* p. 391. For a discussion of comparable scenes that implicitly equate female castration with the chopping off of a woman's hands, see Praz, p. 266, on d'Annunzio's use of this motif. See also the Grimm fairytale entitled "The Girl Without Hands," in *The Complete Grimm Fairytales* (New York: Random House, 1972), pp. 160–66.

43 Macdonald, *Lilith,* p. 389. For a discussion of *Lilith* from a different (and more ameliorative) perspective, see Auerbach, pp. 38–39.

44 The biblical story of Salome omits the violent punishment that Wilde's play inflicts on her; see Matthew, 14:1–11. For other versions of Salome's tale—a plot that obsessed the nineteenth century—see Joris-Karl Huysmans, *Against the Grain* (1884), a text to which Wilde was deeply indebted; Stéphane Mallarmé, *Hérodiade* (1869); Gustave Flaubert, "Herodias" in *Three Tales* (1877); Heinrich Heine, *Atta Troll* (1843); Jules Laforgue, *Moralités legendaires* (1887); and pictorial representations by Georges Henry Regnault, Lucien Levy-Dhurmer, and Gustave Moreau. In *Aesthetes and Decadents of the 1890s,* ed. Karl Beckson (New York: Vintage, 1966), Beckson reprints the passage from Huysmans, a meditation on Gustave Moreau's painting *Salome,* which partly inspired Wilde; the Huysmans's passage characterizes Herodias's daughter as, among other things, "the symbolic incarnation of world-old Vice, the goddess of immortal Hysteria . . . a monstrous Beast of the Apocalypse, indifferent, irresponsible, insensible, poisoning, like Helen of Troy, all who come near her, all who see her, all who touch her" *(Aesthetes,* p. 277). An extended analysis of Wilde's *Salome,* Beardsley's illustrations, and other versions of the story is offered in Elliot L. Gilbert, "Tumult of Images: Wilde, Beardsley, and *Salome," Victorian Studies* 26:2 (Winter 1983): 133– 59. Even in the early years of the twentieth century, artists were still brooding on this femme fatale: Richard Strauss set Wilde's text to music in *Salome* (1905) and W. B. Yeats concluded his "Nineteen Hundred and Nineteen" with the apocalyptic observation that "Herodias' daughters have returned again" *(CP* 208).

45 *Salome,* p. 68.

46 Stoker, *The Lair of the White Worm* (London: Arrow, 1963), pp. 132, 133. Further references will be to this edition, and page numbers will be included in the text. For an analysis of *The Lair* from a different perspective, see Auerbach, p. 25. For a discussion of Haggard's association of snakes and femmes fatales, see Etherington, p. 79, and for a more general review of the fin-de-siècle propensity to brood on serpentine females, see Dijkstra, *Idols,* pp. 305–13.

47 As if to emphasize the sexuality of the scene, just before this horrifying denouement, Lady Arabella has torn "off her clothes, with feverish fingers, and in full enjoyment of her natural freedom, stretched her slim figure in animal delight. Then she lay down on the sofa—to await her victim!" (179).

48 For more extended analyses of the ways in which homosocial male bonding functions to enforce the "proper" social order, see Eve Sedgwick, *Between Men: English Literature and Male Homosocial Desire* (New York: Columbia University Press, 1985), and Claus Thewelheit, *Male Fantasies, vol. 1: women, floods, bodies, history,* trans. Stephen Conway (Minneapolis: University of Minnesota Press, 1987). American and British modernist texts that can be set specifically in this tradition include T. S. Eliot's "Sweeney Agonistes" (1927), which hints at dark secret connections between sex and sacrifice; D. H. Lawrence's pseudo-primitive "The Woman Who Rode Away" (1928), which concludes with an eroticized scene of ritual (female) sacrifice; and William Faulkner's gothic "A Rose for Emily" (1924), which turns on "Miss Emily's" necrophiliac rela-

tionship with her onetime lover and culminates in the more disguised but equally sexual "violence of breaking down [a] door" (in Faulkner, *Collected Stories* [New York: Random House, n.d.], p. 129). In connection with Faulkner's tale in particular, as well as with *She*, it is also useful to consider Praz's discussion of the Princess Belgiojoso, who was supposed to have kept the embalmed corpse of her young lover in a cupboard of her villa at Locate. See Praz, pp. 121–22.

49 All quoted by Cohen, pp. 114, 119, 232.

50 Cohen, p. 24.

51 Kipling, "The Vampire," *Poems*, pp. 251–52. Etherington calls attention both to Haggard's erotic frankness and to his ambivalence toward what he called "the baleful sun of desire," noting that the "closest he came to levity about sex in any of his writings is this little verse from his jotting book for 1885:

> Holy Mother we believe
> Without sin thou didst conceive
> Holy Mother thus believing
> May we sin without conceiving [.] [Etherington, p. 13]

52 See Said, *Orientalism* (New York: Vintage, 1979), esp. pp. 84–92.

53 On the Orient in general as a representation of "Otherness," see Said, p. 21 and passim.

54 For a discussion of the thematic and symbolic significance of the idea of hieroglyphs, see John T. Irwin, *American Hieroglyphics* (New Haven: Yale University Press, 1980), and Eric Iverson, *The Myth of Egypt and Its Hieroglyphics in European Tradition* (Copenhagen: Gec Gad, 1961). For "the vast underground network," see James Hamilton-Paterson and Carol Andrews, *Mummies: Death and Life in Ancient Egypt* (New York: Penguin, 1979), p. 185. Some of the accounts of archaeological expeditions produced by the explorers themselves are strikingly similar to Haggard's narratives of tomb and burial-chamber penetration in, say, *King Solomon's Mines* and *She*. Compare, for instance, this passage from G. Belzoni's *Narrative of the Operations and Recent Discoveries within the Pyramids, Temples, Tombs and Excavations in Egypt and Nubia* (London: J. Murray, 1822):

> the entry, or passage where the bodies are, is roughly cut in the rocks, and the falling of the sand from the upper part or ceiling of the passage causes it to be nearly filled up. In some places, there is not more than a vacancy of a foot left, which you must contrive to pass through in a creeping posture like a snail, on pointed and keen stones, that cut like glass. After getting through those passages, some of them two or three thousand yards long, you generally find a more commodious place, perhaps high enough to sit. But what a place of rest! surrounded by bodies, by heaps of mummies in all directions, which, previous to my being accustomed to the sight, impressed me with horror. The blackness of the wall, the faint light given by the candles or torches for want of air, the different objects that surrounded me, seeming to converse with each other, and the Arabs with the candles or torches in their hands, naked and covered with dust, themselves resembling living mummies, absolutely formed a scene that cannot be described. [Quoted in Hamilton-Paterson and Andrews, pp. 185–86]

55 Yeats, "All Soul's Night" and "Supernatural Songs, X: Conjunctions" (*CP* 224, 287). On the popular fascination with "mummy wheat"—grain found in Egyptian tombs that was widely (but erroneously) believed to be still capable of germinating—see Hamilton-Paterson and Andrews, pp. 204–05. For two representative potboilers which turn on the fin-de-siècle fascination with both Egypt and femmes fatales, see Richard Marsh, *The Beetle* (1897), reprinted in *Victorian Villainies*, ed. Graham Greene and Hugh Greene (New York: Viking, 1984), and Bram Stoker, *The Jewel of Seven Stars*

(1903; London: Jarrold's, 1966). In the first of these works, a group of Londoners are threatened by a shape-shifting Arab (alternatively a man, a woman, and a giant beetle), the emissary of a deadly, obscene, and ancient "cult of Isis." In the second, the mummified, two-thousand-year-old Egyptian "Queen Tera" plans to resurrect herself in England. (For a discussion of *The Jewel of Seven Stars* from a different perspective, see Roth, *Bram Stoker*, pp. 66–74.)

56   On the *incoherence* of Islam, see Carlyle, who, while glorifying Mohammed, defined the Koran as "a wearisome confused jumble" *(On Heroes, Hero-Worship and the Heroic in History* [1841; Lincoln: University of Nebraska Press, 1966] p. 64). On more sophisticated (though equally anxious) views of Islam, see Said, esp. pp. 151, 209–10; as Said observes, the Orientalist studies of, say, William Muir *(Life of Mahomet* [1858–1861] and *The Caliphate, Its Rise, Decline and Fall* [1891]) represented, on the one hand, "enormous labors," and led, on the other hand, to a number of conventionally nervous conclusions, such as Muir's declaration that "the sword of Muhammed, and the Kor'an, are the most stubborn enemies of Civilization, Liberty, and the Truth which the world has yet known" (p. 151); for Balfour, see Said, pp. 32–33.

57   Peckham, *Victorian Revolutionaries: Speculations on Some Heroes of a Culture Crisis* (New York: Braziller, 1970), p. 179.

58   See Peckham, p. 184.

59   Mannsaker, "The Dog That Didn't Bark," in *The Black Presence in English Literature*, ed. David Dabydeen (Manchester: Manchester University Press, 1985), p. 125.

60   Tennyson, "Locksley Hall," 1.184.

61   On Haggard as Egyptologist, see Cohen, p. 103; on Lang, Haggard, and *She*, see Cohen, pp. 180–82, and Etherington, p. 52.

62   Cohen, p. 120.

63   Etherington, p. 17.

64   See Etherington, p. 39, and Cohen, pp. 104–05. Richard Hall, a British government official, ransacked the Zimbabwe ruins to find evidence that—as most European observers long insisted—some culture other than an African one had built the impressive stone structures; for a brief discussion of this point, see Patrick Brantlinger, *Rule of Darkness: British Literature and Imperialism, 1830–1914* (Ithaca: Cornell University Press, 1988), pp. 195 and 292, note 61.

65   Haggard may also have been inscribing anxieties about Islam when he arranged for the British explorers' servant *Mahomed* to be sacrificed in the hotpotting episode.

66   Cohen, p. 27.

67   Etherington, pp. 34, 17.

68   The British Society for Psychical Research was founded in 1882, and during its first decade it numbered among its members such eminent figures as Gladstone and Balfour, as well as Tennyson, Ruskin, Lewis Carroll, and J. A. Symonds; both Yeats and Conan Doyle (who wrote his massive *History of Spiritualism* in 1926) were among the most famous converts to the cause. See Russell M. and Clare R. Goldfarb, *Spiritualism and Nineteenth-Century Letters* (Cranbury: Associated University Presses, 1978) and Ruth Brandon, *The Spiritualists: The Passion for the Occult in the Nineteenth and Twentieth Centuries* (London: Weidenfeld and Nicolson, 1983).

69   Yeats, a sometimes ambivalent admirer of Madame Blavatsky, thought that, along with his hero William Morris, she "had more human nature than anybody else," adding that "To her devout followers she was more than a human being" (Brandon, p. 237). More tellingly, Annie Besant's biographer notes that Besant "was converted to Theosophy at the height of her career as a materialist, an atheist, an anathematised advocate of birth-control, and a feminist crusader in all the new advanced movements. The precipitating factor in this astounding conversion was the controversial, masculine Helena P. Blavatsky, whom she eventually replaced as the most important

figure in the mystical, occult Theosophical Society"; see Arthur H. Nethercot, *The Last Four Lives of Annie Besant* (Chicago: University of Chicago Press, 1963), p. 11.

70 See Emanie Sachs, *"The Terrible Siren": Victoria Woodhull (1838–1927)* (New York: Harper, 1928), p. 46; also p. 19: "nearly all the free lovers were Spiritualists. But in Victoria Woodhull at her zenith, religious ecstasy, free love and Spiritualism met and merged."

71 Sachs, p. 52, and M. M. Marberry, *Vicky: A Biography of Victoria C. Woodhull* (New York: Funk & Wagnalls, 1967), p. 4.

72 Quoted by Sachs, p. 122.

73 Sachs, p. 76. For the supportive reactions of such suffrage leaders and Stanton and Anthony to Woodhull's "Memorial," see chap. 3 of this volume, pp. 83–84, as well as Sachs, pp. 78–80, 80–81.

74 Quoted by Sachs, p. 136.

75 Whatever the facts of the Beecher-Tilton scandal—and it involved alarming counter-charges against Woodhull and Claflin—the prophetess of free love convinced Beecher's sister Isabella Beecher Hooker and his brother the Reverend Thomas Beecher (though not his more conservative sister Harriet Beecher Stowe) that they must be "true to Woodhull"; see Sachs, pp. 188–89.

76 Quoted on the title page of Sachs.

77 Quoted by Sachs, pp. 118–19.

78 Sachs, p. 298.

79 Johann Wolfgang von Goethe, *Faust,* tr. Louis MacNeice (abridged version; New York: Oxford University Press, 1960), pp. 298, 303.

80 For a summary and discussion of these theories, see Jane M. Oppenheimer, *Essays in the History of Embryology and Biology* (Cambridge, Mass.: The M.I.T. Press, 1967), p. 121. For a useful analysis of the ways in which "procreation theories" can be seen both as "creation mythemes" and as projective representations of sexual dominance/subordination, see James Hillman, "On Psychological Femininity," in Hillman, *The Myth of Analysis: Three Essays in Archetypal Psychology* (Evanston, Ill.: Northwestern University Press, 1972), esp. pp. 217–54.

81 Sims is quoted in G. J. Barker-Benfield, *The Horrors of the Half-Known Life: Male Attitudes toward Woman and Sexuality in Nineteenth-Century America* (New York: Harper Colophon, 1976), p. 95.

82 Barker-Benfield, p. 95.

83 See B. I. Balinsky, *An Introduction to Embryology* (Philadelphia: W. B. Saunders, 1960), pp. 14–15. For a somewhat different interpretation of this medical history, see Thomas Laquer, "Orgasm, Generation, and the Politics of Reproductive Biology," in *Representations* 14 (Spring 1986): 1–41.

84 See *Myth, Religion, and Mother Right: Selected Writings of J. J. Bachofen,* trans. Ralph Manheim with a preface by George Boas and an intro. by Joseph Campbell, Bollingen Series 84 (Princeton: Princeton University Press, 1967), passim.

85 Jane Ellen Harrison, *Prolegomena to the Study of Greek Religion* (New York: Meridian, 1955), p. 497.

86 Sigmund Freud, *Totem and Taboo,* in *The Basic Writings of Sigmund Freud,* trans. and with an intro. by A. A. Brill (New York: Modern Library, 1938), p. 921. Freud's biographer, Ernest Jones, points out that, just when the psychoanalyst was at work on *Totem and Taboo,* he published a short paper entitled "Great is Diana of the Ephesians," exploring "a remarkable instance of the continuity in religious worship": the phenomenal endurance, into the twentieth century, of a cult of "a Mother-Goddess" at Ephesus. See Jones, *The Life and Work of Sigmund Freud: 1901–1919, The Years of Maturity* (New York: 1955), p. 349.

87 D. H. Lawrence, "Matriarchy," in *Assorted Articles, Phoenix II: Uncollected, Unpublished,*

and Other Prose Works, collected and ed. with an intro. and notes by Warren Roberts and Harry T. Moore (New York: Viking, 1968), p. 549. For a more extended analysis of the effects of both matriarchal imagery and revised "creation mythemes" on Freud, Lawrence, and other modernist male thinkers, see Sandra M. Gilbert, "Potent Griselda," in *D. H. Lawrence: A Centenary Consideration,* ed. Peter Balbert and Phillip L. Marcus (Ithaca: Cornell University Press, 1985).

88 H. D., unpublished manuscript of *The Gift,* Beinecke Library, Yale University; quoted by permission of Perdita Schaffner.

89 Mary Baker Eddy, *Science and Health* (Boston: First Church of Christ, Scientist, 1875), p. 592; Haggard, *King Solomon's Mines* (Barre, Mass: Imprint Society, 1970), p. 179. Further references will be to this edition, and page numbers will be included in the text.

90 Mary Austin, *Earth Horizon* (Boston: Houghton Mifflin, 1932), p. 344.

91 For a useful discussion of *She* and the figure of the mother, see Etherington, p. 89; as Etherington observes, even without the later evidence provided by *Ayesha, the Return of She,* "Ayesha can be interpreted as a mother in disguise. She is an older woman [to say the least!] who is all-powerful, wise, and knowing. She is totally devoted to the young object of her affection. She will do anything . . . to advance his interests. She will not allow any young woman to take him away from her. Thus . . . she accords well with many a young man's perception of a dominating mother."

92 Haggard's mother published *Myra: or the Rose of the East,* a tale of the Afghan War in nine cantos, in 1857, and Haggard commented, as an adult, that she "opened to my childish eyes that gate of ivory and pearl which leads to the blessed kingdom of Romance." See Cohen, p. 22.

93 On Haggard's explicit antifeminism, see Etherington, p. 125, and Haggard, "A Man's View of Woman," *African Review* 22 (Sept. 1894): 407–08.

94 Leo was born in 1856, a date that, as Grinstein notes (p. 395), is omitted from some modern editions of *She.* He would, therefore, reach his twenty-fifth birthday and inherit the matriarchal sherd in 1881, the year in which Cambridge admitted women students to the same Previous and Tripos examinations (though not the same degrees) as men. In 1884 Oxford allowed women to take the same examinations as men in certain fields; for more on this, see Penny Griffin, ed., *St Hugh's: One Hundred Years of Women's Education at Oxford* (London: Macmillan, 1986), pp. 20–21; and Ann Phillips, ed., *A Newnham Anthology* (Cambridge: Cambridge University Press, 1979), pp. 5–19.

95 Etherington, p. 21; see also Etherington, pp. 21–22, for a more general discussion of the relationship between Schreiner and Haggard.

96 On Schreiner's attitude toward Haggard, see chap. 2 of this volume, pp. 51–52. On the more general issue of the relationship between feminism and accelerated nineteenth-century depictions of the femme fatale, Peter Gay has argued that "that pervasive nineteenth-century theme . . . the devouring female . . . was only incidentally a reaction to the campaign for women's rights" but, more centrally, a reflection of "universal, timeless masculine concerns"—an oddly ahistorical argument for so eminent a historian; see Gay, *The Tender Passion,* vol. 2 of *The Bourgeois Experience: Victoria to Freud* (New York: Oxford University Press, 1986), p. 417. In *The Femme Fatale* Virginia Allen cites a letter to the *Atheneum* which was found among D. G. Rossetti's papers and which would seem, almost by itself, to refute Gay's argument: "Lilith, about whom you ask for information, was evidently the first strong-minded woman and the original advocate of women's rights," declared the writer (identified by Allen as "one Ponsonby A. Lyons"). "At present she is the queen of the demons" (Allen, p. 196).

97 Cixous, "Sorties . . .," in Hélène Cixous and Catherine Clement, *The Newly Born*

Woman, trans. Betsy Wing (1975; Minneapolis: University of Minnesota Press, 1986), pp. 63–64.

98 Freud, *The Question of Lay Analysis*, trans. Nancy Procter-Gregg (New York: W. W. Norton, 1950), p. 61; Ashley Montagu, *The Natural Superiority of Woman* (New York: Collier, 1974), p. 237.

99 Lewis Wurgaft, *The Imperial Imagination: Magic and Myth in Kipling's India* (Middletown, Conn: Wesleyan University Press, 1983), pp. 49–52; as Wurgaft also observes, the English attributed a more nearly western and therefore more virile temperament to the Muslims and Sikhs of the hills (see pp. 46–47).

100 Wurgaft, pp. 49, 52. Wurgaft is quoting Maud Diver, *The Englishwoman in India* (London: W. Blackwood, 1909), pp. 168–69.

101 See Wurgaft's illuminating discussions of Lalun in "On the City Wall" as "mother and seductress" and of Trejago's quasi-sexual wound in "Beyond the Pale" (Wurgaft, pp. 101–03 and 138–39).

102 Quoted in Wurgaft, p. 136.

103 Wurgaft discusses *Mother Maturin* on pp. 135–36 and in a note on pp. 197–98. To be sure, Kipling's adventure story-cum-Bildungsroman *Kim* (1901) may at first seem to be the exception that proves this rule: the heroes of *Kim* include not only the English orphan Kimball O'Hara but also such native figures as the horse-dealer Muhbub Ali, the jewel seller Lurgan Das, the Tibetan mystic Teshoo Lama, and, most important in this context, the Bengali spy Hurree Babu. But the mutual participation of all these characters in the "Great Game" of British espionage strengthens them through a homosocial bonding which wards off any threat that might be posed by the native *feminine*, while their journeys up and down the Grand Trunk Road take place in a kind of timelessly asexual latency period. Even after he has become "a man," for instance, Kim definitively rejects the erotic advances of the polyandrous Woman of Shamlegh, and the novel ends happily with the lama's conviction that he "has won Salvation for himself and his beloved"—Kim (see Kipling, *Kim* [New York: Bantam, 1983], p. 261).

104 Barker-Benfield, p. 122.

105 Barker-Benfield, p. 96; see also Barker-Benfield, pp. 101–02, for Sims's experiments with black slave women and, later, with Irish immigrant women. As this historian observes, "Sims's career was devoted to countering the dark power of woman, of overcoming his hatred by his use of the knife" (p. 107).

106 Quoted in Sachs, pp. 161–62.

107 Sir Richard Burton, *The Sotadic Zone* (New York: The Panurge Press/Kama Shastra Society, n.d.), pp. 117–18, 20. "Kama Shastra" (Sanskrit) means "the law of (erotic) love"; we are grateful to Barbara Metcalf for her assistance with this phrase and with other issues relating to orientalism. Burton's lapse into Latin—*patiens* for passive, *agens* for active—represents, incidentally, a characteristic move of sexologists up to and including Freud, who spoke in a key letter to Fliess of remembering a glimpse of *"matrem . . . nudam,"* and declared in *The Case of Dora: A Fragment of an Analysis*, that "J'appelle un chat un chat," disingenuously *not* calling "a cat a cat" in his native German; see *Dora*, intro. by Philip Rieff (New York: Collier, 1963), p. 65.

108 Burton, pp. 48, 23, 51, 52, 60, 88. Specifically, Burton observes that "Syria and Palestine, another ancient focus of abominations, borrowed from Egypt and exaggerated the worship of Androgynic and hermaphroditic deities," adding that "the old Nilotes held the moon to be of 'male-female sex' " and that "Isis also was a hermaphrodite" (p. 51); in addition, he reports that, when worshipping the "bearded Aphrodite," the sexes "exchanged habits and here the virginity was offered in sacrifice" (p. 60).

109 Said, p. 196. Said discusses western notions of oriental sexual perversion through-

out *Orientalism:* see, for example, pp. 102–03, 162, 167, 187, 190; his analysis of Flaubert's attitude toward the Egyptian dancer Kuchuk Hanem offers particularly interesting insights into the western construction of the "Oriental woman" (pp. 186–87), and his analysis of "Oriental sex"—"the association is clearly made between the Orient and the freedom of licentious sex . . . the Orient was a place where one could look for sexual experience unobtainable in Europe" (p. 190)—is also very useful.

110 Preface to *The Sotadic Zone,* p. 10.

111 We are grateful to Anne McClintock for drawing our attention to some of the gender imperatives dramatized in this romance. On the power of Haggard's imaginative projection, see Etherington, who argues that some of Haggard's writings may "have directly molded the self-image now cultivated by the scions of old African families," noting that in 1982, "When Sobhuza II of Swaziland was buried . . . international wire services reported that his body was carried to 'a hidden cave between twin peaks known as 'Sheba's Breasts' " (p. 109).

112 A number of verses in the "King Bolo" series are included in letters from Eliot to Aiken and Pound that are held at the Huntington Library, Pasadena, and elsewhere; we are grateful to Ronald Bush for calling these materials to our attention and for sharing them with us. For an analysis from a different perspective of the intersection of sexual and racial issues in this period, see Sander L. Gilman, "Black Bodies, White Bodies: Toward an Iconography of Female Sexuality in Late Nineteenth-Century Art, Medicine, and Literature," *Critical Inquiry* 12:1 (Autumn 1985): 204–42.

113 Kipling, *Poems,* pp. 379–80; emphasis ours. Kipling's implicit comparison of the British Empire to the lost civilizations of "Ninevah and Tyre" prefigures Balfour's later allusion to "the petty span of the history of our race" (Said, p. 32). For a similar discussion of "Recessional," see Eric Hobsbawm, *The Age of Empire: 1875–1914* (New York: Pantheon, 1987), p. 82. Although Hobsbawm argues that "it is an anachronism and a misunderstanding to present the history of the peoples and regions brought under the domination and influence of the western metropoles primarily in terms of resistance to the west" in these years (78), he concedes that, for western colonists, "imperial triumph raised both problems and uncertainties" (82), adding that "if empire . . . was vulnerable to its subjects," it was also "vulnerable to the erosion from within of the will to rule" (83).

114 Freud, *The Interpretation of Dreams,* pp. 489–90.

115 See Etherington, "Rider Haggard, Imperialism, and the Layered Personality," passim; for an extended but slightly different analysis of this dream; see also Grinstein, pp. 392–422.

116 During the years when he was working on *The Interpretation of Dreams,* the first of his "own immortal works," Freud related comparable anxieties to Wilhelm Fliess; on October 3, 1897, as he was beginning to "discover" the Oedipus complex, he told his friend about a dream (which he regarded as highly significant) in which "an ugly, elderly but clever woman who told me a great deal about God and hell" and who "was my instructress in sexual matters, and chided me for being clumsy and not being able to do anything (that is always the way with neurotic impotence: anxiety over incapacity at school gets its sexual reinforcement in this way) . . . washed me in reddish water in which she had previously washed herself (not very difficult to interpret. . . .)"; see Freud, *The Origins of Psychoanalysis: Letters to Wilhelm Fliess,* trans. Eric Mosbacher and James Strachey (New York: Basic Books, 1954), pp. 219–20.

117 Joseph Conrad, *Heart of Darkness* (New York: Norton Critical Edition, 1971), p. 8. All references will be to this edition, and page numbers will be included in the text.

Although, according to Ian Watt, Conrad claimed to find Haggard's work "too hor-
rible for words" (Watt, *Conrad in the Nineteenth Century* [Berkeley: University of California Press, 1979], p. 43), the Polish novelist had Marlow confess in *Chance* (1912)
that "We are the creatures of our light literature much more than is generally suspected"; see Joseph Conrad, *Chance* (New York: Doubleday, Page, 1926). p. 288.
Christopher S. Nassaar traces and analyzes *Heart of Darknesss* as Conrad's response
to *Salome* in "Vision of Evil: The Influence of Wilde's *Salome* on *Heart of Darkness*
and *A Full Moon in March*," *Victorian Newsletter* 53 (Spring 1978): 23–27.

118 Pursuing a different Haggard source, Etherington discusses the relationship be-
    tween *Heart of Darkness* and *King Solomon's Mines* (but not *She*) on p. 113.

119 For some recent discussions of Conrad's attitude toward imperialism (which usually
    do not take into account issues relating to gender), see Benita Parry, *Conrad and
    Imperialism* (London: Macmillan, 1983); Hunt Hawkins, "Conrad and the Psychol-
    ogy of Colonialism," in *Conrad Revisited: Essays for the Eighties*, ed. Ross C. Murfin
    (University, Ala.: University of Alabama Press, 1985), pp. 71–87; and Brantlinger,
    Rule of Darkness, pp. 255–74.

120 Kipling, "The Female of the Species," *Poems*, p. 423.

121 Yeats, Introduction to *Oxford Book*, pp. xxx–xxxi.

122 Barker in Yeats, *Oxford Book*, pp. 436–37.

Chapter 2

EPIGRAPHS: Andrew Rosen, *Rise Up, Women!: The Militant Campaign of the Women's
Social and Political Union 1903–1914* (London: Routledge & Kegan Paul, 1974), p.
166; "The White Women," *The Collected Poems of Mary Coleridge* (London: Rupert
Hart-Davis, 1954), pp. 212–14; Matilda Joslyn Gage, *Woman, Church and State* (1893;
Watertown, Mass.: Persephone Press, 1980), p. 21; Elizabeth Cady Stanton, from the
"Speech to the International Council of Women, 1888," reprinted in *Feminism: The
Essential Historical Writings*, ed. Miriam Schneir (New York: Random House, 1972),
p. v.

1 Wilson's *A Casebook of Murder*, quoted in Daniel Farson, *Jack the Ripper* (London: Michael Joseph, 1972), p. 28.

2 Walkowitz, "Jack the Ripper and the Myth of Male Violence," *Feminist Studies* 8:3 (Fall
  1982): 543–74.

3 Walkowitz, pp. 563, 574.

4 Linda Gordon, *Woman's Body, Woman's Right* (New York: Penguin, 1977), p. 120. Also
  see the discussion of the Contagious Disease Acts in Peter Gay, *Education of the Senses*,
  vol. 1 of *The Bourgeois Experience: Victoria to Freud* (New York: Oxford University
  Press, 1984), p. 174.

5 To be sure, as Walkowitz explains in *Prostitution and Victorian Society* (Cambridge:
  Cambridge University Press, 1980), turn-of-the-century suffragists' "acts of arson,
  window breaking, and tearing up of golf links were part of a real sex war, whose
  explicit political precedent may be traced to the campaign against the C. D. acts" (p.
  255).

6 Quoted in Susan Kingsley Kent, *Sex and Suffrage in Britain, 1860–1914* (Princeton:
  Princeton University Press, 1987), p. 28. Kent's chapter on "Sex War" provides indispensable background on suffrage rhetoric in this period.

7 For a discussion of this, see Gay, *Education of the Senses*, p. 194.

8 Quoted in Gail Cunningham, *The New Woman and the Victorian Novel* (London: Macmillan, 1978), p. 1; and quoted in Gerd Bjørhovde, *Rebellious Structures: Women Writers and the Crisis of the Novel 1880–1900* (England: Norwegian University Press, 1987),
  pp. 133–34.

9 Swiney, *Woman and Natural Law* (1912), is quoted by Kent, p. 165.

10 A general discussion of Haggard and Schreiner appears in Etherington, *Rider Haggard*, pp. 21–27. Letter to J. Stanley Little, quoted in Cohen, p. 90*n*.

11 D. L. Hobman, *Olive Schreiner* (London: Watts & Co., 1955), p. 42; quoted in Cohen, p. 90*n*.

12 Quoted by Donald Stone, *Novelists in a Changing World* (Cambridge: Harvard University Press, 1972), p. 52.

13 Schreiner, *The Story of an African Farm*, intro. by Doris Lessing (1883; New York: Schocken Books, 1976), pp. v–vi. Further references will be to this edition, and page numbers will appear in the text.

14 Stein, *Tender Buttons* (1914) in *Selected Writings of Gertrude Stein*, ed. by Carl Van Vechten (New York: Vintage Books, 1972), p. 475.

15 DuPlessis describes how Schreiner evokes traditional stories of religion and romance only to disrupt them in "The Rupture of Story and *The Story of an African Farm*," *Writing Beyond the Ending* (Bloomington: Indiana University Press, 1985), pp. 20–30; Elaine Showalter also links the fragmentation of Schreiner's novel to its original subtitle—"A Series of Abortions"—in *A Literature of Their Own* (Princeton: Princeton University Press, 1977), p. 199. Also see Bjørhovde, *Rebellious Structures*, which argues that *The Story of an African Farm* combines the local color story, the Bildungsroman, and the social criticism or problem novel in a "hybrid" form that seeks to serve Schreiner's aesthetic, political, and philosophical concerns (pp. 25–49).

16 Quoted in Ruth First and Ann Scott, *Olive Schreiner* (London: Andre Deutsch, 1980), p. 53. Also see the discussion of Schreiner's family background in Barbara Scott Winkler, *Victorian Daughters: The Lives and Feminism of Charlotte Perkins Gilman and Olive Schreiner*, Michigan Occasional Paper 13 in Women's Studies (Ann Arbor: Women's Studies Program, The University of Michigan, 1980) p. 10.

17 Our critical vocabulary here is indebted to Paul Ricoeur, *The Symbolism of Evil*, trans. Emerson Buchanan (New York: Harper & Row, 1967).

18 Emily Brontë's heroine's speech in chapter 12 of *Wuthering Heights* is discussed in *The Madwoman in the Attic*, chap. 8.

19 Lessing, "Introduction," *The Story of an African Farm*, p. 9.

20 Dan Jacobson, "Introduction," *The Story of an African Farm* (New York: Penguin, 1971), p. 7.

21 Significantly, when Waldo later meets up with his stranger outside the African farm, he is struck by the disparity of their class identifications, a disparity that fills him with self-revulsion and a sense of hopelessness: see DuPlessis, pp. 23–24.

22 Schreiner, *Undine* (1928; New York: Johnson Reprint, 1972), p. 363.

23 Schreiner, *Woman and Labour* (1911; London: Virago, 1978), p. 79. Further references will be to this edition, and page numbers will appear in the text after the citation *WL*.

24 See the excellent discussion of Schreiner's obsession with female "littleness" in Kathleen Blake, *Love and the Woman Question in Victorian Literature* (Sussex, England, and Totowa, N.J.: The Harvester Press and Barnes & Noble, 1983), pp. 217–22; Showalter discusses Schreiner's association of grotesque obesity with the stereotypical female role in *A Literature of Their Own*, p. 196.

25 Helene Moglen analyzes Brontë's death during pregnancy in *Charlotte Brontë: The Self Conceived* (New York: W. W. Norton, 1976), pp. 241–42.

26 Quoted in First and Scott, p. 83.

27 Showalter, p. 195.

28 Johannes Meintjes, *Olive Schreiner: Portrait of a South African Woman* (Johannesburg: Hugh Keartland, 1965), p. 26. See also *The Letters of Olive Schreiner 1876–1920*, ed. S. C. Cronwright-Schreiner (London: T. Fisher Unwin, 1924), pp. 31 and 76, where

Schreiner describes the "comfort" and "stimulation" she received from Emerson's *Essays*. Emerson's crucial work on "Woman's Suffrage" is reprinted in *History of Ideas on Woman: A Source Book,* ed. Rosemary Agonito (New York: Paragon Books, 1977), pp. 207–21.

29 Quoted in First and Scott, p. 121.

30 The connection between feminization and colonization has been discussed by Margaret Atwood in *Survival* (1972) as well as by Elaine Showalter in *A Literature of Their Own* and Barbara Charlesworth Gelpi, "A Common Language," *Shakespeare's Sisters,* ed. Sandra M. Gilbert and Susan Gubar (Bloomington: Indiana University Press, 1979), pp. 269–79. On Schreiner's feminism and anti-imperialism, see Jane Marcus, "Olive Schreiner: Cartographer of the Spirit, a Review Article," *The Minnesota Review* 12 (Spring 1979): 58–66.

31 Darwin, *The Descent of Man* (1871; Princeton: Princeton University Press, 1981), pp. 326–27. The significance of Darwin's theory is discussed by Elaine Showalter in *The Female Malady: Women, Madness, and English Culture, 1830–1980* (New York: Penguin, 1985), p. 122.

32 Vogt, *Lectures on Man: His Place in Creation, and in the History of the Earth,* ed. James Hunt (London: Longman, Green, 1864), p. 81. In *Idols of Perversity,* Bram Dijkstra analyzes what he calls the "race-and-sex equation" in Vogt's theories (pp. 166–67).

33 Harrison, *Separate Spheres: The Opposition to Women's Suffrage in Britain* (London: Croom Helm, 1978), pp. 75–76 and 97.

34 Mill's analysis of women's "slavery" is discussed by Gay, *Education of the Senses,* p. 175. See also the discussion of the link between feminism and antislavery in Richard J. Evans, *The Feminists: Women's Emancipation Movements in Europe, America and Australasia 1840–1920* (New York: Barnes & Noble Books, 1977), pp. 48–49. Of course, the first convention at Seneca Falls was inspired at least in part by the fact that Elizabeth Cady Stanton and Lucretia Mott, delegates to the World Anti-Slavery Convention in London, had been refused seats and denied the right to speak there.

35 Reprinted in the *Norton Anthology of Literature by Women,* ed. Sandra M. Gilbert and Susan Gubar (New York: W. W. Norton, 1985), pp. 253 and 344.

36 The 1853 letter to Mrs. Jameson appears in *The Letters of Elizabeth Barrett Browning,* ed. Frederic G. Kenyon (New York: Macmillan, 1897), 2:110–11, and is discussed in Helen Cooper, "Working into Light: Elizabeth Barrett Browning," *Shakespeare's Sisters,* p. 72.

37 Rosen, *Rise Up. Women!* p. 166.

38 Cott, *The Grounding of Modern Feminism* (New Haven: Yale University Press, 1987), p. 26.

39 See A. James Hammerton, "Feminism and Female Emigration, 1861–1886," in *A Widening Sphere,* ed: Martha Vicinus (Bloomington: Indiana University Press, 1980), pp. 52–71, and Auerbach, *Woman and the Demon,* pp. 124–26.

40 Quoted in Auerbach, *Woman and the Demon,* pp. 125–26.

41 For a discussion of the success of feminist organizations in areas where "there were no established institutions against which the feminists had to fight," see Evans, p. 62.

42 Holtby, *The Land of Green Ginger* (Chicago: Cassandra Editions, Academy Press 1977), p. 293.

43 Robins, *The Convert* (Old Westbury, N.Y.: The Feminist Press, 1980), p. 149.

44 Nightingale, *Cassandra* (Old Westbury, N.Y.: The Feminist Press, 1979), p. 29.

45 Gardiner, *The Hero as Her Author's Daughter: Jean Rhys, Christina Stead, Doris Lessing* (Bloomington: Indiana University Press, forthcoming), p. 19 of the manuscript.

46 B. Kipling, "The Little Pink House," *The Pall Mall Magazine* (August 1894): 616–24.

47 Lessing, "Impertinent Daughters," *Granta* 14 (1984): 51–68.

48 Dinesen, *Out of Africa* (1937; New York: Random House, 1965), p. 264.

49 Dinesen, *Out of Africa*, pp. 265 and 180.
50 Judith Thurman, *Isak Dinesen: The Life of a Storyteller* (New York: St. Martin's Press, 1982), p. 286, and Isak Dinesen, *Letters from Africa, 1914–1931*, ed. Frans Lasson and trans. Anne Born (Chicago: University of Chicago Press, 1981), p. 281. Dinesen's vision of Africa as a place of personal freedom from sex roles recurs in Beryl Markham, *West with the Night* (1942; San Francisco: North Point Press, 1983), as Markham's epigraph from *Henry IV*—"I speak of Africa and golden joys"—and her recollections of a childhood spent hunting in Kenya intimate.
51 Dinesen, *Letters from Africa*, p. 259.
52 Quoted in Rosen, *Rise Up, Women!*, p. 78.
53 *Cassandra*, p. 53.
54 Christabel Pankhurst's comments appear in the *Suffragette* (28 March 1913), and Wilding Davison is quoted in Rosen, *Rise Up, Women!*, p. 200. See also our analysis of the Cat and Mouse poster in *The War of the Words*, p. 78.
55 Kent, p. 97. Kent also reiterates claims that Emmeline Pankhurst "placed a taboo on marriage for her followers" because "she regarded marriage as 'fraternising with the enemy' ": p. 84.
56 To Havelock Ellis (29 July 1884), *The Letters of Olive Schreiner*, p. 36; to Havelock Ellis (10 Feb. 1885), *The Letters of Olive Schreiner*, p. 59.
57 Phelps, "The Higher Claim," *Independent* 23 (5 Oct. 1871): 1. We are indebted to Alice Falk for bringing this quotation to our attention.
58 Waisbrooker, *A Sex Revolution* (1894) is excerpted in *Daring to Dream: Utopian Stories by United States Women, 1836–1919*, ed. Carol Farley Kessler (Boston: Pandora Press, 1984), p. 189–90.
59 Fuller, *Woman in the Nineteenth Century* (1855; New York: W. W. Norton, 1971), p. 121.
60 Stanton, *The Woman's Bible* (1898; Seattle: Coalition Task Force on Women and Religion, 1974), part 1, p. 79.
61 Stanton, *The Woman's Bible*, part 1, pp. 44, 47, and part 2, p. 22.
62 Quoted in Vicinus, *Independent Women: Work and Community for Single Women, 1850–1920* (Chicago: University of Chicago Press, 1985), p. 259. In 1928, Ray Strachey described the "religious fervour" of the militants, and in 1935, Helena Swanwick called the women's movement "proufoundly religious"; both in Kent, pp. 184 and 3.
63 Mayreder, *A Survey of the Woman Problem*, trans. Herman Scheffauer (Westport, Conn.: Hyperion Press, 1913), p. 16.
64 Mayreder, p. 44; Austin, "The Basket Maker," *The Land of Little Rain* (1903), reprinted in Austin, *Stories from the Country of Lost Borders*, ed. with an intro. by Marjorie Pryse (New Brunswick, N.J.: Rutgers University Press, 1987), p. 95.
65 Gage, pp. 234, 241.
66 Gage, pp. 241, 21.
67 Eliot, *The Mill on the Floss* (1860; Boston: Houghton Mifflin, 1981), book 6, chap. 7, p. 361.
68 Stanton, *Feminism: The Essential Writings*, p. v; Jewsbury's letter and her relationship to Jane Welsh Carlyle are discussed in Lillian Faderman, *Surpassing the Love of Men* (New York: William Morrow, 1981), pp. 164–66. Stanton's and Jewsbury's futuristic rhetoric is strikingly similar to Olive Schreiner's in the parable "Three Dreams in the Desert" (1890), which was read aloud by suffragists in Holloway and which, Gerd Bjørhovde has shown, presents a vision of a "future heaven on earth" when "man and woman walk together as equal partners, and only the collective effort of all of them . . . can lay the foundation of that utopia" (pp. 56–57).
69 West, "So Simple," a review of *The Consumer in Revolt* by Teresa Billington Greig, *Dreams*, and *Dream Life and Real Life* by Olive Schreiner, and *The Naked Soul* by Louise

Heilgers in *The Freewoman* (12 Oct. 1912), reprinted in *The Young Rebecca: Writings of Rebecca West 1911–1917*, ed. Jane Marcus (New York: Viking, 1982), p. 70.

70 For a very different, eroticized fantasy of female power, see George Egerton, "A Cross Line," *Keynotes and Discords* (London: Virago, 1983), pp. 1–36, where a woman imagines herself seductively performing on a stage before hundreds of entranced men.

71 *The Collected Poems of Mary Coleridge*, pp. 212–13.

72 According to Gary Scharnhorst in *Charlotte Perkins Gilman* (Boston: Twayne Publishers, 1985), Gilman observed that Schreiner is "a great thinker. Such minds as hers, appearing from age to age, clarify and rearrange the world's thoughts. She is essentially a poet, both in the sense that the poet is a seer, and in the musical majesty of her forms of expression" (p. 12).

73 Gilman, "Parasitism and Civilised Vice," *Woman's Coming of Age: A Symposium*, ed. Samuel D. Schmalhausen and V. F. Calverton (New York: Horace Liveright, 1931), pp. 110–26; quotation on p. 114.

74 Gilman, *Herland* (New York: Pantheon Books, 1979), pp. 2 and 4. Further references will be to this edition, and page numbers will appear in the text. Of course, Gilman's volcano is situated not in Africa but in South America.

75 See also the discussion of the relationship between *The Princess, Princess Ida*, and *Herland* in *The War of the Words*, p. 89.

76 Rabkin, *The Fantastic in Literature* (Princeton: Princeton University Press, 1976), p. 8.

77 Gilman, *Woman and Economics* (1898; New York: Source Book Press, 1970), pp. 70 and 330. Further references will be to this edition, and page numbers will appear in the text preceded by the citation *WE*.

78 See both Mary A. Hill, *Charlotte Perkins Gilman: The Making of a Radical Feminist, 1860–1896* (Philadelphia: Temple University Press, 1980), pp. 264–72, and Scharnhorst, pp. 46–47. Gilman dedicated *The Man-Made World* (1911) to Ward.

79 Denton Cridge's *Man's Rights* appears abridged in *Daring to Dream*, pp. 75–94. Raphael's "The Myth of the Male Orgasm" is reprinted in *Issues in Feminism*, ed. Sheila Ruth (Boston: Houghton Mifflin, 1980), pp. 19–21. For an analysis of utopian strategies of reversal exploited by feminist writers, see Daphne Patai, "Beyond Defensiveness: Feminist Research Strategies," *Woman and Utopia*, ed. Marleen Barr and Nicholas D. Smith (New York: University Press of America, 1983), pp. 148–69.

80 See Sherry Ortner, "Is Female to Male as Nature Is to Culture?" in *Woman, Culture and Society*, ed. Michelle Zimbalist Rosaldo and Louise Lamphere (Stanford: Stanford University Press, 1974), pp. 73–83, as well as Annette Kolodny, "Honing a Habitable Languagescape: Women's Images for the New World Frontiers," in *Women and Language in Literature and Society*, ed. Sally McConnell-Ginet, Ruth Borker, and Nelly Furman (New York: Praeger, 1980), p. 194.

81 Gilman, *His Religion and Hers* (1923; Westport, Conn.: Hyperion Press, 1976), p. 46.

82 Sanger and Goldman are discussed throughout Gordon, *Woman's Body, Woman's Right;* see chap. 1 for a discussion of Besant. For an analysis of the problematics of maternity in contemporary culture, see Rich, "Motherhood in Bondage," *On Lies, Secrets, and Silence* (New York: W. W. Norton, 1979), p. 196.

83 Gilman, *The Yellow Wallpaper* (Old Westbury, N.Y.: The Feminist Press, 1973), p. 15.

84 For a discussion of "The Yellow Wallpaper" in this connection, see *The Madwoman in the Attic*, pp. 89–92.

85 Quoted in First and Scott, p. 179.

86 See Joyce Avrech Berkman, *Olive Schreiner: Feminism on the Frontier* (St. Alban's, Vermont: Eden Press Women's Publication, 1979), passim.

87 Gilman, *With Her in Ourland, Forerunner* 7 (1916) :155. For a discussion of the eugenics and birth-control movements led by Margaret Sanger and Marie Stopes in terms

of an "ultra right" radicalism that was directed against "the excess fertility" of working-class, black, and Catholic populations, see Germaine Greer, *Sex and Destiny* (New York: Harper & Row, 1984), pp. 295–328.

88 See the discussion of black female sexuality and specifically the analysis of "Hottentot genitalia" that illuminates the intellectual sources of Schreiner's racism: Gilman, "Black Bodies, White Bodies: Toward an Iconography of Female Sexuality in Late Nineteenth-Century Art, Medicine, and Literature," *Critical Inquiry* 12:1 (Autumn 1985): 204–42.

89 Giddings, *When and Where I Enter: The Impact of Black Women on Race and Sex in America* (New York: Bantam, 1985), p. 66. For an analysis of black women's resentment at suffragists' strategies which, in the words of Ida B. Wells, only "confirmed white women in their attitude of segregation," see Angela Y. Davis, *Women, Race and Class* (New York: Vintage, 1983), pp. 110–26. For a discussion of the limits of white women's identification with the black liberation movement of the sixties, see Catharine R. Stimpson, *Where the Meanings Are* (New York: Methuen, 1988), esp. pp. 33–37. Gordimer, "Afterword: 'The Prison-House of Colonialism,' " a review of Ruth First and Ann Scott's *Olive Schreiner,* reprinted in *An Olive Schreiner Reader: Writings on Women and South Africa,* (London and New York: Pandora, 1987) pp. 225–26.

90 In "Three Women's Texts and a Critique of Imperialism," *Critical Inquiry* 12:1 (Autumn 1985): 243–61, Gayatri Chakravorty Spivak argues about fiction from *Jane Eyre* to *Wide Sargasso Sea* that the interiority of the female (white) heroine excludes the native female from any significant subjectivity.

91 Letter to Havelock Ellis (9 Nov. 1888) in *The Letters of Olive Schreiner,* p. 146, discussed in Joyce Avrech Berkman, *Olive Schreiner: Feminism on the Frontier,* p. 9.

92 Auerbach argues that, although the Herlanders' society originated out of war, they are supposedly pacifist; see *Communities of Women* (Cambridge: Harvard University Press, 1978), pp. 162–53.

93 Quoted by Kent, p. 105. For a discussion of the causes of Gilman's antagonism to the medical establishment and specifically to those Victorian physicians who identified women's ambition with sickness, sterility, and race suicide, see Showalter, *The Female Malady,* chap. 5.

94 DuPlessis, *Writing Beyond the Ending,* pp. 66–83.

95 Delany, *Writing Woman: Women Writers and Women in Literature Medieval to Modern* (New York: Schocken, 1983), p. 171.

96 Gay, *Education of the Senses,* p. 168. Gay claims, too, that the "medical literature of the bourgeois century, right down to 1914 and even beyond, runs counter to the revelations of the sexual pleasure that diaries, journals, fictions, and surveys disclose and that psychoanalytic investigations can substantiate" (p. 164).

97 Quoted and discussed by Cott, pp. 48–49.

98 Jeffrey Weeks, *Sex, Politics and Society* (Burnt Mill, Harlow, Essex: Longman Group, 1981), p. 167.

99 For discussions of these and related works, see Cunningham, passim, and Lloyd Fernando, *"New Women" in the Late Victorian Novel,* passim.

100 Quoted in Cunningham, p. 77.

101 Gissing, *The Odd Women* (1893; London: Virago, 1980), chapter 6.

102 "Ellis Ethelmer," *Life to Woman* (1896) is quoted and discussed by Kent, p. 110.

103 Quoted in Cott, p. 35.

104 Mayreder, p. 75.

Chapter 3

EPIGRAPHS: Baudelaire, "Richard Wagner and Tannhäuser in Paris," in *The Painter of Modern Life and Other Essays,* trans. and ed. Jonathan Mayne (London: Phaidon

Press, 1964), pp. 122–23; Swinburne, "Sapphics," in *The Works of Algernon Charles Swinburne* (Philadelphia: David McKay, n.d.), pp. 82–83; Duncan, *My Life* (New York: Liveright, 1927), p. 10; H. D., "Tribute to the Angels," *Collected Poems, 1912–1944,* ed. Louis L. Martz (New York: New Directions, 1983), p. 554.

1 Both quoted in Sachs, *"The Terrible Siren",* pp. 78–80, 80–81.

2 *The Complete Works of Kate Chopin,* ed. Per Seyersted, with a foreword by Edmund Wilson (Baton Rouge: Louisiana State University Press, 1969), p. 733. Further references to works by Chopin (except *The Awakening*) will be to this edition, and page numbers will be included in the text, preceded by the citation *CW.*

3 Reviews of *The Awakening* in *The Mirror* 9 (May 4, 1899), *The Providence Sunday Journal* (June 4, 1899), and (by Cather) in *The Pittsburgh Leader* (July 8, 1899) are all included in Margaret Culley, ed., *The Awakening: A Norton Critical Edition* (New York: W. W. Norton, 1976), pp. 146, 149, 153.

4 See Per Seyersted, *Kate Chopin* (Oslo: Universitetsforlaget, and Baton Rouge: Louisiana State. University Press, 1969), p. 175.

5 Quoted in Seyersted, p. 176.

6 Quoted in Seyersted, p. 181.

7 See Cather, as quoted in Culley, p. 153.

8 For useful analyses of the distinctions between nineteenth- and twentieth-century feminist attitudes toward female sexuality, see Cott, pp. 41–49, 150–52. Although Cott argues that "Schreiner was also a prophetess of women's sexual release" (p. 41), she adduces statements by a number of early twentieth-century feminists whose radical advocacy of women's "sex rights" aligned their views more nearly with those of Woodhull or Chopin.

9 See Seyersted, p. 33. Seyersted declares that "It was apparently Victoria [Woodhull] that Kate Chopin met," but by the early seventies Woodhull had long been defining herself as "Mrs. Woodhull," whereas her sister, Tennessee Claflin (also known as "Tennie C. Claflin"), went by the name "Miss Claflin." In addition, Tennessee Claflin was always described as "fussy, pretty, talkative," while Woodhull appears to have had a more majestic and commanding presence. For further details about the differences (and similarities) between the notorious sisters, see Sachs, passim.

10 Quoted in Seyersted, p. 51.

11 Review in *The Los Angeles Sunday Times* (June 25, 1899), quoted in Culley, p. 152.

12 Daniel S. Rankin, *Kate Chopin and Her Creole Stories* (Philadelphia: University of Pennsylvania Press, 1932), p. 175.

13 The equation of *fin de siècle* with *fin du globe* is wittily made in Oscar Wilde's *The Picture of Dorian Gray:* " 'Fin de siècle,' murmured Sir Henry. 'Fin du globe,' answered his hostess. 'I wish it were *fin du globe*,' said Dorian with a sigh. 'Life is a great disappointment.' " (*The Writings of Oscar Wilde,* 3:326.)

14 On Chopin's reading, see Seyersted, passim, but especially pp. 25 (for her reading of Austen and Charlotte Brontë, among others), 63 (for her familiarity with "Whitman, Flaubert, Zola, Swinburne, and Wilde"), 52 and 101 (for her admiration of Jewett and Freeman), and 206 (for her familiarity with *The Yellow Book*).

15 *At Fault* is included in *The Complete Works of Kate Chopin,* 2:741–880.

16 For "sad and mad and bad," see the review from the *St. Louis Post-Dispatch* (May 20, 1899), quoted in Culley, p. 149.

17 On the New Woman novel, see chap. 2 of this volume as well as Showalter, *A Literature of Their Own,* pp. 182–239; and Lloyd Fernando, *New Women in the Late Victorian Novel,* passim.

18 For a discussion of Chopin's involvement in "local color" writing, see Seyersted, pp. 80–83; although, as we have noted, Chopin did admire Jewett and Freeman, Seyersted cites an interview with Daniel Rankin in observing that "she refused to be

considered a local colorist and resented being compared as such to [George Washington] Cable and Grace King" (p. 83).

19 On Chopin's "delightful sketches," see the review from the *Chicago Times-Herald* (June 1, 1899), quoted in Culley, p. 149. For an incisive analysis of one aspect of the social criticism formulated in Chopin's sketches, see Anna Shannon Elfenbein, *Women on the Color Line: Evolving Stereotypes and the Writings of George Washington Cable, Grace King, Kate Chopin* (Charlottesville: University Press of Virginia, 1988), pp. 117–57.

20 Linda Dowling, "The Decadent and the New Woman in the 1890's," *Nineteenth-Century Fiction*, 33:4 (March 1979): 450.

21 Holbrook Jackson, *The Eighteen Nineties: A Review of Art and Ideas at the Close of the Nineteenth Century*, with an intro. by Karl Beckson (1913; New York: Capricorn, 1966), pp. 29–30.

22 For "sex-distinction," see Schreiner, *Stories, Dreams, and Allegories* [London: 1924], pp. 156–59; Carpenter discusses "the sex-passion" (with approval) in chap. 1 of *Love's Coming of Age.*

23 Schreiner, *Stories*, pp. 156–59; but on Schreiner's attitude toward sexuality, see also Weeks, *Sex, Politics and Society*, p. 167: "Influenced both by [Havelock] Ellis and Edward Carpenter, with both of whom she was on close personal relations, Schreiner's work was clearly within the feminist radical tradition which, while recognising 'inherent differences' dictated by reproductive divisions and hence the rationale of separate functions, stressed the importance of female eroticism in its own (not male) terms."

24 Kathryn Oliver, writing in *The Freewoman* (Feb. 25, 1912, p. 252), quoted in Weeks, p. 164.

25 Grant Allen, "The New Hedonism," *Fortnightly Review* (March 1894), quoted in Jackson, p. 28. The "new Hedonism," declares Allen, "was to recreate life, and to save it from [a] harsh, uncomely Puritanism."

26 See Schneir, *Feminism*, p. 154.

27 *Venus and Tannhäuser* is included in Beckson, ed. *Aesthetes*, pp. 9–46.

28 In his portrayal of the extreme unction administered to Emma Bovary, Flaubert describes the priest stroking oil "upon the eyes that had so coveted all worldly goods . . . upon the nostrils that had been so greedy of the warm breeze . . . Upon the mouth that had spoken lies . . . upon the hands that had taken delight in the texture of sensuality. . . . upon the soles of the feet, so swift when she had hastened to satisfy her desires." See Gustave Flaubert, *Madame Bovary*, ed. and with a substantially new translation by Paul de Man (New York: Norton Critical Edition, 1965), p. 237. Further references will be to this edition, and page numbers will be included in the text. For Aleister Crowley, see "Ode to Venus Callipyge" and other poems, in Crowley, *White Stains*, ed. John Symonds (London: Duckworth, 1973; first published in 1898 "in an edition of 100 copies, most of which were destroyed in 1924 by H. M. Customs"), p. 50 and passim.

29 Acton (1857, 1865), quoted in Gay, *Education of the Senses*, p. 153.

30 Stanton, in *Elizabeth Cady Stanton, As Revealed in Her Letters, Diary and Reminiscences*, ed. Theodore Stanton and Harriot Stanton Blatch, 2 vols. (1922) 2:183, 210; quoted in Gay, *Education of the Senses*, p. 119.

31 Blackwell, in *The Human Element in Sex: Being a Medical Inquiry into the Relation of Sexual Physiology to Sexual Morality* (1884, 1894), p. 14; quoted in Gay, *Education of the Senses*, p. 159.

32 Mosher's survey is discussed in Gay, *Education of the Senses*, p. 136. Gay also cites a range of other European and American authorities who affirmed the reality of female eroticism: he quotes, for instance, the "eminent Scottish gynecologist, J. Matthews Duncan" as believing that "in women desire and pleasure are in every case present, or are in every case called forth by the proper stimulants" (*Education of the*

Senses, p. 135); he notes that the French doctor Auguste Debay thought "women's 'sexual system' is more 'extensive' than the man's; her imagination is livelier, her sensitivity greater. Hence she 'trembles, shudders under the amorous embrace and savors pleasure during the whole time that sexual excitement lasts' " (Gay, *Education of the Senses,* p. 151); and he cites the assertion of the American sociologist Lester Ward that "All desires are alike before nature—, equally pure, equally respectable. . . . Nature knows no shame. She affects no modesty" (Gay, *Education of the Senses,* p. 131).

33 Woodhull is quoted in Sachs, pp. 219, 222–23. For further discussion of the "free love" movement in the nineteenth-century United States, see Hal D. Sears, *The Sex Radicals: Free Love in Victorian America* (Lawrence: The Regents Press of Kansas, 1977), and Taylor Stoehr, *Free Love in America: A Documentary History* (New York: AMS Press, 1979).

34 Carpenter, *Love's Coming of Age,* pp. 26, 9, 22.

35 "More massive and diffuse"; this characterization of Ellis's belief is from Paul Robinson's excellent chapter on the sexologist in Robinson, *The Modernization of Sex: Havelock Ellis, Alfred Kinsey, William Masters and Virginia Johnson* (New York: Harper & Row, 1976), p. 18; significantly (though Robinson does not note this) the concept echoes Auguste Debay's beliefs, as they are reported by Gay (see note 28, above). For the theories of Cixous and Irigaray, see, for example, Cixous in Cixous and Clement, *The Newly Born Woman,* p. 94: "Women have almost everything to write . . . about the infinite and mobile complexity of their becoming erotic . . . [about] woman's body with a thousand and one fiery hearths"; and Irigaray, *This Sex Which is Not One,* trans. Catherine Porter (French ed., 1977; Ithaca: Cornell University Press, 1985), p. 28: *"woman has sex organs more or less everywhere.* She finds pleasure almost anywhere" (emphasis Irigaray's).

36 Eddy, *Science and Health,* p. 517.

37 Both quoted in Sachs, pp. 273 and 219.

38 Dowling observes that though "Whitman and 'Whitmania' . . . are scarcely mentioned in New Woman fiction, [they] were . . . persistently invoked . . . to explain the New Woman phenomenon" for "not only had the poet of 'barbaric yawp' hymned the new primitivism sought by the decadent spirit, he had promised simultaneously that sex . . . would be the means by which conventional culture would be transcended" (Dowling, pp. 451–52).

39 Seyersted, p. 62.

40 *The Awakening,* chap. 30; since there are so many different editions of this novel, all references will be to chapter numbers and will be given in the text.

41 Wolff, "Thanatos and Eros: Kate Chopin's *Awakening,*" *American Quarterly* 25 (Oct. 1973): 463.

42 Thornton, *"The Awakening:* A Political Romance," *American Literature* 52 (March 1980): 51.

43 Ibid., p. 64. Even those writers who analyze the feast more sympathetically tend to be perfunctory, bewildered, or both in their treatment of the event. Bernard J. Koloski, for instance, the first critic to identify the lines from Swinburne quoted by one of the dinner guests, reads the scene entirely in terms of those lines as Edna's Swinburnian "Song Before Death" (see Koloski, "The Swinburne Lines in *The Awakening,*" *American Literature* 45 [1974]: 608–10). Only Seyersted, still Chopin's most perceptive critic, defines the party as "a sensuous feast with subtle overtones of a ritual for Eros" (Seyersted, p. 157).

44 Cather, review of *The Awakening,* in Culley, pp. 153–55; Helen Taylor, Introduction to *The Awakening* (London: The Women's Press, 1978), p. xviii; Warner Berthoff, *The Ferment of Realism: American Literature, 1884–1919* (New York: Free Press, 1965), p.

89; Seyersted, p. 161; Stanley Kauffman, "The Really Lost Generation," *The New Republic* 155 (Dec. 3, 1966): 22, 37–38; Otis B. Wheeler, "The Five Awakenings of Edna Pontellier," *The Southern Review* 11 (1975): 118–28.

45 Thornton, p. 51; Cather (in Culley), p. 154; Wolff, pp. 453–54.

46 See, for instance, "Feminine Secret Societies," in Eliade, *Myths, Dreams, and Mysteries: The Encounter between Contemporary Faiths and Archaic Realities,* trans. Philip Mairet (New York: Harper Torchbooks, 1967), pp. 214–18.

47 Brontë, *Wuthering Heights,* ed. William M. Sale, Jr. (New York: Norton Critical Edition, 1972), p. 107; J.732, in *The Poems of Emily Dickinson,* ed. Thomas Johnson, 3 vols. (Cambridge: Harvard University Press, Belknap Press, 1955). Further references will be to this edition, and poem numbers will be included in the text, preceded by *J.*

48 For an essay which explores the paradoxically positive aspects of the privatized world of nineteenth-century women, see Carroll Smith-Rosenberg, "The Female World of Love and Ritual: Relations Between Women in Nineteenth-Century America," *Signs* 1 (Autumn 1975): 1–29.

49 See Veblen, *The Theory of the Leisure Class* (1899; New York: Modern Library, 1931), passim, but especially chap. 3 ("Conspicuous Leisure"), 4 ("Conspicuous Consumption"), 6 ("Pecuniary Canons of Taste"), and 7 ("Dress as an Expression of the Pecuniary Culture").

50 For a more ambivalent depiction of the American vacation hotel, see the first five chapters of Edith Wharton, *The Buccaneers* (New York: Appleton, 1938), and our discussion of Wharton's own attitude, chap. 5 of this volume, p. 129.

51 Cott, *The Bonds of Womanhood: "Woman's Sphere" in New England, 1780–1835* (New Haven: Yale University Press, 1977).

52 On "Great Time," see Eliade, *The Myth of the Eternal Return, or Cosmos and History,* trans. Willard R. Trask, Bollingen Series 46 (Princeton: Princeton University Press, 1954).

53 Although we are suggesting that "Mariequita" or "little Mary" evokes just the theological orthodoxy from which Edna will seek to flee, in a discussion of Balzac's "The Girl with the Golden Eyes," Shoshana Felman claims that "Mariquita" *[sic]* is a Spanish slang term for an effeminate man, a point which (if it has relevance here) would certainly complicate Chopin's erotic plot; see Shoshana Felman, "Rereading Femininity," *Yale French Studies* 62 (1981): 30–31.

54 Besides Chopin's overt and covert allusions to the power of Aphrodite, there are, of course, several other echoes of the Phaedra story in *The Awakening,* notably the seaside setting of much of the novel, the passion of an older married woman for a single younger man, and the suicide of the heroine.

55 Suzanne Wolkenfeld, "Edna's Suicide: The Problem of the One and the Many," in Culley, p. 220.

56 *Collected Works of Pierre Louÿs* (1896; New York: Shakespeare House, 1951), p. 178.

57 Schreiner, *The Story of an African Farm,* p. 271; Wharton, *The House of Mirth* (1905; New York: New American Library, 1964), pp. 338, 342.

58 The crucifixion imagery at the end of *The Awakening* may be subtly reinforced by the fact that, when Edna encounters Victor at the beginning of chapter 39, the young man is hammering nails into the porch: "I walked up from the wharf . . . and heard the hammering," she says.

59 D. L. Demorest, ["Structures of Imagery in *Madame Bovary*"], in the Norton Critical *Madame Bovary,* p. 280; Flaubert, letter to Louise Colet (March 3, 1852), ibid., p. 311.

60 Sartre, ["Flaubert and *Madame Bovary:* Outline of a New Method"], in Norton Critical *Madame Bovary,* p. 303; ibid., note 3.

61 See Swinburne, "The Triumph of Time," l. 257; Whitman, "Out of the Cradle Endlessly Rocking," l. 168, and "Song of Myself," ll. 452, 199–224; and Swinburne, "The

Triumph of Time," l. 265. Portions of this last poem do, however, foreshadow the denouement of *The Awakening:* disappointed in love, the speaker dreams of a suicide by drowning, and imagines himself first casting off his clothes and then being reborn in the sea:

> This woven raiment of nights and days,
>   Were it once cast off and unwound from me,
> Naked and glad would I walk in thy ways,
>   Alive and aware of thy ways and thee;
> Clear of the whole world, hidden at home,
> Clothed with the green and crowned with the foam,
> A pulse of the life of thy straits and bays,
>   A vein in the heart of the streams of the sea. [281–88]

62 For a more extensive (and slightly different) discussion of Chopin's use of Whitmanesque imagery, see Elizabeth Balkman House, *"The Awakening;* Kate Chopin's 'Endlessly Rocking' Cycle," *Ball State University Forum* 20:2 (1979): 53–58.

63 Friedrich, *The Meaning of Aphrodite* (Chicago: University of Chicago Press, 1978), p. 1.

64 Wagner, *Tannhäuser,* Paris version (1861), trans. Peggie Cochrane (London: The Decca Record Co., 1971), Act 2; Swinburne, "Laus Veneris," in *The Poetry of Swinburne,* with an intro. by Ernest Rhys (New York: Modern Library, n.d.), pp. 13, 16; Morris, "The Hill of Venus," in *The Collected Works of William Morris* with an intro. by his daughter May Morris, vol. 6, *The Earthly Paradise: A Poem IV* (London and New York: Longmans Green, 1911), pp. 295, 303; Beardsley, *Venus and Tannhäuser in Aesthetes,* pp. 37, 46.

65 Friedrich, passim, but esp. pp. 33–35, 132–48.

66 Woolf, *A Room of One's Own* (New York: Harcourt Brace, 1929), p. 69. For further discussion of Sappho's freedom, see also Woolf, "A Society," in *Monday or Tuesday* (New York: Harcourt Brace, 1921), and pp. 224–25 in this volume.

67 *Theogony,* in *The Poems of Hesiod,* trans. with intro. and comments by R. M. Frazer (Norman: University of Oklahoma Press, 1983), p. 36.

68 On Harrison and Duncan, see Jill Silverman, "Introduction to 'Andre Levinson on Isadora Duncan,' " *Ballet Review* 6:4 (1977–78): 4. Silverman notes that Harrison also "guided the young dancer through the Greek collections at the British Museum," and adds that "Harrison's . . . glorification of matriarchal structures in archaic Greece . . . undoubtedly influenced the early development of Duncan's art." On Duncan's mother and Chopin, see Elizabeth Kendall, "Before the World Began," *Ballet Review* 6:4 (1977–78): 24. For Duncan on Aphrodite, see *My Life,* pp. 113–14.

69 The passage from H. D. that we have cited here is, of course, a late one, but its celebratory tone is prefigured by the tone of a number of earlier references to the goddess; see, for instance, "Fragment Forty-one" (from *Heliodora,* 1924), with its invocation of "Aphrodite, shameless and radiant" (*Collected Poems,* p. 182), and "Songs from Cyprus" (in *Red Roses for Bronze,* 1931), with its characterization of Aphrodite as "her who nurtures, / who imperils all" (*Collected Poems,* p. 281).

70 On Woodhull's recantation, see Sachs, p. 294, quoting Woodhull's claim in 1880 that she "has been most unrighteously associated with what is known by the name of Free Love. No viler aspersion was ever uttered. No greater outrage could be inflicted on a woman."

71 "Coming, Aphrodite!" in Cather, *Youth and the Bright Medusa* (1920; New York: Vintage, 1975). Further references will be to this edition, and page numbers will be included in the text. This story also exists in a somewhat bowdlerized version which was published as "Coming, Eden Bower!" in the *Smart Set* (August 1920). For a de-

tailed study of variants between these two texts, see the appendix to *Uncle Valentine and Other Short Stories: Willa Cather's Uncollected Short Fiction, 1915–1929*, ed. Bernice Slote (Lincoln: University of Nebraska Press, 1973). Perhaps the two most significant changes are the title change and the change in the opera that Eden Bower stars in: in the *Smart Set* version, she sings Clytemnestra in Straus's *Elektra*, while in the book version she sings Aphrodite in Erlanger's *Aphrodite*, based on Louy's novel. Both changes suggest Cather's consciousness of the erotic centrality of Aphrodite in the story she really wanted to write. For further background information, see Slote's introduction to *Uncle Valentine*, pp. xxi–xxii.

72 C. Rossetti, "Eve," in *The Complete Poems of Christina Rossetti*, ed. and intro. by R. W. Crump (Baton Rouge: Louisiana State University Press, 1979), 1:156–59; D. G. Rossetti, "Eden Bower," in *The Collected Works of Dante Gabriel Rossetti* (London: Ellis and Scrutton, 1886), 1:308–14.

73 D. G. Rossetti, p. 308.

74 On Cather's sexual ambivalence, see James Woodress, *Willa Cather* (New York: Pegasus, 1970), pp. 86–87, 91–94, and Sharon O'Brien, *Willa Cather: Emerging Voice* (New York: Oxford University Press, 1987), chap. 6, "Divine Femininity and Unnatural Love," pp. 117–46.

75 Lowell, "Venus Transiens," in *The Complete Poetical Works of Amy Lowell*, with an intro. by Louis Untermeyer (Cambridge: Houghton Mifflin, The Riverside Press, 1955), p. 210.

76 Rukeyser, "The Birth of Venus," in Rukeyser, *Body of Waking* (New York: Harper & Row, 1958), p. 44.

77 Sexton, *Words for Dr. Y.*, ed. Linda Gray Sexton (Boston: Houghton Mifflin, 1978), pp. 38–39.

78 Woolf, *Mrs. Dalloway* (1925; New York: Harcourt Brace, 1953), p. 47.

79 For a characterization of female desire that Lawrence also very likely uses to represent what he regards as the inappropriate clitoral orgasm, see, for instance, *The Rainbow*, chap. 11; *Women in Love*, chap. 24; and especially *The Plumed Serpent*, chap. 26. Note, for example, "The throes of Aphrodite of the foam . . . The beak-like friction of Aphrodite of the foam, the friction which flares out in circles of phosphorescent ecstasy" that Lawrence censures in chap. 26 of *PS*.

80 See "Female Coercion," "Volcanic Venus," and "What Does She Want?", in *The Complete Poems of D. H. Lawrence*, ed. Vivian de Sola Pinto and F. Warren Roberts (New York: Penguin, 1977), pp. 538–39.

81 Stevens, "The Paltry Nude Starts on a Spring Voyage," in *The Collected Poems of Wallace Stevens* (New York: Alfred A. Knopf, 1955), pp. 5–6.

Chapter 4

EPIGRAPHS: Lubbock, *Portrait of Edith Wharton* (New York and London: Appleton-Century, 1947), pp. 1–2; James, quoted in R. W. B. Lewis, *Edith Wharton: A Biography* (New York: Harper & Row, 1975); Lubbock, p. 11; Wharton, quoted in Lewis, p. 238.

1 James is quoted by Lewis, pp. 247 and 320; on p. 323, the biographer comments that "these tempestuous periods obviously gave James's rhetorical soul a great deal of pleasure; yet even allowing for James's love of hyperbole, his image of being seized and carried off in the talons of some monstrous female bird of prey might well carry for the post–Freudian (or even post–Jamesian) reader a suggestion of something bordering on sexual panic."

2 "Correct pictures": Burton Rascoe in 1922, comparing Wharton with Willa Cather (who "is a poet in her intensity and . . . Wharton is not"); quoted in Judith Fryer,

Felicitous Space: The Imaginative Structures of Edith Wharton and Willa Cather (Chapel Hill and London: University of North Carolina Press, 1986), p. 368, n. 27. "A limitation of heart": Lionel Trilling, "The Morality of Inertia," in *Great Moral Dilemmas*, ed. Robert M. MacIver (New York: Harper & Row, 1956), p. 39; later in this essay, an attack on *Ethan Frome*, Trilling speaks of Wharton's "cold hard literary will."

3 Wharton and Ogden Codman, Jr., *The Decoration of Houses* (New York: Scribner's, 1897), p. xxii. Further references will be to this edition, and page numbers, preceded by the citation *Dec.*, will appear in the text.

4 Wharton, *A Motor-Flight Through France* (New York: Scribner's, 1908), p. 1. Further references will be to this edition, and page numbers, preceded by the citation *M-F*, will appear in the text.

5 Lubbock, pp. 5–6.

6 See Ammons, *Edith Wharton's Argument with America* (Athens: University of Georgia Press, 1980), passim, but esp. p. ix: "Her fiction records her public argument with America on the issue of freedom for women over more than three decades" and p. 3, on "her argument with American optimism."

7 "Good Americans": Fryer, p. 175, quoting Wharton, "Gardening in France," n.d., p. 1, Wharton Archives, Beinecke Library, Yale University, New Haven, Conn. "A houseful": Lubbock, pp. 49–50.

8 Wharton, *French Ways and Their Meaning* (New York: Appleton, 1919), p. x. Further references will be to this edition, and page numbers, preceded by the citation *FW*, will appear in the text.

9 Both remarks quoted in Lewis, pp. 279 and 292.

10 Quoted in Lewis, pp. 204, 224.

11 See Lewis, p. 262.

12 James, *The Bostonians*, ed. Alfred Habegger (1886; Indianapolis: Bobbs-Merrill, 1976), p. 318.

13 Wharton, *A Backward Glance* (New York: Scribner's, 1934), p. 60. Further references will be to this edition, and page numbers, preceded by the citation *BG*, will appear in the text.

14 Quoted in Lewis, p. 486.

15 Lubbock, p. 187.

16 Quoted in Lewis, p. 483.

17 Quoted in Lewis, p. 444.

18 See Wharton, *Fast and Loose: A Novelette by David Olivieri*, ed. and with an intro. by Viola Hopkins Winner (Charlottesville: University Press of Virginia, 1977), passim. Further references will be to this edition, and page numbers, preceded by the citation *FL*, will appear in the text.

19 "Xingu," in *The Collected Short Stories of Edith Wharton*, 2 vols., ed. and with an intro. by R. W. B. Lewis (New York: Scribner's, 1968), 2:212. Further references to Wharton's short stories will be to these volumes, and page numbers, preceded by the citations *S* I or *S* II, will appear in the text.

20 Other Wharton stories which satirize scribbling women or intellectual women include "The Pelican" (about a female platform speaker who is a Verena Tarrant-like figure), "The Angel at the Grave" (for a discussion of which, see *The War of the Words*, chap. 4), "April Showers," and "Expiation," all included in *The Collected Short Stories*.

21 Lubbock, pp. 27–28.

22 Quoted in Lewis, p. 132.

23 See Virginia Woolf, *Three Guineas* (New York: Harcourt, 1938), passim.

24 Wharton, *The Age of Innocence* (1920; New York: Scribner's, 1968), p. 305. Further references will be to this edition, and page numbers, preceded where necessary by the citation *AI*, will appear in the text.

25 Quoted in Lewis, p. 136.

26 Wharton, *The House of Mirth* (1905; New York: Signet, 1964), p. 313. Further references will be to this edition, and page numbers, preceded where necessary by the citation *HM*, will appear in the text.

27 In *A Backward Glance*, for instance, Wharton mentions her early interest in "the wonder-world of nineteenth century science," specifying her familiarity with "Wallace's 'Darwin and Darwinism', and 'The Origin of Species'," as well as with the works of "Huxley, Herbert Spencer, Romanes, Haeckel, Westermarck, and the various popular exponents of the great evolutionary movement" (94). Even her recently published love letters to Morton Fullerton are dotted with references to reading of this sort; see Alan Gribben, " 'The Heart Is Insatiable': A Selection from Edith Wharton's Letters to Morton Fullerton, 1907–1915," *The Library Chronicle of the University of Texas* 31 (1985): 7–71; we are grateful to Catherine Bancroft for bringing this publication to our attention.

28 Veblen, *The Theory of the Leisure Class*, p. 83.

29 Wharton's vision is often so bleak that even her admirer Louis Auchincloss has commented about *The House of Mirth* that society in this novel "is a bit too harshly drawn. I cannot believe that some member of Lily's family would not have come forward to help her in the end or that she would not have found a man to love her instead of a prosey prig" ("Afterword" to the Signet edition, p. 348).

30 Lewis, p. 262.

31 Lubbock, p. 8.

32 Veblen, pp. 167–87.

33 Maud Howe Elliott, "a daughter of Newport's literary patroness, Julia Ward Howe," quoted (and characterized) in Louis Auchincloss, *Edith Wharton: A Woman in Her Time* (New York: Viking, 1971), p. 12.

34 Quoted in Auchincloss, *Edith Wharton*, pp. 48–49. Lewis reports an incident which also sheds considerable light on Teddy's character (and his wife's dilemma): "Once at Lenox, walking with Walter Maynard a few paces behind Edith, he pointed ahead and said: 'Look at that waist! No one would ever guess that she had written a line of poetry in her life' " (Lewis, p. 272).

35 Emphasizing both her family's hostility to authorship and her own nineteenth-century origins, Wharton adds that "In the eyes of our provincial society authorship was still regarded as something between a black art and a form of manual labour. My father and mother and their friends were only one generation away from Sir Walter Scott, who thought it necessary to drape his literary identity in countless clumsy subterfuges, and almost contemporary with the Brontës, who shrank in agony from being suspected of successful novel-writing" (*BG*, 68–69).

36 For Wharton's brilliant account of her childhood habit of "making up," see *BG*, 32–39, 42–43.

37 Lewis, p. 26; Lewis also notes, later, that Fullerton "addressed her at times as *'Cher ami'* " and that James pointed to "a certain masculinity, a toughness of mind, in the very texture of" *The Custom of the Country* (Lewis, p. 350).

38 Quoted in Lewis, p. 45.

39 Quoted in Lewis, p. 70.

40 James, "The Velvet Glove," in *The Complete Tales of Henry James*, 12:1903–10, ed. and with an intro. by Leon Edel (Philadelphia: Lippincott, 1964), pp. 259, 265. Citing Leon Edel, R. W. B. Lewis agrees that the story is "packed with echoes of Edith Wharton" and that there is "a note of hostility" in it, "as though James were warning Edith Wharton to confine herself to her lavish social existence and not to poach on his literary grounds." But he adds that Wharton herself "rejoic[ed] in the story and prais[ed] it" (Lewis, pp. 254–55). For support of the last point, see *BG*, pp. 308–09.

41 Lewis, p. 83.
42 Wharton, *Summer* (1917; New York: Perennial, 1979), p. 235. Further references will
    be to this edition, and page numbers, preceded where necessary by the citation *S*, will
    appear in the text.
43 Included in *An Olive Schreiner Reader: Writings on Women and South Africa*, pp. 107–
    08.
44 See, for instance, Cynthia Griffin Wolff, *A Feast of Words: The Triumph of Edith Whar-*
    ton (New York: Oxford University Press, 1977), pp. 82–84, and Ammons, pp. 10–
    12.
45 Veblen, p. 205.
46 Wharton, *The Writing of Fiction* (1925; New York: Octagon, 1966), p. 89.
47 Eccles. 7:4; Matt. 6:28; Luke 12:27.
48 Both Wolff and Fryer associate Lily Bart with art nouveau lilies. Wolff connects
    Wharton's heroine with the "repeated floral motif" of art nouveau, noting that "there
    is a latent sexuality in the art nouveau woman," and mentioning Loie Fuller's "Lily
    Dance" (pp. 114–15). Fryer also suggests the links between Lily Bart, "the symbolic
    Woman of the American Renaissance murals, the decorative woman of Art Nouveau
    [and] Loie Fuller's 'lily' " (p. 77).
49 Veblen, p. 362.
50 Ammons argues that Lily is "blotted out" because "she refuses to marry, an action
    that not only makes her useless to the society Wharton portrays, but also, and for the
    reasons Gilman and Veblen outline, threatening" (p. 30). But Wharton's analysis seems
    to us to be subtler than this critic realizes: Lily's only "refusals" are unconscious ones,
    while the pathos of the novel arises from her conscious *complicity* in (rather than
    rebellion against) her own commodification.
51 For a discussion of other contemporary fictional heroines to whom Wharton may be
    intertextually alluding, see Elaine Showalter, "The Death of the Lady (Novelist):
    Wharton's *House of Mirth*, in *New Critical Perspectives on Edith Wharton*, ed. Harold
    Bloom (New York: Chelsea House Press, 1986), pp. 145–46.
52 Quite early in the book we are told that, after Lily's bankrupt father has died, her
    impoverished mother "studied" the girl's beauty "with a kind of passion, as though it
    were some weapon she had slowly fashioned for her vengeance" (*HM*, 37).
53 Wharton might here be elaborating on Veblen's claim that the "servant or wife should
    not only perform certain offices and show a servile disposition but it is quite as im-
    perative that they should show an acquired facility in the tactics of subservience—
    a trained conformity to the canons of effectual and conspicuous subservience" (p.
    60).
54 See Austen, *Northanger Abbey*, chap. 10, in which Henry Tilney laughingly tells Cath-
    erine Morland that, in matrimony as in dancing, "man has the advantage of choice,
    woman only the power of refusal."
55 Ammons argues that the hallucinatory infant gives an optimistic cast to Wharton's
    conclusion: "In the arms of the ornamental, leisure-class Lily lies the working-class
    infant female, whose vitality succors the dying woman. In that union of the leisure
    and working classes lies a new hope" (p. 43). Similarly, Showalter sees the baby hal-
    lucination positively, as a sign of "solidarity and community" (p. 152). But consider-
    ing the bleak skepticism of the plot Wharton has constructed here, there is little
    reason to interpret Lily's imagining of Nettie's baby as anything but an ironic epi-
    phany of this heroine's own, immitigable loss.
56 See *HM*, p. 174, in which the narrator, speaking of the way in which Gerty's hopes
    for a love relationship with Selden are dashed by Lily's "self-betrayal," comments that
    "The mortal maid on the shore is helpless against the siren who loves her prey"; what

Wharton suggests, at the same time, is that the siren may herself be rendered "helpless" by her love for "her prey."

57 Showalter, pp. 152–53; although we applaud this insight, we do not entirely agree with Showalter that "Lily dies—the lady dies—so that [women like Gerty Farish and Nettie Struther] may live and grow" (p. 153). On the contrary, we are trying to demonstrate that, in the Veblenesque society Wharton explores, such women, though admirable, are no more potentially redemptive (for other women) than Lily herself is.

58 See Ammons, pp. 27–28.

59 See *An Olive Schreiner Reader,* p. 63.

60 *An Olive Schreiner Reader,* pp. 87, 94, 99.

61 Veblen, pp. 188, 22.

62 Veblen, p. 42.

63 Dimock, "Debasing Exchange: Edith Wharton's *The House of Mirth,*" in Bloom, *Edith Wharton,* p. 130. For a somewhat similar discussion—in this case, an analysis of *The House of Mirth* as a "stock market allegory"—see Wayne H. Westbrook, "Lily-Bartering on the New York Social Exchange in *The House of Mirth,*" *Ball State University Forum* 20:2 (1979): 59–64.

64 See Veblen: "woman even comes to serve as a unit of value" (p. 54).

65 On Bertha as Jane's double in *Jane Eyre,* see Gilbert and Gubar, *The Madwoman in the Attic,* pp. 336–71.

66 For another, slightly different Wharton exploration of a woman's serial polygamy, see "The Other Two," whose heroine triumphantly serves tea to her present husband and her two former husbands, all the time "diffusing about her a sense of ease and familiarity in which the situation lost its grotesqueness" (*S* I, 396).

67 Wharton *The Custom of the Country* (New York: Scribner's, 1913), pp. 79–80. Further references will be to this edition, and page numbers, preceded where necessary by the citation *CC,* will be included in the text.

68 For a discussion of the supernatural (and *fatale*) connotations of the name "Undine," and of Wharton's familiarity with Friedrich de La Motte-Fouqué's novella *Undine* (1811), see Richard H. Lawson, "Undine," in Bloom, *Edith Wharton,* pp. 29–38.

69 At the same time, however, in the course of her portrait of May, Wharton offers an incisive analysis of the way in which costume functions in this period even for apparently indifferent American women. Contemplating his wife, Archer is "struck again by the religious reverence of even the most unworldly American women for the social advantages of dress." And he adds, " 'It's their armor . . . their defense against the unknown, and their defiance of it' " (*AI,* p. 197).

70 On this "slip," see Lewis, p. 430.

71 Wharton, *The Fruit of the Tree* (New York: Scribner's, 1907), p. 281; Ammons contextualizes this interestingly, p. 52.

72 See Veblen, p. 205: "The outcome of the [requirements of pecuniary reputability] is a strengthening of the general conservative attitude of the community."

73 On the anthropological rhetoric of *The Age of Innocence,* see, among others, Ammons, pp. 143–44, and Fryer, pp. 130–42, esp. Fryer's point that Ellen Olenska "is what anthropologist Mary Douglas would call a 'polluting person,' who is always in the wrong. She has 'simply crossed some line which should not have been crossed and this displacement unleashes danger for someone' " (pp. 138–39).

74 Quoted in Lewis, p. 155.

75 Lewis suggests that Wharton "changed Archer's first name, just before publication, from Langdon to Newland to bring it closer to her own middle name, Newbold" (p. 431).

76 For a somewhat different discussion of the echoes of *Portrait of a Lady* in *The Age of Innocence*, see Wolff, pp. 312–14.

77 Lubbock, pp. 228–29.

78 Auchincloss, "Afterword," *HM*, p. 348.

79 See, for instance, Ammons, p. 15: Wharton "had to move beyond the misandry that repeatedly distorted her work." We want to argue, however, that Wharton's work was in fact strengthened by her sardonic (and often vengeful) portrayals of the nomen—fools or knaves—produced by the culture she so savagely critiqued.

80 Quoted in Auchincloss, *Edith Wharton*, p. 88; see also Lewis, pp. 306–07: throughout most of the Wharton marriage, Teddy's "job in life had gradually become that of managing his wife's large estate and overseeing the many needs of The Mount," but by the summer of 1911 the "greater part of that function was . . . about to be taken from him. . . . Little wonder that a few months before, Dr. Dupré, an expert in nervous diseases, had predicted grimly that M. Wharton would end by killing himself."

81 Lewis records Wharton's crucial role in liberating Fullerton from blackmail by a former mistress of his; see pp. 263–64.

82 Besides covertly assisting James by engineering a fake "advance" on royalties for his last novel, Wharton tried more openly to help him by arranging a financial gift for his seventieth birthday, a gift he angrily refused; see Lewis, pp. 339–43.

83 Quoted in Lewis, p. 131.

84 Quoted in Lewis, p. 237.

85 *An Olive Schreiner Reader*, p. 99.

86 "A calamity": quoted in Lubbock, p. 148; see also Wharton's statement, quoted by Lewis on p. 252, that "I wonder, among all the tangles of this mortal coil, which one contains tighter knots to undo, and consequently suggests more tugging and pain, and diversified elements of misery, than the marriage tie."

87 Quoted in Lewis, p. 396.

88 Ammons argues (pp. 62–63) that the recurrent pattern of sevens gives a kind of fairy-tale, or more accurately *anti*fairy-tale, quality to *Ethan Frome*.

89 In *Edith Wharton: Orphancy and Survival* (New York: Praeger, 1984), Wendy Gimbel points out that "In *Ethan Frome*, the displaced sensibility ends paralyzed in the frozen farmhouse of a Terrible Mother" (p. 166).

90 Wharton, *Ethan Frome* (New York: Scribner's, 1911), p. 11.

91 For a more detailed reading of this aspect of *Summer*, see Sandra M. Gilbert, " 'Life's Empty Pack': Notes Toward a Literary Daughteronomy," *Critical Inquiry* 11 (Spring 1985): 355–84.

92 Quoted in Lewis, p. 249.

93 Lewis, p. 238.

94 Lewis, p. 238.

95 Quoted in Lubbock, p. 20.

96 Lewis, p. 421.

97 Lewis, p. 420.

98 Lewis, p. 420.

99 See Lewis, p. 342; also Wolff, p. 226: Wharton "knew with justified certainty" that her private papers would eventually become the basis upon which a biography would be built. . . . [and] she did prepare a packet of papers labeled 'for my biographer.' It contained a variety of letters, many from doctors, and it constituted an almost formal brief defending her decision to obtain the divorce."

100 Lewis, p. 203; Lewis comments that "The Life Apart" was Wharton's "rendering of the phrase from Ronsard which was currently haunting her and which she added here in parentheses: *'L'Ame Close'* " (p. 203). Wolff notes that "In view of [Wharton's]

unusual caution, it is interesting that she did not destroy either the Love Diary or the Beatrice Palmato fragment. . . . Something in her seems to have whispered: let them discover that I, too, have lived" (p. 226).

101 Quoted in Lewis, p. 222.

102 On Wharton's subversive and at least covertly feminist use of the ghost story, see Allan Gardner Smith, "Edith Wharton and the Ghost Story," in Bloom, pp. 89–97,

103 Quoted in "An Autobiographical Postscript" to *The Ghost Stories of Edith Wharton* (New York: Scribner's, 1985), p. 276.

104 See note 86 above.

105 In *A Backward Glance* Wharton recalls James's parodic improvisations on English genealogies, improvisations that may well have inspired this passage in "Mr. Jones": motoring through the countryside around Lamb House, James "would murmur [quaint names] over and over to himself in a low chant, sometimes creating characters to fit them, and sometimes whole families, with their domestic complications and matrimonial alliances, such as the Dymmes of Dymchurch, one of whom married a Sparkle, and was the mother of little Scintilla Dymme-Sparkle, subject of much mirth and many anecdotes" (249).

106 It is interesting, here, to consider that "Jones" was Wharton's "maiden" (that is, her patrilineal) name, and that, as a long-time admirer of the works of Poe, she had always been fascinated by the trope of "purloined letters"; see, for instance, her use of letters not only in *The House of Mirth* (where Bertha Dorset's letters are crucial to the plot) but also in such a novella as *The Touchstone* and such stories as "The Muse's Tragedy" (1899), "The Letter" (1904), "The Letters" (1910), and "Pomegranate Seed" (1936).

107 To be sure, the first wife in "Pomegranate Seed" is not presented as especially sympathetic: Wharton characterizes her as a "distant, self-centered woman" (*S* II, 763).

108 See *The War of the Words*, chap. 4.

109 Wharton, *Madame de Trêymes and Others: Four Novelettes by Edith Wharton* (New York: Scribner's, 1970), p. 61.

110 See Alfred Lord Tennyson, "Lancelot and Elaine," in *The Idylls of the King, The Complete Poetical Works of Tennyson* (Boston: Houghton Mifflin, 1898), p. 398, lines 1268–69. For an exploration from a very different perspective of the "unsayability" or undecidability associated with Lily Bart, see Frances L. Restuccia, "The Name of the Lily: Edith Wharton's Feminism(s)," *Contemporary Literature* 28 (Summer 1987): 223–38.

111 Quoted in Sachs, p. 135.

112 See Lewis, p. 257.

113 Wharton, *Artemis to Actaeon* (New York: Scribner's, 1909), p. 59.

114 For the complete text of "Terminus," see Lewis, p. 259; for Wharton's own discussion of her (and James's) admiration for Whitman, see *BG*, p. 186.

115 Lewis suggests that Wharton entitled this poem "Terminus" in order "to indicate both that the experience occurred in a station hotel and that it marked a temporary end" to her relationship with Fullerton (p. 259).

116 For the complete (albeit fragmentary) text of "Beatrice Palmato," see Lewis, pp. 544–48. Although most of Wharton's erotic "confessions" were obliquely hinted at or transcribed in secret documents, one of her more public (though still relatively guarded) statements was her expression of admiration for Isadora Duncan in *A Backward Glance:* associating the "joyful *abandon*" of the Aphroditean dancer with "Keats's glorious bacchanal" (p. 322), she wrote, "That first sight of Isadora's dancing was a white milestone to me," adding that it evoked for her the luminous, springtime moment *("Es war der Lenz!")* when Siegmund and Sieglinde first make love in Wagner's "Walkyrie" (*sic;* p. 322).

117 See Lewis, p. 548.
118 Lewis, p. 548. Interestingly, Wharton's last novel, *The Buccaneers,* was to depend on a comparable (though less sensational) liberation of female desire. Summarizing the "plot" outline of that work, Cynthia Griffin Wolff reports that this last Wharton fiction was to end with a young American woman breaking free of her marriage to an oppressive English aristocrat and achieving erotic fulfillment with the man she had illicitly and adulterously loved. As Wharton mused on the ending she had already contrived, Wolff notes, she composed "the last lines in her personal diary," lines in which this staid and conservative writer wrote her final ideas about writing. The beginning of a novel was, said Wharton, like "A ride through a spring wood," the middle like "The Gobi Desert," and the end like "A night with a lover." The consummation devoutly to be wished, the illicit ending toward which she wished her career would tend (though she would not let it tend), was obviously that unsayable "night with a lover."
119 Lewis, p. 544.
120 See "Pomegranate Seed," *S* II, pp. 785–87.
121 On the "exorcism" of Ellen Olenska, see Ammons, pp. 143–45, and Fryer, pp. 138–39.
122 James, *The Portrait of a Lady,* ed. Leon Edel (Boston: Riverside, 1963), p. 353.
123 See Fryer, p. 127. In addition, Lewis notes that Archer finds himself below Ellen's window in 1907, just "the moment when Edith first settled in Paris," and that he "reminds himself . . . that he is only fifty-seven years old—Edith Wharton's exact age in 1919 when she wrote the larger part of the novel" (p. 432).

Chapter 5

EPIGRAPHS: Marvell, "The Garden" (1681) in *The Poems and Letters of Andrew Marvell,* ed. H. M. Margoliouth, 3d ed. rev. Pierre Legios with E. E. Duncan Jones (Oxford: Oxford University Press, 1971), 1:53; Finch, "The Introduction" (1689) in *The Poems of Anne Countess of Winchilsea,* ed. Myra Reynolds, Decennial Publications of the University of Chicago, 2d series, vol. 5 (Chicago: University of Chicago Press, 1903), p. 6; Beard, *On Understanding Women* (1931) in *Mary Ritter Beard: A Sourcebook,* ed. Ann J. Lane (New York: Schocken Books, 1977), p. 139.

 1 Cather, "My First Novels [There Were Two]" in *On Writing,* with a foreword by Stephen Tennant (New York: Alfred A. Knopf, 1949), p. 91. Further references to the essays in this edition will appear in the text, with page numbers preceded by the citation *OW.* The motives behind Cather's later decision to relegate *Alexander's Bridge* to the third volume of the complete edition of her works and thereby to identify it with the early *April Twilights* are analyzed by James Woodress in *Willa Cather: A Literary Life* (Lincoln: University of Nebraska Press, 1987), p. 222.
 2 Gelfant's ground-breaking essay "The Forgotten Reaping-Hook: Sex in *My Antonia*" (1971) is reprinted in Gelfant, *Women Writing in America: Voices in Collage* (Hanover and London: University Press of New England, 1984), pp. 95–116. Throughout this chapter we are indebeted to the pioneering biographical work done by Sharon O'Brien, whose *Willa Cather: The Emerging Voice* established both the literary and the psychological contexts of our discussion (for O'Brien's analysis of Cather's lesbianism, see especially pp. 127–41); Fetterley, "*My Ántonia,* Jim Burden, and the Dilemma of the Lesbian Writer," in *Gender Studies: New Directions in Feminist Criticism,* ed. Judith Spector (Bowling Green, Ohio: Bowling Green State University Popular Press, 1986), pp. 43–59. In his biography, Woodress disagrees with O'Brien's and Fetterley's characterization of Cather as a lesbian and argues instead that she yearns "for the pre-puberty years of sexual innocence," a point that is at least partially qualified by his

argument that "Her greatest failing as an artist is her inability to depict heterosexual adult relationships affirmatively" (pp. 127 and 299). In "Cather and Her Friends," however, Woodress uses Lillian Faderman's definition of lesbianism to characterize Cather's relationship with Isabelle McClung; see *Critical Essays on Willa Cather*, ed. John J. Murphy (Boston: G. K. Hall, 1984), pp. 81–95.

3 *The World and the Parish: Willa Cather's Articles and Reviews, 1893–1902*, ed. William M. Curtin, 2 vols. (Lincoln: University of Nebraska Press, 1970), 2:698. Further page references will be to these volumes, and page numbers, preceded by the citation *WP* 1 or *WP* 2, will appear in the text.

4 Although, of course, *The Awakening* itself was not a commercial success during Chopin's life, Cather frequently described the woman writer as a commercially profitable and prolific artist, while she saw the male artist as rarefied and marginalized. See, for example, our discussion of "The Willing Muse" (1907) in *The War of the Words*, pp. 174–76.

5 Curtin uses as an epigraph to his *World and the Parish* Cather's recollection of Jewett's most important advice: "One of the few really helpful words I ever heard from an older writer, I had from Sarah Orne Jewett when she said to me: 'Of course, one day you will write about your own country. In the meantime, get all you can. One must know the world *so well* before one can know the parish' ": see the 1922 "Preface" to *Alexander's Bridge* (Boston: Houghton Mifflin, 1922), p. vii. For a general discussion of the common "conservatism" of Wharton and Cather, see Lillian D. Bloom, "On Daring to Look Back with Wharton and Cather," a review essay in *Novel* 10 : 2 (Winter 1977): 167–78.

6 "Willa Cather Talks of Work" in the *Philadelphia Record*, New York, August 9 (1913), reprinted in *The Kingdom of Art: Willa Cather's first Principles and Critical Statements, 1893–1896*, ed. Bernice Slote (Lincoln: University of Nebraska Press, 1966), p. 448. Further references will be to this edition, and page numbers, preceded by the citation *KA*, will appear in the text. The phrase "the end of everything" captures both the positive feelings Cather articulated about the prairie and the negative sense upon which she also elaborated.

7 *Lincoln State Journal*, Nov. 2, 1921, p. 7, quoted in O'Brien, p. 68.

8 See O'Brien, pp. 43–44 and 93.

9 Ibid., p. 93.

10 Woodress, p. 139. Woodress also examines Cather's 1912 romantic attachment to a Mexican boy named Julio (pp. 6–8).

11 Michel Gervaud, "Willa Cather and France: Elective Affinities," *The Art of Willa Cather*, ed. Bernice Slote and Virginia Faulkner (Lincoln: University of Nebraska Press, 1974), pp. 65–83.

12 Cather, "The Novel Démeublé," *Not Under Forty* (New York: Alfred A. Knopf, 1936), p. 51. Further references to essays in this edition will appear in the text, with page numbers preceded by the citation *NUF*.

13 Bernice Slote explains that Cather had "three not wholly compatible drives: one was to win out with a career, to be a success in a world of mostly men, in a time when women rarely tried and even more rarely succeeded; another was to be the artist, as great an artist as she might be; and a third was to be a Virginia lady like her mother" ("Introduction," Willa Cather, *Uncle Valentine and Other Short Stories*, ed. Slote, pp. xiii–xiv). In addition, Patricia Lee Yongue describes Cather's "preference for brilliant velvets and satins associated with theatrical and aristocratic costume"; see "Willa Cather's Aristocrats (Part I)," *Southern Humanities Review* 14:1 (Winter 1980): 49.

14 See Baym, *Woman's Fiction: A Guide to Novels by and about Women in America, 1820– 1870* (Ithaca: Cornell University Press, 1978), passim.

15 Cather, *My Ántonia* (Boston: Houghton Mifflin, 1970), p. 211. Further references will

be to this edition and page numbers will appear in the text, preceded by the citation *MA* when necessary.

16 Cather, *One of Ours* (New York: Alfred A. Knopf, 1940), p. 134. Further references will be to this edition, and page numbers will appear in the text. Enid's temperance activism recalls Carry Nation's ax-wielding in Kansas saloons as well as the militancy of the 1880 Kansas Woman's Christian Temperance Union, which put in place the first state prohibition amendment.

17 Cather, *The Old Beauty and Other Stories* (New York: Random House, 1976). Further references will be to this edition, and page numbers, preceded when necessary by the citation *OB*, will appear in the text.

18 See our discussion of Hawthorne's reaction against the feminization of American culture in *The War of the Words*, pp. 142–46.

19 *Cather's Collected Short Fiction*, ed. Virginia Faulkner with an intro. by Mildred R. Bennett (Lincoln: University of Nebraska Press, 1970), p. 152. Further references to this story will be to this edition, and page numbers will appear in the text.

20 Cather's admission about her early imitation of Henry James appears in Flora Merrill, "A Short Story Course Can Only Delay, It Cannot Kill an Artist, Says Willa Cather," *New York World*, April 19, 1925, Section 3, p. 1.

21 Elizabeth Sergeant, *Willa Cather: A Memoir* (Lincoln: University of Nebraska Press, 1963), pp. 68–69. O'Brien discusses the "dubious pleasure" Cather must have had reading James's condescending reply (pp. 308–09), but Woodress claims it gave her "a keen satisfaction" (p. 180). Cather's critique of the "Advanced American Woman" sounds very much like the attack on Edith Wharton by Paul Bourget that we discussed in chap. 4 of this volume.

22 Woodress, pp. 158–63.

23 O'Brien, p. 148.

24 Sergeant, p. 33.

25 O'Brien discusses this comment in the context of Cather's later remark, "Well, of course there are 'boys' books' and 'girls' books,' but I prefer the books that are for both (WP 1, 337)," p. 84. See "Tommy, the Unsentimental," "The Enchanted Fluff," "On the Gulls' Road," and "The Treasure of Far Island" in Cather, *Collected Short Fiction*, pp. 473–82, 69–78, 79–94, and 265–82. Cather chose as narrator "the boy" Niel Herbert in *A Lost Lady* because she wanted to "produce the effect [the main female character] had on me" (Woodress, p. 340).

26 Quoted by T. J. Jackson Lears, *No Place of Grace: Antimodernism and the Transformation of American Culture, 1880–1920* (New York: Pantheon Books, 1981), p. 104. It is worth noting that one of Cather's most prominent female contemporaries—both an anthropologist and a fiction writer—also internalized ideas about women's authorial inferiority. Mary Austin, in whose house Cather composed parts of *Death Comes for the Archbishop*, claimed that "Poetry is a man's game. Women are only good at it by a special dispensation as men are occasionally good at millinery"; see Austen, *The American Rhythm: Studies and Reexpressions of Amerindian Songs* (1923; Boston: Houghton Mifflin, 1930), p. 12.

27 See, for example, Cather's discussion of "Miss Brontë who kept her sentimentality under control" and "Jane Austen who certainly had more common sense than any of them and was in some respects the greatest of them all" in *KA*, 409. Woodress summarizes a 1931 letter about Woolf, in which Cather observes that Woolf had fairly stated the disadvantages of being a woman writer (p. 423). In addition, he discusses Cather's dislike of Amy Lowell (p. 239).

28 Millay, "Childhood Is the Kingdom Where Nobody Dies," *Collected Poems* (New York: Harper & Row, 1956), p. 286.

29 Although O'Brien claims that Cather moved "from male identification to female

identification" (p. 425), we are arguing that both the male and female literary traditions she inherited continued to influence her fiction.

30 Latrobe Carroll, "Willa Sibert Cather," *The Bookman* 53 (May 1921): 212, and cited in O'Brien, p. 73.

31 Cather, *The Song of the Lark* (1915; Lincoln: University of Nebraska Press, 1978), p. 301. Further references will be to this edition, and page numbers will appear in the text. On the female *kunstlerroman*, see Ellen Moers, *Literary Women* (New York: Doubleday, 1976), pp. 257–60; and Linda Huff, *A Portrait of the Artist as a Young Woman* (New York: Ungar, 1983), pp. 81–102. On Cather's advertising wishes, see Woodress, p. 274.

32 According to Woodress, despite the authorial attributions on the title page of these two works, Cather substantially wrote both texts: pp. 194–95 and 248–50. See also L. Brent Bohlke, "Willa Cather and *The Life of Mary Baker G. Eddy*," *American Literature* 54:2 (May 1982): 288–94.

33 Tocqueville, "Fortnight in the Wilderness," in George Wilson Pierson, *Tocqueville and Beaumont in America* (New York: Oxford University Press, 1938), p. 245.

34 See Barker-Benfield, *The Horrors of the Half-Known Life*, p. 6, for a discussion of Lawrence's *Studies in Classic American Literature* and Garland's *Other Main Travelled Roads*.

35 Beer, *The Mauve Decade: American Life at the End of the 19th Century* (New York: Alfred A. Knopf, 1926), pp. 93–94.

36 Lewis, *The American Adam: Innocence, Tregedy and Tradition in the Nineteenth Century* (Chicago: University of Chicago Press, 1955), pp. 1 and 5; Fiedler, *Love and Death in the American Novel* (New York: Stein and Day, 1966), pp. 211, 210, and 339.

37 Lewis, *American Adam*, pp. 101 and 129; Fielder, "Come Back to the Raft Ag'in, Huck Honey!" in Fielder, *An End to Innocence: Essays on Culture and Politics* (Boston: The Beacon Press, 1955), p. 144.

38 Smith, *Virgin Land: The American West as Symbol and Myth* (Cambridge: Harvard University Press, 1950), p. 254.

39 Cunliffe, "The Two or More Worlds of Willa Cather," in *The Art of Willa Cather*, ed. Slote and Faulkner, especially pp. 33–34.

40 Smith, p. 260.

41 For a discussion of the similarity of Cather's and Cooper's response to the American frontier, see John J. Murphy, "Cooper, Cather, and the Downward Path to Progress," *Prairie Schooner* 55:1–2 (Spring-Summer 1981): 168–84.

42 We are grateful to Richard Brodhead for sharing part of an essay on regionalism that will appear in the *Cambridge History of American Literature*, ed. Sacvan Bercovitch, p. 24 of the typescript. For a discussion of the centrality of women writers in the regionalist tradition, see Josephine Donovan's examination of the works of Annie Fields, Harriet Beecher Stowe, Rose Terry Cooke, Elizabeth Stuart Phelps, Sarah Orne Jewett, and Mary E. Wilkins Freeman in Donovan, *New England Local Color Literature: A Woman's Tradition* (New York: Frederick Ungar, 1983).

43 Turner, "The Significance of the Frontier in American History," in Turner, *The Frontier in American History*, with a foreword by Ray Allen Billington (Huntington, N.Y.: Robert E. Krieger, 1976), p. 4

44 Cather, *O Pioneers!* (Boston: Houghton Mifflin, 1941), p. 15. Further references will be to this edition, and page numbers will appear in the text, preceded by the citation *OP* when necessary.

45 Jim also tries to see the Burdens' farmhands as desperado cowboys and similarly fails to keep himself from realizing that they are, in fact, "the sort of men who never get on, somehow, or do anything but work hard for a dollar or two a day" (p. 68).

46 Turner, p. 11.

47 Welty, "The House of Willa Cather," in *The Eye of the Story: Selected Essays and Reviews*

(New York: Vintage Books, 1979), p. 47. Also see Dorothy Van Ghent, *Willa Cather* (Minneapolis: University of Minnesota Press, 1964), especially pp. 8–9.

48 Cathy Luchetti in collaboration with Carol Olwell, *Women of the West* (St. George, Utah: Antelope Island Press, 1982), pp. 31 and 35. See also the description of the "more equal footing" of pioneer spouses in Joanna L. Stratton, *Pioneer Women: Voices from the Kansas Frontier,* intro. by Arthur M. Schlesinger, Jr. (New York: Simon and Schuster, 1981), p. 57.

49 Turner, p. 3.

50 Kolodny, *The Land Before Her: Fantasy and Experience of the American Frontiers, 1630– 1860* (Chapel Hill: University of North Carolina Press, 1984), pp. 8–9.

51 See Cather's preface to *The Best Stories of Sarah Orne Jewett,* reprinted in *OW,* pp. 47– 59. For further analyses of Jewett's vision of women's artistry, see Josephine Donovan, *Sarah Orne Jewett* (New York: Frederick Ungar, 1980), especially pp. 99–121 on *The Country of the Pointed Firs;* and Elizabeth Ammons, "Jewett's Witches," in *Critical Essays on Sarah Orne Jewett,* ed. Gwen L. Nagel (Boston: G. K. Hall, 1984), pp. 165– 84.

52 Martin, "The Drama of Memory in *My Ántonia, PMLA* 84 (March 1969): 304–11.

53 Although Mrs. Shimerda is presented by Jim as a garrulous troublemaker and miserable housekeeper, at the end of the first book she is as shrewd as she is shrewish, triumphing in arduous circumstances by imposing a legal fine on a farmhand who beat up Ambrosch and by appropriating one of Mr. Burden's cows. In addition, Jim's disdain of her sour-dough bread and dried mushrooms merely reflects his own provincialism.

54 For the Mead quotation we are indebted to Shoshana David, who brought it to to our attention.

55 Like Lou's spouse, Oscar's wife refuses to allow Swedish to be spoken at home, in her case because she is "ashamed of marrying a foreigner" (p. 99).

56 For a discussion of the critics who view the book as "split" between "Alexandra" and "The White Mulberry Tree," see Woodress, pp. 231 and 247.

57 Emil asks himself, "Why did she like so many people . . . ?" (p. 179) and later admonishes her, "Sometimes I think one boy does just as well as another for you" (pp. 229–30). In addition, Marie's discussion of "Frank's other wife" (p. 198)—the woman whom he would desire but whom she could never become—suggests that perhaps Emil is her "other" husband.

58 John J. Murphy suggests a relationship between Keats's "The Eve of St. Agnes" and *O Pioneers!* in "A Comprehensive View of Cather's *O Pioneers!*," *Critical Essays on Willa Cather,* ed. Murphy (Boston: G. K. Hall, 1984), p. 124.

59 O'Brien, p. 442.

60 Jewett, "A White Heron," reprinted in Jewett, *The Country of the Pointed Firs and Other Stories,* ed. Mary Ellen Chase, with an introduction by Marjorie Pryse (New York: W. W. Norton, 1981), p. 239. Cather's language also evokes Tennyson's "She took the speckled partridge flecked with blood" and Hopkins's "The Windhover."

61 See Renza's analysis of Jewett's allusions to a "sexual-biblical war" in Renza *"A White Heron" and the Question of Minor Literature* (Madison: University of Wisconsin Press, 1984), p. 83.

62 What both Alexandra's and Carl's explanation does not take into account when they construct a stereotypical portrait of Marie as a destructive Eve or femme fatale is Frank's own admission of his guilt, his realization that "he was to blame. For three years he had been trying to break her spirit" (p. 266).

63 *Letters of Sarah Orne Jewett,* ed. Annie Fields (Boston: Houghton Mifflin, 1911), p. 246.

64 Miller, *"My Ántonia:* A Frontier Drama of Time," *American Quarterly* 10:4 (Winter 1958): 481.

65 Lerner, *The Creation of Patriarchy* (New York: Oxford University Press, 1986), p. 5.

66 Freud's view that "In young women erotic wishes dominate the phantasies almost exclusively" and that "in young men egoistic and ambitious wishes essert themselves plainly enough alongside their erotic desires" appears in "The Relation of the Poet to Daydreaming" (1908), in *On Creativity and the Unconscious,* trans. I. F. Grant Duff (New York: Harper & Brothers, 1958), p. 44. The significance of this passage for women writers and feminist literary critics is analyzed by Nancy K. Miller, "Plots and Plausibilities in Women's Fiction," reprinted in *The New Feminist Criticism,* ed. Elaine Showalter (New York: Pantheon, 1985), pp. 339–60.

67 Chodorow, *The Reproduction of Mothering* (Berkeley and Los Angeles: University of California Press, 1978), esp. p. 169. It is, of course, significant in this regard that Jim Burden is provided with a "Grandfather" whose speech—partly because it is reserved for the most solemn occasions—seems both mysterious and important to Jim. On this aspect of the pastoral elegy, see also Sandra M. Gilbert, "The American Sexual Poetics of Walt Whitman and Emily Dickinson," *Reconstructing American Literary History,* ed. Sacvan Bercovitch (Cambridge: Harvard University Press, 1986), pp. 123–54.

68 For a discussion of the "masculinity complex," see *The War of the Words,* pp. 184–89.

69 For a discussion of Ong on the "father speech" of Latin and Greek, see *The War of the Words,* pp. 243 and 252–54.

70 Gelfant, p. 103.

71 The original version of *My Ántonia's* "Introduction" appears in Cather, *Early Novels and Stories* (New York: Literary Classics of the United States—Library of America, 1987), pp. 711–14.

72 Both stories appear in *Youth and the Bright Medusa,* pp. 67–122 and 151–80. Further references will be to this edition, and page numbers, preceded when necessary by the citation *YBM,* will appear in the text.

73 Cressida Garnet's coach is described as "a vulture of the vulture race, and he had the beak of one" (*YBM,* 75) and Siegmund Stein is presented as "a credit to the garment trade" (*YBM,* 168). See Woodress, p. 283, for a fair-minded discussion of charges that Cather was anti-Semitic. The Jewish Mrs. Rosen in the brilliant autobiographical story "Old Mrs. Harris" (in *Obscure Destinies* [New York: Vintage, 1974], pp. 75–190) is clearly a mentor for the aspiring heroine.

74 Cather, *A Lost Lady* (New York: Vintage Books, 1972), p. 172. Further references will be to this edition, and page numbers will appear in the text.

75 Cather, *My Mortal Enemy* (New York: Alfred A. Knopf, 1926), p. 60. Further references will be to this edition, and page numbers will appear in the text.

76 Woodress, p. 385.

77 About her most Catholic novel, *Death Comes for the Archbishop,* Cather herself noted in a letter that "a story with no woman in it but the Virgin Mary has very definite limitations" (quoted in Woodress, p. 396). As Woodress remarks, however, this statement is not accurate about the novel, and in *The War of the Words* we discussed female imagery in the novel (see p. 251). Mary Austin criticizes Cather's sympathy for the archbishop's desire to build a French cathedral in a Spanish town because "It was a calamity to the local culture"; see *Earth Horizon,* p. 359.

78 Cather, *The Professor's House* (New York: Vintage Books, 1953), pp. 36 and 79. Further references will be to this edition, and page numbers will appear in the text. In *The Machine in the Garden: Technology and the Pastoral Ideal in America* (New York: Oxford University Press, 1967) Leo Marx makes a point about *Huckleberry Finn* that could also be made about *The Professor's House:* specifically, he argues that it "joins the

pastoral ideal with the revolutionary doctrine of fraternity" in a "total repudiation of an oppressive society" (p. 338).

79 Woodress discusses the meetings between Cather and Lawrence, pp. 353 and 364.

80 Our interpretation of the retreat from sexuality effected by the domestic and spiritual rituals of Cecile and Jeanne Le Ber differs from other feminist valuations of these characters. See, for example, Fryer, *Felicitous Space* esp. pp. 326–42.

81 Not only did Cather's adherence to historical sources in such novels as *Death Comes for the Archbishop* and *Shadows on the Rock* contradict her own earlier statement about the necessity of originality in the artist, but such reconciliation scenes as the portrait of herself as a young child at the end of *Sapphira and the Slave Girl* are curiously divorced from the plots to which they are attached. See also the discussion of *Lucy Gayheart* as a retelling of Bram Stoker's *Dracula* from a female point of view in Susan J. Rosowski, *The Voyage Perilous: Willa Cather's Romanticism* (Lincoln: University of Nebraska Press, 1986), pp. 219–31.

82 For an earlier use of Venus, see "On the Gulls' Road," *Collected Short Fiction*, pp. 79–94.

83 Leon Edel, *Literary Biography* (Bloomington: Indiana University Press, 1959), pp. 99–122.

84 We wish to thank Judy Peck for making available to us a photocopy of Willa Cather's will. The passage quoted appears in the seventh article. In terms of the "unsayable," the original "Introduction" of *My Ántonia* is especially poignant, for there Jim Burden hands his manuscript not to another man but to a woman who admits that Jim "had had opportunities that I, as a little girl who watched [Ántonia] come and go, had not" and who goes on to confess that "My own story [about Ántonia] was never written" (Library of America edition, pp. 713–14).

Chapter 6

EPIGRAPH: Mary Barnard, *Sappho: A New Translation* (Berkeley: University of California Press, 1973), no. 38; Renée Vivien, "Landing at Mytilene," in *At the Sweet Hour of Hand in Hand,* trans. Sandia Belgrade ([Weatherby Lake, Mo.]: The Naiad Press, 1979), p. 25; H. D., *Notes on Thought and Vision & The Wise Sappho* (San Francisco: City Lights Books, 1982), p. 67; Gertrude Stein, "Stanzas in Meditation," in *The Yale Gertrude Stein,* ed. Richard Kostelanetz (New Haven: Yale University Press, 1980), p. 405.

1 Carpenter, *Love's Coming of Age,* p. 123.

2 See Faderman, *Surpassing the Love of Men,* especially p. 252, and Smith-Rosenberg, "The New Woman as Androgyne: Social Disorder and Gender Crisis, 1870–1936," *Disorderly Conduct: Visions of Gender in Victorian America* (New York: Oxford University Press, 1985), pp. 245–96.

3 Foucault, *The History of Sexuality,* vol. 1, p. 101, is discussed by Weeks in *Sex, Politics and Society,* p. 108.

4 Ellis *The Psychology of Sex,* p. 224; Carpenter, *Love's Coming of Age,* p. 126; Carpenter, *the Intermediate Sex* (1908; New York and London: Mitchell Kennerley, 1912), p. 73.

5 Carpenter, *Intermediate Sex,* pp. 72–73.

6 Carpenter, *Love's Coming of Age,* p. 198.

7 Hall, *The Well of Loneliness* (1928; New York: Avon Books, 1981), pp. 79 and 267. Further references will be to this edition, and page numbers will appear in the text.

8 Benstock, *Women of the Left Bank: Paris, 1900–1940* (Austin: University of Texas Press, 1986), p. 78.

9 Hall's dedication refers to herself, her first lover "Ladye" (Mabel Veronica Baten),

and her lifelong companion Una Troubridge. For background information, see Richard Ormrod, *Una Troubridge: The Friend of Radclyffe Hall* (London: Jonathan Cape, 1984).

10 Besides Benstock's *Women of the Left Bank,* standard texts on expatriate literary culture include Malcolm Cowley's *Exile's Return* (New York: Penguin Books, 1976); Samuel Putnam, *Paris Was Our Mistress* (New York: Viking Press, 1947); Ernest Hemingway, *A Moveable Feast* (New York: Scribner's, 1964); Janet Flanner, *Paris Was Yesterday,* ed. Irving Drutman (New York: Penguin Books, 1979); and Robert McAlmon and Kay Boyle, *Being Geniuses Together: 1920–1930* (Garden City, N.Y.: Doubleday and Company, 1968). In addressing this subject, we have profited from the work-in-progress of Elyse Blankley.

11 Discussed by Weeks, p. 105.

12 See the discussion of Moore's preface to *Muslin* (London, 1932) in Fernando, *"New Women" in the Late Victorian Novel,* p. 85.

13 Dijkstra, *Idols of Perversity,* p. 152.

14 We have discussed the vampiric lesbian in *The War of the Words,* pp. 27–28, 30–31. Besides Lawrence's "Ego-Bound Women" (in *The Complete Poems,* p. 475), see the sinister portrait of the lesbian in *The Rainbow* (1915), chap. 12.

15 From Elizabeth Robins's remarks on Sappho in *Ancilla's Share* (1924; Westport, Conn.: Hyperion Reprint Edition. 1976), pp. 124–27 to Katherine Mansfield's portrait of a sexually ambiguous and repulsive woman in "At the Bay" (1922; reprinted in *The Collected Stories of Katherine Mansfield* [1945; Newark: Penguin Books, 1981], pp. 205–45, esp. 217–20), a number of modernist texts by women participate in the prevailing "homophobia" of the period.

16 Stein, "Patriarchal Poetry" (1927) appears in *The Yale Gertrude Stein,* ed. Kostelanetz, pp. 106–46. Further references to poems in this volume will be preceded by the citation *YGS,* and page numbers will appear in the text.

17 de Pizan, *The Book of the City of Ladies,* trans. Earl Jeffrey Richards (New York: Persea Books, 1982), p. 68.

18 Woolf, Monday, 21 December 1925, entry in *The Diary of Virginia Woolf,* ed. Anne Olivier Bell with Andrew McNeillie, 5 vols. (London: The Hogarth Press, 1980), 3:51.

19 The indispensable background for the history of the lesbian tradition in literature is Faderman; on Philips, see pp. 68–71. Significantly, Elizabeth Barrett Browning's only mention of a female precursor in "A Vision of Poets" is Sappho, and Christina Rossetti's "Sappho" (1846) and "What Sappho Would Have Said Had Her Leap Cured Instead of Killing Her" (1848) were excised from her collected work by William Michael Rossetti. We are indebted to Dolores Rosenblum for this information. Sidney Abbott and Barbara Love, *Sappho Was a Right-on Woman* (New York: Stein and Day, 1972); Pat Califia, *Sapphistry* (Tallahassee, Fla.: Naiad Press, 1980).

20 An unpublished paper by Anne Winters describes the shift from T. W. Higginson's male pronouns (1871) to J. A. Symonds's female pronouns (1873). These and other translations are reprinted in Henry Thornton Wharton, *Sappho,* 3d ed. (London and Chicago: John Lane and A. C. McClurg, 1885), pp. 51–61.

21 Duncan, *My Life,* pp. 116–22; Millay, "Sappho Crosses the Dark River Into Hades" and "Of what importance, O my lovely girls, my dangers" in *Collected Poems,* pp. 293–94, 451–53; Teasdale, "To Cleis (The Daughter of Sappho)," *Helen of Troy and Other Poems* (New York: Macmillan, 1922), pp. 88–89; Robins, *Ancilla's Share,* p. 125. David M. Robinson quotes Teasdale's "Phaon and the Leucadian Leap" in *Sappho and Her Influence* (1924; New York: Cooper Square, 1963), pp. 227–28; he also mentions Mrs. Mary Robinson's, Mrs. Heman's, and Mrs. Estelle Lewis's use of Sappho. For a further discussion of Dinesen's costumes, see chap. 8 of this volume.

22 Woolf, "A Society," *Monday or Tuesday,* pp. 9–40. Marcus, "Liberty, Sorority, Misogyny," in *The Representation of Women in Fiction,* ed. Carolyn G. Heilbrun and Mar-

garet R. Higonnet, Selected Papers from the English Institute, 1981, n. 7 (Baltimore: Johns Hopkins University Press, 1983), p. 87. The proliferation of Anglo-American scholarly investigations, translations, and biographies of Sappho in the late nineteenth and early twentieth centuries cannot be exaggerated: Edwin Arnold's *Poets of Greece* (1869), T. W. Higginson's essay on Sappho in the *Atlantic Monthly* (1871), J. A. Symonds, *Studies of the Greek Poets* (1873), Henry Wharton's *Sappho* (1885), Maurice Thompson's "The Sapphic Secret" in *Atlantic Monthly* (1894), J. R. Tutin's *Sappho* (1903), Peter Hille's biography (1904), Edward Storer's translations (1908), J. M. Edmonds's *Sappho in the Added Light of the New Fragments* (1912), Mary M. Patrick's *Sappho and the Island of Lesbos* (1912), the Egypt Exploration Society publication (volume 13) of the *Oxyrhynchus Papyri* (Part 10; 1914), Arthur S. Way's translation *Sappho and the Vigil of Venus* (1920), Edmond's *Lyra Graeca*, for the Loeb Classical Series (1922), and Arthur Weigall's *Sappho of Lesbos* (1932) represent an incomplete list.

23 Woolf, "A Society," p. 31. See "Affable Hawk's" review of Arnold Bennett, *Our Women* and Otto Weininger, *Sex and Character* in *The New Statesman* (Oct. 2, 1920): 704, and Virginia Woolf's exchange with him (Oct. 9, 1920): 15–16, and (Oct. 16, 1920): 45–46. The quotations are taken from the second letter.

24 Sitwell, *Selected Letters: 1919–1964,* ed. John Lehmann and Derek Parker (New York: Vanguard Press, 1970), p. 116.

25 Woolf, *A Room of One's Own,* p. 113.

26 Cather, "Three Women Poets," *Nebraska State Journal* (January 13, 1895), is reprinted in *The World and the Parish,* 1:147.

27 We are grateful to Lawrence Lipking who shared with us his work-in-progress on the different ways in which poets have reinvented Sappho's "Second Ode." See his *Abandoned Women and Poetic Tradition* (Chicago: University of Chicago Press, 1988), pp. 57–126, as well as his "Aristotle's Sister: A Poetics of Abandonment," *Critical Inquiry* 10:1 (Fall 1983): 61–81.

28 Bogan, *A Poet's Alphabet: Reflections on the Literary Art and Vocation,* ed. Robert Phelps and Ruth Limmer (New York: McGraw-Hill, 1970), p. 429. See also Carman Bliss, *Sappho: One Hundred Lyrics,* intro. by Charles G. D. Roberts (Boston: L. C. Page, 1903).

29 Elaine Marks, "Lesbian Intertextuality," in *Homosexualities and French Literature,* ed. George Stambolian and Elaine Marks (Ithaca: Cornell University Press, 1979), pp. 353–77.

30 See a discussion of this work in O'Brien, p. 135.

31 Blankley, "Return to Mytilene: Renée Vivien and the City of Women," in *Women Writers and the City: Essays in Feminist Literary Criticism,* ed. Susan M. Squier (Knoxville: University of Tennessee Press, 1984), pp. 45–67. More recently, Karla Jay has devoted a chapter of *The Amazon and the Page: Natalie Clifford Barney and Renée Vivien* (Bloomington: Indiana University Press, 1988) to Sappho's influence on Vivien and Barney (pp. 61–80). Also see Benstock, especially pp. 277–90; George Wickes, *The Amazon of Letters: The Life and Lovers and Natalie Barney* (New York: G. P. Putnam's Sons, 1976); Jean Chalon, *Portrait of a Seductress: The World of Natalie Barney,* trans. Carol Barko (New York: Crown Publishers, 1979); and W. G. Rogers, *Ladies Bountiful* (New York: Harcourt Brace and World, 1968). Useful background information on Barney and Vivien also appears in Jeannette Foster, *Sex Variant Women in Literature* (1956; Baltimore, Md.: Diana Press, 1975), pp. 154–73, and in Bertha Harris, "The More Profound Nationality of their Lesbianism: Lesbian Society in Paris in the 1920's," *Amazon Expedition,* ed. Phyllis Birkby, et. al. (Washington, N.J.: Times Change Press, 1973), pp. 77–88.

32 Vivien, *A Woman Appeared to Me,* trans. Jeannette H. Foster (1904; The Naiad Press, 1979), p. 34.

33 Mario Praz discusses the lesbian femme fatale in *The Romantic Agony,* pp. 236–40 and

260–61, as does Faderman in *Surpassing the Love of Men*, pp. 269–75. Both outline the importance of a sado-masochistic Sappho for Baudelaire, Verlaine, Louÿs, Daudet, D'Annunzio, and Swinburne. Also see Foster, *Sex Variant Women in Literature*, pp. 76–80, 104, and 114. Both Blankley and Benstock (cited above) view Vivien in terms of her resistance to this image, as does Pamela J. Annas, " 'Drunk with Chastity': The Poetry of Renée Vivien," *The Female Imagination and the Modernist Aesthetic*, ed. Sandra M. Gilbert and Susan Gubar (New York and London: Gordon and Breach, 1986), pp. 11–22.

34 A recitation by San Giovanni, Sappho's avatar in *A Woman Appeared to Me*, p. 17; Gayle Rubin, "Introduction," *A Woman Appeared to Me*, p. viii.

35 Vivien, *A Woman Appeared to Me*, p. 15; "Lucidity," *Muse of the Violets*, trans. Margaret Porter and Catherine Kroger ([Bates City, Mo.]: The Naiad Press, 1977), p. 26.

36 Colette, *The Pure and the Impure*, trans. Herma Briffault (1932; London: Penguin Books, 1971), p. 71.

37 Charles Baudelaire, *The Flowers of Evil/Les Fleurs du mal*, ed. Wallace Fowlie (New York: Bantam, 1964), pp. 106–07. We have departed somewhat from this translation. Also see Marcel Proust, "A propos of Baudelaire," in *Baudelaire: A Collection of Critical Essays*, ed. Henri Peyre (Englewood Cliffs, N.J.: Pentice-Hall, 1962), pp. 123, 126.

38 Algernon Charles Swinburne, *Selected Poetry and Prose*, ed. John D. Rosenberg (New York: Modern Library, 1968), pp. 329. Also see Swinburne's poem "On the Cliffs," pp. 249–62. Dolores Klaich sees Vivien as victimized by Swinburnean decadence in *Woman + Woman* (New York: Simon and Schuster, 1974), p. 174.

39 Rubin's introduction to *A Woman Appeared to Me* provides an indispensable introduction to Vivien, pp. iii–xx; Nina Auerbach discusses the relationship between the female and the demonic in Pre-Raphaelite painting and in Swinburne's poetry in *Woman and the Demon*, pp. 74–81 and 104–06. Vivien's pseudonym is also discussed by Sandia Belgrade, "Introduction," *At the Sweet Hour of Hand in Hand*, p. xv, and in chap. 5 of *The War of the Words*, where *The Beguiling of Merlin* is reproduced.

40 Vivien, "The Disdain of Sappho," *The Muse of the Violets*, p. 46, and "I shall be always a virgin," p. 44. We will be using this volume, as well as the Naiad Press edition of *At the Sweet Hour of Hand in Hand*, unless otherwise indicated, for the Naiad Press translations of Vivien's poetry make possible the teaching and study of Vivien in this country. Those who wish to see the original will find the volumes collected in *Poèmes de Renée Vivien*, published by Alphonse Lemerre in 1923–24 and reprinted in facsimile by the Arno Press in 1975 in one volume.

41 Vivien, "Sappho Lives Again," in *At the Sweet Hour*, p. 3.

42 Vivien, "Union," *The Muse of the Violets*, p. 73.

43 The best analysis of Sappho's poetry in terms of the "illusion of perfect union, [the] inevitability of parting" is Eva Stehle Stiger's "Romantic Sensuality, Poetic Sense: A Response to Hallett on Sappho," *Signs* 4:3 (Spring 1979): 465–71, quotation on p. 467. Adrienne Rich addresses the issue of lesbianism as the preferred eroticism in "Compulsory Heterosexuality and Lesbian Existence," *Signs* 5:4 (Summer 1980): 631–60.

44 Vivien, "For Andromeda, she has a beautiful recompense," *The Muse of the Violets*, p. 36.

45 Vivien's "Chanson" is translated in *The Muse of the Violets*, p. 24; thanks to a gift from Elin Diamond, we have taken the original, "Sonnet," from *Etudes et Préludes* (1904; Paris: Regine Deforges, 1976), p. 24; *Poèmes de Renée Vivien*, 1:10–11.

46 Vivien's "Invocation" is translated in *The Muse of the Violets*, pp. 58–59; the original appears in *Cendres et Poussieres* (1902; Paris: Regine Deforges, 1977), pp. 2–4; *Poèmes*, 1:43–44.

47 Although Vivien's verse dramas—"La Mort de Psappha" (The death of Sappho), "Atthis delaissée" (Attis abandoned), and "Dans un verger" (In an orchard)—have not yet been translated into English, they are available in French in *Poèmes,* 1:88–93, 2:129–44.

48 Vivien's "Sappho Lives Again" appears in *At the Sweet Hour,* p. 2, but we have departed from this translation with the help of Star Howlett.

49 Vivien's "Landing at Mytilene" and "Toward Lesbos" are translated in *At the Sweet Hour,* pp. 25–26 and 64–65, but we have departed from this translation with the help of Star Howlett. Vivien is quoted by Jay, p. 108.

50 The most recent biography of H. D. is *Herself Defined: The Poet H. D. and Her World* by Barbara Guest (New York: Doubleday, 1984), esp. pp. 118–20, 123–26. Also see H. D., *Tribute to Freud* (1945–46; New York: McGraw-Hill, 1974), pp. 49–50.

51 Symonds, *Studies of the Greek Poets,* 2 vols. in 1 (New York: Harper & Brothers, 1882), 1:310.

52 H. D., *Palimpsest* (1926; Carbondale: Southern Illinois University Press, 1968), p. 84.

53 Ibid., p. 94.

54 Martz, introduction to *H. D.: Collected Poems,* pp. xxi–xxiii. Susan Friedman has informed us that the Francis Wolle's account of H. D.'s life records a visit to Lesbos that the poet took with her mother in the early twenties, a trip H. D. apparently found overwhelming; see *A Moravian Heritage* (Boulder: Empire Reproduction & Printing Company, 1972), p. 58.

55 H. D., "Fragment 113," in *H. D.: Collected Poems,* pp. 131–32.

56 H. D., "The Wise Sappho," in *Notes on Thought and Vision & The Wise Sappho,* pp. 57–58.

57 See the excellent discussion of Sappho's poetry in Friedrich, *The Meaning of Aphrodite,* pp. 107–28; see also Eileen Gregory, "Rose Cut in Rock: Sappho and H. D.'s *Sea Garden,*" *Contemporary Literature* 27 (1986): 525–52.

58 "Calypso," *H. D.: Collected Poems,* pp. 388–96; *Trilogy* (1944; New York: New Directions, 1973), p. 153; *Hermetic Definition* (New York: New Directions, 1972), p. 29.

59 Friedman, *Psyche Reborn* (Bloomington: Indiana University Press, 1981), p. 10. Adalaide Morris has noted that the existence of women poets like Sappho, Nossis, and Telesilia illuminates H. D.'s attraction to classical literature (unpublished "Prospectus for Gender and Genre Session on H. D.," a talk given at the MLA Convention, 1982).

60 H. D., *Trilogy,* p. 63.

61 *H. D.: Collected Poems,* p. 109.

62 Ostriker, "The Poet as Heroine: Learning to Read H. D.," in *Writing Like a Woman* (Ann Arbor: University of Michigan Press, 1983), pp. 7–41.

63 Hugh Kenner describes Pound's use of Sappho in "The Muse in Tatters," *The Pound Era* (Berkeley and Los Angeles: University of California Press, 1971), pp. 54–75. H. D.'s poems on the problem female socialization poses for the woman poet are discussed by both Thomas Burnett Swann, *The Classical World of H. D.* (Lincoln: University of Nebraska Press, 1962), pp. 109–21, and Vincent Quinn, *Hilda Doolittle* (New York: Twayne, 1967), pp. 43–46.

64 *H. D.: Collected Poems,* pp. 181–84, 173–75.

65 Willis Barnstone discusses Sappho's poetry in this context; see *The Poetics of Ecstasy: Varieties of Ekstasis from Sappho to Borges* (New York: Holmes and Meier, 1983), pp. 29–41.

66 DuPlessis, "Romantic Thralldom and 'Subtle Genealogies in H. D.' " in *Writing Beyond the Ending,* pp. 66–83.

67 H. D., *HERmione* (New York: New Directions, 1981), p. 173; H. D., *Bid Me to Live* (New York: Grove Press, 1960), pp. 51, 55, and 138; H. D., *Tribute,* p. 16. D. H.

Lawrence captures this "frozen" quality in two of his fictionalized portraits of H. D.; the priestess of Isis in *The Man Who Died* (1929, 1931) and Julia in *Aaron's Rod* (1922).

68 H. D., "The Wise Sappho," in *Notes on Thought and Vision*, pp. 58–59.

69 Adrienne Rich has written about the collaborative vision H. D. shared with Bryher on Corfu in "Conditions for Work," *Working It Out*, ed. Sara Ruddick and Pamela Daniels (New York: Pantheon, 1977), p. xix. H. D., *The Gift* (New York: New Directions, 1982), p. 142; *Tribute*, pp. 56 and 130. Also see the discussion of female friendship in Louise Bernikow, *Among Women* (New York: Crown, 1980), pp. 165–92.

70 That Lowell was influenced by H. D. is apparent from *Tendencies in Modern American Poetry* (New York: Macmillan, 1917), in which Lowell defended H. D.'s verse, which she also published in three Imagist anthologies. See, for instance, "A Decade" and "Opal" in *The Complete Poetical Works of Amy Lowell*, pp. 217 and 214.

71 *The Complete Poetical Works of Amy Lowell*, p. 459.

72 Yourcenar, *Fires*, trans. Dori Katz (1957; New York: Farrar Straus Giroux, 1981).

73 Barnes, *Ladies Almanack* (New York: Harper & Row, 1972 [1928]), "Foreword." Further references will be to this edition, and page numbers will appear in the text.

74 In this context, it is interesting to note that Sylvia Beach was called "Mrs. Shakespeare" by the artists who frequented her bookshop, "Shakespeare & Co."

75 Barnes, *Nightwood* (1936; New York: New Directions, 1961), p. 143. Further references will be to this edition, and page numbers will appear in the text.

76 Jean Gould, *Amy: The World of Amy Lowell and the Imagist Movement* (New York: Dodd, Mead, 1975), p. 152.

77 Ormrod, *Una Troubridge*, p. 163.

78 Faderman, *Surpassing the Love of Men*, pp. 70–72.

79 Benstock, *Women of the Left Bank*, p. 17.

80 Quoted in Andrew Field, *Djuna: The Life and Times of Djuna Barnes* (New York: G. P. Putnam's Sons, 1983), p. 104.

81 Stein, *Lectures in America* (1935; New York: Vintage Books, 1975), p. 54. Further references will be to this edition, and page numbers, preceded by the citation *LIA*, will appear in the text.

82 Weininger, *Sex and Character* (London and New York: William Heinemann and G. P. Putnam's Sons 1906), p. 66. Otto Weininger's influence on Stein has been discussed by Catharine R. Stimpson, "The Mind, the Body and Gertrude Stein," *Critical Inquiry* 3:3 (Spring 1977): 489–506, and by Marianne DeKoven, *A Different Language* (Madison: University of Wisconsin Press, 1983), p. 137.

83 Stein, *Everybody's Autobiography* (1937; New York: Vintage Books, 1973), p. 77. Further references will be to this edition, and page numbers, preceded by the citation *EA*, will appear in the text.

84 Lawrence uses this phrase in *Women in Love*, chap. 25.

85 James R. Mellow, *Charmed Circle* (New York: Praeger, 1974), p. 326.

86 Stimpson, "The Mind, the Body and Gertrude Stein," p. 499.

87 Stein, *The Making of Americans* (New York: Harcourt, Brace and World, 1962), pp. 281–82. Further references will be to this edition, and page numbers, preceded by the citation *MOA*, will appear in the text.

88 Stein's statement in *What Are Masterpieces* is quoted in *Gertrude Stein's America*, ed. Gilbert A. Harrison (Washington, D.C.: Robert B. Luce, 1965), p. 63.

89 *The Autobiography of Alice B. Toklas* in *Selected Writings of Gertrude Stein*, ed. Van Vechten, p. 66. Further references will be to this edition, and page numbers will appear in the text preceded when necessary by the citation *AABT*.

90 Stein, "Ada" in *Geography and Plays* (1922; New York: Something Else Press, 1968), pp. 14–16.

91 In *Memoirs of a Dutiful Daughter*, trans. James Kirkup (New York: Harper & Row,

1974), p. 113, Simone de Beauvoir records a similar shock when she exclaims over her childhood friend, "I loved Zaza so much that she seemed to be more real than myself."

92 For background on Toklas's early life, see Linda Simon, *The Biography of Alice B. Toklas* (Garden City, New York: Doubleday, 1977), pp. 7–17 and 20–39.

93 Stein, "Didn't Nelly and Lilly Love You?" in *As Fine as Melanctha,* Yale Edition of the Unpublished Writings of Gertrude Stein, gen. ed. Carl Van Vechten, vol. 4 (New Haven: Yale University Press, 1954), p. 230. Further references will be to this edition, and page numbers, preceded by the citation *AFAM,* will appear in the text.

94 Stein, *Two: Gertrude Stein and Her Brother,* Yale ed., vol. 1 (New Haven: Yale University Press, 1951), p. 2.

95 Stein, "Miss Furr and Miss Skeene," in *Selected Writings of Gertrude Stein,* pp. 561–68; quotation, p. 563.

96 Bridgman, *Gertrude Stein in Pieces* (New York: Oxford University Press, 1970), pp. 210–11. Like all critics of Stein, we are indebted to this meticulous, brilliant work. The name "Gertrice and Altrude" was found in the manuscript of "Lend a Hand" (Yale no. 269) by Wendy Steiner, *Exact Resemblance to Exact Resemblance* (New Haven: Yale University Press, 1978), p. 187.

97 Burke, "Gertrude Stein, the Cone Sisters, and the Puzzle of Female Friendship," in *Writing and Sexual Difference,* ed. Elizabeth Abel (Chicago: University of Chicago Press, 1982), p. 236.

98 Stein, *Fernhurst, Q.E.D., and Other Early Writings* (New York: Liveright, 1971), p. 58.

99 Ellen Moers was one of the first critics to interpret Stein's student essay "In the Red Deeps" in light of her identification with George Eliot; see *Literary Women,* p. 254.

100 Quoted by Bridgman, *Gertrude Stein in Pieces,* p. 149n.

101 Stimpson, "The Mind, the Body, and Gertrude Stein," pp. 496–97.

102 DeKoven, *A Different Language,* p. 136.

103 After Stimpson's essay in *Critical Inquiry,* a number of critics have explored Stein's language and her sexuality, including Elizabeth Fifer, "Is Flesh Advisable? The Interior Theater of Gertrude Stein," *Signs* 4:3 (Spring 1979): 372–83. Also see Linda Simon, *The Biography of Alice B. Toklas,* pp. 101, 107–08.

104 We are grateful to Roger Gilbert for obtaining a copy of "Film Deux Soeurs qui ne sont pas soeurs" from the Beinecke Library, Yale University.

105 Stein, *Ida* (1941; New York: Vintage, 1968), p. 10.

106 Jayne L. Walker, the author of *The Making of a Modernist: Gertrude Stein from "Three Lives" to "Tender Buttons"* (Amherst: University of Massachusetts Press, 1984), has also produced a bibliography of Stein criticism, "Gertrude Stein," in *American Women Writers: Bibliographical Essays,* ed. Maurice Duke, Jackson R. Bryer, and M. Thomas Inge (Westport, Conn.: Greenwood Press, 1983), pp. 117–33. Wendy Steiner, *Exact Resemblance to Exact Resemblance,* and Marjorie Perloff, "Poetry as Word and System: The Art of Gertrude Stein," in *The Poetics of Indeterminacy* (Princeton: Princeton University Press, 1981), pp. 67–108, have been especially influential.

107 Schmitz, *Of Huck and Alice: Humorous Writing in American Literature* (Minneapolis: University of Minnesota Press, 1983), p. 178.

108 Ibid., pp. 195 and 189.

109 Barney's remarks appear in her "Foreword" to *As Fine As Melanctha,* p. xvi.

110 Stein, "Sonnets That Please," *Bee Time Vine,* p. 220; "Susie Asado," *Geography and Plays,* p. 13; "Brim Beauvais," *Yale Gertrude Stein,* p. 158–59.

111 Stein, "Mrs. Whitehead," *Geography and Plays,* p. 155.

112 Schmitz, *Of Huck and Alice,* p. 195, and DeKoven, *A Different Language,* pp. 18–24.

113 Quoted in John Malcolm Brinnin, *The Third Rose: Gertrude Stein and Her World* (Boston: Little, Brown, 1959), p. 290.

114 Stein, *How To Write* (Paris: Plain Editions, 1931), p. 73.

115 Stein, *A Novel of Thank You,* Yale ed., vol. 9 (New Haven: Yale University Press, 1958), p. 30.

116 Stein, *Painted Lace,* Yale ed., vol. 5 (New Haven: Yale University Press, 1955), p. 139.

117 Benstock, *Women of the Left Bank,* p. 185.

118 Freud's phrase "His Majesty the Baby" appears in "On Narcissism" (1914) in *The Complete Works of Sigmund Freud,* ed. James Strachey (New York: W. W. Norton, 1986), 14 : 91.

119 Quoted in James Mellow, *Charmed Circle,* p. 326.

120 "A Transatlantic Interview" is quoted by Betsy Alayne Rayn in *Gertrude Stein's Theatre of the Absolute,* Theatre and Dramatic Studies, no. 21 (Ann Arbor, Mich.: UMI Research Press, 1984), p. 33.

121 Benjamin Reid provides the best example of an outraged critic in *Art by Subtraction: A Dissenting Opinion of Gertrude Stein* (Norman: University of Oklahoma Press, 1958).

122 McAlmon reprints part of this review in *Being Geniuses Together,* p. 231. Also useful is the interview with Berthe Cleyrergue (Natalie Barney's housekeeper) where she says of Stein, "She frightened me. She dressed very strangely with long skirts that trailed along the ground and with her short cropped hair I took her for a man. When I learned that she was a woman, I said: 'That's not true' " ("The Salon of Natalie Clifford Barney: An Interview with Berthe Cleyrergue" by Gloria Feman Orenstein, *Signs* 4:2 [Spring 1979]: 489).

123 Thomson, who said of his collaborator Gertrude Stein, "She didn't work with me, and I didn't work with her" (see Betsy Alayne Ryan, *Gertrude Stein's Theatre of the Absolute,* p. 34), is quoted by Carl Van Vechten in "A Stein Song," one of the prefaces to *Selected Writings of Gertrude Stein,* p. xx.

124 Anderson, from "Four American Impressions," rpt. in *Gertrude Stein: A Composite Portrait,* ed. Linda Simon (New York: Avon Books, 1974), p. 72; Wilder, "Introduction," *Four in America* by Gertrude Stein (New Haven: Yale University Press, 1947), pp. xiv–xv; Porter, "Gertrude Stein: A Self-Portrait," *Harper's* 195 (Dec. 1947): 522, and *The Days Before* (New York: Harcourt, Brace 1952), p. 43. In *When This You See Remember Me: Gertrude Stein in Person* (1948; Westport, Conn.: Greenwood Press, 1971), W. G. Rogers sees her as a "monk" (p. 43). Most recently, in a review essay Catharine R. Stimpson has compared Gertrude Stein to the ghost of King Hamlet in "Reading Gertrude Stein," *Tulsa Studies in Women's Literature* 4:2 (Fall 1985): 265.

125 Stein, "Reread Another," *Operas and Plays* (Paris: Plain Edition, [1932]), p. 125.

126 Bridgman quotes "Left to Right" in *Gertrude Stein in Pieces,* p. 201.

127 Stein, "Before the Flowers of Friendship Faded Friendship Faded," *Writing and Lectures 1911–1945,* ed. Patricia Meyerowitz (London: Peter Owen, 1967), p. 270.

128 Perloff's essay is included in a volume of Stein criticism forthcoming from the University of California Press, intro. by Martha Banta and ed. Karen Rowe.

129 See, for example, the excellent essay by James E. Breslin, "Gertrude Stein and the Problems of Autobiography" in *Women's Autobiography,* ed. Estelle C. Jelinek (Bloomington: Indiana University Press, 1980), pp. 149–62.

130 Rogers, *When This You See,* p. 33. Yet, after Stein's death, even the deferential Toklas explains about the "paragraph in *The Autobiography*" on James Joyce that it was "written because I insisted it should be said" (To Donald Sutherland, 30 Nov. 1947, *Staying on Alone: Letters of Alice B. Toklas,* ed. Edward Burns [New York: Liveright, 1973], p. 91).

131 Bridgman, *Gertrude Stein in Pieces,* p. 235. See Brinnin's discussion of *Blood on the Dining-Room Floor* and *Four in America* as aspects of Stein's troubled meditations on creativity in this stage of her career (*The Third Rose,* pp. 312–15). In the film *When*

This You See Remember Me (dir. Perry Miller Adato, Contemporary/McGraw-Hill Films, 1971), Samuel M. Steward begins to stutter and hesitate when he hints that Alice B. Toklas may have participated in the creation of Stein's art more than either Stein or Toklas wanted to admit.

132 Bridgman casts doubt on the authorship of both "Ada" and *The Autobiography of Alice B. Toklas* in *Gertrude Stein in Pieces*, pp. 209–17.

133 Stimpson, "Gertrice/Altrude: Stein, Toklas, and the Paradox of the Happy Marriage," in *Mothering the Mind*, ed. Ruth Perry and Martine Watson Brownley (New York: Holmes & Meier, 1984), p. 130.

134 *The Alice B. Toklas Cook Book* (1954; New York: Anchor Books, 1960), p. 39. Further references will be to this edition, and page numbers will appear in the text preceded by the citation *ABTCB*. The lax structure of Stein's subsequent *Everybody's Autobiography* is not comparable to the tightly organized *The Autobiography of Alice B. Toklas*, although the later work was clearly influenced by the *Autobiography's* more simple, anecdotal style.

135 Simon, *The Biography of Alice B. Toklas*, pp. 305–06. Although Simon quotes the *Times* reporter and analyzes White's distrust of Toklas's legends about the past, she argues about *The Autobiography of Alice B. Toklas* that "there is no evidence that [Toklas] wrote her own autobiography in 1932"; see p. 186. Toklas, *What Is Remembered* (New York: Holt, Rinehart and Winston, 1963), p. 17. Further references will be to this edition, and page numbers, preceded by the citation *WIR*, will appear in the text.

136 Sedgwick's letter is quoted in Brinnin, *The Third Rose*, p. 309.

137 Schmitz, *Of Huck and Alice*, pp. 215, 217.

138 Quoted by Brinnin, *The Third Rose*, p. 285.

139 Brown, "Sappho's Reply," in *Lesbian Poetry*, ed. Elly Bulkin and Joan Larkin (Watertown, Mass.: Persephone Press, 1981), p. 136; Rukeyser, "Poem Out of Childhood," p. 3; Shockley's story appeared first in *Sinister Wisdom* 9 (Spring 1979): 54–59. Karla Jay notes that Vivien's and Barney's reinvention of Sappho "is closely allied to the impulse which led Judy Grahn in *The Highest Apple* to recreate Sappho's life" (p. 122). Also see "Invocation to Sappho" in Elsa Gidlow, *Sappho Songs* (Mill Valley, Calif.: Druid Heights Books, 1982), pp. 1–2.

140 Kizer, "Pro Femina," in *Psyche*, ed. Barbara Segnitz and Carol Rainey (New York: Dell, 1973), p. 131; Griffin, "Thoughts on Writing," *The Writer on Her Work*, ed. Janet Sternburg (New York: W. W. Norton, 1980), p. 115; Morgan, "Lesbian Poem," *Monster* (New York: Vintage, 1972), p. 73.

141 Sarton, "My Sisters, O My Sisters," *Selected Poems of May Sarton*, ed. Serena Sue Hilsinger and Lois Brynes (New York: W. W. Norton, 1978), pp. 192–93.

142 For an example of the rejection of Stein, see Jane Rule, *Lesbian Images* (1975; Trumansburg, N.Y.: Crossing Press, 1982), pp. 71–72. Diane Wakoski's poem, "My Trouble," is typical in its identication of Stein with "grand / stony ideas" and Toklas with embroidery or baking and secretarial skills; see *Smudging* (Los Angeles: Black Sparrow Press, 1972), p. 39.

143 Broumas and Miller, *Black Holes, Black Stockings* (Middletown, Conn.: Wesleyan University Press, 1985), p. 7. Further references will appear in the text.

144 Hershman, "Making Love to Alice," in *Lesbian Poetry*, ed. Bulkin and Larkin, p. 235.

Chapter 7

EPIGRAPHS: Pankhurst, *The Suffragette*, Aug. 7, 1914, quoted in Theodore Roszak and Betty Roszak, eds., *Masculine/Feminine* (New York: Harper, 1969), p. 97; Lawrence,

Studies in Classic American Literature (1923; New York: Viking, 1964), p. 92; Austin, "Sex Emancipation Through War," *The Forum*, 59 (May 1918): 609 (further references to this work will appear in the text, with page numbers preceded by the citation "SE"; we are grateful to Nancy Cott for calling this essay to our attention); quoted in Eric Leed, *No Man's Land: Combat & Identity in World War I* (New York: Cambridge University Press, 1979), p. 163.

1 Eliot, "Gerontion," *Collected Poems 1900–1962* (New York: Harcourt, 1970), p. 30. Further references to poems by T. S. Eliot, with the exception of *The Waste Land*, will appear in the text, with page numbers preceded by the citation *CP*.

2 On the war's grim psychological consequences for men, major texts include Paul Fussell, *The Great War and Modern Memory* (New York: Oxford University Press, 1975); Leed, *No Man's Land: Combat & Identity in World War I*; and Jon Silkin, *Out of Battle: The Poetry of the Great War* (Oxford: Oxford University Press, 1972).

3 Bradbury, "The Denuded Place: War and Form in *Parade's End* and *U.S.A.*," in *The First World War in Fiction*, ed. Holger Klein (London: Macmillan, 1976), pp. 193–94.

4 In addition to the obviously emasculated characters in Eliot, Hemingway, Ford, and Lawrence, many other war victims—for instance, Ford's Christopher Tietjens (in *Parade's End*) and Aldington's George Winterbourne (in *Death of a Hero*)—suffer from the sensibility, if not the reality, of sexual crucifixion, while, like Eliot's Fisher King, those famous prewar noncombatants, Joyce's Stephen Dedalus and Leopold Bloom, whose story was not fully told until *after* the war, also suffer (in *Ulysses*) from psychic impotence, just as if they too had been through the war's no man's land of battle.

5 On this subject, see Nancy Cott, "Passionlessness: An Interpretation of Victorian Sexual Ideology, 1790–1850," *Signs* 4:2 (Winter 1978); see also chaps. 3 and 4 of this volume, passim.

6 Sassoon, *Selected Poems* (London: Faber, 1968), p. 28. Further references to poems by Sassoon will appear in the text, with page numbers preceded by the citation *SP*.

7 Owen, *The Collected Poems of Wilfred Owen* (New York: New Directions, 1965), pp. 41 and 59; since Owen's poems were published posthumously, the dates given here are dates of composition; all other dates are dates of publication. Further references to poems by Owen will appear in the text, with page numbers preceded by the citation *CP*.

8 Rosenberg, *The Collected Poems of Isaac Rosenberg*, ed. Gordon Bottomley and Denys Harding, with a foreword by Siegfried Sassoon (New York: Schocken Books, 1949), pp. 85–86. Further references to poems by Rosenberg will appear in the text, with page numbers preceded by the citation *CP*.

9 Lawrence, *The Complete Poems*, pp. 741–43. Further references to poems by Lawrence will appear in the text, with page numbers preceded by the citation *CP*.

10 Kelly [Kelly-Gadol], "Did Women Have a Renaissance?" in *Becoming Visible: Women in European History*, ed. Renate Bridenthal and Claudia Koonz (Boston: Houghton Mifflin, 1977).

11 Brittain, *Testament of Youth* (1933; London: Fontana/Virago, 1979), p. 143. Further references will be to this edition, and page numbers, preceded by the citation *TY*, will appear in the text.

12 Quoted in Auerbach, *Communities of Women*, p. 162.

13 Pope, "War Girls," and Nina Macdonald, "Sing a Song of War-Time," both in *Scars Upon My Heart: Women's Poetry and Verse of the First World War* (London: Virago, 1981), pp. 90 and 69. The historian Arthur Marwick quotes an article from the London *Daily Mail* which lists "some of the new occupations for women": "they were, tramway conductors, lift attendants, shop-walkers, bookstall clerks, ticket-collectors, motor-van drivers, van guards, milk-deliverers, railway-carriage cleaners, window-cleaners, dairy workers, shell-makers." (Arthur Marwick, *The Deluge: British Society and the First World War* [Boston: Little, Brown, 1965], p. 89.)

14 Woolf, *Three Guineas*, p. 39. Further references will be to this edition, and page numbers, preceded by the citation *TG,* will appear in the text.

15 See Fussell, "A Satire of Circumstance," in *The Great War*, pp. 3–35.

16 Hynes, "The Irony and the Pity," *TLS*, Dec. 18, 1981: 1469.

17 Brooke, "Peace," and Seeger, "I Have a Rendezvous with Death," both in *A Treasury of War Poetry: British and American Poems of the World War, 1914–1919*, ed. George Herbert Clarke (New York: Hodder & Stoughton, 1917), pp. 246–47; many other poems in this volume also support Hynes's point.

18 Leed, pp. 18–19. The one exception to this point was the heroism, indeed the exaltation, associated with the (unprecedented) air war in this period: both Allied and German "Aces" were idolized, a notable example being Manfred von Richthofen, the famous "Red Baron" who led Germany's "Flying Circus" and who was (significantly) a cousin of D. H. Lawrence's wife, the former Frieda von Richthofen. Like medieval knights, many of the "Aces" knew each other by name, recognized each other's aircraft (for example, von Richthofen's notorious red plane), and chivalrically jousted with each other high above the trenches (although, according to some testimony, their "dogfights" were often unnerving and chaotic). See, for instance, the introduction to Wings [Capt., R.A.F.], *Over the German Lines* (London: Hodder and Stoughton, 1918), whose author (identified only as "Another Hand") writes that "though individual heroism daily adds lustre to the records of every branch of His Majesty's Forces, yet it is in the work of the youngsters who man the 'airy navies grappling in the central blue' that what romance is left to war is chiefly to be found" (pp. ix–x). See also Cyril Falls, *The Great War* (New York: Putnam, 1959), p. 106 ("The airmen were adventurous, high-spirited and gay"), and, for a general history of the air war, Edward Jablonski, *The Knighted Skies: A Pictorial History of World War I in the Air* (New York: Putnam, 1964), esp. p. 73.

19 Leed, p. 19.

20 Ford, *Parade's End: Consisting of Some Do Not . . . , No More Parades, A Man Could Stand Up, The Last Post* (1924, 1925, 1926, 1928; New York: Vintage, 1979), pp. 486–87, 434. Further references will be to this edition, and page numbers will be included in the text.

21 Aldington, *Death of a Hero* (London: Chatto & Windus, 1929), p. 429. Further references will be to this edition, and page numbers, preceded by the citation *DH,* will appear in the text.

22 Graves, *Goodbye to All That* (1929; London: Cassell & Co., 1957), p. 114. Further references will be to this edition, and page numbers, preceded by the citation *GAT,* will appear in the text.

23 Leed, p. 20.

24 Carrington, quoted by Leed, pp. 14–15.

25 Similarly, Christopher Tietjens meditates that, preparing his men to go "up the line," he is "Getting cattle into condition for the slaughterhouse. . . . They were as eager as bullocks running down by Camden Town to Smithfield Market. . . . Seventy per cent of them would never come back" [ellipses Ford's, p. 362].

26 Du Bois, "Essay Toward a History of the Black Man in the Great War," in *Writings* (New York: The Library of America, 1986), pp. 879, 880, 881, 882, 887. Further references will be to this edition, and page numbers, preceded by the citation *W,* will appear in the text.

27 In "The Souls of White Folk" (1920), Du Bois commented further that in "the awful cataclysm of World War, where from beating, slandering, and murdering us the white world turned temporarily aside to kill each other, we of the Darker Peoples looked on in mild amaze" (*Writings*, p. 927).

28 Morrison, *Sula* (1973; New York: Bantam, 1975), pp. 6, 7.

29 Mabel Darmer, quoted by David Mitchell, in *Women on the Warpath: The Story of the Women of the First World War* (London: Jonathan Cape, 1966), p. 161.

30 Auerbach, p. 187.

31 See Blatch (the daughter of Elizabeth Cady Stanton), *Mobilizing Woman-Power* (New York: The Womans Press [sic], 1918), p. 86; Blatch is also quoted and discussed in J. Stanley Lemons, *The Woman Citizen: Social Feminism in the 1920s* (Urbana: University of Illinois Press, 1973), p. 15; the War as Santa Claus is in Mitchell, p. 211. "War compels women to work. That is one of its merits," declared Blatch (p. 90).

32 Barry, "We Enjoyed the War," *Scribner's* 96 (1934): 280. Further references will be to this edition, and page numbers, preceded by the citation "WEW," will appear in the text.

33 Dunbar-Nelson, "Negro Women in War Work," in Emmett J. Scott, *Scott's Official History of The American Negro in the World War* (Chicago: Homewood Press, 1919), p. 395. Further references will be to this edition, and page numbers, preceded by the citation "NW," will appear in the text.

34 Ward, *England's Effort: Letters to an American Friend* (New York: Scribner's 1916), p. 35. Further references will be to this edition, and page numbers, preceded by the citation *EE*, will appear in the text.

35 *The Maryland Suffrage News* is quoted in *The Monthly News of The Conservative and Unionist Women's Franchise Association*, October 1915 (held in Leonard Woolf's file on World War I, University of Sussex Library). Other American comments on what Austin called "sex emancipation through war" include Mrs. Henry Wade Rogers, "Wanted— The Woman's Land Army!", *The Forum* 59 (May 1918): 621–28 ("The woman of tradition, whose domestic obligations prevented her from any wider interests, is fast disappearing" [621]); Anne Emerson, "Who's She in War Work," *The Forum* 59 (June 1918): 745–48 ("Today SHE is everywhere" [745]); "Make Re-Construction Real-Construction," by the Editors, *McClure's* 51:2 (Feb. 1919): 15–16, 52 (reclamation of lands not currently farmed "will offer work to the returned soldier that will keep him from trying to get back the job which Sadie Callahan now has and wants to keep" [52]); Cleveland Moffett, "Is a Woman's War Coming?", *McClure's* 51:2 (Feb. 1919): 24, 53, 58 ("In 1910 we had not less than eight million wage-earning women, in 1919 we have nearly ten million among whom are numbered a million and a half war workers. . . . And if men try to force them back there will come a wage struggle between the sexes as violent as the suffrage struggle" [24]); Fred C. Kelley, "Regarding a Certain Sex," *McClure's* 51:3 (March 1919): 31–32 ("the War almost completely uprooted the last remnant of the old aristocratic idea that it is cute and clever for a young woman to be weak or helpless" [31]); and even an ad for AT&T in *McClure's* 51:1 (Jan. 1919) proclaiming that "Woman has made herself indispensable to the Nation's war activities" (45). We are grateful to Judy Peck for obtaining many of these texts.

36 Mitchell, p. 380.

37 Mitchell, p. 380.

38 Marwick, p. 89.

39 See Gail Braybon, *Women Workers in the First World War: The British Experience* (London: Croom Helm, 1981), pp. 46–47; and Mary Cadogan and Patricia Craig, *Women and Children First: The Fiction of Two World Wars* (London: Gollancz, 1978), pp. 32–33. About the United States, one source remarks that "With the coming of World War I and the mushrooming of the armed forces, white women flocked into jobs hitherto primarily male and black women entered areas such as textiles traditionally the preserve of white females. At war's end nearly 10 million women were employed" (James J. Kenneally, "Women in the U.S. and Trade Unionism," in *The World of Women's Trade Unionism*, ed. Norbert C. Soldon [Westport, Conn.: Greenwood Press, 1985], p. 72). For further information, see Mitchell; and Maurine Weiner Green-

wald, *Women, War and Work: The Impact of World War I on Women Workers in the United State* (Westport, Conn.: Greenwood Press, 1980).

40 *Scars*, p. 7.

41 Matthews, *Experiences of a Woman Doctor in Serbia* (London: Mills and Boon, 1916), p. 72; quoted by Elizabeth Cookson, "The Forgotten Women: British Nurses, VADS and Doctors across the Channel" (unpublished paper written for David Savage at Lewis and Clark College; we are grateful to Ms. Cookson and Prof. Savage for sharing this material with us).

42 Wharton's notes on her *"ouvroir"* and other charities, as well as her program for "Heroland," are held at the Beinecke Library of Yale University; for more general discussions of her war work, see Wharton, "The War," in *A Backward Glance*, pp. 336–60, and R. W. B. Lewis, "The War Years: 1913–1918," in *Edith Wharton: A Biography*, pp. 339–415.

43 Quoted in Woolf, *Three Guineas*, p. 51.

44 John Kipling's letter of Sept. 19, 1915, is reproduced in Elliot L. Gilbert, ed., *"O Beloved Kids": Rudyard Kipling's Letters to His Children* (New York: Harcourt Brace, 1983), p. 220.

45 For a discussion of the hostility to women fostered by the war in *German* soldiers, see Klaus Thewelheit, *Male Fantasies: volume 1: women, floods, bodies, history*, passim.

46 Quoted in Cadogan and Craig, p. 92.

47 Kipling, "Common Form," *Rudyard Kipling's Verse: Inclusive Edition, 1885–1926* (Garden City: Doubleday, Page, 1927), p. 446. See also "The Children: 1914–1918," pp. 590–92.

48 *The Short Stories of Katherine Mansfield* (1927; New York: Ecco, 1983), pp. 600–601.

49 Leed, pp. 15–16.

50 Included in the anthology *Salt and Bitter and Good*, ed. Cora Kaplan (London: Paddington, 1975), pp. 187–89.

51 On this subject, see also the somewhat sardonic depiction of "the gold-star muzzers" in F. Scott Fitzgerald, *Tender Is the Night* (1934), in *Three Novels of F. Scott Fitzgerald* (New York: Scribner's, 1953), pp. 161–62.

52 *A Treasury of War Poets*, p. 238.

53 Quoted by Woolf in *Three Guineas*, p. 182. It is worth noting, however, that Woolf believes Shaw was exaggerating. (See her extended footnote on the same page.)

54 *Scars*, p. 88.

55 See Sinclair, "Victory," in *The Tree of Heaven* (London: Cassell, 1917), passim; and Wharton, *A Son at the Front* (New York: Scribner's 1923), passim; for Wharton's enthusiastic correspondence, see Louis Auchincloss, *Edith Wharton: A Woman in Her Time*, pp. 113–14. Further references to Sinclair's novel will be included in the text, with page numbers preceded by the citation *TH*.

56 Rosenberg, p. 209; for Owen, see both the poem and the notes in *Poems*, pp. 55–56.

57 cummings, "my sweet old etcetera," *The Complete Poems of e.e. cummings* (New York: Harcourt, 1972), p. 276.

58 "The Farcical History of Richard Greenow," in Huxley, *Limbo* (New York: Doran, 1920). Further references will be to this edition, and page numbers will be included in the text; for a more extensive discussion of this novella, see *The War of the Words*, pp. 131–36.

59 *A Farewell to Arms* (1929; New York: Bantam, 1949), p. 76; *The Sun Also Rises* (New York: Scribner's, 1926), pp. 38 and 31.

60 Lawrence, "The Ladybird," in *The Short Novels of D. H. Lawrence* (London: Heinemann, 1956), 1:17.

61 West, *The Return of the Soldier* (1918; London: Virago, 1980), p. 144.

62 Sayers, *Busman's Honeymoon* (1937; New York: Avon, 1968), p. 316.

63 Woolf, *Mrs. Dalloway*, pp. 85–87. Further page numbers will be included in the text, preceded, where necessary, by the citation *MD*.

64 Kipling, "Mary Postgate," in *A Diversity of Creatures* (London: Macmillan, 1917), pp. 438–41. An even more horrifying fantasy about a figure who seems at first to be a nurse but turns out to be a murderess is related in Wyndham Martyn, "The Vulture Woman," *The Forum* 59 (Jan. 1918): 69–76.

65 Leed, p. 47.

66 Leed, p. 45.

67 See Marwick, pp. 107, 111.

68 It seems significant that in *Lady Chatterley's Lover* Ivy Bolton becomes Clifford's perversely sexual nurse, and significant too that Mellors's estranged wife Bertha has the same name as one of the war's principal guns—the "Big Bertha."

69 Lawrence, *The Complete Short Stories*, volume 2 (1922; New York: Viking), esp. pp. 343–44 and 373.

70 Gibson, "Bacchanal," in Brian Gardner, ed., *Up The Line To Death: The War Poets, 1914–1918* (London: Methuen, 1976), p. 145.

71 *Scars*, p. xxxv.

72 *Scars*, pp. 12, 35, and 2.

73 The Prefect of Constanza, who, according to Marwick, was "very widely quoted" (Marwick, p. 98).

74 Lorine Pruette's comment on "the joy of women in wartime" is quoted by Lemons, p. 15; Sinclair's poem is cited in Mitchell, p. 129. We are grateful to Harriet Blodgett for calling to our attention a number of other memoirs by women which also make this point; see, for instance, Dorothy Lawrence, *Sapper Dorothy Lawrence* (London: John Lane, 1919).

75 Sinclair, "The War of Liberation: from a Journal," *The English Review* 20–21 (June–July 1915): 170–71, quoted by Cookson.

76 Mrs. St. Clair Stobart, "A Woman in the Midst of War," *The Ladies Home Journal* (Jan. 1915), p. 5; B. G. Mure, "A Side Issue of the War," *Blackwood's* (Oct. 1916) p. 446; *A War Nurse's Diary* (New York: Macmillan, 1918), p. 59; all quoted by Cookson.

77 Thurstan, *Field Hospital and Flying Column: Being the Journal of an English Nursing Sister in Belgium and Russia* (London: Putanam's, 1915), pp. 141–42; quoted by Cookson.

78 Wharton, "extraordinarily exhilarating": *Fighting France* (New York: Scribner's, 1915), pp. 48–49; "jolly picnic lunches": *A Backward Glance*, pp. 351–52; "reading a great poem": *Fighting France*, p. 25.

79 Wharton, *The Marne* (New York: Appleton, 1918), p. 111.

80 Emerson, *Ruth Fielding at the War Front* (New York: Cupples & Leon, 1918), p. 154. We are grateful to Maranda Loewengard for calling this volume—and others like it—to our attention; there were, in fact, a number of "war" adventures written for children and teenagers, including at least one other Ruth Fielding book (*Ruth Fielding in the Red Cross*) and a whole series of books about "the boy allies"—e.g., *The Boy Allies with the Navy* by Ensign Robert L. Darke (for example, *The Boy Allies on the North Sea Patrol, or Striking the First Blow at the German Fleet*) and *The Boy Allies with the Army* by Clair W. Hayes (for instance, *The Boy Allies on the Somme, or, Courage and Bravery Rewarded*).

81 Cather, *One of Ours*, pp. 416 and 291.

82 Hall, *Miss Ogilvy Finds Herself* (London: Heinemann, 1934), "Author's Forenote." Further references will be to this edition, and page numbers, preceded by the citation *MO*, will appear in the text.

83 Hall, *The Well of Loneliness* (London: Cape, 1928), pp. 315, 319, 320–21. Further references will be to this edition, and page numbers, preceded by the citation *WL,* will appear in the text.

84 Porter, *Pale Horse, Pale Rider* (1936; New York: Modern Library, 1939), p. 198. Further references will appear in the text, with page numbers preceded by the citation *PH.*

85 See Lowell, *The Complete Poetical Works,* pp. 209–18, and 237–41; see also Stein, "The War," in *The Autobiography of Alice B. Toklas, The Selected Writings of Gertrude Stein,* pp. 135–81; also, "Lifting Belly," in *The Yale Gertrude Stein,* pp. 4–54.

86 See Nigel Nicolson, *Portrait of a Marriage* (London: Weidenfeld & Nicolson, 1973), pp. 105 and 112.

87 Thurstan, *Field Hospital,* p. 174.

88 See Holtby, *The Crowded Street* (1924; London: Virago, 1981), passim.

89 Fussell, p. 272.

90 Graves and Thomas are quoted by Fussell, p. 274; Owen, p. 106.

91 Leed, p. 200.

92 For the female "imbecile," see Owen, p. 138, and for the homoerotic significance of "lads," see Fussell, pp. 282–83.

93 The description of no man's land as "chaotic," etc., is from Owen, p. 160; Freud, "Reflections Upon War and Death," in *Character and Culture* (New York: Collier, 1963), pp. 109–13.

94 cummings, *The Enormous Room,* with an introduction by Robert Graves (London: Jonathan Cape, 1930), pp,. 182, 163, 167, 178. Elsewhere, cummings's disaffected view of the war is succinctly summarized by the fellow-prisoner called Mexique: " 'Every-body run a-round with guns. . . . And by-and-by no see to shoot everybody, so everybody go home. . . . I t'ink lotta bullsh-t' " (p. 194).

95 Lawrence, *Kangaroo* (New York: Viking, 1923), pp. 261, 265.

96 Quoted by Cadogan and Craig, p. 38.

97 As DuBois suggested, the war had a comparably "consciousness-raising" effect on black American soldiers; see his "Essay Toward a History," p. 895: "They [black soldiers] began to hate prejudice and discrimination as they had never hated it before. They began to realize its eternal meaning and complications. Far from filling them with a desire to escape from their race and country, they were filled with a bitter, dogged determination never to give up the fight for Negro equality in America. If American color prejudice counted on this war experience to break the spirit of the young Negro, it counted without its host. A new, radical Negro spirit has been born in France, which leaves us older radicals far behind. Thousands of young black men have offered their lives for the Lilies of France and they return ready to offer them again for the Sunflowers of Afro-America."

98 Atherton, *The White Morning* (New York: Stokes, 1918), 165, 137, 146 (cited in an unpublished paper entitled "The Mud in God's Eye: World War I in Women's Novels" by Tamara Jones; we are grateful to her and to Gayle Greene of Scripps College for bringing this text to our attention). Further references will appear in the text, with page numbers preceded by the citation *WM.*

99 Woolf, *The Years* (New York: Harcourt, 1937), pp. 287, 292. Further references will appear in the text, with page numbers preceded by the citation *Y.*

100 See *A Room of One's Own,* pp. 100–01.

101 H. D., *Trilogy,* p. 163.

102 Eastman, "Now I Dare Do It," in Blanche Cook, ed., *Crystal Eastman on Women and Revolution* (New York: Oxford University Press, 1978), p. 240. Further references to writings by Eastman will appear in the text, with page numbers preceded by the citation *CE.* See also Schreiner, "Woman in War," in *Woman and Labor* and Gilman's

comments on the Great War in the excerpt from *With Her in Ourland* included in Ann J. Lane, ed., *The Charlotte Perkins Gilman Reader* (New York: Pantheon, 1980).

103 For Robins, see Lemons, p. 20.

104 This Woolf manuscript is in the Berg Collection of the New York Public Library and is quoted by permission of Quentin Bell.

105 *Bernard Shaw's Plays*, ed. Warren S. Smith (New York: W. W. Norton 1970), p. 147.

106 Wharton, *A Son*, pp. 423–26. Willa Cather records a comparable (and equally encoded) empowerment of the living by the wartime dead in *The Professor's House*, where the sacrificed Tom Outland gives meaning to Prof. St. Peter's existence; see chap. 5 of this volume, pp. 206–10.

107 Mansfield, *The Journals of Katherine Mansfield* (1927; New York:; Alfred A. Knopf, 1954), pp. 43–45, 49. Further references will be to this edition, and page numbers, preceded by the citation *J*, will appear in the text.

108 H.D., *Bid Me to Live*, pp. 145–46.

109 The manuscript of "The Thorn Thicket" is held at the Beinecke Library of Yale University, and is quoted by permission of Perdita Schaffner.

110 Fussell, for instance, includes Yeats in the "long and impressive roster of major innovative talents who were not involved with the war." The others, in Fussell's view, are Woolf, Pound, Eliot, Lawrence, and Joyce. See Fussell, pp. 313–14.

111 *The Collected Poems of William Butler Yeats*, p. 153. Further references will be to this edition, and page numbers, preceded by the citation *CP*, will appear in the text.

112 See James E. Miller, Jr., *T. S. Eliot's Personal Waste Land* (University Park: Pennsylvania State University Press, 1977), p. 19.

113 Quoted in T. S. Eliot, *The Waste Land: A Facsimile and Transcript of the Original Drafts Including the Annotations of Ezra Pound*, ed. and with an intro. by Valerie Eliot (New York: Harvest, 1974), p. 1. Further references to this book will appear in the text, with page numbers preceded by the citation *Facs*. We should note here that, though we do not wish to enter into debate about what some commentators call "the homosexual interpretation of *The Waste Land*," we think the argument about the dead Verdenal's significance as a friend to Eliot, first advanced by John Peter and later elaborated by James E. Miller, is virtually incontrovertible, even if largely circumstantial.

114 Grover Smith, *The Waste Land* (London: Allen & Unwin, 1983), p. 102.

115 Smith, pp. 106–07,

116 See John Peter, Grover Smith, and G. Wilson Knight, quoted and discussed in Miller, pp. 71, 76, and note 17, p. 169.

117 Miller, p. 62.

118 Read, in *Up the Line to Death*, p. 88.

119 Posthumous citation of Verdenal, quoted in Miller, p. 21.

120 See our discussion of Woolf's review in *The War of the Words*, p. 133.

121 Woolf, *Jacob's Room* (New York: Harcourt, 1923), pp. 175–76.

122 For Eliot's "King Bolo" poems, see chap. 1, note 112 of this volume.

123 For a discussion of the connection between women's war work and their achievement of the vote, see Marwick, pp. 95–105.

124 On the gender implications of shell shock, see Elaine Showalter, *The Female Malady*, pp. 189–94. On male fragility, see also Blatch, who asserted that men "should be . . . favored" in the workplace because "they are few, they are precious, they should be wrapped in cotton wool" (p. 112).

125 Mitchell, p. 389. On women's emancipation, and in particular their change of costume during the war, see also Barry, p. 281: "This was the time when silk stockings, hitherto worn at parties only, came in for daytime wear—and flesh-colored ones at that. Underwear ceased to have sleeves, corsets went out, the habit of spending and

of living for the moment came in." A comparable point is wittily made in Jean Renoir's film *The Grand Illusion* (1937); when the French and British prisoners of war on whom the movie focuses receive a trunkful of women's clothes to wear in a transvestite show they are planning, they comment on the radical ways in which feminine styles have changed during the course of the war:

> "It's not just their dresses that are short. They've cut their hair."
> "Short hair?"
> "It must be like going to bed with a boy."
> "When we can't keep an eye on them, women do foolish things."

Less censorious about costume change, an article attacking women for spending too much on clothes during wartime expresses admiration for "the war-dressed woman," who wears "a sort of military upper garment, with a compromise in trousers, half skirt, half bloomer" and who "is still a romantic sort of figure . . . a woman embarking on a new form of adventure" (Baroness Franciska von Heddeman, "The Extravagance of Women's War-Clothes," *The Forum* 59 [April 1918]: 407).

126 Pound, "Hugh Selwyn Mauberley (Life and Contacts)" in *Personae: The Collected Poems of Ezra Pound* (New York: New Directions, 1926), p. 191.

127 West, "Autumn and Virginia Woolf," *Ending in Earnest: A Literary Log* (New York: Arno, 1971), pp. 212–13. On the "decline" of feminism after the first world war, see chap., 2 of this volume as well as Nancy Cott, *The Grounding of Modern Feminism*, passim.

128 Mary Borden, *The Forbidden Zone* (London: Heinemann, 1929), pp. 59–60; quoted by Cookson.

129 The manuscript of Vivien Haigh-Wood Eliot's "The Paralysed Woman" is held by the Bodleian Library, Oxford.

130 Sanguine though she was, even Mary Austin conceded that "Some of the freedom gained by this war will have to be surrendered at the end of it" ("Sex Emancipation," p. 617).

131 Quoted in Cadogan and Craig, p. 47.

132 Lemons, p. 22.

133 Plath, "Getting There," *Ariel* (New York: Harper & Row, 1965), p. 37.

134 H.D., *Tribute to Freud*, p. 77; Pastan, "In the Old Guerilla War," *The Five Stages of Grief* (New York: W. W. Norton, 1978), p. 15; Rich, "The Images," *A Wild Patience Has Taken Me This Far* (New York: W. W. Norton, 1981), pp. 3–5.

Chapter 8

EPIGRAPHS: Lawrence, *Fantasia of the Unconscious* (London: Martin Secker, 1923), p. 87; Stein, "A Long Dress," *Tender Buttons*, in *Selected Writings of Gertrude Stein*, ed. Carl Van Vechten, p. 467; Joyce, *Ulysses* (New York: Random House, 1934), p. 515; Bishop, "Exchanging Hats," *The Complete Poems 1927–1979* (New York: Farrar Straus Giroux, 1983), p. 200.

1 Nicolson, *Portrait of a Marriage*, pp. 105–06.

2 Woolf, *Orlando* (1928; New York: Harvest-Harcourt Brace Jovanovich, 1973), pp. 308–09. Further references will be to this edition, and page numbers will appear in the text.

3 See Rose and Mitchell, "Introduction I and II," Jacques Lacan, *Feminine Sexuality: Jacques Lacan and the école freudienne*, ed. Mitchell and Rose, trans. Rose (New York: W. W. Norton, 1982), pp. 1–57.

4 Ackroyd, *Dressing Up: Transvestism and Drag: The History of an Obsession* (New York: Simon and Schuster, 1979), p. 95.

5 Dijkstra, "The Androgyne in Nineteenth-Century Art and Literature," *Comparative Literature* 26:1 (Winter 1974): 62, 73.
6 Gautier, *Mademoiselle de Maupin* (New York: Boni and Liveright, n.d.), p. 277. Balzac, *Seraphita,* Afterword and Foreword by Patricia Werthheim Abrams (New York: Freedlieds Library, 1986).
7 See Freud, "Female Sexuality," in *Sexuality and the Psychology of Love,* ed. Philip Rieff (New York: Collier Books, 1963), pp. 196–97.
8 For background on "uniforms," see Lawrence Langner, in *The Importance of Wearing Clothes* (New York: Hastings House, 1959), who notes that in ancient Greece "women were not permitted . . . to wear more than three garments at a time. In Rome . . . the law restricted peasants to one color, officers to two, commanders to three. . . . In the reign of Charles IX of France, the amount and quality of ornamentation of clothing was regulated according to the rank of the wearer, and most of these laws remained in force until the French Revolution. In England Henry VIII insisted that a countess must wear a train both before and behind, while those below her in rank might not have this distinction" (p. 179). The first of Yeats's visionary "Fragments," though probably intended as a comment on the Industrial Revolution, mythologizes the transformative power of the spinning jenny: "Locke sank into a swoon; / The Garden died; / God took the spinning-jenny / Out of his side" (*The Collected Poems of W. B. Yeats,* p. 211).
9 Moers, *The Dandy: Brummell to Beerbohm* (New York: Viking, 1960), p. 283.
10 Wilde, "More Radical Ideas Upon Dress Reform," *The Writings of Oscar Wilde,* 5 vols. in 1, pp. 146 and 151.
11 Moers, p. 295.
12 Beerbohm, "A Defense of Cosmetics" in *Aesthetes,* ed. Beckson, pp. 59–60. Beerbohm also argued that "men have not the excuse of facial monotony, that holds in the case of women. Have we not hair upon our chins and upper lips?" (see p. 59).
13 Beerbohm, "A Defense of Cosmetics," p. 51.
14 On Eltinge, see Martha Banta, *Imaging American Women: Idea and Ideals in Cultural History* (New York: Columbia University Press, 1987), pp. 269, 272–73; also see Ackroyd, p. 112.
15 Quoted in Moers, p,. 327.
16 Bloomer's remarks are quoted in the entry for her in *Notable American Women 1607–1950: A Biographical Dictionary,* ed. Edward T. James, Janet Wilson James, and Paul S. Bayer, 3 vols. (Cambridge: Harvard University Press, Belknap Press, 1971), 1:180.
17 Wilde, "More Radical Ideas Upon Dress Reform," p. 152.
18 Letter to Gerrit Smith, Dec. 25, 1855, quoted in Robert E. Riegel, "Women's Clothes and Women's Rights," *American Quarterly* 15:3 (Fall 1963): 391.
19 Stanton, *Eighty Years and More (1815–1897): Reminiscences of Elizabeth Cady Stanton* (New York: European Publishing Co., 1898), p. 201.
20 Stanton, p. 202.
21 Walker, *Hit* (New York: The American News Company, 1871), pp. 66–69. See also Helene E. Roberts, "The Exquisite Slave: The Role of Clothes in the Making of the Victorian Woman," and David Kunzle, "Dress Reform as Antifeminism: A Response to Helene E. Roberts's 'The Exquisite Slave: The Role of Clothes in the Making of the Victorian Woman,' " in *Signs* 2:3 (Spring 1977): 554–69, 570–79.
22 [Mary E. Walker], *Unmasked; or The Science of Immorality.* To Gentlemen. By a Woman Physician and Surgeon (Philadelphia: Wm. H. Boyd, 1878), p. 98. This is a quote from a letter written by Mary E. Tillotson of Vineland, N.J. We would like to thank Bernard Horn for making this text available to us.
23 Charles McCool Snyder, *Dr. Mary Walker: The Little Lady in Pants* (New York: Vantage Press, 1962), pp. 29, 47.

24 Joyce, *Ulysses,* p. 524. Further page numbers will appear in the text.
25 Bullough, *Sexual Variance in Society and History* (New York: Wiley-Interscience, 1976), pp. 554–55.
26 See, for example, Carolyn G. Heilbrun, *Toward a Recognition of Androgyny* (New York: Alfred A. Knopf, 1973), p. 95, and Suzette Henke, *Joyce's Moraculous Sindbook: A Study of Ulysses* (Columbus: Ohio State University Press, 1978), pp. 7, 93, and 194–97; and more recently, Bonnie Kime Scott, *Joyce and Feminism* (Bloomington: Indiana University Press, 1984), esp. pp. 156–83.
27 See Kate Millett, *Sexual Politics* (New York: Avon, 1970), pp. 336–61. Discussing Genet, Millett suggests that "as she minces along a street in the Village, the storm of outrage an insouciant queen in drag may call down is due to the fact that she is both masculine and feminine at once—or male, but feminine. [And thus] she has . . . challenged more than the taboo on homosexuality, she has uncovered what the source of this contempt implies—the fact that sex role is sex rank" (p. 343). See also Maria Ramas, "Freud's Dora, Dora's Hysteria: The Negation of a Woman's Rebellion," *Feminist Studies* 6:3 (Fall 1980): 472–510, for a useful analysis of the connections between sex role, sex rank, and sadomasochistic fantasies. Ramas suggests that heterosexual desire cannot be separated from "what psychoanalysis terms 'primal scene' phantasies. These phantasies are sadomasochistic in content and have rigidly defined masculine and feminine positions. They are, perhaps, the most profound ideology, precisely because they are eroticized" (p. 478).
28 Davis, "Women on Top," *Society and Culture in Early Modern France* (Stanford: Stanford University Press, 1975), pp. 129–30.
29 On Joyce's politics during the Great War, see Colin MacCabe, *James Joyce and the Revolution of the Word* (New York: Barnes and Noble, 1979), pp. 158–71.
30 Stoller, *Sex and Gender* (New York: Science House, 1968) pp. 214, 177. Significantly (in view of the connections we have been examining between sex role, sex rank, and transvestism), Stoller asserts that "Fetishistic cross-dressing is almost non-existent in women"; see *The Transsexual Experiment: Sex and Gender, Vol. 2* (New York: Jason Aronson, 1976), p. 143.
31 Stoller, *Sex and Gender,* pp. 214–15.
32 It is quite clear that Joyce is referring consciously and sardonically to the turn-of-the-century idea of the New Woman. He even introduces a bit of comic dialogue for "a feminist" who comments on Bloom's fantasied achievements as a political leader (p. 472):

>   A Millionairess: *(Richly.)* Isn't he simply wonderful?
>   A Noblewoman: *(Nobly.)* All that man has seen!
>   A Feminist: *(Masculinely.)* And done!

33 Moore, "Albert Nobbs" in *Celibate Lives* (1918; New York: Boni and Liveright, 1927), pp. 80–81. Further references will be to this edition, and page numbers will appear in the text.
34 Lawrence, "The Fox," *Four Short Novels,* pp. 114, 130. Further references will be to this edition, and page numbers will appear in the text. "Tickets, Please," which Lawrence wrote during World War I, is an interesting mirror image of "The Fox." For a discussion of the latter, see chap. 7 of this volume.
35 Eliot, *The Waste Land: A Facsimile and Transcript . . . ,* ed. Valerie Eliot, pp. 140, 148. Further references will be to this edition, and page numbers will appear in the text. In *Crome Yellow* (1921), Aldous Huxley presents a portrait of Madame Sesostris *(sic)* as a transvestite man who poses as a gypsy fortune-teller in order to seduce an innocent village maiden; interestingly, according to Grover Smith, this character in Hux-

ley's roman à clef was based on Bertrand Russell, a close friend and mentor of Eliot and his wife Vivienne (see Smith, pp. 67–68).

36 It is interesting to consider the connection between Bram Stoker's *Dracula* and the upside-down bats described in "What the Thunder Said" (p. 145). In early drafts of *The Waste Land* these were "a [man] form" which "crawled head downward down a blackened wall" (p. 75), and Valerie Eliot has noted the link between this figure and the scene in *Dracula* where the count crawls in a similar way (see Leonard Wolf, *The Annotated Dracula* [New York: Clarkson N. Potter, 1975], p. 37n29). Count Dracula is, of course, a dead man who must depend for sustenance on the blood of living women; after he has converted his female victims to vampires, moreover, they prey on infants, unnaturally reversing woman's maternal role. Finally, *The Waste Land*'s "voices singing out of empty cisterns and exhausted wells" (p. 145) are reminiscent of the voice of John the Baptist, who was the victim of yet another "woman on top"— Herodias's unruly daughter Salome. For further discussion of these works, see chap. 1 of this volume.

37 See D. G. Rossetti, "Jenny," in *Poems*, ed. Oswald Doughty (London: J. M. Dent and Sons, 1957), pp. 63–72.

38 See our discussion of Vernon Lee and Henry James in *War of the Words*, pp. 214–15.

39 Hemingway, letter to Col. Buck Lanham, 12 June 1948; quoted in Carlos Baker, *Ernest Hemingway: A Life Story* (New York: Scribner's, 1969), p. 460; Hemingway, *The Garden of Eden* (New York: Scribner's, 1986). Further references will be to this edition, and page numbers will appear in the text.

40 Lynn, *Hemingway* (New York: Simon and Schuster, 1987), pp. 38–46. Although Lynn does not particularly explore the point, Hemingway's ambivalence toward gender blurring is further highlighted when the early, incomplete story "The Last Good Country" is juxtaposed with *The Garden of Eden*. In "The Last Good Country"—a positive tale of which *The Garden* may be seen as a negative version—Nick Adams's younger sister Littless (modeled, according to Lynn, on Hemingway's sister Ursula) demonstrates her loyalty to Nick by cutting off her hair and explaining that "Now I'm your sister but I'm a boy." See "The Last Good Country," in *The Complete Short Stories of Ernest Hemingway: The Finca Vigia Edition* (New York: Scribner's, 1987), pp. 504–44; see also Lynn, pp. 56–58.

41 Woolf, *A Writer's Diary*, ed. Leonard Woolf (New York: Harcourt, Brace and Company, 1954), pp. 48, 49; T. S. Eliot's description of James Joyce as "ethically orthodox" appears in *After Strange Gods* (London: Faber and Faber, 1934), p. 38.

42 Barrett Browning, *Letters of Elizabeth Barrett Browning to Mary Russell Mitford, 1836–54*, ed. Meredith B. Raymond and Mary Rose Sullivan, 3 vols. (Winfield, Kansas: Wedgestone Press, 1983), 2:7; Robert and Elizabeth Barrett Browning, *The Brownings' Correspondence*, ed. Philip Kelley and Ronald Hudson, 4 vols. to date (Winfield, Kansas: Wedgestone Press, 1984–), 1:361. We are grateful to Alice Falk for bringing these passages to our attention.

43 Schreiner, *From Man to Man* (1925; London: Virago, 1982), p. 226.

44 Nightingale, *Cassandra*, p. 53; Schreiner, *Stories, Dreams, and Allegories*, pp. 156–59. For further discussion of Schreiner's work in this connection, see Joyce Berkman, "The Nurturant Fantasies of Olive Schreiner," *Frontiers* 2:3 (Fall 1977): 8–17.

45 de Beauvoir, *The Second Sex*, trans. H. M. Parshley (New York: Bantam, 1961), p. 47.

46 Habegger, "A Well Hidden Hand," *Novel* 14:3 (Spring 1981): 197–212.

47 Habegger, pp. 198–99, 202.

48 Grand, *The Heavenly Twins* (New York: Cassell, 1893), p. 453. Further references will be to this edition, and page numbers will appear in the text.

49 Cather, *My Ántonia*, pp. 149–50; Richardson, *The Tunnel* in *Pilgrimage 2* (New York: Popular Library, 1976), p. 148.

50 Nin, *Ladders to Fire,* in *Cities of the Interior* (Chicago: The Swallow Press, 1974), pp. 37–38.

51 Moore, *Jirel of Joiry* (New York: Paperback Library, 1969), p. 7. "Jirel Meets Magic" is reprinted in *More Women of Wonder,* ed. Pamela Sargent (New York: Vintage Books, 1976), pp. 3–52. Also see Moore's *Judgment Night* (1952) in which the armored heroine, Juille, fights for her father, who had "used to want a son" (New York: Paperback Library, 1965), p. 6. For a more extensive discussion, see Susan Gubar, "C. L. Moore and the Conventions of Women's Science Fiction," *Science Fiction Studies* 20:1 (March 1980): 16–27. Moore may be drawing upon the broadside ballad tradition discussed by Tristram Potter Coffin: see *The Female Hero in Folklore and Legend* (New York: Seabury Press, 1975), p. 191.

52 Photographs and an interview with Dorothy Arzner appear in *Women and the Cinema: A Critical Anthology,* ed. Karyn Kay and Gerald Peary (New York: E. P. Dutton, 1977), pp. 12, 16, and 167; 153–68. A photograph of Bonheur's "Permission de Travestissement" is reprinted in Karen Petersen and J. J. Wilson, *Women Artists* (New York: Harper Colophon, 1976), p. 77. This permit from the police raises the interesting subject of cross-dressing and the law. Morton L. Enelow's argument, summarized by Ralph Slovenko, is that: "Exhibitionism, voyeurism and transvestism are lumped together by the law and viewed as 'public nuisance offenses' " punishable as acts disturbing or alarming to the public. See "Public Nuisance Offenses" in *Sexual Behavior and the Law,* ed. Slovenko (Springfield, Ill.: Charles C. Thomas, 1965), p. 278. But a comprehensive history of the law and transvestism apparently still needs to be written.

53 Ackroyd argues persuasively that the "unacknowledged potency" of Elizabethan and Jacobean female impersonation on the stage "accounts in part for the closing of the theatres during the Puritan Commonwealth. Certainly everything changes as a result of that suppression and, after the Restoration and the reopening of the theatres in 1660, another drama emerged. . . . In an age of literal representation, and at a time of male-dominated commercialism, cross-dressing seemed a peculiarly alien and threatening activity. It was fit only to be laughed at—which is, of course, exactly what happened" (pp. 95–96). On film and transvestism, see Rebecca Bell-Metereau, *Hollywood Androgyny* (New York: Columbia University Press, 1985). On *Yentl,* see Garrett Stewart, "Singer Sung: Voice as Avowal in Streisand's *Yentl,*" *Mosaic* 18:4 (Fall 1985): 135–58.

54 Photographs of Sarah Bernhardt playing Hamlet, the Duc de Reichstadt, and Pelléas appear in Joanna Richardson, *Sarah Bernhardt and Her World* (London: Weidenfeld and Nicolson, 1977), pp. 161, 168, and 179. For a discussion of Marlene Dietrich's exploitation of military uniforms, see Alexander Walker, "Marlene Dietrich: At Heart a Gentleman," *Sex in the Movies* (Baltimore: Pelican Books, 1969), pp. 88–93.

55 Nin, *Ladders to Fire,* p. 38.

56 Secrest, *Between Me and Life: A Biography of Romaine Brooks* (London: Macdonald and Jane's, 1976), p. 8.

57 Hall, *The Well of Loneliness,* (1928; New York: Avon, 1981), pp. 52, 204–05. Further references in this chapter will be to this edition, and page numbers will appear in the text.

58 See Susan J. Wolfson, " 'Their She Condition': Cross-Dressing and the Politics of Gender in *Don Juan,*" ELH 54 (Fall 1987): 585–617; see also Cecil Lang, "Narcissus Jilted: Byron, *Don Juan* and the Biographical Imperative," in *Historical Studies and Literary Criticism,* ed. Jerome McGann (Madison: University of Wisconsin Press, 1985), pp. 143–79.

59 See Elaine Showalter, *A Literature of Their Own,* pp. 248–49, and Virginia Spencer Carr, *The Lonely Hunter: A Biography of Carson McCullers* (Garden City, New York:

Doubleday, 1975), pp. 159, 167, and 338. See also *The War of the Words* (pp. 186–87) on Djuna Barnes's portrait of Barney in *The Ladies Almanack*, pp. 7–8, where Barnes explains about Saint Musset that she had "developed in the Womb of her most gentle Mother to be a Boy," and "when she came forth an Inch or so less than this," she had the audacity to explain to her father that she was "more commendable" than the son he desired "seeing that I do it without the Tools for the Trade."

60 See Phyllis Rose, *Woman of Letters: A Life of Virginia Woolf* (New York: Oxford University Press, 1978), pp. 192–93. For a discussion of Woolf's love of women, see Blanche Weisen Cook, " 'Women Alone Stir My Imagination': Lesbianism and the Cultural Tradition," *Signs* 4:4 (Summer 1979): 718–39.

61 See Smith-Rosenberg, "The New Woman as Androgyne," pp. 245–96; and Esther Newton, "The Mythic Mannish Lesbian: Radclyffe Hall and the New Woman," *The Lesbian Issue: Essays from Signs*, ed. Estelle B. Freedman, Barbara C. Gelpi, Susan L. Johnson, Kathleen M. Weston (Chicago: University of Chicago Press, 1985), pp. 7–26.

62 Freud, "Some Psychological Consequences of the Anatomical Distinction between the Sexes," *Sexuality and the Psychology of Love*, p. 187.

63 Dinesen, *Seven Gothic Tales* (New York: Vintage Books, 1972), p. 43. Also see the discussion of clothing in Dinesen, "Daguerrotypes," *Daguerrotypes and Other Essays*, trans. P. M. Mitchell and W. D. Peters (1951; Chicago: University of Chicago Press, 1979), p. 26. Dinesen's wardrobe is discussed by Judith Thurman, *Isak Dinesen* pp. 160–61, 196–97, 367–68.

64 Susan Leonardi, "A Dangerous Thing: Somerville College and the Somerville Novelists, 1912–1922," Ph.D. diss. University of California, Davis, 1986, p. 31. A photograph of Dorothy Sayers, "in a characteristically mannish costume and hat," appears in Janet Hitchman, *Such a Strange Lady* (New York: Avon, 1975), p. 96.

65 Stein, *Selected Writings of Gertrude Stein*, pp. 469, 51.

66 Stein, *Wars I Have Seen* (London: B. T. Batsford, 1945), pp. 48–49.

67 Stein, *How To Write*, p. 27.

68 Stein, "Talks to Saints or Stories of Saint Remy," in *Painted Lace*, Yale Edition of the Unpublished Writings of Gertrude Stein, ed. Van Vechten, vol. 5, p. 111. We are indebted here to conversations with Tom Boll, who brought the significance of this text to our attention.

69 Joyce, *A Portrait of the Artist as Young Man* (New York: Modern Library, 1928), p. 252.

70 Eliot, introduction to Barnes, *Nightwood*, pp. xi–xvii.

71 Miller, *T. S. Eliot's Personal Waste Land*, pp. 31–32.

72 Barnes, *Nightwood*, p. 146. Further references will be to this edition, and page numbers will appear in the text. The best critical treatment of this novel appears in Louis F. Kannenstine, *The Art of Djuna Barnes* (New York: New York University Press, 1977), pp. 86–127.

73 Barney, *The One Who Is Legion* (London: Eric Partridge, 1930); see the discussion of this work in Benstock, *Women of the Left Bank*, p. 298.

74 H.D., *Bid Me To Live*, p. 62.

75 H. D., *Tribute to Freud*, pp. 180–81.

76 H.D., *End to Torment*, ed. Norman Holmes Pearson and Michael King (New York: New Directions, 1979), pp. 11, 33–34, 41, 45, 46–47, 51–52; see the discussion of H. D.'s bisexual imagery in Susan Friedman and Rachel Blau DuPlessis, " 'I had two loves separate': The Sexualities of H.D.'s *Her*," *Montemora* 8 (1981): 7–30.

77 H. D., *Helen in Egypt* (1961; New York: New Directions, 1974), pp. 10, 263, 300. Further references will be to this edition, and page numbers will appear in the text.

78 Eliade, *Mephistopheles and the Androgyne*, tr. J. M. Cohen (New York: Sheed and Ward, 1965), pp. 113–14.

79 See Carpenter, *Intermediate Types among Primitive Folk: A Study in Social Evolution* (New York: Mitchell Kennerley, 1914), passim; Carpenter, *The Intermediate Sex,* passim.

80 On Carpenter's influence on Bloomsbury and specifically on Woolf, see Barbara Fassler, "Theories of Homosexuality as Sources of Bloomsbury's Androgyny," *Signs* 5:2 (Winter 1979): 237–51.

81 Delavenay, *D. H. Lawrence and Edward Carpenter* (New York: Taplinger, 1971), pp. 190–235.

82 Harris, "The More Profound Nationality of Their Lesbianism: Lesbian Society in the 1920's," *Amazon Expedition,* p. 79.

83 Victoria Glendinning, *Vita: The Life of V. Sackville-West* (New York: Alfred A. Knopf, 1983), p. 106.

84 Anderson, "The Man Who Became a Woman," *Horses and Men: Tales, Long and Short, from Our American Life* (New York: B. W. Huebsch, 1923), p. 207. Further references will be to this edition, and page numbers will appear in the text. See also Lonna M. Malmsheimer, "Sexual Metaphor and Social Criticism in Anderson's *The Man Who Became a Woman,*" *Studies in American Fiction* 7:1 (Spring 1979): 17–26. We are grateful to Karyn Riedell for bringing this text and several others to our attention.

85 West, *The Dream Life of Balso Snell,* in *Two Novels* (New York: Noonday Press, 1963), pp. 21–22; after murdering a man and experiencing a terrible fear, the protagonist relinquishes his knife and feels "like a young girl"; he imitates a girl's flirtation with sailors; and he finally ends up violently sick. For a discussion of *Miss Lonelyhearts,* see *The War of the Words,* pp. 40–43.

86 Farrell, "Just Boys," *The Short Stories of James T. Farrell* (New York: Vanguard Press, 1937), p. 49.

87 Genet, *The Thief's Journal,* Foreword by Jean-Paul Sartre, trans. Bernard Frechtman (New York: Grove, 1964), pp. 49 and 100.

88 Ackroyd, p. 147. Interestingly, in 1961, Lawrence Durrell translated Emmanuel Royidis's *Pope Joan* (1886; New York: E. P. Dutton, 1961), a novel about the legendary female pope in which the pregnancy of the cross-dressed pontiff causes, among other things, a plague of locusts, and Joan herself is told by an angel that she must choose between "the eternal fire of hell for your unlawfulness" and "premature death and disgrace upon earth" (pp. 143, 141). For other visions of transsexuality as "bizarre and threatening," see Gore Vidal, *Myra Breckenridge* (Boston: Little, Brown, 1968) and Philip Roth, *The Breast* (New York: Holt, 1972).

89 Brown, *I Want What I Want* (New York: G. P. Putnam's Sons, 1967), p. 223.

90 Friedman, *Hermaphrodeity* (New York: Alfred A. Knopf, 1972), p. 26. Further references will be to this edition, and page numbers will appear in the text.

91 Fiedler, *Freaks: Myths and Images of the Secret Self* (New York: Simon and Schuster, 1978), p. 341.

92 McCullers, *The Ballad of the Sad Cafe and Other Stories* (New York: Bantam, 1981), is discussed in *The War of the Words,* pp. 104–12; O'Connor, "The Temple of the Holy Ghost," *The Complete Stories of Flannery O'Connor* (New York: Farrar Straus, 1971), pp. 236–48.

93 Le Guin, *The Left Hand of Darkness* (New York: Walker, 1969), esp. p. 17: "For it was impossible to think of him [Estraven] as a woman . . . and yet whenever I thought of him as a man I felt a sense of falseness." For a revision of an early story about Winter, in which Le Guin uses "she" instead of "he" to describe her androgynes, see her "Winter's King," *The Wind's Twelve Quarters* (New York: Harper & Row, 1976), pp. 85–108.

94 Brophy, *In Transit: an heroic cyclic novel* (1969; New York: G. P. Putnam's, 1970), pp. 81, 89.

95 Rich, "Diving into the Wreck," *Diving into the Wreck: Poems 1971–1972* (New York:

W. W. Norton, 1973), p. 24. Joanna Russ, *The Female Man* (New York: Bantam Books, 1975); Maxine Hong Kingston, *The Woman Warrior* (New York: Alfred A. Knopf, 1976).

96 Gould, *A Sea-Change* (New York: Simon and Schuster, 1976), p. 129.
97 Jong, *Fanny* (New York: New American Library, 1980), p. 61.
98 Oates, *A Bloodsmoor Romance* (New York: E. P. Dutton, 1982), pp. 244 and 594.
99 Benmussa, *The Singular Life of Alfred Nobbs,* tr. Barbara Wright, in *Benmussa Directs* (London and Dallas: John Calder and Riverrun Press, 1980), p. 120.
100 Plath, *Collected Poems,* ed. Ted Hughes (London: Faber and Faber, 1981), pp. 245, 247.
101 Plath, *The Bell Jar* (New York: Harper & Row, 1971), p. 124. From *Jane Eyre* and *The Mill on the Floss* to Kate Chopin's *The Awakening* and Margaret Atwood's *Surfacing* (1972), ruining, tearing, or throwing away clothes is a persistent metaphor for defiance of sex roles, but Plath, especially in her poems, presses it further than most of her precursors and contemporaries.
102 Schor, "Dreaming Dyssymetry: Barthes, Foucault, and Sexual Difference," *Men in Feminism,* ed. Alice Jardine and Paul Smith (New York: Methuen, 1987), p. 100.
103 Schor, p. 105.
104 Heath, "Male Feminism," *Men in Feminism,* pp. 6 and 7.
105 Derrida, *Spurs,* trans. Barbara Harlow (Chicago: University of Chicago Press, 1979), pp. 103, 105. Further references will be to this edition, and page numbers will appear in the text.
106 Quoted in Robert Scholes, "Reading like a Man," *Men in Feminism,* p. 212.
107 Cixous in Cixous and Clement, *The Newly Born Woman,* p. 85.
108 Furman, "The Politics of Language: Beyond the Gender Principle?." *Making a Difference: Feminist Literary Criticism,* ed. Gayle Greene and Coppelia Kahn (London and New York: Methuen, 1985), p. 59; Kamuf, "Writing Like A Woman," *Women and Language in Literature and Society,* p. 285.
109 Jacobus, *Reading Women,* p. 15.
110 Jacobus, p. 13.
111 Schor, *Men in Feminism,* p. 103.
112 Showalter, "Critical Cross-Dressing: Male Feminists and the Woman of the Year," *Men in Feminism,* p. 130.
113 Schor, *Men in Feminism,* p. 98.
114 Heath, *Men in Feminism,* p. 25 and 28.
115 Ross, "No Question of Silence," and Nelson, "Men, Feminism: The Materiality of Discourse," both in *Men in Feminism,* pp. 86 and 159.
116 Gates, private conversation with the authors at the MLA Convention, 1987. The current controversy was interestingly prefigured by a debate about androgyny that took place among feminists in the early seventies after the publication of several important works on the subject, including Carolyn G. Heilbrun's *Towards a Recognition of Androgyny* and Nancy Topping Bazin's *Virginia Woolf and the Androgynous Vision* (New Brunswick, N.J.: Rutgers University Press, 1973). For various views of the matter, see the special androgyny issue of *Women's Studies,* 2:2 (1974), edited by Nancy Topping Bazin.
117 Ackroyd, p. 120.
118 Miss Manners [Judith Martin], *San Francisco Chronicle,* Dec. 18, 1987.
119 Morris, *Conundrum* (London: Faber and Faber, 1974), pp. 9, 10, 28, 50.
120 Olds, "Outside the Operating Room of the Sex-Change Doctor," in *Powers of Desire: The Politics of Sexuality,* ed. Ann Snitow, Christine Stansell, and Sharon Thompson (New York: Monthly Review Press, 1983), p. 300.
121 *Sun,* 5 : 39 (Sept. 29, 1987) and 6 : 2 (Jan. 12, 1988). On "Le Funelle," a "wallet-size

paper funnel that enables a woman to urinate like a man—standing," and the "Baby Bonder," a "biblike garment with breast-shaped protuberances into which ordinary baby bottles have been inserted" so that men can nurse their infants, see Barbara Roessner, "Breast-Feeding for Men: A Techno-fix for the Nurturing Father," San Francisco *Chronicle* (March 20, 1988), *Sunday Punch,* p. 5.

122 Phillips, *The Pregnant Man* (Garden City: Doubleday, 1978), pp. 33–4.

123 Lynn, *The Woman Who Loved the Moon and Other Stories* (New York: Berkeley Books, 1981), pp. 123. Further references will be to this edition, and page numbers will appear in the text. We are indebted to Alice Falk for bringing this text to our attention.

124 Churchill, *Cloud 9,* rev. ed. (New York: Methuen, 1984). Further references will be to this edition, and page numbers will appear in the text.

Index

Individual titles of works are listed under the names of the authors.

Acknowledgments

The authors gratefully acknowledge permission to reprint material from the following sources: From "Consorting with Angels," by Anne Sexton, from *The Complete Poems of Anne Sexton*, copyright © 1981, Hougton Mifflin; from "Consorting with Angels," by Anne Sexton, from *Live or Die*, copyright © 1966, reprinted by permission of Sterling Lord Literistic, Inc.; from "Tribute to the Angels," by H. D., from *Collected Poems 1912–1944*, copyright © 1983, reprinted by permission of New Directions Publishing Corporation; from "Prayer to My Lady of Paphos," by Sappho, from *Sappho: A New Translation*, trans. Mary Barnard, University of California Press, 1973, copyright © 1958 by The Regents of the University of California; excerpt from "Exchanging Hats" from *The Complete Poems* by Elizabeth Bishop, copyright © 1979, 1983 by Alice Helen Methfessel, copyright © 1956 by Elizabeth Bishop, reprinted by permission of Farrar, Straus and Giroux, Inc.; from "Rider Haggard's Heart of Darkness," by Sandra M. Gilbert, from *Coordinates: Placing Science Fiction and Fantasy*, ed. George E. Slusser, Eric S. Rabkin, and Robert Scholes, Carbondale: Southern Illinois University Press, 1983, and also from *Partisan Review*, Summer 1983; from "The Second Coming of Aphrodite: Kate Chopin's Fantasy of Desire," by Sandra M. Gilbert, from *Kenyon Review*, Summer 1983, and also (in a slightly different version) from *Kate Chopin's The Awakening and Selected Stories*, selected and with an introduction by Sandra M. Gilbert, Penguin, 1984; from "She in *Herland*," by Susan Gubar, from *Coordinates*, ed. Slusser et al.; from "Soldier's Heart: Literary Men, Literary Women, and the Great War," by Sandra M. Gilbert, from *Signs* 8:3 (1983); from "Costumes of the Mind: Transvestism as Metaphor in Modern Literature," by Sandra M. Gilbert, from *Critical Inquiry*, Winter 1980; from "Sapphistries," by Susan Gubar, from *Signs* 10:1 (1984); from "Blessings in Disguise: Cross-Dressing as Re-Dressing," by Susan Gubar, from *The Massachusetts Review* 20:1, 3 (1981); from "Landing at Mytilene," by Renée Vivien, from *At the Sweet Hour of Hand in Hand*, trans. Sandia Belgrade, Naiad Press, copyright © 1979, reprinted with the permission of the publisher.